America's Corporate Art

Post45 Florence Dore and Michael Szalay, Editors
Post•45 Group, Series Board

America's Corporate Art
The Studio Authorship of Hollywood Motion Pictures

Jerome Christensen

Stanford University Press
Stanford, California

Stanford University Press
Stanford, California

© 2012 by the Board of Trustees of the Leland Stanford Junior University. All rights reserved.

All images from *Grand Hotel* are Copyright MCMXXXII in the United States by Metro-Goldwyn-Mayer. All images from *The Crowd* are Copyright MCMXXVIII in the United States by Metro-Goldwyn-Mayer. All images from *Little Caesar* are Copyright MCMXXXI Warner Bros. Pictures, Inc. All images from *Gold Diggers of 1933* are Copyright MCMXXXIII Warner Bros. Pictures, Inc. All images from *Boys Town* are Copyright MCMXXXVIII in the United States by Loew's Incorporated. All images from *Mrs. Miniver* are Copyright MCMXLII in the United States by Loew's Incorporated. All images from *Battleground* are Copyright MCMXLIX in the United States by Loew's Incorporated. All images from *Singin' in the Rain* are Copyright MCMLI in the United States by Loew's Incorporated. All images from *The Band Wagon* are Copyright MCMLIII in the United States by Loew's Incorporated. All images from *Executive Suite* are Copyright MCMLIV in the United States by Loew's Incorporated. All images from *The Fountainhead* are Copyright MCMXLIX Warner Bros. Pictures, Inc. All images from *Vertigo* are Copyright © 1958 by Alfred J. Hitchcock Productions, Inc. All Rights Reserved. All images from *Batman* are © 1989 Warner Bros., Inc. All images from *JFK* are © 1991 Warner Bros. Regency Enterprises V.O.F. & Le Studio Canal+. All images from *You've Got Mail* are © 1998 Warner Bros. All images from *Bonnie and Clyde* are Copyright MCMLXVII by Warner Bros.-Seven Arts, Inc. and Tatira-Hiller Productions. All images from *Pinocchio* are © Copyright MCMXL Walt Disney Productions, Inc. All images from *Toy Story 2* are Copyright © MCMXCIX Disney Enterprises, Inc./Pixar Animation Studios.

Use of the WB in Shield Logo by permission from Warner Bros. Entertainment Inc. "MGM Logo" © METRO-GOLDWYN-MAYER TM & © 2011 METRO-GOLDWYNMAYER STUDIOS, INC. ALL RIGHTS RESERVED. Courtesy of MGM Media Licensing. "RKO Mark" Courtesy of RKO Pictures. "Universal Logo (1930s)" Courtesy of Universal Studios Licensing LLC. "Columbia Pictures 1942 Logo" Courtesy of Columbia Pictures.

No part of this book may be reproduced or transmitted in any form or by any means, electronic or mechanical, including photocopying and recording, or in any information storage or retrieval system without the prior written permission of Stanford University Press.

Printed in the United States of America on acid-free, archival-quality paper

Library of Congress Cataloging-in-Publication Data

Christensen, Jerome, 1948- author.
  America's corporate art : the studio authorship of Hollywood motion pictures / Jerome Christensen.
     pages cm. -- (Post 45)
  Includes bibliographical references and index.
  ISBN 978-0-8047-7167-2 (cloth : alk. paper) -- ISBN 978-0-8047-7863-3 (pbk. : alk. paper)
  1. Motion picture studios--California--Los Angeles--History. 2. Motion picture authorship--California--Los Angeles--History. 3. Motion picture industry--California--Los Angeles--History. 4. Hollywood (Los Angeles, Calif.)--History. I. Title. II. Series: Post 45.
  PN1993.5.U65C525 2012
  384'.80979494--dc23
                                2011027422

Typeset by Bruce Lundquist in 10/15 Minion

Contents

	Acknowledgments	vii
	Introduction	1
1	The Rackets: Entertainment Inc. and the Warners Gang (1928–1939)	24
2	MGM and the Invention of the Postwar Era: *Mrs. Miniver* and *Battleground* (1940–1949)	105
3	"'Til the Stars Go Cold": *Singin' in the Rain*, *The Band Wagon*, and *Executive Suite* (1952–1954)	157
4	Ownership and Authorship: Warners' *Fountainhead* and Hitchcock's *Vertigo* (1949–1958)	210
5	Saving Warner Bros.: *Bonnie and Clyde*, the Movements, and the Merger (1964–1968)	245
6	Post-Warners Warners: *Batman* and *JFK*; *You've Got Mail* (1989–1998)	280
7	The Conscience of a Corporation: Toys United the Disney-Pixar Merger, and the Assertion of "Cultural" Authorship (1995–2010)	314
	Notes	341
	Index	371

Acknowledgments

After the third iteration of a graduate seminar testing the explanatory power of the hypothesis that the studio, not the director, screenwriter, or even producer should be regarded as the author of Hollywood motion pictures, a couple of graduate students presented me with a placard intended for my office door. It read: "Jerry Corp: Inquire Within." The sign was a joke, but a telling one, not only because I had slipped into ventriloquizing corporations in order to affirm the movies' projections of their interests, strategies, and obsession, but also because the enterprise that I warily began in the 1990s did eventually turn into a truly corporate project, which has absorbed many voices and many ideas from those and subsequent seminars, contributions which I have amplified and synthesized into a narrative and an argument that, I hope, will vindicate my students' confidence and zeal.

I simply could not have completed this book without the enthusiasm, generosity, and challenges of the numerous superb graduate students I have had the good fortune to teach at Johns Hopkins in the 1990s, Vanderbilt from 1998 to 2003, and at University of California, Irvine, from 2003 on. At the risk of inadvertently omitting someone, let me gratefully list the names of those former graduate students who made memorable contributions: Jared Gardner, Cathy Jurca, Abigail Cheever, Courtney Berger, Mark McGurl, Matthew Sewell, Jason Gladstone, Lisa Siraganian, Kyle Dawson Edwards, Ellen Levy, Brian Rajski, and Matthew Mieskoski. John Williams and Matthew Harrison each read several unmercifully long chapters—shorter and better now, thanks to their penetrating comments. I want to give special thanks to a handful of former graduate students, who have been my partners in the classroom and whose own work and critical judgments have been crucial to the development of my argument: J. D. Connor, Charles Dove, Drayton Nabers, and Michael Szalay. Connor and Szalay have been extraordinarily helpful in editing the final draft.

I have been the beneficiary of encouragement, criticism, and advice from many friends and colleagues over the years. Thanks to my unfailingly patient, if occasionally sardonic, friend Sam Girgus for always being there; to Scottie Girgus for making sure there was, indeed, there; to Jack Murray, who never complained if a hike up Ampersand became the occasion for a monologue on the morning's groggy idea; to Leo Braudy, whose comments and conversation notably improved the postwar chapters; to Jonathan Auerbach, whose own work has been an example to me of innovative film scholarship; to John Belton, a scholar of immense knowledge of Hollywood movies and operations, whose help on the Hitchcock chapter was critical; to Steve Mailloux, whose dinner got cold many times as, over a beer or two, he queried me gently about the logic of my claims and the form in which I made them; to Richard Grusin, an intellectual and emotional mainstay during my first year at Vanderbilt and thereafter; to Vicki Silver, a ready ear and a penetrating critical intelligence; to Mark Goble, whose work and conversation were both enlightening; to Clifford Robinson for his steadying influence; to Larry and Linda Ziff, for morale boosts along the way; to Richard A. Price, for his generous elaboration of Pixar corporate policy; to Victor Friedman, whose as yet unpublished analysis of the Pixar-Disney contract was vital to the final chapter; to Nora Ephron for graciously agreeing to be interviewed; to William Epstein for seeing the importance of in-laws to Bonnie and Clyde; to Laura Dwelley who did the market research for Chapter 6; to Janet Kobrin, Vice-President and Senior Intellectual Property Advisor at Warner Bros.; and to Ken Reinhard, Lee Patterson, Marshall Brown, Jay Williams, Michael Warner, Alladi Venkatesh, Robert Mitchell, Garth Jowett, and Virginia Wexler for many remembered kindnesses and support.

I want to offer special thanks to Tom Schatz, who was there at the beginning of this project and, providentially, at its conclusion, and whose work set a standard that I did my best to emulate.

My thanks for research assistance and institutional support along the way to: Mark Daniels, Collections Associate Hall of History and Father Flanagan House; the Humanities Center at Wayne State University; the English departments at Williams College, Duke University, Yale University, the University of Washington, and the University of Southern California; the English Institute; the USC Warner Brothers Archives; the American Academy of Motion Pictures Arts and Sciences; the Wisconsin Center for Film and Theatre Research; and the Billy Rose Theater Library at Lincoln Center.

I am grateful for the assistance, encouragement, and patience of Emily-Jane Cohen, Sarah Crane Newman, Rob Ehle, Emily Smith, and Andrew Frisardi at Stanford University Press.

And, as always, I am deeply and abidingly grateful to Carol Burke for her loving support throughout this long project.

America's Corporate Art

Introduction

> Man keeps on calling new things by old names—the work of the machine is manufacture; the contract of employment concerns masters and servants; the corporation, a device by which a group gets things done, is still a person.
>
> Walton H. Hamilton, "Our Social Responsibilities"

i. Corporate Art, Studio Allegory, Corporate Identity

Midway through *Fortune*'s profile of Metro-Goldwyn-Mayer in 1932—the first in the career of that primer on making and spending to be devoted to a Hollywood motion picture studio—the half-flattering, half-mocking tone of its analysis of the studio's history, structure, and personality shifts to a different key, as the article boldly heralds the advent of a new art form:

> MGM is neither one man nor a collection of men. It is a corporation. Whenever a motion picture becomes a work of art it is unquestionably due to men. But the moving pictures have been born and bred not of men but of corporations. Corporations have set up the easels, bought the pigments, arranged the views, and hired the potential artists. Until the artists emerge, at least, the corporation is bigger than the sum of its parts. Somehow, although our poets have not yet defined it for us, a corporation lives a life and finds a fate outside the lives and fates of its human constituents.[1]

Poets had not yet defined the fateful life of the corporation, but, as the writers of *Fortune* well knew, the Supreme Court had done its best. Since the landmark Santa Clara case of 1886, which nonchalantly declared the corporation to be a person, a series of judicial decisions had generously invoked the due process clause of the Fourteenth Amendment to expand the life of the corporation outside the lives and fates of its human constituents and to ensure the right of this prodigy of industrial capitalism to pursue profit undistracted by the threat of government intervention.[2] In the trough of the Great Depression, *Fortune* decided to promote the potential of the Hollywood motion picture studio to exercise cultural leadership at a time when such leadership seemed crucial to the future of capitalism. For *Fortune*, the condition for the emergence of cinematic works of art, and therefore for faith in the future of a capitalist system capable of transcending merely commercial concerns, was not money or technology or even individual genius, but the corporate organization of the studio. It may or may not be that, according to the criteria of the academy, Hollywood motion pictures qualify as art. No matter. *Fortune* does not promise that Hollywood motion pictures will be admired as art or that they will be preserved as art; it simply affirms that if any do, they will count as instances of corporate art. The conviction that the corporate organization provides the social condition for art is more important than evidence of any motion picture's fulfillment of the traditional aesthetic criteria by which paintings or poetry or concertos are evaluated.

Corporate art should not be confused with a house style, as important as the latter is for the establishment of a brand identity in the eyes of the audience. As *Fortune*'s profile of MGM argues, the look and feel of MGM motion pictures was largely the concoction of Irving Thalberg, vice-president in charge of production, but Thalberg's efforts to implement a consistent house style served a house strategy, which MGM's motion pictures both represented and, with tactical adjustments to contingent circumstances, performed. Whether corporate art is represented by General Motors' commissioning of massive murals painted by Diego Rivera in the courtyard of the Detroit Institute of Arts in 1932 or Warners' hiring of Howard Hawks to direct *Scarface* the same year, the key to understanding that art is to plumb the strategic intention of General Motors and Warners, not Rivera or Hawks. Corporate art always counts as a tool of corporate strategy—that is, as one of a set of actions taken to attain competitive advantage which are coordinated and implemented by executives, who can successfully claim the authority to interpret the intent of the corporation and project a policy that will advance its particular interests, whether financial, social, cultural, or political. Those interests are invariably diverse and necessarily specific to the individual corporation insofar as they are framed within a highly competitive environment. No doubt a major interest is making a profit, for without profit a corporation cannot survive. Yet to state that a motion picture studio pursues profit, even that its dominant goal is the maximization of profit, tells us nothing about what kind of business it is and what its objectives are. Only individual movies understood as corporate performances and restored to the social, economic, and political environment in which they competed and which they endeavored to mold, simultaneously identify the studio's business as they attempt to accomplish its objectives.

Strategy should not be confused with ideology, although each addresses ways in which economic interests condition or inform the cultural productions of corporations in a capitalist system. Ideology, however, operates at a higher level of abstraction; its operation is subject to no person's intention or control. Corporate strategy is intended by the artificial person who the corporation is. For strategy to develop and be implemented there must be agents who can consciously interpret corporate objectives and devise the specific means to accomplish them. Ideology does its work well on constructions that function at the same level of generality, such as "the corporation," or "corporate capitalism" or "the motion picture industry," but does not explain, let alone command, particulars such as the individual movies of MGM or Paramount or Warners. When it comes to film theory the concept of ideology has often been employed as a fail-safe device for the selection of movies as apt examples or symptoms or vehicles. As a consequence of its abstraction, most ideological critique discovers the belief system it already knows must be there. Fulfillment of its tasks does not require the interpretation of texts as instances of a deliberate, variable, and focused strategy that aims to define, explain, consider, or advance the particular interests of a specific corporation—in this case a studio. One Hollywood studio may resemble other studios in its use of technology, the terms of its contracts, and the size of its reels, but each makes movies that mean different things and advance different objectives. Those meanings and those objectives are only made intelligible by alert, informed interpretation of the circumstantially grounded, strategically oriented, and tactically effective individual motion pictures that MGM, Warners, Paramount, Universal, Disney, and Columbia have produced from the classical era to the present day.

As *Fortune* suggests and this study hopes to demonstrate, the motion picture studio is the exemplary modern corporation. Each studio motion picture has the capacity to represent the general conditions of corporate personhood and expression even as it allegorically represents and pragmatically advances the particular interests of the specific studio. The Hollywood studio is a business that does its business right there on the screen as the projector rolls.

During the so-called classical era of Hollywood (roughly from the incorporation of Metro-Goldwyn-Mayer as a fully owned subsidiary of Loew's Inc. in 1924, to 1967, when Jack Warner completed the sale of Warner Bros. to Seven-Arts Productions), the five integrated major motion picture companies—Paramount, Loew's, Warner Bros., Twentieth-Century Fox, and RKO—each an owner of a studio, a distribution agency, and a number of first-run theaters, colluded to exercise oligopolistic control of the film industry and to restrain competition by restricting producers' access to resources and markets and exhibitors' choices among products. Despite "gentlemen's agreements" among the majors, which were designed by Will Hays, head of the Motion Picture Producers and Distributors of America, to ensure cooperation among the principals, the studios did compete aggressively over market shares, especially after the crash in 1929, which imposed a new economics of scarcity on American businesses large and small. Each member of the oligopoly strenuously sought to differentiate itself from the others by acquiring what John Sedgewick and Michael Pokorny call "a monopoly on uniqueness." The burden of that differentiation fell, of course, on the studios, which made the products that engaged consumer interest and solicited their loyalty. In order to "attenuate the risks associated with film consumption," each studio incorporated "a bundle of design features which aroused and satisfied a set of expectations among filmgoers," such as "stars, genre, director, sequels, and production company."[3] The differentiation among the studios was not merely a matter of electing a certain style. MGM was the studio of stars, as part of a strategy conducted by a management that had more autonomy, more longevity, and more prestige than any other group. It was the preeminent producers' studio, and despite its status as a subsidiary of Loew's, which controlled the purse strings and administered both distribution and exhibition, MGM made movies that constructed a corporate whole of which it was the predominant part. Its capital was management capital: a reliable profitability based on managerial capacity to make stars on the screen before our eyes and to feature them in narratives in which the role of the individual star and the social, political, and economic value of the entertainment he or she provided were consistently confirmed.

The long-standing opposition between MGM, the studio of stars, and Warner Bros., the studio of genres, structures the narrative and organization of this book. MGM not only never made a gangster movie that could compete with *Little Caesar* (1931) or *The Public Enemy* (1931), it never even tried. Even when MGM did directly mimic Warners, as in its musical *Dancing Lady* (1933), the differences between the studios' take on economic need, individual desire, group opportunity, and company success were unmistakable—differences that expressed MGM's irrepressible commitment to use every motion picture it produced as an occasion to elaborate a studio identity which its customers would recognize, approve, and internalize. The careful control of the process of individuating each picture in conformity with what *Fortune* would call a "common denominator of goodness" (*AFI*, p. 325), within a large population of motion pictures, each of them individuals, some of them stars, is part of the production and marketing model that made MGM strong and enabled it to succeed Paramount as the leading studio in Hollywood—the production company most responsible for establishing and maintaining the oligopolistic equilibrium that was classical Hollywood.

The success of Irving Thalberg's and Louis B. Mayer's strategy for consolidating a studio monopoly on uniqueness depended on a massive investment in the cultivation of "outstanding personalities" into what Leo Rosten called "monopolies on themselves."[4] MGM became the studio of stars so that it might establish itself as the star studio—an intangible value that may not have shown up in the box office receipts for every MGM product but which accrued to the company's earning power and long-term profitability. The executives at MGM did not imagine that the studio's pictures were uniformly important—their budgets established their place in the hierarchy with ruthless precision—but it was central to the house ideology that pictures authored and owned by MGM and that appeared under the MGM trademark were more important, *better*, than Warner Bros. or Paramount or Fox films, regardless of the budget. That conviction fueled studio ambitions to establish an MGM taste among moviegoers and an MGM community among both its customers and employees. MGM motion pictures were characteristically and deliberately allegorical. They provided the immediate pleasures of watching charismatic stars performing in skillfully constructed narratives, even as they invited viewers to understand the arrangement of pleasures as the expression of a studio strategy that alert viewers could appreciate, of a studio ethos of quality entertainment in which, as faithful customers, they could participate, and, finally, of a corporate politics, to which they, as well-meaning citizens, could subscribe. *Dancing Lady* is a movie that imitates Warners, but it is also a movie about why, even in imitating Warners, MGM remains itself, innately superior to its competitor. *Boys Town* (1938) tells the story of the struggle undergone by Father Flanagan to establish a town for parentless boys outside Omaha, Nebraska, but it also represents Boys Town as a commonwealth of young performers under the benign leadership of a man who, despite the collar, resembles the paternalistic L. B. Mayer, who is a master of public relations and whose dream of an entertainment community free of the trammels of the state (and the church), dependent only on the goodwill of the public, the movie symbolically fulfills. *The Wizard of Oz*, a hotbed of allegorical meanings, paints a picture of the paternalistic leader as a former peddler who rules by bluster and deceit. Eventually, he is rescued from his impotent seclusion by the combined forces of three eccentric talents, who in support of a youthful star, form a successful unit that proves its merit to succeed the superannuated "Wizard," just as the Freed unit would eventually succeed Mayer as custodian of MGM's signature genre, the musical comedy.

Warners was the studio of genres. As we shall see in Chapter 1, the predominance of the gangster picture in the early 1930s was not incidental. Among all the studios, Warners had the least separation between ownership and management. The gangster movies worked out the strengths and weaknesses of that organizational compression through the model of the gang and the figures of Scarface and Rico. Thalberg and Mayer could adhere to the productionist model as the basis for their relative autonomy within Loew's. But the Warner brothers had more on their minds, and we can understand what that was only by careful study of the individual pictures that Warners used to conduct its business. Gangster movies are allegories of organizational imperatives and, even more distinctively, of distribution: how to get your product into speakeasies and nightclubs and how to keep your competitors out—problems that were of little immediate concern to MGM. One way that gangsters achieved their ends was through intimidation, a strategy adopted by Warners when it launched its controversial gangster cycle in 1931, which both allegorized the company as a gang and attempted to intimidate the other members of the Motion Pictures Producers and Distributors Association, just as Rico intimidates Little Arnie Lorch, the owner of the Golden Palm. Warner Bros., the only studio besides MGM not to go into receivership during the Great Depression, is the ideal complement to Metro as a subject for this allegorical history because Warners was antithetical to Metro in its management structure, its unapologetic assembly-line attitude toward production, its fervent commitment to story before stars, its general disdain for an ideal of quality derived from literature or the legitimate stage, its urban feel, its utilitarian look, its journalistic urgency, and its New Deal politics. As I have already stated, the Warners of the 1930s is characterized by its mastery of genres—an association so strong that, as we shall see, Jack Warner waxed wrathful over the persistence of Hollywood cycles, not because there were too many newspaper pictures or gangster pictures or musicals but because the cycles were sustained by studios like RKO and producers like David O. Selznick, who copied the Warner Bros. original genre pictures. An "original genre picture" sounds like a contradiction in terms, but even if the origination of a genre was not the self-conscious objective of the studio when it went ahead with *Little Caesar* or *42nd Street*, in retrospect the emergence of such Warner Bros. films involved less an individualized offering among the studio's roster than an act of speciation, a creation of a new kind of movie that punctuated the equilibrium of the industry as effectively as Warners' introduction of sound technology, its predatory raids on stars under contract to Paramount, or the studio's break with the Motion Picture Association of America's silent tolerance of anti-Semitic business practices in Nazi Germany. The credit for recognizing the impact of generic invention as a kind of speciation goes not to Warners, however, but to Universal's *Frankenstein* (1931): its self-consciousness about producing the first entry in a new "horror" genre (forgetting, of course, a precedent or two) is evident in the staged prologue to the narrative but also in the deliberate allegorization of the studio's ambitions to create a new species of entertainment in the narrative itself.

Studio allegories often address multiple audiences—an overdetermination of meaning that, for *Fortune* at least, was most compelling in *Grand Hotel* (1932), the preeminent symbol of MGM's symbolizing genius. A studio like MGM or Paramount that thinks in pictures may find certain dramatic situations, such as Lady Belden's flower show in *Mrs. Miniver* (MGM, 1942), convenient vehicles for allegorizing its corporate strategy. A studio may use allegory to admonish its employees and punish its stars; it may exhort the president of the United States to alter policy; it may allegorize its formidable institutional power to appease its creditors and dismay its competitors. During the classical era the appearance on the screen of the studio logo—MGM's lion, Paramount's mountain, Warners' shield, RKO's radio tower, Fox's searchlights, Disney's fairy castle—fused the statement of studio ownership with a claim of studio authorship. When the lion roars MGM speaks. If the lion fiercely announced a proprietary inclusivity, it also jealously guarded a carefully defined exclusivity. No studio but MGM could have made *Grand Hotel* or *Captains Courageous* (1937). MGM could never have produced *Little Caesar* even if L. B. Mayer had both Edward G. Robinson and Mervyn LeRoy under contract. *Too Hot to Handle* (Warners, 1933) and *Batman* (Warners, 1989) are definitive Warner Bros. pictures—although definitive of a studio which, under the pressure of fundamental changes in technology, in personnel, in the demographics of moviegoers, in the economics of filmmaking, and, most of all, in the corporate form, has been altered past recognition by its founders. Nonetheless, it is as important for a student of Hollywood to know that *The Big Sleep* (1946) was a Warner Bros. feature as it is to know that Howard Hawks directed the picture. It is vastly more significant that *Marie Antoinette* (1938) is an MGM feature and part of the legacy of Irving Thalberg than that the film was directed by W. S. Van Dyke: if not for the posthumous influence of Thalberg the film would not have been made; if Thalberg had lived Van Dyke would never have directed it.

That *Morocco* (1930) was made by Paramount may appear to be a fact of less significance than that Josef Von Sternberg directed and that Marlene Dietrich and Gary Cooper starred in the film—but it seems that way only because *Morocco was* made by Paramount. As a later Paramount motion picture, *Sunset Boulevard* (1950), would argue, in Hollywood only at Paramount were the directors and their stars more important than the studio (not to mention the screenwriters)—a hierarchy that was integral to Paramount's identity. Cecil B. de Mille's *Ten Commandments* (Paramount, 1956), a Cold War updating of his 1923 silent epic, is about a sacred text in the Judeo-Christian tradition; in addition, it is itself a sacred text in the Paramount canon of brand-lore, the set of films that ponder the conception, founding, consolidation, and transformation of the Paramount brand, including *The Cheat* (1916), *The Covered Wagon* (1925), *The Virginian* (1929), *Love Me Tonight* (1932), *Christmas in July* (1940), *Road to Utopia* (1946), and *Sunset Boulevard* (1950).⁵

If, to entertain an impossibility, *The Philadelphia Story* (MGM, 1940) had been made, scene by scene, shot by shot, star by star, by Warners rather than MGM—introduced by Warner Bros.' crest rather than by the rubric of MGM's roaring lion—the film would mean something entirely different. *The Philadelphia Story* as we have it is saturated with Metro's corporate intention to justify the ways of Louis B. Mayer, studio head, to Nick Schenck, the boss of Loew's Inc. Like *The Jazz Singer* (Warners, 1927), *Gabriel over the White House* (Cosmopolitan/MGM, 1933), *Bullets or Ballots* (Warners 1934), *Boys Town* (MGM, 1938), *The Grapes of Wrath* (Twentieth-Century Fox, 1940), *Pinocchio* (Disney, 1940), *Twelve O'Clock High* (Fox, 1949), *The Fountainhead* (Warners, 1949), *Singin' in the Rain* (MGM, 1952), *Psycho* (Shamley, 1960), *Jaws* (Universal, 1975), *Invasion of the Body Snatchers* (United Artists, 1978), *Toy Story* (Pixar, 1995), *Toy Story 2* (Pixar, 1999), *Shrek* (Dreamworks, 2001), and *Minority Report* (Dreamworks, 2002), *The Philadelphia Story* is a significant instance of studio authorship because it, like they, is a motion picture deeply involved in analyzing the concept of the corporation and in marketing that concept to an audience that the studio aspires to incorporate in order that it may achieve its social, economic, and political objectives. *The Philadelphia Story* is not, however, a motion picture that had long-term consequences for the strategic position or financial health of the studio as did *Grand Hotel*, *Mrs. Miniver*, or *Singin' in the Rain*, or as *The Jazz Singer*, *Little Caesar*, *Bonnie and Clyde*, *Batman*, or *You've Got Mail* did at Warners, where each of those motion pictures punctured an equilibrium established among the studios and became an instrument of what we can loosely call the evolution of the industry from classical Hollywood to New Hollywood and beyond.

The Concept of the Corporation is the title of Peter F. Drucker's landmark 1946 study, which endeavored to unhitch the corporation from its moorings in state charters, Supreme Court decisions, and abstract theories of corporate personality. No need to look back, Drucker claimed, since World War II had established "beyond any doubt" the "large corporation as the representative institution of America today." No empirical corporation matters as much as the concept of the corporation "organized in such a way as to be able itself to function and to survive as an *institution*, so as to enable society to realize its *basic promises and beliefs*, and to enable *society* to function and to survive." As the single most "dynamic element" of American society, the concept of the corporation has become the preeminent "symbol through which the facts are organized in a social pattern."⁶

Fourteen years before Drucker proclaimed the corporation's chief social importance as a symbol, *Fortune* had discovered that symbolizing power exercised at MGM by the executive vice-president in charge of production, Irving Thalberg. As we shall see in Chapter 1, the magazine figures Thalberg, star executive, as both camera and projector, producer and spectator—a division of functions that he mobilized to refine MGM's "common denominator of goodness," and thereby create his brand loyal customers. Thalberg does not claim to be the studio author; he famously takes no screen credit at all. Thalberg, in *Fortune*'s canonical interpretation, is the agent of the studio who best impersonates its purposes and practices, and who enables the structuring self-reflection that is MGM's singular mode of authorship. Although there was no Thalberg at Warners, an anti-Thalberg appears in the gloaming of Jack Warner's reign: Warren Beatty uses *Bonnie and Clyde* (1967) both to represent and to exploit studio dysfunction in a Hollywood where credit means everything because it is the brand, not the sound stage or the real estate or the superannuated Jack Warner, that remains of Warner Bros. And it is in the brand that moviemakers and movie executives will henceforth live, move, and have their being.

From the perspective of Drucker, corporate theorist, Thalberg developed his executive discipline in order to create customers for MGM motion pictures. From the perspective of Roland Marchand, cultural historian, by distilling a "common denominator of goodness" which deeply resonated with a struggling middle-class audience often forced to align with denominators of the commonest sort, Thalberg was creating MGM's soul. Marchand's important study, *Creating the Corporate Soul*, examines the connection between the professionalization of modern marketing and corporate America's response in the 1920s and 1930s to widespread discontent with a massive increase of corporate size and power unaccompanied by any regard for the public welfare. Progressives charged that if the corporation is, as the courts had ruled, indeed a person, it is a person without a soul.[7] If we have our eyes on the PR men who became expert soul makers for the corporations that hired them, we can read soul making as an allegory of the increasing sophistication and cynicism of modern product managers in exploiting any pretext to invest corporations with pathos. But marketing itself, as distinguished from either advertising or merchandising, may be reasonably read as an allegory of something like soul making, insofar as the project of marketing involves the establishment of the social legitimacy of a company that seeks to make customers for its products rather than simply make products it can somehow sell to a consumer. As making a shareholder into a stakeholder involves the establishment of a connection to the company based on a perception of its value independent of the Friday's closing stock price, so making a consumer into a customer involves the establishment of a connection to the corporation, which is also dependent on the perception of its value apart from the immediate appeal of the glistening commodity it puts on the shelf.

The common denominator between soul and value is *personality*—a term with innumerable associations that was used by marketers to humanize the spiritual astringency of *soul* and to spiritualize the commercialist connotation of *value*. In the 1920s and 1930s the phenomenon of "personality" became an instrument to synthesize a new kind of corporate capital. In his iconoclastic book *The Folklore of Capitalism* (1937), Thurman Arnold ponders consequences of the irrepressible tendency of the "folk" to personify what we now call the culture of organizations:

> Not only do organizations acquire personalities, they also acquire three-dimensional substance. Thus habits and disciplines and hopes of a great organization are given a money value. Capitalized earning power is called "property" and then is treated as if it could be moved from place to place and sold. Then people dealing with these imaginary personalities deal with them as if they owned this sort of property. Without this alternate reification and personification of the same things a corporate structure could not exist and do business under a money economy.

From one perspective corporations are personified; they become individuals with personalities, who acquire substance by their possession of "goodwill" (the economists' compromise with the term *soul*). From an alternate perspective they "are storehouses of tangible property" that can be sold down to the bare walls before the walls themselves are sold. The reification (or, perhaps, commodification) of goodwill as capitalized earning power enables it to be sold as property by the very personality that is constituted by nothing but the goodwill attributed to it. Nonetheless the seller retains its personality as an "earning capacity" (or brand), which somehow has value above and beyond the market value of its material property. Arnold illustrates the strange logic that follows from this structure with the remark that "to say that the Baltimore and Ohio Railroad Company owns the Baltimore and Ohio Railroad is like saying that the United States Marine Corps owns the United States Marines."[8] It would seem impossible for the Baltimore and Ohio Railroad Company to own the Baltimore and Ohio because the Baltimore and Ohio Railroad Company *is* the Baltimore and Ohio. Ordinarily, it would seem absurd that an organization could at once be itself and yet be a property of itself. But it is not absurd. The corporate person owns itself in a way that no other persons do—except, crucially, movie stars. The corporation, like a star, is, in form if not necessarily in fact, a monopoly on itself. It can authorize its agents to complete the sale of itself, its rolling stock, its autographed images, its buildings, its recorded performances, while still remaining itself, a singular subject which exists apart from those agents and despite those sales—a subject which has as its representatives those managers who have exercised their dexterity to create intangible value out of numerals in a ledger, or light and shadows on a screen. The goodwill that increased the intangible, material capital of the motion picture studios lay in the studios' capacity to manufacture goodwill for other companies or causes with practiced efficiency.

Goodwill, personality, soul, star—all are human terms for intangible values, for earning power, and for endlessly replenishable managerial capital. Classically, the profit motive drives the entrepreneur as he pursues ever more efficient transactions and, consequently, provides greater returns to the corporate shareholders on their investments. From Drucker's perspective—which we shall alternately call a *strategic*, a *managerial*, or a *marketing* perspective—it is the *institutionalization* of profitability as managerial capital which enables the executive to act effectively as agent of the corporate principal to assure that future revenue will be sufficient for the long-term survival of the firm. To attain profitability is to invest in producing the capital (capitalized earning power, goodwill, brand equity) that will enable the manager to render uncertainty as intangible value, to convert intangibles into wealth, and to exploit that wealth as an opportunity for the corporation to take risks—risks which are vital to an aggressive society for which a stationary economy is a threat to prosperity. A management perspective embraces the view that "management has replaced capital . . . , management reflects ([or] 'determines') societal and economic prerogatives in the broadest sense . . . , and at the centre of all societal and economic prerogatives is . . . the capitalist corporation."[9]

No company in America in the 1930s had a better claim to represent that fundamental shift in the concept of the corporation than MGM, which was formed not by a group of investors but by a management team that had organized the company as the production subsidiary of Loew's Inc. and, critically, renounced shares in the company in order to take percentages of the profit, which would improve, not simply as the annual revenue of the company rose but as profitability—that is, not its annual profit but its long-term capacity to return profit—increased. The MGM executives' primary, self-defined responsibility was not to manage the studio's relations with distributors, its allocation of resources, or the moods of its stars but to strengthen the MGM brand. Their management was so successful that although the MGM studio has, since the deaths of Thalberg and Mayer, been managed and mismanaged, bought and sold, dissolved and revived, only to be wrecked by debt and recently put on the block again, and although the MGM soul expired long ago, its brand retains its value in a world of mutating profit centers that neither Thalberg nor *Fortune* could have foreseen but for which they had astutely prepared. If it is true that in 1946, after the smoke had cleared from the battlegrounds in Europe and the Pacific and large companies had proved the vital importance of their capacity to organize society in successful defense against the nation's enemies, the corporation could legitimately claim to be the most representative institution in American society, it is equally true that from the beginning of the sound era, until approximately the postwar era, the Hollywood motion picture studio and especially MGM could plausibly represent themselves as what Will Hays called "the epitome of civilization and the quintessence of what we mean by 'America.'"[10] Hays could say such a thing not because it was actually true, however truth is measured when press agentry warbles its fond hyperboles, but because, more than any other major corporation, the Hollywood studio had and has the art of successfully marketing itself as a virtual star.

By 1949, however, the law, the Supreme Court, and the talent agents had intervened in that market, and when MGM under its new vice-president in charge of production, Dore Schary, turned to a new *Battleground* (MGM, 1949), the terrain had altered so dramatically that MGM's strengths proved to be weaknesses. It was one thing to model the concept of the corporate studio on the star, which was merely a form, when stars were safely under seven-year contracts to the studio; it was another when, after the war, the stars incorporated themselves and drastically diminished the capitalized earning power of the studios. By the 1950s MGM was caught in a struggle between two warring camps, the Freed unit and the Schary coalition: the former committed to retooling MGM's signature genre, the musical comedy—especially *Singin' in the Rain* and *The Band Wagon*—in order to stage a resistance to a diminished future by exhausting its imagination in its effort to revive the glory of the studio, the latter using *Executive Suite* as the vehicle to help save the company by prospecting a future of enlightened management and ill-defined innovation.

MGM barely survived, while Warner Bros. thrived. Warners had never tied its fate to the vicissitudes of stardom and the elixir of self-replenishing intangible capital. It preferred to put its faith in technology, in its capacity to be independent of any of its properties, and, under the cunning leadership of the brutally unsympathetic Jack Warner, its willingness to make the deals that would sacrifice ownership for a lingering control. The first half of this book is ruled by MGM, with appearances by Warners as conservative Metro's chief antagonist. The second half belongs largely to Warner Bros., as party to mergers and acquisitions which left the studio bereft of its connection to the past but healthy in its financials and ripe for rejuvenation: first, by a charismatic producer, Warren Beatty, who could exploit Jack Warner's willful depreciation of the asset in order to commandeer the Warners brand, and later, by a charismatic CEO, Steve Ross, who, as acknowledged master of the art of the deal, could deploy the studio as the marketing arm to use *Batman* to assert the transcendence of the Warners brand and beguile the management of Time Inc., the largest entertainment corporation in America, into outfoxing itself at the negotiating table. Finally, Gerald Levin, Ross's successor, who was infatuated by technology, handicapped by his unreflective faith in his acquisition of Ross's mastery, mistook the effective use of *You've Got Mail* (1998) to manipulate the stock market as the creation of capital, and happily completed the worst merger deal in the history of corporate America.

ii. The Studio Authorship Thesis:
Authorship, Strategy, Functionalism

Positions on the authorship of studio films tend to cluster antithetically: at one pole are auteurist, so-called romantic accounts of authorship which stipulate that some actual individual's contribution, whether director, screenwriter, or producer, qualifies her to be credited as author despite her limited participation or control; at the other extreme are materialist and collectivist accounts that render some apparatus or set of industrial conditions or group as the functional equivalent of the individual author.[11] This book identifies a more comprehensive alternative, a person who is not actual but who nonetheless qualifies for the status of the intending author: the corporate studio itself. With the phrase *corporate studio*, I include those Hollywood production companies that were actually incorporated (such as Samuel Goldwyn Inc. and MGM until the end of the 1930s), those that were the production subsidiaries of larger corporations (Twentieth Century-Fox Film Corporation, RKO Radio Pictures Inc., Paramount Pictures Inc.), the one that straddled that distinction (Warner Bros.), and production companies that shared the structure, practices, and objectives of the major studios (Universal Pictures, Selznick International, and United Artists after 1950). Organizational commitment to "the concept of the corporation" as "a social institution organizing human efforts to a common end" is decisive in determining studio authorship, not strict adherence to any particular organizational form (*CC*, p. 12). Different organizations make pictures that have different objectives and meanings, not mere differences in style—a truth that cannot be deduced from a flow chart or a biography of an executive, or a table of revenues, or a theoretical model of the development of finance capitalism, or a policy statement from Will Hays or Jack Valenti, but must be discovered by close examination of the particular motion pictures that are each corporation's individualized speech. To state the studio authorship thesis in its full extension: no adequate understanding of the artistic achievement, social role, and economic objectives of Hollywood motion pictures can be attained without interpretation of individual movies. There is no interpretation without meaning, no meaning without intention, no intention without an author, no author without a person, no person with greater right to or capacity for authorship than a corporate person, and, finally, no corporate person who can act without an agent.

Although versions of the studio authorship thesis have been developed by filmmakers and studios from the mid-1930s to the present, it has attracted few adherents among those who study Hollywood motion pictures. As Richard Maltby declared in 1998, "there has . . . been a fairly clear division between a practice of textual analysis that has either avoided historical contextualization or engaged in it only minimally, and economic film history that has largely avoided confronting the movies as formal objects."[12] A review of major histories of the industry confirms Maltby's generalization. For example, Howard T. Lewis's *The Motion Picture Industry* affirms that "no attempt to understand the present problems of the American motion picture industry can be even partially successful without some appreciation of the character of the development out of which the present situation evolved."[13] Lewis gives a useful account of the background of the industry and illuminates each sector of its organization: production, distribution, and exhibition. But he rarely names an individual film. Leo Rosten's splendid *Hollywood: The Movie Colony, the Movie Makers* takes as its premise that Hollywood is "an index of our society and culture," and aims to lay bare the social mainsprings and the economic framework of a community that is "significant because of the product it manufactures and the symbolic function it serves to millions of men" (*H*, p. 6). Rosten's results are revelatory, especially regarding the often neglected, somewhat elusive role of producers in the manufacture of motion pictures, but by forsaking any study of the movies that those producers actually made, the social scientist scants the cultural dimension of his subject. In her indispensable 1944 study, *Economic Control of the Motion Picture Industry*, Mae D. Huettig asserts that "the structure of the major companies is important because there is a real and direct connection between the way in which they are set up, the kind of people who run them, and the kind of films produced."[14] Yet Huettig's predominant interest in structure rather than strategy is satisfied by classifying the releases of individual studios; she does not analyze the movies themselves. Maltby's generalization regarding the segregation of film criticism from economic film history also applies to key works that appeared in the 1980s and 1990s, such as Thomas Schatz's *The Genius of the System*, Maltby's own *Hollywood Cinema: An Introduction* (with Ian Craven), Douglas Gomery's *The Hollywood Studio System*, and the multi-authored *History of the American Cinema*. Of those valuable histories, Schatz's impeccable producer-oriented study, which makes a strong case for studio executives as the "chief architects of a studio's style," has had the most influence on this book. Most recently, in his illuminating study *Production Culture: Industrial Reflexivity and Critical Practice in Film and Television*, John Thornton Caldwell has skillfully employed an ethnographic approach to develop what he calls an "industrial auteur theory," which applies to the above the line/creative personnel (that is, those who contribute to the conception and direction of the picture—as opposed to below-the-line personnel who execute others ideas) and an "industrial identity theory," which applies to the above the line/business personnel for whom "screenplays are also business plans." Because Caldwell's "analytical task . . . is to make sense of film/video workers who function as part of a very different 'post-network' industrial world," he is not concerned to make sense of the movies themselves. Instead he commits himself to "considering cinema within the diverse contexts of electronic media"—an important task, brilliantly handled, but one that sharply diverges from the project undertaken here.[15]

Even though Huettig does not attempt analysis of individual films, she recognizes the importance of the project. "The facts," she writes, "indicate clearly that there is a connection between the form taken by the film and the mechanics of the business, even if the connection is somewhat obscure" (*EC*, p. 55). Four and a half decades after Huettig's book, *The Classical Hollywood Cinema*, by David Bordwell, Janet Staiger, and Kirsten Thompson, attempted to dispel that obscurity regarding the connection by applying a functionalist model of explanation to the industry that has been immensely influential, even hegemonic. This landmark study understands the Hollywood film industry during the classical era as comprising companies that shared a specific mode of production and that manufactured standardized industrial commodities—that is, motion pictures—which conformed to "integral and limited stylistic conventions" that emerged from and fed on Hollywood production practices.[16] According to that study, by the mid-1920s feature filmmaking had evolved from the individualistic enterprise of the early silent era into an industrial system organized on quasi-Fordist principles of mass production. Supervised by an inflexible hierarchy of managers, propelled by a rhythm of technological innovation and standardization, characterized by a coherent, yet variable repertoire of "ideological/signifying practices," and driven to maximize profit, the motion picture industry produced, distributed, and exhibited marginally differentiated commodities for mass consumption.

Classical Hollywood Cinema combines extraordinary attention to film form with an equally impressive analysis of the industrial system. But because "meaning" is incidental to the mode of production, questions of authorship or what *Fortune* would call "art" are not relevant. As Dirk Eitzen states in an early review of *Classical Hollywood Cinema*, the form of Hollywood motion pictures follows industrial function not individual intention. What an owner, manager, or worker wants to do or thinks he or she is doing has little bearing on what is finally done. In defense of *Classical Hollywood Cinema*'s functionalist premise, Eitzen argues that while the book does show how innovations in lighting and sound technology produced changes in Hollywood film style, it insists on "a clear discrepancy between the motivations for innovation and the actual causes of change. It was the *consequences* of inventions that determined their 'success,' and consequences, though they were deliberately sought, could very rarely be fully anticipated."[17] Among competing innovations by Hollywood practitioners, it was the system, not the individual inventors or even their managers, which determined what eventually succeeded: "The innovations that won out were always those that fit best into the established 'modes' of practice and production" ("E," p. 77). For the functionalist any supposed motive, whether individual or corporate, is a secondary effect of the dynamism of an industrial system that is fundamentally a technology for efficient self-reproduction by means of profit-maximization.

The symmetries of functionalist systems propagate most neatly if individual Hollywood corporations are amalgamated into the general category of the "film industry." The term *industry* conveniently designates "a group of firms producing products that are close substitutes for each other."[18] That an industry exists does not presuppose that it is the consequence of deliberate planning. From the perspective of classical economics, the behavior of a group of firms scales up from the behavior of an individual firm: there is a market demand for a certain kind of product; a firm can fulfill that demand more cheaply than the open market; it therefore makes sense that a group of firms would emerge to make the same product and probably more cheaply than one firm alone, since costs would be saved in terms of proximity to resources and customers. As the story to the Justice Department might go, it should be no surprise that the supply of products among all the firms in the industry would automatically seek and find a level that would dictate a floor on prices throughout the industry. For classical economics, whatever coordination occurs among the firms that constitute an industry is a function of the price mechanism, not the consequence of a plan shared among the producers.

Since the turn of the twentieth century, however, the term *industry* has usually been reserved for a group of firms that have some kind of formal relationship. Unlike a corporation, neither a firm nor a group of firms has the status of a person before the law, which is to say that when an industry is personified (as "Hollywood" regularly is in the pages of *Classical Hollywood Cinema*) and assigned "wants" or "needs," that trope is a metaphorical extension of the chartered status of the corporate person—a device that actually *has* wants and needs. Firms with shared interests do establish associations or councils, appoint representatives, agree on objectives, collaborate on policies, and hire specialized individuals to speak on behalf of their industry. The organization of the group of the major firms that constituted the American motion picture industry was more advanced than most in the 1920s as a result of the formation of Motion Picture Producers and Distributors Association (MPPDA) in 1922, with Will Hays as its director. As a result of Hays's skillful agency, journalists in the 1930s could reliably learn what the motion picture industry "thought" by consulting him. Or they could survey an aggregate, such as the studio heads or the members of the Academy of Motion Picture Arts and Sciences.

In *The Grand Design* Tino Balio distinguishes outmoded accounts of Hollywood as virtually controlled by the Wall Street financiers who owned the studios from "revisionist" accounts that "rest more or less on contemporary critiques of finance capitalism that focus on corporate hegemony." Like Bordwell, Staiger, and Thompson, Balio cites as his authority Alfred D. Chandler's *Visible Hand* (1977), which

> defined the modern business enterprise as having two specific characteristics: "It contains many distinct operating units and is managed by a hierarchy of salaried executives." Motion-picture firms took on the first characteristic during the teens and the twenties when they integrated both horizontally and vertically. As they grew in size, these firms became managerial, which is to say, they rationalized and organized operations into autonomous departments each headed by a professional manager.[19]

Such thinking has long ceased being revisionist. Well before Balio consecrated *Visible Hand* as the foundation on which contemporary histories of Hollywood should build, Martin J. Sklar argued that Chandler's functionalist thesis that increased efficiency of operation naturally selected large-scale, well-coordinated corporations for dominance of the economy echoes the Darwinian apologies made on behalf of the corporate system in the early years of the century by "pro-corporate partisans," who defended the social dislocation attendant on the rapid transition to a new, highly organized system of industrial production and market control as "simply a matter of submission to 'objective' laws of economic evolution."[20] William G. Roy has distilled the terms of the "major underlying debate" among contemporary historians and theorists of the modern corporation: those who insist that "the economy operates according to an economic logic based on efficiency" are opposed by those who are convinced that it "operates according to a social logic based on institutional arrangements, including power."[21] Roy's own case histories of individual corporations rising to dominate entire industries in the early decades of the twentieth century indicates that the efficiency of the business organization was rarely decisive. The success of particular corporations in specific industries was contingent on both the mix and mastery of the actual actors involved and the concrete material and political opportunities available for exploitation.

As established by judicial decisions and charters granted by federal and state governments, corporations of the late nineteenth century, according to Roy, constituted a "new type of property, socialized property," which was distributed among a number of owners who are strangers to each other and to the operations of the company in which they have a financial stake. The socialization of property entails that the "variable" rights, entitlements, and obligations are not only in relation to an "object itself but also in relationship to other individuals," including the board of directors, managers, workers, and customers; and also to the state, which must take an active role in defining and enforcing property rights. Consequently, Roy argues, "the major corporations as a form of property set within a broader institutional structure [are] shaped by the dynamics of power at least as much as by efficiency" (*SC*, p. 11). By committing to the anti-intentionalist efficiency thesis, by overvaluing technological determination, and by undervaluing the studios' strategic exercise of power, functionalist film scholars typically construct a history of unintended but preordained consequences. Getting the story right requires that we learn how corporate enterprises determined what they wanted, to reconstruct what corporate actors did to get what they needed—for example, spend money, exert influence, conspire—in order to acquire what they wanted, and to pay close attention to the ways in which interested representations *of* and *by* corporations helped achieve corporate objectives.

There are three distinct kinds of power that corporations deploy to achieve their objectives. The most evident kind Roy calls, after Weber, "behavioral power": "the visible overt behavior of the power wielder in the form of a command or request" (*SC*, p. 13). *Behavioral power* is the kind of power that could compel an actor, such as Clark Gable or Claudette Colbert, who is under contract to one studio, to report to work for another as a "loan"; it is the kind of power that would require George Cukor to shoot *A Star Is Born* (Warners, 1954) in Cinemascope rather than the preferred academy ratio; the kind that would keep potential scandal involving Rock Hudson out of the newspaper; and the kind that might be exercised by a congressional committee in the form of a subpoena summoning studio executives to testify regarding communist infiltration of the motion picture industry.

Corporate power is also structural—that is, embedded, ordered, expansive, and indirect. According to Roy, those corporate actors who possess structural power have an "ability to determine the context within which decisions are made by affecting the consequences of one alternative over another" (*SC*, p. 13). *Structural power* is the kind of power more or less systematically exercised by oligopolies such as the Motion Pictures Producers and Distributors Association; it is the power engineered by lawyers drawing up corporate contracts with investors and independent agents that mystify the relations between the gross revenue and the net profit; the kind exerted by the Office of War Information to assure the projection of a consistently optimistic image of the war effort.[22]

It was the motion picture companies' formidable symbolic power, however, that distinguished them among the leading corporations and earned them an influence out of proportion to the magnitude of their revenues or capital reserves. Each studio projected its preferred identity and screened its ambitions by marketing commodities that proposed plausible versions of the world, then, now, and in the future. As David Riesman argues in *The Lonely Crowd*, more than any other cultural medium it was Hollywood that constructed the characterology of the modern American individual, that sold the concept of personality (or "other-direction"), and that minted imitable prototypes of appealing personalities, which the studios mobilized on their screens.[23] The symbolic power generated by individual studios and channeled through the agencies of the MPPDA, the Academy, *Variety*, *The Hollywood Reporter*, *Fortune*, *Time*, *Life*, *Look*, *Photoplay*, the Hearst newspaper chain, and so on created the mystique of Hollywood as one of the handful of political, financial, commercial, and cultural institutions within the national imaginary—along with Washington, the national press, Wall Street, and Madison Avenue—which had the capacity to mold, manipulate, and mobilize public opinion.

To strategically exercise behavioral, structural, and, above all, symbolic power has always been the ambition of the major and minor Hollywood studios. This book departs most decisively from the premises of functionalist film scholarship and the procedures of traditional film criticism in its conception of how strategy is developed within the corporation and how corporate strategy projects institutional power. In the functionalist study *Strategy and Structure*, Alfred D. Chandler, Jr., acknowledges that one finds that changes in corporate "strategy... called for changes in structure," but typically adds that such changes, according to Chandler, "appear to have been in response to the opportunities and needs created by changing population and changing national income and by technological innovation.... The prospect of a new market or the threatened loss of a current one stimulated geographical expansion, vertical integration, and product diversification."[24] For Chandler and the school of economic history he launched, then, strategy is fundamentally reactive and adaptive to changes—"opportunities and needs"—created by the external environment. By establishing, realigning, or reinventing appropriate functions, structure *operationalizes* strategy.

Kenneth R. Andrews has argued that it is the task of the corporate strategist to interpret corporate discourse in order to discover and implement the intention it conveys. Whereas "business strategy" defines the "choices of product or service and market of an individual business," "corporate strategy" applies to "the whole enterprise" as "the pattern of decisions in a company that determines and reveals its objectives, purposes, or goals, and defines the range of business the company is to pursue, the kind of economic and human organization it is or intends to be and the nature of the economic and non-economic contribution it intends to make to its shareholders, employees, customers, and communities." The signification of a business strategy provided by any single decision or by any single employee becomes part of corporate strategy only when a manager, who understands himself as the intended interpreter of corporate purpose, deduces from "decisions observed, what the pattern is and what the company's goals and policies are." Corporate strategy cannot be inferred from any single action that alters the way something is done ("Why did you decide to change the office software system?"), or that can be referred to any individual such as, say, the writer of a mission statement ("What exactly did you mean by saying our mission was 'the general welfare?'"), or referred to the innovator of a product line ("Does this mean that all our shorts have to be baggy?"), or even referred to the CEO ("What was the *real* reason we merged with AOL, Mr. Levin?"). Sounding like a new critic, Andrews urges that because the "essence of the definition of strategy... is *pattern*... it is the unity, coherence, and internal consistency of a company's strategic decisions that position the company in its environment and give the firm its identity, its power to mobilize its strength, and its likelihood of success in the marketplace."[25] Corporate employees become effective executives insofar as they are able to discern a pattern and, discounting the professed intentions of the actual agent of any particular decision, make a decision consistent with the operant intention of the whole to mold an environment in which the company can achieve its objectives.

Andrews's corporate executive interprets a set of decisions as establishing the strategy authored by the corporation, which he then impersonates in order to render a decision in keeping with corporate intentions. Impersonation is the norm for successful performance in the corporation as, Barry King argues, it is in the theater and motion pictures:

> The process of character representation through impersonation entails that the actor should strive to obliterate his or her sense of identity in order to become a signifier for the intentionality inscribed in character. Such obliteration returns the project of intentionality to the level of the narrative itself, which is usually "authored" reductively in terms of the director's or playwright's "vision," rather than as a meaning emergent from a collective act of representation. The full participation of the actor in the narrative as character thereby depends upon the suppression of the literary conception of the author.[26]

If we substitute "corporation" for "collective," "executive" for "character," and "strategy" for "narrative," we are on firm ground. In the late 1920s and early 1930s, Irving Thalberg *personified* MGM, but so did Clark Gable, Louis B. Mayer, Cedric Gibbon, Joan Crawford, and Leo the Lion. Most people would have agreed that Clark Gable was the personification of MGM. If Gable were to have said, "I am MGM," however, that claim would have invited rebuttal from numerous quarters: the New York office, the shareholders, even the PR agent for Spencer Tracy. The personification of a studio is an identification that people may recognize, but not one to which anyone must consent. A personification does not bear corporate authority and cannot enunciate strategy. A personification of the studio is, ultimately, an element of the corporation's brand, one of the cluster of associations people make when they hear the name "MGM" or "Disney." Thalberg, Mayer, and Selznick impersonated MGM at various times, the latter filmmaker with a touch of the irony that flared during Warren Beatty's conversations with an aged Jack Warner when Beatty claimed Warners as his own proprietarial trademark, as if to predict that studio authorship, though merely nominal, would survive studio owners, who are merely old, merely mortal.

iii. Summary of Chapters

The chapters that follow are arranged roughly chronologically. Chapter 1 uses readings of MGM and Warner Bros. motion pictures from 1928 until 1939 to illuminate the way the two studios developed their identities in a struggle to attain competitive advantage during the Depression and under the rules of engagement established by the Motion Pictures Producers and Distributors Association, the Production Code Administration, and, eventually, the federal government. The predominant theme that emerges from the corporate liberal entente of the first New Deal involves the relation or competition between the motion picture industry and the government in providing protection—whether as a form of social insurance or as a protection racket—to a distressed populace. The chapter is organized by the elaboration of the autotelic mechanism by which *Fortune* figures Thalberg's successfully self-reflexive management, by analysis of the trope of social adjustment that MGM proposes as a device to divert potential conflict between the masses and the classes, and by illustrating the trope of commutability that characterizes the particular form of collectivism embraced by Warner Bros., the New Deal studio.

Chapter 2 explores the implications of *Fortune*'s return to MGM in 1939, this time to examine the dynamics of the relationship between Loew's and its subsidiary and to evaluate Louis B. Mayer's record as the studio head after the decline and death of Thalberg. The first two sections of the chapter engage *Mrs. Miniver* as MGM's chief statement of the importance of breeding for the creation of stars and for asserting the authority of the studio in the postwar era. The second section examines the chief cinematic exponent of change at postwar MGM, *Battleground*, the pet project of the studio's new vice-president of production, Dore Schary. *Battleground* tested whether the studio of *Meet Me in St. Louis* could remain relevant to the veterans of the war and restore its lost audience. It broke with MGM conventions by embracing a Cold War liberalism that stressed the importance of tolerance toward our former foes, vigilance toward our new ones, and the central role of motion pictures as the vehicle for the global spread of American popular culture.

Chapter 3 looks at MGM's response in the 1950s to a continued decline in revenue and to the bitter rivalry within the studio between those talents in the renowned Freed unit, which retained allegiance to the entertainment values that the retired Mayer had long embraced, and those who were aligned with Schary, a believer in the progressive mission of the studio to represent and even to solve contemporary social problems. Neither Freed nor Schary veered from MGM's core identity as the studio of the stars, however; and it is through reflection on the complex process of making, maintaining, reviving, and disciplining stars that *Singin' in the Rain*, *The Band Wagon*, and *Executive Suite* think through mortal threats to the continued existence of the studio.

Chapter 4 examines the terms on which independence as a director, a star, and a studio could be achieved in the 1950s. It begins with Warners' *The Fountainhead*, directed by King Vidor, which exploits the Ayn Rand novel as the opportunity to investigate the ways in which the modern corporation can achieve autonomy on the same terms as a work of modern architecture. The chapter then turns to a reading of Hitchcock's *Vertigo* as an allegory of the director's own struggles for independence in the 1950s under the guidance of Lew Wasserman, his powerful agent from MCA.

Chapters 5 and 6 unfold the contributions of three motion pictures, *Bonnie and Clyde*, *Batman*, and *You've Got Mail*, to the transformations undergone at Warner Bros. in the aftermath of the sale of the studio to Seven Arts Productions in 1967, during the negotiations over the merger with Time Inc. that were brought to a successful conclusion by Steve Ross, CEO of Warner Communications in 1989, and during the subsequent courtship of Steve Case and AOL by Gerald Levin and Time Warner in 2000. The essay on *Bonnie and Clyde* situates the motion picture in the context of a handful of cultural and political movements during the late 1960s: the New Sentimentality, the New Left, the New Wave, and, finally, the New Hollywood, which the motion picture inaugurated by its example of an organizational style that could exploit the chaos that the studio system had become and its demonstration that, in the absence of viable institutions, "institutionality" could be achieved by imaginative marketing and canny brand management. The sections of Chapter 6 on Ross and Levin both demonstrate how blockbuster motion pictures could be used as highly effective instruments of persuasion in the course of merger talks that depended on a mystification of the actual, book value of Warner Bros. by its CEO. *Batman* is a rescue fantasy that convinced Time Inc. that Warners could rescue *it*. *You've Got Mail* is a takeover fantasy that, like many, imagines itself as a merger of true minds.

Chapter 7 makes the case that the merger agreement between Pixar and Disney in 2006 executed a significant revision in the corporate form by the assertion of "cultural authorship." The chapter initially engages the vexed issue of corporate criminal liability in relation to the distinction between the author, whom this book invokes, and the corporate speaker, whom the U.S. Supreme Court lavishes with constitutional rights in *Citizens United v. Federal Election Commission*. The Roberts Court has recognized the corporation as a rights-bearing citizen, but it is a citizen without a conscience. The remainder of the chapter examines the *hermeneutic* relations between Pixar's *Toy Story* and *Toy Story 2* and *Pinocchio* in order to argue that it is by means of a reading of *Pinocchio*'s oddly evasive representation of the transformation of an artificial person into a real boy that Pixar was able to provide an alternative teleology for toys and for the animation studios whose culture they allegorize: not to become a real boy but to become a real conscience for the artificial person named Disney to whom Pixar belongs.

The Rackets
Entertainment Inc. and the Warners Gang (1928–1939)

> There is a very general tendency to over-emphasize the moral and educational influence of the motion pictures. . . . The sole purpose of the commercial motion picture is to entertain.
>
> Irving Thalberg[1]

> [The executives at MGM] all point to the harm they could do me by putting me out in bad pictures, which is only too true. They also tell me that it would do them no harm, as they are so organized that they would go on just the same, but that I would suffer irreparable loss.
>
> Lillian Gish to her lawyer[2]

i. Be a Camera

"Metro-Goldwyn-Mayer, largest of 124 subsidiaries owned by Loew's Inc. is a corporation devoted exclusively to the business and the art of producing moving pictures." So states *Fortune* as it begins its 1932 corporate profile of Metro-Goldywn-Mayer—its first devoted to a Hollywood studio.[3] An inventory of MGM's fifty-three acre plant, its army of employees, the names and salaries of its stars, and its box office receipts fills the page. And then the author pauses to explain why those facts and figures are worthy of attention: "For the past five years, Metro-Goldwyn-Mayer has made the best and most successful moving pictures in the United States." Why was this the case?

> It may be luck. It may be the list of MGM stars, vastly the most imposing in . . . "the industry." It may be MGM's sixty-two writers and eighteen directors. It may be MGM's technicians, who are more numerous and more highly paid than those of MGM's competitors. It may be Irving Thalberg—Norma Shearer's husband. If no one in Hollywood knows the reason for MGM's producing success, everyone in Hollywood believes the last. Irving Thalberg, a small and fragile young man with a suggestion of anemia, is MGM's vice-president in charge of production. The kinds of pictures MGM makes and the ways it makes them are Irving Thalberg's problems. He is what Hollywood means by MGM.[4]

To think of MGM is to think of Thalberg, the man who, to his peers, personifies the studio. *Fortune* will affirm that sentiment. From the outset of the business magazine, in February 1930, hard upon the crash of the stock market, it had invested in the genre of the corporate profile. Characteristically, the *Fortune* profile individuates its corporate subject by identifying it with one or more of its agents, the executives responsible for setting company policy and achieving the company's objectives.[5] Although Thalberg was the chief executive neither of MGM (that would be Louis B. Mayer) nor of Loew's Inc., the company of which MGM was the corporate subsidiary (Nicholas Schenck had this role), he was the executive most responsible for molding MGM's corporate personality as the studio of personalities. Thalberg introduced the "galactic" strategy of loading MGM films with expensive stars; he regularly ordered costly retakes to assure that each picture met his (MGM's) standard of quality. It was not an easy job. MGM had abundant talent at its disposal, but the vice-president in charge of production had to "know how to focus all this talent." Thalberg succeeded because he had a way with "ideas, [which] are the seeds of motion picture production—the most valuable commodity in Hollywood—Ideas for whole films, Ideas for episodes, Ideas for a single scene. . . . [In Hollywood] men get huge salaries for generating and sifting Ideas. Mr. Thalberg gets the hugest" (*AFI*, pp. 314–15).[6] Thalberg performed those tasks with mechanical efficiency. "For Irving Thalberg's brain is the camera which photographs dozens of scripts in a week and decides which of them, if any, shall be turned over to MGM's twenty-seven departments to be made into a moving picture. It is also the recording apparatus which converts the squealing friction of 2,200 erratic underlings into the more than normally coherent chatter of an MGM talkie" (*AFI*, 313). Converting the studio's "squealing friction" of idea after idea, of idea against idea, into the talkie's "coherent chatter" would be pointless if there were no good reason to expect audience approval. To complete the circuit of the conversion of ideas into talkie and talkie into money required that Thalberg turn his attention from the known talents of the studio—writers, directors, designers, and producers—toward the audience, the frequent and occasional moviegoers who were the customers for MGM's product.[7] And so, after a day in which Thalberg's efforts seemed to "follow no pattern whatsoever," Thalberg left the studio for his home and his own private Bijou: "The chatter of Mr. Thalberg's working day is replaced at night by an electric silence in which, pallid and intent, he performs the trick of dividing his brain into two parts. One part, reading a script, turns it into a moving picture; the other part watches this imaginary picture and, probably because it is so much like the conglomerate brain of fifty million other U.S. cinemaddicts, tells Mr. Thalberg with an astonishing degree of accuracy whether or not the picture is good" (*AFI*, 317–18). Hollywood *personified* MGM as Thalberg. Irving Thalberg merited that singular distinction because, according to *Fortune*, when he was alone, left to his own marvelous devices, the executive effectively *impersonated* the studio as a feedback mechanism that integrated production, distribution, and exhibition. He made the movie in half of his brain (the studio one) and distributed it to the other half (the exhibitor one), where he showed it to himself as a faithful representative of the mass audience.[8] Faithful in his way, that is: Thalberg's objective, MGM's objective, was not merely to anticipate an audience's judgment of what was good; it was to *form* an audience's sense of what was good—what *Fortune* calls its "taste." Universal Studio may profitably have dramatized the construction of patchwork monsters by egoistic obsessives who mix seething chemicals and ignite flashing electrodes; with the exception of Todd Browning's scandalous *Freaks*, greenlit by Thalberg in 1932, however, MGM would generally abstain from horrifying its susceptible public by putting monsters or freaks on the screen. *Fortune* imagines, however, that behind the screen, generating and gratifying the taste of the American middle class, is an uncanny hybrid of camera and projector, which is Thalberg's freakish brain, more efficient in producing its effects than any scientific gadget would be. This is no casual invention on *Fortune*'s part. Thalberg is *Fortune*'s version of "the structure of the mechanism which controls the public mind,"[9] as public relations pioneer Edward Bernays had called it in his 1928 provocation entitled *Propaganda*. When *Fortune* declares that Thalberg "represents a new psychological type of power, which must be distinguished if you would understand the age," it speaks on behalf of the corporate person whom Thalberg personifies; it creates "the public mind" on which it operates and from which it profits (*AFI*, p. 319).

After considering the challenges that confront public relations experts, Bernays formulates what would become the first principle of modern marketing: "To make customers is the new problem. One must understand not only his own business—the manufacture of a particular product—but also the structure, the personality, the prejudices, of a potentially universal public" (*P*, p. 65).[10] Bernays boasts that the expert public relations professional can solve business's new problem because he can manipulate "public opinion with a fair degree of accuracy by operating a certain mechanism" and thereby create a customer subject to his control (*P*, p. 48). Bernays is not forthcoming about what, exactly, that "mechanism" is.[11] Where Bernays is vague *Fortune* is vivid: Thalberg becomes the mechanism he operates in order to exercise a control that goes beyond the transient manipulation of public opinion. Instead he tests the audience's responsiveness by means of extensive previews and the acuteness of his own sensorium in order to exploit the power of motion pictures not only to appeal to an audience but to create customers by adjusting an audience's temperament, inducing people to take on new personalities that resonate with, even mimic, the MGM stars they see onscreen and in fan magazines.[12] *Fortune*'s conceit captures the truth that for Thalberg making good pictures meant delivering the kind of quality product that the public had come to expect from MGM because MGM had itself established the taste by which it was to be judged. *Fortune* calls that quality a "common denominator of goodness," which prevails in MGM films because Thalberg's "fine eye for contour and polish" assures that "the quality and texture of Miss Shearer's gowns for some drama of the haut monde can be compared with the quality and texture of the hippopotamuses that Mr. Thalberg hired for Tarzan" (*AFI*, p. 325). Although the comparison flirts with the comic, it is not promiscuous. *Fortune* would not make the same claim about Paramount. No one would dare compare the quality and texture of the furs draped on Marlene Dietrich in *Blonde Venus* with the quality and texture of Margaret Dumont's hippopatamine bosom in *Duck Soup*.

Fortune's adoption of the figure of a hierarchical organization composed and supervised by a self-reflexive corporate mind to represent MGM attests that the studio had successfully made the business magazine a customer (and publicist) for its brand, for the conceit recapitulates the bravura opening of *Grand Hotel*, MGM's banner production of 1932, to which the article respectfully refers.[13] *Grand Hotel* begins with an overhead pan of female telephone operators speedily connecting calls amid the chatter of their workplace (Figure 1.1).

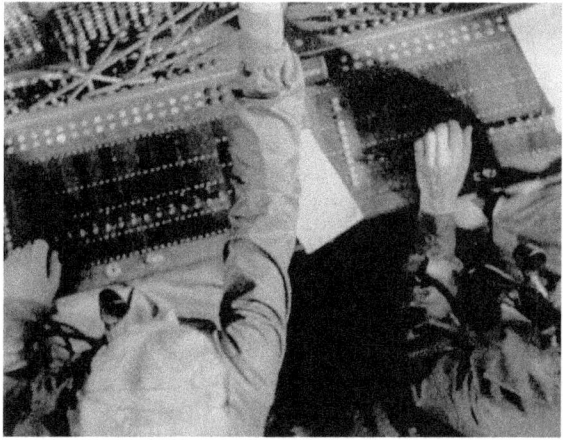

Figure 1.1

A cut connects the scene of the networkers to a montage sequence of the networked telephone users, who are individualized by faces and messages and by their isolation in telephone booths—a supposed privacy already penetrated by the camera and intermediated by montage, and that will soon be dissolved by a network of indirect connections (Figures 1.2 and 1.3). We move to a nearly eye-

Figure 1.2

Figure 1.3

Figure 1.4

Figure 1.5

level long shot of the bustling hotel lobby (Figure 1.4), which is followed by a medium close-up of Dr. Otternschlag (Figure 1.5), who, like Thalberg at MGM, visually *focuses* the noisy activity. He does this by being a disinterested observer, and by commenting, "People coming and going, but nothing ever happens." Then there is a cut to a majestic shot from the ceiling of the hotel, a perspective that could only be contrived by the sophisticated tools of a studio, composing in its ambit all the workers and guests, masters and servants, rooms and corridors into a reassuring pattern of concentric circles (Figure 1.6). The shot and space order people's apparently random comings and goings. This extraordinary shot not only represents the design that comprehends all the action that will ensue, but unlike any other shot from the Thalberg era, it reflexively refers to the camera that, transcending the action, makes it possible for that design to be recorded and projected.

The camera renders the Grand Hotel as a business that is more form than firm, an institution which in Paul Vinogradoff's words, "has an existence of its own—a life which transcends the lives of the individuals engaged in it." We should ask the same question of *Fortune* that Vinogradoff asks of the law when it faces the problem of a company that lives such a transcendent life: "How is [*Fortune*] to deal with such superindividual undertakings?" And we ought to give exactly the same answer for *Fortune* as Vinogradoff does for the law: "The usual expedient is to assimilate [such superindividual undertakings] to live persons. We assign to them a will, i.e., the faculty of taking resolves in the midst of conflicting motives; a governing brain and nerves, in the shape of institutions and agents; a capacity for the promotion and the defense of interests by holding property, performing acts in law, and exercising rights of action in courts."[14] As for the law, so for *Fortune*, which represents each company it profiles in person; we may attribute to it the mental traits and physical capacities of actual humans. I add "in the process" because no matter how legal realists repudiated the sterile debate between artificial entity theorists (those who saw the corporation as a construction of the state) and natural entity theorists (those who regarded the modern corporation as an organic development in the evolution of capitalism), and sought sheerly functional justifications for legal rights acquired by the modern corporation, no one—not even John Dewey in his famous call in 1926 to eliminate "the idea of personality until the concrete facts and relations involved have been faced and stated on their own account"—could forestall the attribution of human traits to the corporate person.[15] Dewey's sensible advice to abstain from indulging in the idea of personality could not prevent the popular perception that a description of a person with no human sympathies or any regard for community standards of behavior is a description of a person without a soul. That corporations feared the consequences of such a widespread perception was, as Roland Marchand demonstrates in his magisterial *Creating the Corporate Soul*, amply confirmed by increased investment in public relations aimed at rehabilitating their humanity *before* the market crash.[16] In 1937 Thurman Arnold would argue that any truly realistic account of the role that corporations play in American society would have to consider the anthropomorphism to which they have been subject, the apparently ineradicable tendency of people to personify groups of men and women working together as one gigantic human being. For Arnold, to acknowledge that there is what Dewey calls "social reality . . . back of or in corporate action" entails the recognition that most people must have an idea of personality in order to organize social facts into an intelligible pattern. *Fortune* did not need Arnold to inform it that a folklore that venerates the idea of personality and a business that capably manufactures new personalities adequate to whatever social facts might emerge are vital to the continued legitimacy of capitalism. *Fortune*'s essay is a self-conscious contribution

Figure 1.6

to that folklore, and self-reflexive to the degree that it celebrates the genius of a man who concocts personalities that people will admire and animates them in stories that people will believe—and who can do so not only because he knows what they want but, more important, because he sells to no one what he has not already sold to himself as the self-created customer of his wares. Just as *Fortune* establishes that Thalberg's executive undertaking on behalf of MGM is a making, it urges that his making is a marketing: Thalberg only oversees movies that can be marketed *as* MGM movies—movies packaged with "so high a sheen that it sometimes constitutes [the movies'] major box office appeal" (*AFI*, p. 325)—movies, that is, packaged the way that the Grand Hotel packages its customers, and the way that *Grand Hotel* lustrously packages its stars, and, not incidentally, the way that *Fortune*, resplendent with brilliant graphic art, handsomely packages its corporate executives.

Fortune's version of Thalberg spins the romantic myth of the myth maker himself. To understand the studio's double-minded "business and the art of producing moving pictures" is to acquire special insight into the value added to economic life by the modern corporate form. The ability of the corporation to *attract* capital did not matter most to *Fortune*; rather, it was the ability of the corporation to *make* capital, independently of the active involvement of its shareholders.[17] Thalberg does not triumph through the system or despite the system; he triumphs without a system: "He doesn't spend time making infinitesimal calculations because he is an artist, and an artist with a blank canvas to fill doesn't begin by marking off squares. He begins with instinct and checks his results with a meticulous sense of values. He is a stickler for results but he cannot be a stickler for plans. Even so with Irving Thalberg" (*AFI*, p. 315). Thalberg may not be constrained by a system, but he *is* given a canvas:

> MGM is neither one man nor a collection of men. It is a corporation. Whenever a motion picture becomes a work of art it is unquestionably due to men. But the moving pictures have been born and bred not of men but of corporations. Corporations have set up the easels, bought the pigments, arranged the views, and hired the potential artists. Until the artists emerge, at least, the corporation is bigger than the sum of its parts. Somehow, although our poets have not yet defined it for us, a corporation lives a life and finds a fate outside the lives and fates of its human constituents. (*AFI*, pp. 318–19)

The corporation supplies the easel, tools, and impersonal perspective that are the sufficient conditions for the emergence of the modern, managerial artist, whose artistry, answerable to "the great consistency which is not the policy of Thalberg or Mayer or Schenck but the policy of MGM," is to organize the parts into an intelligible, even beautiful representation of the corporate form, to create a corporate personality that will arouse the energies and shape the activities of "its human constituents." All would agree that those constituents include the shareholders and the salaried employees. Thalberg enlisted the customers who come to the theater to be entertained by MGM's moving pictures and to pay for the experience of MGM's marketing of itself—*happily* pay, because, as adherents of the MGM brand, they appreciate its elaboration as if they held stock in the studio.[18] As beneficiaries of MGM's "goodness," the customers may receive no financial reward for MGM's corporate success, but ideally they are induced to believe that fealty to the new brand world that Thalberg has wrought will buffer them from the shocks of reality, or, failing that, in the words of the pathetic Mr. Klingelein in *Grand Hotel*, provide "moments of happiness that compensate for all the misery of the past."

ii. Be a Clown

MGM's most potent early representation of its motion pictures as the medium for the construction of its public was the 1928 film *The Crowd*, an investment by Thalberg in the studio's reputation for commitment to quality before innovation.[19] In the sound era, but not of it, *The Crowd* has the look and feel of a conscious anachronism. MGM's cautious decision to maintain a watchful silence in the wake of Warners' 1927 *The Jazz Singer* doomed the picture to belatedness.[20] Nonetheless, *The Crowd*'s aggressively plastic visual style, which vividly renders the public and private technologies (the elevators, the revolving doors, the bus routes, the tunnel of love at Coney Island) with which the modern city's masses are organized, and its narrative, which efficiently typifies the plight of a person caught up in the modern urban crowd, combine to give the film an immediacy that *The Jazz Singer* can not rival. If the picture looks back toward a silent art made obsolete by Jolson's announcement, "You ain't heard nothin' yet," its plot nonetheless seems premonitory of a collective reversal of fate that *The Jazz Singer* could not imagine.

In retrospect *The Crowd*'s study of the downward spiral of a feckless hero, who falls from his seat in a gridded office of diligent clerks to the streets thronged by the downcast unemployed, seems to portend the crash and depression that would soon follow. The signs are inexact, however. The hardship of John Sims (James Murray) may appear to be a symptom of a social order that stringently rations success and provides no protection for those who fail, but *The Crowd* does not represent its protagonist's calamity as the effect of a general economic crisis. John may be, as his director, King Vidor, called him, "an ordinary fellow [who is] just one of the group," but he is no "everyman" representative of the multitude.²¹ John has a job. He then loses it. John is not sacked for economic reasons, however; he isn't sacked at all. He foolishly quits his job in despair of performing it after the death of his young daughter, who has been run down by a truck before his horrified eyes. To those watching *The Crowd* in 1928, John's subsequent depression would have been plausible as a response to a traumatic accident. Few would have interpreted the picture as prefiguring a financial crash; fewer yet would have acted on those signs by taking steps to protect themselves.

There were few economic forecasters who predicted the stock market crash of 1929. One year before the release of *The Crowd*, Halsey, Stuart, and Company, which already had a considerable financial stake in the motion picture industry, prepared an optimistic prospectus on the soundness of the motion picture industry as an investment for bond financing:

> The present is reassuring. But what of the future for this great industry which no less an authority than the director of the United States Bureau of the Budget has ranked as fourth in the whole country, while it is still scarcely thirty years of age? What are the prospects for further expansion? And what is the probability that its present popularity and patronage will be maintained?
>
> Every survey of the situation indicates promising conditions ahead. The fundamental human desire for entertainment, the urgent need for recreation and surcease from the dull routine of factory and office, is most certainly not going to diminish greatly in the near future. Moreover, the motion picture will doubtless increase in its ability to compensate for the drabness of modern industrial life.²²

The chief problem that *The Crowd* presents is how to assess the concluding scenes at the vaudeville show where the bereft John, his wife, and his son are momentarily reunited as a family in laughter and absorbed into a laughing audience. How are we to appreciate the value—moral, political, economic—placed on this transitory merger of atomized individuals into a contented collectivity? John's willingness to spend his meager paycheck on entertainment would seem to endorse the analysis of Halsey, Stuart. But what does it mean for him? Is his attendance at the show an imprudent distraction from the real problems that he and his family face? Or is his satisfaction of "the fundamental human desire for entertainment" a wise buy, fair compensation for his pain and suffering?

Those adult concerns are altogether alien to the young John, whom we first see seated alongside other boys on a village fence, the camera panning as each youth speculates on his future. John boasts that, born on the Fourth of July, he is, as his father has told him, destined to be a big man. The boast seems comical both because his ambition is so familiar—the intertitle compares his youthful recitations, piano playing, and choir singing to "Lincoln and Washington!"—and so unlikely: many dream but few fulfill those dreams. The disparity between John's idea of himself and the opportunities available to him is dramatized in the subsequent, harrowing scene where he learns of the death of his father, who was the authority on his prospects and, potentially, the guide to achieving them. That scene is quickly followed by a grown-up John's arrival in New York to occupy a desk among hundreds of identical desks in a large firm in a towering skyscraper, where he, like everyone else, enters endless numbers in a ledger (Figure 1.7).

Nonetheless, John does not abandon his sense of his own specialness, nor its basis in what Walter Lippmann in *Public Opinion* had called "stereotypes," the culturally imprinted categories that systematically form each person's experience.[23] If small-town America provides a roomy culture that enables the individual to choose from an inventory of traditional stereotypes in order to model his imaginary world, in the big city, where the world is already organized down to the most intimate details, the stereotypes have been abbreviated into slogans and clichés that invoke desired effects while occluding the enabling causes. *The Crowd* is the story of an individual who has no sense of narrative. John cannot stick with his plans because he is reflexively and comically responsive to the signs that surround him and stimulate him to action by offering him stereotypes with which to conform. When John, exhausted on his return from a first date with Mary (Eleanor Boardman), who is delivered to him by a revolving door, reads an ad on the subway that urges marriage, he summarily proposes. Later the newlyweds are mutually embarrassed when they read a magazine that refers to a baby, as if they sense that the ad expresses the thoughts of each of them before they can be voiced. Sure enough, a baby soon follows, delivered not by the stork but by *Collier's* magazine.

Figure 1.7

When taken to task by his wife about his lack of advancement, John resorts to his signature cliché: "Wait till my ship comes in." Mary bitterly compares her husband's stalled lot to that of his former crony, Bert (Bert Roach), a bachelor, who ascends to the position of manager. Apart from his bachelorhood, there are no clues to explain why Bert succeeds. We are probably meant to take John's explanation, "that Bert is always playing up to the bosses," as sour grapes. But there's no way to know, since we see nothing of Bert that distinguishes him from John or nothing that distinguishes John from anyone else in the office, except that John steals time from his ciphering to craft jazzy product names and jingles on stray bits of paper in response to "a newspaper advertisement that commands him to use his 'genius' to come up with an advertising slogan." Although this game is not, as Robert Lang suggests, "the film's answer to the problems it stirs up," it does come close enough to imply that the bureaucratic workday contains multitudes of utopian solicitations.[24] John does not keep his mind on his work, but then again there is no evidence that he *has* a mind except when he is distracted from that work. Seated at desk 137 he sports in the gaps that perforate even the most monotonous workday. We might be tempted to say that John's playing is bad for his career, except that he has no career. No one has: there is no evidence that the other salaried clerks are rewarded for conscientious performance of their mindless duties. *The Crowd* represents the business, not in light of its economic activity, but in terms of its principle of organization, which orders men in ranks and disciplines them to abstract tasks—a business not that much different from the entertainments at Coney Island, where John and Mary go on their first date. The amusement park is organized to direct crowds toward regimented pleasures and to sort out couples for the greater good of social reproduction.

Besides his "instinctive equipment" for crafting slogans, the only other distinctive trait that John has is his zeal to impress one and all by entertaining with sleights of hand or by playing the ukulele. But he's not very good at either tricking or picking. On one occasion, however, his fancied skills spontaneously combine. After strumming his ukulele on the beach, John brags to his wife, "I feel another slogan coming on."[25] Sure enough, out pops a slogan that he feels sure would win a contest sponsored by a household soap. In the one means-end narrative in the film that links an act with potential success, Mary challenges John to enter the slogan, "Sleight o' Hand, the Magic Cleaner," in the contest. He does. As if by magic their lives instantly brighten when he wins first prize: five hundred dollars. As his wife prudently performs her own computations of income and outlay, John returns to the

Figure 1.8

apartment laden with gaudy gifts for her and the two children. Swept away by John's exuberance, she joins him at the window of the apartment, where they display the merchandise to their children, who are playing across the street (Figure 1.8). The children respond to their parents' calls by running toward them. John sees the approach of a truck. Too late, he shouts to his young daughter to stay back. She runs in front of the truck, whose driver honks a warning—although an eyewitness who shared the point of view of the movie audience would surely attest that the truck swerves *toward* the running child, that it even seems to pursue her (Figure 1.9). The girl is struck, goes into a coma, and eventually dies. The accident unhinges John. The death crushes him.

Figure 1.9

Since his youth John has inhabited a world of stereotypes of success. Now that John has found himself actually fulfilling one he suffers catastrophe. In a dire irony the long prophesied arrival of his ship brings disaster in its wake. And "no wonder," writes Lippmann, "that any disturbance of the stereotypes seems like an attack upon the foundations of the universe. It is an attack upon the foundations of *our* universe, and where big things are at stake, we do not readily admit that there is any distinction between our universe and the universe (*PO*, pp. 63–64). Stripped of his fortifying stereotypes, John quickly descends into what can only be called subjectivity, for it is a mental state that is his and his alone. When, traumatized by his grief, John returns to his job, he cannot work. Vidor employs expressionist technique to render John's own mind on the screen: a whirl of ghostly numerals, which then dissolve into a flashback of the accident (Figure 1.10). In that distraction John finds himself as his own separate fantasy, different from those around him and, consequently, indifferent to the routine tasks before him. The narrative finally has come to invest in John's uniqueness as much as he had, but on the condition that his singularity is the sign of derangement.

Figure 1.10

John's daughter's death is doubtless the occasion for his shock and subsequent depression. But who is to blame for the accident? It is inviting to pin it on the protagonist. The option is so tempting that one of the best critics of the film comments that winning the advertising contest "results in a binge of consumption that gets the baby girl killed."[26] I doubt that any viewer watching *The Crowd* could have predicted that John's "binge of consumption" would be followed by a crash. Neither could John. Anyone, however, might have predicted that some children in the city would run heedlessly into the street and be hit by a moving vehicle. Such a prediction would rely not only on anecdotal knowledge about cities and children but on statistics kept by both the government and by insurance companies—neither of which would likely have recorded many, if any, instances of traffic accidents caused by "binges of consumption." It is natural, as David Hume would say, for the effect of the collision to induce a craving for a cause. Hume, however, would encourage us to look for the "cause" in the most contiguous object, which in this case is surely the truck motoring down the street, not the doll displayed in the apartment window. The one person best capable of predicting the crash (because it is imminent) and thus best capable of preventing the crash (because it is not determined) is, arguably, the truck driver. I say "arguably" because the truck driver's lawyer might attempt to argue that the man lost control of the truck because of defective steering or brakes, problems that are the responsibility of the trucking company. The company lawyer might see it another way and counter that implication of liability by accusing the father and mother of contributory negligence. The point here is not to reach a verdict. The point is to argue that the case could be argued. To assume that John is responsible (as in some sense *he* surely does) is to succumb to the temptation to fill in the cause-effect linkages that the film rigorously refuses to represent, relying instead on our stereotypes, moral and political, or, in this case, moral (the evil of consumption) masking as political (the subjection of citizens as consumers).

John offers no argument. After the accident the crazed man accosts a policeman, but only to urge that he quiet the crowd, not to charge the truck driver with reckless homicide. The policeman patrols the street, but he does not enforce the law. John does not think to make a claim for compensation or even to file a complaint. Apparently, among the various stereotypes that constitute John's world there is none called "insurance" or "law" that he would expect to provide him compensation or justice. And that's peculiar, for John is employed by an insurance company. That fact is revealed obliquely when, on the sad day of the company picnic cruise after John's resignation, a ship does come in, with a huge banner draped along its side announcing, in a panning shot, "Atlas Insurance Co. Fifteenth Anniversary Picnic" (Figure 1.11). This is a world, then, in which insurance exists not as a contextual probability, but as the actual product of the firm where John worked at the time of his daughter's accident: those were actuarial tables on John's desk.[27] John works for an insurance company but evidently he has no insurance of his own. Before the crash, immunized by stereotypes of singularity and good fortune, John never imagined that an accident could happen to him; after the crash, deranged and depressed, he cannot imagine a compensation for the loss that he has suffered.

Figure 1.11

The defect in imagination is key. John could not have predicted—and nor could the insurance company—that a street accident would befall him. But he might have imagined that some kind of accident would happen. In *New Deal Modernism*, an important study of the political imagination of modernist literature during the New Deal, Michael Szalay illuminates the aggregative calculus of "all forms of insurance." The "individual's imagined experience of susceptibility to 'risk,'" he explains, "serves as the principal means by which actuarial science situates persons within population groups. At its heart, risk identifies the frequency with which a given outcome will occur in a given target group. As a measure of probability, risk is not predictive for the individual per se." If it works well, insurance induces in the individual a contingent identification with a represented type (white male; twenty-nine; married with two children; low-income urban office worker), in order to situate that person within a population group made something more than a crowd because each person has the same imagined experience of susceptibility by means of the common denominator of the stereotype. Szalay adds that the meaning of an accident is its transgression of "an individual's imaginative capacities, his ability to predict or foresee future states."[28] John's daughter's accidental death "incapacitates" him for his specific task, which is manipulating numbers that predict future states, and for any task that involves projecting a future beyond the event of his daughter's death. I fence off "incapacitates" because the causal connection between the daughter's death and John's depression is no clearer than the liability of the truck driver for the child's death. Although she certainly shares in his grief for the death of their daughter, Mary does not become incapacitated. John's prosperous brothers-in-law treat him with contempt when he refuses the job that they have reluctantly offered him. We are not led to doubt that John suffers, but there is apparently no organic basis for his misery or his inability to hold down a job. That does not mean that the accident was not the cause of John's depression, however; and if it was or could be proved to have been, the trucking firm could be held liable for damages, not only for the death of the child but for the trauma that follows.

John's symptoms closely parallel those associated with what, in the second half of the nineteenth century, came to be called traumatic or, alternatively, accident neurosis, which became "epidemic" in Great Britain subsequent to the widespread introduction of railway travel. The epidemic spiked in response to the passage of two acts by Parliament: the 1846 Campbell Act, which "mandated compensation for families of victims killed in accidents caused by the negligence of a third party" and a later extension of the act "to include compensation for victims of railway accidents." Allan Young quotes a treatise by a railroad surgeon that claimed "the British public was fully aware of the provisions of the Campbell Act, and people involved in railway accidents were now unable to think of injuries in isolation from their monetary significance."[29] The "official doctrine in accident medicine after World War I [was that] it was not the accident, but actually the insurance itself that caused psychic injuries." That "disorder" would be mockingly called "compensation neurosis" by those convinced that were there no prospect of indemnification there would be no trauma: "A compensation neurosis is a state of mind, born out of fear, kept alive by avarice, stimulated by lawyers, and cured by a verdict," according to one physician, intent on proving that the trauma reported by so-called victims represented imaginary damage, which does not merit compensation.[30]

John has all the symptoms of trauma neurosis but one: he makes no claim for monetary compensation—neither for his daughter's death nor for his own psychological reaction. Although John's reserve does not protect him from his family's scorn, it would go a long way toward maintaining sympathy for him among a healthy, tax-paying audience. John's grief may be excessive, but the lack of a monetary claim is a sign of the sincerity of that grief. The audience need make no decision regarding the actual cause of John's illness because there is nothing at stake in determining that cause. Still, even though John claims no injury, his case does not entirely escape the widespread influence of the struggle for indemnification, which had resulted in its own curative narrative. Suppose we take the skeptics at their word and conclude that John's incapacitation is psychogenetic, and, therefore, as the train engineer shouts to the abandoned Princess Jeannette at the end of *Love Me Tonight* (Paramount, 1932), "that's not a railroad problem!" What makes trauma neurosis paradoxical is that even though the struggle for indemnity is not the conscious motive for John's malingering, given the case histories of other trauma neurotics, there is good reason to expect that indemnification would produce a cure. It does not matter whether the sufferer is sincere or not; compensation is designed to erase the psychic deficit that trauma records, even if that deficit cannot be ascribed to the actions of a specific agent, such as a truck driver, with legal responsibility for his actions.

That John did not imagine an accident could happen is a failure of the insurance business. Insurance may not be responsible for protecting John's daughter from harm, but it is responsible for convincing him that she is susceptible to harm—not for moral reasons but because insurance has the same objective that any other business, including MGM, has: to create customers. The indemnification that the insured person contracts to receive for an accident is not exactly exchange value for the loss of an irreplaceable individual arm, leg, or daughter; it is compensation for the individual's willingness to imagine his vulnerability as part of a population, a willingness signified by his investment of a premium that will be paid in the future should an accident happen or when death does occur.[31] The settlement of the claim represents the appropriate cost (appropriate because agreed upon by the entire population of those who have taken out insurance) of restoring the injured individual to the crowd and the predictable, commonly denominated future. Thus, *The Crowd* argues that motion pictures succeed at doing what insurance fails to accomplish.

Betrayed by stereotypes of singularity, after his calamity John loses his place in the crowd and therefore his sense of a future. When John refuses the job his brothers-in-law hand out, Mary angrily condemns him with the great American stereotypes for failure: "You bluff, you quitter." She slaps him, and sends him away with the curse, "I'd almost rather see you dead." He shambles to a nearby railroad bridge and almost takes her up on the suggestion. Unable to jump and warmed by the love and admiration of his son, John instead finishes his wife's series of accusations—"bluff" and "quitter"—with "clown." Though he is shut out of job after job, John's ability to juggle finally lands him work costumed as a clown and sandwiched between signs to which he attracts attention by his sleight of hand. Of course it is ironic that the John who had earlier mocked a sign-toting clown has become one himself. The irony is not derisive, however. John had jeered that the man's "father probably thought that he would be president." As had John's. But that stereotype of ambition has been demolished. No one watching the film can cling to the fantasy that with a break here or there John could have become president—or even office manager. Neither the size nor the complexity of the firm is an indicator of internal mobility. As *Fortune* will pithily observe in its 1934 profile of the Metropolitan Insurance Company, "the biggest company in the world is a company of pigeonholed men."[32]

Except for the missing paycheck, then, the loss of a desk job at the insurance company hardly counts as a disaster. If there were unemployment insurance to tide him over, or medical insurance to afford him help, John might be better off. There is neither unemployment insurance nor medical insurance in the pre–New Deal world of *The Crowd* and its audience, but because this is MGM's world, John is better off anyway. Later, in the depths of his own private depression, a chastened John discovers what so many subsequent MGM characters would learn, that no matter how desperate you are and no matter how far your fall, there is a clown to catch you. In his new job John does not write advertisements, he has become one: a juggling clown slapped between sandwich boards, which read, "I Am Always Happy Because I Eat at Schneider's Grill" (Figure 1.12).

Figure 1.12

It is unlikely that anyone would believe in the truth of that slogan. The difference between an "I" who might be John and the "I" who is a stereotypical clown is that the stereotype protects us and him against the threat that verifiable facts and plausible narratives present to those beliefs that make us and him safe and happy.[33] By entertaining the public, John engages his fellows in the collaborative act of creating what business consultants would now call "a brand identity" intended to become integral to the dining experience. John will happily keep his job until Schneider's changes its marketing strategy. Even should that occur, however, the MGM brand promises that John will always be able to find a job because there will always be work for a clown, as long as people want and need to be entertained.

At the end of the day John's reward for being entertaining is to be entertained—at least in the version of the film that has come down to us. In his autobiography King Vidor recalls that "when the picture was finished, we had a difficult time deciding on an ending. We made seven of them, and tried out each one at sneak previews in small towns. Finally the picture was sent out with two endings, so that the exhibitor could take his choice." The majority of exhibitors selected "the realistic ending [which] showed Murray [John] with his wife and child sitting in the audience of a variety theater, laughing at a clown. . . . A perfectly natural finish for the story of Mr. Anyman" (*TIS*, pp. 152–53).[34] Vidor's "we" is not an example of false modesty. Raymond Durgnat, who is committed to an auteurist account of Vidor's work and career, glosses the plural pronoun here as "MGM, and Vidor too." Although Durgnat might have conjoined "Thalberg" with "Vidor," it is clear that when Vidor speaks as "we" he utters a corporate plural on behalf of the studio.[35] However the decision to allow the exhibitors to choose between two endings was reached, the process cannily enlisted them as collaborators in the corporate judgment of what was right for this MGM picture. Of the two versions eventually distributed, the one that, surprisingly, lost out included a happy ending in which John managed to turn his talent for a slogan into a successful advertising career. Consecration of advertising as a redemptive option would have transformed it from the medium of a utopian solicitation into a medium for actually fulfilling the fantasies it promotes.[36] MGM's *The Crowd* is interested in advertising as a mode of entertainment and, more globally, in entertainment as the preferred compensation for past accidents as well as the best social insurance against accidents in the future. Unlike Atlas Insurance, an unreliable place to lodge one's hopes for the future, the theater compensates people for the drabness of their lives by giving them the feeling of safety.

For MGM, the audience at a show, preferably an MGM motion picture show, is the telos of the crowd and its problems. Lippmann would certainly agree. In his dark sequel to *Public Opinion*, *The Phantom Public*, which appeared the year before the release of *The Crowd*, he equates people who vote at periodic elections with an audience at a staged melodrama and identifies the cinema, rather than the theater, as the most powerful medium for controlling an audience—an audience whose wishes are passively fulfilled as they are "reeled off on the screen."[37] Although Lippmann recognizes the cinema as a potent instrument for forming public opinion, he ultimately turns to Washington, not Hollywood, to find the initiative to use that technology effectively. The remedy for a society in which the "governing forces are so imperfectly recorded," he argues, must be "a social organization based on a system of analysis and record," what he calls a "machinery of knowledge"—"intelligence bureaus" where experts can do "intelligence work" (*PO*, pp. 239–49). By 1932, writing during the trough of the Depression, on the eve of the New Deal, and from a position well on Lippmann's left, Reinhold Niebuhr could see no progress on the intelligence front. He decried the "lack of social intelligence in all of our economic groups," and gloomily concluded that "power is never checked by the voluntary action of those who hold it but only by raising power against it. . . . In our situation the powerful groups are not intelligent enough to yield under pressure, and the laborers are not intelligent enough to provide the pressure." The lack of social intelligence by both sides is ominous. "Our social danger is increased," Niebuhr warns, "by the absence of any deeply rooted cultural traditions among us. All human societies are a compound of political relationships and cultural traditions. Of the two the latter are the tougher and serve to hold a society together long after political and economic relations may have been reduced to chaos by the inexorable march of events.... [But now] we are held together mechanically by our means of production and communication."[38] Niebuhr's gloomy analysis takes a strange turn. Why derogate the binding force of the "means of production and communication" unless fastidious adherence to the organic metaphor counts more than actually preventing "chaos"?

As *The Crowd* shows and as MGM movies will persistently argue, people *are* held together by popular culture, which contributes to the prevention of chaos by "mechanically" organizing the crowd into an audience and compensating it for a life otherwise drab except for accidents that frighten or disable. *The Crowd* represents the theater as having the capacity to relieve the care of the impoverished and the forlorn, who spend their dimes and quarters to watch comedians performing pratfalls. Similarly, while watching MGM movies in which some mishap occurs, the individual may imagine that he or she is susceptible to risk but nevertheless experiences that act of imagination as a member of an audience having the same experience. The key to this imaginary solution to an imaginary problem is the term *experience*. Clinical evidence suggests that the trauma neurosis that follows from losing a child or from any other serious accident is not caused by some feature of the accident itself but is an overdetermined effect of the "accident experience," which in *The Crowd* includes the exhilaration of displaying the goods, the shock of the impact of the truck, the oppression of the noise of the crowd, and the desperate feeling of impotence at the bedside of a dying child. Attendance at the theater cures trauma by canceling the individual experience of victimage with a social experience of integration. People spend tangible coins for intangible compensation, and everyone is better off for the exchange. It does not matter whether or not the trauma is authentic, for if it can be relieved by indemnification, the theater will do the job that Atlas Insurance will not do. Recall Halsey, Stuart's prediction that "the motion picture will doubtless increase in its ability to compensate for the drabness of modern industrial life." MGM represents itself as a mainstay of the corporate liberal project newly undertaken by leading corporations, which, as Jeffrey R. Lustig writes, "were no longer simply tools of production or means for amassing profits. They were charged with maintaining social health and cohesion, and said to be responsible for 'that habitual sense of solidarity which is the foundation stone of democracy.'" They had fashioned themselves as "'vital institutions' of social life" that contribute to what Herbert Croly regarded as the fulfillment of the promise of American life: the individual's being provided with "room for 'distinction' within an organized world."[39]

The curative narrative of indemnification is carefully crafted. In a dissolve from a reconciled John and Mary laughing together after dancing to a popular tune playing on their Victrola, we see them still laughing while seated with their son in the audience of "a show." Then there is a cut to a shot of two clowns giving each other body blows on stage. This is followed by a cut back to the audience, where John solicitously slaps the back of the stranger in the seat beside him to stop a coughing fit brought on by his convulsive laughter. John's day labor of juggling for the crowds has lifted his spirits and given him the cash and confidence to try to win Mary back. The music restores them as a couple; the show returns them as a family to society. The violence that the clowns perform dramatically evokes and, by typifying, comically distances the humiliating slap that John had received from his wife that morning. John's equally strong slapping of his coughing neighbor echoes his wife's blow. It is the kind of blow that John might want to return to Mary or give to Bert (whom the stranger resembles); but, mediated and typified by "the show," the slap can be *communicated* to a stranger. When John had first entered the job market his fate was foretold by the portentous intertitle: "We do not know how big the crowd is, and what opposition it is . . . until we get out of step with it." The double rhyming of the slap that had abjected John brings him back into step with the crowd. John loses his debilitating depression according to a thoroughly behaviorist psychology that repudiates inwardness in favor of the recovery of a social self.

To the scriptural question urgently revived by the modern crowd, "Who is my neighbor?" *The Crowd* answers, "The person sitting next to you at the show." The demonstration is completed when John, prompted by his wife's discovery in the playbill of his "Sleight o' Hand" jingle, illustrated with a juggling clown, proudly shows the advertisement to his new neighbor. In response to the man's question, John nods and points to himself (Figure 1.13). It may be that John is taking credit for being a successful writer of ad copy; it may be he is taking credit for being a clown. Either way, he is not endorsing the product; he is exploiting his implication in the brand in order to seek what in fact he acquires, an endorsement of himself. The theater, then, provides the institutional space and the facilitating conventions for the interactive, social performance of self. But, as the camera demonstrates, pulling back sublimely to reveal

Figure 1.13

row upon endless row of people who are always happy because they clown at the show, only the motion picture can comprehensively represent that individual act as enabled by the organization of individuals in a place of entertainment where no harm can come. Richard Maltby could have been writing about the last scene of *The Crowd* when, in *Harmless Entertainment*, he argues that in Hollywood motion pictures "the camera's presentation encourages the viewer's participatory identification with the performances it presents at the same time that it demonstrably reveals itself as artificial."[40] *The Crowd* extends the analysis, however, by manifestly identifying entertainment with an organizational principle, the telescoping of "family, community and society—three different scales of organism"—into a theatrical topography that unfolds "a longed-for unity of microcosm and macrocosm."[41] Finally, the motion picture forcefully associates that principle of unification with the particular corporate organization that is responsible for the artifice that entertains an audience that sees itself represented on a screen aggressively claimed by the MGM trademark.

iii. Be a Gangster: MGM and Warners—The First New Deal

The Crowd represents a stateless world. Except for the brief appearance of a useless policeman, nothing suggests that in New York or any other American city there is a government that might offer security against traumatic public events or remedy systemic social dysfunction. The Crash of 1929 and the ensuing depression, of course, prompted ideas of radical social and political change among both the populace and the elite. The year of *Fortune*'s profile of Thalberg, 1932, was also a year of revolutions: a silent "corporate revolution" was announced in the pages of Adolf A. Berle and Gardiner Means's study *The Modern Corporation and Private Property*; another, the uprising of the bonus marchers camped on the Anacostia in Washington, D.C., was averted; and yet a third was under production for the screen as MGM's dream of what Franklin Delano Roosevelt's election might lead to: *Gabriel over the White House*.[42]

Walter Wanger, having recently been signed by Thalberg as a producer at MGM, began work with the script for *Gabriel over the White House* in January 1933 under the patronage of William Randolph Hearst, whose Cosmopolitan Productions company had been affiliated with MGM since the founding of the studio, and who stepped in with financing when Thalberg had a heart attack at Christmastime.[43] With the connivance of Loew's chief, Nick Schenck, Mayer soon began reorganizing the studio into a unit production system that would displace Thalberg from his position of centralized authority. Thalberg wrote to Schenck in protest, but he had neither the power to deter him nor the energy to stay and fight. On the advice of his doctors, in early March Thalberg left for a European vacation. Consequently, there was little studio supervision of the production of *Gabriel*.[44] Hearst, who had aspirations to influence the new president's policies, rewrote some of the political scenes in line with his recent editorials.[45] When Mayer did finally see a print, he was aghast at its apparent mockery of his friend in the White House, the very lame duck, Herbert Hoover. Initially, Mayer ordered the print to be locked up; he then sent it to Will Hays, who insisted on retakes, some of which responded to Mayer's concerns, some of which responded to objections from the White House.[46] Wanger had to abandon his plan of coordinating a four-city opening on inauguration day and the picture did not open until late in March.[47]

Gabriel over the White House, which celebrates a president who seizes dictatorial powers in order to confront domestic and international crises, was the most ardently fascist motion picture released by any Hollywood studio during the 1930s. That it escaped widespread denunciation attests to the appeal of aspects of the fascist agenda for both conservatives and liberals desperate to escape from the social and economic crisis that the Depression had brought about.[48] That Hearst would espouse dictatorial measures would have surprised no one: as the "chief" of a privately held corporation that gave him unrestricted access to the front page of many of the nation's most influential newspapers, he did not need to practice subterfuge. It may count as a surprise that no representative of FDR ever objected to his association with the dictatorial rule of the president, Judd Hammond. FDR may have abstained because the picture cleverly seized every rhetorical and iconic opportunity to associate Hammond's politics with the precedent of Lincoln, but more likely it was because Hammond's militant rhetoric was in accord with FDR's own exhortations during the 1932 campaign, such as his famous radio-address reference on April 17 to "the forgotten man at the base of the economic pyramid" and his invocation of "the infantry of our forgotten army," as if a corps of men stood ready to be mobilized to whatever ends the chief executive should deem appropriate. Mayer's complicity was another matter. *Gabriel over the White House* made it to the screen, not only because of Hearst's clout and FDR's approval, but also because the studio head saw, when he and Hays stripped away the most provocative segments of the film, the congruence of *Gabriel*'s authoritarian dream state with the kind of corporate community that MGM imagined itself to be.

Gabriel's vision of the state's wise aggrandizement of civil society under authoritarian rule also anticipates a non-MGM production, Ronald Coase's 1937 essay "The Nature of the Firm," an adjustment of classical liberal economic theory that, unlike Hearst's editorials, remains influential. *Gabriel* and "The Nature of the Firm" are mutually illuminating texts, for although neither mentions the word *corporation*, each adumbrates a justification for the predominance of the corporate form in a liberal economy. Coase begins by restating the principle that sustains classical economic thought: "The normal economic system works itself. It is under no central control, it needs no central survey. Over the whole range of human activity and human need, supply is adjusted to demand, and production to consumption, by a process that is automatic, elastic and responsive." That's true in theory, Coase comments, but it is also true that in the real world there is such a thing as economic planning.[49] Coase quotes the colorful statement of surprise by a colleague who is committed to orthodox laissez-faire theory, saying that "we find 'islands of conscious power in this ocean of unconscious co-operation like lumps of butter coagulating in a pail of buttermilk'" ("NF," p. 387).[50] Endeavoring to account for those lumps, Coase defines the firm as an organization that allocates the "co-ordinating function" of the market to the entrepreneur who does the planning that such co-ordination requires. Yet it is one thing to acknowledge the empirical fact that organization exists as a site where planning occurs; it is another thing altogether to explain why there should be a firm in *the first place*, for if, as the laissez-faire economist believes, "production is regulated by price movements, production could be carried on without any organization at all."

From that radical premise Coase deduces that "the distinguishing mark of the firm is the supersession of the price mechanism." This supersession makes sense because "the operation of a market costs something. . . . By forming an organization and allowing some authority (an 'entrepreneur') to direct the resources, certain marketing costs are saved. The entrepreneur has to carry out his function at less cost, taking into account the fact that he may get factors of production at a lower price than the market transactions which he supersedes, because it is always possible to revert to the open market if he fails to do this" ("NF," p. 40). Coase solves his initial problem by deducing that firms are organized in order that entrepreneurs may save money by coordinating transactions more cheaply than the open market, which enables them to diminish uncertainty over the future by making long-term contracts with purchasers of their products or services.[51] Improving the efficiency of the market is a reason both necessary and sufficient for firms to exist.

"What follows?" Coase queries. And then, reversing his initial question as to the reason for the existence of firms, he asks, "Why, if by organizing one can eliminate certain costs and in fact reduce the cost of production, are there any market transactions at all? Why is not all production carried on by one big firm?" As answers, he offers three contingencies: (1) increasing costs of organizing additional transactions within the firm may occur; (2) the entrepreneur "fails to place the factors of production in the uses where their value is greatest"; (3) the "supply price of one or more of the factors of production may rise, because the 'other advantages' of a small firm are greater than those of a large firm" ("NF," pp. 42–43). Apart from those contingencies, however, there is no good reason, "for all those areas in the economic system where the direction of resources was not dependent directly on the price mechanism could be organized within one firm" ("NF," p. 45). They are thus forcibly organized in *Gabriel*, but with the corporate supplement to the laissez-faire theory of the firm: the concrete embodiment of that organization in the charismatic figure of the leader, whose authoritative voice, thanks to the radio, fills the air, expanding the reach of the firm called "the state" beyond all merely physical limits.

In Coase's rationalization of the firm, if cost savings were to vanish there would be no good reason not to dissolve the firm and revert to the baseline normalcy of the market system. In the real world, of course, that rarely happens. For one thing, the choices are seldom so stark: the entrepreneur's claim on the future gives him a considerable temporal cushion between a plan, its implementation, and the playing out of all its economic consequences. For another, once given authority, as Alfred D. Chandler argues, it will be in the interest of the manager to exercise that authority to the end of preserving his own position, not to maximize profit.[52] And who is to stop him—especially if, like Judd Hammond, he has tanks? The passive constructions that Coase employs—"authority is allowed to an entrepreneur"; a "system of relationships . . . comes into existence"—are striking, for they elide crucial bits of information that would make sense of his story. What exactly is "conscious power" and to whom does it actually belong? Is it lodged in the entrepreneur or in the person or group that has the authority to "allow" authority to an entrepreneur? How did, does, and should that allowance occur?

Gabriel, I shall try to show, supplies answers to those questions, and it appeared five years before Coase's essay. But before turning to the motion picture, it is important to observe that Coase's model of the firm is distinguished, not only by its attention to the issue of transaction costs, but also by its interest in what, since the work of A. O. Hirschman, we have come to call "exit strategies." In *Exit, Voice, and Loyalty*, Hirschman contends that organizations may be classified according to how they enable a customer or employee to respond to a perceived decline in the quality of a product. There are two fundamental types: those organizations that encourage exit and those that respond to voice. Exit belongs to the economic realm because "the customer who, dissatisfied with the product of one firm, shifts to that of another, uses the market to defend his welfare or to improve his position; and he also sets in motion market forces which may induce recovery on the part of the firm that has declined in comparative performance."[53] The same option is, theoretically, open to the employee who cannot in good conscience carry out an executive's order because he believes it departs from the purpose of the organization: he can look for a job elsewhere. Intelligent firms make exit relatively easy, if not desirable, because they recognize that such departures provide information that enables firms to recuperate from an otherwise unperceived deterioration of quality or performance.

If exiting is a clean datum—he stopped buying; she left her job—voice, according to Hirschman, "is a far more 'messy' concept because it can be graduated all the way from faint grumbling to violent protest; it implies articulation of one's critical opinions rather than a private 'secret' vote in the anonymity of the supermarket; and finally, it is direct and straightforward rather than roundabout. Voice is political action par excellence." For the firm, voice—a customer's angry letter or a line manager's memo objecting to a change in materials, for example—can be anything from an irritant to a disruption. In general, economic organizations do not prize dissent. The classic example of intolerance is Henry Ford's firing of managers who proposed rationalizing accounting procedures at Ford Motor Company. The promise of cost-cutting was less important to Ford than the perceived challenge to his authority. In the political realm, however, where the vocal negotiation of positions is the norm and where a member is expected to speak up before he opts out, "exit has often been branded as *criminal*, for it has been labeled desertion, defection, and treason" (*EVL*, pp. 16–17).

Hirschman's idea of the "exit" nicely fits Coase's model of the firm, insofar as customer dissatisfaction has to do with costs. For Coase the firm itself is formed as the result of the entrepreneur's exit from the open market in response to the perception that the costs of transactions exceed their utility. To voice objections to the operations of the open market would be futile because said market functions only insofar as it is not subject to the whim or will of any individual agent. The firm's internalization of transactions is both an organization and an individuation: after it economizes on transactions it will be distinct from other firms in the same industry and deal directly with those firms in a more specialized and predictable market, where the relative costs of competition or cooperation can be more exactly calculated. The firm's individuality is wholly contingent on the entrepreneur's success in controlling cost. Just as the customer's appropriate response to a newfound disparity between price and quality would be to exit and seek an alternative vendor, so, eventually, the appropriate response of the entrepreneur coordinating a firm that fails to achieve lower transaction costs would be to engineer the "exit" by the firm of its own individual existence and its return to the open market. For a consumer to voice dissent over matters of quality would make no sense to the manager of a firm unless the drop in "quality" at issue could be translated into revenue.[54] "If the market in which the firm sells is highly competitive, that is, full of highly knowledgeable buyers," the recuperative mechanism will fail, and "the firm will be competed out of business in short order" (*EVL*, p. 25).

Although *Gabriel over the White House* has all the trappings of a political film, the narrative soon establishes that it has a thoroughly economic orientation. The picture begins with documentary footage of parades and cheering crowds in Washington, D.C., at the inauguration of the new president Judson Hammond (Walter Huston). Even if the election has not been bought, the newly sworn-in president has. At the inaugural ball he boasts that he is a creature of the party and jovially acknowledges his debts to his guests, who half-jokingly promise to collect. Hammond soon settles into laissez-faire cronyism and blithe indifference to the Depression and the army of the unemployed (a slightly displaced version of the march of the Bonus Army, which occupied the banks of the Anacostia in the summer of 1932 until they were dispersed at Hoover's order by U.S. Army troops under the leadership of General Douglas MacArthur), which is marching on Washington to get relief. In a brilliant contrivance, the turbulent outside enters the president's office by way of a radio news announcement, which reports on the approach of the unemployed as the oblivious Hammond, on hands and knees, plays with his nephew, who searches for candy that the president has hidden in his office. The scene (which will be recapitulated without the radio voiceover in the 1938 movie *Boys Town*) dramatizes Hammond's infantile insensibility to a political movement that, hungry for work and for justice, menaces the game of greed he plays with his cronies.

As in *The Crowd* and a number of MGM films of the 1930s and 1940s (*The Nuisance, Captains Courageous, Boys Town, The Wizard of Oz, Random Harvest,* and *Madame Curie*), an accident precipitates a drastic change in the direction of the narrative. Here an automobile crash with Hammond at the wheel that leaves him in a coma allegorically represents both the crash of the economy brought on by reckless presidential indifference and the massive change that must occur for the government effectively to engage the challenges—both domestic and international—that are facing it. Like the truck crash in *The Crowd*, this accident signals that the narrative will be bereft of any plausible causal account of how a transformation could occur in the normal operations of the state. At the brink of death Hammond is visited by a mysterious, curtain-stirring light, which revives him as a new man: somber, decisive, incorruptible, even visionary. Otherwise, the appearance of light—named Gabriel, the angel of the Annunciation, by Hammond's assistant—illuminates nothing; it is an image of the enigma of the agency that effects transition from market to firm. No accident, the epiphany, however, is saturated with intentionality: it is purpose conferring purpose without any clear motivation for doing so. The explanation of how, in Coase's terms, "power" takes on "consciousness" in the firm is neatly represented by the momentous visitation in *Gabriel*; for the visitant is the apparition of the fabled invisible hand of classical economics, which arouses the comatose president as the chosen instrument for the repair of the price mechanism. *Gabriel* visualizes classical economics as a providential theology whose telos is the *incorporation* of a strong leader and, through his agency, of the state.

The transformed president suspends the give and take of politics by decreeing extreme measures. When the disgruntled cabinet members conspire for Hammond's impeachment, the president's personal secretary appears to distribute resignation letters. Each member signs, thereby exiting the government and the narrative. The renovated president sees dangers where earlier he had not even noticed issues. Three command his attention: the "soldiers in the army of the unemployed," who are marching on Washington; the failure of the nations of the world to pay their war debts to the United States; and the pervasive menace of the gangsters led by the immigrant Nick Diamond. The first two threats are long-term consequences of World War I; the last is the result of what Hammond calls "the cesspool known as the Eighteenth Amendment." Prohibition, he intones to Congress, has "fostered an evil force, the greatest enemy of law and order the country has ever known, the racketeer, a malignant cancer eating up the health of the American people." Each of those dangers threatens the survival of the nation, now conceived as identical to the state as it is embodied in the figure of President Hammond.

After the gangsters kill John Bronson, the leader of the unemployed, for refusing their "protection," Hammond travels to Baltimore to meet with the marchers, whom he wins over by promising to enlist them in "the army of construction," where they will be subject to military discipline and given productive jobs to perform until the economy rights itself and they can be "rotated back into industry." When Hammond meets legislative resistance to his request for "funds for the rehabilitation of America," he calls a special meeting of Congress, declares a state of national emergency and assumes dictatorial powers. Even though a compliant Congress has repealed the Eighteenth Amendment, Hammond imperiously summons the gangster Diamond to the White House. When Hammond tells the jauntily turned-out Diamond that he wants to talk about the bootlegging business, the gangster amiably jokes, "I guess you and I are the only Americans who have any business left." The force of the allegorical concept is so strong at this point that despite the fact that there must be other businesses in Baltimore, New York, and even in far-off Los Angeles, the racketeer's claim seems literally true. There are only two businesses left in America, and the chief executives of both are facing off in the West Wing. In his defense Diamond claims, "I am where I am today because of public approval." True or not, such a claim could be expected to have no effect on Hammond, who was democratically elected, but who is now formidable not because of public support but because he has control of the levers of power available to the leader of a corporate state.

Diamond sophistically asserts his legitimacy with the relativistic trope, "On my trucks it's bootleg. On a silver tray on Park Avenue, it's hospitality." A liberal in spats, Diamond has offered Hammond a way out of the impasse that would economize on the cost of law enforcement, a maneuver which had recently been prescribed by Thurman Arnold, who, in the *Yale Law Journal*, had argued that the problem of cleaning up the gangs is merely a problem of "social adjustment," and that "we could by one stroke of the pen socially adjust thousands of persons by calling bootleggers by the term 'liquor merchants.'"[55] Hammond grasps the principle but alters the application. There will be no new deal with Diamond. Why bother? With one stroke of the pen the president can socially adjust thousands of persons by calling *government employees* by the term "liquor merchants." Hammond explains, "I had hoped we could make a bargain, but you seem to have other ideas. The bootlegging business involves a sum of money aggregating several hundred thousand dollars. The American people need that money. I warn you, Diamond, the American government is going to muscle in on your racket." As head of a rival "racket," Hammond warns that the state intends to enforce its monopoly on the means of violence in order to achieve a similar monopoly on the liquor business. No sooner does Diamond leave than Hammond establishes state liquor stores in every city in America. Diamond retaliates by bombing one of the stores, provoking Hammond to declare, "Nick Diamond has declared war on the United States." A posse in tanks blows up the gang's headquarters, arrests Diamond and his henchmen, tries them, and speedily executes them. Gangsters gone. Prohibition gone. The government has eliminated costly rackets by turning the nation's citizens into the state's customers.

In taking on the ambassadors of Europe, Asia, and South America, whose aggregated wealth, accumulated at the expense of the American people, is as much of an offense as the criminal proceeds of the gangsters, Hammond follows the inexorable logic of the firm, which has no policy that can be debated, only the single objective of eliminating costly market transactions. In a replay of the famous bombing tests conducted under the leadership of Billy Mitchell in 1921, Hammond invites the gaggle of ambassadors to watch a display of American airpower, staged to extort debt repayment from their governments. By cutting financial entanglements and retrieving alienated wealth to recapitalize the state, Hammond ensures that America Inc. is the only game in the world. It's a great racket.

For the laissez-faire economist, the firm remedies the costliness of the market by serving as a device for the internalization of commercial transactions and for engineering the supersession of politics—that is, the costly contest over the right to determine the good and over the best way to distribute goods. As Mussolini, a favorite of Hearst and Henry Luce, would later declare in *The Corporate State*, fascism is the realization of a corporate state imagined as capable of economizing on the friction of political opposition and of preventing misplaced investments by incorporating all external transactions within its domain.[56] The signal difference between cost-effective fascism as Mussolini describes it and the government foreseen by the classical economist is that the economist refuses to imagine any government at all. *Gabriel* takes Mussolini's side, as, not for the last time, MGM veers into an absolutist reverie that concocts a world in which it could prosper without competition.

The corporate state has purged its gangsters. But why gangsters, rather than, say, longshoremen or bankers? And what gangsters did MGM have in mind? By January 1933 Al Capone was in Alcatraz. FDR had promised to seek the repeal of the Volstead Act as soon as he took office. If the representation of the menace that gangster Nick Diamond presents is an exaggeration, it is not a singular exaggeration. Sounding a good deal like Hammond, Walter Lippmann declared, "The people know that they are beset by organized criminals who operate on a scale which has horrified the civilized world. They know that unless they master this evil it will master them. They know that a generation of city children is growing up in an atmosphere where racketeering has become an established institution."[57] Part of the danger was the difficulty of distinguishing legitimate businesses from criminal enterprises—an ambiguity concentrated in the slippery word *racket*. Legally speaking, rackets were and are organizations that achieve their commercial objectives by force or the threat of force—that is, extortion. Usually, *rackets* was a synonym for organized crime, which characteristically compelled legitimate businesses to pay "protection" money to ward off the harm that they threatened. *Threat of force* covers a lot of territory, however; and *racket* was often applied to any business that exploited its market power to intimidate its rivals in order to secure an unfair advantage in the market. More loosely yet, to call a business a racket was to slur any unusually prosperous business that could be suspected of having some kind of edge. The sliding signification of racket, then, not only expressed an epistemic fuzziness in the legal concept of extortion that was exploited by gangsters and prosecutors alike (especially after the passage of the RICO law),[58] but also enacted the ease of transit from criminal organizations to the corporations, whose "growth, consolidation, and organization" the rackets emulated. As David E. Ruth has demonstrated, the comparison between gangs and big business was common in the late 1920s and early 1930s. For example, *The Saturday Review* wrote in 1933, "Crime, like industry, if it is to flourish on a large scale, must depend on the perfectly coordinated efforts of sundry groups of specialists, each group under central direction, knowing just when and where and how it is to function."[59] Such a description of organizational efficiency tightly fits the gangs depicted in Warners' cycles of gangster films of the 1930s, including *Scarface* and *Little Caesar*—films that feature sociopathic protagonists, who conceive plans, assign duties, accomplish objectives, and struggle to climb to the top of the organizational ladder.[60]

It would be unwise to take Warners' gangster films as accurate representations of contemporary urban criminal organizations—and certainly not in Chicago, gangster capital of America. As Mark H. Haller has shown, Hollywood's favorite prohibition gang, the Capone gang of Cicero, Illinois, was not organized as a centralized hierarchy but as an array of illegal enterprises—gambling, bookmaking, dog racing, beer distribution, auto and truck dealing—under the supervision of four senior partners, Al Capone, his brother Ralph, Jack Guzik, and Frank Nitti, who coordinated their operations and shared in the profits.[61] It was the Capone gang in name only and that because Capone was so successful in promoting himself. The gang itself was a laterally complicated organization. Its structure was more fraternal and territorial than the patriarchal and arboreal pattern featured in charts of most corporate organizations. As the reach of the gangs systematically extended during Prohibition, that relatively inefficient partnership-based form of organization was retained out of what Haller describes as a temperamental preference for the friction and risk involved in the continual deal making that the form demanded. Transactions were not understood as costs but as occasions for the exertion of power. Few business deals were struck without a gun or two in the room, and violent force was always an option, though seldom a preference. Haller comments that "violence is destabilizing and not an effective method for partnership enforcement. A person with a reputation for violence is less likely to be accepted as a partner by successful entrepreneurs. Who, after all, would wish to jeopardize his life or health if he could pursue a successful career without doing so?" ("IE," p. 223). Warners answers: "Rico Bandello and Tony Camonte—that's who."

Warner Bros. was ready to give that answer because the company was a partnership among the brothers Harry, Albert, and Jack. Harry was the titular leader, but though he could open the purse strings he could not close them without the general agreement of the other top executives—that is, his brothers: Jack, who ran production, and Albert, who handled distribution in the office with Harry. At Warners, friction occurred at the edges of the defined areas of responsibility because questions of authority could never be fully settled. At MGM, friction occurred within a defined hierarchy: Thalberg was formally Mayer's subordinate; Mayer was Schenck's. Schenck answered to Loew's board of directors and the banks. Although Thalberg or Mayer could be taken as Jack Warner's equal when competing for a table at the Copacabana or a box on the rail at Santa Anita, finally, despite their clout, Thalberg and Mayer were employees: Thalberg could be reassigned; Mayer could be forced to resign. Jack was an owner. His position was secure. And his mentality was predatory.

When *Gabriel* targets gangsters, its makers had Warners in mind. Not only was there mutual implication between the terms *gangsters* (or *pirates*) and *Warners* in the Hollywood lexicon, but the summit meeting between Nick Diamond and Judd Hammond carefully revised the scene in *Little Caesar* in which Rico has his audience with Big Boy, the boss of the underworld, after Rico's bold leadership has vaulted him into preeminence in the gang. He meets Big Boy in a room flush with Warner Bros. ritz. A cartoon version of a Park Avenue plutocrat, the boss brandishes none of the mobster's tools of intimidation: no revolver bulges under his dinner jacket; no greenbacks litter his desk. What captures Rico's eye and excites his admiration is a painting on the wall (Figure 1.14):

> *Rico*: I bet all this trick furniture set you back plenty.
> *Big Boy*: Well, they don't exactly give it away with cigar coupons.
> *Rico*: I'll tell the world . . . well, look at that!
> *Big Boy*: You like it?
> *Rico*: I sure do. It's elegant.
> *Big Boy*: That cost me $15,000.
> *Rico*: Fifteen thou . . . ? (*Whistles.*) Boy them gold frames sure cost plenty of dough.

The display of art is the most conspicuous distinction between the lowlife gangster and his upper-crust boss. Because of what Chester I. Barnard calls "the fictiveness of authority" in an organization, such a display is crucial to the construction of Big Boy's qualification to rule, for "the executive functions . . . have no separate concrete existence. They are parts or aspects of a process of organization as a whole. . . . It is a matter of art rather than science, and is aesthetic rather than logical."[62] That sounds as much like Thalberg as it does Big Boy.

As we have seen, *Fortune* constructs the genius of Thalberg, his unifying vision and supervisory authority at MGM, out of the metaphor of aesthetics that the studio consistently flaunts. In *Little Caesar*, there is no evidence that Big Boy actually has any feeling or judgment, only that he can give the appearance of an aesthetic sense by metonymy: his proximity to art makes him seem a man of taste to Rico. Metonymy is all a boss needs in Warners' gangster films, where nobody looks too closely at the paintings hanging in the gilded frames on the walls of the rich and powerful and where taste both signifies and mystifies the fundamental and ineradicable difference between Rico and Big Boy, which is class.[63]

Figure 1.14

Rico may have been enthralled by gold frames and gone soft over a dancer, but not Warners. In the early 1930s the Warner brothers were an aggressive, effective unit, straining at the formalities that bound them to their peer studios. The maneuvers that David Ruth calls "the fundamental business strategies explored by the inventors of the gangster . . . growth, consolidation, and organization" were exactly the strategies implemented by Warners (*IPE*, p. 43). *Little Caesar* was not only about business strategy, it was a crucial element in a concerted strategy undertaken by Warners in late 1930 and early 1931 without consulting Big Boy or his minions. On January 14, 1931, Warner Bros. bought five full pages of advertising in *Weekly Variety*, which climaxed in a half-pager with the screaming banner, "LITTLE CAESAR PANICS B'WAY," and which gloatingly quotes from both the *Daily Mirror*'s headline, "Doors Are Smashed at Strand in Rush to See Gang Film," and *The Evening World*'s report that *Little Caesar* "cause[ed] two riots at N.Y. Strand." On the same day *Variety* headlined, "Studios Seethe as WB Reported Grabbing Chatterton, Bancroft, Powell, Bennett and after Coleman." Constance Bennett, who was under contract with Pathe, was free to make a couple of films a year "outside." But Ruth Chatterton, George Bancroft, and William Powell were still under contract with Paramount, as was Ronald Coleman with Goldwyn. In approaching those stars, Warners, *Variety* reports, had broken "the gentleman's agreement in existence for five years . . . one of those trade understandings which cannot be transcribed in writing. It restricts one studio going after another's personalities until the expiration of contracts in a common cause not to unduly jack up salaries" (*V*, January 14, 1931, p. 3). The so-called "gentlemen's agreement," like the unwritten agreement made by the Chicago gentlemen named Al Capone and Bugsy Moran to honor territorial boundaries between the North and South Sides, could not be transcribed because it was illegal, a combination in restraint of trade in clear violation of the Sherman Anti-Trust Act.[64] In attempting to anticipate the conclusion of the stars' contracts, Warners was doing nothing criminal according to the laws of the United States or even those of California; and *The Motion Picture Herald* had reported that Will Hays disavowed any authority over the conflict because, it being only an informal understanding, no agreement existed between members of the Producers Association. That didn't stop *Variety* from labeling the tactic "star stealing" and "personality larceny." It seemed like a deliberate provocation to a gang war. The January 21 *Variety* included a two-page ad: page 24 announced that Constance Bennett would appear in *Jackdaw Strut* in the 1930–31 Warners program; page 25 reveled in the violent excitement generated by *Little Caesar*, featuring a photo of crowds outside the Strand headlined with the question, "What would you give for mobs like this banging at your door?" On page 3 *Variety* reported that "Harry M. Warner in a dignified and business-like announcement last week denied, in refutation of many reports, that Warner Brothers was engaged in any 'war' with a competing picture company." The article reported that the "trade admired the announcement by Harry Warner, but couldn't see it his way. Reports are that the slowly rising battle between the Warners and Paramount is now in the open." On page 5 appears a news item that lacks references to the story item on page 3. It details how Warners will "discard stories for or substitute personalities into 15 pictures already announced on this year's program with exhibitors to get these films under their present contracts. The move is radical in picture annals and comes about following the recent acquisition of 'name' people by WB." It also includes a more complete list of the acquisitions: "Ruth Chatterton, George Bancroft (probable), Constance Bennett, Kay Francis, William Powell, E. G. Robinson, and Bebe Daniels." By February 11, under the headline "Rules About 'Raids,' etc.," *Variety* had reversed its field and was reporting that "despite universal impression, there neither is nor has been a 'gentleman's agreement' between coast picture producers over the engagement of talent." Instead there was merely a question of whether Warners had violated the bylaws of the Hays organization by creating "dissatisfaction" in stars at an "unusual" period before the expiration of their contract with another studio.[65] In April *Variety* reported "'piracy' pact soon due": "Star and Personality Thefts to Stop as per Understanding—Recent Hollywood Meetings Started 'Gentlemen's Agreement'" (*V*, April 8, 1931, p. 3).

The treaty ended the "war" but not before Warners had bruised the other gentlemen in the industry, both by raiding Paramount and by launching a new "gangster film wave," which made the studio money and made its recent acquisition, Edward G. Robinson, a star. Warners also managed to get plenty of ink for the other personalities it had signed and to enhance its reputation as an aggressive studio ready to take advantage of the equivocal position of the cartel before the law in order to "hold-up," first, Paramount and then, through Paramount, the other major studios in order to advance its own short-term interests.[66] While it lasted, Warners' muscling in on Paramount and its exploitation of loopholes in the Hays agreement was a good racket—and it cost the studio nothing except the willingness to make another "gentlemen's agreement"—evidence that in Hollywood, as in Chicago, "the new crimes such as racketeering were easy, safe, and 'continuously profitable'" (*IPE*, p. 60).

Even though the pirate raids had stopped by April 1931, Warners did not desist from trucking with gangsters. Warners' "gangster film wave" persisted through *Public Enemy* (1931), and, finally, *Scarface* (1932), the most lurid and murder-infatuated of the three. *Gabriel over the White House* is a movie about gangbusting, but it so exaggerates the threat of the gangsters that, Hearst's fantasies notwithstanding, *Gabriel* only makes sense as an MGM picture if we understand the studio defending its own interests by standing up for the industry against a predatory Warners, which had cozied up to the new administration but whose gangster films and gangster behavior threatened the concert of interests and the security of the code that had been established by the industry to appease the moralists while reinforcing the collusive bonds among the studios.[67]

Studio concern regarding the application of a gangster image to Hollywood was well founded. As Louis Pizzitola reports, "at the time of *Gabriel*'s release, William Irving Sirovich, a congressional representative from New York, was pushing for a resolution calling for a broad-based investigation of 'financial, operative, and business irregularities and illegal actions by interests inside and outside the motion and sonant pictures industry.'" The resolution was defeated on May 12, 1933, because of publicity in the Hearst papers estimating the potential cost of a congressional investigation based on information acquired from the Federal Trade Commission by order of the White House (*HH*, pp. 297–98). Suspicions of Hollywood business practices would not die, however, in part because the same language was used by racketeers and moguls. Mae Huettig commented on the industry's struggle to shed a reputation for extortionate practices:

> The market of films is affected by two groups of trade practices: those governing the sale of films by distributors to exhibitors and those governing exhibition. In the first

group are the highly controverted practices of block-booking, blind buying, and designated play dates. In the second group are the interrelated restrictions known as protection, or clearance, zoning, and over-buying. (The term "protection" was given up by the industry when gang racketeering began using it in conjunction with shake-down practice.)[68]

Nevertheless, Huettig continues, "the term is an apt one. It means just what it says in that the objective is protection of one group of theatres against competition from others" (*EC*, p. 125).

The protection policies of Judd Hammond and Will Hays were in accord with the condemnation of what business associations had dubbed "cut-throat" competition—a designation reserved for firms that sought to attract more customers by setting their prices below industry standards.[69] During the Hoover administration, Gerard Swope, chief executive officer of General Electric, had led an attack on antitrust laws that prohibited combinations of businesses that could regulate prices in favor of a "vision of a cartelized economy run by trade associations"—a dream of no competitive pricing and emancipation from the Sherman Act that President Hoover repudiated as "the most gigantic proposal of monopoly ever made in history" (quoted in *NDPM*, pp. 41–42). The New Deal seemed to fear economic anarchy more than monopoly, however. The National Industrial Recovery Act [NIRA] in April 1933 established the apparatus "of self-governing trade associations that would write their own codes of law and enforce them through public power with a minimum of governmental supervision" (*NDPM*, pp. 42–44). Ten days before passage of that legislation, the Hays Office had advocated its own proposal that would "pool all [motion picture production] under a single governmental commissioner"—a radical option much closer to Judd Hammond's corporatist preferences than to those of Gerard Swopes. Faced with the NIRA, the Hays Office produced its own code, which FDR approved after rescinding his order giving "the NRA [National Recovery Administration] the unique right to modify the motion picture code." As a result of what might be called the Studio Security Act of 1933, the Hays Office walked off with the oligopolistic authority to write its own codes with the guarantee of no interference from the NRA.[70]

iv. Be a Dancer

In October 1932 *Variety* ran a headline that read, "Jack Warner Burns at Cycles," which was an odd lead because Warners had been the chief target of numerous complaints about film cycles that surfaced in the trades during the early 1930s. Jack didn't have in mind genre cycles, whether westerns or gangster pictures, however; his target was "unscrupulous producers who imitate original ideas." He cited the successful Warner Bros. originals, such as *The Blessed Event* (1932), which had been followed in the same year by Universal's *Okay America* and RKO's *Is My Face Red?* "in the columnist trend"; and the blistering *I Am a Fugitive from a Chain Gang* (1932), which seems to have triggered the release of RKO's *Hell's Highway* (1932) and Universal's *Destination Unknown* (1933), "chain gang stories" (*V*, October 4, 1932). The chief culprit Warners had in mind was David O. Selznick, who got executive producer's credit at RKO on both *Is My Face Red?* and *Hell's Highway*—evidence that he had a hand in ripping off the subjects from Warners that the studio had earlier ripped from the headlines.

When Selznick accepted Mayer's appeal that he move to MGM early in 1933, the imitation didn't stop, which was not unusual: there was heavy demand for product at the majors (the five companies, MGM, Warners, Paramount, RKO, and Fox, which owned studios, distribution agencies, and theaters) and only so many original ideas—many of which, unfortunately, happened to belong to rivals. Following *Dinner at Eight* (1933), Selznick's next big production was *Dancing Lady* (1933), a picture that must have made Jack Warner burn. The immediate objects of Selznick's attention were *42nd Street* and *Gold Diggers of 1933*, Warners' hugely successful efforts to reanimate the musical. *42nd Street* had been completed in November 1932, but was held back from release until the grand promotion of "The 42nd Street Special," a seven-car train, illuminated by lights spelling out the name of the studio and the picture, whose arrival in Washington was timed to coincide with Roosevelt's inauguration. Largely, one supposes, because of the tremendous success of *42nd Street* and in expectation of imitators in the wings, *Gold Diggers of 1933* (the third remake of Avery Hopwood's play *The Gold Diggers*) was hurriedly released on May 27, 1933.[71] Just a few weeks later *Dancing Lady* went into production, proof that the new cycle of musicals had begun.

Dancing Lady begins with the arrival of a group of tuxed and tight, gowned and giddy uptown swells descending on a burlesque theater in the Bowery to be entertained by a chorus of beauties strutting from the stage onto the ramp that circles through the audience, where, on cue, they all begin to strip. The camera, serving as the eyes of a rich admirer, adheres to the Joan Crawford character as she unzips and drops her skirt to reveal her tights beneath. She is then abruptly relieved of her blouse by a customer. Before she can recover her composure the cops arrive to haul the girls away to night court, where, before a lively audience that includes the slumming swells, they are charged with indecency. When the

Crawford character is arraigned, she is unrepentant. She identifies herself as Janie Barlow and defends herself aggressively to the owl of a judge:

> *Janie*: If you'd walked the street looking for a job and hadn't anything to eat for a week, you'd do a strip tease too.
>
> *Judge*: You mean to tell me that in a city like this, burlesque dancing was the only work you could find?
>
> *Janie*: It was the only dancing I could find.
>
> *Judge*: Did it have to be dancing?
>
> *Janie*: Yeah, it had to be dancing.
>
> *Judge*: Why?
>
> *Janie*: Because I'm a dancer.
>
> *Judge*: Who's the defendant here?
>
> *Janie*: I don't know who's the defendant, but I'm the victim. I don't see any girls pulled in here for pushing pencils around on paper or massaging a typewriter. I'm a dancer, and I'll go on bein' one when I get out of here.

If a customer had missed the credits and, from the tawdry opening, suspected that Crawford was on loan-out to Warners, she would now know that she was watching an MGM picture. The judge believes there are many jobs in the city, but for Janie there is no option except a job dancing. For the judge there is a difference between burlesque dancing and other forms of dancing: the former, aka "strip tease," is indecent and therefore illegal; the practitioners of the tap, the waltz, and the ballet do not appear before the bench. Janie, however, does not discriminate among dance forms; she identifies herself as a dancer; therefore whatever she performs, wherever she does it, it is dance. Because for Janie there is no way to tell the dance from the dancer, it is merely social prejudice that "victimizes" her by criminalizing her profession. If Janie is credible, it is because she is played by Joan Crawford, herself plucked from the chorus and whom we recognize as a star.[72] Being Joan Crawford does not make her credible about all things: we need not believe her if she were to claim that she can be trusted with another woman's husband or that it was she who shot her ex-husband at his beach house. At MGM, however, there is a special relationship between being a star and being a dancer. As *Grand Hotel* amply demonstrates, being a dancer is as different from working as a secretary as being a member of the galaxy at MGM is different from laboring on the assembly line at Warners. Janie doesn't dance for money or fame; she dances because *it is* who *she is*. To be a dancer is to be differentiated as a species, like being a star, like being an artist, and, ultimately, as *Fortune* genially affirmed, like being a corporation. The judge, less than impressed, sends her to jail anyway.

After her rich admirer, Todd Newton (Franchot Tone), springs her, Janie joins him for dinner. When she asks him why he paid her fine he cheerily answers, "That's my business: investments." Her reply draws a line: "Sorry to tell you, but I'm the kind of investment that don't pay." She insists that she is determined to succeed on her own. Still, she listens to his advice: "Don't forget, what is striptease downtown is art on Broadway." Newton sounds just like Nick Diamond, when, in *Gabriel*, he cracks to President Hammond, "On my trucks it's bootleg. On a silver tray on Park Avenue, it's hospitality." The writers for *Dancing Lady* would have seen *Gabriel over the White House*. By the time we get to *Boys Town* (1938) and *The Wizard of Oz* (1939), the connection between what I shall call MGM's social adjustment trope and its first enunciation (if, indeed, *Gabriel* was the first) will be attenuated past reckoning. While the signature slogan of a company—such as "progress is our most important product" or "better living through chemistry," or "ars gratia artis"—can usually be tracked back to the public relations man, such as Howard Dietz at MGM, who devised the leonine and Latin logo, it is impossible to trace the path by which a particular trope lodges in the corporate mind and gradually becomes characteristic of its public speech. Nevertheless the trope of social adjustment does become conspicuous among a set of pictures across the decade of the 1930s that have nothing in common except that they were produced by MGM. The trope of social adjustment is the way the social intelligence of MGM expresses itself.

Like Nick Diamond, Janie refuses the deal she is offered—not because she's a gangster but because she *knows* she's a dancer, not a stripper, and not a prostitute. Such epistemic certainty and moral fortitude are all but unknown among the dancers at Warners. Dorothy Brock (Bebe Daniels) in *42nd Street* turns down the *quo* insinuated by her timid "angel," Abner (Guy Kibbee), but she's happy to accept his *quid*—on behalf of the show, herself, and her insolvent lover (George Brent). There's nothing compromising about taking the money itself. People work for money. There's no other good reason. And you can't work without money. There's nothing accidental about the angel in a Warner Bros. musical. The traffic in women that surrounds a production is designed to seduce rich men to invest in a show and turn commerce into capitalization. As the producer, Barry (Ned Sparks), says of Angel Abner, "His interest is our principle." When an angel gets his new protégé, as Abner does at the end of *42nd Street*, he's getting exactly what he pays for, "Anytime Annie" (Ginger Rogers), who is honest enough to admit that, despite Abner's support, she's not good enough for the lead but who is not scrupulous enough to repudiate his sponsorship. Prostitution and promiscuity are at the core of the dancing profession. Nonetheless, there are discriminations to be made: in *Gold Diggers of 1933*, Carol (Joan Blondell) and Trixie (Aline MacMahon), posing as Polly (Ruby Keeler), who is the objectionable fiancée of "Brad Roberts" (Dick Powell), take gifts as escorts but they will not take money for sex. In one sense they are saved by the Production Code, which, unusually, is in concert with their moral inclinations. In another sense they are enriched by the Production Code: by resisting the exchange of money for sex, they get a better deal: marriage for sex. And they get to keep the money too.[73]

Janie is untroubled by moral complications: she would not make "Anytime Annie's" sacrifice nor would she accept the deal offered by Abner in *42nd Street* or Bradford in *Gold Diggers of 1933*, or even by her own Todd Newton. She takes the tip without paying the tout. "I'm not goin' back to the joint," she tells her roommate. "I'm through dreaming. I'm gonna start doin'. I'm goin' up where it's art: uptown." And she does. By way of a quick montage sequence and the uptown express Janie makes her way to the hall where Patch Gallagher (Clark Gable) is rehearsing his new Broadway show, *Dancing Lady*. She cannot get in the door and reports the rebuff to Newton. This time he offers to write a letter to the producers on her behalf. When she asks, "How do you cut in?" he answers with impeccable cunning, "I'll do it for art's sake." It is an offer that Janie cannot refuse—at least without raising the doubt that anyone would support her art for art's sake. As *Dinner at Eight* had toyed with the lion heart of MGM's trademark, turned into a comically pretentious aspic centerpiece, so *Dancing Lady* toys with its equally ostentatious slogan, "ars gratia artis." This is serious play. It is not that the scene requires us to take seriously what Newton says. The scene requires us to believe that Janie believes it—to accept that it is somehow possible, even necessary, not only to Janie's success but to her *appeal*, that Newton would believe that her dancing is an art that could be subsidized for art's sake. So for MGM. "Ars gratia artis" is just a slogan, but it is a necessary slogan for a studio that bases its distinction on its willingness to avow that belief and to maintain the credibility of that claim as the basis of its identity. *Art* is a term of art for MGM. The executives at MGM do not yearn to make pictures that are works of art; they are happy to conclude that a picture is art if it is made by MGM.

Well into rehearsals Gallagher confronts the trio of writers of *Dancing Lady* and derides the show (probably with Hearst in mind) as "standard Spanish American War stuff. You can't get by with that sort of thing today. You've got to give them something out of modern, everyday life. Something out of the city streets." He tells them he wants the whole thing rewritten. Gallagher sounds a lot like Barney Hopkins, the producer in *Gold Diggers of 1933*, when Hopkins described his vision of a new, socially relevant show to the girls. When Gallagher declares, "Give them the slums, burlesque shows, riveting machines, a girl who beats time to the city's rhythm, a girl crazed to dance. Get it?" a writer objects that the current lead, Vivian Warner (Gloria Foy), could not handle that role.[74] Gallagher agrees. He has already decided to drop her in favor of Janie Barlow, the girl whose talent and grit inspired his new story (Gallagher does not admit to having seen *42nd Street* or *Gold Diggers of 1933*). So Gallagher drops a girl named "Warner" from a show with a script that sounds like it was pilfered from a writer's office at Warner Bros. This is MGM, where invocation of "the slums, burlesque shows, riveting machines," does not announce topicality, what *Fortune* would later call Warners' exploitation of "sensational happenings in the lives of everyday people." At Warners "the stories became the stars."[75] At MGM the topical inheres in the self-reflexive, slightly mocking reference to Warners' recent precedent. At Metro the *stars* are the stars. When Gallagher pulls Janie into his office and informs her, "You're through with the unit: I want to put you in the top spot," he gives her the lead because she is *better* than Warner. We do not get to see that she is better; it's not necessary: Janie is better than Warner because she is "the Duchess," and the Duchess is Joan Crawford. In a cutaway one member of the chorus asks another, "How'd that Barlow get to take Warner's place?" The other cattily replies, "Didn't you ever hear of poisonality?" A star's poisonality, *especially* Joan Crawford's, is death to those who merely have talent.

The word *modern*, which would signal realism at Warner Bros., turns out to announce stylish fantasy at MGM. When Gallagher's show does open it begins with Janie and Fred Astaire (Fred Astaire) in evening clothes paired for an irresolute tap number, which ends with the duo transported on a magic cloud over ocean and mountain to Bavaria, where, in a beer garden among the quaintly costumed burghers, they give a sudsy rendition of "The Beer Song," a vestige of the nineteenth century. Eventually, Janie returns to New York and modern times, but it's nothing like the throbbing, dangerous, and lonely metropolis represented in the finales of *42nd Street* and *Gold Diggers of 1933*. Although there are plenty of girls to populate the faux Busby Berkley numbers that follow, Astaire has left the picture. Janie is awkwardly featured alone. *We* know that she is crazed to dance because she has declared it to nearly everyone she has met, but there's no way the theater audience would know it as they watch the kaleidoscopic finale, which is capped by the duchess riding high on a painted pony, wholly separated from the carousel of chorus girls.

When Gallagher says to Janie, "So, dancing is your racket," he means it as a compliment. The word *racket* simultaneously combines and individualizes all forms of business. In Gallagher's argot (which Gable carries with him from picture to picture) *racket* is the word for what a person does best or must do, what he or she can put over, profit from, and should stick with. A racket is talent matched to a career or, to borrow from Warren and Dubin's hit number from *42nd Street*, it may just be the one habit that you can't break. When, after the show, the duchess asks her fiancé, "Believe now that dancing is my racket, Todd?" the question is thoroughly rhetorical. The whole picture has been devoted to proving that proposition and preparing for the inevitable moment when Janie would abandon wealth and privilege, even if, as Newton promises, she can "have [her] cake and eat it too," for Broadway, where she can have her boss as lover and her racket as art.

At Warners, where class matters, the social adjustment trope was disused or mocked. One could conjecture that Warners chose *Midsummer Night's Dream* as its highbrow picture of the 1930s in order to conjoin the commutability that is the Shakespearian mode of mischief with Warner Bros.' principle of economy. Poet and studio teach, respectively, lovers and stars the moonlit lesson of how easily surrogates will serve and how absurd it is that mechanics like Bottom or Cagney would rise above their class, except in a dream. The commutability test was proposed by John Thompson as a way to isolate the traits or characteristics of an actor that significantly contribute to his or her performance by "the [mental] substitution of one actor for another, in order to observe not merely *if* a difference in meaning results but *which* difference results."[76] If we could exchange Clark Gable for James Cagney, Thalberg for Zanuck, Mayer for Jack Warner, would Warners still be Warners? Whatever the outcome, the process would be less disturbing to Warners, which understood itself as the antithesis of MGM, whereas Metro understood itself as incomparable. At Warners commutation was not just a thought experiment; it was a cost-effective operating principle for managing resources, including actors; it was an egalitarian political principle that manifested itself as a general populist suspicion of class difference and as collective expressions of solidarity; it was a democratic ethic that governed individual behavior; and it was a trope that animated narrative permutations. When commutation fails—when, for example, Rico, stuck on himself, begins to think that he is irreplaceable, and when, stuck on Joe, he cannot be happy with Otero as his substitute—catastrophe occurs. As the shocking ease with which the studio accepted the departure of Darryl F. Zanuck, the one rival to Thalberg as the most brilliant film executive in the history of Hollywood, attests, at Warners no one is irreplaceable. There's always Hal Wallis or someone like him ready to step in.

Gold Diggers of 1933 is as keenly interested in commutation as it is in what a dollar can buy. The credit sequence that introduces the Warners players starts with a shot of a disc on which a ring of stars frames the image of a classical bust over the imprint "1933"—a facsimile of the Morgan silver dollar, omitting only the legend "e pluribus unum." A hand pulls the disc away to reveal another. It too is snappily withdrawn to reveal in sequence images of the principal performers superimposed on the disc and ringed with stars. Then there is another shot of the 1933 dollar, which is swiped away to disclose Fay (Ginger Rogers) in close-up, bedizened with a necklace and a stole composed of what appear to be gold dollars. The "coins" freely adapt the design of the silver peace dollars, but because they are stamped with 1933 these gold coins alchemized from silver could only have been minted by Warner Bros., for the U.S. Treasury never minted a gold coin of that design and minted no silver dollars at all that year. Fay begins to belt out, "We're in the money," with her eyes looking the camera "right in the eye," just as she exhorts the audience to do with "the landlord." During the reprise of the song, the camera pans down the chorus line, catching each smiling girl as she unmasks herself, until it reaches the end of the line and a close-up of Fay again, who has commuted from the left of the line to the right. The camera then pulls back to capture the entire chorus dancing before a wall of giant, overlapping dollars, until it stops before a portal through which march head-on a procession of chorus girls, each given a flattering, brief close-up as she passes before the camera. Fay reappears at the end of the line, and, marvelously, breaks into a pig Latin rendition of "We're in the Money," which recodes the English by commuting the end of the word to the front, demonstrating that the message of cocky confidence is a technical trick. "We" is no true *unum* formed from the *pluribus* of words and music, dancers and the dance; it is the effect of the synchronization of Dubin's words with Warren's music and of the moving image of Fay's lips with the sound that comes out of the theater's speakers. "We" may not really be "in the money"; we is not even really "we."

When Janie Barlow first appears in *Dancing Lady* she is performing a striptease. The cops raid the joint and tell her to put her dance clothes back on. After she is released from jail she changes into a nice outfit and then another and another: they are her clothes not because she can afford them but because Janie is Joan Crawford. Poverty is a plot device, not a material fact. The chorus girls for *Gold Diggers* are not wearing much more than Janie, but when the police arrive they tell the girls to take the clothes off. It's not indecency that's the issue, it's a failure to pay the bills. FDR has taken the nation off the gold standard. Where will the gold diggers find gold to dig? When, in the next scene, we are introduced to the three impoverished chorus girls who will become the focus of the narrative, they are still undressed, bundled up together in a single bed. They remain *deshabille* until Fay arrives wearing a figure-flattering dress on loan from her boss and informs them that Barney (Ned Sparks) is once again putting on a show. The girls—Polly (Ruby Keeler), Trixie (Aline MacMahon), and Carol (Joan Blondell)—improvise a competition to decide who will be the one to get to wear Fay's dress in order to approach Barney about jobs. Each chooses a cab company—Yellow, Checker, Red Top—as they run to the window of the apartment. Carol's cab appears first, so she wins the right to borrow Fay's borrowed dress to wheedle Barney for jobs for each of the girls. The prior police seizure of props on behalf of someone is redressed by an expropriation of property on behalf of everyone. A showgirl begins in the chorus, and despite whatever circumstances may combine to remove her from the line, her formation sticks. A show closes: the girls share an apartment, a bed, a dress, a name, a costume, a number. In a Warners musical a girl can climb from chorus to solo, but it is the Warners rule of commutation that someone pays for what the others get. When Carol, who has won the right to approach Barney, telephones to break the news that he's going to put them in the show, her tearfulness suggests she is relieved but also that she has suffered something, not as a victim (only men are victims in this picture) but as part of a quid pro quo on behalf of the group. Carol's reward for her sacrifice is a featured performance as the torch, for which she qualifies by having acquired, like Jack Robin, née Jackie Rabinowitz in *The Jazz Singer* (Warners, 1927) "a tear in [her] voice" (Figure 1.15). Carol's consolation inheres in the extension of the rule of choric commutation: if you pay for what you get paid for, everyone else also gets paid for what you get paid for (eventually). A measure of solidarity cushions the sacrifice.

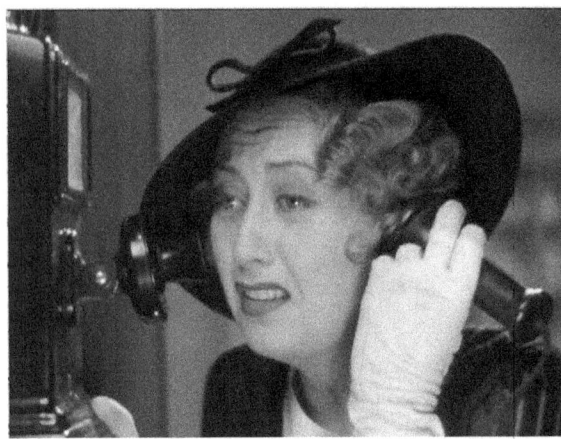

Figure 1.15

Following the format of new comedy, the rest of the narrative spins out from the claim of the young songwriter, Brad Roberts (Dick Powell), who tells his girlfriend Polly that he can easily acquire the fifteen thousand dollars he has promised to invest in the show. The necessary intergenerational conflict hangs upon a case of mistaken identity. Brad's banker brother, Lawrence Bradford (Warren William), who strenuously disapproves of his younger brother's theatrical ambitions, visits the girls' new apartment to bribe Polly away from her engagement with Brad, but he mistakes Carol for Polly. Trixie sees a way to exploit the confusion and improvises a racket on the spot. She phones out for a pair of expensive hats. Affecting surprise when they are delivered, she indirectly threatens the elder Bradford with noncooperation unless he pays for the hats. It's extortion, of course, but no more than what the elder Bradford had expected when he tried to bribe the girls, and no more than he had practiced when he threatened to cut off his brother's trust fund. He has his methods; showgirls have theirs. Bradford willy-nilly commutes between extracting terms and submitting to them. The farcical elements of the plot contribute to the sense of the trio of girls as a robust female unit, which is organized so as to hold its own against the personifications of a dynastic capital that is personally and politically untouched by the financial crisis and capable of reparations from these moneymen on behalf of the real men lost to war and depression.

The farce is resolved by a double act of framing. The first is Trixie's idea. In revenge for Bradford's fulminations that showgirls are "parasites, chiselers, gold diggers," they strip the dead-drunk Bradford in Carol's apartment, tuck him in her lingerie-strewn bed, and exploit his hangover in the morning to extort money from him for "the night's lodging." Trixie supplies Roberts the pen with which he signs a check to Polly for ten thousand dollars. Later, when Roberts learns from the newspaper that his brother has married the real Polly Sawyer (or, as the headline has it, has "married 'Polly Sawyer'"), he returns to Carol, who admits the hoax, and tells him, "Your check. That's on exhibition there on the wall" (Figure 1.16).

Roberts has not stopped payment as Carol expected, but then he did not need to, since the check is made out to "Polly" as payment for services supposedly rendered by a person who is actually Carol. Once framed, the check has become money aestheticized—which, not coincidentally, travesties the prepossessing use by Big Boy of his tasteful painting to overawe Rico in *Little Caesar*. The ten thousand dollars that Bradford signed away for "a night's lodging" (which is literally all he got) demonstrates the banker's easy access to reserves of capital completely closed to showgirls. Carol's exhibition of the check on the wall neutralizes that distance by taking the money out of circulation and transforming capital into what would be called "art" at MGM. Warners can't represent a facsimile of the Morgan dollar or the ten thousand dollars in greenbacks that Brad plunks down on Barney's desk; but the studio can frame and hang a check for ten thousand dollars on the wall so that, as the song goes, "you can look that guy right in the eye." Carol's mock aestheticization is a version of Warners' commutability: substituting the check that pays for

Figure 1.16

art for the artwork itself and the signature of the patron for that of the artist. The trope repudiates the reference of the ten thousand dollars to any service rendered or product supplied, to anything or anybody. The check cannot be cashed unless it is endorsed, and it cannot be endorsed unless the frame is broken. And even then, who will endorse the transaction and turn this dream of paper into gold? It is made out to "Polly" and given to Polly as a wedding present, but as Bradford says, it can only be cashed when Carol endorses it (Figure 1.17). By this time it is clear that the deconstruction of identity has unraveled so far that "Polly Parker" can sign no proper name without committing fraud.

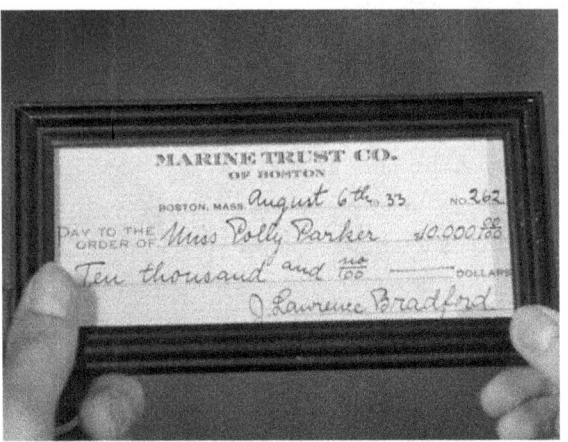

Figure 1.17

Dancing Lady is a conspicuously voiceless movie by A. O. Hirschman's standards. At the literal level, there are no vocal numbers until we reach the final show; moreover, though Joanie is steadfast in her refusal to be placed in a reciprocal relationship with Todd Barlow, she is completely uncritical of Patch Gallagher, who claims to tire of her insistent expressions of gratitude and her fawning eagerness to hold his coat for him. Not only does Vivian Warner exit without a word, Todd Newton does so too: the conversation in which Janie finally rejects him occurs offstage. There is plenty of talking back to Barney in *Gold Diggers*, but the most vociferous demonstration is the "Forgotten Man" number itself, which restores discourse to spectacle. The narrative has been completed—the Jills all have their Jacks—and what could have been conflict between classes turns out to be the usual marriage across genders. The finale reopens the picture, however, by explaining suppressed class conflict that has been displaced to the marriage plot cannot be so easily sublimated. The grooms that the girls accept are silver substitutes for the once golden men now missing because unemployed and unemployed because their service to the nation has been forgotten and uncompensated. By breaking through the frame and talking back to its audience, the motion picture reassigns what Charles Eckert would call displaced agency back to its place, to *you* sitting in a seat in the theater.[77] The first words of the picture, "We're in the money"—celebrate the illusion of the cheerful collective: the *pluribus* is all one, big, happy *unum*, flush with the silver that will turn their dreams to gold. The finale drops the cheerful hug of the first-person plural for an assertive second-person singular and plural. From the first recitative of Carol under a street lamp, to the plaint of the African-American woman leaning from her window, to the cadence of the marching soldiers, "The Forgotten Man" is addressed to "you," an audience that is the individual-citizen-assembled-as-a-public: "You took him from the plow," "you put a rifle in his hand." The "Forgotten Man" invokes World War I, but not as a traumatic historical accident. Crucially, Carol does not ask for sympathy. We are told, "Forget your sympathy," because sympathy for the man enables us to distance him by entering into an imaginary transaction in which we pay a price of sentiment in order to be free to go about our business. The address to a pluralized "you" attempts to overcome the resistance of the singular "you" to acknowledge its involvement in an ineradicable network of social relations deformed by poverty but not reducible to cash transactions: "Forgetting him, you see, means you're forgetting me, like my forgotten man." You are the one who has forgotten and, in doing so, you have become like the forgotten one. Your ticket buys you a few laughs, a couple of catchy tunes, more than a couple risqué shots of chorus girls, Busby Berkeley's glamorous symmetry, and a summons to accept your political responsibility for sending men off to war and your financial responsibility for restoring a fractured society.

v. Be a Racket: Warners and MGM—The Second New Deal

In the 1930s, *Fortune* profiled two "metros" of that decade: in 1932, Metro-Goldwyn-Mayer, the leading studio in Hollywood, and in 1934, Metropolitan Life, "the biggest company in the world." *Fortune* introduces its examination of Metropolitan Life with a statement as perspicuous as it is methodologically central to the magazine's project: "It seems quite clear that the biggest company in the world must have offered the world something it wanted very badly. It must have conducted itself in a way that the world approved. And at the same time it must have learned pretty well how to get along in the world. In other words, if you study the Metropolitan you may expect to discover a good deal about the world itself."[78] That claim extends the reach of the magazine's inaugural ambition to become "a national institution, perhaps the greatest of all institutions which are concerned with criticism and interpretation," by taking as its subject an industry, which is "*a* world itself."[79]

Fortune congratulates Metropolitan on having been lucky enough to be an insurance company during the Depression (people have been more anxious about security, but people have also been healthier), and on its special good fortune in having been subject to laws that have prevented it from suffering the kind of catastrophes that have befallen other less regulated businesses. *Fortune* does not mean the laws of probability, which are a sound enough basis for a business, but the legal code imposed on insurance companies by the state of New York in 1905 to curtail the exploitation of customers' gullibility and the free exercise of executives' cupidity. Even the magazine that means business has to approve the result of the state's regulation. "One reason why the life-insurance business has so sturdily weathered the depression is its sound foundation of laws.... Despite their early squawks and yowls, you can find no stronger defenders of the insurance code today than the insurance officers themselves. They generally agree that the best way to restore public confidence in an indicted industry is to have a thorough investigation followed by regulation which tends to make operations more public.... The code made the Metropolitan" ("MLIC," p. 131).[80] *Fortune*'s profile of the Metropolitan instructs its business readers in the New Deal catechism that Metro, like Metropolitan, has already learned: codes are good for business both as public relations and as devices that challenge managerial ingenuity. It is the moral of *Fortune*'s story of Metropolitan Life's good fortune under the constraints set by the Armstrong Commission that, had conditions been different in 1905—had the government been more enlightened, had insurance companies been more foresightful, had their been a business magazine like *Fortune*—it would have been possible to sell the insurance code to insurance companies in the same way that insurance companies sell ordinary life to its customers. For, as *Fortune* enjoins, "insurance must be sold."

Fortune's examination of the Metropolitan divides between the New York office, where the top executives plot financial strategy and the actuaries calculate risk and concoct policies, and the field—Omaha, Kennebunkport, Los Angeles—where the Metropolitan's salesmen beat the pavement, knock on doors, and work their jaws to get people to buy those policies. The actuaries produce numbers that are massaged into policies. But salesmen do not sell policies by the numbers; they know that information is not an economic offering, whereas protection is. The willingness of the customer to buy does not depend on the capital reserves of Metropolitan; the sale depends on the customer's confidence in the Metropolitan brand. That brand, as *Fortune* observes, has been carefully constructed to be "protective—its men and its buildings exhibit a fortress-like solidity." In a metaphor of mythic reassurance Metropolitan calls itself "the light that never fails." The iconic manifestation of that slogan is the search light beaming forth from the tip of Metropolitan's headquarters building, seven hundred feet above Madison Avenue in New York—a fortress of protective stereotypes graphically represented in the advertising space that Metropolitan purchased in magazines like *Fortune* and in the brochures squadrons of salesmen distributed. The promotion of the brand did not cease at the moment of sale, however, for the sale is only the promise to pay the first premium. To prevent "lapsation" and keep the premiums coming, Metropolitan agents were instructed "to call at a home at the same time each week to ensure familiarity and contact. In the process of collecting premiums, insurance agents listened to the problems, concerns, and hopes of their client"—thereby making her (for it was the wife of the breadwinner who answered the door) part of a community of Metropolitan policyholders—a brand community—that would supplement or, ideally, replace traditional social affiliations, such as fraternal organizations, and increase Metro community's sense of the strength of their purchased security, which, like risk, can only be found in numbers.[81]

What salesmen promise and what clients think they buy usually exceeds what they actually acquire.

> The buncombe in life insurance ... lies in the way in which it is sometimes sold. The commodity that the life-insurance companies offer is usually called Protection with a capital P (or Financial Independence with a capital F, or Security with a capital S—see almost any insurance advertisement).... Facts lead to the observation that, our social system and our economic life being what it is, the people cannot afford to buy anything approaching genuine, absolute Protection from even the great fortress of life insurance. Not that the life-insurance business really pretends to offer absolute protection. But its salesmen, in print and speech, often use the word Protection with lavish tongues. ("MLIC," p. 49)

Fortune imagines absolute protection as a kind of insurance ideal—which, like always being happy when you eat at Schneider's, is insurance that people cannot afford to buy and that insurance companies do not really pretend to offer. At a time when the average annual salary was seventeen hundred dollars, the average compensation received by 55 percent of Metropolitan's beneficiaries was three hundred fifty dollars: "What the beneficiaries can do with such sums is, plainly, a matter of circumstance. On the one hand, they may support themselves for a few months, a year, until new adjustments can be made. On the other, they may be of decisive importance, or it may merely be convenient. Only one thing is certain: for the average man it cannot even suggest an absolute Protection against death" ("MLIC," p. 51). *Fortune* does not intend to expose the truth behind the ugly lie of life-insurance salesmen, because there is none. "The life-insurance salesman will often try to sell you the policy that brings him the highest commission. But no matter what the salesman succeeds in selling you—you will get full insurance value for what you pay" ("MLIC," p. 49). The New York State code guarantees that you get what you pay for, even though you can never buy what you want and you will rarely acquire what you expect.

Fortune's corporate story serves the overriding objective of promoting the readjustment rather than the abolition of the institutions of capitalist society. That project depends on the imaginative deployment of what, in *The Folklore of*

Capitalism, Thurman Arnold would call the "trick of personification" by which institutions such as large-scale firms could take on the traits and capacities of persons and attract public support by the strategic profession of "ideals."[82] In its general effect, the "trick of personification is similar to the trope of social adjustment that Arnold identified in 1932: by the use of a rhetorical device a phenomenon moves from a lower to a higher status. The difference lies in attitude and agency. Social adjustment might require the act of a legislature or the signature of a president; the "trick" of personification *may* be deliberately legislated or cannily promoted but it need not be; it is a widespread habit of mind and tongue among people who tend to give familiar things, such as a group of people with obscure powers, such as the capacity to raise enough money to build a railroad, the attributes of a person. Arnold's version of the trick of personification, which can be played by people on themselves, moots the long-standing chicken-and-egg debate between "artificial entity" and "natural entity" theorists *and* humbles the rational prescriptions of the realists.[83] For Arnold it is *natural* (that is, inevitable) that the *artifice* (that is, trick) of conferring a fictive personhood on a firm would occur. Knowing the truth is of little use, for fiction is, in general, more potent than truth. But if the artifice of personification is natural and institutional persons are potent fictions, the acquisition of an appealing personality does not happen automatically, nor does it endure without careful attention. Anticipating Peter F. Drucker's management theory during the postwar era, Arnold insists that the security of the corporate person depends on the fabrication of ideals to which it credibly commits, for "without ideals," Arnold writes, "the institution loses its personality and appears to the public as a mere group of people doing various little things in a very imperfect way. It does not matter to the security of the institution that the ideals are not 'true.' It is only important that they fit into the vague emotional notions of that part of the public whose acceptance is vital to the power of the institution, and without which it fails."[84] The security of institutions in a democracy depends on their capacity to make people feel secure.

That's why we have gangsters. A 1934 *Fortune* article entitled "Crime and the New Deal" announces that "the federal government is on the run to rescue a nation hard pressed by organized crime." The nation is hard pressed because gangsters have wised up:

> The end of prohibition was . . . the end of beer running as the major example of national lawlessness. Into precisely what new channels the liquor gangs directed their superabundant energies is a matter of speculation. Some of them, glad of a chance to get out of the racket safely, retired on their earnings. Some of them stayed

in the liquor business. But the old violence and bloodshed are no more. They hijack a truckload of legitimate liquor every now and then for old times' sake, but for the most part they go in for such bloodless chicanery as evading revenue taxes and counterfeiting labels. Some of them have gone in for the multitudinous rackets—milk, poultry, dry cleaning, labor union, and so on—which sprang up during prohibition and still seem to flourish, New Deal or no New Deal.[85]

This new era for gangsters forecasts a new, more ambiguous era for the New Deal, which will mean a new and unwelcome era for the Hollywood studios whose cooperative, even favored relationship with the Roosevelt administration had quickly turned suspicious and adversarial—especially at Warner Bros.

Warners' *Bullets or Ballots* (1936) is an artifact of the Second New Deal that understands the new New Deal as a racket, just like any other racket, though a more powerful and efficient one. The picture begins with a shot of a theater marquee. The camera tilts to a chauffeured car pulling up to the curb; then there is a cut to two well-dressed men buying tickets. They are interested only in the bottom half of the double feature, "the crime picture": *The Syndicate of Crime*. Inside, as the film rolls, we crosscut from the screen, which maps the insidious network of the rackets, to the men's faces as, driven by an urgent voiceover, *The Syndicate of Crime* sounds an alarm to the public about the menace of the rackets.

> They rob the American people of fifteen billion dollars. Huge sums extorted from the business man. A steady flood of pennies, nickels, and dimes drained from the purses of the homeowner, the laborer, and the housewife. [*Cut to a visual of a New York market.*] On the East Coast, perishable foods: a quarter of a cent levied on every head of lettuce, a cent on artichokes, a fraction of a cent on every type of produce. [*Cut to a tracking shot of stationary boxcars.*] When wholesalers refuse to pay tribute, the racketeers prevent them from moving shipments. Hundreds of carloads of fresh vegetables rot on sidings.

We see the reenactment of several instances of extortion: gangsters compel a storeowner to house pinball machines that suck the nickels out of the pockets of schoolboys; they light kerosene-drenched steaks on delivery trucks as a warning to wholesalers who resist giving them a piece of the action. One of the watching men, "Bugs" Fenner (Humphrey Bogart), who has already seen the movie, pokes his companion and says, "Wait until you catch the character who takes you off." The friend, identified by the film as the gangster boss Al Kruger (Barton MacLane), is then treated to a dramatization of his own trial for extortion. When he is acquitted, the disgusted judge scolds the jury for destroying "the confidence of law-abiding people in the integrity and justice of the American court." The *Syndicate of Crime* ends with the impassioned address of its producer, Ward Bryant (Henry O'Neill), crusading newspaperman, who announces to the audience that although he and his family have been threatened with death unless he stops making these movies, he will continue his attack on the racketeers and their "entrenched" directors, "who laugh at your laws [and] make a joke of your courts. They rule by the fear of their bullets. They must be smashed by the power of your ballots."

The narrative accelerates when Fenner fulfills his death threat by shooting Bryant, even though Bryant has been warned off by Kruger. We then shift to a cabaret where Johnny Blake (Edward G. Robinson), a plainclothes cop exiled to the Bronx for his zeal in arresting criminals, is reading a news account of the crime. Lee Morgan (Joan Blondell), the cabaret owner and an intimate friend of Johnny's, stops by the table to talk about the murder. They are interrupted by a "mug," whom Johnny manhandles and tosses through a plate glass door for failing to show him the proper respect. A special grand jury, alarmed by the death of the newspaperman, decides to make Officer McLaren (Joseph King), a friend of Blake's, chief of police with extraordinary powers to break the rackets. Soon Blake is fired from his job. After he demonstrates his resentment by punching McLaren at a prizefight, Blake is asked by Kruger, who trusts Blake's honesty, to join the gang and review the rackets to check for weaknesses and inefficiencies. Blake accompanies Kruger to the center of the operation, where piles of cash are received, counted, and then distributed. Blake gets a rundown of the operation. Fenner grows increasingly suspicious of Blake's conversion. Soon the police raid the rackets. When Kruger carries a satchel of cash to the mysterious "directors" of the racket, rich and ostensibly respectable businessmen, he is warned to secure his operation. Blake assaults a policeman on the street and is hauled into jail, where he meets secretly with McLaren. We learn what almost everyone in the picture and in the audience has already suspected: Blake is working undercover for the police.

After his release, Blake fights off that suspicion by proposing that the gang enter the numbers game, which, he promises, will produce revenues that more than compensate for the recent losses to the police. Kruger is satisfied, but Fenner is not. He kills Kruger and attempts to take over the gang. In a tense confrontation, Blake manages to convince everyone he has the support of the big bosses, which turns out to be true. The bosses appoint him to deliver their cut. He then arranges for a police raid of the racket's hideout to precede his appointed delivery of the cash to the directors at the Oceanic Bank. He visits the bustling headquarters, records the serial numbers of the bills he is to carry to the bosses, and deposits the list in a trash basket for the police to retrieve after he has departed. He then signals McLaren to begin the raid. Fenner, who is informed by a sentinel that Blake tipped off the police at the hideout and provided with Blake's location by the unwitting Morgan, hunts Blake down and shoots him. The wounded Blake returns Fenner's fire and kills him. He staggers to the street, where he is picked up by Lee Morgan, who, oblivious to Blake's wounds, takes him to the Oceanic Bank. Blake makes his delivery to the directors, then crawls to open the door to admit the waiting police. Having transferred the money with the serial numbers on his note, Blake dies in the arms of McLaren, but not before he tells the chief that the bullet in his body from Fenner's gun is a match for the bullets that killed Kruger and Bryant, the newspaperman. Blake has already killed the murderer; he expires, having closed the case.

Bullets or Ballots is a complicated movie. It is also, I shall argue, the pivotal Warner Bros. motion picture of the mid-1930s, in part because, as Drayton Nabers first suggested, it is a movie that is *designed* to be pivotal.[86] The title offers a choice between violence or the law as a method of dealing with this "modern gangster." Surprisingly, given the studio's progressive politics and the proscriptions against depictions of gunplay by the Production Code, *Bullets or Ballots* eschews legal methods and advocates direct, violent action. Ruth Vasey observes that Joseph Breen had advocated that the industry "promote a new kind of criminal who was soft-spoken and had the appearance of a gentleman: 'Instead of showing an eagerness to kill, he is eager to avoid killing, preferring to use his wits to gain his ends rather than to use weapons, to resort to scheming rather than to violence.'"[87] How about scheming and violence? To defeat the gangsters of the new school, who hide behind the letter of the law, the police deliberately behave like gangsters of the old school, and the picture reverts to the "old genre of the gangster," even as it represents the criminal threat as a corporate form of organization run by men who do not carry firearms. That reversion to what Richard Maltby has called the "generic impulse to provide an individualistic, heroic solution to the problem [of corruption] it produces" is just one of the apparent contradictions in a "fissured film" that portrays its hero simultaneously as a cop who denounces the rackets and as a gangster who promotes them, and which portrays criminals in a way that may make them less glamorous and imitable but also "more respectable, and less readily distinguished from the society around them." Maltby takes up the claim by Comolli and Narboni that "such cracks expose the ideology they express," arguing that "the film's internal tension is directly attributable to the operation of the Hays Code" (*HE*, pp. 119–24).

Maltby's account of causation is not wrong, just insufficiently specific to distinguish the fissures in *Bullets or Ballots* from symptomatic contradictions in any number of Hollywood films after 1934. In his penetrating commentary on the *Bullets or Ballots* DVD, Dana Polan individuates the way the Hays Code operates in this instance by elaborating a familiar thesis that goes something like this: Warner Bros. eagerly embraced this historical moment, this cusp between the old and the new, as a pretext to revive the gangster film, once boffo at the box office, but shelved after the outcry over *Scarface.* Adapting the successful tactic of *G-Men*, starring James Cagney, which had been released the previous year, the studio outflanked the Hays Office by taking the point of view of the police while turning the police into a type of gang, a trick performed without regard to its political implications, but instead somewhat cynically designed to provide the kind of excitement that had made gangster films so popular at the beginning of the decade. Polan does not vigorously press this claim, but he does provide some distinctive evidence when he mentions one scene that appeared in early versions of the docudrama at the beginning of the picture but that was later dropped: it depicted gangsters coming into the office of a businessman named "Hays" (therefore, the "Hays Office"), and strong-arming him. Polan comments, "Undoubtedly, it was felt that you couldn't have a scene where Will Hays or someone named like Will Hays is also giving in to the pressures of gangsters." Just as undoubtedly, it was felt that you would like to have such a scene. Why? Perhaps, as an edgy joke regarding the incapacity of the Hays Office and its elaborate Production Code to protect the film industry from a gangland threat somewhat more brutal than the Catholic Church's Legion of Decency. More likely it was because gangster infiltration of the film industry had already occurred. By 1936 gangsters Willie Bioff and George Brown had muscled their way into the film industry, taken over the International Alliance of Theatrical Stage Employees (IATSE), the major Hollywood craft union, and begun extorting protection money from several studios, if not directly from Hays himself.[88] Polan does not pursue the real-world allusion in that direction, however. He is more interested in how the self-conscious remodeling of a genre that had been integral to the studio's brand identity is registered in the theatricality of the film. He usefully calls our attention to the numerous representations of scenes of spectatorship. He also conjectures that the repeated staging of confrontations between the characters Blake and Fenner could be read as serious contests between the actors Robinson and Bogart for primacy at the studio. Of course, that interpretation has to welcome irony, since although Robinson (barely) wins in the picture, Bogart wins in reel life.[89]

Because Polan never settles on a single agent responsible for what he considers to be the film's complex industry-reflexive meaning, his argument gives considerable indirect support for the studio authorship thesis, for throughout his commentary it is Warners' intention on whose behalf these various agents work and their sense of Warners' interests that guide their decisions on what to cut and what to keep. Unfortunately, Polan's version of a studio thesis is not compatible with his mimetic thesis—that the movie reflects a shift in the nature of criminal activity from "the lone gangster" to the rational, number-manipulating organization. If there ever was such a species as "the lone gangster" (something of a contradiction in terms) he had long been replaced in the public mind by the image of the highly articulated criminal organization, most popularly associated with the Capone gang. As David E. Ruth has amply demonstrated, from the mid-1920s onward the press had published numerous exposés of the rackets, and the theme of the "modern gangster" had been well established by the time *Little Caesar* made it to the screen in 1931. In 1926 Edward H. Smith published an article in *The New York Times* with the title "Crime Has Now Evolved as a Big Business." In the *New York Times Magazine* Raymond Daniell observed in 1930 that "the gang has oriented itself to contemporary conditions, and, while it touches the lives of ordinary citizens as closely as ever, it does so with more finesse and less violence. It is less painful to pay a few extra cents for your artichokes . . . than it is to be thumped on the head with a lead pipe and have your valuables and cash removed. It comes to about the same thing economically."[90] After repeal of the Volstead Act in 1933 some bootleggers made their way into other rackets that were already organized and so managed with relative ease. With repeal the government was ready to call "gangsters" "liquor salesman," but once liquor became a commodity just like any other, the gangsters wanted to deal in more commodities than just liquor, so they reorganized to exploit all commerce. *Fortune* called them racketeers, they called themselves businessmen. That identification would disturb MGM. Not Warners. As *Bullets or Ballots* shows, the studio, like its commutative characters, will readily exploit equivalancies: racketeers are businessmen, as businessmen are racketeers.

Just as there was no major change in the structure of criminal organizations in 1935–36, there was no perceptible criminal emergency either. In "Crime and the New Deal" *Fortune* informed its select readership that despite the highest homicide rate in the civilized world, a "crime bill estimated at $13,000,000 a year and some 400,000 Americans who regularly engaged in criminal activities," "there is no crime wave" ("CND," p. 56). It explains the "paradox" with the assertion that "the statistics don't make a crime wave because there is nothing new about them." *Fortune* does not devote much ink to the rackets, but not because there's no racketeering: "because it is an indirect form of crime, because its victims seldom complain to the police, and because many semi-legitimate businessmen actually welcome the racket as a way of getting ahead of competitors, racketeering statistics are extremely incomplete." Racketeering can look a lot like the market power exercised by a monopoly or a cartel that—perhaps with the encouragement of the NRA (National Recovery Administration)—squeezes out those "chiselers" who engage in the commercial violence of "cut-throat competition" in order to put a floor under prices. *Fortune* concludes that there is just not enough evidence to determine whether racketeering is "more or less prevalent today than in the past" ("CND," p. 59).

Bullets or Ballots is no help. There is almost no crime in this crime picture. Crimes are alleged and imaginatively dramatized in the docudrama *The Syndicate of Crime*. But even though we see the judge censoring the jury for acquitting Kruger, we are shown no evidence (even in reenactments) that would indicate he is guilty of any crime at all. Kruger complacently dismisses Fenner's worries about the effects of the newspaperman's picture: "The public has been played for suckers for so long they'll never wake up. Who threatened Bryant? He can't hurt us without the evidence and he isn't going to get any." Fenner, all too susceptible to the movie, foolishly murders Bryant anyway. Without that murder there's no *Bullets or Ballots*, for without it the grand jury has no interest in investigating the rackets, and, by extension, the public has no interest in a motion picture about the rackets. Even so, with the exception of the DA, we never see the public aroused about *breaking* the rackets; on the contrary, the few glimpses of representatives of the public we get in montage sequences show their eagerness to *participate* in the rackets by buying tickets in the numbers game. That looks like a doubling of Warners' cynicism: not only does it use the danger of the rackets as an excuse to mount an old-fashioned crime picture, but it plays its audience for suckers by pretending that its motion picture will have some positive effect on law enforcement. Warners crosses up the Hays Office all right, but to conclude that it double-crosses its audience is to miss the distinctive touch of Warner Bros. irony, an irony that certainly aims to deflate the idealism of Bryant and—not incidentally—the New Deal, while at the same time acknowledging that the public is not a sucker after all, for the infiltration of the rackets into business is good for business—is, in fact, business itself.

There are only two examples of extortion in this film about the rackets. In one instance, the cops, warrantless, wreck Fenner's business and then brag about their use of the crooks' own tactics. In the other instance, Fenner's boys try to strong-arm Lee into surrendering the numbers game that she and Nellie LaFleur (Louise Beavers), her former maid, are conducting in the Bronx and Harlem. Lee, who is running an illegal racket, is hardly in a position to complain to the police. Her success depends on taking a percentage from a lot of little businesses in the Bronx and then merging Nellie's business in Harlem with her own. She should know that when the bigger racket takes over the smaller it is just following the logic of increasing efficiency and cutting costs. As Raymond Moley perspicuously commented in 1930, "The reason the racket is so hard to stop is that it looks like normal life."[91] The racket looks like normal life to the jury that acquits its boss, and it even looks like normal life to the racketeer who has made his way to the top of the organization. Kruger, the boss, carries no gun, threatens no one, and pays his own way into the movies. He is not a crook pretending to be a businessman; he *is* a businessman, which, paradoxically, is why he is so vulnerable both to Blake's bravura sales pitch *and* to Fenner's bullets. Blake's ideas for making more money make sense, so why would he be treacherous? Fenner will make more money as part of the organization even though he suffers in the short term, so why would he want to ruin a good thing?

Not-so-secret sharers, the abnormal Blake and Fenner cannot focus on business because they are driven to solve the mystery of their existential unhappiness. Stung by the murder of Bryant and exalted by the confidence of McLaren, Johnny thinks he is risking his life in a search for hard evidence that will put both the racketeers and their corporate overseers in jail. But, unknowingly, he is also searching for the bullet with his and Fenner's names on it. The suspicious Fenner spends most of the film trying to find proof that Johnny is a double-crossing cop. Fenner succeeds. Johnny is convinced that he has found evidence of a high-level conspiracy. If, unlike Fenner, Johnny does not succeed in his investigation, it is because, although he has obtained what he was after, what he thinks is evidence will not convict anybody of racketeering.

Once Johnny has been initiated into the hideout of the mob, where men busily stack currency retrieved from the betting customers and count up untaxable revenue, the narrative continues as if the sheer counting of money and keeping of records are crimes and as if all Johnny has to do is connect the dirty hands in that scene with the clean hands of the unseen directors. Johnny knows that what he sees is a criminal enterprise, but to any other observer the scene might look like the backroom of a highly profitable business. We don't see any criminal activity; directors have not committed any crime except that of receiving money they haven't earned. There is no implication that it is stolen money. It *may* be extorted money, but extortion remains to be proved. Blake is entirely focused on establishing a chain of evidence that connects the underworld with legitimate business. He records the serial numbers of the currency on a slip of paper, which the cops retrieve in the faith that the numbers will connect the money he subsequently delivers to the banker and his cronies with Kruger's gang. Even if the mere possession of money that is suspected of having been extorted would count as a crime, however, there is a bad fracture in the chain of evidence: Blake himself delivers the money; he's a cop, now a dead cop. He will never testify. What jury is going to believe that he did not plant the serial numbers? After all, he planted himself in the gang and roundly denied it to everyone except McLaren. It is no cure for skepticism that the picture makes a big deal of the only real evidence for a crime, which the dying Blake supplies when he carries Fenner's bullet lodged in his gut to McLaren. The bullet is proof that the same gun killed Bryant and Kruger. So what? Fenner is already dead at Blake's hand. By closing the case with his dying breath, Blake ensures that the public will know that at least one crook got his just desserts in receiving bullets for bullets; but, on reflection, the melodrama also looks like a diversion from the grim realization that, equipped with Blake's so-called evidence, a DA would be unlikely to win a jury's ballots for convicting anyone else.

If the contest is between bullets and ballots, bullets win without question. But they do not win much. Even the most trigger-happy cop can't shoot everybody. Moreover, it is a little odd that the lawman chooses bullets not in the *absence* of ballots but in *contempt* of ballots. And it is odd that the only character who is actually associated with ballots is the murderous Fenner. When Blake walks in on the gang after Kruger's murder and finds Fenner seated at Kruger's desk, he asks, "Say, what is this, an election?" Fenner replies, "It's already been held." "And you're it," Blake rejoins while pointing his cigar at Fenner. Fenner nods. "Any objections." Blake voices some, and by the time he has finished he has effectively overturned the result of the "election" by lying to the men about his appointment with the secret bosses. It is unlikely that any ballots were cast, of course. The point, however, is that even the psychopathic Fenner invokes an election as the basis for his authority, while Blake dismisses it. As we have seen, the relation of Big Boy to the gang in *Little Caesar* is opaque, a social hieroglyph figured by the painting whose aesthetic quality Rico could never grasp. The *agency* of the upper-class directors is equally enigmatic in *Bullets or Ballots*. How, exactly, did they go about influencing the jury during Kruger's trial? How would they carry out their threat to the life of Kruger? These are men who would not even touch a gun, let alone fire one, and no one knows that they exist except Kruger. Their agency may remain murky, but the *function* of the secretive directors at the Oceanic Bank for Kruger's gang is considerably clearer: they provide protection for the racket that enables it to operate without fear of indictment and prosecution.

In making *Bullets or Ballots* Warners never got close to reading the headlines. The screenwriters seem to have spent more time watching early Warner Bros. films than poring over the story on which the picture is nominally based.

Bullets or Ballots is a remake of *Little Caesar* with the elegant variation of splitting Rico between Blake and Fenner. Blake gets Rico's criminal ingenuity, his rhetorical gifts, his vanity, and his repressed homosexuality; Fenner gets Rico's hatred of double-crossers and his proclivity to deal with enemies by shooting them. Fenner's assassination of Bryant, like Rico's more hotheaded murder of McClure, galvanizes the police. In this version of the story it is Fenner who gets Otero as his sidekick, or at least George E. Stone, the actor who played Otero in 1931. The real difference between *Little Caesar* and *Bullets or Ballots* is that the power of homosocial bonding, which eventually disables Rico's intention to shoot Joe Massera (Douglas Fairbanks, Jr.), migrates to the law's side of the street. Although Lee, the owner of the cabaret, adores Blake, Blake tells Lee it could never work out; he is married to his job. The personification of that job turns out to be McLaren, a man with godlike power, who selects Blake as his agent of subversion, and who, with smoke rising from his pipe, secretly meets his man in the intimacy of a dark jail cell meant for one, and who later cradles the dying Blake in his arms. The predatory Fenner goes after Lee's operation and Lee herself, forcing on her an unwanted kiss. What she wants—Blake—she won't get. Her affection for Blake is hopeless: he cannot protect her when Fenner threatens to take her numbers game away from her; he cannot provide her the protection from the police that Fenner offers, because he *is* the police. If Fenner defeats Blake, Lee gets to keep the numbers game and Fenner. If Blake wins she loses the numbers game and Blake—and probably goes to jail with the rest of the gang.

Polan has pointed to the incongruity of the scenes at Lee's cabaret, which, in a narrative that otherwise has all the stylistic and thematic traits of a film noir, are brightly lit and cheerful, punctuated by comical appearances of the ever-drunk or distracted Frank McHugh, who plays Herman, Lee's bagman. Despite the fact that Lee mistakenly enables Fenner to find Blake and kill him, this *femme* is not really *fatale*, just ignorant, hurt, and impetuous. Lee is a commuter from the Warner backstage musical days with which Joan Blondell was, of course, closely identified. Lee's partner is Nellie, a black woman, formerly her maid, who first appears accompanied by a black chauffeur and bodyguard carrying a satchel loaded with the day's revenue from the game in Harlem.

In his commentary Polan worries whether, despite the racial stereotyping of Nellie, there is any way to classify this representation as "progressive." He settles on the moment when Nellie summons her black bodyguard to eject Fenner's henchman as one that might have caused discomfort to southern racists. Maybe. There's no need to guess at what the good folks in Little Rock would have thought, however. Warners progressivism is a specific studio formation, which here must be gauged in relation to its return to a former act of racism, *The Jazz Singer*. In his compelling essay, "Blackface, White Noise," Michael Rogin argues that in their breakthrough picture the Warner brothers chose to represent blackface as the vehicle for Jewish assimilation into the world of entertainment in order that they could appropriate "jazz" from the African-American musicians who invented it. The mammy-loving, Jewish jazz singer "with the tear in his voice," could thus claim an authentic Americanness. That expropriation followed from a racism so profound that there could be no sense of a wrong done, for unlike the white ethnic, the Negro was nothing more than a black Other, perpetually unassimilable and therefore always available for exploitation by blackface masquerade.[92]

Bullets or Ballots preempts Rogin's indictment not by a defense of its action but by an attempt to redress the error. When Nellie, swathed in fur and glittering with diamonds, arrives in Lee's office, she says to her former boss, "You're going to get rich from [the numbers]." But later in the scene, when Nellie, busy putting a wave in Lee's hair, says she would like to come back to her old job and take care of her, Lee responds, "No, Nellie, you've graduated. You keep managing the Harlem end. You thought of this game, and you're the one who deserves to get rich from it." Nellie objects, "Sometimes I wish I'd never thought of it." Nevertheless, she resigns herself to her success and her obligations. The two women are the only characters who have measurably "progressed," and, though the picture cannot relinquish the notion that a successful black woman would be nostalgic for her days in service, in principle the two women, black and white, are commutable as managers. Nellie does not owe her graduation to someone's redescription of hairdressing as "art"; she ascended by partnering with Lee to build an organization based on her own idea.[93] Rather than being an example of MGM's social-adjustment trope, this is the trope of authorship: the products that follow from your idea become yours; in turn, you become responsible for them. Recognizing its own responsibility, Warners attempts to make some redress for the cultural expropriation that capitalized *its* graduation by acknowledging the African-American authorship of an efficient racket that requires no muscle to operate because it is purely a matter of numbers.

Nicknamed "policy," the numbers game was a well-organized gambling operation, as illegal in New York as in Cleveland or Atlanta. Unlike other forms of the racket, which involve extortion of retailers who do all the work of production and distribution, long-term profits in the numbers game required a percentage payoff to the shop owners, who collect the money and make the payouts. Unlike the other indirect forms of the racket, where customers may be completely unaware that they are being taxed to pay off the extortionate gamblers who provide protection to honest businessmen, in the numbers game the number is the commodity and each individual purchase both directly approves the game and indirectly approves the organization that makes it possible. Each purchase is, in that respect, a ballot in favor of the racket, which could not exist without wide popular support. The nickname of the numbers game, "the poor man's insurance," contains more truth than sarcasm. Most poor people could not afford any insurance at all. Although the odds are against you in the numbers game, they are—like the actuarial tables that tilt the whole life policy inexorably to the profit of the insurance company—still odds. And you can beat them. The numbers game pays off at six-hundred-to-one to a person who can afford to spend the money, whereas insurance pays off anywhere from thirty-thousand-to-one, if you are lucky enough to die the day after you pay your first premium, to about five-hundred-to-one, if you have the stamina to keep up your payments and the misfortune to live a long life. Short or long—either way you don't get to spend it. You are boxed up in your payout as they lower you six feet under. When you hit the numbers, however, the money's right there at your local tobacco store or hairdresser, hot to be spent or invested in more numbers.

Or that is the way it should be. As we have seen in *Fortune*'s profile of Metropolitan Insurance, insurance salesmen are able to sell security because the company projects an image of security: its fortresslike headquarters, its conservative investments, and, most of all, its capital reserve. For the numbers to be successful the payoffs must be predictable and immediate: if your number hits, you want your money right away. A corner grocery story that tries to run its own game could be wiped out by one big winner, and even a small organization like Lee's, which has revenue of about twelve thousand dollars a week, could get seriously hurt if the numerals of a local telephone exchange turned up as the last four numbers of the total bet on the winner in the fifth race at Belmont. A slow or partial payoff and the same grapevine that accounts for your prosperity will quickly dry up and starve you of players. And that's where a large, tightly managed criminal organization like Kruger's comes in. For a reasonable percentage on each ticket, it will make sure that mom and pop will never come up short. They'll pacify the police and handle the money. They offer protection and they provide it. They offer security and provide it. Kruger's racket serves a purpose for its salesmen and customers substantially the same as Metropolitan's executives serve for its salesmen and customers. The primary difference is that one racket is illegal, the other respectable. In the big picture Lee is lucky that Fenner tried to enlist her in an expanded organization, and if she can stay out of jail, there is no reason to think that she won't thrive as a member of the syndicate—whoever runs it.

The numbers game is progressive. As Nellie jubilantly proclaims, "The boys at the pool halls are spending their money on numbers instead of dice. And when a colored boy stops crap shooting that's something." Nellie and Lee's racket takes men out of the poolrooms and alleys, where they shoot craps, and into the corner grocery, where they buy a number and maybe a cigar or an apple. Despite its programmatic commitment to the direct action of an automatic weapon rather than the indirect action of the ballot box, with *Bullets or Ballots* Warners indirectly endeavors to compensate for the studio's expropriation of jazz, the major innovation of black culture, by its acknowledgment of the numbers game as the major innovation of black commerce—an innovation that efficiently sublimates tangible commodities into intangible numbers, which enables the involvement of disparate, independent neighborhood businesses in a vast syndicate, of all social classes in a single racket, and which, like no other business in America, offers everyone the same access to the game and the same chance to risk their money. The numbers game is, therefore, much more progressive than another recently introduced racket: social security.

Upon signing the Social Security Act into law on August 14, 1935, FDR announced, "We can never insure one hundred percent of the population against one hundred percent of the hazards and vicissitudes of life, but we have tried to frame a law which will give some measure of protection to the average citizen and to his family against the loss of a job and against poverty-ridden old age."[94] No absolute protection—fair enough. But the original bill only provided benefits to the worker. There were no dependent or survivor benefits for the spouse and minor children. Moreover, the social security bill sent to Congress did not provide social insurance. The Social Security Administration, set to begin withholding money in 1937, the same year it would begin distributing benefits, would never have sufficient reserves to make good on all its obligations, whereas social insurance can only be viable if there are adequate capital reserves.[95] The effectiveness of social security depends on no new radical innovation in the relations of property; on the contrary, it depends only on that traditional and generally uncontested characteristic of the state: the power to tax, that is, what some might call the power to extort from employees and employers regular "contributions" to the fund.

In the pages of *The Journal of Business* in April 1933, Ralph Cassady, Jr., examined the block booking policy of the major studios. He generalized that theater circuits owned by the major producers "are granted protection over the theaters of the independent. Protection, a marketing device peculiar to the motion picture industry, has evolved out of necessity due to the unique nature of the product." "Unique" is an exaggeration, of course. Protection was the primary marketing device of the insurance industry and the rackets. Indeed, when Cassady goes on to discuss the likelihood of breaking up the control of the major producers, he sounds a great deal like Kruger talking about the sleeping "suckers":

> It is a well-known fact that the public is perennially apathetic concerning matters only indirectly involving their welfare. The independent exhibitors, on the other hand, have a real interest. Theirs is of a rational nature. As a result they have brought to the attention of the Federal Trade Commission and Department of Justice several of the questionable trade practices. As an indirect result of their efforts many suits have been filed against the major companies under the anti-trust laws.... Out of this array of lawsuits may come the relief for which the independent is clamoring and the public, despite its lethargic attitude, may also benefit.[96]

Cassady's projections became almost immediately obsolete with the passage of the National Industrial Recovery Act. By June, *Fortune* could optimistically urge that "the Sherman Act and the Clayton Act and the general body of anti-trust legislation has served its purpose and outlived its period and that some combination not in restraint of trade, but in restraint of unregulated production and competition, has become an evident necessity."[97] FDR's engineering of the National Recovery Administration promised relief from anxiety for the major studios on the political front. Its subsequent repudiation by the Supreme Court fed a growing disillusionment on the part of Roosevelt with the corporate liberal goals of the cartelization of industry, cooperation between business and government, and self-regulating markets.[98] Pivoting his artillery as he launched the Second New Deal, the president announced hostilities with "financial and industrial groups, numerically small but politically dominant" and attacked "entrenched greed," the "minority in business and industry" who seek "to control and often do control and use for their own purpose legitimate and highly honored business associations; they engage in vast propaganda to spread fear and discord among the people—they would 'gang up' against the people's liberties."[99]

This attack on corporate strategies of "association" had real consequences for the stability of the film industry. For Warners it was a presidential double-cross. "Harry had been persuaded by Jim Farley to back Roosevelt in 1932," *Fortune* reported at the end of 1937, "and what happened? The New Deal, as Harry sees it, pays off its friends with the Sherman Act and causes him to lose his theatres."[100] The loss to which Harry refers involved a complex deal in which a small stockholder managed to send the Skouras chain of theaters in St. Louis into receivership and then bankruptcy. Despite Warners' controlling interest and strong bond position in the Skouras company, it was frozen out of the management contract, which was awarded "to one Harry Arthur." In retaliation Warners instructed its agents to "nail 'any can in St. Louis.' This turned out to be the Shubert-Rialto and the Orpheum theaters." Not only did Warners deprive the Skouras chain of Warner Bros. pictures, its new theaters "turned up with first-run contracts for RKO and Paramount pictures too." Arthur sued the three majors under the Sherman Act. It was claimed (and denied) that Warner had strong-armed Paramount into joining the boycott of Arthur by threatening to upset Paramount's control of the theaters in Detroit, then a delicate situation because Paramount was going through bankruptcy.

> Judge Moore, a recent appointee, hearing his first major case, charged the jury in a vein that seemed to expect a conviction, and his charge has been called a Magna Charta of the industry by independents. The jury, taking a less sensational view, acquitted. Whereupon the government sued all over again in a civil action, which it later abandoned only to try a third time (on the same grounds) in the New York courts. By then Harry had been hounded enough. He recently sold his Skouras holding to the Arthur crowd, gave them a ten-year contract for Warner pictures, and moved out of St. Louis altogether. ("WB," p. 212)

In real life a judge urged conviction of the three companies, but the jury brought in an acquittal; in *Bullets or Ballots* a judge is depicted scolding a jury for failing to convict a man for extortion: the scenarios are as similar as corporate combinations that restrain trade and gangland racketeering. From Warners' perspective the major difference was that the federal government tenaciously, even obsessively, pursued the motion picture companies, not the racketeers. By 1936 the Roosevelt administration had abandoned the strategy of cooperation in favor of the application of muscle. And Warners, though it won in court, settled in order to buy protection from further prosecution. Big rackets tend to drive out small rackets, and under the New Deal the federal government had become the biggest racket of all. In being double-crossed by the president, Warners felt at home. It was familiar with a world in which betrayal is normal and everybody is part of a racket. The beleaguered studio did not name the feds as racketeers: to do so would just have invited more trouble. Thus, at the literal narrative level, *Bullets or Ballots* reads as an account of the dissolution of the evil of the rackets, even as, at the implied social and economic levels, it reads as an indirect defense of the rackets as "progressive": illegal businesses that mimic the legitimate business of insurance, that penetrate markets beyond the reach of a publicly held company, and that do a better job than the federal government of involving blacks and women in the management of its operations. At the level of character and generic affect the motion picture reads as a regression by the disillusioned studio to the violent melodrama of "cops" versus "crooks," which *Little Caesar* had proved would bring the "mob" to the theater. The spectator, we may imagine, is gripped with suspense as the wounded Blake staggers toward the Oceanic Bank to fulfill his mission at the cost of his life. It is unlikely if any of the suckers in the paying seats care whether the rackets are actually broken or, if broken, they will revive under cleverer ownership, capable of covering its tracks and massaging its numbers

vi. Be a Boy

Boys Town begins with two title cards imprinted with this dedication:

> This is the story of Father Flanagan and the City for boys that he built in Nebraska. There is such a place as Boys Town. There is such a man as Father Flanagan.
> This picture is dedicated to him and his splendid work for homeless, abandoned boys, regardless of race, creed, or color.

We can get a fair sense of the place of *Boys Town* within the MGM canon during the late 1930s by substituting: "Wizard" for "Father Flanagan" and "Oz" for "Nebraska," and by putting a "no" before each "such." *Boys Town* and *The Wizard of Oz* represent the yin and yang, the Rooney-Garland, the Spencer Tracy–Frank Morgan, the reality-illusion of MGM's prestige productions during the late 1930s. Follow the yellow brick road out of Munchkinland and you will eventually wind up in the Emerald Kingdom ruled by a bashaw of buncombe. Follow the long strip of asphalt out of Omaha, however, and you'll reach the black-and-white city for boys under the benign rule of a wise priest. The films complement each other. For one thing, the priest's authority, like the Wizard's, is wholly grounded in his mastery of public relations. For another, *Boys Town* and *The Wizard of Oz* are both films about character: its nature, its formation, and its use. Both evoke a place elsewhere: the former a greenbelt town, the latter an Emerald City. Most important, each film is structured as an argument to prove a simple world-grounding proposition: for *Boys Town*, "There's no such thing as a bad boy"; for *Oz*, "There's no place like home." Those propositions are complementary because in the world persuasively imagined by MGM in the late 1930s there is no such thing as a bad boy because some place this side of the rainbow there *is* a place like home. In *Boys Town* that home is no less protective and productive for being an institution, and no less an idealization of the corporate community of MGM for being presided over by Father Flanagan rather than Louis B. Mayer.

Boys Town opens with a bleak image of a vast building where many men live out their lives but which no man calls home. A dark mass, turreted with search towers, it is the image of a prison, which is also the image of the state. The connection between prison and state is made with the force of a verdict when the warden visits the death-row cell of a condemned killer to induce him to confess to his crime before his imminent execution. In another cell a black man is singing, "Sometimes I feel like a motherless child." Agitated, the convict beseeches, "Can't you stop his singing?" The warden (Orville Caldwell) puts his hand on the man's shoulder and replies, "You confess. He sings." The warden wants a confession, not to mitigate the man's punishment, but to justify justice as the state administers it. Although the prisoner appears remorseful, when the warden announces to the accompanying journalists, judge, and priest (who, it will be disclosed, is Father Flanagan), "This man wants to admit his debt to the state," the prisoner is roused: "What's that? My debt to the state?" The judge (Addison Richards) replies, "If you'd done this sooner that debt wouldn't have been so big." The condemned man indignantly responds: "Is that what this is all about? You're going to take my life because I owe the state somethin'? Where was the state when a lonely, starving kid cried himself to sleep in a flop house with a bunch of drunks, tramps, and hoboes? Is that when that debt started? . . . One friend, . . . one friend when I'm twelve years old, and I don't stand here like this." In that indictment of the state, Father Flanagan (Spencer Tracy) hears the tragedy of a bad man who once was a good boy, a boy who needed but failed to find one friend. Monopolist of the means of violence, the state is the ultimate creditor and implacable in enforcing the payment of debts when they become due. And what is a friend? He is not someone who will absolve a debt, for as the warden says it is not a matter of relieving debt altogether, just of diminishing or perhaps of distributing that debt. Flanagan will take on the debt for his charges—not to redeem it, for it is the New Deal thesis of *Boys Town* that debts can never be, perhaps should never be, finally redeemed. For if friends diminish debt, debt knits together friends, in observance of "the basic idea of society and of the nation itself that people acting in a group can accomplish things which no individual acting alone could even hope to bring about."[101]

The priest's ripening intention to befriend homeless youths is resolved by an accident on his return to the urban "refuge" that he runs for "drunks, tramps, and hoboes." He tries to break up a scuffle among a bunch of boys on the street. A window is broken, and the shopkeeper whose window it was, joins a delicatessen owner who is missing a sausage to press charges against the boys. Notably, the criminal charges are for accidental damage and for the theft of food. In accident and hunger, the extremes of contingency and necessity meet by excluding a middle terrain of calculation and criminal malice.

As Flanagan says of the breakage: "It was a free-for-all. Any boy could have done it." The crimes are not the consequences of individual will but the kind of incidents that inevitably occur in the Hobbesian world of the street where adolescent boys run free, brawl, and steal. That world is highly generalized: no signs specifically associate the urban environment either with Omaha in 1917, when Boys Town was founded, or with America in 1938 (suffering through a hard recession that badly shook the New Deal), when *Boys Town* was made. The social conditions for juvenile delinquency are characterized negatively, indeed, almost entirely by a single negative: the absence of parents. The boys fight in the streets because they have no parents. The boys are hungry because they have no parents. At their arraignment, no family members appear on behalf of any of them. That parental absence turns out to be providential, however, for it allows Father Flanagan to assume the role of the boys' advocate and mount a successful defense: the shopkeepers relent, and the judge releases the boys into the priest's custody.

Warners' *Crime School* (1938) was *Boys Town*'s chief competitor. A sidebar in the exploitation materials provided to exhibitors for *Boys Town* recommends that theater owners not tie their marketing to the "'kids' crime school' pictures and similar juvenile tough-guy roles . . . [because] 'Boys Town' is not a crime school nor a place where vicious juvenile delinquents are confined. . . . Boys Town is a story of moral, physical and spiritual juvenile regeneration."[102] "Regeneration," not "reform." *Crime School* had been Warners' spin on the successful formula established in *Dead End* (Goldwyn, 1937). Once again a group of streetwise boys get themselves into trouble; once again the promising but misdirected leader of the group disappoints his patient, hardworking sister. In Warners' variant, however, the leader and his buddies are sent off to reform school for retaliating against a fence who has cheated them out of a fair return on the property they stole. The boys have problems but the drawbacks of the so-called reform school are even greater, since it is run by a cruel and corrupt warden (Cy Kendall). The problem with the state-run school is not structural but administrative, just as the boys' delinquency is as much a failure of leadership as it is of poverty. Both sets of social problems are addressed by an employee of the state, Deputy Commissioner Mark Braden (Humphrey Bogart), who provides tough love to the boys in order to induce them to regulate their behavior and who cleans up the reform school by first demanding more money from the state and then by uncovering the warden's embezzlement. *Crime School* is hardly a leftist film: it does not imagine a world where the slums are cleaned up or where reform schools are unnecessary; it does imagine a penal system in which reform is possible, not through heroic efforts but through the exertion of bureaucrats who perform their duties responsibly. Typically for Warner Bros. (see Cagney's *Mayor of Hell* from 1933), *Crime School* represents a thoroughly social world where individual behavior counts in a group and where the charisma of a gang leader qualifies him for the kind of professional effectiveness that is demonstrated by a "reformed" Bogart (he had been cast in the role of the psychopathic gangster in *Dead End*) as reforming warden of the reform school.

Unlike the bonded toughs in the Warner Bros. films, the boys fighting in the beginning of *Boys Town* only *seem* ganglike. In reality they are just a bunch of kids thrown into the streets and made guilty by an incidental association that has not reached the level of any kind of organization and indeed would never do so without the intervention of a "father." In other MGM youth films of the late 1930s task-oriented groups may temporarily substitute for a missing family, but no organization is permitted actually to displace the family. In *Captains Courageous* (MGM, 1937), the spoiled rich boy Harvey Cheyne (Freddie Bartholomew) falls into the sea. When he is rescued he becomes part of a close-linked world of men. He learns respect for authority and the importance of self-sacrifice when he goes on a fishing voyage that inevitably ends as the transformed youth returns to the safe harbor of his wealthy father. In *The Wizard of Oz*, the parentless Dorothy (Judy Garland) forms a crew of specialists who save a kingdom; yet her real objective is to return home to her aunt and uncle. In *Babes in Arms* (1939), the youths belong to a community that, in the absence of improvident parents, provides the youths with some protection from absolute want and, worse, the tender mercies of the state as represented by the cruel social worker (Margaret Hamilton). Although the kids successfully band together to put on a successful show without parental supervision, Mickey Moran (Mickey Rooney) eventually arranges for this father to be reintegrated into show biz with his paternal dignity intact. In *Boys Town* the streetwise boys are as footloose and family free as the scarecrow, the tin man, and the lion—and just as much in need of someone, good priest or fake wizard, to help regenerate a character signally deficient in the virtues.

Although *Boys Town* is readily recognizable as an MGM film by virtue of its resemblance to other members of the studio genre of the entertainment commonwealth, it is also, like *Bullets or Ballots*, recognizable as an artifact of the Second New Deal. *Boys Town*'s unusual attention to economics is surely owed to the contribution of Dore Schary, a New Deal Democrat, who earned his first story and screenplay credits (along with Eleanor Rankin and John Meehan) for the picture. Despite the research that Schary and director Norman Taurog conducted on the site of the actual Boys Town, the story deviates considerably from the historical record (despite a marketing campaign that, like the printed prologue, invests heavily in the fidelity of the film to the reality of Boys Town), especially in how it portrays the means and methods that Flanagan used to construct Boys Town. With the moral-regeneration plot foremost in mind, the film, predictably enough, looks like an endorsement of a beneficent private corporation's efforts to compensate for the failure of the state to provide for the welfare of people so socially marginal that they do not count as citizens. The economic plot, however, introduces an antithetical line of figuration that represents Boys Town not merely as a corporation that redresses governmental ineffectiveness but as an institutional metaphor for the welfare state itself as its contours and protocols were emerging during the Second New Deal.

According to the official history of Boys Town, Father Flanagan acquired ninety dollars to pay the first month's rent "during a visit with a friend whose name is unknown, but very likely was the local Jewish attorney Henry Monsky." Because Monsky, who apparently never collected on his loan, desired confidentiality, Father Flanagan stipulated to the screenwriters that the original benefactor not be identified as Monsky or as a lawyer. In the film the rent for Father Flanagan's initial home is financed by a friend named Dave Morris, who is not a lawyer but the owner of the pawnshop whose window had earlier been broken by the boys.[103] Crucially, the money does not come in the form of a gift but a loan. After the boys have been released from legal custody Flanagan enters the shop and asks Morris for a loan of a hundred dollars to enable him to rent a home for the boys. Morris asks, "What security have you got?" Flanagan offers a watch that Morris rejects as worth less than sixty-five cents. "Have you got anything else?" Flanagan produces a cheap toy given to him by one of the boys he rescued from the brawl. Morris objects, "That's a ten cent toy!" He asks, "Have you got any other security?" Flanagan answers, "Every boy who becomes a good American citizen is worth ten thousand dollars to the state. That's a fact. I have good authority for it." Morris doesn't seem impressed by Flanagan's fact. He asks, "Couldn't you make a good American for fifty dollars?" Flanagan sticks to his initial request, and his pitch eventually persuades Morris, who gives Flanagan the hundred dollars and keeps the toy as "security." Flanagan promises, "I'll redeem it someday with interest." Morris is skeptical enough to ask Flanagan to sign a note, but is sentimental enough to rescind the request immediately. Indeed, because Flanagan needs furniture for the new home, Morris accepts fifty dollars back from the priest as downpayment on the price of one hundred sixty dollars that Flanagan has negotiated. The peculiar transaction ends with Morris's half-exasperated, half-resigned exclamation, "Fifty dollars of my own money as downpayment on my own furniture!"

This is a confidence game turned into a performance of public relations that retains the form of the con while bearing none of its sting. Morris is manipulated into placing confidence in the purveyor of a plan he doesn't fully understand. He is not exactly deceived, however, for he collaborates in the fiction of being fooled in order that he may be manipulated into doing something that, without Father Flanagan's marketing ministry, he would not know he wanted to do. The circularity of the transaction would seem to be a recipe for disaster, but it proves to be a miracle of rare device, like the "security" of the child's toy (token of the good in all children and the child in all men) that Flanagan periodically redeems. Here's how it works: Flanagan uses Morris's initial loan to get started. Other loans follow and are repaid. When Flanagan appeals to Morris for more money to relocate the expanding community from a cramped urban tenement to a massive rural campus, his friend and financer sets the conditions that Flanagan must meet to secure a new loan. He meets them, and the buildings rise. The buildings fill with boys. And Flanagan borrows more to erect more buildings to meet the demand of the youths who plead for admission. The more Flanagan borrows, the better off he is; the deeper his debt, the larger his edifices. As Boys Town prospers, so does Morris. Each time he appears to negotiate a new loan, he arrives in a new car and wears ever more expensive-looking clothes. Although ostensibly a pawnbroker, Morris is certainly no usurer: after Flanagan's promise to redeem the child's toy there is no more mention of interest on his loan. The prosperity he achieves is an indirect benefit of being the agent for the circulation of capital through debt, donation, repayment, and deeper debt, which is the cycle of Boys Town's expansion. The process by which this occurs represents the action of the Keynesian "multiplier." Keynes theorized that in a situation of vast unemployment, "the expenditure of, say, $100 by government would ramify through the economy with the effect of an expenditure of twice that sum, or even more. The precise multiplier depended on persons' 'marginal propensity to consume.'"[104] Morris donates nothing, but the hundred dollars he loans Flanagan is, as Keynes predicted, quickly multiplied in the consumption of the unemployed boys, for furniture, food, tools, and building materials. In *Boys Town* the capacity to become and sustain a self-governing community depends on the implementation of a Keynesian fiscal policy, which called for a drastic reduction in the interest rate and the stimulation of output by "increasing aggregate purchasing power" by means of deficit spending.[105] Boys Town thrives by running a regenerative deficit which funds an increased expenditure with direct benefits for the boys and indirect benefits—economic and social—for the community at large.

The "collateral" of the child's toy is a token of the personal credit that Father Flanagan has with Morris. Expansion of Boys Town will require more money, drawn from sources with which Father Flanagan has no connection and to which he cannot make his pitch directly. The continuing success of Boys Town depends on the development of a device that has the formal and symbolic function of the toy but that can be represented to a dispersed and anonymous populace. A brand is such a device. Flanagan's branding moment occurs when, as the symbolic first act of the new institution, he helps the boys hang a crude sign on the rundown house that will be the first quarters for the community. They then pose by the sign for local news photographers (Figure 1.18). In a gesture that anticipates the problems that Flanagan will have in getting good press, when the newspaper prints the photo it crops the sign from the frame. From then on, Flanagan will manage the brand more carefully. At the next home "Father Flanagan's Home for Boys" will be crisply inscribed over the door (Figure 1.19). Eventually, "Father Flanagan's Boys Home" will be embossed in stone above the entrance to the town's brick administration building (Figure 1.20). The sign is not an address, but a proprietary claim, which warrants Flanagan's representation of the community to outsiders as the Boys Town brand: the open campus, the commitment to self-government, and, crucially, its logo, the famous statue of the Homeless Boy that greets all visitors (Figure 1.21).[106] That statue is

Figure 1.18

Figure 1.19

Figure 1.20

Figure 1.21

Figure 1.22

as integral to the brand identity of Boys Town as the sacrosanct roaring lion is to MGM. We can be sure of that because the two are ostentatiously paired: an image of the Boys Town logo with the MGM trademark superimposed concludes the movie that the leonine MGM trademark introduces (Figure 1.22).[107]

That Boys Town is organized under a corporate brand rather than rationalized by a supervening state makes the difference between this community and what Erving Goffman grimly calls a "total institution." Otherwise, Goffman's description of such an institution corresponds fairly closely with Father Flanagan's establishment: "First, all aspects of life are conducted in the same place and under the same single authority. Second, each phase of the member's daily activity is carried on in the immediate company of a large batch of others, all of whom are treated alike and required to do the same thing together. Third, all phases of the day's activities are tightly scheduled. . . . Finally, the various enforced activities are brought together into a single rational plan, purportedly designed to fulfill the official aims of the institution."[108] The differences are critical, however. Boys Town is not a prison. The boys are citizens, not inmates: they are governed not by trustees but by officials whom they elect. Although the first group of boys is remanded to Flanagan's custody by a judge, no boy is compelled to stay; as we shall see, it is crucial that there are no external walls to keep malcontents in or supplicants out.

The most important distinction between Boys Town and a prison is that Father Flanagan founds his home for boys not on an imperative of the state but on the truth of a single proposition: there's no such thing as a bad boy. Unlike a prison, membership in Boys Town is not physical, restricted to those boys on the campus, but credal, available to all of those individuals anywhere and everywhere who make a commitment to Boys Town that follows from their belief in an institutive assertion about reality. If someone falsifies Father Flanagan's proposition, "There is no such thing as a bad boy," he or she falsifies Boys Town. Boys Town is thus an *absolute*, not a total institution. The security of an absolute institution is only as good as the customer's belief in the truth of what the brand attests. One bad boy can spoil the institution, not because boys are apples or an institution is a barrel, but because that's the condition that Flanagan has established in order to justify his plea to a public on whose conviction he depends in order to obtain the donations he needs to pay down his debt and sustain Boys Town.

Flanagan's task is not at all like the reformist challenge faced by the warden in *Crime School*, but it does resemble the brand-management challenge posed by David F. D'Allesandro, former CEO of John Hancock, who expansively defined a brand as "whatever the consumer thinks of when he or she hears your company's name."[109] Whereas the trademark is protected by statute, the brand is not. The trademark authenticates the provenance of the commodity for a potential purchaser. The brand manager understands that his customer is not merely someone who purchases a commodity or even whistles an advertising jingle; it is anyone and everyone who believes in, that is, who credits the brand. Only the diligent and imaginative effort of the managers of a business can hope to control the connotations of a company in the minds of everyone who thinks about it. Flanagan must do so in order to prevent the propagation of unintended and unwanted associations that have the potential of falsifying the essential proposition that distinguishes the Boys Town brand and qualifies it for financial support. Hence the life of this priest, like the life of a marketing manager, is a life of continual brand warfare. The terms of that battle are laid out when, in response to Flanagan's appeal for a large loan to finance the relocation of Boys Town to the countryside, Morris sets the condition that Flanagan must first obtain the support of the previously skeptical newspapers, for he knows that without good publicity Flanagan will never receive donations sufficient to repay the loan.

Father Flanagan knows that his proposition that "there is no such thing as a bad boy" cannot be falsified by good data, only by bad publicity. The test case is Whitey (whose name, as we shall see, is no accident), an unruly youth who has been reluctantly conscripted into the community at the request of his criminal brother. Whitey is played by Mickey Rooney, featured actor of the astonishingly lucrative, low-budget Andy Hardy series and fresh from supporting Spencer Tracy in *Captains Courageous*. The studio promoted *Boys Town* as Rooney's crossover film, what the exhibitor's sheet calls "his elevation to stardom." The movie is an account not only of how stardom is achieved but also of its social and political significance. The brash Whitey is contemptuous of all he sees during his tour of the community, which soon reciprocates his rejection. His repudiation is first marked when he goes to the town barbershop and high-handedly demands a haircut from Moe, the one Jewish kid in the community (he dons a yarmulke at lunch and says his grace in Hebrew). The Jewish boy plays a trick on Whitey in the barber's chair: instead of patting aftershave onto his face he lathers him with black shoe polish (Figure 1.23). When the oblivious Whitey is mocked by the rest of the boys he gets furious with Moe and blackens his eye in revenge for making him look like "a mammy singer."

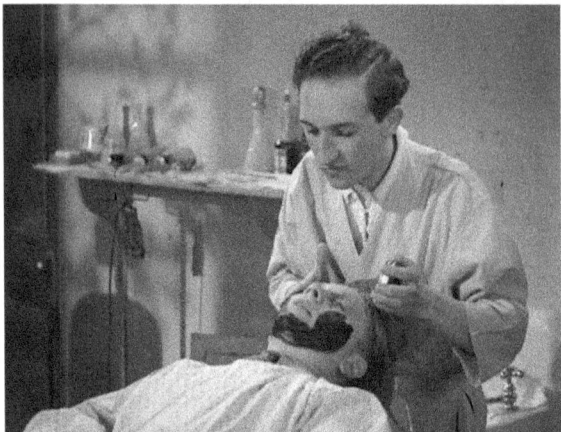

Figure 1.23

Whitey had gotten what he asked for. Not only had he mocked Moe earlier, but on Whitey's arrival he had aped the supplicating posture of the "Homeless Boy" statue, the community's highly visible logo, by raising his arms in a similar gesture and belting out, "Mammy! Mammy!"—mocking the icon and the community it represents by associating the trademark with Jolson's famous stance and plaint (Figure 1.24). Moe simply takes the implications of Whitey's jape and applies the blacking to Whitey's face, thereby transforming a performed act of distinction into an imposed stigma, which racializes Whitey by making him a black mommy's boy in a white daddy's town.

Figure 1.24

As Michael Rogin has shown, the jazz singer's blackface had, through the career of Jolson, become the privileged vehicle for representing and, indeed, enacting the assimilative aspirations of the Jewish moguls. Here the blackface is conferred by a Jew on a "Whitey." It is not the means of his assimilation into the society—it does not make him Jewish or black—nor does it ostensibly have anything to do with what Rogin and Flanagan call making an American, insofar as that is an ethnicized or racialized category. Rogin insists on the priority of psychological need, arguing: "The mammy singer asks for unconditional love by pretending to be what he is not" (*WN*, p. 183). When, standing next to the statue, Whitey extends his arms and belts out, "Mammy, Mammy!" he is not asking for unconditional love; he is mocking the piteous plea for fulfillment of that need he imagines the statue represents. And if pretending, he is pretending to be what we will learn that he actually *is*: an entertainer. At this point in the film, however, Whitey's routine, which mocks the trademark image of the institution, wins no one over. Whitey's readiness to travesty the sentimental figure of need is the visible sign of the threat that he poses to the community and that will almost be fulfilled when he later gets tangled up with his felonious brother. Regeneration of Whitey will mean his incorporation into Boys Town; and the incorporation of Whitey into full citizenship in Boys Town will mean the synthesis of the student, the citizen, and the entertainer into a new person. *Boys Town* shows what kind of educational work political activity can perform and what kind of political work entertainment can accomplish, not only in making an American but in forging what Dewey calls "the Great Community." As we have seen, MGM's marketing campaign for *Boys Town* directly takes on Warners' *Crime School*. Correspondingly, the studio's interest in the mammy-singer trope in *Boys Town* is less in appropriating the minstrel tradition than it is in expropriating the trademark of the professional entertainer from Warners—ancestral home of Jolson—on behalf of Mickey Rooney and of a new vision of the social ontology of the entertainment community which MGM alone represents.

Whitey is a braggart and a smart aleck, who rubs everyone the wrong way except for Pee Wee, the community mascot, who takes him for the great guy that he says he is. Pee Wee's admiration will become the standard that Whitey will eventually have to meet. Undaunted by the community's disapproval of his swaggering cynicism, when Whitey learns of the upcoming election for mayor of Boys Town he decides to launch a campaign complete with bold publicity and brash promises. The campaign concludes on the day of the election when he leads a small, makeshift band in a brassy march down the aisle of the assembly hall: MGM on parade (Figure 1.25). The hoopla confounds the decorum of the occasion. When Whitey, unabashed, takes the stage, his boastful oratory momentarily stuns the audience. The institutional process trumps Whitey's spectacle, however, as he loses by a landslide to the crippled boy (compared by Flanagan to FDR), who is the candidate anointed by the outgoing mayor.

Pee Wee remains infatuated. He chases Whitey around as if the boy were one of the pieces of candy that Father Flanagan

Figure 1.25

hides until it can be used to reward good behavior, or as if he were one of those bright shiny toys that John Sims bought with his contest winnings. If the latter simile seems strained, it is nevertheless justified by the "result" of Pee Wee's worship. On leaving the charmed precincts of Boys Town in pursuit of Whitey—who, humiliated by the boys' rejection, has packed his bag and made his getaway—Pee Wee inevitably becomes the victim of an accident; struck down by an automobile, he goes into a coma. Despite the fact that Whitey discouraged Pee Wee from following him, and despite the fact that an impartial observer might be inclined to question the due diligence of an institution that has no fences or gates to keep children from wandering onto the highway, the guilt falls on Whitey, who, like John Sims, flees what he cannot cope with. The premise has not changed from the street fight at the beginning of the film: a boy is bad only by accident. Guilt over an accident initiated Whitey's regeneration. Another accident brings him back to Boys Town when he is rescued by Flanagan after being inadvertently shot in the leg by his brother during a robbery. If invulnerable walls mark the total institution of the prison that we see at the outset, a vulnerability to imminent accident marks the perimeter of the absolute community.

The film climaxes with Boys Town's counteraction of the state's ineffectiveness in protecting the community from the bad consequences of its neglect by the spontaneous decision of the boys to police its perimeter. When the boys learn that the runaway Whitey has gone to the tavern where his brother's gang is holed up, there is no deliberation or vote as to whether to call the authorities. They amalgamate as a posse into which Father Flanagan himself eventually merges; and, in a scene that anticipates the unsettling nocturnal march of the showbiz children in the 1939 *Babes in Arms*, they march as one with the corporate intention of performing what could be called either a citizenry's arrest or vigilante justice by taking vengeance on those who had sullied the good name of Boys Town. No police are in sight. At first the posse directs its hostility toward Whitey, who is assumed to be an accomplice. But if Whitey has had a divided allegiance, he quickly makes up his mind and, with his brother's encouragement, allies himself with Flanagan and the boys by giving up his brother. Without becoming a squealer, Whitey nonetheless affirms a greater love than a boy has for his brother, thereby claiming his citizenship in Boys Town. The warden had said of the black convict: "You confess. He sings." Whitey, turned virtuous stool pigeon, overcomes that racial distinction and his own self-division: in his outpouring of the truth to the good Father, he "sings like a canary." The mammy singer has become a pappy singer.

In rescuing Whitey, the posse rescues Boys Town. Just as the regenerated Whitey finally comes to perceive and know the indirect benefits of the Boys

Town system, so will the public come to perceive those benefits through the agency of the press that reports Whitey's innocence. An enlightened public will then certainly rescue Boys Town from bankruptcy by automatically making the donations necessary to meet the deadline. Soon the community reassembles to stage another election. The outcome is no surprise. Whitey is elected mayor in recognition of his service to the community—not that he has helped hoe the field or cart the bricks, but that he has proven he is not a bad boy (or perhaps avoided having been proven to be bad) and thus restored the credibility of the brand on which the future prosperity of Boys Town depends. Yet the changes in Boys Town are at least as great as those in Whitey. Whitey's first grab for power had been backed by the radical innovation of a brass band and a parade. The community's response had been as much a rejection of the meretricious hoopla of the show as it had been of Whitey personally. When Whitey enters the hall for the climactic election of the new mayor he has not even announced himself as a candidate. He enters alone, without a band. He doesn't need one. The band is already in the hall, now apparently incorporated as part of the electoral process (Figure 1.26). Whitey is elected mayor by an acclamation solicited by Father Flanagan, who commands the stage and cues the fanfare. The indirection of the secret ballot or even the raising of hands has been abandoned in favor of the most direct mechanism that MGM can imagine: election by audience response. The finale reads as a cynical sophistication of the conclusion of *The Crowd* that submerges politics in cultural collectivism and demonstrates that the aim of an election is for the electorate to be entertained by a troupe of performers and for each citizen to be invited to his own participation in the show.

Figure 1.26

The "true" story of Father Flanagan's success props a Bernaysian fantasy of social control on a protection racket that extorts money from members of an audience in payment for the provision of the belief that they are protected from harm. We don't know the name of the company in the movie that owns a string of newspapers in the Midwest, but we do know the name of the company that through *Boys Town* advertises Boys Town and, no doubt, produced a bonanza of voluntary contributions to Father Flanagan's community: MGM. Mayer, who in 1936 had called motion pictures "the greatest molder of public opinion that ever existed," surely understood the larger claims that this motion picture made (*MD*, p. 290). *Boys Town* is public relations for Boys Town, but it is also public relations for MGM. In *Fortune*'s 1935 article examining the soundness of the new Social Security Administration, the magazine diagnosed the problem faced by a federal government that took on new, paternal functions yet remained committed to liberal democracy:

> Ideally a government with fatherly views of its responsibilities to its citizens should have fatherly authority to determine just what those responsibilities should be. But the government of the United States, though assuming the paternal obligation, remains the nephew rather than the ancestor of its citizens. It remains, that is to say, a democratic government, subject in it legislative assemblies to the will of any group of its citizens sufficiently homogeneous in either condition or need or both.[110]

Boys Town solves that problem by rendering democracy as a spectacle that homogenizes all parties and groups into a vast audience and by representing to *its* audience the prudent government of the citizenry as a problem in public relations, which, when artfully managed, will provide the wise father—modeled, no doubt on Louis B. Mayer—with sufficient authority to protect the faithful: those Americans who believe that there is no such thing as a bad boy and there is no such thing as a bad MGM picture.

vii. Be a Dreamer

Spencer Tracy in a collar, Mickey Rooney shedding his toughness with his tears: *Boys Town* was a sure thing. *The Wizard of Oz*, with its massive production budget and lack of bankable stars, was a horse of a different color. More than any other film under Mayer's regime *Oz* was designed to prove that Mayer could make the grand Thalbergian gesture. Mayer, who had been the subject of rumors predicting his imminent departure from the studio, had a need to assert his power. Making an expensive, Technicolor box office winner was the ideal vehicle.[111] With *Oz* he executed a double maneuver: he hired the dependable and efficient Mervyn LeRoy, long a mainstay at Warners, and advanced him to the head of the queue of producers at the studio.[112] He then appointed Arthur Freed as uncredited assistant producer to shadow both LeRoy and director Victor Fleming and report to him on a daily basis (*GS*, p. 263–64).

Frank Baum's novel was freely, even licentiously adapted for the screen. There is very little framing narrative in Baum, and no characters that correspond to Miss Gulch or Professor Marvel. If MGM had been Fox, if Mayer had been Zanuck, and if the screenplay had been written by Dudley Nichols rather than the MGM writers colony, *Oz* might have been given a Depression updating: the adaptation would likely have involved the sheriff, summoned by Miss

Gulch, arriving to dispossess Dorothy's aunt and uncle of their farm. Instead *Oz* induces an instant hatred for an unattractive and unpleasant woman who has been bitten in the leg by a dog she was attempting to chase from her garden. The mortgage is not at stake; nor is the callousness of capitalists under indictment: just a dog, and an order from the sheriff to apprehend it. Miss Gulch's rabid indictment of the dog as a "menace to society" could not be expected to sway the audience. Neither in long shot nor close-up can little Toto be mistaken for Little Caesar. Not only do we weigh the attested damage of the unseen bite against the visual image of cute Toto, but we must weigh the claims on our sympathy by the affectionate family of Aunt Em, Uncle Henry, Dorothy, and the hired help against that of a "society," which is not completely abstract only insofar as it is represented by the gruesome Miss Gulch. "Society" means as little as "law" to Dorothy, whose response to Miss Gulch's threat is to accept personal responsibility—she volunteers to go to bed without supper—but not personal liability: the damage to Miss Gulch means nothing to her, nor does the law that the injured woman invokes.[113]

Aunt Em has earlier told Dorothy to "find yourself a place where you won't get into any trouble"—an instruction that is the bridge to the film's theme song, "Over the Rainbow." More effective than the music, the twister would seem to fulfill her wish by depositing her, Toto, and the house in Oz. But of course Dorothy does not get exactly what she wishes. She does get into trouble in Oz. She learns that the twister that has swept her to this all but edible Technicolor fairyland has dropped her house on a witch. When the Wicked Witch of the West (Margaret Hamilton) arrives on the scene and wrathfully inquires, "Who killed my sister? Who killed the Wicked Witch of the East, was it you?" Dorothy replies, "No it was an accident. I didn't mean to kill anybody." Now, in Kansas this might have been prelude to the kind of lawsuit for damages that Miss Gulch has threatened. In Oz, however, although there may be trouble, there is no law; people can "cause accidents," if not with impunity at least without threat of suits for damages. The Wicked Witch menacingly replies to Dorothy, "I can cause accidents, too," before she suddenly disappears. The witch's claim is hollow, of course. She can fly through the air on a broom and survey the kingdom; she can write ultimata in the sky; she can dispatch legions of slaves at her command. She has a power to cause things to happen unrivaled by anyone else in the kingdom. Yet she cannot cause accidents—no one can who sets herself to do so. In the film the privilege of causing accidents belongs to Dorothy alone, just so long as she is radically innocent of any intention to do so. As it is by an accident that Dorothy kills the Wicked Witch of the East in an act of domestic violence, so she accidentally terminates the Wicked Witch of the

West by dousing her with a bucket of water. The Wicked Witch may appear to have a statelike monopoly on violence in Oz. But to innocent Dorothy is given the greater capacity, a countervailing monopoly empowered by the capacity to cause—inadvertently—fatal accidents.

MGM was a lot like Oz in that regard: no protection for those who did not merit it. The scene in Munchkinland where the Wicked Witch threatens, "I can cause accidents, too," ends with her sudden disappearance in a cloud of smoke and flame—an expensive theatrical trick that resulted in a gruesome accident to the actress Margaret Hamilton. The technicians knew that the shot would be risky: Hamilton had to move backward to a small trap door, and, as the elevator descended, she needed both to avoid the flames and to ensure that her bulky costume would not be caught in the apparatus. After many rehearsals, they got the shot; everything worked fine. But the director Victor Fleming insisted on a backup; and this time an accident did happen. Hamilton got caught in the machinery and suffered first-degree burns over her arm. Uninsured and uncompensated, she left the set and spent the next six weeks in bed. She resisted orders to return to the studio, but she also rejected advice from friends to sue. Hamilton recounted to Aljean Harmetz that when she was later asked to do another risky scene involving fire, she refused: "I said that if Mr. Mayer had been me, the studio would have the biggest suit of its life on its hands. I said, 'I'm not suing you because I know enough about this business to know I won't work again if I do sue. But I won't go near fire again. You can terminate me if you like." It was a good decision not to sue, a good decision not to go near fire again, and a good idea to compel the studio to choose deliberate termination rather than to let it happen accidentally. Hamilton was replaced by her understudy Betty Danko. Danko, who rode the witch's broomstick to which was attached a pipe for expelling smoke, was also injured when on the third take the pipe exploded. She was hospitalized for eleven days. So far as we know, neither Hamilton nor Danko was really a witch. Neither deserved to suffer. No one cheered when either woman was burned. Yet the innocence of the studio that caused the accidents remained as impregnable as a heroine's virtue in a fairy tale. None of the various accidents on the set (with the exception of Billie Burke's sprained ankle) was reported; none delayed the shooting schedule; and none cost the studio or its underwriters a dime. It is the studio's privilege and power, as the dominant company in a company town, to cause accidents with impunity. This is how monopoly works on the ground: it hurts people who are impotent to obtain justice.

By now it should be no surprise that an MGM motion picture would represent its focal character as saying, "It was an accident. I didn't mean to kill anybody." As we have seen, the exculpation of institutions from accidental damage had been MGM's story throughout the First New Deal; and the studio continued to stick to the story in the face of the Justice Department's revival of antitrust prosecution of the motion picture industry in 1938 on the grounds that Paramount and others were a "menace to society," an oligopoly designed systematically to produce good consequences for itself and bad consequences for those who are not part of the combination. The representation in *The Wizard of Oz* of a split between the innocent "I" who unintentionally causes accidents and the wicked "I" who claims the power deliberately to do so describes an agent whose effectiveness depends on her innocence of bad intentions but whose strength requires the repudiation of those who hold authority in the world of Oz. The dominion of the Wicked Witch of the West looks like a nightmare version of totalitarianism (Russian in dress, Nazi in style). Conversely, the Emerald City looks like a cross between a fantastic version of the corporate liberal imperium as it might have been imagined by the New Deal and a slightly exaggerated version of a Hollywood studio. On the one side, the broadcast of the commanding voice and the care taken to hide a ruler whose physical presence is ludicrously incommensurate with his projected power suggests FDR. Yet the rendering of a paternalistic corporate enterprise that is expert at makeovers but incapable of protecting itself except by promoting the illusion of wizardry with expensive apparatus and awe-inspiring special effects suggests MGM's own culture.

The baring of the device triggers a change of regime. Toto helps out by tugging aside the veil, but the illusion of wizardry is definitively dispelled when the master is compelled to recognize the nobility of his servants. He cannot, however, simply say the words, "I recognize your brains are as good as mine." The creatures have learned not to trust his assurances. He has to back up his words with greater magic, namely, the MGM trope of adjustment, here engineered with help from the prop department, which has furnished the wizard with testimonials and medals, that he can claim are authorized by institutions chartered in "the land of 'e pluribus unum'" and which he uses to transform the scarecrow–tin man–lion trio into full-fledged persons. The gesture is just another con, of course, but it does acknowledge the rule of law: the same rule of law that Miss Gulch invoked on her behalf against a biting dog; the same rule of law that sustains the Social Security Administration in its assurances to the wage earners of America that they can be protected from an uncertain future without staging accidents and waging lawsuits; the same rule of law that the film will finally, idiotically, disavow by magically conducting Dorothy back to Kansas in a state of blissful forgetfulness that an outstanding sheriff's order cannot be suspended by clicking the heels of ruby slippers.

The Technicolor allegory of the wizard's abdication has more bite than the black-and-white piety of Dorothy's homecoming. There is no election for the wizard's replacement: as in *Boys Town* it has become obvious who deserves to rule. By recognizing the virtues of scarecrow, tin man, and lion, the wizard has acknowledged a speciation of talents that forms a new aristocracy: complementary talents organized fraternally, happily collaborative, adept at improvisation, tested by struggle, and ready to rule. In other words, the trio is a fictionalized version of the creative team assembled not by Mayer or by LeRoy but by Arthur Freed, which included Freed, Harold Arlen, and Yip Harburg.[114] That team would provide the template for the talent package called the "Freed unit," which would emerge out of the production of *The Wizard of Oz* and eventually come to dominate the studio's production facilities and define its corporate image during the postwar years. It was Freed and Harburg who prevailed on behalf of the original script by Noel Langley (who had been removed from the film in June 1938) over LeRoy's resistance. It was the trio, led by Freed, which successfully opposed Mayer's decision after the first sneak preview, to drop "Over the Rainbow" from the film. It would be Freed, not Mayer, who, as the master of his own imperium in the Metro imperio, would become the standard bearer for quality at MGM. If we care to locate the mogul in the allegory, we should recall that it was Louis B. Mayer, not FDR or Irving Thalberg, who, like the Kansas wizard portrayed by Frank Morgan, started out in life as a peddler and who bragged about his associations with the "crowned heads of Europe." And if anyone is likely to fly away to exile in a balloon, it is Mayer, a mogul of vast assurances and petty betrayals. As it was, the beleaguered mogul would hang on during the 1940s as MGM sank to fourth place among the majors in "the annual net profits sweepstakes."[115] Mayer would not resign, however, until the spring of 1951, after a bitter fight with the newly empowered Schary. His departure was less like the wizard's embarkation than the witch's evanescence: "so abrupt that almost none of his surviving executives can remember exactly what took place. One minute he was in the studio, the next minute he was gone" (*MD*, p. 463).

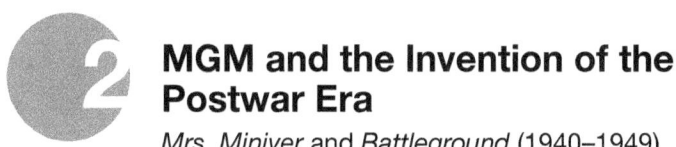

MGM and the Invention of the Postwar Era
Mrs. Miniver and *Battleground* (1940–1949)

i. In the Name of a Rose

Determining when the postwar era started is not the same as dating the end of the war. The end of a war is an empirical event. In the modern era, however, the postwar has been a figure of grand strategy. Leaders achieve a conceptual breakthrough, which is propagated through the news media in order to bring about a tidal shift of belief in the populace. In *Hollywood Goes to War*, S. Clayton R. Koppes and Gregory D. Black declare that

> the tide of war began to shift about October or November of 1942. "This is it," people sang out. The United States mounted its first offensive in the European theatre, in North Africa, on November 6, and though the news from Kasserine Pass was bad, we were finally giving it to the Nazis. We scored a victory at Guadalcanal. And there was another morale-boosting event of great symbolic significance—Eddie Rickenbacker, the World War I ace, was found alive after drifting for twenty-four days on a raft. We could feel at last that victory would be ours, perhaps as early as 1944.[1]

As Dwight D. Eisenhower recalled in his memoirs, *Crusade in Europe*, the perception of a turning point was necessary to provide political cover for the long range planning of the military objective of an invasion of northwestern Europe.[2] The press's willingness to share and propagate that perception provided the base in public opinion on which to build a postwar strategy. In the United States, safe from bombing or invasion, the shape and conduct of the war—and particularly the 1942 offensive in North Africa—were attuned to the registration of public opinion about the war. Koppes and Black can legitimately mix the results of battles with symbolically significant rescues because for the United States victory over the foreign enemy and over the demos were radically implicated: in a liberal democracy, especially one that is fighting because it *chooses* to fight, military latitude is constrained by political imperatives, which in turn are quantified as public opinion. Eisenhower recalls that Britain had no choice but to mobilize to fight a total war that fused homefront and battlefront.

Although Eisenhower suggests that Pearl Harbor had convinced the American people that their "survival" demanded entry into a global war, he shows that from a military perspective the reasons that the United States could *choose* to enter the war and the reasons it *needed* to enter the war were virtually identical and had nothing to do with survival. Despite the sporadic successes of the New Deal, there remained an untapped reserve of industrial capacity, unemployed labor, technological ingenuity, and military know-how that mobilization for war would exploit, completing that "revolutionary transformation" of the nation that the New Dealers had aspired to engineer during the 1930s (*CE*, 3–4). At least since planning for the Lend-Lease Act was initiated in December 1940, President Roosevelt had begun developing a duplex strategy that would respond to Great Britain's desperate struggle, while advancing a postwar political strategy that targeted the preference system of the British empire. FDR's capacity to juggle ostensibly incompatible political and military aims was the hallmark of a wartime diplomacy that always had the postwar embedded within it as a regulative idea.[3] The revolutionary transformation that Eisenhower regarded as a wartime necessity was exploited by Roosevelt as an opportunity to take strategic advantage of the peace.

Those Hollywood executives not in uniform followed Roosevelt's lead. No more than the other leading American industries had Hollywood distinguished itself by its preparations for war. Planning for the postwar would compensate for that neglect. And at this crux MGM assumed its rightful place as industry leader. Since the decline of Paramount in the 1930s, MGM had become a synecdoche for the industry in the mind of the public, for whom Hollywood meant stars and MGM meant "more stars than there are in heaven," as the studio flacks boasted. Because of its numerous stars, MGM's involvement in the career of the war was especially conspicuous. The death of Carole Lombard, the war work of Clark Gable, the airborne leadership of James Stewart, the ardor for service of Robert Montgomery, the enlistment by a stubborn Mickey Rooney, and the clandestine heroism of Greta Garbo—all affected not only the continuity of production in the war years, but also jeopardized the dominance of a studio so deeply identified with its stars. Like the transition to sound, which had ruined the careers of silent stars and annulled the investments of the studios, the prospect of a transition to a new era sounded a note of mortality. Because stars, unlike cameras, sound stages, and studio lots, were not subject to depreciation, the death of a star, whether by bullets on the battlefront or by indifference on the homefront, was a dead loss.[4]

During the war the output of combat films among the majors—discouraged by the Office of War Information—was generally low (*HGW*, pp. 48–81).

Making rousing battlefront pictures was largely the business of the "minors" such as Columbia and Universal and the poverty-row studios Monogram and Republic. Even so, MGM was slow to come to terms with the Nazi threat. Well after Harry Warner had challenged the restraints that the fascist-friendly Joseph Breen, chief of the PDA, was imposing on pictures that cast the Nazis in an unfavorable light, Mayer resisted all attempts by his writers and directors to propagandize on behalf of the Allies, and maneuvered to keep access to German and Italian markets open as long as possible. Once the war began, MGM settled into a mix of war-themed melodramas, comedies, and, of course, musical fantasies, with a few combat films thrown into the mix. The genre of movies most congenial to MGM during the war, however, was a set of movies that focused, not to say obsessed, on the bonded themes of breeding and grooming. Most involved animals. Almost all involved a setting or characters that could easily be identified as British. Indeed, those breeding motion pictures symbolically extended the homefront to Great Britain, and in doing so, they connected the fate of MGM to the fate of England. The British focus was unsurprising. Under Thalberg and Selznick, MGM had cozied up to the classics of British literature and regularly employed some of the leading talents of the British stage and film industry. Mayer was both a notorious anglophile and an avid horse breeder—passions that fused in a string of films he developed—beginning with *Thoroughbreds Don't Cry* (1937)—in which British actors are associated with the themes of breeding and grooming in order both to prove their pedigree for stardom in Hollywood and to confer class on MGM productions. Among the British stars in the stable were Freddie Bartholomew, Ronald Sinclair, Roddy McDowell, and, supremely, Elizabeth Taylor, who was groomed for stardom in a trio of wartime films that featured grooming: *Lassie Come Home* (1943), *National Velvet* (1944), and *The White Cliffs of Dover* (1944). For MGM stardom chronically carried a class connotation—not as a matter of ownership or of power but as an attainable aristocratic status. Class meant good breeding. Regardless of which was tenor and which was vehicle the mutual implication of starmaking and horse breeding was indubitable.

Thoroughbred's Don't Cry is the most bizarre member of the group. It tells the story of a British boy, Roger Calverton (Ronald Sinclair), who travels to the United States with his uncle Sir Peter Calverton (C. Aubrey Smith) and their racehorse, whose success at the track represents the only chance for the family to achieve financial security. The uncle dies from a sudden heart attack after watching his horse lose a race, and the young laird is forced to employ Timmy Donovan, the brash young American, played by Mickey Rooney, as his jockey. Though Roger had initially been repelled by Timmy, under the pressure of their common mission, they soon warm to each other. The crucial and exhilaratingly perverse scene occurs when the lads are alone in a closed bedroom, where Timmy has persuaded Roger to take his pants down to his knees and lie prone on his stomach, while the jockey sits athwart the young foreigner and rubs him down with liniment. The sexual innuendo is manifestly felt by the characters: as Timmy forcibly massages Roger, Cricket West (Judy Garland), the daughter of the landlady, appears outside the closed door of the bedroom to serenade the two boys with her ukulele. Timmy, embarrassed by Cricket's proximity and yet determined to keep Roger face down on the mattress, farcically ricochets between door and bed, until Cricket finally bursts in and interrupts the boys' intimate play. From a certain theoretical perspective, the scene, which balances one male riding another with a female who both enables the play and frustrates its consummation, presents a perfect example of the homosocial triangle. But where studio authorship affects our interpretation is in the necessity to describe the scene, not as one between men or even between boys, but as one between child actors. And not only child actors, but a budding American star and a British actor who is being groomed to replace the box office darling, Freddie Bartholomew, who was in the middle of contract negotiations with the studio. The sexual implications are as much cross species as they are homoerotic: in attempting to mount Sinclair, Rooney is in the position of mating with a horse, a British thoroughbred (the title *Thoroughbreds Don't Cry* does not refer to the horse but to its owner), in order to symbolically inseminate him with the drive that will make him a winner or, failing that, with the seed that will breed another more dynamic child star to add to Mayer's stable.

So intensely normative was the horse-breeding trope in MGM's natural philosophy that the racist and eugenic implications of *Florian* (1940), which celebrated the Lippizaner stallions, a breed born black but that magically turned pure white, could be overlooked by Mayer and his subordinates, even in 1939.[5] *Mrs. Miniver* (1942) has no horses. Nonetheless, it belongs within that group of films in which themes of Englishness, good breeding, and the cachet of aristocracy combine. Indeed, *Mrs. Miniver* applies unprecedented tension to those themes by connecting from the very opening credits the fate of MGM as a studio to the possibility of postwar Anglo-American hybridization. In pursuing that strategy of developing a special relationship that would later enable it to achieve its commercial objectives, MGM was tracking FDR's effective combination of wartime strategy—subsidizing its ally—with postwar planning: opening Great Britain's markets to U.S. goods. But there was another issue that concerned Metro: the continued pressure by the Roosevelt Justice Department for the divorce of production from distribution among the majors. Thus MGM could imagine itself both as a winner in relation to FDR's anti-British strategy, which promised to destroy the imperial preference system and open international markets, and as a potential loser insofar as the vertical integration of Loew's mimicked the structure of British imperial control. Like the studio's lawyers, *Mrs. Miniver* insinuates that the hierarchical social system has no necessary economic consequences. The motion picture masterfully renders the dear, antique feudal *form*, not as a system of class exploitation, but as a common cultural heritage that needs a transfusion of the vital sap that only MGM's middle-class melodrama can provide.

ii. Choosing *Mrs. Miniver*

Mrs. Miniver depicts the entry of Britain into the war through the experience of a village that overcomes superficial class distinctions to unify in the face of a common threat. The focus is on the life of what the prologue calls an "average middle-class family," the Miniver family: Mrs. Miniver (Greer Garson); Clem (Walter Pidgeon), the father; Vin (Richard Ney), the college-age son; and two accessory juveniles, Toby (Christopher Severn) and Judy (Claire Sandars). The Minivers move from a happy state of bourgeois getting and spending to an earnest involvement in the war at every level: Vin leaves Oxford to enlist in the RAF; Clem, an architect, joins the shore patrol and assists in the evacuation at Dunkirk; and while Clem is away at Dunkirk, Mrs. Miniver confronts a downed German airman and captures him in her kitchen. The war also transforms the lives of other members of the village: Carol Belden (Teresa Wright), the granddaughter of the dowager Lady Belden (Dame May Whitty), hurriedly marries Vin in order to take advantage of a brief leave; the grocer (Reginald Owen) becomes an air warden; after the annual conferral of the Belden Challenge Cup for the finest rose, Lady Belden opens her house to the villagers fleeing German air attack. The film concludes with a stirring eulogy for the dead, delivered by the vicar in the ruins of the village church, that dedicates the community to the greater cause of the "people's war."

There are surprises: the death by air attack that was feared for Vin Miniver, a youthful pilot, instead befalls his recent bride; Mr. Ballard (Henry Travers), the working-class winner of the Belden competition for the best-bred rose in the village, is killed by German bombardment moments after he steps forward for his trophy. In the big picture, however, those local surprises are no surprise; they starkly dramatize the shared vulnerability of the community under a potent and indiscriminate threat. In the state of total war to which Great Britain is subjected there is no immunity from danger and, apart from fallout shelters, no refuge from the rain of German bombs.[6] As a film directed toward American audiences, the message would seem clear: not only are Americans supposed to feel sympathy for the British, who display great pluck in the face of such terror; but America's situation is analogous to theirs insofar as even civilians, and thus potentially mainland Americans, are endangered by a ruthless and fanatical enemy. The traditional MGM message coincides with the path of patriotic prudence: Americans should elect the integration that the British have been forced to adopt.

Such a message was deemed necessary to arouse public interest in the European theater. Although the administration regarded the threat in Europe as more dangerous and of greater strategic consequence than the aggression of the Japanese, the focus on Pearl Harbor as the rationale for American entry into the war and the impact of the promotional machinery of Douglas MacArthur had focused public opinion on the Pacific Theater as the crucial arena.[7] Where the allocation of resources—the willingness of the populace to buy war bonds and to undergo shortages of commodities—was concerned, the administration could not afford to ignore Congress, and a biennially elected Congress was constitutionally incapable of ignoring public opinion. But it is important to distinguish between public opinion and morale. The former is a political quotient, the latter a military necessity. In Great Britain morale—the determination to endure, the readiness to fight—was an issue for the entire population, which, suffering intense bombardment, could not afford the luxury of opinions about either the wisdom of the war or the prudence of its leaders in conducting it. For Eisenhower, staff morale was fundamentally a troop-related issue, since the troops had to face inevitable delays in engaging with the enemy and would doubtless suffer temporary setbacks on what the commanders regarded as the inexorable push to victory (*CE*, pp. 299–300). When there is a difference of opinion about when and where morale is important a poll will not help; the decision lodges with the supreme military commander.

Mrs. Miniver would not have taken the shape it did had Americans been subject to the same peril as the British. The film articulates the ideology of a liberal society alarmed into action but secure from fundamental threat. It represents the opportunity to choose as authentic and inalienable. The objects of choice change during the film, but the right to an opinion and the freedom to choose are represented as *necessary*—one cannot choose not to choose. That formal necessity takes on the criteriological force of identifying characters as individuals, who are the enemies of the unindividualized enemy. The film investigates what makes choice necessary for all individuals in liberal societies and what directs that choice toward its proper object. *Mrs. Miniver* manifestly affirms that art is sufficient to the task; propaganda can only spoil. So great was Mayer's resistance to propagandizing, even in the days subsequent to Pearl Harbor, that he insisted (futilely, it turned out) that the scene in which Mrs. Miniver confronts a feral Nazi pilot be balanced by the introduction of a good Nazi.[8] Mayer's stipulation was not pro-Nazi but pro-choice. We might, even should, choose to hate the Nazis, but it is certain that we ought to *choose*.

Mrs. Miniver is not free from the propagandist's impulse, however. Propaganda is baldly present in the closing eulogy, a stirring call to national unity written by the director William Wyler and the actor Henry Wilcoxon, who plays the vicar, the night before shooting the final scene—a speech applauded by both Churchill and Roosevelt (*TT*, 236). But propaganda also operates in an allegorical discourse that has to do not with the public and its opinions of the war effort but with the Hollywood community, which would read the film as more than a story of the war: a prooftext of Mayer's continued power and of the likelihood of MGM's survival in the postwar era.

The issues are clearly framed in the 1939 sequel to *Fortune*'s Depression-era article on MGM, "Loew's, Inc.," which examines the larger corporation, directed by Nicholas Schenck, of which Mayer's MGM was the subsidiary.[9] The article justifies its timing in relation to the recent release of the last (and successful) movie that Irving Thalberg had launched before his death, *Goodbye Mr. Chips* (1939), starring Robert Donat and introducing Greer Garson to American audiences. Although the article reports that "Metro's gross revenue from film rentals has been consistently higher than that of other studios" and acknowledges Metro's continuing popularity, it cautions that "Metro pictures, while still possibly the most successful in the world, have recently been failing to make their customary splash in the trade." The failure to make a splash is not, according to the article, due to a lack of promotional savvy but to a decline in quality, which interests *Fortune* not as an issue in aesthetics but as a problem of what it calls "responsibility": "The recent crop of turkeys has not been reassuring. Insofar as this constitutes a problem for Mr. Schenck, he can hardly turn solely to Mr. Mayer, for it might be Mr. Mayer's fault. It is certainly Mr. Mayer's responsibility" ("L," p. 335). Although the article repeatedly protests that there is no reason for Schenck to worry, its report on the "antitrust problem" posed by the suit launched by Assistant Attorney General Thurman Arnold nonetheless identifies a set of ominous circumstances for Schenck not to worry about. And if Schenck truly does not worry, that could be no comfort to Mayer, the person "responsible" for the decline in MGM's quality. Schenck's presumed peace of mind might very well have been owed to his authority, should the antitrust action fail and decline continue, to fire or demote his studio head or, should the antitrust action succeed, to divest himself of MGM and concentrate on distribution and exhibition. Either way Mayer loses, and MGM, as the world knows it, vanishes.

Fast upon the challenge of *Fortune*—the foremost representative of the highest class of "trades"—in the year ahead Mayer would undertake to assure that Schenck *would* turn to him, and he would do so by absolving himself of fault while accepting full responsibility. His vehicle will be *The Philadelphia Story* (1940), a film over which he exercises complete control: he buys the rights to the play from Katherine Hepburn for the large sum of $150,000 and casts her—an actress of indisputable quality, despite her reputation for being "box office poison"—in the lead. He accepts Hepburn's choice of the despised George Cukor to direct, persuades her to accept Cary Grant's condition for co-starring, and shrewdly recruits James Stewart to replace the demurring Clark Gable, Hepburn's choice for the role of the reporter. The result is a critical and popular triumph. But, as *Fortune* instructs, such success counts less toward acquiring Schenck's confidence than does the argument that the film makes for the integrity and effectiveness of the studio. That argument is quite coherent: through the agency of a mysteriously gifted director and with the resourceful assistance of a loyal photographer and a talented writer, initially bankrolled by the publisher of *Spy* magazine, the purblind star of the household is saved from an alliance with a vain and stupid capitalist, who shows himself to be less a public-spirited leader than a slave to public opinion, which is formed and marketed by *Spy*. The goddess is humbled and brought back to the fold to star in the performance of her wedding. Behind the action are two authorizing figures. First, there is the figure of the mogul, the absent father in whose home-studio the action takes place. Like Mayer, he is a philanderer who has been supporting the theatrical career of an attractive young woman but returns to his estranged wife and family on the eve of the scheduled wedding. In a brutal exchange with his daughter, he both denies fault for his daughter's unhappiness and accepts anew his responsibility as head of the household. Second, there is the publisher of *Spy* magazine, which either qualifies as a gossip magazine that is a base organ of the trade or represents a parody of *Life* magazine, a publication of the same Luce Corporation that publishes *Fortune*. At the end, no one remains in the employ of *Spy*, and the performance of the wedding is splendidly brought off under the benign eyes of the rightful chief, Mr. Lord. The studio knows quality, the studio produces quality, and the studio is of such quality that it would be insane to sacrifice it to ignorant businessmen or venal gossip mongers.[10]

The wedding may be carried out in the studio under the eyes of its head, but it is also produced in front of the camera of the publisher of *Spy*, whose photos freeze the action and conclude the film. That it ends thus proves the resolute clarity of the film as an allegorical argument directed to the New York office of the studio. For *Fortune* had insisted that gossip had an independent and powerful status as the measure of Metro's slump. *Fortune* admits that it is a "volatile thermometer," but adds, "Hollywood gossip is itself sometime a hard business factor, in its effect on people in the industry" ("L," p. 335). For *The Philadelphia Story* to deny *Spy* would recast its deliberate argument as a fantasy of a world in which studio productions are mounted without reference to the public that, in the last analysis, registers their quality. By refusing to cast out *Spy*, the film acknowledges the power of publicity to mediate motion pictures and the public while insisting on an economy of publicity: there will always be publicity, but MGM, staffed by unparalleled talent and supervised by a responsible father-mogul, can render that publicity benign. Pace Stanley Cavell, *The Philadelphia Story* is Mayer's dream: one big happy family preserved in pictures by Mayer's MGM for the pleasure and edification of the American middle class.[11]

Yet to make an argument that represents the pacification of gossip is not the same as pacifying gossip. And even if *The Philadelphia Story* could, perhaps even did, persuade Schenck that he should continue to turn to Mayer, succeeding with that argument could not dissipate all the perils that faced the studio. Despite Schenck's own powerful arguments at the antitrust hearings in 1940, the five majors were forced to sign a consent decree to abandon certain anticompetitive practices in order to fend off a judicial ruling that would potentially require the disassembly of their vertically integrated companies. Moreover, although *The Philadelphia Story* carried away two Oscars, it missed the best picture and best female actress. Oscars went to Donald Ogden Stewart and James Stewart—both ingloriously *writers*: one the film's writer and the other the actor who played the writer. Even those second-tier awards were exceptions for MGM in a barren period at the annual Academy Awards ceremony.

Once again, the industry's notable indifference may not have been Mayer's fault but it was his responsibility. In retrospect we can see that it was a problem insoluble in the only terms that Mayer, who had become the studio's sole managerial star, could frame it. MGM was the Cadillac of the studios and could make only Cadillacs. It pursued a Fordist approach to motion picture making, except instead of Model Ts, the studio was producing (or pretended it was producing) only luxury cars, and those with almost no perceptible changes in the annual product line. Alfred Sloan's account of his strategic considerations regarding annual styling changes as CEO of General Motors sheds a bleak light on Mayer's predicament: "The degree to which styling changes should be made in any one model run presents a particularly delicate problem. The changes in the new model should be so novel and attractive as to create demand for the new value and, so to speak, create a certain amount of dissatisfaction with past models as compared with the new one, and yet the current models must still be capable of giving satisfaction to the vast used car market."[12] The difference between MGM and General Motors was not merely structural; it inhered in the kind of products each manufactured. General Motors made hardware, stylized, to be sure, but with a useful life sufficiently long to permit trade-ins and resale, with profits for the seller at every transaction. MGM, as *Fortune* notes, made an "ephemeral product" ("L," p. 336). There were no such things as used films and no venue for rerunning old movies until the advent of television.

Because of its product's ephemeral nature, a more exact analog to MGM's predicament is that of what Richard S. Tedlow has called "the great Cola wars." Tedlow identifies two phases in Pepsi-Cola's eventually successful struggle to wrest a substantial market share from the beverage industry's monopolist, Coca-Cola, both involving strategic breakthroughs by Pepsi executives but both made possible by Coca-Cola's identitarian commitment to an unchanging and intangible standard of quality. The first was the decision, made in the 1930s, to double the size of a nickel bottle, a pricing strategy that successfully attracted Depression-era consumers. But the paradigmatic breakthrough for Pepsi occurred after the war, when it pursued a strategy of market segmentation designed to enhance the prestige of the beverage, not for all consumers but for the expanding youth market it effectively denominated "the Pepsi generation." Because the identity of Coca-Cola's equally ephemeral product depended, as did MGM's, on a nondemonstrable faith in a product of superior quality with universal appeal, the industry leader was, if not defenseless against Pepsi's marketing strategy, extremely vulnerable, as the record of its declining market share in the 1950s, 1960s, and 1970s shows. Coca-Cola was effectively trapped not by its mode of production (identical to Pepsi's) but by its skillfully marketed corporate identity as a "brand beyond competition." Whatever the options available to it in the 1930s or even the late 1940s, by the time Pepsi's postwar campaign showed ominous signs of success, Coca-Cola could no longer *choose* to remain inflexible, it could only be Coca-Cola by *being* inflexible. The proof of this evolved law of Coca-Cola marketing was forcibly made by the debacle of the introduction of New Coke in 1985—one of the most notorious disasters in the history of marketing, so severe that the company, in peril of destroying its brand name, abolished the product within months, reverted to its classic status, settled for its stabilized domestic share, and renewed its concentration on the expansion and saturation of the global market.[13]

Like Coca-Cola, MGM was a prisoner of its performative commitment to quality. Although there were good economic reasons for market segmentation, Mayer made adjustments grudgingly and on his own terms. B pictures meant Andy Hardy pictures—cheaper productions, formulaic plots—but these were nonetheless star vehicles that targeted the same middle-class audience as the representative MGM features. Later, when Mayer had aged and weakened, Schenck finally gave Dore Schary free hand to produce grittier, topical films. By then it was too late: television had segmented the market for good, transforming films from ephemeral objects into software, fungible commodities that, as sixteen-millimeter prints, videotapes, laserdiscs, and DVDs, could be endlessly exchanged and plugged in to various kinds of hardware. Given that market segmentation would destroy the studio it was designed to save, the only strategic alternative for Mayer was the one he took (the same one Coca-Cola took): expansion of the global market for MGM films, each a quality product.

"It would be impossible to overstate the simplicity of Coca-Cola production," *Fortune* observed.[14] Reproducing the quality of flavored syrup is far easier than sustaining the quality of feature films.[15] The predicament of MGM was not the effect of the Hollywood mode of production; nor was it attributable to its own unit production system. It was predominantly the consequence of the studio being identifiable with a studio style, a commitment to production values that gave it "the highest per-picture budget in the industry" ("L," p. 343) and that, according to market logic rather than industrial logic, became the value of the studio in the eyes of its audiences, its employees, and such chroniclers of the industry as the trade press and the gossip rags. *Fortune* comments on the invariability of the "general lines" of Mayer's picture making and attributes it to the studio's "ringing faith in the star system," which, long MGM's strength, has paradoxically become its chief weakness, for the investment in creating a star "imposes penalties on the star's casting thereafter": most damagingly, the need to make pictures that are "more often vehicles than stories." Other studios were caught in similar predicaments in the 1930s, but the predicaments were *merely* similar. Each studio had its own sectarian faith. Despite prevailing federal suspicions of Hollywood conspiracies, Mayer could not learn how to solve his predicament by emulating Warner Bros. or Paramount or Twentieth-Century Fox.[16]

A journalist, not a strategist, the writer of the *Fortune* article does not recommend market segmentation to Nick Schenck. Indeed, despite its iconoclastic air, the essay accepts the same premise that Mayer had made his own: MGM is MGM only insofar as it makes quality pictures. It diverges only in that it fails to see what Mayer knows in his bones: those quality pictures would be made only under Mayer's direction; MGM is Mayer. But what prevents the making of quality pictures? What exactly constitutes the domain of Mayer's responsibility? Recognizing MGM's distinctiveness, *Fortune* provides a diagnosis of the ills of a studio whose decline, though real, is not to be measured in box office receipts or profits and whose reluctance to change is psychological rather than infrastructural:

> Naturally there is no issue of taste or social conscience to be raised by this timidity; but there is a question of studio morale. Since the ingredients of a successful picture are nothing but people and ideas, an atmosphere of courage and inventiveness can be just as vital to a studio as a chestful of contracts for stories and stars. Many Hollywood gossips believe that the recent series of Metro fiascos can be traced to a decline in morale. ("L," p. 343)

With the introduction of considerations of morale, *Fortune* identifies another, distinct audience for Mayer to address allegorically: not the public for whom MGM pictures are ephemeral commodities that they choose because of the perceived value of the productions, the stories, and the stars; not the New York office, for whom a film may be an argument for continued confidence in the importance of the studio and in the competence of the boss of that studio: but the studio itself, the craftspeople who build, wire, and light the sets; the writers who must "twist" the best stories "out of recognition to fit expensive reputations"; the producers and directors, and the publicists, who must convince the gossips that it is false "that Metro, like Paramount before it, has passed its prime." The difference between the first two audiences and the third is the difference between the *management of opinion*, public or corporate, and the *production of morale* in the studio and its feedback apparatus. That difference corresponds to a difference between persuasion, which influences choice, and propaganda, which instills or confirms a faith impervious to evidence. By insisting on the importance of morale, *Fortune* renders MGM as a distinctive cultural unit, subject to the same kind of threats to its identity and answerable to the same kind of compelling rhetoric as a nation immersed in total war—in other words, the corporate equivalent of Great Britain. The rhetoric of opinion and of propaganda systematically differ: the opinion argues, propaganda transforms; the former means and the latter does; opinion plans for a possible future and propaganda represents plans in order to dictate the future; opinion presents a star, propaganda makes a star; opinion might lead to selection for an Oscar, propaganda *claims* an Oscar. Those differences are as clear as that between black and white, or, rather the difference between choosing black or white and being compelled to see black as red. Although Mayer persistently refused to propagandize his audiences, to avert the perception of decline he would nonetheless try to revive the faith of the believers. *Mrs. Miniver* was the chosen vehicle for Mayer to vindicate MGM's commitment to quality, both in the eyes of its public audience, whom the film endeavors to confirm in its choice, and in the hearts and minds of the Hollywood faithful, for whom the film will attempt to devise its future and performance quality.

Mrs. Miniver begins with separate choices being made by Mrs. Miniver and her husband, Clem, in different scenes: she jumps off a London bus to return to a shop and purchase an expensive hat; he secretively buys an even more expensive roadster. Those impulsive purchases, subsequent marital deceptions, and mutual revelations are rendered comically—the war has not yet broken out. But the point of these opening scenes is a serious one; they establish a social context in which conspicuous consumption is regarded indulgently as a guilty pleasure. In the train carriage on her return from London with the hat safely in tow, Mrs. Miniver engages a vicar in a discussion of the morality of buying expensive things and discovers, to her relief, that he shares the same weakness for luxuries: he carries home the trophy of a box of cigars. Though caught up in the shopping spirit, the vicar nonetheless confesses his foreboding of the future war. Mrs. Miniver responds to this evocation of the threat of war by asking, "Oh, then, you are expecting trouble?" "I think it has already arrived," rejoins the vicar as their moment of intimacy is broken by the arrival of the aged Lady Belden, who expostulates against the rudeness of middle-class women who crowd the shops to buy what they cannot afford. "I don't know what this country is coming to," she complains. "Everyone trying to be better than their betters. Mink coats and no manners. No wonder Germany's arming." That contempt separates her from the affective community bound together by a consumerist ethos and identifies her as a "trouble" analogous in some way to the threat of war. Although the affective community of consumers is here represented only by Mrs. Miniver and the vicar, we soon learn that even those working-class people who cannot afford to practice conspicuous consumption are knit with the middle class through the network that consumption creates. For example, the high regard in which Mr. Ballard, the bashful village stationmaster, holds Mrs. Miniver is, he admits, based solely on observing her comings and goings from the London train. And she only goes to London to shop.

The picture dramatizes other moments of choice involving consumption. When Vin returns from Oxford, the superficiality of his conversion to socialism is depicted both by his facile pronouncements—mere opinions—and by the conspicuous acquisition of a new pipe. Typically middle class. But the consumptionist imperative spans class boundaries. The working class may not buy hats, roadsters, cigars, or pipes, but they do buy groceries. In another scene, a short argument between Mr. Foley, a grocer, and a customer, regarding the seemliness of the entry by Mr. Ballard, the humble stationmaster, entry of his rose into the competition for the prestigious Belden Challenge Cup, ends with the customer threatening to take her business elsewhere and with the grocer answering with a bit of MGM corporate philosophy: "My opinions have got nothing to do with the quality of my merchandise, Mrs. Atkins." It is true that the working-class woman must have groceries, whereas Vin does not need a pipe; but what is common to both scenes is the disconnection of consumption from either an ascriptive social status or deeply held political beliefs.

Styles of consumption are linked to a developmental theory of personality when, on the eve of Vin's vacation from Oxford, Mrs. Miniver discusses Vin's enthusiasms with his two younger siblings while she spoons out their porridge. Asked by one of the children, Toby, whether Vin is still a vegetarian, Mrs. Miniver answers, "I doubt it, darling. . . . That was just a phase he was going through." The boy asks, "What's a phase?" His sister Judy explains, "It's just a thing people go through." What women know in the blood must be taught to men—a lesson here swallowed with the nursery meal. Through the intimate ritual of consumption female biology becomes male history. Toby greets his mother's assurance that he is going through a phase right now, by exultantly shouting, "I'm going through a phase, I'm going through a phase!" This is a truly celebratory moment in which a story of human development or, perhaps, transformation is being happily internalized by its male audience. Although Mrs. Miniver's phasal theory smacks of kitchen-sink Freudianism, it is in fact studio-lot Freudianism, accommodated to Hooverian economic philosophy. Individual psychology, that is, recapitulates the business cycle; adolescence is a phase just as the Depression was thought to be. It is important here to insist that development *or* transformation is at issue, because it is not yet settled whether the phasal model is progressive, leading to some stage that could be called maturity, resulting in a fundamental change of attitude, or merely successive like the phases of fads and fashion.

This question is soon answered. Having shaved off his mustache ("After all, one can't waste too much time on the vanities of life") and acquired a pipe, Vin also affects a new set of convictions: "I think I've developed a social consciousness," he admits to his parents. When asked what that means, he vaguely explains, "Recognition of my fellow man." The phasal model not only ironizes the claims to a social consciousness but discounts Vin's claim to have *developed* it. Vin's social consciousness has been assumed like any other accessory that an Oxford undergraduate might acquire—and is tolerated as such by his doting parents, even when he inveighs against "the class system that exists in this country," and particularly the remnants of the "feudal system," of which Lady Belden is "the living proof." He brandishes these views over tea on the terrace of his parents' well-appointed home and aggressively presses them on Carol Belden, who has come to appeal to Mrs. Miniver that, on behalf of tradition, she persuade Mr. Ballard, the stationmaster, to withdraw his rose, named "the Mrs. Miniver," from competition for the Belden Challenge Cup. Already warmed to the task of critique, Vin accuses Carol of treating Mr. Ballard as "a vassal, as it were. Milady," he scornfully adds, "must be offered no competition." Vin's rude attack on tradition in general and Lady Belden in particular embarrasses his parents but does not daunt Carol, who retorts by characterizing his social consciousness as mere "talk," which she contrasts to action. She counters his sloganeering with the example of her own regular philanthropic excursions to the slums of London.

We should suspect some dialectical subterfuge here. That an ardent defense of charity in preference to a vaguely leftist "social consciousness" should emanate from the studio that made *Boys Town* is probably no surprise. Yet the success of that film was to *equate* social consciousness with philanthropy. It is something of a shock to have philanthropy opposed so starkly to social consciousness, even by MGM. Significantly, among the various aspects of Vin's "phase," only his social consciousness is challenged. No one mocks his pipe (indeed, his father, who has no discernible political opinions, smokes one). Unlike buying a pipe, assuming a social consciousness implies a progressive future that would, even in Vin's simplistic terms, change the extant social structure, if only by eliminating the last vestiges of the village's feudal past. His parents, wiser in the ways of the world, see what he does not: the destruction of so-called "feudal" privileges would involve them in its train (as it would the nouveau barons of Hollywood). The film benignly tolerates pipe smoking, not because the habit is intrinsically valuable, but because it is "one of the vanities of life," like a hat or a roadster, a consumption item to which its audience can aspire to purchase. Every phase that Vin or anyone else goes through will be marked, not only by the acquisition of some accessory set of opinions, but by the acquisition of a consumerist icon. Contextualized, among the appurtenances that Vin picks up at Oxford, "social consciousness" is fundamentally no different from a pipe; it is not a conviction but an accessory to be indulged, which deserves condemnation only when it motivates censure of those manners ("Manners are everything, aren't they?" Vin asks sarcastically) that make guilty feelings lovely.

Carol shows her good manners by withdrawing her request that Mrs. Miniver deter Mr. Ballard (with Vin as her foil, Mrs. Miniver has been spared voicing an opinion on the matter). If Vin does not convince anyone with his critique of feudalism, his assertion of the value of "competition" has a talismanic power to override tradition. In one sense nothing could be more natural: the value of competition, its preservation, is an American value of long standing. But for a studio that has been subject to investigation for its anticompetitive practices, it is rather an odd turn. The key here is that competition is being asserted in the context of a challenge that has social consequences but no evident political or economic effects. The feudal system of ownership and power can remain in place while prestige can be reallocated among the parties, rather like the annual competition for the Oscars.

What I have called Mrs. Miniver's "phasal theory" has broader import than to reconcile her to Vin's stirrings of social consciousness. The war too can be regarded as a phase. Although the war suspends conspicuous consumption (no more trips to London or even to the grocer once the bombs start falling), the assault will surely cease; and one fine day the shops will open again. Whatever the private qualms of its board of directors, MGM had no choice except to convey optimism. If the Office of War Information did not dictate content, and if its criteria for what should be on and off the screen were little more scientific than Joseph Breen's, it did successfully regulate attitude and combated films that were defeatist. Yet it was up to the studios to concoct the fiction by which optimism could be made plausible. They had good reason to do so, since the future of the motion picture industry lay in the international markets, especially Great Britain—and any boost to the morale would eventually translate into a boost in MGM's profits. Optimism was easy for MGM to project, for it was a tenet of the studio creed that was although people and nations go through phases, the need for entertainment remains constant.

Vin's phase of social consciousness lasts just until he falls in love with Carol under the moonlight the evening of the day of their meeting. Soon thereafter, both the undergraduate ideal of making a difference in society (if only by talk) and the domestic ideal of life with Carol are trumped by the overriding difference that the war makes and by an imperative call to action. From the perspective of phases the acquisition of a wife looks relatively trivial, just another accessory casually acquired for the phase of the war or the even more limited period of a leave between duties. Carol admits to some doubt regarding Vin's commitment. Before they are betrothed, she tells Vin that he is "a crazy boy, and I was not sure the craze would last." Events will moot her doubts.

Thus far everything that I have said about the film could have been said about the screenplay for *Mrs. Miniver*. This is an important point, since, as we shall see—as Mrs. Miniver makes us see—the literariness of the film is crucial to its identity as the flagship in MGM's war line as well as to the scope and power that *Mrs. Miniver* understands itself to have. The film's distinguished director, William Wyler, had a distinctive visual style. Wyler, already known for his collaborations with the cinematographer Gregg Toland in the dramatic use of deep focus, adapted his style in this film to prefigure Carol's death. Wyler's use of deep focus is most in evidence in his Wellesian employment of the staircase in the Minivers' house as a prominent background feature even when there is no movement on the stairs and the second-story landing is empty. In the scene establishing the dramatic potential of those shots, Clem steps to the first landing to adjust the clock in the right of the frame, leaving the other half of the frame to the empty staircase (Figure 2.1). As in *Citizen Kane*, the use of deep focus with no anchoring figure in the background portentously prepares for a later moment or scene in which the composition will be balanced and thus increases the significance of whatever will appear to complete the composition. That moment arrives when Vin mounts the stairs toward his mother and fiancée, who now fill that vacant space (Figure 2.2). When he reaches the two women, he stands between them and asks, "Which way am I to turn?" He turns, naturally, to the embrace of his mother. That choice saves Vin, who recognizes that single individual who is permanent and beyond phases, and dooms Carol, who is subordinated to the status of a pipe or mustache, an opinion, or a mere love interest. The eventual death of Carol, which Vin's choice portends, prevents Vin from relinquishing the phase of his love for her. It will be the mother, Mrs. Miniver, who transports Carol on the dark road to the scene of her fatal wounding by stray bullets during a dogfight, bullets from a plane that could be German, could be English—could be Vin's.

Figure 2.1

Figure 2.2

Vin's choice would have merely oedipal resonance were it not that the film leaves no doubt that it is the right choice: not only the choice that anyone would reasonably make, but the choice no one could refuse to make. That there is nothing psychological, the effect of mere development, involved in Vin's choice is argued by the dramatization of an oedipal drama in the episode of the downed German airman, a demonic Peter Pan, who has been shot from the sky and has fallen in Mrs. Miniver's garden. While the men are away on combat and rescue missions she discovers the wounded, sleeping airman in the bushes and attempts to grab his pistol. He revives and compels her to take him to her kitchen, where he commands that she feed him with bread and milk. Eventually he faints from his wound (let's call it castration) and she seizes the pistol (the phallic substitute). Having infantilized him, she gives him an opportunity to recant and accept her loving, maternal guidance; but he defies her with a burst of Nazi ideology, and, having proved himself the bad, propagandized son, is taken off by the police to a captivity from which he will be released when he can no longer do harm. As the one person in the film who is immune to Mrs. Miniver's charm, the febrile Nazi aptly receives the punishment of being immured rather than phased.

Phasal logic does not psychologize the social. Vin's turn to his mother at the top of the stairs is more like a tropism of the soul than a movement of the mind. Phasal logic *economizes* the psychological and the social by submitting both dispositions to a ratio of consumption. *Mrs. Miniver*'s salience is to incorporate the oedipal as a monitory fable of frozen development to be contrasted with the real life, average, middle-class family going through its normal and normative phases. By representing the oedipal drama out of sight of the men, the film purifies the choice that Vin makes. Vin chooses Mrs. Miniver not because she is his mother, but because she is Mrs. Miniver. As does everyone else in the film. And to choose Mrs. Miniver, I shall argue, is to choose MGM, which, under the guidance of L. B. Mayer, has made Greer Garson into Mrs. Miniver and makes Mrs. Miniver into *Mrs. Miniver*.

I have spoken with some poetic license of a "tropism of the soul." When Vin does not know where to turn, *we* know where he will turn because the telos for all turns in the film is Mrs. Miniver. This truth is established in the crucial early scene when Mr. Ballard, the stationmaster, invites Mrs. Miniver into his office, with the invitation, "I've got something to show you, something very special." Mrs. Miniver has just returned late from her shopping trip to the city, where she had surrendered to second thoughts and returned to the store where she suppressed her desire for a hat. On returning she finds the hat is gone and registers an expression of puzzled disappointment. But the canny sales clerk returns from the back room and crows, as she brandishes the hat, "We knew you'd come back." Slightly embarrassed, Mrs. Miniver explains, "I know it's foolish and extravagant, and I don't know what my husband will say, but I've simply got to have it." She needn't have bothered to explain. Another sales clerk, participant-observer to a scene that she has seen many times, hurries over to help stuff the hat in a box. Knowing that the strength of her desire is in inverse proportion to its duration, Mrs. Miniver approves of the bustle, "Yes, wrap it up quickly, before I change my mind."

The scene in the stationhouse is a subtle but critical revision of the acquisition of the hat during the opening scene. Mr. Ballard positions her before his mantle, and at first she does not know what it is she is to look at—there's nothing to anticipate because there's nothing for sale in the stationhouse. In the next shot the camera closes to a shot of Ballard and the rose on his mantle, while Mrs. Miniver is offscreen left. Mr. Ballard's eyes swivel from the direction of the offscreen Mrs. Miniver toward the rose. The camera cuts to a close-up of Mrs. Miniver's face from an as-yet-unmotivated point of view as she recognizes the rose, then crosscuts to a close-up of the rose, and back to Mrs. Miniver as she exclaims "Oh, Mr. Ballard!" (Figures 2.3 and 2.4). Cut to Ballard and rose: "It's my masterpiece." Then cut back to Mrs. Miniver looking at the rose: "How lovely!" The crosscutting produces, not only a montage of attraction (a tropism of souls) between Mrs. Miniver and the rose, but a reverse-angle sequence: Ballard watches her look at the rose; the spectator participates in the exchange of points of view between Mrs. Miniver and the rose (Figures 2.5 and 2.6). The crosscutting between the rose and Mrs. Miniver produces an exchange of looks between two subjects: we learn that it is the rose that looks at Mrs. Miniver looking. It is as if the rose's look is transferred

Figure 2.3

Figure 2.4

Figure 2.5

Figure 2.6

to Mrs. Miniver so that she will have the power compellingly to look. This application of reverse angle as crossbreeding is consummated when, under the eye of an ecstatic Mr. Ballard, Mrs. Miniver, having exclaimed, "I think it's the most beautiful rose I've ever seen," leans forward to take the fragrance of the rose and suffers a delicious *petit mort*.

More than looking is involved, however; a particular *quality* of looking comes into view. Though officially filmed in black and white, another color appears in *Mrs. Miniver*. Before his investment in the dynamic opportunities provided by deep focus, Wyler had made his reputation in part as a director who could convincingly film color in black and white: the scarlet of Bette Davis's dance dress in Warners' *Jezebel* (1938) is every bit as vivid as the bright red of the scarf that the working-class woman brandishes after the successful mutiny in Eisenstein's *Potemkin*. In *Mrs. Miniver*, color breaks through when Mr. Ballard introduces Mrs. Miniver to the rose that will bear her name. It is not just a rose, and certainly not a black rose, but a red rose that immediately appears to the spectator's eye. "And the color! I adore red roses!" Mrs. Miniver exclaims, corroborating what is right before our eyes. The manifest redness of the rose is the metaphorical production of blood, through breeding. Wyler, it may be said, exploits the formal surplus value of never quite pure black to produce something like another color on the spectrum. We do not stop to think. Propagandized by the mise-en-scène, we look at Mrs. Miniver looking at a red, red rose. Something like the power to look and the apparition of redness are bonded in a forcible idea—call it *quality*—that exceeds impressions of the sense. As we have seen, stardom is one of those phenomena. "What goes to make a rose is breeding and budding and horse manure, if you'll pardon the expression. And that's where you come in, ma'am," the awkward Mr. Ballard explains to his paragon. Ballard does not merely explain the way the rose has become beautiful, he describes the process that has occurred in front of our eyes. The reciprocal transfer of affective power between Mrs. Miniver and the rose instances breeding, a process which the naming of the rose "Mrs. Miniver" completes as a particularly forceful deployment of MGM's trope of social adjustment. No longer is it enough, as Mickey Moran jauntily explains in *Babes in Arms*, to "freshen the rose." An altogether new rose must be bred. Masterful breeding explains the beauteous power that the rose has for Mrs. Miniver, the enhancement of that power by Mrs. Miniver, and, not at all incidentally, the fully bloomed power of Greer Garson, who, picked by Thalberg to replace the retired Garbo and the aging Crawford, here, under Mayer's eye, and as proof of *his* power, fully realizes the stardom planned for her.

Although the motion picture aims to depict the condition of total war, it frames within that war a contest of quite a different kind: the annual flower show, which climaxes with the conferral of the Belden Cup on the finest rose bred in the community—a cup that has "traditionally" gone to Lady Belden herself, whose entry, indeed, had never before been challenged. There is something of a scandal here in diverting interest from winning the war to winning a flower show (see the earlier debate between the bell ringers regarding the decorum of continuing the annual show during the war). One might suspect that both Lady Belden's and MGM's scales of values have gone awry. The studio would seem to be more interested in manners, how values are scaled, than it is in the turbid ebb and flow of armies on a darkling continent that will decide the fate of Europe. It seems safe to assume that if a British filmmaker other than Michael Powell and Emeric Pressberger were making a war film, it would not focus on flower contests. But that's just the point. It is the enabling and advantageous fiction of *Mrs. Miniver* that British filmmakers were *not* making films.[17] In *Mrs. Miniver* consideration is never given to canceling the flower show—no more than there had been to canceling the Academy Awards ceremony. Nor had the Academy Awards vanished from the calculations of the beleaguered Mayer, all too aware that the Oscar for the best picture had recently eluded his grasp. It is an allegorical characteristic of a certain privileged class of motion picture that their extradiegetic aims, such as an aspiration for Oscars, must be "invisible" to the public and yet both unmistakable and compelling to the studio and to the trade—not just in the promotion of the picture but in the picture itself. Here the paradox that a society at total war could still appreciate the value of a flower show is not merely apparent; it is *aggressively* apparent. The war suspends consumption, but not choice, the liberal virtue that consumption puts into play better than constitutions and governments. *Mrs. Miniver* modifies the perception of total war to include and justify a realm of symbolic practices such as flower and star breeding and competitions such as the Belden Challenge and the Academy Awards. In part, the film can get away with such diversion because of one social indicator that distinguishes total war from America's more limited involvement. In Great Britain the need for manpower was so imperative that all women under thirty had been conscripted for war work, but not in the United States. *Mrs. Miniver* does not so much falsify the British situation as Americanize the notion of war work to include award competitions.

In *Mrs. Miniver* the rose must be nonblack for the same reason that the setting of the film is non-American. Although most commentators on the film mention the competition, none mentions that it clearly recalls the War of the Roses, which is a favorite Hollywood figure for the kind of epochal divisive strife in Great Britain that the Civil War enacted and represents in American history.[18] The flower show pits two houses against each other, but the competition is relieved of its sting by being rendered as thoroughly feudal. *Mrs. Miniver* does not advocate that feudalism ought to be overturned in the name of democracy (which gets no hearing in the film) but that competition ought to be conducted according to a feudal or studio model of challenge between the red rose of Ballard (whose champion is its namesake, Mrs. Miniver) and the white rose of Lady Belden (who champions herself and the tradition that she embodies). Mr. Ballard may look like a class upstart, but in fact he does not challenge Lady Belden's prerogatives. Nor does Lady Belden, however aristocratic she is in demeanor and sentiments, speak for a class; she speaks on behalf of a tradition of manners that the flower show perfectly epitomizes. One does not shut down the theaters or the flower shows during the war because, as the great theorist of manners as national ideology Edmund Burke first argued, those theaters where national culture has been bred in the bone remain the most effective instruments for maintaining morale during an extended national crisis.[19] Mayer's version of this notion is that the flower show is a necessary entertainment—necessary not as a distraction but because it performs quality.

The protocol of the Belden challenge dictates that a choice must be made. Lady Belden has learned that *she* must choose. Before she is called upon to ascend the dais, Lady Belden turns to Mrs. Miniver, complaining, "You've such a way of looking at people." Mrs. Miniver's potent look is doubled by the red rose that catches Lady Belden's eye and compels her choice (Figure 2.7). Choice is not the consequence of calculations of the marginal utility of a hat, a pipe, or a roadster. Choice is subject to aesthetic determination, a bred responsiveness to a bred beauty that does not, could not exist in nature, and that makes all nature wonder. Choice translates imperious form into socially consequential action: a recognition based on the power of forms to compel one's choice. With an irony that goes to the core of MGM's studio art,

Figure 2.7

Lady Belden vindicates Vin's notion of social consciousness, not as progressive politics inclined to destroy the class system, but as manners. In choosing Mr. Ballard's flower she recognizes her fellow man, a choice that has no particular political import but does have vast social consequences. Overruling the judges, she sacrifices the immunity of her social status in the exercise of her social authority. She chooses, not democracy (as if any one person could), but to recognize Ballard, a recognition that leaves everything else in place. The recognition of Ballard is in the name of a rose and the name of that rose is "Mrs. Miniver." The rose's redness is virtually identical to the surplus value conferred by its nominal association with Mrs. Miniver; and the transformative power of that hybrid form affects the social realm more effectively than even the Nazi bombs.

The answer to Vin's earlier sarcastic question, "Manners are everything, aren't they?" is in the affirmative: manners *are* everything. A formality without true competition becomes a competition in which form rules—form as the power of beauty, beauty as embodied in the look of Mrs. Miniver–Greer Garson, contracted long-term to MGM. MGM's reinvigorated feudalism models a Burkean utopia where the exercise of good manners and the application of social consciousness come to the same thing: form imposed on social being; manners as the visible embodiment of property; gentle deviations as the guarantee of the permanence of the core. At first glance Lady Belden's demonstration of social consciousness nicely perfects the integration of the village. The rain may fall on the just and the unjust, but the German bombs are not so indiscriminate: not one of the middle-class characters in the film actually dies. Death is depicted only for the child of the aristocracy and the working-class stationmaster. The devastating loss of his new wife has the consolation that it allows Vin to prove that, despite the mockery of his father, he was correct: the age of chivalry is not dead. He proves it by acting the chevalier at the end of the film, when he moves from the side of his mother during the funeral service to join the solitary, bereaved Lady Belden in her pew across the aisle. Although Vin's manners mute the suggestion of his invasion, he does occupy the pew in the name of Miniver. Justified according to its intensity, not its brevity, the marriage of commoner with a pedigreed lady is revised by the circumstances of the war as an alliance that enables a mannerly social adjustment of the Minivers with the house of Belden and a quiet transfer of property, achieving the hybridization prefigured in the credits to the film which cross the rose and the seal of the United Kingdom, which like MGM's logo includes a roaring lion (Figure 2.8). Henceforth Lady Belden's estate, lacking an heir, will pass to the scion of "the average middle-class family," which will survive the war and renovate the ruins

Figure 2.8

of a feudal society. The transfer of affection from Carol to Lady Belden seals the transfer of property from the Beldens to the Minivers and conveys Vin to a manor preserved beyond all phases. The war of the roses ends with a new dynasty confirmed. Guiltless of blood, the house of Miniver reverently assumes the place that the white queen graciously concedes.

In the name of a rose a great deal changes in the world of Mrs. Miniver. In particular, it seems that a change has occurred from a time of changes, of phases, crazes, and fashions, to a new maturity linked to a new proprietorship of the received social architecture. The shift from phasal logic to maturity would appear to represent a contradiction reflecting the filmmaker's usual concession to the prevailing conventions of the classical Hollywood narrative. Yet the contradiction is merely apparent. The shift from phasal adolescence to stable maturity echoes a fundamental problem for an industry such as the motion picture industry, which was conducting its business in what was being called, at the time of the war, "a mature economy," especially an industry that serves the vagaries of the public taste but that must construct a long-term plan to ensure that in the future it will continue to be *the* noble servant of a capricious and demanding public. It is the doctrine of the oligopoly called Hollywood and its chief ventriloquist, MGM, that the entertainment industry must have stability through all the phases. It may appear that only the merest analogy—a flower of rhetoric—links the Minivers' rise with Mayer's postwar planning. Yet Mrs. Miniver's potent look diverts attention from a plot that announces the American design on the postwar future of Great Britain. Mrs. Miniver not only has a son who chooses her, but she also has a husband who has chosen her. As we have seen, Clem Miniver is introduced in a moment of choice: his purchase of the roadster. Mrs. Miniver's splurge on a hat suggests a harmless, indeed appealing, female frivolousness. Clem Miniver's purchase of the automobile, however, indicates that he is an expatriate American. Played by Walter Pidgeon, Clem is the only character in the film who has an unaccommodated (North) American accent. In the scene when he purchases the roadster, Clem betrays his American origins by attempting to dicker with the salesman (he even kicks a tire): the salesman's complete incomprehension indicates a telling cultural difference. Evidence of a similar sort appears when Mr. Foley, air warden and grocer, offers to sell Clem some tins of kippers during a blackout. Clem replies decisively, "I hate 'em." His bluntly colloquial rejection of a staple of the British diet is virtually the only opinion that Clem expresses. Clem's nationality is important to no one in the film (either they don't recognize it or they are too good mannered to mention it), but the mark of the American is important to the project of the film because it links Clem's muted nationality with his profession as an architect.

Although Clem is carrying a roll of blueprints when we first meet him, we learn of no building to which those plans refer. That particular sign remains long unattached, as if waiting for some open land to appear or some demolition to occur. In fact, the first building in which Clem takes a professional interest is directly war-related: he constructs the only bomb shelter to be seen in the film and outfits it with a gas-detection device that he proudly displays to his wife. A potential patent under his belt, Clem later greets the destruction of a wing of his house by Nazi bombing with good-humored stoicism, remarking, "I always meant to do something with that dining room anyway."

The bombing gives Clem a project: to reconstruct and improve a demolished building. The prospect of reconstruction sounds the genuinely American note of the postwar, of an aftermath that will be the responsibility and will accrue to the profit of Americans, who are experienced in reconstruction. When Wyler, under Samuel Goldwyn, returns to the postwar *after* the war, making *The Best Years of Our Lives*, he will become the messiah of Levittown and Dana Andrews will be his prophet. But there is potential, plannable space on Long Island, whereas Great Britain, as Eisenhower recalls in *Crusade in Europe*, presented the problem for American planners in 1942 of a tight little island with barely enough space to fit the men who would man the ships and the planes that would eventually batter the beaches of Normandy (*CE*, pp. 56–57). Something must be torn down in order that something else can be built, but the British do not have the means. The architect is the figure of American planning, an assurance that there is a blueprint that will guide the energies of Yankee know-how and can-do. Were it not for an American perspective this lonely reading of Clem as a figure for the planning of reconstruction might seem farfetched, except that it seems close to MGM's own reading. The studio would follow the 1942 release of *Mrs. Miniver* with the 1943 production of the controversial account of post–Civil War reconstruction entitled *Tennesee Johnson* (1942)—a film so intent on supporting the Southern plantation owners' line on the Johnson era that it stumbled into racism as if by the way. *Tennessee Johnson* testifies to the difficulty of dealing with the possibilities of reconstruction after a war in the historical idiom of the United States, since in that idiom, the term *postwar* gravitated toward the Civil War and the Civil War toward issues of race.

The War of the Roses is another matter. Roses have color but no race—they are never just black and white. No ideological issues are at stake in the Belden competition, for all ideological differences in Great Britain are submerged in the common cause of defeating the Nazis. Clem may be American, but he is no carpetbagger. Like MGM, with its British production company under the volatile direction of Alexander Korda, Clem has his appointed place in the British equivalent of the plantation society before the war, and as long as he minds his manners, there is no reason that the British will greet his plans for reconstruction of a shattered society (and bombed-out movie theaters) with anything other than the gratitude that he deserves.

The renovative mission of Clem fulfills the wish that is one of the most enduring themes of the New Deal: that planning prove its relevance and command social acceptance. Henry A. Wallace gave it one of its most influential formulations in his pamphlet of 1934 entitled *America Must Choose*, a formulation that resonates strongly with the representation of Clem: "It is true," Wallace writes, "that the blueprints of the new order cannot now exist. We are all of us still educating one another to face the fact that we must sacrifice, each of us, some inherited concept, or some childish fable learned at our mother's knee, for the sake of the day to come." Wallace's subtitle is *The Advantages and Disadvantages of Nationalism, of World Trade, and of a Planned Middle Course*.[20] Wallace and MGM may seem strange bedfellows, but in fact, out of all the New Dealers, Wallace would have been the one most sensitive to the way horticultural metaphors are employed in *Mrs. Miniver* to assist the audience in imagining a hybrid, beautiful, new breed. Among the studios, MGM was best able to accept the force of *must* in the title *America Must Choose*, and to appreciate how the war promised to solve the New Deal problem of planning by hybridizing the domestic and the international, by ridding choice of its ideological components, and by locating the middle course in the postwar destiny of the middle class. Having accepted the need to sacrifice and having abandoned "the inherited concept" of restricted competition, the imagined community of *Mrs. Miniver*, which includes both the war-weary characters and the war-ready audience, are ripe to commit to the blueprints for something like a new order.

Nonetheless, one discrepancy mars the correspondence between Wallace's vision and MGM's view. The studio of *David Copperfield* could never be expected to agree that planning for a middle course entailed the sacrifice of "some childish fable learned at our mother's knee." *Mrs. Miniver* clearly marks the disparity between a New Deal vision of planning committed to new forms of community and a Culver City commitment to investment in the old forms on behalf of a feudalized middle class. Although the film nestles the Minivers in the statistical nook of the average, there is enough interest in history among the characters to justify our own historical speculation. Why would the very British Mrs. Miniver have married the American Clem? What could they have had in common? The prologue's announcement of a narrative focusing on the average middle-class family may forestall expectations of the usual Hollywood fare of boy meets girl, boy gets girl, boy gets another girl, and boy learns to settle for the first girl; but in doing so, it calls attention to the peculiarity of that normality. By preventing expectations that the Minivers would quarrel and split, the donnée of seamless domesticity raises questions of how such normalcy came to be. Why, among the multitude of individuals with varying and conflicting desires, did these two come together in such a nice fit of stellar averageness? It could not have been the Miniver look that subjugated Mrs. Belden. However powerful that look is, it is, if not indiscriminate, certainly impersonal: Mrs. Miniver never looks Clem into submission It turns out that the basis for the Minivers' integration, the wedding of British and American culture, is not a visual effect but literature: the shared childhood reading of *Alice in Wonderland*. "It was my first book," Mrs. Miniver offers, as she closes its pages after reading her children to sleep in the fallout shelter. "Really? Mine too," her husband replies.

MGM will trust roses and even stars only so far. Formal abstraction is a tactic for transformation in a crisis, when morale is at stake, not a reliable strategy for a studio that aspires to produce the kind of entertainment that will do the infrawork that *Alice* has done for the Minivers and for English speakers since the late nineteenth century. Even the power of the Miniver look is only a tactical or phasal weapon: the look is a function of style, but for the studio such style is fatally anchored in the biological body of the roseate star, which is subject to age and, increasingly, the unreliability of contracts. Planning depends on predictability; predictability, even for a visionary like Wallace, is a function of history. For MGM, unlike Wallace, history's relevance depends on the authority of tradition; and for MGM what makes possible the continuity of tradition is the abiding power of literature. It is because Clem has not abandoned the fables learned at his mother's knee—because in a real sense he is still imbibing them from his wife—that his blueprints can be trusted to design a new order that will not break with the old. Sacrifice, if you must, Mrs. Belden's old gray head, but spare your culture's stories. For a studio that never shrank from oppression at home or abroad, what Clement Greenberg called the oppressiveness of literary subject matter promised power rather than posing a threat. Transformative moments quell crises. Literature keeps people in line.

In this movie the basis for prediction is *Alice in Wonderland*, which has an appeal that transcends phases and connects the young with the old, the husband with the wife. The same goes for motion pictures. A story-reading heroine, Mrs. Miniver is both Alice grown up and a visible assurance that a return to wonderland is still possible. For MGM the literary is both a proof of Anglo-American identity, justification for a postwar colonization of the United Kingdom, and a talisman against fundamental social change that might threaten the studio's interests—against any change which would not simply be a phase, fashion, or craze. Time proved MGM wrong. As the 1950s would forcibly teach Hollywood, the classics would not hold.

In 1942 that lesson/calamity was still distant. More immediate was the problem of the postwar and the studio's ability to bring about a change in the conditions of production, distribution, and exhibition that would enable it to prosper in a world where the Paramount decree loomed, and where the national broadcasting of television was imminent. What would count as effective change? As we shall see in the next section, the same question motivates the postwar *Battleground*, a project of Dore Schary not of Mayer. By the 1950s, it would become clear that MGM had no answer to the challenge of change. So, it is hardly necessary to try to prove that *Mrs. Miniver*'s demonstration of it is the studio's capacity to transform black into red, accomplishing its goal of colonizing the colonial power. Perhaps it is sufficient to show that the picture accomplished the one goal toward which it clearly aspired: to win, not the Belden Cup, but the Oscar. Many in the trade had associated MGM's losing streak with the substitution of Mayer's vulgar sentimentality for Thalberg's unique sensibility. As *Fortune* argued, in Hollywood symbolic losses are tokens of real failure. How could it be believed that there would always be an MGM if the studio could not capture the prize conferred by the Academy that Mayer had founded and whose annual awards ceremony had long seemed to be a pretext for the industry to pay him fealty? But, as if preordained, the hugely profitable *Mrs. Miniver* ended the barren time, seeming to give the lie to the gossips' murmurs of decline.[21] If not a sweep, MGM nonetheless executed a stunning triumph. That year's Oscars went to *Mrs. Miniver* for best picture, to Teresa Wright for best supporting actress, and, of course, to Greer Garson for best actress, thus vindicating the studio and its chief. The splendor of the moment was, however, almost spoiled by Garson's uncharacteristic volubility. Her acceptance speech ran on for over seven minutes. The moment, the occasion, and the phenomena were saved, however, when the breathless Garson gushed, "I feel just like Alice in Wonderland."[22] Somewhere in the audience, dapper in his tux, flush with the success of his vassals, he who had ordered the painting of the rose, Louis B. Mayer, the Red Queen, smiled.

iii. The American Studio

> Know the enemy, know yourself; your victory will never be endangered.
> Know the ground, know the weather; your victory will then be total.
>
> Sun Tzu, *The Art of War*

The aptly named *Battleground* (1949) is both the story of a major battle between the German and U.S. armies in World War II and the site of a struggle for control of MGM, which, because this was MGM and not RKO or Fox, was not just a competition for executive power between Louis B. Mayer and the new head of production, Dore Schary, but a contest over the studio's identity. Schary, like David O. Selznick years before, had switched from RKO to MGM when he was hired there as a screenwriter in 1938, and, after a sabbatical, appointed as executive producer of the studio's "near A" unit in 1941. Like Irving Thalberg, Schary conspicuously neglected to take the executive producer's credit he earned on some of the most successful pictures he supervised at MGM: *Joe Smith, American* (1942), *Lassie, Come Home* (1943). It was the same with *Bataan* (1943). Although Irving Starr was the producer of record, Schary's fingerprints were all over the picture: he recruited Tay Garnett to direct, and he supervised the picture from script and casting through postproduction. After *Bataan* Schary left MGM again, this time to join Selznick in his new venture, Vanguard Pictures. When Selznick closed down Vanguard in 1945, Schary went to RKO, where he was made production chief. Beleaguered by Howard Hughes, Schary was lured back to MGM as chief of production in 1948 with the *Battleground* project in mind.[23] Mayer, who in his own eyes and the eyes of many others, *was* MGM, at least since the death of Thalberg, had opposed *Battleground* from the beginning. In the past that would have meant the end of the project. But Mayer's authority had dwindled in the company, the box office had shrunk, costs had soared. Mayer's long-time foe Nick Schenck had lost confidence in Mayer's ability to lead the studio in the post-Paramount world and had lost his qualms about overruling the studio chief in favor of his vice-president in charge of production. *Battleground* was made, and this time Schary took his producer's credit. Many believed *Battleground* turned the tide for MGM just as it certainly did for Schary (although the conclusive battle in the civil war between Mayer and Schary would not occur until 1951). "'When MGM started," remembered the director George Sidney, "the picture that really made the studio was *The Big Parade*. And then twenty-five years later, Dore came and made *Battleground*, another war story, and it seemed we had a new company."[24]

The terrain on which *Battleground* takes its position is the genre of combat pictures as developed during the war years. *Bataan*, Jeanine Basinger has argued, set the standard for the composition of the unit, the structure of authority, the likelihood of death for the men, and even the order in which the unit members are killed.[25] *Bataan* had Warners-like immediacy. Every person in the theater in 1943, soldier or civilian, would have known what is at stake in *Bataan*, a film that takes its title from the battle of the Bataan peninsula, the staggering defeat of American forces in the Philippines the year before. Just in case, however, the picture provides the exposition to clarify the way the task of the part, the story of an improvised platoon, fits into the crusade of the whole, the epic struggle of the Army of the Pacific. Captain Lassiter, who has been charged to form a patrol from soldiers in a pell-mell retreat from the Japanese attack, explains everything to his new sergeant: "Our orders are to demolish this bridge to prevent a breakthrough. Our job is to keep the Japs from moving their tanks and artillery through here. Stop them any way we can. . . . For as long as we can. The idea is that General MacArthur needs time to reorganize and consolidate down below. If the Japs are able to flank our main army by pouring their heavy stuff through this pass, the Battle of Bataan is going to be all over, too soon." Everyone also knew what had happened: MacArthur had escaped; the men he abandoned either had died or were marched off to the so-called death camps. Everyone in the audience would also know what is at stake ideologically: *Bataan* aimed to boost American spirit while the outcome of the war in the Pacific was still in doubt by providing an example of unyielding defiance and noble self-sacrifice. There was another objective: although the future of the war, like all wars, depended on the bravery of the troops, the outcome of this particular contest in this theater of the world war depended on MacArthur's ability to "reorganize" the army out of the units scattered and shrunken by defeat. *Bataan* aimed to strengthen the conviction of the American public that MacArthur could succeed at his vast enterprise by representing the way "this mixed crew" of soldiers, as the captain calls his men, organizes into an effective fighting unit that will cohere and hold until the last man left standing.

When Sergeant Dane (Robert Taylor) first sees the men he has to work with, he scoffs to his buddy, "How'd you like to draw them in a raffle? 'Are any of the names familiar to you, sergeant,' says the captain. You tell me what difference it makes what their names are? Three months ago they were all jerking sodas, or selling shoes, or punching adding machines. You see a soldier in that lot, Jake? I said soldier." Jake (Thomas Mitchell) replies, "You can't always tell, Sarge. Some of those kids learn pretty good. Kinda quick." They are both right: it makes some difference what their names are, but not much. (For Dane to know that Corporal "Todd" [Lloyd Nolan] was formerly "Burns," a murderer with a good reason to kill him, seems like vital information, but, eventually, along with everyone else, "Todd/Burns" turns his hatred toward the Japanese.) The magical world in which the name of Mrs. Miniver is a talisman has no place on Sergeant Dane's map. The important thing is to get these men organized into a fighting unit.[26] As the group stands at ease in a line before him, Lassiter says, "We have a few minutes to get organized before the Japs send over their reconnaissance planes and they report back, which will give us a little more time to get organized. So, let's get organized." Despite the quick death of the captain, despite the hopelessness of the odds, they do get organized and put up a good, effective fight. If a sergeant can do it, MacArthur can do it. It is inherent in the American character to be able and willing to organize. That quality is manifest from the platoon to the command level. Authority follows the organizer. From the ability of the sergeant to organize a mixed crew into a unified fighting force will come the resources of time and faith for the commander to reorganize the whole into an army with the strength to win.

There is no South Pacific sweat in *Battleground*. The war has turned cold by 1949. The picture tells the story of the stubborn resistance of Squad 2, Platoon 3, of I Company of the 101st Airborne Division, later nicknamed "the bloody bastards of Bastogne," to the last major German offensive on the Western Front— commonly called the Battle of the Bulge—which began in the frigid December of 1944 and continued deep into the snowy January of 1945. At the level of the plot, at stake is the ability of beleaguered American soldiers to hold off the German forces until the weather permits them to be resupplied by air and successfully to counterattack, ending the German hopes of compelling a stalemate that would force a peace negotiated on favorable terms. Most of the audience would know of that objective (and there is a prologue for those who have forgotten), but unlike *Bataan*, whose characters acquire knowledge of their mission at the cost of knowing that they will die in completing it, the characters in *Battleground* do not know exactly why or even where they are fighting. The film is intensely local in its point of reference: one squad, in one platoon, in one company, in one division. Cut off from any reliable sources of information, the men only see the big picture as it is distortedly reflected in the stale reports they read in newspapers sent from home. Cloaked in fog, the GIs rarely glimpse even the small picture, such as the location of the mortar that sends a silent and sudden death or the faces of the enemy lurking in the trees just beyond the clearing. The audience in 1949 would see the big picture, of course, because unlike the audience for Bataan it knew how the war would turn out. But the clarity of the audience's vision of the overall narrative arc may come at the expense of clarity about the ideological import of the narrative in 1949. The soldiers of the 101st Airborne are not still fighting. Are we at war? Will we fight? Why should we? And who are "we"?

We are an audience, of course. But what is an audience? It may be, as MGM urged in 1928, that we, the audience, are a crowd. And if a crowd, perhaps an army. "An army," wrote the British military theorist J. F. C. Fuller in his 1914 text *Training Soldiers for War*,

> is still a crowd, though a highly organized one. It is governed by the same laws which govern crowds, and under the stress of war is ever tending to revert to its crowd form. Our object in peace is so to train it that their reversions will become extremely slow; in other words, we add to each individual a quality known as "moral," so that, when intellect and reason fail man is not ruled by his instincts and sentiments alone, but by the moral which has become part of his nature.[27]

As *Bataan* begins we see a crowd, though nothing like the crowd of interchangeable office workers who throng the streets of New York in MGM's 1928 picture *The Crowd*. This is a rout of dark-skinned and light-skinned, uniformed and civilian men and women who are in flight to save their lives. The narrative unwinds a fantasy of assimilation as organization, of an odd lot of soldiers (including one sailor) who have enough group morale to suppress their differences and overcome their fear in order to collectively stand and fight against a well-trained, well-armed, highly aggressive, and multitudinous enemy on behalf of men they have never seen or will see. Once Dane (who has the charismatic authority that falls to a character played by the only star in the picture) says, "So, let's get organized," the possibility of reversion to the crowd is never seriously entertained. It is too close a fear.

At the beginning of *Battleground* we see an army company marching in close order drill, the tedious, wearing exercise designed to mechanize men into fighting machines (Figure 2.9). This is not boot camp, however. This is a combat unit on furlough, marching in an empty staging area of a camp behind the lines as they await the trucks that they believe will transport them from the war zone and their unit to Paris with its luxuriously individualized pleasures: a compliant girl or a private room with bath. They have been trained. These men are battle-hardened and battle-weary veterans, some ready to be rotated out. But they continue to train. The company returns to the drill of boot camp to ensure that this furlough from danger will not diminish its combat

Figure 2.9

readiness. While the company is practicing, it is showing off. It marches, "two, three, four; right face, two, three, four; about face, two, three, four: SOUND OFF," while chanting its collective good fortune that Jody is back home taking care of their girls' needs, in order to remind itself and whomever is watching, what a combat unit looks and sounds like. It is an impressive demonstration of unit cohesion. Such a demonstration is not, however, an invitation to join. This is not the Big Parade that comprehends every soldier who has been or is about to be on the front. I Company of the 101st Airborne parades itself as a single unit with a single ego. It is an exclusive group; how could a newcomer possibly fit in? That's the question that Jim Slayton, the green replacement who is watching the display, will ask himself. That's the crucial question that *Battleground* aims to answer.[28]

Any newcomer would have to adjust, just like everyone else—that's the heavily documented answer given by *The American Soldier*, which was published in 1949 as the first two volumes of the series *Studies in Social Psychology in World War II*, "prepared and edited under the auspices of a Special committee of the Social Sciences Research Council" and based on data "collected by the Research Branch, Information and Education Division, War Department, during World War II." Volume 2 is called *Combat and Its Aftermath*. In the preface to volume 1, *Adjustment During Army Life*, the authors identify their three audiences, the armed forces, historians, and most important, "social psychologists and sociologists" engaged in "the study of personal and institutional adjustment to new social situations." They distinguish their objective from those social scientists who in "World War I used the tool of psychology to aid in the measurement and classification of human abilities." "Just as World War I gave new impetus to the study of human aptitudes," they write, "so World War II has given new impetus to the study of attitudes." The methods and results may have scientific interest, yet the authors are careful to remind their audiences that "the Research Branch existed to do a practical engineering job, not a scientific job. Its purpose was to provide the Army command quickly and accurately with facts about the attitudes of soldiers which, along with other facts and inferences, might be helpful policy formation."[29] You can exploit aptitudes but you can actually change attitudes.

Battleground shares the predominant concern of *The American Soldier*—how to adjust an individual to the combat unit—and dramatizes many of its specific topics: the problems of integrating a replacement, the collective response to gold brickers and men paralyzed by fear or anxiety, resentment at being reassigned to the front when it is time to be rotated out, attitudes toward officers, noncommissioned officers, and the enemy. The screenwriter of

Battleground, Robert Pirosh, would object to the charge that he had invented incidents or imitated other combat films, insisting that the characters and incidents of the picture emerged out of his own wartime experience in the Bulge. To note the scrupulous accuracy with which *Battleground* dramatizes the findings of *The American Soldier* does not invalidate Pirosh's claims. After all, the Research Branch based its findings on empirical research obtained by asking questions designed to elicit responses on specific topics. Pirosh's engineering of a script from his wartime experiences is the same enterprise moving in a different direction: it starts with the answers that the men gave to the questions that the sociologists asked them. The answers focused on: Layton's anxiety that the men in his new company did not know his name; Hooper's immediate and unforeseen death by mortar attack; the guy who knocked out his teeth with a rifle butt; Sergeant Wallowicz's reaction to Bettis's flight from the line ("Well, I hope he makes it. They should have never sent him back on the line. Some guys just can't take it"); Sergeant Kinney, whom all the men trust and to whom the lieutenant defers; Holley, the hotdog who couldn't quite measure up to the demands of leadership. The questions were: What does a replacement go through in trying to fit in with a veteran unit? What was the weapon that the soldiers most feared? How did the other men in the unit respond to men who fabricated injuries or illness in order to get pulled from the frontlines? Whom do infantrymen most respect, noncommissioned or commissioned officers? Will men unnerved by the imminence of a violent death nonetheless stand and fight?

Both the research study and the motion picture try to explain how men become adjusted to combat duty. There the convergence stops, for the Research Branch and, through Pirosh, *Battleground*, take sharply different points of view on that adjustment. In their methodological prologue the authors of *The American Soldier* explain,

> The concept of personal adjustment is here viewed from the point of view of the Army command. One might have looked upon adjustment from other viewpoints. For example, irrespective of the needs of the Army command one might have considered adjustment as that adaptation to changing environmental demands which minimized psychological tension or anxiety; or one might have looked at adjustment from the standpoint of the consistency of concern with the democratic values of the larger society; or as conformity to the informal structure of the Army, even when that structure was at odds with military requirements. But it seemed useful, both for the engineering task of serving the Army and for the analytic task of producing these chapters, to view adjustment in terms of adaptation as viewed by the Army command. (*AS*, p. 82)

Battleground has no interest in serving the army. It rigorously avoids taking the commander's point of view. Indeed, the picture only acknowledges the relevance of officers once: when an officer reports to the men of I Company that the German officers who appeared under a flag of parley to demand the surrender of the Americans received from Brigadier General McAuliffe, the defiantly demotic response, "Nuts!" Otherwise, a major accosted in a jeep finds his authority nullified by his failure to explain the meaning of a password to the itchy-fingered GIs. At the company level there is no officer higher than a lieutenant, and he is practically anonymous; he makes few decisions without first checking with his NCO, Kinnie (James Whitmore), who transmits orders with the unreflective confidence that they will be followed.

This picture does not track the process of adjustment to the organization through the experience of the commander, as in Fox's contemporary *Twelve O'Clock High* (Fox, 1949), but through Jim Layton (Marshall Thompson), a fresh replacement and an admiring spectator of the opening drill. The naïve Layton is excited by the prospect of joining the 101st. As he and his buddy Hooper (Scotty Beckett) watch the platoon drill smartly in the mud, Layton holds the badge with the Screaming Eagle up to his shoulder and boasts, "Boy, they know who you are when you walk down the street with that on your sleeve" (Figure 2.10).

It turns out that just about anyone can wear a screaming eagle patch, as Layton learns when he discovers that a squad of soldiers whom he let past his checkpoint while on guard duty on the authority of their patches and their knowledge of the password, "bug," and the countersign, "jitter," were in fact German infiltrators, who, following his helpful directions, destroyed a strategically important bridge.

Figure 2.10

The Germans have our badges and know our passwords. They look like American soldiers, they talk like American soldiers. But that does not make them American soldiers. They are no more American soldiers than a German graham cracker made to taste like a Nabisco graham cracker and sold in a package decorated with a facsimile of the Nabisco brand would *be* a Nabisco graham cracker. There is a difference between authentic and ersatz Nabisco graham crackers. Courts have been established to police that difference and protect registered trademarks from infringement. War between sovereign nations means that no court is in a position to assert its jurisdiction to judge which man legitimately wears the screaming eagle patch and which does not. Patches are not the only device that the army adopted to distinguish the authentic from the fake. It also employed passwords as a suitably flexible code to discriminate friend from foe at the borders (Figure 2.11). In *Battleground*, however, the passwords fail three times. The first time occurs when the Germans penetrate the lines with "jitterbug." The second occurs when a patrol stops a jeep of men in American uniforms, including a major. Challenged for the password, the major correctly gives, "Texas"; and Holley (Van Johnson), challenged in turn, answers, "Leaguer." But trouble follows when Holley, rifle at the ready, stung by the earlier deception, asks the major: "What *is* a Texas Leaguer?" When the best the major can come up with is, "Some kind of baseball term," Jarvess (John Hodiak) asks, "What kind?" Even though a sergeant in the back of the jeep interjects, "A safe hit, just over the infielder," the interrogation continues:

Figure 2.11

> *Jarvess* (*waving gun at sergeant*): Nobody asked you. (*To the major*): How did the Dodgers make out this year?
>
> *Major* (Edmon Ryan, uncredited; *angrily to Holley*): Hey, who's your commanding officer, soldier?
>
> *Holley*: Whoever he is he knows how the Dodgers made out.
>
> *Jarvess*: Let's see your dogtags!
>
> *Major*: What?
>
> *Jarvess* (*aggressively*): C'mon, we're not taking any chances.
>
> *Holley*: Sprechen Sie Deutsche!
>
> *Major*: Hey, what is this?
>
> *Holley*: Was ist dein Namen?
>
> *Major*: What kind of nonsense?
>
> *Holley*: Schnell! Schnell! Namen! Namen! Sprechen Sie!

At that point the sergeant and the major in the jeep produce weapons, and the sergeant tells Holley, Jarvess, and Roderigues to drop their rifles. There is a tense stalemate.

> *Sergeant* (*to Holley*): You! Who's Betty Grable going with?
>
> *Roderigues* (Ricardo Montalban): Cesar Romero.

Sergeant: Shut up!

Driver: Who's the Dragon Lady?

Holley: She's in *Terry and the Pirates*.

Sergeant: What's a hot rod?

Holley: A hopped-up jalopy.

Corporal: Hello, Joe, what do you know?

Holley: Just got back from a Vaudeville show! (*Laughing*): I guess they're okay.

Major (*sarcastically*): Thank you, Sergeant.

Holley: PFC, Major. Praying for Civilian. That's why I believe in being careful. May I suggest, sir, that you study up on baseball?

Major (*smiling*): I guess I'd better. And by the way, you might tell your buddy that Cesar Romero is out. She's married to Harry James. (*They drive off.*)[30]

The scene is notable for the shifting mood of the exchange, which is tense then lighthearted, and whipsaws from one "side" to another, for Holley's stupid shift from English to German (it is bad German, but the Americans do not hear it as bad German, just German), for the range of cultural references, and for the kind of limits on even these American men's knowledge (the major, who wears glasses, does not know a long-time slang term from baseball, but he does have access to the latest Hollywood gossip—rank has its privileges). Finally, neither the command of the passwords nor the ability to speak English nor the knowledge of baseball terms nor Hollywood gossip is decisive, it's the edgily competitive swing of the exchange and the way it is resolved in the seamlessly automatic completion of a call with a response that tips suspicion over into confidence. A mutual mastery of a rhythmic banter like that learned on U.S. playgrounds and practiced as one-upmanship in the enlisted men's barracks and formalized as the uniquely GI marching cadences and calls convinces each side that the other is American. The men do not call out, "What is the difference between revealed and natural religion?" or "What are the main tenets of the Atlantic Charter?" or "What is substantive due process?" No ideas—so nobody can be wrong and none can disagree; only trivia—so all Americans can meet on the common ground of mass culture.

Holley's confident claim that he is careful is deluded. Earlier, he sat by when the group of German infiltrators evaded Layton's challenge; he let the guys in the jeep get the drop on his squad even though they had their rifles ready; and within a few minutes of his encounter with the major his squad is surprised when, while goofing off watching Rodrigues pitch snowballs, a snowball is thrown back with good velocity, a guy comes out of the woods, and "hits" what Rodrigues next pitches "over second base." Holley challenges him, "Sound off, pal. Password?" The accentless soldier points, "Don't you get it? Right over second base. Texas . . ." Holley answers, "Leaguer." That would do it, except the rest of the stranger's squad steps into the clearing. Holley recognizes the lieutenant from the checkpoint the night before, cuts short the conversation, and leads his men a way off before urgently whispering, "Let's get outta here. Those guys are Krauts!" A skirmish ensues in which Rodrigues is wounded and dies buried in the snow that he had so joyously welcomed.

While it is clear that Holley is not careful, it is not clear how being careful would have helped in this last instance. If he had assumed a hostile stance at the approach of the ball thrower, his men would have been cut down by the squad of Germans waiting in the woods. And why should he suspect the snowball thrower? The guy clearly knows the password and what it means. Holley might have interrogated the squad, but we know from the previous scene that all the disguised Germans speak English. It is likely someone would have gotten stuck on the "Hello Joe, what do you know?" routine. But though it works once, that vaudeville routine is not a particularly good test of being an American. For one thing you cannot ask every stranger who gets the password right to stand by for a host of supplemental questions. For another, the GIs are outnumbered, and overt detection of the German ruse would have meant a firefight that Holley's men would have lost. For another, you can't really expect that every GI—someone, for example, who hails from Alabama or Tennessee—would correctly reply, "Just got back from a vaudeville show." So there is no reason to look for an ironclad test that would detect which men in American uniforms are Americans. It is just good luck that Holley recognizes the German lieutenant's face. Of course, he could have made a mistake and his whole squad might have been slaughtered. It is not, however, the picture's objective to expose the careless Holley as a bad soldier but to show him as a *representative* soldier, one who is going to make mistakes and sometimes get men killed—just like generals. Unlike generals, however, Holley is likely to pay for his mistake with his own life.

The picture does not intend a critique of the army's use of passwords; it approves of the equivocation that occurs. The American soldiers are good at fighting the enemy, but, at least in the European theater, they are not so good at detecting who the enemy *is*. The GIs are not much good at discerning differences even by means of their preferred test of applying cultural filters.[31] There are several reasons that *Battleground* approves of this flaw, but at this point let us suggest only one of them: any criterion of Americanness that would press for knowledge beyond the ordained and vulnerable password (which can be intercepted by a radio transmission, extracted from a prisoner, or simply overheard in the dark) in order to exclude the German infiltrators would also exclude the majority of the audience at the picture in 1949: those American adolescents who did not know about vaudeville or those American women who did not know about the Dodgers, and those MGM moviegoers—American, British, *and* German—who had lost interest in Betty Grable, a fading star by 1949.

The way GIs talk in *Battleground* clearly reflects the findings of *The American Soldier* of how American soldiers talked during the war, a discourse which registers the soldier's impatience with those who mouth beautiful ideals. But it also indirectly expresses the theory of morale implicit in the excerpt from Fuller above, which had lapsed, at least among theorists, by 1949. *Battleground*'s position on morale is significant because, although *Battleground* focuses on the soldiers under a wintry siege in 1944, theories of morale have considerable consequences for how citizens are turned into soldiers, how a crowd becomes an army, and how a martial spirit can be maintained in the face of a threat that has global reach. According to Hew Strachan, since 1945 "three generic explanations have been adduced to explain how morale is sustained in the terrifying conditions of industrial war. The first, and dominant one, focuses on the primacy of the small group. Men, it is argued, fight for their mates rather than for their country."[32] In the words of Roy Grinker and John Spiegel, whose *Men Under Stress*, published in 1945, exerted considerable influence on theorists of morale, "The ability to identify with a group and the past history of such identification are probably the most important components of good motivation for combat."[33] Strachan points out several problems with the band-of-brothers theory: it makes no allowance for high casualties, such as those on the Eastern Front in 1941 and Belgium in 1945. As the records document and *Battleground* depicts, casualties of all kinds—from death or wounds, from nervous breakdowns or "pneumonia" were high in the veteran 101st. In the course of this battle, the second squad loses two men to wounds, one to psychiatric exemption, one to medical illness, and two by death—60 percent of the unit. Strachan observes that "the small-group argument, which by definition becomes of increasing importance the more sustained and vicious the fighting, rests on a paradox: such operations erode the very basis on which the unit's morale is said to rest. It has to absorb an increased flow of replacements, many of whom do not survive long enough to become anybody's buddy and whose names and backgrounds the unit's surviving members struggle to recall" ("TMMW," p. 212). Layton's case illustrates the contingencies affecting the integration of a replacement for someone dead or disabled. When he looks for his buddy Hooper in K Company, no one knows the name. Then the sergeant connects it with the guy who took a direct hit by a mortar and whose exploded body was so dismembered that they could not even find his dogtags. The shaken Layton presses his own name on his sergeant when he returns from Hooper's platoon—only to be told,

"Of course, I know your name." The sergeant may know, but, like the makeshift platoon in *Bataan* the unit first assimilates him anonymously —puts him to work digging foxholes, sends him out on sentry duty—and only later learns his name. At the crisis of the battle, the Americans empty the hospitals and absorb the walking wounded in their stand against the Germans. Skeptical of the band of brothers as an idealism justifying exclusion, *Battleground* reveals the unit's tendency to fragment and then shows that despite losses, flights, and squabbles, the second squad hangs together and fights together without rivalry with other units or even without much outspoken hatred for the Nazis.

The second theory of unit cohesion, according to Strachan, is that harsh, punitive measures, such as the execution of deserters, should be imposed in order to deter any men from leaving the lines—a policy ruthlessly employed by the German army, which executed fifteen thousand. The men stayed and fought, unlike the soldiers in World War I, when a more humane approach was taken. The British Army, which had executed 346 men in World War I, abandoned the practice in World War II ("TMMW," p. 215). The nations' different experiences defeat any generalization.

The third way to keep men in line is indoctrination, the inculcation of patriotism and other spiritual values. That approach comprises two of the three wartime objectives for the motion picture industry that the producer Walter Wanger recommended in his 1941 essay "The Role of Movies in Morale," which was published in the *American Journal of Sociology*. Wanger urges that "national morale in a democracy must be built through three channels: (1) by clarifying to the individual his place, responsibilities, and rewards in a great democratic endeavor; (2) by inspiring the individual citizen with enthusiasm and confidence in the principles and purposes of the democracy of which he is a part; and (3) by affording the individual relaxation from the urgent problems which crises impose."[34] Not surprisingly, because he was writing before Pearl Harbor destroyed the isolationist fantasy of U.S. immunity, Wanger, a spokesman for the liberals among Hollywood's executive class, focuses his remarks on the problem of building morale among a civilian population that might be called on to sacrifice lives and treasure to defend against a distant threat. Thus the emphasis on education, the need to construct "a primer of democracy: clear, confident, inspiring." Subsequent experience would teach that education or indoctrination in patriotism would only have limited effects under wartime conditions. Recalling the lessons learned regarding the effectiveness of indoctrination in the two world wars, Strachan remarks that among specialists, "skepticism regarding patriotism or commitment to a set of beliefs generated from outside the armed forces themselves, seems sufficiently great not to be dismissed." He concludes that given the evidence of cynicism toward "political education" among the German and French armies in both world wars, a general consensus has been reached "that political or patriotic instruction is important in getting the soldier to the front, in inculcating the sense of duty which causes him to volunteer or report on mobilization, but is at best implicit rather than explicit when in the field" ("TMMW," p. 214). Likewise GIs. American soldiers overseas were notoriously dismissive of combat films with their canned patriotic messages—partly, one assumes, because many of them had responded with enthusiasm to such films when civilians.

However, Wanger does not restrict his argument to claims regarding filmmaking's value as indoctrination. His inclusion of "relaxation" as an objective of morale building underwrites his assertion that Hollywood's contribution to national morale is irreducible to the message it delivers. Echoing the early Depression-era proclamations of Will Hays and other spokesmen for the industry, Wanger affirms that "entertainment is not a luxury; it is a necessity. Hollywood's contribution to national morale so far has been to provide entertainment to the public in a steady stream. This has not been part of any plan. Movies are made for profit, and profit is made by making movies which satisfy popular tastes. We are serving the public and are dependent upon their nickels and dimes to keep us going. It is impossible," Wanger attests, "to sell them anything they do not want." Wanger shows no concern about supplying the data to back up his statement, which is, after all, an article of the liberal faith: profitable sales follow and fulfill strong wants. As we have seen, the obverse of that truism is the first principle of marketing, which, according to public relations men from Bernays onward, does have some claim to empirical verifiability: namely, that it is entirely possible for an enterprise to create wants in the public for the products that it has to sell—even, perhaps, to plan to do so. In any case, Wanger's ritually self-interested exculpation from any ulterior motives by an industry that has recently consented to abjure from certain business practices in order to avoid prosecution for monopolistic restraint of trade is the prologue to his declaration of the grander ambition of Hollywood: the fulfillment of its patriotic duty: "In the United States the creation of morale must be concerned with an insistent, long-range campaign to inspire the American people with fervor about American life. Our symbols must be vitalized and revived" ("RMM," p. 380).

We have seen how MGM undertakes the project in *Mrs. Miniver* of revitalizing the symbol of the hybrid rose and the lion, which will be shared for all imaginable time by the studio and the British empire. A break with Mayer's MGM in so many other ways, *Battleground* aggressively claims continuity with the studio's reflexive practice of self-revitalization and with the studio's assertion of its synechdochal privilege of being the studio part that stands for the industry whole, just as Hollywood's output of entertainment is claimed by the studio stewarded by Schary as the popular-culture part that stands for the mass-cultural whole that binds the public together in a fervent yet relaxed Americanism on the way to global hegemony. By 1949, whatever propagandistic impulses there had been at MGM to inculcate noble ideals that would get the soldiers to fire their weapons and the civilians to ration their gasoline had expired. No film on World War II in the 1940s posed as more thoroughly uninterested in political instruction than *Battleground*. The ethos of *Battleground*, true to its source in *The American Soldier*, rules out what that study calls "idealistic talk" (*AS*, p. 150), whether that idealistic talk is done by soldiers in combat or *about* soldiers in combat. The narrative democratically dilutes all easy optimisms with a dose of disappointment. All the men think they are going to Paris but in fact they are headed to Bastogne. Pop's letter approving his return to Omaha is in the mail but he is sent to the front before the mail can reach him. Abner signed up for the 101st Airborne, but parachuting into Normandy, he has tramped through the same mud as any other foot soldier.[35] Holley steals some eggs from a Frenchwoman's chicken coop, but every time he attempts to scramble them the call comes to move out; then the one shell that hits the camp lands on the campfire. Jarvess writes a column for *The Sedalia News* exhorting everyone to do his part in the war on fascism and winds up surrounded by the German Army in the Ardennes Forest. Layton objects to Kip's grievance against the rear echelon, that "they just don't care" but later will second the self-pitying refrain. The narrative's ironic structure is devoid of any superior point of view because the GIs are themselves all ironists: Layton's "personal adjustment" involves the acquisition of the ironic attitude that has become second nature to his buddies. Phrases that early on Layton could not or would not speak are later uttered with a sarcasm that may not be standard issue but is the standard effect of months spent at the front, the attitude men take to deal with disappointment and homesickness, to subdue regional, intellectual, and ethnic differences. Getting trained to adopt a common ironic attitude distances what is happening to the soldier in I Company from what is happening to the "I" in the company of soldiers.

The most aggressive assault on inspirational bromides comes, unexpectedly, from the callow Layton, who, as part of his socialization, has quickly picked up a nicotine habit as the objective correlative of a facile fatalism:

> *Layton*: Well, here goes my last butt.
> *Holley*: Don't tell me your problems. Tell the chaplain.

> *Layton*: The chaplain, I forgot. We got nothin' to worry about. Holy Joe is going to pray for us at the Christmas services. They that wait upon the Lord shall renew their strength. Shall mount up with wings as Eagles.... (If the fog lifts.) Shall run and not be weary.... (Unless they have frozen feet.) And they shall walk and not be faint.... (If they don't lose too much blood before the medics come up.)

Layton's sarcasm gets no reinforcement from the squad. The answering silence and the somber glances cast in his direction suggest that he has stepped over some kind of line—maybe by saying what all are thinking but still what no one should say. Kip had earlier griped that "no one cares." But that was just a gripe. Layton has gone too far by equating his individual need for a cigarette with the right to voice a *programmatic* cynicism that counters the idealistic talk of religion with a bleak materialism that challenges the unit's sense of connection to something outside of itself that invests its training and sacrifice with purpose and gives them hope.

When, in the next scene, the chaplain (Leon Ames) addresses the platoon in the fierce cold of a forest clearing and at the nadir of their prospects, he begins by asking, "Anybody here from Ohio?" A handful of men call out their hometowns. The chaplain responds, "I'm from Chillicothe," and asks, "Any of you men Lutherans?" and is answered affirmatively by a half-dozen. "So am I," the chaplain pitches in. "But these services aren't just for Lutherans any more than they're just for men from Ohio. I only happen to be in your area. In other areas there are other chaplains of various denominations and religions. All of us 'Holy Joes' are switch hitters. Earlier this month in Holland I held Hannukah services for some of the men of the Jewish faith." The chaplain finishes warming up his audience with a joke and then gets to the point: "And the sixty-four-dollar question is, 'Was this trip necessary?' I'll try to answer that. But my sermons like everything else in the army depend on the situation and the terrain." The camera tilts to the chaplain's ragbound, frozen feet. "So I assure you, this is going to be a quickie." His slangy, straight-from-the-hip answer to his own question compacts the men's perspective on why they fight with the audience's perspective on why they fought, into a single, unified perspective on why they will continue to fight.

> Well, let's look at the facts. Nobody wanted this war but the Nazis. A great many people tried to deal with them. And a host of them are dead. Millions have died for no other reason than the Nazis wanted them dead. So, in the final showdown there was nothing left to do except fight. There's a great lesson in this. And those of us who've learned it the hard way aren't going to forget it. We must never again let any force dedicated to a super-race or a super-idea or a super-anything become strong enough

to impose itself on a free world. We must be smart enough and tough enough in the beginning to put out the fire before it starts spreading. My answer to the sixty-four-dollar question is, yes, this trip *was* necessary. As the years go by a lot of people are going to forget, but you won't. And don't ever let anybody tell you you were a sucker to fight in the war against fascism. And now, Jerry permitting, let us pray.

But Jerry does not permit. The chaplain cannot be heard over sudden noise of artillery fire. Once again adapting to "the situation and the terrain," he tells the men, "Let us each pray in his own way to his own god."

Some do pray. Some, perhaps, reflect. At first the answer to the sixty-four-dollar question seems simple: "we made the trip because we had to fight." But it gets more complicated as the chaplain shifts to the retrospective claim that the war has been a necessary learning experience; we have learned from this war how to prevent another one. For that reason the soldiers' duty will not end with their active service. They must remember. Jarvess, a journalist in civilian life, also advocates memory, though crucially not as an ideal but as a technique. Faced with the indifference of the other men to the sight of an old woman scrounging food from a garbage can, Jarvess declares his commitment to remember the suffering of the civilian populace of Bastogne. Later he briefly explains to a confused Layton the importance of memory in clarifying behavior that was inexplicable at the time: "Things just happen. Then afterward you try to figure out why you acted the way you did." Afterward: after the battle, then, in 1945, and after the war, now, in 1949.

The duty to remember that the chaplain urges the men to accept (and *Battleground* performs) is in the service of a project, to put out "the fire before it starts spreading." The fire is a force described, not in terms of the size of its population or the number of its armaments, but in terms of its fervent devotion "to a super-race or a super-idea or a super-anything." If, in 1945, the force dedicated to a "super-race" was Nazi Germany, in 1949, the force dedicated to a "super-idea" was the Soviet Union. And the "super-anything"? The chaplain tolerantly invites the men to pray to their own gods after he has implicitly repudiated the one God, an all-powerful force, a "super-anything." An impersonal "God" is the placeholder for whatever super-something is to be invoked by those who would impose force on the free world. The chaplain may speak in the name of "God," but he speaks on behalf of the ideology of no ideology, in other words, Cold War liberalism.

Battleground does not invest in the decline or displacement of religion but in its functional differentiation. Religious service is just one of many tools that can help the individual GI adjust to his buddy, and his nation as the army adapts "to situation and terrain." In this pluralistic form of populism there are in principle as many gods as there are individuals—what connects them is the attitude of reverence adopted by all the men who fill the frame. Some men kneel; one holds his helmet over his heart; more kneel; Holley turns his eyes to the ground; Kip just stares at the men kneeling in front of him. Layton is standing off to the side under a pine. At first he gazes almost straight ahead as the men around him lower their heads. Cut to a close-up of a thoughtful Holley, pondering, who then looks off camera, watching Layton, whom the camera catches glancing right and left at the other men. Layton then looks up, crosses his arms, and lowers his head, like the others. Cut back: Holley is still looking at Layton and then, like Layton, he lowers his head and crosses his arms in imitation of Layton's attitude of prayer. The men never avow beliefs, only affiliations—Ohio, Lutheran, Jewish—and any sense that they have beliefs is just an inference from their presence at the service and the reverent attitude they adopt in response to Holy Joe's invitation to prayer. There is no felt need to know whether the men are actually praying or whether they actually believe in one god or another as long as they look as though they might be praying, might believe, for their reverent attitude is assumed not because they stand under the eyes of God but out of respect for the other men in the company.

Another way of putting this is to say that *Battleground*, a film about men who have mastered their fears and who can be at home anywhere, is an anti-noir. In *Bataan* the platoon occupies a rocky prominence against which the Japanese launch wave after wave of assaults on the American position. The picture belongs to the last-stand genre of *The Lost Patrol* (RKO, 1934), *Beau Geste* (Paramount, 1939), *Gunga Din* (RKO, 1939), and *They Died with Their Boots On* (Warners, 1941). *Battleground*, however, solicits a comparison with film noir throughout. The exhausted soldiers are ready to exit a world of mortal danger and are suddenly recalled to their duty by orders they may not question which send them to a region of constant peril from formidable but unseen enemies, whose hostility is all the more fearsome in that it is utterly impersonal. The fighting in *Battleground* occurs in a forest of error: a thick mist covers the terrain, blending day and night; it masks an enemy that has freedom of movement and effortlessly surrounds the soldiers (Figure 2.12).

In the demonic landscape of the Ardennes the poor, fog-baffled devils of the

Figure 2.12

grounded airborne cast no shadows. When the German soldiers do emerge from the mist they are indistinguishable from comrades-in-arms. They look like GIs, they talk like GIs, they know the GI passwords—so they are easily able to fool the sentries, penetrate the lines, and perform acts of sabotage. Yet whatever confusion the men feel is eventually cleared up. Their alienation is alleviated. Moreover, there is not a hint of paranoia about the Germans. The Germans are uniform thieves, not body snatchers. If their nation has followed the delusional faith of the master race, there is no evidence that these commandos share in that conviction. No rabid captives spout the malignant Aryan doctrine of the downed airman captured by Mrs. Miniver, not even the arrogant officers who are held by the squad during a parley. When the Germans are killed, they do not deliquesce; they become corpses that, apart from their sensible white coveralls, are indistinguishable from American corpses. What makes the German soldier appear American is what makes the soldier from "Dog Patch" appear as American as the guy from Sedalia, Ohio.

There is nothing uncanny about the imposture of the Germans: they have an objective and have chosen the best means of achieving it. The Americans have the objective of breaking out of the surrounding circle of enemies. The fog must lift, but when it does there will be no epiphany. There will be the recovery of a man's shadow cast by the breaking sun and a premonition of the reinforcements on the way (Figure 2.13). And then the sight of C-47s carrying food and ammunition (Figure 2.14). Only those in the audience who had not read their local newspaper could fail to recognize that what the soldiers saw in Belgium in 1945, what Americans saw on the screen at their local Rialto, is exactly what the surrounded Germans saw in Berlin in 1949: salvation from the skies, also delivered by C-47s, also food—but no ammunition this time, excepting the propagandistic triumph of the act itself.

Figure 2.13

Figure 2.14

At the beginning of Universal's version of "The Killers," Anthony Veiller, the screenwriter, quotes Hemingway's dialogue directly as the killers at the lunch counter order Nick to "'go on the other side of the counter with your friend.' 'What's the idea?' Nick asked. 'There isn't any idea,'" one killer brutally replies. That declaration is never challenged in the film, which takes as its premise a world in which ideas have no power to motivate action or constrain passion and where the only "bright boy" is the insurance investigator who solves the crime, constantly reminded that what passes for rationality in his actions serves some deeper drive that he cannot name but that he must obey until he sets the trap that will kill the killers. Holy Joe's sermon implies a predicate: there is no idea, not even the idea that there is no idea—for the very negation of the idea that emancipates the killers from motive or affect enables them to murder according to a standard of efficiency that knows no constraints. Holy Joe's sermon advising that the men "adapt to the situation and the terrain" wisely preaches the worldview of the tactician at the battlefront and the GI in the trenches, for as all Americans know, obsolescence and irrelevance are built-in to any idea that claims permanent authority.

That MGM would make an antinoir is no surprise. The studio never showed any affinity with film noir. *The Postman Always Rings Twice*, released in 1946, was the studio's ostensible attempt to enter a genre dominated by Fox and RKO, among the majors. In retrospect, however, *Postman* has more in common with Warners' *Mildred Pierce* (1945) than with *Street with No Name* (Fox, 1948), *Out of the Past* (RKO, 1947), or *Fallen Angel* (Fox, 1945)—or with *Double Indemnity* (Paramount, 1944), for that matter. Although *Double Indemnity* shares the provenance of a Cain novel, Billy Wilder's picture more closely follows the noir script of sexual intrigue, violence, and betrayal than the studio jobs *Postman* and *Mildred Pierce*, which turn the novels toward investigations of the problems of marketing, of selecting commercial real estate in Southern California, of managing restaurants, and of women attaining financial independence from their husbands.[36] Diverted by the challenge of squeezing every bit of sex out of the figure of Lana Turner that Joseph Breen would allow, Tay Garnett, the director of *Postman*, did not make much of an effort to adapt the Depression-era fable to a postwar environment. The sign "man wanted" hanging in front of the restaurant, which catches the vagrant's eye, does the symbolic work of bridging the decades. *Postman*, like *Mildred Pierce*, *The Big Sleep* (Warners, 1946), and *Scarlet Street* (identified as both a Fritz Lang Production and a Diana Production, 1945)—all films on the cusp of demobilization—are faux noirs, pictures that exploit some of the techniques, motifs, and themes rapidly becoming routinized by the genre. The infusion of noir enables *Postman* and *Mildred Pierce* to acquire the kind of allure that would attract a male audience otherwise uninterested in stories of women's perilous attempts to acquire real estate. The same fuel enables Hawks and Lang to have their films do their double duty as thrillers and as arguments on behalf of the directors' professional agendas of achieving artistic independence through studio ownership.

Unlike those opportunistic projects, *Battleground* has epochal aspirations. As Schary's studio-remaking attempt to produce the exemplary post–World War II film, *Battleground*, as George Sidney testifies, recalls the studio-making *Big Parade* of 1925. If that recollection can claim to restore the studio by exercising the MGM trope of self-reflection, it fundamentally revises the lesson of *The Crowd*, released three years later, by solving the problem of alienation in a way that does not require full-scale commitment to a sociology of distraction. As we have seen, it is the argument of *The Crowd* that the individual in mass society can find no vehicle for the expression of his talent in the bureaucratized office of modern business; nor can that business insure him against the traumatic consequences of accidents that occur in the world outside the office. Entertainment provides a kind of social insurance via the compensation of laughter and the consolation of being part of an audience with others, all safely gathered into a collective forgetting of whatever wounds each has suffered. *Battleground* holds no idea of trauma as a wound to the psyche that cannot be remembered or spoken. The movie is committed to remembering everything. The picture can honestly make that commitment because it has evidence that the training undergone by the modern soldier infuses the morale that protects him from indulging his own separate fantasy of omnipotence or from sinking into abjection. "Entertainment" is not imagined as spectatorial; instead *Battleground* represents entertainment as the practical employment of popular culture to assist in a training that assimilates men from every state and class into a citizen army. And *Battleground* projects that training, which was the wartime responsibility of the army, as the peacetime obligation of the corporate studio applied not only to American men but to men and women across the "free world."

Despite his agon with Metro's founding mogul, Schary has kept the corporate faith. *Battleground* deploys the trope of social adjustment that was the distinctive device of MGM in the 1930s. But this is social adjustment of a different order. Like *The American Soldier*, *Battleground* is a completely adjusted text that has adjustment as its business. That adjustment is self-reflexive. *Battleground* endeavors to adjust MGM to the social reality, the new situation and terrain, that the studio faces in the postwar era: to the perspective of a lost American audience, veterans of the war, who after demobilization began abandoning the cities for the suburbs and the movies for television; to an international situation where former enemies are new allies, and new allies are new markets for the products of Hollywood, products that can help bond the peoples of the free world as citizens of a common culture. Led by MGM, Hollywood would perform this bonding among peoples by adjusting their attitudes—which is not simply a matter of changing opinions or even moods, but, more importantly, adjusting what people say and the way they say it, the clothes they wear and the way they hold their bodies.

In an essay for *This Week* magazine of December 12, 1943, Samuel Goldwyn remarked that "The motion picture is one of the most tremendous forces in the world for influencing public opinion," and exhorted, "It is time Hollywood learned to respect its own power."[37] *Battleground* answers Goldwyn's charge. Like the work of the Research Branch, *Battleground* is an effort in practical engineering, what the market theorists now call "rebranding." It aims to engineer an audience from the half-million soldiers—now veterans—that the Research Branch identified, and recognizes that this requires that MGM adjust to their tastes and expectations. The chaplain conducts a primitive version of market research when he polls the platoon to learn how many men there are from Ohio, how many Lutherans: religious pluralism is the corollary of a market pluralism. The work of the Research Branch has made a science of the chaplain's improvised polling techniques by representing the men that the war took away as tables of data that schematize the opinions they have freely offered. Schary had the wit to see that what was formerly the statistical representation of an army adumbrates a market that could be addressed in the mass as the army had already done and from which customers could be formed. *Battleground* represents its own imagined market as comprising a multitude of men whose sense of their own identity as Americans involves a commitment to the culture that Hollywood screens. For MGM, if not for the Research Branch, however, that multitude includes America's former enemies, whom *Battleground* represents as having their identity formed, at least partly, through American popular culture. *Battleground*'s project is not only adjustment at home but the continuation of what Goldwyn called the "cultural colonization of the world through its movies." That's Schary's gamble. It was a good gamble based on the percentages the Research Branch helpfully supplied. It was a bet that Mayer was not prepared to make, largely because it depended on a methodology Mayer was not prepared to recognize, which was designed to identify an audience that Mayer was not prepared to see. As the declining box offices of 1947 and 1948 made clear, the golden years of the war had been a boom that ended when the veterans returned home, an audience lost to Hollywood.[38] Given the market research already conducted by the Research Branch, Schary had every reason to feel confident. Market research could not guarantee success, but no market research had previously developed such a comprehensive study of the attitudes of such a large population and therefore such an opportunity for an entrepreneur who could rise to the occasion.

Schary's strong commitment to *Battleground* would seem to have been driven at least in part by an identification with Layton, the new man in the unit. Recollecting this period when his relations with Mayer began to fray, Schary represented his situation in terms similar to the replacement's. "We had a good relationship," recalled Schary, "but then inevitably and this I must say is absolutely so—it's inevitable when a new guy comes in and the studio suddenly changes complexion that press guys begin to notice it. . . . And Mayer began to fret and he disagreed with me about a couple of pictures and . . . he just thought I was making a fool of myself" (*LH*, p. 425). "New guy" means that Schary was not only a new executive in a group that had been stable since the 1920s, but that he was a second-generation filmmaker without connection to the founders. Zanuck, then running Fox, was there at the beginning of Warners. When he left, Hal Wallis was his replacement, also there since the sound era began. RKO and Paramount were cautionary examples of what happened to a studio when the founders lost control and the studio went into bankruptcy and receivership. Before Schary, Selznick was the exemplary "new guy" at MGM. His Hollywood pedigree was strong but he strengthened it even more by marrying into the Mayer family. Schary was a different kind of new guy—a liberal in a conservative studio, a writer from the New York stage, an executive whose strongest allegiance was to Schenck, not Mayer. Allegiance to Schenck meant an allegiance to the studio, but not the MGM that Mayer had in mind.

Layton is not any kind of boss and has no boss with which to contend. His arrival does little to change the "complexion" of the unit: he aims to blend in. But to Layton falls the one vocal affirmation in the picture. When the fog lifts, when the men can once again see their shadows, and when the sound of American fighter planes and C-47s is heard throughout the land, Holley gleefully turns to Layton and asks him,

> *Holly*: What was that about eagles?
> *Layton*: They shall mount up with wings as eagles.
> (*Pause, shots of planes and parachutes.*)
> *Layton*: They shall run and not be weary.
> *Holly*: Well, what are we waitin' for?

As we have seen, there is much repetitive speech in the picture, some annoying, some ironic, some so habitual that it is hardly noticed. This is the only time in the movie, however, when someone is asked to repeat something he has said. Holley's question bears no reproach. He does not ask Layton to recant his parody of religious piety. Holley invokes "eagles," not "the Lord." He summons Layton to reverse his irony not so that he will acknowledge the truth of religion but so that he will affirm the truth of an identity believed lost. At one point it seemed enough to Layton to wear the screaming eagle patch; then it became important to be known by his name. But as Layton adjusted himself to his unit, the identity of the 101st Airborne dissipated in the implacable fog. The division endured the humiliation of sinking from air assault pilots to mud-bound infantry; the men had to shed their patches as they approached battle; they suffered the successful imposture by German commandos. Yet it is as if no one cares. And no one does care about Kip or Layton or Holley—not even, finally, Kip, Layton, and Holley. When the sky opens and the ammunition falls it demonstrates the distant care by the nation for a corps beleaguered in its service; a demonstration that recalls the men to the memory of whom they are. They mount "*as* eagles." This invigoration is not proof of the power of God to shower manna on the hungry, but proof of the power of metaphor to deploy an image in order to transform likeness into unity and confer strength on individuals by enabling their recognition that they participate in a corporate identity. The men will mount up with wings like eagles because the 101st Airborne *are* eagles. Layton and Holley witness to a comprehensive image, not a superior ideal. The belief that we mount *as* eagles is distinctively American insofar as it is belief without creed.

Just like fidelity to a brand. Or, to reverse the simile, a brand works just like the metaphor: it translates the individual into one who identifies with the group by means of an image, a noncognitive visual or aural idea that focuses an array of desired associations and invests meaning in official insignia, patches, or trademarks and applies a shared distinction to those individuals (or products) that bear them. *Battleground* teaches the liberal lesson that a belief is a brand and a brand is an identity that a person—American or German—can wear on his sleeve. *Battleground*'s strategy of "rebranding" revives the lapsed potency of a brand by a forcible transfer or expansion of its associations, whether deliberately achieved or not, that attracts new meanings as if it elaborates the core idea that the brand originally bore.

As *Boys Town* had shown, both Mayer and Schary, conservative and liberal, shared a vision of the studio as a corporate community that spoke on behalf of a vision of a society as an imaginary community bonded together by a common culture called entertainment. In this entertainment, entitled *Battleground,* Dore Schary is the agent of MGM's reflexive attempt to rebrand itself as the studio whose pictures can represent the shared aspiration of a postwar generation of Americans to participate in an idea of community uncontaminated by doctrine and uncompromised by an objective: America as a brand that can claim allegiance at home and loyalty abroad. When Layton responds to Holley's request that he speak, he answers not in his own voice but in the voice of the rejuvenated corps, which vindicates its training and proves its unquenchable morale, as, chanting in close formation as I Company, it marches right down the center of the road that will take them home, ready to take on "Jody" and whatever else the future holds (Figure 2.15).

Figure 2.15

Although Schary affirms innovation in the name of adjustment, his voice only acquires authority insofar as he convincingly utters a lapsed corporate intention that belongs to MGM, not just to the new guy and certainly not to the old guy. *Battleground* proved that audiences would watch a war picture. More important, however, it seemed to show that MGM could get men back in the theater. Watching *Battleground*, reviewing the box office receipts, one could imagine that MGM was springing forward on its haunches as a lion, and that though he had abandoned the red rose of the Minivers the tenacious Schary had earned for the studio its red badge of courage.

3. "'Til the Stars Go Cold"
Singin' in the Rain, The Band Wagon, and *Executive Suite* (1952–1954)

i. Star Deterrence

> The Freed unit was a studio within a studio. If I fell a half-day behind schedule, Joe Cohn would be on my back. If Freed fell behind two weeks—nothing. For one thing, nobody knew how he did what he did.
> Armand Deutsch, producer at MGM[1]

A penitential episode in the life cycle of a handful of major stars at the major studios, most of them women, was enduring the star-punishment picture, in which real-world bad behavior or, worse, superannuation was penalized on-screen. As the vehicle of Katherine Hepburn's rehabilitation, *The Philadelphia Story* required her character, Tracy Lord, to acknowledge the justice of all the humiliating criticisms that had been leveled at her by her father and her husband, which were virtually the same criticisms—for example, "prig and perennial spinster"—that had been heaped on the aristocratic Hepburn in the press and in the executive offices of RKO and MGM.[2] In *When Ladies Meet* (MGM, 1941) the judgment of Paris becomes the judgment of MGM mainstay Robert Taylor, who, as Jimmy Lee, confers the prize of his and his studio's golden affection not on Mary "Minnie" Howard, played by Joan Crawford, the dowager queen at Metro, but on Mrs. Claire Woodruff, played by her heiress apparent, the classy import from the breeding ground of royalty, Greer Garson. In *No Highway in the Sky* (Fox, 1951), Marlene Dietrich, an aging movie star whose popularity has declined, plays Monica Teasdale, an aging movie star whose popularity has declined and whose glamour is eclipsed by the cheerful domesticity of the flight attendant Marjorie Corder, played by the perky Glynis Johns. Bette Davis had the best claim to dominate the genre: as the brutally chastened Julie in *Jezebel* (Warners, 1938), Davis vicariously pays for her upstart attempts to dictate contract terms to Jack Warner; in *All About Eve* (Fox, 1950), as Margo Channing, Davis is compelled to adjust to a future of diminished stature; in *The Star* (Fox, 1952) she plays Margaret Elliott, an alcoholic, spoiled actress, well past her prime, who cultivates delusions and resentments and undergoes humiliation after humiliation until she discovers that her happiness lies in marriage and child rearing; and, of course, there's *Whatever Happened to Baby Jane?* (Associates and Aldrich Company, 1962), in which Robert Aldrich, with Davis's enthusiastic and Crawford's reluctant participation, at once sends up and fulfills the star-punishment genre.

Male stars were occasionally selected for the special distinction of a performative punishment. The most famous example is *His Glorious Night* (MGM, 1929), a legendary flop that hastened the end of John Gilbert's career at the beginning of the sound era. After its release, rumors abounded that Louis B. Mayer, who despised Gilbert, arranged that the sound picture would expose and magnify the weaknesses of the silent star. As we shall see, MGM's *The Band Wagon* (1952) goes far to dissipate what remains of Fred Astaire's aura as he plays Tony Hunter, a has-been whose career mirrors Astaire's. That Hunter's and, through him, Astaire's stardom are revived (or is it the other way around?) does nothing to mute the demonstration of the studio power to hustle a career to the verge of irrelevance. *Singin' in the Rain*, perhaps the greatest of Hollywood musicals and certainly the most self-reflexive of all MGM pictures, makes the punishment of a star the conclusive action of its narrative. The studio that had already shoved the despondent John Gilbert out the door and toward an early death, re-creates his home as a set for the spirited number "Good Mornin'," apparently to take advantage of the opportunity of rubbing it in by dancing on Gilbert's couch, if not quite his grave. There is nothing on the screen that suggests studio antagonism toward Gene Kelly, the one confirmed star in *Singin'*, whose most recent picture had brought the Oscar home to MGM. Debbie Reynolds, Donald O'Connor, even June Hagen might achieve stardom, but they have done nothing yet that would have deserved the kind of allegorical degradation that Warners and MGM engineered for Crawford and Davis. They were unlikely to misbehave if they paid attention to what the studio did to Lina Lamont and what it did to Gilbert. A fit genre for the 1950s, *Singin' in the Rain* represents star punishment as a studio option in order to make it unnecessary.

In his autobiography, *Heyday*, Dore Schary goes into some detail about the organizational issues he negotiated with Louis B. Mayer, studio head at MGM, and Nick Schenck, CEO of Loew's, in 1948 before he accepted their offer to return to MGM as executive vice-president in charge of production. One item he did not think he had to negotiate was the end of the unit system, which, he says, Mayer had been ready to discard. Much of the tension that immediately developed between Mayer and Schary, however, had to do with Mayer's reluctance to follow through on his promises. Although the unit *system* was abandoned before Schary's arrival, not all the units were abandoned—a fact that Schary acknowledges only obliquely in his discussion of the three producers of musicals at MGM—Arthur Freed, Joe Pasternak, and Joe Cummings—each of whom had his own stable of talent and was protected by Mayer, who promoted musical projects.[3] In light of their consistently high costs and variable returns, the musical producers needed a patron. Ominously, Schary's charge was to increase profits; and, deplorably, his tastes and his duty converged in black-and-white realism, which cost far less than Technicolor musical fantasies. Many of the musicals of the 1940s had been good pictures—in that they had sophisticated arrangements of new or revived songs and dances that were choreographed to feature the estimable talents of MGMs contract stars: Eleanor Powell, Mario Lanza, Gene Kelly, Frank Sinatra, Esther Williams, Judy Garland, and Mickey Rooney. All had been "quality" pictures, in Robert A. Brady's terms, in that they were uniformly expensive productions that did not yield the kind of box office returns that would have a huge effect on the bottom line of the company.[4] Unfortunately, not all of them were popular. Scott Eyman reports that MGM suffered "huge losses on *Summer Holiday* and *The Pirate*, and . . . minor losses [on] *Good News* and *Words and Music*" (*LH*, pp. 400–401). Nonetheless, Mayer continued to commit large sums of money to their production—notably the half-million dollars that Arthur Freed requested to complete the ballet sequence in *An American in Paris* (MGM, 1951) (*LH*, p. 139). Schary's *Battleground* had made plenty of money, but it did not win the Academy Award. *An American in Paris* did. Its success seemed to vindicate the Mayer commitment to expensive, prestigious musicals—an orientation best exemplified by the house style mastered by the Freed unit, "the studio within the studio." Oscar in hand, Freed, the studio head under the studio head, managed to slough off Schary's supervision in the name of a studio brand identity of which the Freed unit alone could claim custody.

Unlike Warners' *The Fountainhead*, which we will engage in the next chapter, *Singin' in the Rain* is no manifesto. Its agenda is implicit. In that regard it keeps faith with the culturalist, anti-ideological thrust of *Battleground*, but in almost every other way it represents a competitive vision of the studio: it is expressly a studio production that lays claim to being the bearer and conservator of the studio identity, fully in touch with the studio's history, utterly confident that the studio's history is the only history that matters, and completely attuned to the studio's audience—an audience it has created and can re-create, as it has made, and unmade, and sometimes can remake stars. Like *The Fountainhead*, however, *Singin' in the Rain* is a film about credit: who gives it, who receives it, who takes it, and incidentally who deserves it. The issue of credit had long been a vexed issue at MGM. Irving Thalberg was famous for his refusal to take a producer's credit for any of the numerous pictures that he supervised.[5] Dore Schary, who would become the first studio executive since Thalberg to be in a position to take a producer's credit, had been restrained while directing the Rapf-Schary B unit at MGM from 1942–44, but when, after a stint at RKO, he became vice-president in 1948, he was not shy about giving himself credit as producer or executive producer as the case warranted. Challenged by a characteristically disingenuous Mayer for this break with Thalberg's precedent and Mayer's own reticent practice, Schary responded, "L.B., I'll make a deal with you. Change the name of the studio to Metro-Goldwyn-Mayer-Schary and I'll never put my name anywhere else" (*H*, p. 209). Mayer did not appreciate the jest. By the time *Singin' in the Rain* went into production Mayer was gone, though the name "Mayer," not the suggested "Schary," stayed with the studio as a permanent credit to its mogul, sealing the studio's name off as an eponym or, to choose the name that Comden and Green gave to the studio in *Singin' in the Rain*, securing it as a "Monumental" production.

Carol Clover puts the issue of credit front and center in her essay "Dancin' in the Rain," in which she examines the technology and protocol in *Singin' in the Rain* of one person doubling another. Lina Lamont does not greatly mind being dubbed by Kathy Selden, but she does strenuously object to the studio head's decision that the youngster get full screen credit for talking and singing in *The Dueling Cavalier*, the studio's first talking picture. Justice must wait until opening night, when "the curtain behind the lip-synching is jerked away and the true talent—Kathy at the microphone—is now, at last *seen*."[6] As other examples of falsely taking credit or of excessive insistence on receiving credit, Clover cites Arthur Freed's reuse of the earlier songs of Freed and Nacio Brown; his apparent plagiarism of Cole Porter's "Be a Clown" from *The Pirate* for the "Make 'em Laugh" number; his objection to the absence of a credit to the song writers in the advertising for the film; the similarities of the plot of this film to the 1949 *You're My Everything*; and, crucially, the absence of any screen credit for Betty Noyes, the woman who dubbed Debbie Reynolds's dubbing of Lina's singing in the number "Would You" (Jean Hagen who played Lina dubbed Kathy dubbing Lina's speaking voice in *The Dancing Cavalier*). The injustice that Kathy is represented as having had done to her, is essentially the same injustice that is done, without representation, to Noyes. Clover concludes, "so wide is the gap between what *Singin' in the Rain* says and what it does that one is tempted to see a relation between the two—to see the moralizing surface story of *Singin'* as a guilty disavowal of the practices that went into its own making" ("DR," p. 725).

Some might call that inversion of manifest statement and concealed intent "irony" or, as we shall see, "camp." Clover insists on psychologizing the disparity between narrative theme and industrial practice. Regarding the "larger resonances" of this disavowal, she argues "that *Singin' in the Rain*'s morality tale of stolen talent restored is driven by a nervousness about just the opposite, about stolen talent *unrestored*, and that one reason for its abiding popularity is the way it redresses our underlying fear that the talent or art we most enjoy in movies like *Singin' in the Rain* is art we somehow 'know' to be uncredited and unseen. The question," she says, "is what is talent and who it belongs to." And if indeed talent has been stolen, one might add the questions, as Stephen Silverman puts it, "who is culpable for the theft, and who is blocking the restitution?"[7]

The issue of credit *is* crucial to *Singin' in the Rain*, but neither talent nor credit is stolen. Whatever talent means on Broadway or in a community theater in Cedar Rapids, for the Freed unit at MGM, the studio within the studio, a talent that can be stolen is no talent at all. No doubt in *Singin' in the Rain* we see and learn that *credit* has been transferred, but, however unfair, that transference is perfectly legal. The basis of Lina's power, as she gloats to the head of Monumental, R. F. Simpson, is that her contract with the studio gives her control of all the publicity that the studio releases about her and thus guarantees that she will retain credit for the songs that Kathy Selden dubs. Simpson does not dispute the claim. Cowed by her threat to sue in order to enforce the contract, he quickly capitulates to her demands. Betty Noyes, like most singers who dubbed for stars, never managed to acquire contracted rights to credits.

The only documented complaint regarding credit came from a surprising source: Arthur Freed. It was not the credit scroll at the opening of the film that disturbed Freed. Those credits begin, of course, with the familiar MGM trademark of Leo couchant and roaring which, sans sound, had been the contribution of the "G" for Goldwyn constituent of the new studio. Here Leo is buoyed by an unfamiliar orchestral accompaniment, which continues into the next shot of three figures with their backs to the audience and their heads hidden by three umbrellas. As the music mounts, the names of the three actors appear on the umbrellas in a sequence that reflects their relative stature: Gene Kelly, Donald O'Connor, Debbie Reynolds. In synch with the muting of the orchestra, the figures turn, and we see their faces as they stride toward the backtracking camera, singing—what else?—"Singin' in the Rain." As the actors complete the refrain with "Singin', singin' in the rain," and wheel to retreat, the title card "Singin' in the Rain" appears in a slow dissolve over them. The orchestra returns to segue into "You Are My Lucky Star," which accompanies the remaining sequence of credits cards, including the credit:

> Story and Screen Play by
> Adolph Green
> and
> Betty Comden
>
> Suggested by the Song
> "Singin' in the Rain"

This is followed by the credit:

> Songs:
> Lyrics by
> Arthur Freed
>
> Music by
> Nacio Herb Brown

Whatever the sequence or size of the credits, everything proceeds from the song that "suggested" the screenplay—a song by Arthur Freed, who, along with Nacio Brown, wrote it and continued to own it right up until Freed sold his songbook for a mere twenty-five thousand dollars to MGM in 1950, just before Mayer approved a picture to be suggested by the song title. Stanley Donen, who, along with Gene Kelly, is credited with the direction of the picture, complained about the title, which "should never have been *Singin' in the Rain*. Look at the picture. It's not about weather. The theme has nothing to do with rain. The picture is about movies. The title should have been *Hollywood*." Donen may have resented making a picture that has nothing to do with what its name suggests, but, following Donen's logic, since the picture is actually about one particular studio in Hollywood it might have been better entitled *Monumental Pictures*, or, to drop the weak disguise, *MGM*, or, since it is about one particular production unit in that studio, "the studio within the studio," it might have been called *Arthur Freed*. Since "the musical served as Metro's signature genre" as well as Freed's signature genre, however, the picture probably has the title that gives credit where credit is due.[8] Freed had no doubts. When his credit for the music was omitted from the advertising for the picture, he wrote to the employee responsible: "I notice that you omitted the most important credit of the last ten years in not giving credit to those famous writers and composers of screen musicals, Nacio Herb Brown and Arthur Freed. I do not care how much you reduce my credit as the producer, but as an artist I rebel against not receiving proper credit as a lyricist."⁹ Freed fashions his order to alter the ad copy as an ironic statement of rebellion against the decision of a subordinate rather than as a direct threat to dismiss him. The irony may be weak in Freed's use of "famous," but without it he would come off sounding a great deal like the one character in *Singin' in the Rain* who rebels against being deprived of credit: Lina Lamont.

Signaling one's irony was important when using the term *rebel* in the early 1950s. Like *revolt*, *rebel* of course invoked highly charged associations for the red hunters and bashers in Hollywood and Washington. But *rebel* also stirred the executives of the studios, who had been treated to the drama of Schary's usurpation of Mayer at MGM and who had suffered the challenge of "top producers, high-priced writers and directors, and the cherished stars," who, according to Ernest Borneman in his article "Rebellion in Hollywood," have "ventured, one by one into the hazardous world of private enterprise and hopeful profit sharing, clutching the banner of artistic freedom in one hand and an income tax blank in the other."¹⁰ Borneman published his article in 1946. Much had changed by the time *Singin' in the Rain* went into production. A revision of the income tax code bled the profits out of single picture companies. The tightening of distribution outlets squeezed independent production companies. The shrinking of the audience hurt everyone, but it crippled the independents. Those developments slowed the exodus of talent, but they did not alter what Brady called the monopoly power of stars, a power in which MGM had long invested ("PM," p. 132).

It was with some irony that Freed, the establishment producer at the establishment studio, applied the term *rebel* to himself, and it was with similar irony that the Freed unit introduced the term *revolution* in the motion picture. The whirling montage sequence that takes Monumental Pictures from silence to sound in the middle of the filming of *The Dueling Cavalier* is introduced by an insert from a contemporary undated *Variety* (labeled vol. 72, no. 7), with the headline "Revolution in Hollywood," which invokes not only the technological change but also the prospect of an upheaval in the ranks of the Hollywood studios, as Warners crashed the club of the Big Five. Steven Cohan has noted that the omission of the dates from the newspaper pages that follow enables *Singin' in the Rain* to condense 1927, the year of *The Jazz Singer*'s release, with 1929, the year that MGM adjusted to sound by releasing *Broadway Melody*, the "first all-talking, all singing, all dancing musical" (*IE*, p. 222). By that compression MGM gives its counterrevolution credit for what Warner Bros. had wrought—a maneuver consistent with the revisionist historiography of the picture as a whole: the vehicle for the history of Hollywood is the history of

MGM, which, in turn is the history of the musical, which in another, even more tightly reflexive turn, is the history of the recycling of the Freed catalog and of the evolution of the Freed unit.

Singin' in the Rain not only recalls triumphs over adversity, it reflexively reclaims flops as comedy. Nineteen twenty-nine was the year that MGM released both the box office hit *Broadway Melody* and the fiasco *His Glorious Night*, in which John Gilbert idiotically repeated "I love you, I love you, I love you"—the scene that is parodied in the disastrous preview of *The Dueling Cavalier*. The humor here is as self-critical as Don's narration of a life wholly discrepant with the visual truth before the microphone at the opening of *Royal Rascal* that begins the movie. MGM indulged in irony about its own early pretensions, but it always recuperated self-criticism as a feature of its chief, defining, integrative device: a studio self-reflexivity that overcomes minor lapses in taste and decisively distances the studio's products from anything that Warners or Paramount could manage. In the MGM musicals of the 1940s and early 1950s, self-reflexive recycling of product and conferral of self-credit had become formalized as a corporate strategy of brand management, which entailed a history that could be sung to the tune of "Where or When": the MGM musical is a perfection that has always already been reached (Cosmo: "If you've seen one, you've seen them all"), but that is always unfolding (R.F.: "It's a nice idea, but I'll have to wait to see the visuals").[11]

Singin' in the Rain warns that things that happened for the first time in 1927 (or 1929) are happening again in 1952. The headline "Revolution in Hollywood" recalls the high anxiety of the industry in the wake of *The Jazz Singer*'s extraordinary success, but it also evokes the climate of innovation and uncertainty afflicting postwar Hollywood in the wake of the Paramount decision and in the face of challenges to studio hegemony by independent production companies. The headline should also alert the audience to the implicit theme of the imminence of revolution that runs through the costume dramas in which Lockwood and Lamont star. Their plots are glibly encapsulated by Cosmo after Don tells him of the plans to follow *Royal Rascal* with *The Dueling Cavalier*, a "French Revolution story": "Don't tell me," Cosmo replies. "You're a French aristocrat, and she's a simple girl of the people, and she won't even give you a tumbril." Oddly, the supposedly hackneyed Lockwood-Lamont story, as Cosmo tells it, has a conspicuous part for Kathy, "girl of the people," but no part for Lina, glamorous aristocrat. Given the revolutionary allegory Cosmo introduces, we might guess that someone will lose his or her head.[12] Cosmo alone seems to have given a thought to the prospect of decapitation, however. In a further bit of guillotine humor he punctuates his joke by pulling himself by the neck and jumping down from the piano bench, as if through a trap door. He hits the floor instead and makes the most of it by launching into the manic "Make 'em Laugh" number, in which he releases whatever he has bottled up inside him—mostly, it appears, repressed sexual energy. Cohan adds, "That response is not out of line when O'Connor does a bit of sexual play with the headless, genderless dummy; he puts his hand on the dummy's knee suggestively and gets hit in the face for making a pass" (*IE*, p. 159). Cohan does not mention the political cue that precedes the mayhem that follows this "bit," however. In the course of displacing his gay desire Cosmo responds to the (self-inflicted) slap on his face as a provocation to a wild pantomime of beating, slamming, heaving, and, finally, kicking the dummy, which could stand in for multiple fully gendered, flesh-and-blood targets. The similarity of the headless figure to the famed tavern sign featuring a headless torso over the caption "The Silent Woman" cannot help but suggest Lina, whose chief offense is the irritation of her voice. As evidence, note that, as Charles Dove first observed, the sequence of Cosmo's hilarious routine is preceded by Don and Cosmo crossing in front of the set with the couch, which, as we see in a brief pan, is occupied by the headless dummy at one end, a woman in contemporary dress in the middle, and, at the other end, a woman dressed in high Marie Antoinette mode, expensively gowned, and wearing a towering powdered wig that resembles the one favored by Lina Lamont (Figure 3.1). The fleeting visual association of Lina as French aristocrat and the headless dummy helps to explain why Cosmo reacts so violently to the slap on his face. Yet if Cosmo's revenge fantasies focus on Lina, they surely, guiltily, also involve Don. Perhaps his anticipated rejection by his friend, should he avow his feelings, is displaced onto Lina, whom Cosmo does not really want but who is available as a hostile surrogate for all women who are rivals with him for Don's love, including Kathy, who is, however, exempt from his criticism if not his resentment.

Figure 3.1

Despite its lack of narrative connectors the "Make 'em Laugh" number is key to the integration of the motion picture as a studio statement. That claim conflicts with the powerful reading of *Singin' in the Rain* by Cohan in *Incongruous Entertainment*, which argues that MGM's integrated musicals were not so integrated as the conventional wisdom supposes. Especially during the 1940s, and even in a musical so heavily plotted as *Meet Me in St. Louis* (MGM, 1944), music, according to Cohan, was predominantly used in individual, contingently related *numbers* that involved singing, dancing, comedy, and even an interlocutor or two. Those numbers were vestiges of the vaudeville mode of entertainment as nostalgically invoked in *Babes in Arms* (MGM, 1938) and *Singin' in the Rain*, or of the more elaborate showmanship of Ziegfeld's follies. Typically, MGM's recollection of the demise of vaudeville was a way of keeping it alive both in form—as a revue or biopic or a musical within the musical—and in substance: vaudeville tunes and routines were revived (albeit "freshened" as Mickey Moran advised his father in *Babes in Arms* as he planned his comeback). As functions of what Cohan calls the "industrial purpose" of the picture, numbers of "high entertainment value" were aggregated into the movie one by one, here and there, with scant evidence that the featured singers or dancers knew what motion picture they were performing in. Consequently, the story of a boy and a girl meeting, falling in love, overcoming obstacles to their union, and finally marrying, may be the narrative thread designed to integrate the music into the story, but the "big numbers disrupt the integrative form to offer a pleasure other than that of following a story: namely, watching the spectacle purely as spectacle" (*IE*, p. 62).

All audiences enjoyed the spectacles, although, as Cohan argues, we have good reason to believe that a self-consciously gay audience was especially alert to an aesthetic supplement of décor, costuming, gestures, and double entendre in the aggregated numbers that was incongruous with both MGM's targeted middle class and the prevailing heteronormative ideology of the musical. The minority gay audience cultivated what Cohan calls, "an ironic engagement with ideological incongruity through an exaggerated theatricality" or "camp affect"—a fit response by the knowing few to the "house style's own representation of cultural incongruities" (*IE*, p. 45). Cohan affirms that Hollywood musicals are generally characterized by a dialectic between "the contrasting cinematic values of story and spectacle, respectively," and goes so far as to claim that the house style manifest in the dialectical tension of MGM's musicals combines "all the key elements of the MGM brand" (*IE*, p. 45). There were, of course, conspicuously profitable and nonmusical elements of MGM's brand, including the Andy Hardy series, the Mayer vehicles for Greer Garson and Irene Dunne, Clark Gable and Spencer Tracy, and, in the 1950s, the series of pictures that John Houseman produced for Dore Schary. Even within the scope of the musicals, however, Cohan does not associate the "house style" with either MGM's or Loew's corporate strategy. Except for the productions of the Freed unit, Cohen finesses the question of corporate intention by explaining the fit between the "formal tensions" of the pictures and the camp aesthetic as a matter of "correspondence" or "paralleling."

The Freed unit clearly knew what it was doing. "'Freed's fairies,'" as the artists and craftsmen assembled under the producer were called, "could, on the one hand, offer escapist family entertainment seemingly committed to wholesome, normative values through plots, and even numbers, figured around the centrality of a heterosexual couple. On the other hand, the same musicals could deliver a camp affect for an audience who did not align itself with those values and who took great pleasure in the visual strategies with which, as [Matthew] Tinkcom puts it, 'camp style marks a critical commentary upon the narrative of 'heterosexual bonding'" (*IE*, p. 50). The ability of the Freed unit to employ a refined house style to address both the mass audience and the gay audience within the mass audience renders the Freed unit not only as the metonymic studio *within* the studio but also the unit *as* the metaphorical studio, the privileged artificers and custodians of the MGM brand.

For Cohan, *Singin' in the Rain*'s historical and aesthetic distinction in the Freed canon is that it appropriates camp for a mass audience (*IE*, pp. 244–45). The condition of that transformation, I suggest, would have been the recognition by the Freed unit that it had developed a style which comprehended both integration and aggregation as *formal* arrangements in the service of a corporation with which it aggressively identified and on whose behalf it exploited camp affect for its value to the MGM brand as it was recalibrated to suit the tastes of the consumerist audiences of post-Paramount Hollywood. The Freed unit adapted the self-reflexive mechanism that Thalberg first impersonated in order to exploit the camp affect innovated by gay culture so as to create anew the taste by which MGM films would be appreciated and to legitimate its claims to be the avatar of MGM's true identity. The dream of the Freed unit and therefore MGM was that a cinematic style could generate a popular art form, a dream given muscle by the realization both that a cinematic style could not be separated from the technology that was the condition of its making and that the technology could not be separated from the corporation that owned and controlled it. Freed's dream of a capable cinematic style was the dream of a corporate style, and the art generated by that style would be, as *Fortune* prophesied, a fully reflexive, fully corporate art.

Indeed, the polar opposition of aggregationists (splitters) and integrationists (lumpers) is not only critical in the history of the MGM musical, it also defines the history of the theory of the modern corporation to which MGM's self-reflection is a crucial piece of evidence. Integrationists view the corporation as a natural person who exists independent of any interventions by legislatures and the courts and which develops according to an immanent capitalist logic. Aggregationists regard the corporation as an artificial being constructed for financial convenience, whose history is a series of crucial legislative enactments and compelling judicial decisions—"big numbers" that subvert any integrative form that might be imposed on the story of the evolution of the corporate person. The historical relation between these two accounts has been thoroughly nondialectical. As Thurman Arnold showed in the 1930s, one way to understand the peculiar vitality and power of the corporate form is that it can comprehend both perspectives at the same time without attempting an integration that would quench the dynamism that their tension generates.

If we look at the "Good Mornin,'" scene, we can discern how the number performs the integrative function of managing Cosmo's sexual desire by distributing it among the aggregated trio of Cosmo, Don, and Kathy, and applying it constructively to the problem of Lina. Inspired by Cosmo's idea of turning *The Dueling Cavalier* into a musical, the high-spirited dance begins with the friends each performing a bravura turn in different costumes and dancing together in numbers that cross genders or, by leaving out heads, maximize interchangeability by neutralizing gender. By rhyming with the shot that opens the picture before the credits, the turn that the trio do with the raincoats reminds us that headlessness is the default position of studio talent (Figures 3.2 and 3.3).

Figure 3.2

Figure 3.3

After the tumbriling finale of the number, the trio's excitement is quickly dashed by the realization that if they made a musical the squeaking Lina would have to stay in the picture. Cosmo, however, comes up with a solution, which he demonstrates by fronting for Kathy as she sings another chorus of "Good Mornin'" while he mouths the words she is singing, as if they are coming out of his head. For a brief, brilliantly confounding moment, Cosmo, Don's former partner, sings *as* a girl, and not just any girl: as Don's *current* girl. So here it is for all to see: the cross-dressing partner speaks as a woman to his most intimate friend (Figure 3.4). When Don finally understands the rationale for Cosmo's queer demonstration and endorses the idea of dubbing Lina, Kathy expostulates, "Don, you're a genius." Cosmo pouts, "I'm glad you thought of it." Kathy responds, "Oh, Cosmo," and kisses him on the cheek. That's that. The picture has been rescued. Kathy's transfer of credit from Cosmo to Don tidily reciprocates Don's transfer of affection from Cosmo to Kathy. Her kiss acknowledges Cosmo's desire and substitutes for the credit a proxy for what he really wants, therefore cannily taking advantage of the inadmissibility of Cosmo's desire. Cosmo cannot complain, "Why should my right to credit be satisfied by a kiss?" because everyone knows why and no one can say it. Ironically, at the moment of near exposure of what we know Cosmo feels for Don, Cosmo is as far as possible from intimacy with Don: he cannot say what he means to say because the condition of his saying anything, like the condition of Lina singing, is that he does not mean anything at all.[13] He is merely the mechanical medium for another iteration of Arthur Freed's tune.

Figure 3.4

Cosmo innovates his own obsolescence, for once the principle of lip-synching has been proven he will be superfluous. The same could be said about anybody, because the technology of sound reproduction ensures that any head can be separated from the living, breathing body to front a voice including (and this is the joke on both Debbie Reynolds and Betty Noyes) that head which appears to be the source of the voice. Kathy does not ventriloquize Cosmo; Cosmo is in synch with Kathy's utterance because both are following the same score, which is the lyric to "Good Mornin'," written by Arthur Freed. Freed gets the credit for authorship, but the lyric is owned by MGM, which gets the financial return on its 1950 investment in Freed's song catalog. Like *Fortune*'s Thalberg, who makes himself camera and projector in order to channel his audience, Cosmo instrumentalizes himself as the medium for the rescue of the movie, of Lina, of Don, of Kathy, and *of the company*. Cosmo is the proxy of a studio organized as an autotelic recycling machine which successfully instrumentalizes individuals (a star is such an instrument) to achieve its ends. Foremost among those objectives is survival—a feat that vaudeville did not achieve, except insofar as its myth is recalled and its numbers recycled by MGM musicals.

Singin' in the Rain is a story not of technological determinism but of corporate determination: the determination to ensure the survival of the corporation by establishing a basis of profitability. As the final scene of the film shows, it is not technology that ultimately matters but "ownership" of technology and the agency to determine its uses and users. What counts at the end of the picture is the authority to approve the pulling of the ropes to open the curtains—the oldest technology in the theatrical profession. This time it is the Freed unit—as played by Simpson, Cosmo, and Don—not Toto, that pulls the curtain to disclose not a fake wizard operating his own apparatus in his own studio but just another makeshift Dorothy, singing for her supper. Lina vanishes quicker than the Wicked Witch of the West, executed instantly by the revelation that her head has *already* been cut off. It is a hard fate, but revolutionaries should know that they play for high stakes. Because ownership is nothing but control and control is virtually identical with the power to confer or claim credit, when, in Simpson's office, Lina seizes control of herself for herself ("I control my publicity, not you." "Yeah?" "Yeah, the studio's responsible for every word printed about me. If I don't like it, I can sue"), threatens to use her contract to take over the studio ("I could sue you for the whole studio"), and forces Simpson to approve taking Kathy's "credit card off of the screen," she all but signs her own death warrant. Lina's vaunt would not have been taken seriously in 1929; but in the 1950s, surging star independence and the institutionalization of the newfound power of the talent agencies were sufficiently menacing for a studio to imagine that such a transfer might happen and to decide to deter that outcome by making an example that would refresh everyone's memory of the studio's cold-blooded resolution.

Norma Desmond complained about the effacement of the stars that accompanied the switch to sound. No one in *Sunset Boulevard* (Paramount, 1950) argues the point. However mesmerizing, the face—as Norma laments and as Don Lockwood fears—remains insubstantial, a configuration of light and shadows. There is no body without speech and no speech without a head and no head without capital. The advent of sound required the recapitalization of the motion picture industry, which meant reorganization of most studios and, consequently, the involvement of bankers on the boards of directors and even in the executive offices at RKO and Paramount. Bankers have a considerable role in Warners' *Gold Diggers of 1933*, where the financing of a show is the predicament that sets the plot in motion. Except for a very few exceptions, such as the renegade *Our Daily Bread* (1934), MGM protected its audience from the muddle that spreads once you start lampooning bankers. There are no bankers in MGM's *Dancing Lady*, where the financing is handled by a well-heeled stagedoor Johnny. In *Babes in Arms*, the money to finance the show is borrowed from the faded child star, Baby Marie, who is later conveniently removed from the cast by her father without a request for repayment. There is not only no banker, but no mention of money at all in *Singin' in the Rain*, which is a complete credit economy. Both Monumental Pictures and MGM pay in the credit that each asks its audience to extend: the faith that we will finally see the true person behind the voice that comes out of the loudspeakers or that what we are seeing is authentically innovative despite its recuperation of the past. *Singin' in the Rain* deliberately forgets the crisis of recapitalization of the studio that occurred in the industry at the beginning of the sound era in order to focus on a new crisis of recapitalization in the 1950s, when some stalwarts, including Astaire, were aging, and when an even larger number of talented, but blacklisted or tax-afflicted screenwriters, directors, and actors had departed or were about to depart for Europe, Gene Kelly among them.

The Freed unit updated the trope of social adjustment that MGM perfected in the 1930s from a device that enabled the studio to "solve" problems of inequality (the fact that I have less opportunities for success than other people), while finessing issues of class (the fact that almost everyone from my socioeconomic background has less life chances than almost everyone from the background of those who employ people like me) into a mechanism for the recapitalization of the studio that would solve problems of shrinking revenues while finessing the issue of financing. As always, MGM thinks through stars. The difference between the then of the 1930s and the now of the 1950s is that now it understands that it must act through technology. In *Singin' in the Rain* the trope of social adjustment, which had been mastered by MGM, is revised as the *technology* of *cultural* adjustment, which is owned by Monumental Pictures, aka MGM. The change makes things simpler. In *Dancing Lady*, having bailed Janey Barlow out of jail, Todd Newton induces her to join him for dinner. He keeps a little notebook by his side in which, he reveals, he is keeping track of her use of slang and mistakes in grammar. She strikes an indignant pose, but she takes the advice to heart and brings the notebook back to her apartment, where she practices self-correction and successfully standardizes her English. True, getting rid of a few slang words is an easier task than correcting Lina's wretched pronunciation, which is saturated with regional and class indicators, but it is significant in the context of old MGM musicals, which is the context that *Singin' in the Rain* invites us to reconstruct, that Janey Barlow could learn a new manner of speaking sufficiently well that she can enter another social echelon, whereas *Singin' in the Rain* depicts Lina's tutorials as a waste of effort. In *Dancing Lady* there can be a successful social adjustment because there is a society for Janey to measure herself against: a judge in a courtroom, Franchot Tone's sympathetic mother, fellow revelers on a trip to Cuba. The only group that exists outside the studio in *Singin' in the Rain* and for *Singin' in the Rain* is the mass public, which is disdainfully rendered as the audience for the movies, the readers of the fanzines, and the reporters at *Variety*—the world of opinion that fills Lina's head and the argot that spills from her mouth. The only society worth attending to is entirely congruent with the exclusive camp culture to which Don and Cosmo belong and to which Kathy is inducted. The class markings we observe in the picture do not signify social or economic deprivation; they signify cultural abjection. Without any self-awareness that does not reflect what she reads in *Photoplay*, Lina is incapable of readily discerning incongruities; and when she cannot help but notice them, as during the preview of *The Dueling Cavalier*, she takes those incongruities as an offense against the ineffable propriety of her own stardom. She can't make a joke, she doesn't get a joke, and she certainly can't take a joke. She'll never be one of the guys in the way that Kathy proves she can be.

There is no evidence that Don cares about the principle of credit. When he objects to Kathy's treatment, it is Kathy he cares about, no one else; and he cares about Kathy because he cares about Don. From his first encounter with Kathy when he lands in her jalopy, Don makes it clear he needs the authentication that she would bring if he could make her his fan and his alone. Kathy is Don's lucky star because she will be the instrument of his emancipation from the shadow world of the silent screen: he will leave the world of opinion associated with Lina's delusional belief in everything printed in the fan magazines, and he will enter the bright world of reality with the fan who loves him. But Kathy is also lucky to *be* a star and is personally beholden to Don in a way that Lina never could be. Monumental/MGM's choice of a woman to star in the picture who has little acting experience, no training as a dancer, and a voice almost as marked by her geographical origins as Lina's—that is, Kathy, that is, Debbie Reynolds—reinforces MGM's ability to make stars, even out of spare parts. As number after number in *Singin' in the Rain* proves—from the "Singin' in the Rain" during the title sequence to "You Were Meant for Me," to "Make 'em Laugh," to "Good Mornin'," to the "Singin' in the Rain" after the preview, sound technology gives actors speech and therefore heads. As numbers are aggregated in order ultimately to be integrated, so are stars, even if they need to be disaggregated first—a lesson that will be forcefully allegorized in the "Girl Hunt" sequence of *The Band Wagon* the following year.

Integration is not merely mechanical. Kathy could become part of the unit Don-Cosmo because, as the "Good Mornin'" sequence demonstrates, she was educable in camp affect. Kathy learns how to behave in the face of sexual incongruity after the "Good Mornin'" dance number when the trio laughingly recap the "no, no, no . . . yes, yes, yes" exchange or, rather, double exchange from the preview of *The Dueling Cavalier*, when, due to a dropped synch, Don's voice comes out of Lina's head as Lina's voice comes out of Don's. Cosmo starts it off, Kathy picks it up, and then an embarrassed Don catches on and joins in the glee. The three share a camp affect at the irony that even "manly" and "womanly" voices can produce gender confusion in a cinema of sound. Having proven her taste, Kathy is admitted into the exclusive culture of Cosmo and Don. It must be a relief to the entire audience here and, of course, at the end of the movie to take pleasure in the incongruity with its mild criticism of gender conventions, to enjoy our superiority in knowledge to the dramatized audience, and, finally, to be reassured that this cultural initiation has nothing to do with deviant sexual practices. To get the joke is to experience what Cohan has described as the absorption of camp culture into mass culture. We must add that this particular instance of absorption occurs so smoothly because camp culture and an incongruous mass culture are happily synthesized as plain old MGM culture. Of course, the promise of inclusion depends on an unspoken exclusion, just as the promotion of the Freed unit's style as the corporate style depends on the exclusion of other candidates, and just as the universal association of R. F. Simpson, the fictional head of Monumental Pictures, with Arthur Freed collaborates in the exclusion of the real head of the studio, Dore Schary, who is even less of a presence in *Singin' in the Rain* than Betty Noyes. The audience's initiation, however, adjusts them to a corporate culture where new bonds are being formed as part of a new way of doing business on the basis of a new "common denominator" of taste under the auspices of the MGM brand. We exercise this taste when camp affect, its sexual edge blunted, becomes the routine ability to recognize and ironically engage ideological incongruities with some theatricality: as when we begin to whistle "Singin' in the Rain" on a dreary, dripping Monday morning while we pluck from the porch a sodden newspaper with the headline, "Credit Markets Collapse!"

The corporate case conveyed by MGM's "signature genre" is that the studio will endure because it is capable of being disaggregated and remaining the same. Just as the studio within the studio can do without Gene Kelly, Vincente Minnelli, Stanley Donen, John Alton, Roger Edens, Adolph Green, and Betty Comden, so can the studio get by without Arthur Freed. The secret as to how Freed did what he did is that he did not need to do it. He managed an organization that deployed a technology that got it done. That sounds heartless as well as headless. And it was. But just because the corporation was heartless does not mean that it should sound or look so. *The Band Wagon* (1953) responds to *Singin' in the Rain* by explicitly reviving the allegory of body parts as a key to the relation of the formation of the star and the organization of the corporation. The Astaire musical innovates a notion of social responsibility that handily supplements MGM's branded affect in order to give its audience—the initiates and the clueless—a reason they should care whether the studio survives. Social responsibility had not historically been a preoccupation of MGM musicals. The baseline for the social conscience of the musical was set in Warners' *Gold Diggers of 1933*—and not by *The Forgotten Man* number. When, after the disabling of the "juvenile" lead, Barney Hopkins, the producer, urges Brad to abandon his scruples and take the stage, he asks, "Do you know what will happen to these kids if we close the show?" Shamed, Brad capitulates. A similar question is implicitly posed in the 1950s by both *The Band Wagon* and *Executive Suite* (MGM, 1954): "Do you know what will happen to these kids if we close the studio?" Unlike during the Depression, it is not the implied prospect of prostitution to which the impoverished chorus girls (and boys) may have to resort. During this age of abundance it is something worse: television.

ii. Neocorporatism, *The Band Wagon*, and the Charismatic Margin

The term *neocorporatism* was coined by the leftist sociologist and pamphleteer Hal Draper to characterize a set of propositions regarding corporate governance developed in the late 1950s by a group of intellectuals who gathered to study "the Corporation" under the auspices of the Center for the Study of Democratic Institutions in Santa Barbara, California.[14] Draper's other tag, "neoreformers," is also apt because those men self-consciously returned to a problem of business responsibility initially confronted by the corporate liberals of the first New Deal who pursued the implications of *The Modern Corporation and Private Property* (1932), written by A. A. Berle, Jr. and Gardiner Means. Berle's writings in the 1950s also set the terms of the debate at the Center regarding the most effective means to channel the dynamism of the postwar corporation toward socially desirable goals. The neocorporatists developed four distinct approaches to reform: constitutionalism, stakeholder participation, conscience creation, and consensus application. Each approach presupposed Berle's central thesis that the rise of the corporation has changed property from being "a proprietary concept . . . under which a man is protected in the possession of certain things with which he lives" to being a power concept, whereby property provides control over "production and does not express an individual."[15]

Constitutionalizing the corporation meant accomplishing "a legalized incorporation of the economic process and political processes," which entailed the "founding of a new political order on a 'commonwealth of corporations'" (*EUL*, p. 93), in which the same protections would be provided to employees as the U.S. Constitution guarantees citizens. The *stakeholder* approach recognized the claims for consideration by the workforce, by the government, by communities, and by large institutional investors such as pension, insurance, and mutual funds. Berle first proposed the *conscience* model in *The Corporate Revolution in the 20th Century*, where he elaborated an analogy between feudal states and corporate organizations. When feudal rulers faced popular dissatisfaction with the law court's version of justice, they would defuse the conflict by yielding to "a higher law" than their own sovereign will called the "conscience of the king," to whom people could appeal for relief. Berle argued that similar political conditions would impel corporations to develop a "realization of a counter force which checks, and remotely acts upon, and in time may modify in certain areas the absolute power of business discretion."[16] The *consensus* model depended less on transhistorical analogies. Berle predicted that corporate managers would come to respect norms of social responsibility when they realized that retaining power requires a legitimacy earned by adhering to consensus values of the broader political community. The commitment to consensus would be superintended not by a corporation's conscience but by an elite of moral and political arbiters who would be the custodians of what he calls "the transcendental margin," which "is not produced by the movement of capital toward the highest profit or even the movement of effort toward the highest profit.... It is the movement toward abnegation. It turns on something extra-economic in motivation, some philosophical ideal of what a good life is and what a good community is." Berle nominated as custodian of extra-economic ideals "the political scientists," whom he regarded (somewhat implausibly) as having a professional interest "in the state of man's soul" (*EUL*, pp. 52–53, 64).

Although none of the neoreformers' recommendations had any immediate impact, their concerns with corporate social responsibility did not altogether perish with the liberal consensus in the late 1960s. In the 1990s, after several scandals involving trading by insiders and the victimization of outsiders, corporate theorists revived the issue of corporate governance.[17] Berle's hopes for the development of a corporate conscience were partially realized in the ombudsman movement that began in government and corporations in the 1960s. But his prescription of a transcendental margin that would, with the help of a wise elite, guide corporate behavior has found no constituency. Berle was not, I think, wrong in his intuitions. He just sought his evidence from the wrong books: instead of Karl Marx and John Maynard Keynes, he should have been reading Max Weber and Thurman Arnold. If Berle had changed the adjective modifying *margin* from *transcendental* to *charismatic*, he would have escaped some conceptual difficulties that trouble his theory, and, more important, he would have acquired some disciplinary capital by using Weber's sociological concept to challenge Weber's own pessimistic outlook. Berle's late work helps to specify the indispensable place of charisma—not as transcendental but as intangible, not as extrapersonal but as hyperpersonal—in the construction of a corporate organization whose actions have social and political consequences that exceed economic calculation.

"The term 'charisma,'" stipulated Weber in 1925, "will be applied to a certain quality of an individual personality by virtue of which he is considered extraordinary and treated as endowed with supernatural, superhuman, or at least specifically exceptional powers or qualities.... On the basis of them the individual concerned is treated as a 'leader.'"[18] Weber invoked a historical divide between traditional societies where authority was based on personal contact between a charismatic leader and his followers and a depersonalized, modern society characterized by bureaucracies in which authority is exercised by officials who enforce procedures. "Bureaucratic authority," he wrote, "is specifically rational in the sense of being bound to intellectually analysable rules while charismatic authority is specifically irrational in the sense of being foreign to all rules" (*ES*, p. 244). It may have been Weber's difficulty in precisely identifying the difference between spontaneous faith in a truly charismatic leader and contrived faith in a manufactured charismatic leader that led him occasionally to suggest that the charismatic, like the fabled poet, is born rather than made. Weber's equivocations are regarded by Alan Bryman as evidence that the operation of charisma requires a transactional model: the "followers agree to submit to the charismatic leader in exchange for his or her preparedness to meet their needs for salvation etc.... The charismatic leader agrees to bring them benefits provided they are prepared to submit to his or her will.... Each [side] becomes reliant on the other but the exchange is an asymmetric one in the end, for it is the charismatic leader who holds the reins of power."[19] Bryman's focus on an interested exchange propels charismatic authority into the market, where it cannot help but suffer the humiliation of quantification. And surely Bryman errs when he asserts that the asymmetry of power tips the balance to the leader "in the end," for "in the end" the leader will die like everyone else. No charismatic leader dies certain that his charisma will survive as a personal possession bequeathed to child or protégé. Pace Bryman, I shall replace *transaction* with *relation* and *exchange* with *collaboration* in order to align the construction of charismatic authority with the dynamism of those prototypical modern persons, the corporation and the star, as they have evolved in law, in practice, and in theory.

It was Thurman Arnold's insight in 1937 that the peculiar dynamism of the modern corporation was not genetic but the result of the legitimation of a new category of economic value called "capitalized earning power."[20] Peter F. Drucker opined in 1946 that the source of managerial power is not maximization of profit on behalf of the shareholders but increasing profitability, that is, the strategic augmentation of a company's capital of aggregated intangibles in order to create value that had not been invested, borrowed, or earned. Drucker's recognition of managerial capital as the basis for managerial discretion led to his claim in 1954 that management is about creating customers who will buy, not about producing items that might sell. Managing is marketing all the way down.[21] Metro-Goldwyn-Mayer did not need to learn those lessons from Drucker: like the other Hollywood studios, MGM had long been indifferent to its shareholders; moreover, at MGM it was bred in the corporate bones that MGM markets movies not simply for box office but because movies market MGM as the dominant studio in Hollywood. MGM's particular contribution to this short history of corporate theory was the insight that Arnold's aggregate of intangibles is nothing other than star power. Star power is the *charismatic* margin that distinguishes Clark Gable from John Hodiak, Gene Kelly from Dan Dailey, and Fred Astaire from . . . , well, Fred Astaire. As we shall see.[22]

Arnold shared with his fellow legal realists the objective of replacing a scholastic formalism with a functional approach to the law. But he departed from his colleagues by insisting that the power of symbols over people's perceptions of the law, of government, and of corporations cannot simply be dismissed in the name of "reality" or "efficiency." He recognized that symbols are constitutive of that reality and "sought to understand and use them to reshape the public's beliefs."[23] As we have seen in the introduction to this volume, in *The Folklore of Capitalism* Arnold calls the personification of corporations "folk psychology" and shows how that trick of personification enables the accumulation of wealth by rendering "personality" as "goodwill"—an earning power that somehow confers value on a corporation above and beyond the market value of its material property. Thus, half magically, the Baltimore and Ohio Railroad Company is able to sell off all its tangible property and still remain itself. The accounting procedures that recognize goodwill as an intangible value make the corporate person, like Leo Rosten's definition of the star, "a monopoly on itself."

In *The American Economic Republic*, Berle offers his prosaic definition of "the transcendental margin," as "the product of a value system that causes effort and expenditure beyond that calculated as conducive to the personal advantage of an individual or his immediate family group."[24] The use of *value system* in 1964 silently puts the quietus to political "consensus" as a normative engine. We can hear the undersong of Cold War ideology in Berle's claim insofar as he painstakingly avoids the use of the word *ideology* to name what it is that would "encourage individuals to labor and sacrifice for ends aside from their personal advantage" (*AER*, p. 200). Perhaps, however, the definition is more interesting for what is left unsaid. Berle does not say what Arnold should have equipped him to say: because the value system that produces this incalculable margin *is* the corporation there is actually no reason to pointedly avoid using the word *ideology*, since "ideology" has little to do with the way the corporation works. Perhaps, then, a different definition is in order. The corporation is a value system which, if properly managed, systematically generates both a fair financial return on its stakeholders' investment of money, time, and labor and produces a charismatic margin of incorporeal capital that potently solicits extra-economic allegiance. Not its ability to attract capital, but its ability to make capital, to produce a charismatic margin, makes the corporation an extraordinary, exceptional, technically irrational, superhuman person.

As Arnold insisted, no economist's account of the miracle of capitalized earning power can produce the charisma that solicits stakeholder allegiance. The value system that is the corporation must be represented by language or images that symbolize what it is doing in order to get it done. Good will is accumulated as a personal relation between a corporation that symbolically promises and a customer who is promised. The Santa Barbara neoreformers most deeply and symptomatically erred in failing to engage the importance of symbols such as the trademark, the logo, the institutional advertisement, and the mission statement to the operation of the value system that is the modern corporation. Thus their corporate theory is alien in concept and spirit to the brand lingo that was emerging in the 1950s and now dominates the marketing perspective on the corporation.

Procter and Gamble invented brand management in 1931 in order to enable the consumer goods firm to mimic the multidivisional structure successfully installed by Alfred Sloan at General Motors.[25] The first exploration of brand management *strategy* did not appear until the mid-1950s in *The Harvard Business Review*, however, where it was first argued that businessmen should "think of the advertisement as a contribution to the complex symbol which is the brand image—as part of the *long-term investment in the reputation of the brand*."[26] From the perspective of marketers, what Berle called "consensus" was not something out there in the world that directed corporate behavior; consensus was a constituent of the brand, the intangible referent whose rising and falling fortunes would indicate what people—investors, consumers, the media, the government—actually think about when they hear the name of a company.[27] More recently, Marty Neumeier has affirmed that "a charismatic brand [is] any product, service, or company for which people think there is no substitute."[28] And, in fact, there is no substitute, if that's what people think. Because what people think about a company is part of its brand and therefore its value system; you don't need to be a consumer of a company's products to be its customer. Corporations aspire to arrange things so that customers not only succumb to marketing but they actually "buy" the marketing, whether by putting money down to purchase a product or service or by being enlisted as generators of goodwill.

The pattern for that relationship with customers was established by Hollywood, and its most effective vehicle was the star. A star was merchandised as multiple properties: as a moving image in motion pictures, of course, as an image in newspaper ads and lobby placards or on the covers of *Photoplay* and *Life*, or proxied as puffed sleeves or top hats. Auratic artifacts, such as autographed photos, were endlessly replicated, but there was no substitute for the star unless the star had stopped being a star. Barry King incisively distinguished between two kinds of actors: those who are mere personifications of certain attributes, which are mobilized in performance after performance, and those who see their objective as the impersonation of characters as represented in the script.[29] According to that cultural code, the stars of the classical era were personifications. Only a few, such as Paul Muni, the Barrymores, and, perhaps, Bette Davis, qualify as the kind of impersonator that was associated with the legitimate stage. By the 1950s the extraordinary success of the Actors Studio had broken down that code: due to Strasburg's publicity machine the Hollywood stars trained in the Method to fully inhabit their roles became personified as impersonators and, consequently, as Marlon Brando often complained, Method actors were stereotyped as much as the stars of the golden era had been. All stars seem to share the advantages of the corporate form: they are personifications of the set of all the properties attributed to them and the owner of that personification, who can choose to impersonate it on the screen and sell it in the market. By that logic, just as the Baltimore and Ohio Railroad owned the Baltimore and Ohio Railroad, Gable owned Gable and Crawford owned Crawford. Except of course they did not. For most of their careers both Gable and Crawford were under long-term, ironclad contracts to MGM, which dictated their pictures and roles. Leo Rosten's oft-quoted reference to "outstanding personalities," as "monopolies on themselves" was simply a striking metaphor as long as the studios held the stars under long-term contract, which all but a few accepted until the postwar period, when, due to a combination of factors (the Paramount Decree, accelerating costs, aging stars, the rise of the talent agencies, and a general move from a model of vertical integration to a network that Neumeier has praised as "unbundling"), the studios could no longer afford the luxury of a gallery of stars poised for use in the next feature.[30]

No doubt MGM could not make a Gable picture without Clark Gable; RKO couldn't make an Astaire picture without Fred Astaire. But could Warner Bros. make gangster pictures without Cagney? Could MGM continue to make adventure films without Gable? In the 1950s some stars had achieved professional autonomy and economic power by becoming in fact the corporations that they had always been in principle. But the high cost of that autonomy raised the question, even for MGM, of whether any particular star was irreplaceable. Among the handful of ruinously expensive motion pictures made by MGM in the late 1940s and early 1950s, two musicals directly addressed those questions: *Singin' in the Rain*, which clearly answered "no" to "irreplaceable" in 1952, and *The Band Wagon*, which enigmatically answered "yes" in 1953. The anticharismatic, materialist *Singin' in the Rain* is far better known and has been the beneficiary of superb criticism. More pertinent here, however, is *The Band Wagon*, which makes an argument on behalf of the charismatic margin that has better legs than anything the neoreformers brought to the dance.

The Band Wagon depicts the successful rehabilitation of the career of Tony Hunter, a song-and-dance man who has abandoned a dwindling career in Hollywood to return to his first love, Broadway. The studio allegory hangs on the explicit and coded parallels drawn between Hunter and Fred Astaire, who plays the fading star. The opening credits roll over a shot of a pedestal that displays a top hat, white gloves, and a cane—the iconic articles of Astaire's trademark costume. After the director's credit fades from the screen, the camera pans to reveal a posterboard with a picture of Astaire—or rather of Hunter—and then to a room of well-dressed people attending to the sales pitch of an auctioneer as he announces, "Yes, ladies and gentleman, we are in luck here today in Los Angeles. Bullwinkle Galleries has bought up for auction many of the personal effects of your famous movie stars. Today, today, today, is indeed a red letter day: the personal effects of Tony Hunter (Figure 3.5). Some of the potpourri of Mr. Hunter's own personal costumes that he used in his famous pictures. Remember this?" He brandishes a cane above a top hat. "Perhaps the most famous top hat and stick of our generation. Yes, the one he used in *Swingin' Down to Panama* and all his other famous pictures. Let's start the bidding at $5.00. Do I hear $5? Do I hear $2? How about 50 cents? *Anything?*"

Figure 3.5

"Personal effects" is language appropriate to the deceased. Tony Hunter, as we shall learn, is not dead, but he might as well be, for what gave the star life was what gave his effects value: his fame. We begin with irony, then: an event that initially appears to be the commodification of a dead person's belongings is actually the devaluation of a live individual's props. The last plaintive question, which asks if Tony Hunter's personal effects and, therefore, Tony Hunter, are worth *anything*, comically but uneasily suggests another: is Astaire unpropped still Astaire?

Hunter's initial retooling for Broadway involves his acceptance of a role in a pretentious musical adaptation of *Faust*. Before the show can be a go, Hunter has to accept a new partner so that the producer can promote the pairing and acquire financial backing. The partner, played by Cyd Charisse, is Gabrielle Gerard, a classical ballerina who has agreed to descend from the ballet to Broadway. A gaggle of black-tied and bejeweled prospective backers, attracted to the property by Tony and Gabrielle's participation and by the fire-and-brimstone synopsis by Jeffrey Cordova (Jack Buchanan), the director, agree to put up the money for shares in the production. But the pairing of the principals turns out to be a mismatch, the highbrow musical misbegotten. The show bombs, and the shareholders lose their money; but not before the icily restrained Gabrielle thaws under the slow revelation of Hunter's personality, which, she learns, is not to be reduced to a top hat, tails, and a cane. When Gabrielle impulsively visits Tony in his hotel room to apologize for her aloofness (interrupting a tantrum in which he is futilely trying to rend his unbreakable vinyl LPs) she is surprised to discover that the walls are covered with impressionist paintings, which she takes for excellent reproductions. On learning that they are originals, Gabrielle makes the figurative leap of taking Tony's possession of paintings as a metaphorical expression of the individual. She sees Tony as a new person infused with intangible value: there can be no substitute for a Monet, there can be no substitute for a wall of Monets, there can be no substitute for Tony. Of course, the trick here is that exploiting the prestige of high art, as the studio had already proved with *An American in Paris*, is a clever marketing maneuver. Inadvertently, Tony makes Gabrielle a customer for Tony by associating himself with the kind of objects she values in order eventually to reveal to her that he gives value to the paintings, not the other way around.

It doesn't take long. Sitting around with the kids from the chorus and his cronies after *Faust*'s flop, Tony casually offers to sell his paintings to finance the new, entertaining musical revue that the troupe wants to mount. Metaphor becomes metonymy as the gallery of intangible art becomes a storehouse of tangible commodities and Hunter's capitalized earning power is transformed into cash value. Gabrielle observes the speedy alternation from the personification of art *as* Tony to the reification of art as Tony's *property* without dismay. She is undisturbed by the dramatization of Tony as a corporate form. On the contrary, it is the proof that he is a star, which is the demonstration that he and she and everyone else have been seeking all along. The picture argues the thesis that one should not (like, say, Charles Foster Kane) warehouse tangible objects as if they were truly intangibles. It also argues the corollary, that one should be careful (unlike Charles Foster Kane) never to *leave* personal effects behind, because they are valueless unless imbued by a charisma that inheres only in the relation between the star and a fan or another star, or a fan who becomes a star (like Kathy Selden in *Singin' in the Rain*), or a star who becomes a fan (like Gabrielle Gerard). A star, like a corporation, gets to have his cake and eat it too, just as long as he doesn't leave anything on the table when the meal is over. Both star and corporations are institutions that ensure, as much as any person can, that the device of the charismatic margin, not the individual, generates wealth and in doing so destroys possessions by rendering them as incipient transactions.

The recovery of Tony's charismatic margin is accompanied by a new sense of social responsibility: not to the sick or to the poor, but to the talented. Not only does Tony bankroll the show by selling his paintings, he also exploits his "capitalized earning power" at the postflop party to draw upon the reserves of idealism of the youthful cast, who rally around him to offer their energy and labor on the credit of his past successes. As its method for re-creating the Astaire brand, *The Band Wagon* conducts Tony through stages of abnegation: he renounces his film career, he renounces his talent as he prepares for *Faust*, he renounces his paintings on behalf of the troupe and the new musical, and, in that musical, he renounces his "dignity" as he joins a trio of dancers dressed in baby clothes and seated in high chairs.

Hunter's submission to what Phillip Rieff would call "charismatic discipline" pays off in the finale, "Girl Hunt," a fantasy in the mode of the hard-boiled detective fiction of Mickey Spillane. As detective Rod Riley, Hunter strides across a stylized, noirish New York landscape. He is accosted by a beautiful blonde, who falls into his arms and then lures him into a sensual dance. She collapses and then vanishes (Figure 3.6).[31] A man intrudes, bends to pick up a bottle, and is suddenly vaporized. Riley narrates, "There was nothing left of the guy, nothing at all, except a rag, a bone, and a hank of hair" (Figure 3.7). Riley is puzzled; perhaps Hunter is puzzled; but there is no reason that Astaire and the film audience, both witnesses of the prologue in the auction gallery, would not reach the same conclusion: the objects are the man's "personal effects," dream parallels for the gloves, the cane, and the top hat. The parallels are slightly displaced, however. Riley discovers that the rag matches the pattern on a woman's dress, and the hair looks like nothing other than the glossy black pageboy of a mysterious sleek siren. Evidently, Riley's best chance of avoiding the fate of the vaporized man will mean becoming a man who is more than just a Rod, whose power will depend on acquiring feminine properties: properties of a corporate person, not what Berle had called "expressions of the individual."

After Riley pockets the tokens, the blonde disappears, and some goons arrive to rough him up under the direction of "Mr. Big," a mysterious man in a black overcoat and hat, who pitches in by beating Riley with (what else?) a cane. The number, recall, is named "Girl Hunt": while Riley is tracking down Mr. Big, he is also hunting a girl: perhaps the enticing blonde who appears and disappears, perhaps another woman who can solve the riddle of the tokens. He finds a brunette siren and pursues her through stylized sets jammed with Freudian props, such as the bodiless heads of live men and the severed arms of mannequins that confront him in the stockroom of a department store (Figure 3.8). The stunning climax occurs when Riley's bone leads him to the gangster-infested, slickly sexy "Dem Bones Cafe" (Figure 3.9), where Riley finds, once again, the dark haired, long-stemmed woman played by Gabrielle/Charisse, the synthesis of the tokens he bears (Figure 3.10). Riley sees Mr. Big

Figure 3.6

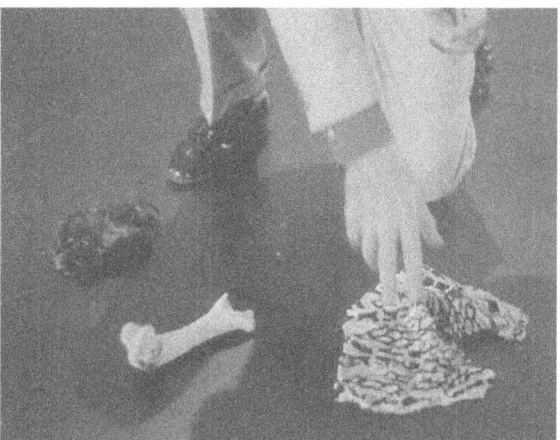

Figure 3.7

Figure 3.8

Figure 3.9

Figure 3.10

Figure 3.11

climb the bandstand, grab a trumpet, and sound the battle cry that summons his gangsters to the attack. Riley fights them off in a strenuously choreographed melee. In the explosive conclusion, he shoots Mr. Big, who slumps into Riley's arms as his coat opens and his hat falls, revealing that the bête noire is a *bête* blonde (Figure 3.11). The menacing brute with the cane and the butterfly of a dreamgirl are identical. But who is it?

"Girl Hunt" ends as Riley, walking alone again on the nocturnal Manhattan street, has his cigarette lit and his match extinguished by the slinky brunette, who takes his arm and strolls off with him as his one and only remaining match. The blonde dies with her identity still a mystery to Riley and to Hunter, for the mystery can only be solved at the level of the extradiegetic referent: Astaire must finally kill off Ginger Rogers. Death to Rogers and the golden age is life to Astaire in the new postnoir world. Death to Rogers is also life to Charisse and to the gang of kids in the chorus. When, after the show, Hunter descends from the dressing room and is surprised by the assembled cast, he learns that finding himself means finding a partner who mediates his connection to a community bonded to him personally by love (each statement in Gabrielle's public profession of love begins with "we") (Figure 3.12). The new company is a company of a different kind: it is not backed by aging swells avid for glamour and a large return on their investments; it is sustained by the contributions of the star, other featured performers, the set designers, and the community of youth who make up the rest of the cast. The finale represents a place where "the world is a stage and the stage is a world" because partnership is not marriage, the kids in the chorus are no one's children, and the corporate "we" is bigger than all of them. There is no way to bequeath one's talent, and no one who has a claim on it. There is no reason to form attachments to personal effects in a corporation of talents, who are members of a value system that has produced its charismatic margin in the figure of Astaire, as its leader, and who in unison sings out the name of its "global brand": "that's entertainment."

Figure 3.12

All will not be well for every person involved in this enterprise, however. *The Band Wagon*'s allegory invites the picture's audience to accept that MGM's capacity to revive a star, Astaire, to make another, Charisse, and to represent corporate harmony proves that MGM still has the capacity to declare itself "Entertainment Inc." Finally, however, MGM is dependent for its ability to demonstrate its corporate potency on agents who are more than allegorical characters: they are stars. Because MGM can only appear through its stars, the triumph of *The Band Wagon* ironically confirms the shift of power from the studio to the star whom *Singin' in the Rain* combatted. In the next decade, ungrateful to their makers, stars (including Fred Astaire, who would subsequently move from studio to studio and from musical to melodrama) would continue to assert an independence that would make them no longer agents of the studio but the principals of their own adaptable corporate structure—and, in turn, examples to us all. The *Band Wagon* tells us that the Faustian deal that each star must strike to achieve charismatic authority and immortal life requires that he or she leave nothing behind. No one can bequeath stardom or inherit the intangible wealth of the charismatic margin. Still there is a utopian promise that *The Band Wagon* makes and that our contemporary cross-platformed and corporate populist entertainment industry seeks to fulfill. When stars become corporations they represent what we can truly become, stars of our own making. We can become persons who construct value systems on the model of the corporate form and who constellate with our friends—old, new, and newest—in a chorus such as Facebook, where more stars glitter than there are in heaven.

iii. Choosing Sides: *Executive Suite*

"If one is successful in one's craft, one is forced to leave it."

David Riesman, *The Lonely Crowd*

On the train from L.A. to New York at the beginning of *The Band Wagon*, Tony Hunter overhears an excruciating conversation between two businessmen who engage in a postmortem about the career of the "has-been," Tony Hunter. If Hunter still has star quality, it is not apparent to those informed observers. Of course, the apparent extinction of Hunter/Astaire's stardom is intended to make MGM's demonstration of its capacity to rejuvenate Hunter and therefore Astaire impressive evidence of the studio's continued potency as it faces an equally uncertain future. But what will happen when Fred Astaire dies? What will happen when Clark Gable, long the "king" of MGM, dies? Who will succeed them? Rejuvenation is one thing, but resurrection is something else.

In "Girl Hunt," the enigmatic objects that Rod discovers are clues as to how a new Astaire image could be assembled by manipulating the dream correspondents of the props that elemented the older, RKO image. The picture, however, stresses Astaire's active involvement in the process. "Girl Hunt" is not *Frankenstein*, though it is close enough to make anyone a little nervous. One could imagine a reading of its allegory that projects a future "Astaire" stitched together out of film clips to compose a segment of an anthology called (after a number from this picture) *That's Entertainment*, or stitched into a commercial in order that he may partner with a vacuum cleaner while he dances on the ceiling. Insofar as charisma depends on the conviction of a personal relation with its possessor, the dying dancer, like the dying dictator or the dying prophet, takes his charisma with him. After Astaire's death we would no doubt agree that Astaire *was* a star but we would not say, even of his digitally generated image, that he *is* a star, let alone that he *will* be a star. The image of Astaire is not mortal, but it no longer represents an ensouled person; the image does not have the intentionality that belongs to both the corporate and the star form, whether that star is an actor like Astaire or an executive like Thalberg. How, then, does a studio with aging stars and executives facing a world changed utterly by the war, the Paramount Decree, television, and the mackerel-crowded drive-in handle succession so as not to leave a dark void where once the star and the studio were? How can the charismatic margin be preserved and the deadening grasp of bureaucracy, the nightmare of Hollywood creatives since Thomas Ince first moved West, be averted? How can the studio arrange that the right person may move from the chorus line to the marquee or ascend from a seat at the foot of the table to the throne at its head?

Executive Suite, MGM's most sustained reflection on the corporation on behalf of corporations, went into production in 1954, just after the studio finally implemented the terms for divorcement that had been negotiated in response to the U.S. Supreme Court's Paramount Decree of 1948. As Dore Schary tells the story, "At about this time MGM, which had been the last of the Mohicans, ran out of legal devices, deterrents, and dodges, and was compelled to divorce the ownership of their theaters, leaving them with their distribution operations and film production activity. This divorcement procedure (largely cosmetic) was designed to prevent production companies that owned theaters from freezing out pictures made by competitors." He adds that "the new arrangement renamed Schenck as president and retained me as a vice-president and head of the studio for MGM. Loew's Inc. became the distribution arm, no longer allied with production. The new alignment brought a flurry of activity in Metro's stock, which led the exchange for a day for reasons that still remain obscure to me" (*H*, pp. 275–76). In Schary's narrative, the divorce, so long opposed, lacked any drama when it finally occurred, which seems strange for a company sliding into hard times. There was that "flurry of activity" in the stock, however. A version of the drama missing from Schary's account emerges in *Executive Suite*, a motion picture about "new arrangements" of executives following the departure of a powerful president, about new policies intended to arrest decline, and about a flurry of activity in the company's stock at the crucial moment. Schary may have said so little regarding MGM's reorganization because *Executive Suite* says it all—and does so even though Schary would have preferred not to be aware of it.

Executive Suite was the third picture produced for Dore Schary by John Houseman, whose *The Bad and the Beautiful* (1952) and *Julius Caesar* (1953) had garnered numerous Oscars, and who had proven to be Schary's dependable ally in the treacherous environment of the studio. *Executive Suite* takes as its subject the succession struggle at a small furniture manufacturer in a company town, Millburgh, Pennsylvania. Like Houseman's earlier movies, it is directly concerned with charismatic authority: how it is acquired, exercised, lost, and revived. As we have seen, similar concerns trouble *Singin' in the Rain* and *The Band Wagon*. *Executive Suite* does not, however, indulge the Freedian fantasy that the studio within the studio is the part that stands for the whole; it understands the Freed unit as one among several competing voices; and it takes as its business the integration of the two principal rivals, the Freed unit and Schary's allies, into a single team organized to confidently face an uncertain future.

At the center of the Cameron Hawley novel is a struggle between two corporate vice-presidents for the right to run the company after the sudden death of its president, who, though once an executive of heroic stature, had begun to show signs of decline, while neglecting to name his successor. The rivals in the picture are Loren Shaw (Fredric March), the calculating comptroller, who considers himself certain to be the next president, and Don Walling (William Holden), the idealistic materials engineer and designer, who enters the fray when no one else will step forward to challenge Shaw. Schary had himself won a fierce contest with Louis B. Mayer for power at MGM three years before. The parallel, should anyone care to draw it, could be expected to flatter Schary's sense of himself as the youthful, reforming executive of the film industry. But the parallel is a rough one—Shaw is more like Nick Schenck than Mayer, who might pass for the expired CEO, Avery Bullard. The former struggle between the aging Mayer and the ambitious Schary does impinge on *Executive Suite*, but as one instance of a more general predicament: the stress that a corporation undergoes when, in the course of things, it must select a successor to a highly effective corporate president. As Oscar Grusky observes, "administrative succession always leads to organizational instability." The prospect of a presidential succession raises questions that trouble almost all organizations: What is the basis of executive authority? Will the organization survive the loss of its leader? As for the question of survival, Grusky comments, "the corporate form of business organization has an obvious advantage over the partnership form, in that the permanent existence of the former, unlike the latter, does not rely on the continued existence of a few persons."[32] *Executive Suite* focuses on the critical question of what the permanence of the person who is the corporation *means* to those persons whose transient existence is caught up in its life, and why that meaning should matter. The picture argues that a vital qualification for the presidency of a company is the capacity to interpret that meaning and communicate it to the multiple groups that make up the stakeholders of the company. The other, equally important qualification that will justify a man's right to be a successor of a charismatic leader will be proof of his potency not simply as a born leader but as a proven innovator, for as we shall see, *Executive Suite* translates the criterion of corporate effectiveness from profit maximization to product innovation, which acquires its unprecedented value as the talismanic device that the modern manager employs to enable a company to succeed itself without suffering the pangs of death.[33] As a study in the affiliation of corporate modernism with managerial innovation, *Executive Suite* is closer to the story of the Herman Miller Company than *The Bad and the Beautiful* is to the life of David O. Selznick, and almost as close as *Boys Town* is to the actual history of Boys Town.

The posthumous vitality of the corporation is dramatized as the narrative of *Executive Suite* silently opens following the prologue, with its arch voiceover by Chet Huntley.[34] The scene begins by establishing a first-person point-of-view shot in which the camera travels from an elevator down the corridor of an office building and through a door into a Western Union office, where the person whose point of view the audience shares orders, dictates, and then sends a telegraph calling a meeting. He signs it "Bullard."

We—the vehicular individual and the transported spectator—exit the building onto a busy urban street, look toward a taxi as if to hail it, and then, struck by momentary dizziness, fall face down, flat on the sidewalk. As a wallet falls into the gutter the spectator sees his hands twitching at the curb. Is the man dead, or is he looking at his hands as we are? The surmise itself dislodges our identification with the inert body and reorients the "we" to include those who go on living. We do not know where the man's soul goes; but we are released from the corpse by a black out, then returned to ourselves by a cut to the conventional third-person point of view, which may be employed to solicit identification but does not induce the sense of incorporation the spectator has just experienced. That *sense* of incorporation that "we" had as "we" traveled in the man's body and saw through his eyes has not provided access to what he thought. The point-of-view shot bore no burden of subjectivity: "we" did not feel anything that the man feels; and, perhaps most important, "we" have no feeling *for* him. Those of us who are "we" see the same thing, share with the vehicular individual the same relation to what is disclosed by the lens that stands in for eyes. And thus "*we*" are momentarily surprised to be aware of living on after the man has died. Only when we individual spectators notice that the first-person point of view has been abandoned do we infer that this singular, impersonal point of view through another person's eyes *was* in fact a distinctive subject position: a *corporate* point of view, which integrates anonymous mentalities and coincides with an individual human being only for an uncertain term. That corporate point-of-view shot will not be repeated in *Executive Suite*. It does not belong to us amalgamated spectators any more than it ever actually belonged to Bullard.

Restored to the third person, the viewer soon learns that Avery Bullard was the powerful president of the publicly owned Tredway Corporation, makers of mass-produced furniture, who was in the process of returning to his corporate offices in Pennsylvania for a meeting, which we have seen him call by telegraph, and at which he had apparently planned to name his preferred successor, thereby to dispel uncertainty and preempt competition among the executives. Seven voting members assemble. With the exception of Julia Treadway (Barbara

Stanwyk), the founder's daughter, and Harold Caswell (Louis Calhern), a shady financier, each is a potential candidate for the presidency: Jesse Grimm (Dean Jagger), grizzled vice-president of production; Walt Dudley (Paul Douglas), the gregarious head of sales; Fred Alderson (Walter Pidgeon), the decent, loyal, but indecisive treasurer; Loren Shaw (Fredric March), the grasping, ambitious comptroller; and Don Walling, the youthful vice-president of design and development. Walling had once been Bullard's favorite because they shared the dream of a progressive, risk-taking company committed to practicing good design and attaining industry leadership. Recently, however, he has found himself marginalized, as Shaw has persuaded the increasingly conservative Bullard to cut back on investment in research and design and focus the resources of the company on the cost-efficient mass production of "priced merchandise," such as the cheaply constructed "KF line." After the chairless meeting breaks up and even before he gets the news of Bullard's death, Walling complains to his wife, Mary (inevitably, June Allyson), of the new dominance of Shaw's bottom-line mentality ("For Shaw, it's improve the profits, not the product") and laments the death of the dream that Bullard had promoted when recruiting him to move to Tredway.

If Shaw were to succeed Bullard, his colleagues could be sure that the company, which had once been rescued from ruin by its charismatic president, would soon be reformed by the bureaucratization of managerial functions, by the abolition of expenditures on research and development, by a downsizing of the labor force, by increasingly intrusive surveillance, and by a concentration of all planning on the single objective of increasing the bottom line. It is easy enough to find that prospect distasteful. Indeed, it may be that Fredric March, who plays Shaw as a version of Richard Nixon (complete with a perspiration problem), makes it too easy. Suppose, however, that Bullard *had* decided to select someone with charisma. How could he be sure it was the real thing? How could the succession have occurred according to the formal procedures of the organization? Weber provides no help. Charisma's inalienable personal quality, which resists transfer and repudiates institutionalization, interdicts charismatic succession. Charisma is not a property but a power—a power neither earned nor deserved but given, like grace. And like grace you cannot inherit or bequeath it. Charismatic authority expires with the bearer, unless it becomes the "charisma of office," a transformation that involves the transfer of the belief in legitimacy from the individual to "acquired qualities and to the effectiveness of ritual acts," such as priestly anointments or democratic elections.[35] Charismatic authority must fail to guarantee its survival beyond the body it inhabits, although the institutions of the state and civil society will routinely claim to have succeeded.

When Walling learns that the dreamer is dead, he quickly allies himself with Fred Alderson in order to keep the dream alive by preventing the bean-counting Loren Shaw from being elected president. The Machiavellian Shaw has, however, been effectively maneuvering to build his own majority among the board of directors. We see him obtain the vote of Caswell through stock manipulation: he has used the newspapers to prop the price of Tredway stock, thereby jeopardizing Caswell's insider, short-selling maneuver, which had created a flurry in the stock's activity; he then offers to loan Caswell stock certificates from the company safe. Shaw gets another vote by blackmailing Walter Dudley, a salesman who is married and whom he catches in a tryst with Dudley's secretary. Bewildered by Shaw's machinations and dispirited by the evidence that Bullard did not want him for the top spot, the elderly Alderson tells Walling that he won't fight for the job. Walling asks, "Who is going to stop him [i.e., Shaw]?" Looking meaningfully at the dynamic young executive, Alderson answers, "If it was five years from now, I know who could."

Later that night Walling's wife, Mary, finds him seated at his desk in his strikingly modernistic study, jammed with interesting objects and signs of creative labor, where he is seated at an architect's desk. She looks over his shoulder at his sketch and comments, "Oh, I like that." Walling pushes the drawing aside and pulls out his projected list of the votes for the presidency. Mary asks, "What about the stockholders?" Without a flicker of a pause Walling answers with the managerial creed espoused by Drucker: "The stockholders had their say when they elected the board." So much for the stockholders (or so he thinks).[36] His wife, concerned at Walling's mood, returns to her theme of independence in words that suggest that she has just finished reading *The Fountainhead*: "Leave Tredway. Design what you want. Build what you want. If it hadn't been for this room the last few months, you couldn't live." Walling is almost persuaded by this advice, replying, "I'm not going to die young at the top of the tower worrying about bond ratings. That's not why I came here. I'm a designer, not a politician—I think." But that's no answer. The question is whether Walling is going to do his thinking on behalf of the company or of his own private interests.

When Alderson recommends that they back the glad-handing Dudley for the presidency, Walling objects that he is in no way the peer of Bullard. Alderson replies, "We're not going to get another Avery Bullard, Don. You've got to make up your mind to that." A less rapt observer than Alderson, however, might conclude that Avery Bullard himself had done his best to ensure that there would never be another Avery Bullard and that, moreover, the company would be better off without one. Mary comes the closest to making that case when Don later tells her that he has changed his mind and will seek the presidency because, he believes, the goals that motivated him to join Tredway can still be accomplished under his leadership.

> *Mary*: That's impossible, Don.
> *Don*: Nothing's impossible.
> *Mary*: Bullard's line, not yours.
> *Don*: The whole company is at stake. Tredway's got to be kept alive.
> *Mary*: Avery Bullard has to be kept alive—isn't that what you mean? You want to sit in his chair, be his ghost. You're even beginning to sound like Bullard.
> *Don*: Oh, stop!

After Don has brushed aside his wife's objections, he pursues the presidency for what he thinks is the good of the company. The problem with his resolution is not, as one might expect, that he cannot separate the interest of the company from his own but that he cannot initially separate either his interest or the company's from Avery Bullard's. Before the election meeting Walling confronts Julia Tredway, daughter of the founder, the company's largest shareholder and the spurned lover of Bullard, in an attempt to gain her support. When he learns that she has taken Shaw's advice to sell all her stock and assign him her proxy in the forthcoming election, Walling attempts to make her see "reason." Stung by her resentment of Bullard, Walling rages that "if she wants to stab a dead man, she should do it in person." He fends off her furious attack and departs—leaving a hysterical, suicidal woman whose opposition he seems to have strengthened by surrendering to his homosocial jealousy and rage. If it were true, as Eric Larrabee and David Riesman urge in "The Executive as Hero," their *Fortune* article on the movie, that Walling's major qualification for the presidency is his "palsy walsy personality," it is not on display in this scene.[37] Walling succeeds only in provoking Julia Tredway into attending the crucial meeting after all, where she does rescind her proxy but only to cast her vote for Shaw personally.

Nonetheless, Shaw surprisingly loses that first round of voting because Shaw's co-conspirator, Caswell, intent on ensuring that he will get the stock to make good what Shaw has promised, has cast a tactical abstention, which costs Shaw a majority. A recess follows. The delay is just long enough for Walling's ally Alderson to return with Grimm. Alderson whispers to Walling, "I thought I could move him, Don. But he's stubborn." Alderson has set the agenda for Walling, which is to move Grimm, to move Tredway, to move Dudley, and to move even Shaw—to move them all if he is to move anyone. The stakes are established when Shaw is induced to make a paltry campaign speech in which he states his conviction that because the purpose of the corporation is to make the highest possible return on stockholders' investments, its president should be a specialist in finance, who, unlike the folks in production or sales or those in research and design, knows how to cut costs to make money. After Shaw has criticized Bullard's recent performance, Walling offers him this paraphrase: "In other words, Avery Bullard was the right kind of man to save this company from this disaster, to build it up and set it on its way. But now we need a different kind of management, one that will dedicate itself to paying the maximum dividends to the stockholders. Is that it?" Shaw assents. And why shouldn't he? That dividend maximizing, charisma routinizing jargon is not only what he would have learned while studying for his CPA, it's the Weberian thesis that he would have learned in Sociology 101. What makes Walling a rhetorician instead of a charismatic is his canny use of Shaw's simplification, not only to expose the man's values as shallow, but as a pretext to offer the lament that Bullard, who had once worked out of pride rather than for the Dow Jones index, had let that pride cut him off from everyone who mattered to the company: workers, employees, his fellow executives.

In the same issue of *Fortune* in which Eric Larrabee and David Riesman published their prickly essay on *Executive Suite* there appears an article by Herryman Maurer entitled, "The Age of the Managers," which, while not mentioning the motion picture, faithfully glosses its message. According to Maurer, "modern management, self-conscious and even introspective, is engaged in constant study, experimentation, and change. The modern managerial breed is preoccupied, above all, with the future—not just the personal future, but the future of the corporation itself."[38] Riesman and Larrabee, meanwhile, don't see the future of the corporation as different from present business as usual, and thus smugly predict that once the idealistic Walling has assumed the presidency, he will find himself negotiating the customary "conflicts and collisions of interest that give business its true drama" ("EH," p. 134). Maurer projects a different future for corporations because corporate America and—as this special section in *Fortune* and cover stories on *Executive Suite* in *Time* and *Newsweek* handsomely attest—the motion picture business project it. A motion picture may not be capable of producing the future, but by depicting the future or even by eloquently invoking it, a studio associates itself with the kind of hypothesizing that, according to Maurer, Drucker, and Walling, is the engine of change. Maurer explains his own role as commentator by pointing to the communications gap between what managers are doing and their ability to explain their role. Although we are in a new era in which we can expect the emergence of an "art of management" free from ascription to production or sales or even finance,

> few managers are entirely free of embarrassment in explaining to employees or to the public the "social" value of profits or in explaining to fellow managers the

"economic" value of decency. This slowness in recognizing the essential unity of a company's multitudinous affairs suggests that managers themselves are not yet fully aware of the logic of the large corporation with its emphasis on doing now whatever will contribute most to the health (i.e., profits) of the corporate community in the future. ("AM," p. 122)

The logic of MGM has led it to the point where its future can be imagined as bound up with its ability to explain the logic of the corporation to its employees, its industry, and its middle-class audience—all stakeholders in a perilous future.

As Walling decries the decline of the Tredway Corporation to his colleagues before the final ballot, he laments that when Bullard lost faith in the future his prideful aloofness made him insensitive to the pride that the company must have in itself. Suddenly, Walling grabs one of the conference-room side tables and brandishes it as a shameful example of the stuff turned out in the cheap KF line. "We're now doing things like this," Walling contemptuously declares. He ferociously yanks off a leg, tosses the table aside, and roars, "This is what Tredway has come to mean" (Figure 3.13). The eruption transfixes his colleagues, who from that moment on are swept along to the election of Walling as president. Larrabee and Riesman dismiss Walling's "frenzied" behavior as throwing "another temper tantrum," even though, as expert sociologists and commentators on popular culture, they must have known that there have been few if any business films since *Skyscraper Souls* (MGM, 1933) that more explicitly represent the tactical manifestation of charisma deployed to claim authority. But if

Figure 3.13

it is charisma that Walling displays, it is not charisma of the Weberian kind. Walling's "frenzy" is not genuine. The audience in the theater knows what the audience in the executive suite does not, that Walling is imitating an action of Bullard's that he learned about earlier in the day from the line foreman down at the plant. In the course of lamenting the decline in the quality of the Tredway product, the foreman had recounted an incident when Bullard grabbed a cheap piece of furniture as it passed him on the assembly line and angrily broke it into pieces. Bullard *committed* an act of unpremeditated violence. He lost his temper then as Walling did later with Julia Tredway. If Bullard's anger was directed at anyone, it could only have been directed in impotent rage at himself for compromising his own standards of quality. Walling, however, *performs* an extemporaneous act of violence by imitating Bullard. Unlike Bullard he is effective. Whatever his rapt colleagues may think or his wife may fear, Walling is not possessed by Bullard. By breaking off the frail table leg, Walling adroitly ironizes Bullard's gesture, which he now uses to demonstrate what a declining Tredway has come to mean over the recent years of Bullard's own management. He boldly highlights the importance of that act as the rupture of the trammels of the cash nexus by embracing the "creative destruction," which, according to Joseph Schumpeter, drives capitalism by "revolutioniz[ing] the economic structure *from within*."[39]

Revolution is, of course, Schumpeter's and Weber's term of choice, not Walling's. As a designer and engineer, he prefers to exhort his followers to technical innovation. As a manufacturer he must orient the company to the customers whose needs it must satisfy. As a marketer, he must make the customers understand what their needs are. His acting in the film combines manufacturing and marketing: he has gathered resources, arranged them, conducted experiments, improvised when necessary, and constructed a character that could move the souls of his customers, the assembled board of directors of the Tredway Company. Appearances to the contrary, Walling is not, as they say at the Actors Studio, acting "from the inside out," as he did during his furious attempt to persuade Julia Tredway. During the scene in the conference room he acts from the outside in: delving within for a memory to motivate his performance and move his audience. But unlike the target prescribed by the Method, the memory is not a traumatic or inspiring moment from his distant past; it is an anecdote, which he reworks into the raw material from which to manufacture a symbolic statement for his audience, just as the company, under his leadership, will manufacture furniture with symbolic import to its customers. By showing how charisma is produced in performance, *Executive Suite* has bared its device to the audience in the motion picture theater who must conclude that William Holden, acting the role of Walling, exploits the same technique. The demonstration is subtler than the "You Were Meant for Me" number in *Singin' in the Rain* but its self-reflexive intent is the same: to prove that exposing a device magnifies rather than dispels its potency. Walling is not the possessed personification of Bullard; nor does he impersonate Bullard by unveiling his own rival vision. Walling is impersonating the company whose intentions he interprets and on whose behalf he speaks. By making explicit the intention of the company to take as its primary objective the manufacture of meaning rather than the maximization of profit, Walling aims to bind producers, sellers, and buyers together in a corporate culture, which, as Gareth Morgan says, "directs attention to the symbolic significance of almost every aspect of organizational life."[40] What goes for Tredway's tables and chairs also goes for MGM's *Executive Suite*, which affirms the studio's corporate identity as a continued commitment to make pictures that adhere to what *Fortune*, in its 1932 profile of the studio, had called "a common denominator of goodness," pictures that bind an audience together in pleasure and for their profit, from which they benefit as stakeholders in MGM's survival.

The executives at MGM, whether affiliated with the Freed unit or with Schary's camp, were ideologically unified in that they, like Walling, did not question the business model of "managerial control," which was of natal importance to MGM, the one studio founded as a management team with no equity stake in the company. Thalberg established the management style that deployed resources in order to exploit social categories like "prestige" or "stardom" as vehicles for the accumulation of symbolic capital that would enable the studio to take more risks than the New York office would normally endorse and that would cushion the consequences of an occasional failure. As employees, the studio executives had no incentive to translate symbolic capital into anything but movies and then from movies into money. The value of the studio on the market was not their concern. But there was more than one style of management in Hollywood and more than one at Loew's Inc., the owner of MGM. As Douglas Gomery has demonstrated in *The Hollywood Studio System*, the history of Hollywood can be written as a straightforward story of profit maximization, which renders it as much the same kind of history as that of any other large, vertically integrated company. Nick Schenck is the protagonist of the Loew's plot, as Barney Balaban is of Paramount's, because, as Gomery insists, the overseers in New York were responsible for the bottom line.[41] By the mid-1950s the liquidation or sale of Paramount, MGM, and Warners was a definite possibility. The decision would be made by financial people in the New York office, which manages the brand equity of the corporation, not the Hollywood studio, which had manufactured what Alexander L. Biel has called "the brand image." The paths of brand equity only lead to those like Loren Shaw, who, Walling fears, is ready to liquidate the company. Walling's bottom line is the company's survival, which is threatened both by the indifference of consumers to its products and by accounting procedures that assign the company a value which can only be realized if it is sold.[42] He invokes the "meaning" of the company as a standard of value by design: he wants a company that *makes* meaning, not one that *counts* meanings; he wants the corporate culture to be the ground from which meaning organically arises, not just one image among others and up for sale like all the others; he wants a commitment to the value of goodness; he wants a company that manufactures quality in quantity.

How do we know goodness when we see it? In *Executive Suite* we first recognize it when we see Walling at work at his desk in his home study. Riesman and Larrabee, in another publication, sneeringly describe the study as "an upper-middlebrow version of Charles Eames' studio (Eames, an architect and furniture designer, was technical adviser to the film) with its collection of little contemporary-chic bibelots like Chinese kites or notion-counter odds and ends" (Figure 3.14). Riesman and Larrabee claim that far from representing the reality of contemporary business, *Executive Suite* actually draws more heavily than "may first appear on the anti-business sentiments of a half-century ago; on half-forgotten longings for a vanished world of rural, craftsmanlike virtues; and hence on assumptions that—far from being 'capitalistic' or contemporary—are actually populist and Veblenian."[43]

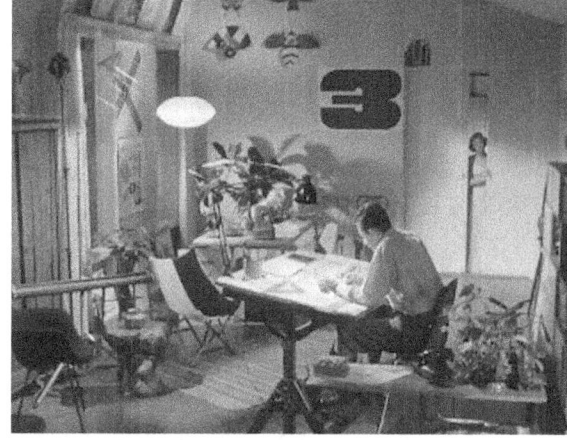

Figure 3.14

There's a great deal of browbeating in Larrabee and Riesman's article, but what does "upper-middlebrow" actually signify? Does it mean that anyone who admires Walling's room belongs to that status niche? Or must we imagine that the room's design stimulates a socio-somatic response in the audience that raises or lowers or simply sets their brows in the upper-middle area? The former option, which specifies the *registration* of taste, is the way of sociology, and would likely be the critics' preference. The latter, which predicates the *formation* of taste, is the way of MGM. No doubt Riesman and Larrabee were right to call attention to the importance of Walling's study, but they were dead wrong to stigmatize it as a refuge segregated from the manly occupations of business, politics, and manufacturing. Larrabee and Riesman dismiss Walling's activity as "doodling," when he is clearly working with his designer's tools, which he puts down only to show his wife his true diversion: vote counting. As for ornaments that Larrabee and Riesman mockingly describe as "*objets de vertu*": they may be craftsmanlike to their eyes, but they have not been crafted. They have been manufactured. Like Astaire's hat, cane, and gloves, Walling's' desk, wall decorations, and chair *do* identify him, but unlike Astaire's props, which are worthless metonyms unless he invests them with his star quality, many of the Eamesian furnishings in Don's study, in the bedroom, and in the living room of the Walling home, could have been selected for purchase by anyone with the money. Indeed, Mary might have selected them from a Herman Miller Furniture Company catalog, which included layouts of attractive and functional arrangements—making it unnecessary for a middle-class family in Pelham or Evanston or Westwood to hire Charles Eames or Ray Eames as an adviser.

How do we know that what we see in the Herman Miller Furniture Company catalog is good? Most people would find it useful to know that in 1940 the model of an organic chair, with a molded plywood shell designed by Eames and Eero Saarinen, won first prize in the category of chairs in a design competition sponsored by the Museum of Modern Art. The goal of the competition, as stated by Eliot Noyes, the director of design at MoMA, was to respond to the development of "a new way of living" with a "fresh approach to the design problems and a new expression. An adequate solution," he observes, "which takes into consideration the present social, economic, technical and esthetic trends is largely lacking."[44] The winners were required to produce full-scale versions of the chairs that would be mass produced by participating manufacturers and sold by select retailers. The Eames and Saarinen chairs presented unforeseen challenges because of the intractable difficulty of molding the plywood and the cost of the tooling required for an acceptable result. Eventually, the chairs were completed, although with compromises, including a high price, which meant, Noyes reported to Alfred Barr, director of MoMA, "The excitement of sitting in them is not going to be a middle-class thrill at this point because the prices are something terrific." Ray Eames recalls, quotes Eames Demetrios, their disappointment that "the Organic chair, intended as an expression of the potential of mass production, had . . . 'become a handmade object' after all"—that is, crafted, which is not what the Eameses wanted their work to be or to mean. The chairs may have represented a "conceptual breakthrough," but they failed to realize the ambition enunciated by Charles Eames: "We wanted to make the best for the most for the least" (*EP*, p. 39). The chairs had been judged the best by the few who enjoyed the opportunity to sit in them, but it would take much more designing, retooling, and experimentation with materials before the middle class could have its turn.

Not until the end of the war would the Eames office enter another molded plywood chair in another MoMA competition. George Nelson, who had recently become the head of design for the Herman Miller Furniture Company, visited the 1946 MoMA show accompanied by D. J. and Hugh DePree, owners of the firm, and persuaded them to compete with the Knoll Furniture Company for the rights to distribute and sell and eventually to produce Eames furniture. Herman Miller won. Charles and Ray Eames were sure the company was a better fit because, as Nelson would later note, "It is a small company operating in a small town and by the owners . . . [that believes]: What you make is important; Design is an integral part of the business; the product must be honest; there is a market for good design." Herman Miller shared the Eameses' conviction that "'what works good is better than what looks good, because what works good lasts.' In other words," Eames Demetrios adds, "the people who had just designed the most revolutionary chair of the 20th century felt that they were better off with a company that took that approach as a given and put it in the marketplace as simply a good chair" (*EP*, p. 109).

Like Tredway, which has its factory and offices in Millburgh, Pennsylvania, Herman Miller was established in a rural setting, in Zeeland, Michigan, in 1905. Like Tredway, Herman Miller successfully produced "traditional 'period' furniture of good quality but uninspired design" (pieces like those that furnish the Aldersons' home in *Executive Suite*). The company began to lose out to competition in the South and worsened after the Crash. By 1930 "Herman Miller's devout Dutch Reform Calvinist president, Dirk Jan De Pree [Mr. Tredway], was praying for guidance because his firm was close to bankruptcy."[45] In 1930 the designer Gilbert Rohde (Avery Bullard) walked into the office of D. J. De Pree (Mr. Tredway) and announced that the furniture that Herman Miller was manufacturing was no longer suitable for contemporary spaces and needs. He was hired to renovate the company, and he did. After Rohde's death, in 1944, Herman Miller considered several modernist designers as a replacement and settled on George Nelson (Don Walling), "who recommended developing a corporate identity, standardizing lines, placing more emphasis on showrooms, introducing catalogs, and targeting architects." Herman Miller did not actually attempt to produce the Eames stamped chairs until 1948, when, after many setbacks, the company learned that manufacturing the metal stamped chairs was beyond its capacity: the cost of retooling the factory to produce the chairs for a mass market would eclipse any profit that the company could expect to make. By the time MoMA exhibited the prototypes of the metal chairs in 1950, however, they were shown alongside chairs with the same shapes but in a completely different material: fiberglass. Because fiberglass requires far less tooling than either plywood or metal, it solved the mass production problem for Eames and Herman Miller, enabling them to achieve their objective of making the best for the most people for the lowest cost.

Fiberglass was also the solution to the problem of developing a new molding process that Walling's team was working on at Tredway when Shaw terminated the research. The remnants that the technicians held closely resembled the mass-produced, inexpensive molded fiberglass chairs designed by the Eames studio that the Herman Miller Company began mass producing in 1950

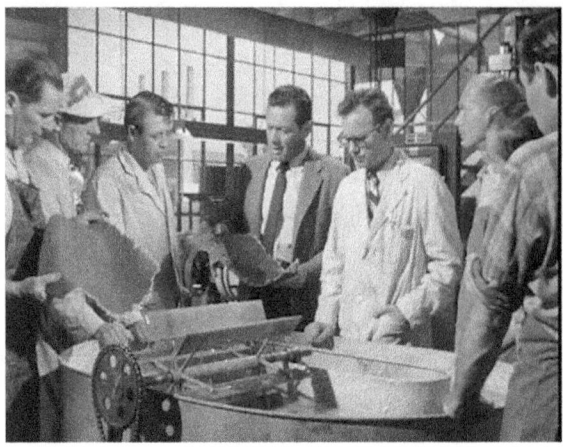

Figure 3.15

(Figure 3.15). At Tredway, however, success will require retooling the *organization* not the machinery.

The connection of Herman Miller with MGM is not incidental but genealogical: Eames was selected as set designer for the only sets that were designed specifically for the movie, in part because when Eames had first relocated to California before the war, he worked as a set designer at MGM under Cedric Gibbons. Thalberg might have cited that connection as proof that MGM's commitment to goodness was not mere sales talk but, through the mass-production techniques of a designer groomed at the studio, was fully assimilated by the American middle-class people, whether they sought their thrills at home in their Eames chair or in the theater. The movie's connection of those fragments in the hands of the disconsolate engineers with the crisis in Tredway's management indicates that by 1954 MGM understood that Herman Miller had come to share Drucker's 1946 insight that mass production is "not a technique but a basic concept of industrial organization that is generally applicable. Its essence," Drucker had asserted, "is the substitution of co-ordination and organization for individual skill. The skill of the individual craftsman is replaced in mass production by the understanding of a basic production-concept and the leadership qualities of the supervisor" (*CC*, p. 30). The objective of making the best for the most people for the lowest cost renders the word *craftsmanlikeness* obsolete except in an ironic sense. Three applications of the basic production concept were learned by Eames and Nelson through trial and error: (1) never let the demands of your chosen materials exceed the capacity of your available tools; (2) the most important tool of a company is its organization, which includes plant and equipment, capital and revenue, executives, shareholders, workers, and customers; (3) the principle of what would later be called "flexible specialization," practiced in the Eames office, should be integrated into an organizational model that can fully exploit the diverse talents of a team of managers (*CRE*, pp. 143–99).

Larrabee and Riesman describe *Executive Suite* as a "nostalgic reverie for the company town—the home of paternalistic order, domestic virtue, and productive work" ("EH," p. 108). This comment is fair to a point. Tredway's past is Herman Miller's paternalistic past. The motion picture takes as its subject the nostalgia of people in Millburgh for a paternalistic company town, because

MGM is its allegorical subject, a studio that successfully marketed such nostalgia in pictures like *Boys Town* and *Babes in Arms* under the leadership of Mayer, who also cultivated the impression that Culver City was itself an orderly, virtuous, and productive company town—a synechdoche for Hollywood, the largest company town in America. No doubt, at a time when the fate of the studio was no longer secure, nostalgia was strong among many executives and employees for the day when nostalgia could make big money. The Freed unit, of course, programmatically exploited nostalgia as a device to recuperate the studio's symbolic capital, its connection to an audience that reflexively related MGM's bright present to its glorious past. The debilitating animosity between Arthur Freed and Dore Schary at MGM, however, threatened to destabilize the studio. After Mayer was forced out, the members of the old guard who revered Mayer and Freed were vocal in their contempt for Schary, who had stepped up his interference in the operations of the Freed unit and weakened his advocacy with Nick Schenk in New York on behalf of Freed's chronically high budget requests. Scott Eyman gives this account of Freed's mounting hostility:

> At the time Mayer left MGM, Freed had three pictures in various stages of production: *An American in Paris, Show Boat,* and *Singin' in the Rain.* All were critical and commercial smashes.... But after Mayer left, both the quantity and quality of Freed's work dropped sharply. He averaged one picture a year from 1953 to 1958, and only *The Band Wagon* and *Gigi* were the equivalent of the work done under Mayer's affectionate supervision. L.B. had created Arthur Freed, schooled him in the art of spending in pursuit of perfection, and had always run interference with Nick Schenck to give his lieutenant the tools he needed. Without L.B., Freed was hobbled. (*LH*, p. 462)

Executive Suite invites us to diagnose Freed's plight as a consequence of the failure of Mayer to conceive of a procedure that would enable a smooth succession from his own patriarchal management style to a system of management that would somehow retain the charisma of the departed mogul and ensure the survival of the company.

Weber had the same problem, according to the sociologist Edward Shils, who faults him both for his restriction of charismatic authority to a past when people were motivated by irrational beliefs rather than by rational interests and for isolating charisma conceptually by insisting on its irrationality and therefore its antithetical relation to bureaucratic authority, which, according to Weber, is "specifically rational in the sense of being bound to intellectually analysable rules." The revolutionary potential of charisma in a traditional society translates into a senseless disruption of "rational economic activity" in a liberal society, a repudiation "of any sort of involvement in the every-day routine world" (*MWC*, p. 52). Shils criticizes Weber's "pronounced tendency . . . to see [the object of attributed charisma] almost exclusively in its most concentrated and intense forms, and to disregard the possibility of its dispersed and attenuated existence." That antithesis is virtually identical to the polarity between spectacular numbers, which are "concentrated and intense forms," and profane narrative, "a dispersed and attenuated existence" that, as we have seen, Steven Cohan identifies as the central tension in the MGM musicals of the Freed era.[46]

Shils argues against Weber that "charisma can become an integral element in the process of secular institutionalization." He proposes that "the authority of the official" in a rule-governed organization has a source in "the perception of a property derived from the 'participation' of the particular official role and its official incumbent in the inclusive corporate body, which is conceived as being under a supreme authority." The subject accepts the legitimacy of an authority "constituted by sharing in the properties of the 'organization as a whole' epitomized or symbolized in the powers concentrated (or thought to be concentrated) at the peak. This is 'institutional charisma; it is not a charisma deduced from the creativity of the charismatic individual. It is inherent in the massive organization of authority. The institutional charismatic legitimation of a command emanating from an incumbent of a role in a corporate body derives from *membership in the body as such, apart from any allocated, specific powers*" ("COS," pp. 203, 206). However, Shils provides no guidance as to how to discriminate a large organization that is charismatic from one that is not.

Both *The Band Wagon* and *Executive Suite* name their dream organization "the company." In the former, the company is both the group of people who have banded together to put on the show and the theatrical company that is formed with the help of Tony Hunter's capital. *The Band Wagon* ties together the fate of a company with the fate of a star—a connection that can be expected to pay off because of the discovered isomorphism of the form of the star and that of the corporation. Each consists of a constructed personality, incorporeal capital that can be converted into property and sold—thereby earning revenue and replenishing the goodwill or earning power that constitutes the originative charismatic margin that attracts the extra-economic allegiance of customers as fans and stakeholders. *The Band Wagon*'s theory foundered on material changes in the industry that drastically altered the nature of stardom. Stardom may work as a metaphor for the corporation, but stardom will no longer work as a dependable device for MGM to replenish its capital. The studio can no longer pretend that stars are chattel whose personalities can be exploited to augment the value of a faded studio identity. *Executive Suite* is as obsessed with intangible value as *The Band Wagon* and recognizes the contribution of stars to the company, but only insofar as those stars make a contribution to the organization and not solely to the aggrandizement of their own personalities. Both motion pictures espouse institutional charisma as a principle of order and value. *The Band Wagon* trumpets the obligation to be entertaining with the assurance that if a motion picture is entertaining it will be good. For Mayer and his adherents there can be no entertainment without stars. A *Grand Hotel* for an era of diminished expectations, *Executive Suite* uses its stars to argue that if a motion picture accepts the responsibility to be good it will be entertaining.

The example of Herman Miller also shows how good design and aggressive management can rescue a company from nostalgia by reinventing it for the future. Even Larrabee and Riesman sourly admit that Walling is something more than a sentimentalist: "Walling is the end-product of that modern process, the institutionalization of institutional advertising—the methods of conscious myth-making through which a company . . . can concoct a new personality for itself in order to make malleable its previous conflicts" ("C-TP," p. 336). We have been arguing throughout that it was the particular ambition of MGM to be the company that institutionalizes institutional advertising and establishes itself as the leading studio by hiring stars that would be identified with the studio and advertise its preeminence. Proof that Larrabee and Riesman are correct and that Walling and *Executive Suite* are the end-products of MGM's process occurs during the election scene, which reorients the residual yearnings of individual executives for charismatic leadership toward the institution itself.

Executive Suite is designed to prove the reviving power not of the charismatic individual but of the principle of teamwork. The proof is made challenging by the number of stars involved in the production, for directing a roomful of stars presents a managerial challenge at least as formidable as organizing a roomful of vice-presidents.[47] Stars are figures of spectacle *within* the narrative, built-in distractions from a Hollywood motion picture's normative project. The minimal claim that each star makes upon the narrative is that he or she must have his or her scene, or number, if you will, when he or she commands the camera. Nicknamed by a reviewer during production "eight stars in a boardroom," *Executive Suite* gives each member of the board of directors a scene apart from the group, all, with the exceptions of Shaw and Julia Tredway, involved in tense conversations with wife or mistress.[48] The critical scene in *Executive Suite*, of course, is the climactic deliberation around the conference table, where Don Walling takes his stand—literally, for he purposefully avoids taking a seat, choosing instead to stand before his colleagues in the space where Bullard's medieval chair had been and where Walling's modern chair will surely be. Here's the rousing finish to Walling's campaign speech, which appeals to the assembled executives not as stars jealous of their prerogatives but as a team of talents:

> We'll have a line of low-priced furniture, a new and different line—as different from anything we're making today as a modern automobile is from a covered wagon. That's what you want, Walt, what you've always wanted: merchandise that will sell because it has beauty, and function, and value? Not because the buyers like your scotch and coming off your production line. A product that you'll be able to budget to the nearest hundredth of a cent, Shaw, because it will be scientifically and efficiently designed. And something you'll be proud to have your name on, Miss Tredway. We're going to give the people what they need at prices they can afford to pay. And as fresh needs come up, we'll satisfy them too with something new and even more exciting. And when we achieve that we're really going to grow. We're not going to die. We're going to live. And it's going to take every bit of business judgment and creative energy in the company: from the mills and the factories right to the top of the tower. And we're going to do it together. Everyone of us. Right here at Tredway.

Walling becomes the voice of the company that celebrates the "beauty, efficiency, and value" that characterize each of the executives around the table insofar as they perform those individual roles in harmony with the others and in adherence to the narrative concept of mass production that the motion picture has worked out. As for executives, so for stars. They are the materials and the team is the tooling.

In his probing and provocative *The Laws of Cool*, Alan Liu defines a team as "the unit of ephemeral identity that most flexibly fuses technologies and techniques into skill sets (called 'innovation,' 'creativity,' or 'resourcefulness') adapted to the changefulness of the global economy." Liu's subject is not the emergence of team culture at the intersection of craft and mass production as a defense against a form of managerial control indifferent to anything but the integers on a balance sheet, but the team as one of the tools with which "diversity management" accomplishes the "*capitalizing* of the concept of culture so that the pure business culture that remains at the end of the process becomes definitive of all culture."[49] It has been a burden of this argument that MGM's project had long been the capitalization of culture in order that its corporate culture could, indeed, become definitive of all culture. In both its imagery and its rhetoric, then, *Executive Suite* extols the virtues of teamwork. Walling plays catcher for his Little League–playing son (Tim Considine), who attempts to throw strikes while pretending to be the New York Yankee pitcher Allie Reynolds. When Don is called away by his research team at the plant, Mary puts on the catcher's mitt and takes his place, slinging the ball back to her son as hard as he's burning them in. Earlier, we had seen Walling on the shop floor with his research team, where he wears an apron and rolls his sleeves up just like the rest of his men. When the experiment was interrupted by a call from above, the team continued with the experiment. At the moment that his son is trying to pitch his team out of a jam in the baseball game that afternoon, Walling runs off to play boardroom politics. But Mom stays, and the game goes on.

Under Walling's leadership, the board of directors will work the same way that Walling's son's Little League team works (there's always a reliever warming up); the same way that a contemporary family works (Mary can step in when Don's called away); and the same way that the family, the workers, and the executives can work together as part of the company team in a company town. The exchange that occurs between Walling and Mary (who has been peeping through the door during her husband's performance) as they walk to the elevator to head home, is about the outcome of the Little League game he missed. Walling says, "Oh, I almost forgot. Who won the game?" "We did." Because we know (Don almost certainly knows since he was the only person in a position to see her) that Mary had been part of the audience for his speech in front of the board, we know that she, like the audience of the board and like the audience in the theater, was included in the "we" of "we'll do it together." And so the board is included in the "we" that she utters at the end: the family includes the business and the business includes the family. Family cannot be understood in the older sense of a business family-owned, operated, and even inhabited—Mom and Pop and Kid living above the store. Don and Mary and Mike are not likely to move into the tower, but they are likely to redecorate it with furniture that looks more like their own, more like the furniture that Tredway will make, more, that is, like the furniture in the Herman Miller catalog, which is the strategic expression of a company committed to the coordination of the home and office by a unified design scheme:

> While the contemporary residential interior has been demonstrating a steady evolution towards a more "workmanlike" kind of space—easier to furnish and take care of—the executive office has been going though an equally interesting development towards the warmth and informality of the well-appointed living room. It has become more and more common, for instance, to find that the conference area in executive offices, is not the desk, but a coffee table flanked by sofas and comfortable chairs. Because of the overlapping nature of the design trends in home and office it seemed appropriate to expand the Herman Miller Collection to include furniture for both types of interiors.[50]

Although the language and imagery of team is prominent in the picture, it is, after all, called *Executive Suite*, not *Executive Team*. *Suite* is a term with its own resonance and ambiguities. In the language of the designers whom the motion picture takes as its exemplars, *suite* has pejorative connotations through its association with an outmoded idiom of design. Here is the paragraph introducing the "Bedroom" section of the Herman Miller catalog of 1952:

> Furniture for the contemporary bedroom has changed its composition greatly in the past half-dozen years. Except for the most retarded end of the market, the bedroom "suite" has become obsolete—housewives have become impatient with the task of cleaning small rooms occupied by seven to ten separate pieces of furniture, and the logical elimination process has gone on to the point where the modern bedroom consists of little more than the beds, a light chair, bedside units and necessary storage. Apparatus for sleeping and dressing in the Herman Miller Collection carries the expression of this trend as far as it can be done in terms of movable units, and it is completely in keeping with the design requirements of the contemporary bed-dressing room interior. (*HMC*, p. 33)

Nothing could be more "retarded" than the faux Gothic style of the Tredway tower, symbol of a faith in which neither secularist designers, no longer dependent on commissions from the Church, nor young families just starting out in towns like Millburgh, can still believe. And no president whose pride carries him into the gloomy suite of rooms from which Bullard ruled his domain, rooms burdened with suites of large, ornate, medieval-style tables, chairs, desks, and sideboards ideally suited for dividing up the spoils brought back to England from the First Crusade, could be expected to maintain his vision of the future. The impatience of the housewife is a sign of that future and of the "logical elimination process" that will mean the replacement of the bulky furniture of the founder with a few lean, streamlined pieces, perhaps a couch and a coffee table for the office and a blond slab of wood balanced on six slender legs and surrounded by eight molded plywood chairs for the conference room. Of course, the set is as Houseman found it. The furniture is MGM's house furniture, perhaps left over from *Ivanhoe* (MGM, 1952) or even from *The White Cliffs of Dover* (MGM, 1944). Only the sets for the Wallings' house were made new for the picture. *Executive Suite* not so subtly argues for a general remodeling. And though it is easy to imagine that the talk of team spirit and the baseball metaphor would not be appealing to Arthur Freed or Roger Edens, it is difficult to imagine them objecting strenuously to a more modern design. But it is almost certainly another meaning of suite, its reference to a set of instrumental pieces organized by a common theme, which would be expected to appeal to the musical sensibilities of Schary's adversaries. *Suite* elegantly suggests that each member of the company is a featured performer who deserves his or her own movement in the company, each individual an instrument perfect in its own way and ordered by a corporate theme. Even though the "we" of the team, like the first-person point of view at the beginning of the picture, might feel coercive to some, the metaphor of the suite, I suggest, is meant to be seductive to those who just do not want to play ball. Specifically, *suite* figures the corporate intention to recruit the Freed unit to the theme of MGM of which Schary is the agent.

Just after Walling has been told to close down his experiment for the second time, he leaves the shop floor and casts his eyes on a gallery of photographs that hang along the walls of the corridor. They are pictures of prize-winning pieces of furniture that Tredway has produced over the years. At MGM, where pictures about pictures have a conspicuous place, this is a scene of some moment. Walling stops before a photo of a thinly disguised Eames cabinet in the style of the one in his home study (Figure 3.16). He then moves on to a settee in the Shaker style that was part of the Herman Miller line. Walling's reflections are interrupted by the line foreman who asks, "Where do we go from here, Mr. Walling? Four years since we've done anything good like that."

Those four years correspond to the span of time between the beginning of work on both *An American in Paris* and *Singin' in the Rain* in 1950 and the production and release of *Executive Suite* in 1954. The connection is deliberate, an implicit admission that the studio has departed from the standard of MGM's last "good" pictures, which were *An American in Paris*, which had been made in 1950 (released in 1951), four years before *Executive Suite*, which was the last musical that Mayer supervised before his forced resignation, and which won the Oscar for best picture in 1952. The last musical that Mayer sponsored was also begun four years before the release of *Executive Suite*: *Singin' in the Rain*, which Freed had assigned to Comden and Green, who began working on the script in May 1950.[51] There is no specific allusion to the Minnelli film in *Executive Suite*, but it does invoke the Kelly-Donen picture. Much has been made of Houseman's decision to renounce a musical soundtrack. He did not ban all music, however. There's the annoying hourly chime of the bells in the tower and a noodling piano in the background

Figure 3.16

at the bar in the Stork Club when Caswell makes his anxious call to Millburgh. *Executive Suite* has no musical numbers as such; its one instantly recognizable tune is embedded so fully into the diegesis that it seems less a dexterous achievement of integration than just another signifier of realism. As Walling crosses through the foyer of his home on his hasty return from the airport to change clothes en route to the decisive meeting, we hear the voice of his son loudly scatting, "Ba de di da da, ba de di da da," to the tune of "Singin' in the Rain." Humdrum. No spectacle at all: we don't even see Mike, dripping wet and wrapped in his bath towel, until Walling has left the house. Yet the music counts. The inclusion of the "number" that is the title song from the motion picture given the greenlight by Mayer in 1950, reputedly over Schary's opposition, soon before the mogul's forced resignation, is neither inadvertent nor incidental. The quotation is an homage to the musical and a generous personal tribute to Arthur Freed, coauthor of the song "Singin' in the Rain," producer of the motion picture, and Hollywood's uncontested leader in recycling his own songs. *Executive Suite* takes one for the team by selecting as its only musical theme the signature tune of the golden age of MGM musicals, thereby making this picture an instrument in the suite created by Freed, sustained by Mayer, and now endorsed by Houseman on behalf of Schary on behalf of the company. But no one who watches the movie needs to know that. Why should they? The MGM audience would recognize the theme, and its delight in hearing the tune scatted by a joyous youth would be undiluted by ignorance of the political work the song is meant to do.

In his attempt to define the distinctiveness of British culture in a period of revolutionary turmoil, Edmund Burke rhetorically asks his readers why it is that when he attends the theater he sheds tears at the death of a king. He replies that it is natural that he should—not because he knows any kings or because his personal interests are connected with their welfare, but because a British culture that is intimately bound up with the theater and with the plays of Shakespeare has trained British subjects to experience and display that reverent grief. The same goes for singing in the shower in a suburban home in mid-century America: it is natural that one should sing or hum or whistle "Singin' in the Rain"—a naturalness manufactured by a popular culture that MGM has had a major role in defining and with which it is identified as a charismatic institution.[52]

By the mid-1950s, however, the infusion of charisma into a corporation is no longer to be called the institution of institutional advertising or the generation of a charismatic margin. As we have seen, in 1955 Burleigh H. Gardner and Sidney J. Levy announced that the end-product of institutional advertising would be brand management. That Gardner and Levy urge that the new task for management is to develop a "guiding, governing product and brand personality that is unified and coherently meaningful" ("P and B," p. 39), such as the personality that the tune of "Singin' in the Rain" evokes, attests to the foresight of MGM's corporate vision during the classical era; but the promotion of that task as everybody's business registers the loss of the studio's uniqueness in the age of television. Schary offers the same defense of obsolescence as Walling: the reinvention of the company's brand image, beginning with a new company theme song that could be shared by the earnest and the camp alike, reconciling adversaries in a new team: not the sentimental "Where or When" but the upbeat "Singin' in the Rain." Freed did not sing along. Schenck did not even hear the music. Schary was canned. The studio dwindled away. From our standpoint, however, the boy's innocent song sounds differently than anyone at MGM could have imagined. "Singin' in the Rain" now reverberates with Stanley Kubrick's perverse use of it to accompany a brutal beating in *Clockwork Orange* (Warner Bros. and Hawk Films, 1971) in order to teach a lesson about the fragility of what we take as natural or common. What once was a tune as jaunty and optimistic as a Herman Miller catalog now lingers as a mottled fragment shored up against the ruin of a company that could not sing its way out of trouble. Thus the lion would lie down like a lamb.

4 Ownership and Authorship
Warners' *Fountainhead* and Hitchcock's *Vertigo*
(1949–1958)

i. Delirious Warner Bros.

In his 1896 essay "The Tall Office Building Artistically Considered," Louis Sullivan famously asserts, "It is the pervading law of all things organic and inorganic, of all things physical and metaphysical, of all things human and all things superhuman, of all true manifestations of the head, of the heart, of the soul, that the life is recognizable in its expression, that form ever follows function. *This is the law.*"[1] Sullivan's may not have been the first enunciation of the functionalist thesis, but it was likely the most potent. The slogan "form follows function" was taken as law for the River Rouge Plant and for the Lever Brothers Building, by Frank Lloyd Wright and by Ayn Rand. According to the modernist narrative, functionalism dictated the aesthetic for the skyscrapers of New York and Chicago. According to the complementary modernizing narrative advanced by Alfred D. Chandler, Jr., functionalism was also the one law for the kind of large business enterprise that commissioned and occupied those gleaming boxes: the modern corporation.[2] As the modern corporation is the organizational form that capital takes in the industrial age, so is the towering lattice of silicon and steel the organic expression of and enabling vehicle for the operation of that form.

Sullivan and his modernist heirs no longer lay down the law. According to Robert Venturi and Denise Scott Brown, the postmodernist shift to a new architectural paradigm involved less a violation of Sullivan's law than a conviction that it never had been nor could be obeyed, that "form follows function" could not explain "the manifestation" of the skyscrapers it celebrates. "Functionalist architecture was more symbolic than functional. It was symbolically functional. It represented function more than resulted from function. It looked functional more than [it] worked functionally.... But the symbolism of functionalist architecture was unadmitted. It was a symbolism of no symbolism" (quoted in *FD*, p. 14). Venturi and Brown do not intend a moral criticism of functionalist architecture, as if modernist theorists and modernist architects were to be condemned for a lack of candor. Their argument presupposes a rhetorical criticism of functionalist architecture as a discourse of authority—a discourse more about making law than about discovering it, and one reliant on a programmatic figuration. By claiming that architectural functionalism was not only symbolic but also that it owed its persuasiveness to the *occultation* of its symbolism, Venturi and Brown identify the signifying practice of architectural functionalism, its public speech, as allegorical. Venturi and Brown do not, however, suggest who might be the allegorist of the material expression of the corporate form. Warners' *Fountainhead* does: the corporation itself. In *The Fountainhead*, the folklore of capitalism becomes the studio lore of modernism.

The script for *The Fountainhead* (1949) adapted Ayn Rand's successful 1943 novel (she had produced an earlier script adapting the novel for Warners in 1944). Rand's contract with Warner guaranteed her the right to approve all changes to the script.[3] Given a veto over the studio's nomination of an actor to play Howard Roark, the uncompromisingly independent protagonist of the novel, Rand ultimately accepted Gary Cooper. The studio assigned King Vidor to direct. Vidor's long-standing struggle for artistic control had become excruciating when, having departed Metro in the mid-1940s, he signed on as David O. Selznick's choice to direct the grandiose Western *Duel in the Sun* (Selznick Studio and Vanguard Films, 1946). After seven and a half months of grueling conflict with the obsessively intrusive producer, he resigned from the picture. When Vidor signed a three-picture deal with Warners in 1948, he brought with him a frustrated ambition to resuscitate his career on his own terms. In the making of *The Fountainhead* Vidor's career converged for the first time with Cooper's. Cooper had been one of the biggest box office stars of the 1930s and early 1940s, when he split his time among Paramount, Warners, Goldwyn, and Columbia. Like so many other actors, directors, scriptwriters, and producers, as the war wound down he went independent, first with Leo Spitz, William Goetz, and Nunnally Johnson to form International Pictures, a short-lived, IRS motivated production company; and then, after selling out to Universal in 1946, signing up to make *Good Sam* (1948) for Leo McCarey under the aegis of his IRS-motivated production company, Rainbow Productions (*GC*, pp. 191–95, 201). The cheerless comedy sank and the reputation of the aging Cooper followed.

Jack Warner, head of production, had his own agenda. Since the departure of long-time executive producer Hal Wallis in 1944, driven out in part by Jack's usurpation of credit for the unexpected success of *Casablanca* in 1942, Warner had gradually assumed more creative control at the studio, moving his name around in the credits (sometimes putting his name above the credits as "presenter," sometimes listing himself at the end as "producer") to take personal responsibility for Warner Bros. films. Jack had long chafed under the dominion of his brother Harry, who held the purse strings. The HUAC hearings in the fall of 1947 first brought together Warner, Rand, and Cooper as witnesses eager to speak out on behalf of American principles and to help the committee root out leftists suspected of contaminating the motion picture medium with a collectivist ideology. The authority that Vidor, Cooper, and Rand attained at Warners was scalable. Jack signed the contracts and, with Harry's approval, set the budget. Vidor could pick his project. Cooper could choose his director and his script. Rand had complete control over the script and had approval over the cast. So who was the author of *The Fountainhead*? Warner had to honor the contracts. Vidor was constrained by Rand's script, Cooper by Rand's script and Vidor's direction. Rand had the authority to insist on maintaining the integrity of her novel in her script but failed to achieve authority over its visualization—most crucially the designs of the buildings selected to represent Roark's achievements.[4] By agreeing to work together on *The Fountainhead*, the independents Vidor, Cooper, and Rand exchanged the *fact* of autonomy for an opportunity to represent the *idea* of autonomy.

In *The Concept of Corporate Strategy*, Kenneth R. Andrews asserts that "the pattern of goals and policies, rather than the separate substance, is the source of the uniqueness that ideally should distinguish every company from its competitors." He adds, "Especially when values visibly affect economic choices, the special character of a company becomes apparent to its employees and customers."[5] Andrews does not specify what those values might be. He need not, for the demonstration that "values visibly affect economic choices" *is* the value that trumps mere economic considerations as the manifestation of a company's special character, its brand. A strong, visible brand, according to the gospel of marketing, is its own reward.[6] *The Fountainhead* tells the story of a man, Howard Roark, who not only prefers his own company but also *becomes* his own company, Howard Roark. His brand is who he is. Howard Roark never fails to take the opportunity visibly to demonstrate his subordination of economic choices to values and to assert his "special character." Warner Bros., the most cost-sensitive major studio in Hollywood, was notoriously reluctant to permit values to affect economic decisions. Not this time. Having postponed production from the height of the novel's popularity in 1944, Warners was taking a risk in bringing it to the screen in the postwar era. Most have regarded it as a bad bet: the film has the reputation of being a commercial failure. As Robert Spadoni shows, however, Warners did in fact achieve some commercial success by launching a massive marketing campaign for the opening of *The Fountainhead*, which boosted box office revenues.[7] The unusual investment in front-end marketing, which placed a premium on the first weeks of the first run, must have cut into the net profits; and the prominence of the marketing campaign must have magnified the speed with which the film vanished from the nation's screens, thus leaving the perception of financial loss.

Why would Warners have taken that financial risk? Why revive the shelved *Fountainhead* project in 1948, when, despite the afterglow of wartime prosperity, the future of the studio looked bleak? What difference did the delay make? In 1944 King Vidor was under contract to MGM. Robert Burks, the cinematographer responsible for the expressionist style, was just getting his start and would have been an unlikely choice for this important project. And in 1944 the war would have been an imperious factor. Anticollectivist, the novel, as Spadoni shows, was recognizably anti-Nazi in that "Roark calls collectivists 'gangsters' and 'dictators' and 'tyrants' and 'emperors.' In the film he calls them not one of those names" ("GO," p. 223). By the time the film went into production the Nazis were no longer a problem. The communists were. Yet despite the advent of the Cold War and the tumult of the HUAC trials, the film makes no explicit reference to communism.[8] But then *The Fountainhead* does not mention any of the threats by the U.S. government to property rights, such as the recent Paramount Decree. Rand made no attempt to adapt the narrative to the political, social, or economic circumstances in which it would appear. The film itself supplies no reason why Warners would have revived it in 1948 or any other year. The expressionist camera angles, lighting, and sets, the antinaturalist acting style, as well as the hyperbolic rhetoric of timeless truths—all contribute to abstract the film from any material context that might condition its meaning. Nonetheless, the "imperative" to abstraction that *The Fountainhead* obeys "comes from history"—from, that is, as Clement Greenberg argued, "the age in conjunction with a particular moment reached in a particular tradition of art," or if not quite art, of motion picture making.[9] The moment reached here is not the achievement of an inexpressive purity of form that surrenders to the limits of its medium. Nor does the film break with a "realistic illusion [that is] in the service of sentimental and declamatory literature" ("TNL," p. 27). Yet *The Fountainhead* pursues abstraction all the same: an abstraction of the narrative mode of classical cinema in the service of the *idea* of the purity of the work and its maker. Spadoni has acutely observed that unlike Hollywood films that typically have psychologically motivated characters and character motivated narratives, "the force at the center of [*The Fountainhead*] is *ideologically* motivated causality" ("GO," p. 225). What goes for the narrative also goes for the narrators. Ideological motivation enchains not only the characters in the film but also the agents—screenwriter, director, producer, cinematographer, studio head—who contribute to the telling of the story. He or she must act as if motivated only by ideology if *The Fountainhead* is to realize its historically specific objective, which is disinterestedly to contradict anybody—collectivists, HUAC, trustbusters, stockholders, the critics, or the public—who doubts that a person, a skyscraper, a film, or a company can stand on its own, as the concrete manifestation of a self-conditioned idea, its special character. In its frenzied commitment to aggressive self-display, its delirious association of the ideology of individualism with the soaring presumptuousness of the skyscraper, and its dependence for narrative coherence on the lobotomizing of a hero made so iconic that no thinking could possibly stain the stark purity of the idea that drives him, *The Fountainhead* occupies its own peculiar genre, which, after Rem Koolhaas, we may call "Warner Bros. Manhattanism."[10]

In the context of Warners' brief, lurching postwar return to the gritty crime and social-problem films that had made its reputation in the 1930s, the hyperbolically stylized, author-congested *Fountainhead*, which preaches that the only social problem is society itself, sticks out like a demented skyscraper. The film uses the story of an architect's temporarily thwarted but ultimately triumphant career as the basis for a turgid melodrama of ideas: the battle between egoistic individualism (good) and altruistic collectivism (evil). Battered by the vulgar, who have been trained to despise genius, the conviction of the young architect, Howard Roark (an ersatz Frank Lloyd Wright), is fortified by his dying mentor (modeled on Sullivan), who gasps out the dogma of functionalism: "The skyscraper is the greatest invention of man. The form of a building must follow its function. New materials demand new forms. A new building cannot borrow another's shape just as one man can't borrow another's soul. Every new idea must come from the mind of one man." This becomes gospel for Roark, who relentlessly pursues his ambition to build what he wants and as he wants, regardless of the vicious journalistic attacks of Ellsworth Touhy (Robert Douglas), fawning architectural critic for Gale Wynand's (Raymond Massey) powerful tabloid *The Banner*, where he insidiously promotes beaux art decadence, and despite blandishments to compromise served up by the parasitical Peter Keating (Kent Smith), Roark's former fellow student at architecture school. When it becomes clear to Roark that he cannot build without sacrificing the purity of his vision, he takes a laborer's job in a marble quarry. He is spied there by the voracious Dominique Francon (Patricia Ryan), with whom he soon shares a fadeout. On his successful return to New York, Roark is cultivated by Wynand, now married to Francon, who convinces him to build his dream home, a Cold War Xanadu. In order to acquire the commission to build the large-scale Cortland housing project, Keating offers to front for Roark, whose reputation for independence would disqualify him. Although Keating vows to execute Roark's radical design, he soon surrenders to the combined forces of Touhy, the owners, and his architectural colleagues, who spoil Roark's austere conception by slapping on academic frills and furbelows. With Francon as his accomplice, Roark blows up the project. Touhy then mounts a crusade against Roark. Wynand, who has lost the last semblance of his power to manipulate public opinion, finally capitulates to save his newspaper. Roark is put on trial for wanton destruction of another man's property.

The narrative wastes no time on petty legalisms. The trial scene begins with Roark's summation to the jury, which concludes with this prophecy:

> I know what is to come according to the principle on which it was built. We are approaching a world in which I cannot permit myself to live. My ideas are my property. They were taken from me by force, by breach of contract. No appeal was left to me. They had a claim on me without my consent. They forced me to serve them.... I came here to say that I do not recognize anyone's right to one minute of my life, nor to any part of my energy. The world is perishing from an orgy of self-sacrifice. I came here to state my terms. I do not care to live by any other. My terms are a man's right to exist for his own sake.

Roark's terms are good enough for the jury, which acquits him. Later, the defeated Wynand, who has closed his newspaper, brusquely presents a contract to Roark authorizing him to design and build the Wynand Building. After Roarke departs, Wynand shoots himself offscreen, his dead hand that grips the revolver falling in close-up on the signed contract that will enable Roark to build according to his own principles. The film ends with Roark, the godlike object of our gaze, astride the top of the skyscraper, awaiting the arrival of Francon, now Mrs. Roark.

But what is the point? Are we to endorse the modernist slogan that form must follow function or the antithetical, Kantian claim made in Roark's peroration to the jury that a man has a right to exist for his own sake? How could a film that speaks such a contradiction imagine itself to be coherent? The mating of the two injunctions only makes sense, as the film's Manhattanism makes sense, in terms of Warner Bros.' monopolistic impulse to exploit unexamined possibilities for countering the worst consequence of the 1948 Paramount Decree: a challenge to the relevance of the studio. *The Fountainhead* is in the business of fabricating a new scenario of corporate transformation: a change from the idea of a firm justified by its economic functionality into the idea of an organization as a person who can claim the right to exist for its own sake. That scenario was given real-world traction by a little-known but crucial revision of the legislative code which set the terms for certain privileges that businesses can claim. *The Fountainhead* defends monopoly, but not in the terms by which the Paramount case was prosecuted, defended, or decided. Instead it advances a revisionary conception of what *Fortune* in 1938 called "proprietary monopoly," one that not only involves the control of patents but that also lays claim, on the grounds of a novel definition of corporate identity, to the absolute right to ownership of one's ideas and the products that emanate from them.[11]

Copyright and patents are protected by the U.S. Constitution; trademarks are creatures of the common law and federal code. That law was dramatically altered by congressional passage of the Trademark Act of 1946, popularly known as the Lanham Act—a federal statute that heralds the postwar rollback of New Deal regulatory policies by a Congress newly impatient with organized labor and indulgent of the prerogatives of big business. Following Harry Aubrey Toulmin's contemporary analysis, the various provisions of the bill that would have mattered to the film industry can be briefly itemized: making trademarks generally incontestable after a five-year period; providing for registration of "secondary meaning" marks, which, over time, have become distinctive of the applicant's goods; permitting assignment of a trademark without simultaneous assignment of the entire business in which it is used.[12] By making it possible for descriptive or generic marks and secondary meanings, such as the particular trade dress associated with a product, to become incontestable after five years, the statute substantially expanded the domain of distinctive, authenticating characteristics and gave the trademark what amounted to perpetual life. By making possible the assignment of the trademark without the business and vice-versa, the code implicitly applied a "two worlds" model to corporate organization: the phenomenal world of the business that can be bought and sold; the intangible world of the corporate form that is instantiated by the trademark and computed as goodwill. The effect of those revisions in the code was dramatically to increase the value of the trademark, which had become a form detachable from the capital assets of the company and which could accrue new attributes and traits. Under common law the trademark designates only a commodity's provenance. The Lanham Act established the grounds for the trademark to become a commodity that could be bought and sold and that, by the accretion of secondary meanings, could develop a legally protected personality. As the Justice Department's brief opposing the legislation forecast, the Lanham act statutorily legitimated and expanded the scope of proprietary monopoly. In doing so it ensured that henceforth corporate politics would be the politics of identity.

Form, we have been instructed, follows function. Yet the only scene in *The Fountainhead* that actually dramatizes that modernist thesis occurs far away from the metropolis, in the New Hampshire quarry where Roark seeks to purge his disgust with society by absorption in hard labor. When Francon first spots her man, Vidor uses a hyperbolically telescopic point-of-view shot to close in on Roark's sinewy arms pressing a throbbing jackhammer deep into the hard rock (Figure 4.1). We do not need to dwell on the symbolic implications of the image, for the commentary quickly follows when Roark, having been called once to Francon's summer home to repair a marble tile she has deliberately spoiled, intuits Francon's "need," returns later and rapes her, thereby staking his claim to ownership by an act of violence.

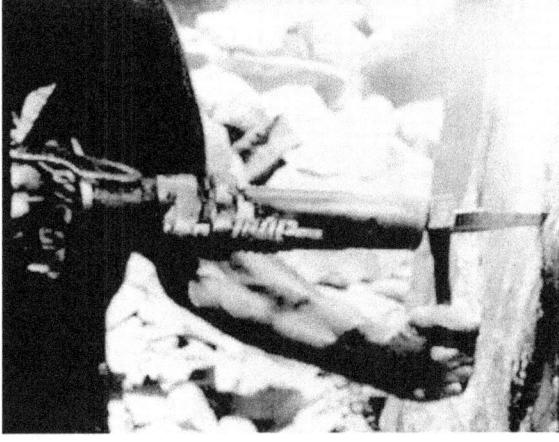

Figure 4.1

The narrative represents Roarke's sublimation of physical brutality as not simply the effect of shifting from laborer back to architect, but as a fundamental change in the conception of a person. It does so by executing a turn that *Fortune* did not foresee: the imagination of the corporation as star, a turn consequent on both the Lanham Act's legislated redescription of corporate identity as intrinsic to the trademark rather than to the business and, more locally, on the postwar shift in industrial conditions that made it possible for stars to be corporations. In his 1941 study of the industry, Leo Rosten famously described "outstanding personalities" as "monopolies on themselves."[13] Rosten does not make it clear who actually holds the monopoly: the individual actor who signs contracts as the personality, or the studio that, under the terms of the contract, is able to dispose a star personality at will by assigning her to productions without consultation, to manipulate her image as it sees fit, and even to loan her to another studio for a lucrative fee. By the late 1940s, however, when the studios' capacity to control its employees had waned, and when, through their agents at the Music Corporation of America (MCA)—especially Lew Wasserman—actors such as James Stewart and directors such as Alfred Hitchcock had begun to exert new authority over their careers, the star system as it had been constituted was jeopardized: the personality of James Stewart was a monopoly on himself by himself.[14] *The Fountainhead*'s conception of the autotelic genius is a star model without a star system—a position that Warners could embrace just insofar as it followed that the star studio could exist without the studio system. Through its mouthpiece Roark/Cooper, *The Fountainhead* makes the case that the star is a transcendental corporate form with a proprietary monopoly over its distinctive traits, understood as occupied, not acquired, and elaborated, not constructed. That position would receive legal recognition in the judgment of the United States District Court for the Eastern District of the State of New York in *Haelan Laboratories Ind. v. Topps Chewing Gum Inc.* (1953), which established, at least for the state of New York, the celebrity's right to be protected against exploitation of his or her voice, image, or persona.[15]

Warners made *The Fountainhead* as Roark builds the Wynand Building, to assert its identity as a skyscraper soul.[16] The vindication of that claim occurs in the courtroom after Roark's climactic speech and acquittal, when the audience—that is, the mind of the public—breaks into applause at the verdict. Indeed, the jury has become nothing more than an audience itself by delivering a verdict that effectively nullifies the indictment by absolving Roark of his admitted crime—not because of extenuating circumstances but because of a collective opinion that circumstances do not apply to Roark, who successfully claims monopoly rights over the expressions of his personality. Of course, the applause does not matter to Roark, who has never sought public approval; his only aspiration is to build buildings. And the public does not build. The real achievement of Roark's self-vindication occurs in the response of the one man who does not applaud the verdict, the defeated Gale Wynand. The courtroom scene neatly exhibits the difference between advertising, a powerful rhetorical appeal that sells a product or person to a credulous public, and marketing, which, by demonstrating an enterprise's capacity to sell its product, creates (or in this case re-creates) a customer. Roark's success in obtaining an acquittal on his own terms creates Wynand, the capitalist who makes building possible, as the customer for what will not be (as he lugubriously intones) "the last skyscraper in New York" but the first skyscraper that will be a free-standing work of art.

In a drastic break with the novel, which lists the various businesses that will occupy the new building and whose rents will pay off the costs of its construction, the movie lobotomizes the proposed Wynand Building, which is emptied of any kind of commercial enterprise and cut off from its former owner, who, unlike the novel's Wynand, conveniently commits suicide and leaves only his authorizing signature on the architectural contract.[17] The Wynand Building will no longer be a "banner" advertising a newspaper intent on arousing the populace to phony crusades but what Wynand, addressing Roark, calls, "a monument to your spirit." A monument to Roark made by Roark, this skyscraping "automonument" presents, in Koolhaas's words,

> a radical, morally traumatic break with the conventions of symbolism: its physical manifestation does not represent an abstract ideal, an institution of exceptional im-

portance, a three-dimensional, readable articulation of a social hierarchy, a memorial; it merely *is* itself and through sheer volume cannot avoid being a symbol—an empty one, available for meaning as a billboard is for advertisement. It is a solipsism, celebrating only the fact of its disproportionate existence, the shamelessness of its own process of creation. (*DNY*, p. 100)

In the Warner Bros. film, if not the Rand novel, the Wynand Building, unlike the noisome newspaper that fertilized it, is frozen speech which disinterestedly celebrates the idea of its impersonal origin. The Wynand Building neither rapes nor sells. Without function, the skyscraper's form follows the phallus as utterance follows the form of thought. *The Fountainhead* revises Sullivan's modernist credo on behalf of a *corporate* modernism: form follows form. The form of the artifact does not follow from the function to which an interested agent, human or institutional, would apply it; it expresses the form of the principal, the towering corporate person, in whose spirit and according to whose intention the object was made.

How do we know that the film makes an assertion on behalf of a corporate person? Surely, *The Fountainhead* instructs us to look for the architect of the film, the person whose idea it expresses. As I have suggested, authorship might be assigned to multiple sites of what, as we have seen in Chapter 1, Ronald Coase called "conscious power." When Roark stands on the top of the skyscraper, who or what does he stand for?

The held shot of the contract on Wynand's desk shows two signatures: Roark's and Wynand's reciprocal acceptance of the terms of Wynand's transfer of all of his authority to Roark. A pistol is placed on the document—not to persuade but to seal (Figure 4.2). Cut to an extreme low-angled shot of the rising skyscraper. Then cut again to the sign in front of the building. The camera lingers long enough for us to read the black letters on a white background: "The Wynand Building: The Tallest Structure in the World," and so on (Figure 4.3). There are other such signs earlier in the picture—or at least parts of them, as Roark, shut out from commissions, patrols the large construction sites in the city. In each case we see only the bottom of the sign where the names of the architects are inscribed. Here we see an entire sign that lists the contractors

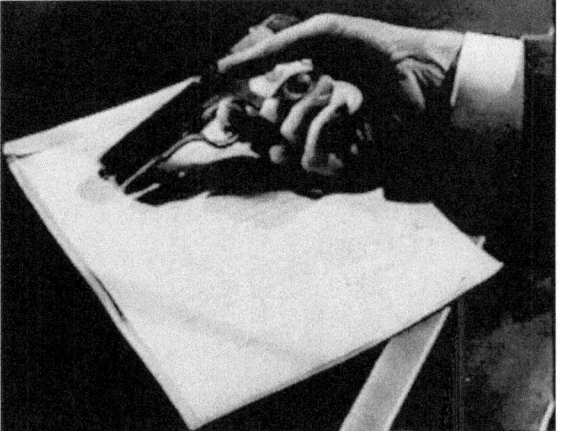

Figure 4.2

Figure 4.3

Figure 4.4

Figure 4.5

who have collaborated to build the skyscraper. Both in its placement at the end of the film and in its form—black letters on a white background that first entitle the work and then indicate the importance of the various contractors by the sequence and by the size and boldness of the lettering—the sign mimics the credits of a motion picture. The display reads as a statement of corporate authorship, for the authority to assign credit attests to a corporate capacity to integrate conscious powers in the completion of a work. *The Fountainhead* insists that it is indeed a work, not a commodity, for the film, like the skyscraper, is intended to be the iconic assertion of the corporation's identity as an ensouled form. Or so we must infer from the self-reflexivity of the image, for what's missing from the credits in front of the Wynand Building as from those at the beginning of the film—in which the contractors who contributed to the making of the film are surveyed—is the specification of the designing mind. As we complete the figure, moving from vehicle to tenor, the camera itself moves, tracking in and tilting down to close in on a gray plaque beneath the large sign on which is inscribed in white letters, "Howard Roark, Architect" (Figure 4.4). It is a self-credit by the man who "states his own terms." Gone is the black, cursive script, mimetic of a signature that had earlier graced Roark's office door (Figure 4.5). Earlier, Wynand had adhered to his identification of Roark as the architect of the Cortland Apartments, despite Roark's denials by asking the rhetorical question, "You think I pick artworks by their signatures?" The abandonment of the facsimile of the signature in favor of the bold block imprint overrides the realm of the personal in which the struggling Roark had been mired, and most pointedly, the preceding image of the countersigned contract on which Wynand lays his pistol after shooting himself.[18] Emancipated from patronage, the incorporated Roark needs no identification but his iconic product. The camera then veers downward and to the side to capture Francon's admiring glance and track with her to the elevator that will take her to her man atop the skyscraper.

That plaque with Roarke's company name, which is given pride of place as the lowest and (because of the framing and camera movement) last credit, and which is disconnected from the others by position, font, and color, matches no credit at the beginning of the film. It points us forward, that is, down and later, to another credit, also composed of white letters on a field of gray, which is the last frame on the last reel of exposed celluloid: "The End," accompanied by the Warner Bros.' credit (Figure 4.6). Roark's representativeness is formally settled not by an authorial signature but by a proprietary trademark. What difference does a signature make to claims of authorship? Not the signature but the right to authorize signatures counts, not even the credit but the power to credit oneself, a right and a power that may be assumed by Jack Warner as agent in this instance but assumed only on the condition that it is finally referred to the principal, the corporate author itself, which can only appear as a trademark, never as a signature. Warner Bros. superintends the symbolic economy of credit as Roark superintends the construction of the skyscraper. The studio claims *The Fountainhead* as its own utterance by virtue of its being the fountainhead from which the work flowed. Like Roark, Warner Bros. has made a monument to its own spirit. The audience staring up at the plaque on the screen gazes at the studio's work and admires, if not enjoys, what in a happy moment Gale Wynand called "the wonder of ownership." If it is the assertion of the romantic genius that authorship is ownership, it is the trademarked genius of the postwar corporation as Warner Bros. imagines it that creates the basis for a new era of proprietary monopoly by troping ownership as authorship.

Figure 4.6

ii. Curatorial Corporatism

> The producer pushes; the consumer pulls.
>
> David Riesman, *The Lonely Crowd* (1950)
>
> This ain't no museum!
>
> Abe Warner, "Warner Brothers"

Donald Spoto gives this account of *Vertigo*'s inaugural action: "San Francisco detective John 'Scottie' Ferguson (James Stewart) discovers his acrophobia (a pathological dread of heights) when a police colleague falls to his death during a rooftop chase. The condition leads to vertigo, a psychosomatic illness which produces dizziness and a sensation of drifting in spinning space—a frightening but strangely pleasurable sensation."[19] As vertigo is predetermined by acrophobia, so the acrophobia would seem to be predetermined by something—physical or psychological—in possession of this man before we see him hanging from the gutter of a high building. Those original spectators of *Vertigo* who had seen the explicitly psychoanalytic *Spellbound* (Vanguard, 1945) might have expected the narrative in *Vertigo* similarly to involve a return to, revelation of, and release from that secret—classically Freudian, classically Hollywood—predetermination. Despite the intervention of a psychiatrist, however, such a pat conclusion does not occur here. The return is not to Scottie's past but to Madeleine's; the revelation is not of a childhood trauma but of an adult contrivance; and the release is a cure that kills. *Vertigo* is not a psychoanalytic film that regards the world from the perspective of Freudian theory or whose plot can be reduced to a symptom of the psyche. On the contrary, *Vertigo* is a sociologically informed film that shows how psychoanalytic tropes can be deployed as tools of mystification.[20] *Vertigo* is a film about agency—about how things get done and undone—specifically, an allegory of the transformation of motion picture authorship into a new type of agency with a potent social character of unprecedented independence, an agency called "Alfred Hitchcock," which was structured as a remarkably proficient version of the corporate—let's call it "bilateral monopolism"—and which was managed by a shrewd proprietor of formidable insight and power: Lew Wasserman, head of the Music Corporation of America (MCA) in the 1950s, and then the studio head of Universal Pictures.

In *Vertigo* Alfred Hitchcock establishes a peculiar relationship between his spectatorial protagonist and the implied spectator of the motion picture. If we think of acrophobia as a disorder in which a perception of physical depth appears to the perceiver as the representation of something else, itself unseen, the motion picture would seem to attempt a difficult, perhaps impossible thing: to reproduce that vertiginous confusion between perception and representation in a medium where the perception of depth is always propped on some technical device, and is, therefore, already a representation under the control of someone, himself unseen (Figure 4.7). It is hard to keep in mind such disparity between perception and representation. Here is Robin Wood's analysis of the mechanics: "The sensation of vertigo is conveyed to the spectator by the most direct means, subjective shots using a simultaneous zoom-in and track-back that makes the vast drop telescope out before our eyes.... The sensation has been explained ... by psychologists as arising from the tension between the desire to fall and the dread of falling—an idea worth bearing in mind in relation to the whole film."[21] Although Wood acknowledges that the means of conveying the sensation are technical, he clings to a psychological explanation, perversely attributing to the psyche what belongs to physics, to the mind what belongs to the brain, and to the Freudian father what belongs to the Edisonian camera. Hitchcock's push-pull shot may be an apt metaphor for a disabling ambivalence, but it even more precisely images the oscillation between the physical and the psychological. The shot is a perfectly balanced rendering of a state of imbalance, a vivid presentation of the duplicity of cinematic representation: seeing flat things as deep, seeing moving things as still, seeing past things as present, seeing right before our eyes what we know to be false.

The slippage between the psychological and the physical is dramatized in the scene following the suspended prologue, where, in the cluttered apartment of his friend Midge, Scottie celebrates the advent of "tomorrow." "Tomorrow," he exclaims, "the corset comes off tomorrow. I'll be able to scratch myself like anybody else, tomorrow. I'll be able to throw this miserable thing [he waves his cane] out the window. I'll be a free [wince] man." Midge attempts to temper Scottie's expectation by giving him an education in gender. "You'd be surprised

Figure 4.7

by how many men wear corsets," she replies. Scottie tries to change the subject by turning his attention to the undergarment that Midge is sketching for a newspaper ad (Figure 4.8). When he gingerly touches it with his cane and asks, "What's this do-hickey?" Midge replies in a tone of mocking tolerance, "A brassiere, Johnny. You know about such things. You're a big boy now." Scottie's denial of what he knows evidently has something to do with his conception of a man as being free from feminine traits. Midge's encouragement that Johnny admit what he knows as a "big boy" is of a piece with her "motherly" advice that Scottie *adjust* to his vertigo. She concedes that experts believe some kind of revolutionary shock might eradicate the destabilizing condition of acrophobia, but she discourages Scottie from betting on the long shot. "You've got it, and there's no getting rid of it," she declares, skeptical that he'll find a cure for his physical condition, let alone for the condition of being subject to conditions.

Scottie will try to get rid of "it," however. He practices by getting rid of other things: the cane, the corset, and, most conspicuously, his job. Reminding Midge that he is a man of "independent means, well, fairly independent anyway," he explains his decision to quit the police department, abandoning his ambition to rise to chief, by his apprehension that, sitting at his desk, he might drop a pencil and suffer vertigo while bending over to pick it up. That's clearly a tongue-in-cheek alibi. But an alibi for what? Not, Midge declares, for guilt over an act he has committed, since the death of the fellow officer was not Scottie's fault. Scottie does not dispute her, and nothing we have seen refutes her. Yet even though the death of the patrolman was not Scottie's fault, the patrolman, his subordinate, was his *responsibility*. As Gavin Elster, beholden for his executive position to his wife's family, remarks, "One assumes responsibilities." As Elster will demonstrate, however, the ruthless man will use all his cunning to dispose of

Figure 4.8

them. With knowledge of the events that will befall Scottie, we may reasonably conjecture that what is intolerable for the "fairly independent" man is being responsible for something that is not one's fault, afflicted with guilt for effects that one has not caused. The equivocation between fault and responsibility, where responsibility wants to confess to an imagined fault and fault wants to be free of responsibility, also tracks a mutual implication of physical altitude and organizational advancement—that is, between something we would want to call "literal" and something we would want to call "figurative" height. To be at fault without responsibility would mean discarding all those jobs, people, and things that cripple intentions and hobble freedom—a project that Scottie tragically completes at the end of the picture.

We do not understand a man like Scottie by investigating his personal past. We must examine him in light of a set of social conditions that mass produce men whom the audience of the mid-1950s would recognize as typical. "In an earlier day the audience was given a story of the hero's work-minded rise to success. Today the ladder climbing is taken for granted or is seen in terms of breaks, and the hero's tastes in dress, food, women, and recreation are emphasized—these are, as we have seen, the frontiers on which the reader can himself compete, while he cannot imagine himself in the work role of the president of the United States or the head of a big company."[22] That forecast of Scottie's predicament appeared in David Riesman's *The Lonely Crowd* (1950), where he announces the emergence of the "social character" of the other-directed person, whose "conformity is insured by their tendency to be sensitized to the expectations and preferences of others." The other-directed person follows in historical sequence, the "tradition-directed people" and the "inner-directed people." According to Riesman, the conformity of the latter type of person, who had dominated American society since the nineteenth century, is ensured by his "tendency to acquire early in life an internalized set of goals" (*LC*, p. 9) and to acquire "a psychological gyroscope" that enables him to maintain "a delicate balance between the demands upon him of his goal in life and the buffetings of the external environment." With the decline of the birth rate and the prospect of abundant goods, "increasingly, *other people* are the problem, not the material environment." The inner-directed person's "gyroscopic control is no longer sufficiently flexible.... The other-directed person must be able to receive signals from far and near.... This control equipment, instead of being like a gyroscope, is like a radar" (*LC*, p. 25). Riesman imagines that, despite the advent of the other-directed person, there is a sizeable remnant of inner-directed types, who, because of the power of "social institutions [to] harness different motivations, springing from different character types, ... may be compelled to behave in one way although their character structure presses them to behave in the opposite way" (*LC*, p. 7). Riesman describes the consequence of that imbalance, which defeats gyroscopic regulation as "a psychic cost" (*LC*, p. 25). Hitchcock names it "vertigo."

iii. Art, Bilateral Monopolism, and the Fate of Fading

To reverse a famous statement from a tale of another wandering Scott (told by Walter Scott), when John Ferguson, formerly of the San Francisco police force, decides to keep his appointment with Gavin Elster in the "mission district," it is clear that the history of his life has ended and its romance has begun. It took the shock of battle and the anguish of betrayal to awaken Edward Waverley to his estate as a man in the civic life of the nation. The shocking discovery of his impotence in the performance of his duty convinces Scottie that he is not the man he thought he was. The ideal of an autonomous and potent masculinity is constantly evoked in the landscape of San Francisco: evoked by bridges Scottie cannot cross, cranes he cannot operate, and towers that he cannot climb (including one named "Coit"). As Scottie admires Elster's prints of the vanished, gay San Francisco, the executive nostalgically contrasts his luxuriously useless position with the lot of the founding dynasts, a world of "color, excitement, freedom, and power." The same nostalgia will later be expressed during antiquarian Pop Liebel's (owner of the Argosy Bookstore) narration of the history of Carlotta Valdes's seizure, exploitation, and sequestration by her Anglo lover, whose "freedom and power" consisted in his ruthless abandonment of the Spanish dancehall girl on whom he begat his love child. The patriarchal myth subjects modern "big boys" to an inimitable precedent. If freedom conjoined with power constitutes a lost state of virile plenitude, the psychic cost of belatedness is the sense that now freedom can be only negatively defined as emancipation from responsibility and power—a moral that, we know, Scottie is primed to accept.

The film leaves two questions tantalizingly open: Why does Elster construct the scenario he does in order to involve Scottie in his plot to murder his wife? Why does Madeleine enchant Scottie? The first question asks us to surmise how someone could anticipate another person's reaction to words and sights. The second asks us to understand what it is that Scottie experiences. The former asks us to put ourselves in the place of a character who combines the functions of producer, writer, and director; the latter asks us to identify with the actor under direction. To conjecture why Elster chose Scottie is directly analogous to understanding why Hitchcock eventually chose James Stewart rather than Cary Grant to play the role. The two actors were cast as Hitchcock's versions of the antithetical Riesmanian types: Grant, the other-directed ad man, Roger Thornhill, in *North by Northwest* (MGM, 1959), whose initials are R.O.T. (the O, Roger says, stands for "nothing"); Stewart, the inner-directed John Ferguson, who Midge placates with the phrase "O Johnny O" ("Johnny" as the core of a person externalized and balanced by ciphers). To substitute one for the other was to fundamentally change the subject. It is hard to visualize Grant in the role of Scottie (perhaps renamed "Cockney") without also imagining him using other-directed radar to pick up on the peculiar signals he is getting; conversely, it is hard not to imagine Stewart swooning into the role of the fictional Kaplan in *North by Northwest*. In *The Philadelphia Story* (MGM, 1940), the only screen pairing of Grant and Stewart, it is Grant who, as C. K. Dexter Haven, plays a benign version of the Elster figure; Macaulay Connor, Stewart's character, tries to act up to his part in the contrived "front story" but loses his balance by falling for Tracy Lord as an ideal of femininity conjured into divinity by Haven's mocking eloquence. Cary Grant had an immunity from life's bruising that James Stewart lacked. Stewart's characters, precariously embodied, were consistently figured as spanning two worlds: war and postwar, here and elsewhere. He was the actor that Hitchcock would recognize as Scottie's type, just as Elster would recognize Scottie as the type who would be the ideal agent to realize his scenario.

Of course, when we first meet Elster we don't know that he has developed a scenario, just that he has a problem with a wandering wife named Madeleine and a conviction that Scottie is the person to solve it. We hear him ask the fundamental question, "Scottie, do you believe that a someone from the past, someone dead, can take possession of a living being?" Scottie answers with a vigorous "no." But the suggestion has been planted. Scottie stays skeptical, but he does stay to hear Elster out. The scene ends with Elster's appeal to Scottie, "Look, we're going to an opening at the opera tonight. We're dining at Ernie's first. You can see her there." And see her he does. A cut to Ernie's, a track in through the door, then a cut to Scottie at the bar leaning back in his seat. Then a series of intricate cross-cut shots which present Madeleine to the eyes of the furtive Scottie and to us, the even more furtive audience. The sequence concludes with, once again, a shot of Scottie at the bar, which fades to a black screen followed by a shot of Scottie in his car on the job the next day, hooked on looking at Madeleine. To some extent the audience's willingness to accept Scottie's instantaneous fascination rests on the extradiegetic analog to this scene of Stewart's look at another blond actress, Grace Kelly, who presents herself as if she were a fold-out fashion plate in *Rear Window* (Paramount, 1954). As Robin Wood observed, however, the diegetic basis for Scottie's enchantment is, crucially, the fact that "Madeleine is presented in terms of the work of art" (*HFR*, p. 384). As she enters the bar, she is casually framed by a doorway and then, after a posed profile, fleetingly framed by a mirror as she and Elster exit (Figure 4.9). Ostensibly, Madeleine has no more self-consciousness than any beautiful woman presenting herself.[23] Smitten by the effect of art, we might, like Scottie, initially overlook the *terms* of art, in part because at least one term is missing: a work of art presupposes an artist; and there is no evidence of one here.

We do not have to wait until Judy's revelation of Elster's contrivance for a dramatic reactivation of "the terms of the work of art." Scottie follows Madeleine to the Palace of the Legion of Honor, where he sees her in a place where works of art are displayed, silent and motionless as a statue, seated in contemplation of the portrait of a woman (Figure 4.10). We could easily imagine coming upon such a woman in a museum gallery, frozen in a fair attitude,

Figure 4.9

Figure 4.10

and suspecting she is, for one reason or another, *acting* engrossed, merely posing as a woman absorbed in a painting. We will later learn that this is true. Scottie is troubled by no such suspicion, however. Elster has disposed him to see something other than theater here, to see the attitude as evidence of Madeleine's possession by the portrait. Madeleine not only seems to belong in the place where works of art are displayed, she seems to belong to the portrait of Carlotta, her attitude referring to the painting, her presence that to which the painting refers.

The work that art does is conveyed to the viewer, however, by editing and the movement of the lens, which do not adopt Scottie's point of view but do render the intensity with which he registers the correspondences among the images and objects under his gaze. The camera hyperbolically zooms in on the bouquet of forget-me-nots lying on the bench by the seated Madeleine and then tilts to the image of an identical bouquet that the woman holds over what would be her lap. After a cut the camera zooms in to a close shot of the twist that holds Madeleine's hair in place, and then shifts to the portrait where it again zooms in on an all but identical bun in the darker hair of the painted woman. We may infer that Scottie sees in the spiraling space (echoing his recent pursuit of Madeleine through the streets of San Francisco) an objective correlative for the dizzying push-pull of vertigo, or that he experiences it and its doubling as the oscillation between "it is" and "it is not," "you have it" and "you do not have it" that, according to Freud, characterizes castration anxiety.[24] We may infer because, even though we are still innocent of Elster's design, *we* know that we are being *directed* to infer. Hitchcock's manipulation of our point of view dramatizes the disparity between how we, the spectators, are compelled to *read* the correspondences and how Scottie *experiences* them.

Because the identity—indeed, the existence—of the *metteur en scène* is occluded, Scottie's vertiginous experience of the scene forces him to conclude that both Madeleine's mimicry and her rapt attitude are authentic responses to a portrait that possesses her, as if from the dead. To credit the force of that binding is to be bound in turn. That Scottie would reach such a conclusion should be no surprise, for his experience is only one instance of a power of coercion that, since Plato, has been attributed to all art. Retrospectively, it is clear that Elster's installation in the palace has "ionized" Scottie, for we can infer that, like the Socrates of the *Ion*, the author of this scene conceives that art achieves its effect by a suspensive force that enchains its viewer—perhaps not all viewers at all places and at all times, but doubtless a certain type of viewer susceptible to vertigo and impelled to hang silently in rapt belief.[25] Elster's design successfully captivates the viewer of that viewer who poses as captivated. Not so for the viewers of the viewer of the viewer—that is, for the audience—who are distanced from the scene by the visible hand of Hitchcock, who efficiently analyzes the mimetic technique that mystifies Scottie. By *conveying* the mechanics of possession rather than *triggering* it, Hitchcock shows a truly Socratic disdain for artistic representation: its irrational force, its ideologically imposing force (Figure 4.11).[26]

Hitchcock's deconstruction of the power of art fittingly occurs in a museum, that unique public place where a framed picture can be hung and a person can dwell for hours in contemplation while she herself may be the object of a person's prolonged observation. The museum not only certifies what is art; it has an institutional power to "harness different motivations, springing from different character types" (*LC*, p. 29), and organize them in galleries of associations and potential identifications. The effect can be sublime. But as Hitchcock shows and Elster knows, that rapt suspension is strictly an institutional effect. Although the portrait of Carlotta Valdes invokes the terms of art, its actual contribution to the attainment of Elster's objective is as a prop not an agent. Gavin Elster, the "hidden persuader," accomplishes the suspensive enchantment to which poetry and painting aspire, its institutional effect, without getting any credit; indeed, producing the institutional effect of art depends on the one *not* getting credit for the installation.[27] In that sense Elster is no Hitchcock, if by Hitchcock we mean the director whose distinctive signature visual style is on display in the museum, just as it was in the serpentine pursuit of Madeleine through the streets of San Francisco, and will be in the climbs up the mission tower.

Midge's reaction to Scottie's enthrallment is personal and professional, not philosophical. When we first see her in her apartment-studio, she is seated drawing at her desk, surrounded by examples of her commercial art, which are mostly illustrations of the kind of clothes that someone who wanted to look

Figure 4.11

like Madeleine would wear and of the hidden devices that would form her figure. Although reproductions of Miros hang on her walls, this is a workshop not a museum. Midge makes her living by making pictures for magazines and newspapers that she can sell because *they* sell. Scottie ignores her pictures and is indifferent to making a living. Later, after Madeleine's visit, he returns. As Midge initially tried to persuade Scottie to accept the reality of his disease, so now after evidence that Scottie is willing to expend his health on the future of an illusion, she tries to jolt him into an acceptance of reality by disenchanting *Carlotta*. When Midge mentions that she has gone back to her "first love, painting," and refers to Scottie's disdain for her commercial work, he confirms her by joking, "I always thought you were wasting your time in the underwear department." She then invites him to view an easel painting. "Do you want to see?" He takes it in from bottom to top, slowly comprehending a parody of the Carlotta portrait with Midge's bespectacled face mounted on the Spanish beauty's shoulders, which aims to demystify the *Carlotta* by showing that it too was an advertisement designed to sell Scottie on a dream (Figure 4.12).[28] Seeing only what he definitely does not want to see, Scottie replies, "That's not funny, Midge. No, not funny at all," and leaves.

Midge's shock does not cure Scottie. She might have done better to *buy* the *Carlotta*, and, even better, had Scottie watch her bid on that painting and others like it at an art auction, as Roger Thornhill does in *North by Northwest*. There Hitchcock's satire of art is direct. He has Thornhill demystify the special privilege of paintings by his insouciant disregard for either their mimetic power or their aesthetic qualities. Thornhill succeeds where Midge fails because, improvising to save his own life rather than to change someone else's, he treats the painting of "this seventeenth-century master" as just another com-

Figure 4.12

modity—the institutionally specific form of the commodity that sustains the art market—and by doing so he renders all the art on display as commercial. Because the paintings are packaged in golden frames like the portrait that Big Boy hangs in his office in *Little Caesar*, when the audience at the auction looks at them, we can imagine that they think they are seeing money (just as Roger had earlier ordered a box of chocolates wrapped in gold foil for his secretary on the principle that she'd like it because she'd think "she is eating money"). Had Midge compelled Scottie to see the *Carlotta* as a piece of property rather than a charmed possession, the romance might have ended right there.

The romance does unravel later, when the reflection of "Carlotta's" necklace in Judy's mirror betrays it not as a magical possession but as currency given in payment by one person to another for services rendered. Judy triggers the disillusionment when, after "fixing [her] face," she asks Scottie to come to the mirror and secure the clasp on the ruby pendant, the one accessory of Carlotta's that he has omitted from his makeover. Scottie fumbles the catch, then asks, "How do you work it?" The answer is another question, which rephrases Midge's challenge, "Don't you want to see?" "Can't you see?" Judy asks, inadvertently inviting Scottie to see how "it" has been worked from the beginning. Recalling not only the scene at the museum but the way the scene was seen, the lens initially zooms in on the reflection of the pendant; then there is a match cut to its painted counterpart; and then the camera tracks back from the pendant to the scene of Madeleine absorbed in the painting. Scottie puts things together by taking the scene apart: the zoom followed by the track back analytically breaks down the push-pull of the "vertigo" shot, revealing how it works.[29] Closing the clasp closes the investigation as Scottie, whose face comprehends the mirror, sees how he had been framed by Elster.

That Scottie can work things out better in Judy's room at the Empire Hotel than in a museum is no surprise. Hotels are prominent in Hitchcock's films of the 1950s: from *The Man Who Knew Too Much* (Paramount, 1956) to *To Catch a Thief* (Paramount, 1955), from *Vertigo* to *North by Northwest*, from *Psycho* (Shamley, 1960) to, well, nowhere, for the shift from the metropolitan Phoenix Hotel at the opening of *Psycho* to the backcountry motel, like the shifts from first-run movie houses to lonely televisions and from suspense to shock, executes a fundamental alteration in Hitchcock's conception of his project. In *Vertigo* alone the name of the hotel invites allegorization: "Empire" is assuredly the name for the state of subjugation experienced by both the real Judy (not Madeleine), subsidized by Scottie so that he can fulfill his fantasy without resistance, and the real Carlotta (not the portrait), the Hispanic mistress of an imperious Anglo lover who kept her for his pleasure in the McKittrick Hotel.

It is also tempting to allegorize the Empire Hotel as the type for the Hollywood studios with which Hitchcock had contracted, whether RKO, Warners, or Paramount. Paradoxically, however, what makes the connection inviting is its elusiveness: nothing much happens in this hotel that looks like filmmaking, or at least like filmmaking in the classical mode. Activities associated with the motion picture business do occur here, however. An independent producer identifies a promising starlet, an exclusive performance contract is struck, a makeover occurs, rehearsals follow, and a screen test is passed when the starlet is bedded. The implication, I suggest, is not that the hotel is what had been known as a studio but that a studio, reduced to its postclassical essentials, is not much more than a temporary residence for stars on a single picture contract or an agency that subcontracts labor to specialists in underwear departments, who are responsible for realizing what the director wants by selecting costumes, applying make-up, and finding locations. The association of empire with such an organization may look either ironic, if you have in mind the waning studio system, or prophetic, if you are attuned to the moves made by Lew Wasserman on behalf of the emergent MCA/Universal and his most prized client, Alfred Hitchcock.[30]

Wasserman launched MCA's spectacular rise to power on the so-called "blanket waiver" he secured in 1952 from the Screen Actors Guild, which exempted the company from the rule that prohibited a talent agency from also operating as a production company and enabled MCA both to assemble talent packages for the networks and to ensure that Revue, its own television production company, would have unique access to that talent. Although MCA was investigated for possible violations of the Sherman Antitrust Act, its anticompetitive practices were fundamentally different from the ones that had provoked the antitrust prosecutions of Paramount and the rest of the Hollywood majors, which had systematically obstructed the access of small studios and independent producers to distribution networks and had dictated the kind and cost of the product available to unaffiliated exhibitors. MCA succeeded not by vertical integration but by *bilateral* integration. Functionally, MCA became a new form of distribution company disguised as a talent agency. The product it distributed was not movies but stars. MCA contracted with stars on the promise that it could deliver jobs in the movies and television; it contracted with studios and networks to deliver packages of stars for specific projects, which Revue then produced. MCA redefined the agent from one who worked on behalf of an actor or actress to one for whom actors, actresses, even stars, worked; it restrained trade by making sure that those stars would be unavailable to the studios and networks unless they dealt with MCA. In *Bottlenecks of Business* Thurman Arnold had described the Sherman Antitrust Act as the great "balance wheel" of the American economy.³¹ MCA simulated the regulatory effect of that balance wheel as a two-handed engine, which sold actors to itself as Revue.

No director navigated the hotel era of Hollywood filmmaking more successfully than Hitchcock, its diagnostician, in large part because he was one of the foremost beneficiaries of MCA's self-aggrandizement. Hitchcock had begun to establish his own independence in the industry with *Notorious* in 1946, which had been sold by David O. Selznick, his indifferent patron, to RKO. The new contract enabled Hitchcock to produce his own picture. Hitchcock refused a producer credit, however. No name appears. That peculiar convention was revived in 1947 with *Rope*, Hitchcock's first film after the expiration of the Selznick contract and the first motion picture made by Hitchcock as a partner with Sidney Bernstein in Transatlantic Productions as part of a four-picture deal with Warners. When Cary Grant suddenly backed out, the *Rope* project was saved by the intervention of Lew Wasserman. Wasserman had acquired Hitchcock as a client by default, in 1945, when MCA absorbed the Hayward-Deverich agency, which had acquired Hitchcock as a client when it absorbed the rolls of the agency of Myron Selznick, David's brother. Lew Wasserman connected Hitchcock with Stewart, another client, and solved the problem of financing Stewart's participation by persuading the actor to accept a percentage of the box office in lieu of a portion of his normal salary. It was with *Rope* that Hitchcock first claimed a possessory credit, which stipulated that the film be released as "Alfred Hitchcock's *Rope*." Wasserman subsequently closed a string of extraordinary deals, all of which retained Hitchcock's possessory credit and none of which credited a producer: first, a deal with Paramount for five pictures—*Rear Window*, *To Catch a Thief*, *The Trouble with Harry* (Paramount, 1955), *The Man Who Knew Too Much*, and *Vertigo*—which guaranteed their reversion to Hitchcock's ownership after eight years; next, a single picture deal with MGM for *North by Northwest*; and then, a lucrative connection with Universal, which became MCA's own studio in 1962 and in which Hitchcock had an ownership stake.

In 1955 the television anthology series *Alfred Hitchcock Presents* was packaged by MCA under the rubric of Hitchcock's newly formed television production company, Shamley Productions. The anthology series was sold to CBS by MCA, packed with MCA clients, enriched by MCA-sponsored merchandizing tie-ins in various media venues, and annuitized by MCA's acquisition of the syndication and the residual rights previously overlooked or undersold by the studios and the professional guilds. Hitchcock made spectacular money on the deal. He would later use that capital to finance the production of *Psycho*. As usual, MCA made money on both ends: a commission on the talent that went out and a profit on the revenue that came in. The setup was a Wasserman production for which he did not seek credit. Eventually, the Justice Department of President Kennedy tried to force credit on him by preparing an indictment of MCA in 1962 for intent to restrain trade. By that time, however, Wasserman was happy to shed the talent agency in order to deflect the government's indictment. He was fully prepared to run Universal International Pictures and exploit the codependency of film and television—a strategy which Hitchcock's enterprises epitomized.[32]

Writing about the arch representations of Hitchcock that precede and follow episodes of *Alfred Hitchcock Presents*, Thomas M. Leitch comments that each role that Hitchcock assumes in the introduction is "designed . . . to reveal the host's carefully groomed public personality as the one constant term in a weekly game of charades which is in turn the one constant in a series of ironic melodramas." Leitch argues that the host's address to his audience skillfully integrates "Hitchcock the director with Hitchcock the public figure," so that "whenever we attempt to look behind Hitchcock the impresario, we find Hitchcock the creator, and vice versa."[33] He convincingly concludes that the prominence of this oscillation between figure and ground dramatizes the standoff between the prevailing theories of film authorship. The "overdetermined status" of what I shall call Hitchcock's bilateral persona "suggests that revisionist theories of authorship that present the author as nothing more than an effect of the apparatus, like the realist theories of representation they are meant to correct, are telling only part of the story" ("OC," p. 69). The ambiguity of the possessory credit similarly exemplifies the distinctive dynamics of the Hitchcock persona that Leitch has shrewdly formalized. From one perspective "Alfred Hitchcock's" is simply a trademark that identifies the provenance of whatever title follows, a credit justifiable as preventing the product from being confused with imitations and as a marketing device that would likely increase the box office by building Hitchcock's brand. Yet the possessory credit could also reasonably be regarded as a claim that Hitchcock is the author of the motion picture, the generative mind responsible for its creation. Precisely that reading would provoke an attempt by the Writers Guild of America in 1966 to seize control of the allocation of possessory credits on the grounds that the prevailing conventions inevitably led to the suppression of the contribution to the picture of the individual screenwriter, who should be credited as the real author because all feature production starts with a script. More generally, the SWG claimed that because the possessory credit had historically been given only to directors, it had the malign effect of officializing the auteur theory, regardless of the particular circumstances of the attribution.[34] Doubtless, when the conventional "Warner Bros. Presents" preceded the exceptional "Alfred Hitchcock's *Rope*," the former tended to slide toward a claim of ownership and the latter toward authorship, but the effect was only relative: the apostrophe fell well short of a "by" as in *Rope,* by Alfred Hitchcock or *Mr. Smith Goes to Washington* (Columbia, 1939), by Frank Capra—credits that never appeared on the screen.

Hitchcock would subsequently testify, "I consider the possessory use of my name as of extraordinary value to the producing company as well as to myself."[35] It is unlikely that Hitchcock regretted any inferences that he was in some way the author—a way that would be worked out by Andrew Sarris's version of the auteur theory as the evidence of a signature style imposed on material locked into industrial formulas.[36] In 1946, however, Hitchcock owned only his name and a partnership in International Productions; and, as we have seen in our examination of Warner Bros.' management of *The Fountainhead,* authorship in classical Hollywood had always been contingent on ownership—a relation even more strenuously asserted in the 1950s as the importance of the studios as production companies diminished and as the importance of the motion pictures stored in the studio vaults increased. The success of Hitchcock's claim to possessory credit in the four-picture deal with Warners was due as much to the fact that International Productions, in which he was a partner, was the production company of record for *Rope* (International, 1948) and *Under Capricorn* (International, 1949) and a stakeholder in the pictures' success, though not an owner of the pictures themselves. Hitchcock did own his name. He *almost* owned *Rope.* The possessory credit, like the four-picture contract itself, was the negotiated recognition of the value of that stake by Warners, which nonetheless retained control of the films that "Alfred Hitchcock's" introduced. That ownership relation would change during the postwar years, when Hitchcock moved from hotel to hotel. Right up until the paradigm-shifting *Psycho* he used both film and, later, television to model a corporate authorship. Wasserman's negotiated acquisition with Paramount of the eventual return of the movies to Hitchcock's ownership was, of course, a major accomplishment of ownership. But the most telling evidence of Hitchcock's strategy for constructing a corporate author capable of giving credit rather than continuing a celebrity relationship that strengthened his *claims* was his consistent rejection of the producer credit, a programmatic omission that marked out, well beyond the director's or screenwriter's or cinematographer's scope, a Thalbergian domain of impersonal control over and identification with the entire process, which, as the unfolding of *Alfred Hitchcock Presents* demonstrated, could be occupied by Alfred Hitchcock himself, by Joan Harrison, or by any other duly appointed, that is, credited agent who would be faithful to the Hitchcock brand and the corporate intention it expressed.

Vertigo was the last of the five pictures Hitchcock made for Paramount that would revert to his control. It is the one picture to meditate the nature of a legacy, to question its own status as a work of art, and to imagine the combination of factors that would enable Hitchcock's capital to accumulate rather than deteriorate—chief among them the formation of an institutional infrastructure. *Vertigo* undertakes those tasks from an imagined position of corporate authorship, which is *virtually* the same position from which the bilateral figure of Hitchcock was constructed by Shamley Productions for *Alfred Hitchcock Presents*. As a television production company, Shamley was efficient. But in 1957 it was not sufficiently capitalized to produce motion pictures, let alone to distribute them, and would not be until Hitchcock partnered with Wasserman at Universal in 1962 to take advantage of the television unit and produce *Psycho* under the Shamley rubric. Hitchcock and Wasserman, uncredited producers, shared a commitment to a form of corporate authorship best described as curatorial: the corporation assumes responsibilities for the acquisition and exhibition of art objects within an institutional framework that will preserve their commercial value. *Vertigo* most comprehensively models bilateral authorship among Hitchcock's movies of the 1950s: on the one hand there is the mobilization of the *Ion* scenario by Elster, the curator of Madeleine, who acquires her and exhibits her according to the terms of art; on the other, there is the visible but unrecognized labor of people like Midge whom Elster must employ to fabricate the illusion: whenever we look behind Elster we see Midge, and whenever we look behind Midge we see Elster. Supervising both is the corporate author that Hitchcock imagines here and will eventually establish, as, ironically, he becomes the junior partner to his agent at Universal International Pictures, thus making him "fairly independent" and in a position to "mix commerce with work that was true to the art-film vision" (*VMHC*, p. 18).

Scottie's repudiation of Midge is of a piece with his resignation from the police department, which is one department among many in *Vertigo*'s San Francisco. Especially prominent is Ransohoff's boutique, where, in specialized workshops, expert women fashion brand-new, marketable females, designed to attract the masculine eye, then to be brandished as accessories, and, finally, to be undone by an early obsolescence. Recall that Midge and Scottie respectively propose shock and gradualism as alternative approaches to the "cure" that would enable Scottie to go up and to grow up. In that early scene, Midge also mentions a kind of raising that is neither gradualist nor exactly shocking when she describes the "revolutionary uplift" of the brassiere that momentarily captures Scottie's curiosity. Now we are not meant to take "revolutionary" entirely seriously; it is advertising hyperbole: the so-called revolution endangers no person or institution. The fetishizing of the revolutionary (and the cantilevered bosom) is as American as Madison Avenue. Midge's wry citation of the slogan reminds us that there is no eternal feminine, just as there is no eternal automobile. Each model is the fulfillment of an ideal; yet in mid-century America neither my true love's eyes nor my Chevrolet's fins will last beyond the morrow (see "Hedren, Tippi"). But the slogan is also an insider's joke, calling attention to the bosom of the full-figured Kim Novak—whose breasts when she first appears as Judy are conspicuously uplifted but notoriously braless. Unlike Midge, Judy does not waste her time in the underwear department. Not that Scottie comments on the difference. He cares that the breasts are raised, not how they are raised. He commands that Judy's hairdo be changed to match Madeline's; it would not occur to him (or, likely, to Elster) to apply his hands to the job, except when writing the check to pay for what others have produced.

Although Hitchcock did not dress or paint Kim Novak, he did take an avid interest in Edith Head's designs for Madeleine's clothes and in the technical problems that the film raised. Moreover, Hitchcock created unnecessary problems, as if to set challenges for himself and his crew. One was the staging of the two death scenes on the bell tower of the Mission San Juan Batista, which reverberate to Midge's joke about "revolutionary uplift." The formidable tower first defeats Scottie, but he finally wins through, triumphantly mounting the steps, as if rising out of the depths of his paralyzing obsession (Figure 4.13). The most notable aspect of the actual mission chosen for the location is that, unusual among surviving California missions, San Juan Batista lost its bell tower in a fire earlier in the century. The bell tower was restored by movie magic. The still from the movie shows a bell tower constructed on the Paramount

Figure 4.13

back lot, which has been matted onto the image of the mission (*VMHC*, p. 64). Rationales have been offered for Hitchcock's choice of San Juan Batista, but the likeliest reason is that he wanted a mission with no tower, a gelded building, which his technical assistants—the men and women in the underwear department—could repair by designing a matte to be employed in a process shot that would produce a revolutionary uplift—a quasi satire of the depth model in which the film indulges.

To press that line of argument would be to do violence to a film that, finally, is no satire. However critical *Vertigo* may be of the agency of painting in forcing our eyes wide shut, the picture never fully disinvests from the pathos of art, which is not merely the pathos of possession but that of permanence. The thoroughly practical Elster exploits that pathos, but his curatorial ambition, exhausted by the successful acquisition and exhibition of Madeleine, does not extend to preservation at all, which he leaves to Scottie as an obligation unfulfillable in part because of the vertigo that disables him from performing either his duty or desire, and in part because he refuses to recognize the institutional support that is a condition for preservation and even more so for the restoration that must be undertaken when the attempt to preserve and protect fails.[37] Hitchcock takes up that project with the foresight of Elster, the tools of Midge, the passion of Scottie, and with the knowledge that failure awaits him. The endurance of the Palace of Legion of Honor as an institution emancipated from market considerations guarantees that each visitor to the palace is a member of posterity. Not so for the movie audience, whose living memory was the final screen for almost all motion pictures. After World War II the stopgap practice of reissuing box office winners to meet an insatiable demand dramatically slowed, as the industry shifted to low-budget features and big-budget gambles. In the early 1950s there was one chance to see most movies, and then they were gone; cans of films on flammable, unstable nitrate were left in studio vaults to rot or be destroyed.[38] The television industry, which helped destroy the studios, saved motion pictures from abandonment by creating a secondary market for Hollywood products, especially for color movies that would help sell color televisions. Nonetheless, not all survived. And because the reproductive requirements for television were not demanding, especially where color was concerned, departures from the original, whether through intent or by neglect, were the norm.

For Wasserman or Hitchcock, who shared a commitment to preservation, this was not so: preservation in the name of empire for Wasserman, whose objective of evacuating a deal-driven agency to rehabilitate a lackluster studio flouted the conventional wisdom by reversing the emigration of the moguls from the world they had made; preservation in the name of legacy, and even, perhaps, in the name of art for Hitchcock. He could only imagine betting on a future with the prospect of security that a corporation sempervirens could extend and, more particularly, with the assurance of curatorial good faith that only a proven master of money and men could plausibly make. Scottie assumes the responsibility of preserving Madeleine. But he cannot deliver anymore than can the archivist at Paramount. The prevailing color process, Eastmancolor, was subject to fading within a few years. Technicolor prints, Hitchcock's medium, were vulnerable to deterioration in storage. Tape transfers preserved only the information that the medium coded as essential. The perishability of films was in part a side-effect of the practicality of the industry. In part it was an effect of the lowbrow cultural status of the product. Ultimately, it was an effect of film's fatal materiality. We can give reasons for the canonicity of Homer and Keats and argue about the contingency of their stature, but the possibility of permanence is the very condition of such arguments, for what persists of Homer or Keats is not a book but a text, a script for the performance of identification independent of any physical manifestation. Chemistry underlies the visual and the plastic arts, however; whether tempera or oils, Praxiteles or Minnelli, it is the colors that go first.[39]

Like the Frigidaire, Kim Novak was a color-coordinated product. Harry Cohn had branded his star by supplying her with an ensemble of lavender outfits with which she had been identified since she had signed her initial contract with Columbia. When he loaned her out to Hitchcock he first tried to ensure that Novak's costumes would reflect the Columbia color scheme. Repulsed, he nonetheless pressed on—with equal futility—by suggesting that his star play the role as a blonde with a lavender rinse so that she would bear the Columbia brand. Novak herself was less demanding about the color of her clothes than Cohn. Anything but gray, she told Hitchcock. Hitchcock listened. And gray she got. As sensitive to the chromatics as to the pneumatics of Novak, Hitchcock got what *he* wanted from Edith Head, his costume designer, a somber gray business-suit tailored with nuances that would elude all but a lover's eye and would usurp the control of Novak's appeal from the vulgar Cohn by coordinating it with the distinctive style of eroticism that Hitchcock had commercialized as his own.[40]

Gray is one of five dominant colors—gray, green, lavender, brown, and black-and-white—in a motion picture that uses them systematically to compose what Roland Barthes would call its *studium*, a pattern of expressive and increasingly symbolic hues.[41] The primary color (though not one of *the* primary colors) is green: the jade green of the gown that Madeleine is wearing when she first comes to life for Scottie at Ernie's; the soft green of Judy Barton's sweater when Scottie confronts her at the hotel; the metallic green of the Bentley that she drives through the streets of San Francisco; and, almost finally, the oppressive green of the mammoth sequoias in a deep forest glade, barely pierced by light, where the detective interrogates Madeleine in order to penetrate her somnambulism:

> *Scottie*: What are you thinking?
> *Madeleine*: Of all the people who've been born and who've died while the trees went on living.
> *Scottie*: Their true name is *sequoia sempervirens*—always green, ever living.
> *Madeleine*: I don't like it.
> *Scottie*: Why?
> *Madeleine*: Knowing I have to die.

It is a poignant moment, in part because Madeleine has already passed from green to gray to a gravely elegant black-and-white; in part because although the thought that Madeleine divulges is presumably scripted, not her thought at all, her response to Scottie's unscripted botanical tag is, nonetheless, true for Madeleine and, ironically, true for Judy.

Both women are coded as very mortal beauties when they first appear in garb tinted a green that mimics the color of life. In what is perhaps a gesture to the Kim Novak trapped within the Judy who is entering once more the trap of Madeleine, lavender is selected as the color of the dress that Judy chooses to wear to Ernie's when she still has a choice. Lavender will not do for Scottie, however, who insists on the purgatorial gray that recalls the Madeleine of the Palace of the Legion of Honor and that invokes the melancholy persistence of a life already given over to death. The transfiguration of Judy and the resurrection of Madeleine occur in the hotel. Donald Spoto quotes Hitchcock,

> For that hotel room . . . I deliberately chose a hotel on Post Street that had a vertical green sign outside. I wanted her to emerge from that room as a ghost with a green effect, so I put a sliding glass in front of the camera, blurred at the top when she first appears. We raised this glass as she came toward Scottie. In other words, he saw her first as a ghost, but with the proximity she became clarified and solid. (*DFG*, p. 330; Figure 4.14)

We do not see what Scottie sees. For Scottie the room is lit by the sign of Empire, and the green light that it casts is the illusion of a man's freedom and power to revive his past and fulfill his dreams. For us the room is lit by Hitchcock, and the figure that materializes on the screen is Hitchcock's ideal, the

Figure 4.14

imaginative fusion of Grace Kelly, Kim Novak, Judy Barton, and Madeleine—always Madeleine. There is no better example in the classical Hollywood cinema of Samuel Taylor Coleridge's definition of the symbol, which is "characterized by the translucence of the eternal through and in the temporal. It partakes of the reality which it renders intelligible; and while it enunciates the whole, abides itself as a living part in that unity of which it is the representative."[42] This Madeleine may touch us, but she is no ghost; like the symbol she is an apparition: an emergent figure and a passing presence, what Barthes calls the *punctum* of the movie, which pricks us. And though we see this figure on film, and though she touches us, this has never been, so there is nothing to regret as the figure passes in front of the camera and solidifies into flesh.

At least that's my guess at what I would have seen were I in the audience at *Vertigo*'s exhibition in 1958. If only I knew for sure. I was just young enough not to care about missing *Vertigo*, to enjoy *North by Northwest*, and to be forbidden to see *Psycho*. I read Spoto while I was preparing to teach *Vertigo* for the first time in the early 1990s. When I read that paragraph I returned to my sixteen-millimeter reduction and confirmed my memory of what I had seen in that dark hotel room, which (it was true) was not a green but a dimly blue effect, a color that had made no sense to me and that I had now learned was the wrong color. Green was the right color both because it formally invoked Scottie's first sight of Madeleine, and, vitally, because it conferred the aura of immortality, "ever-green, ever-living." Scottie failed doubly to accomplish by restoration what he had failed to preserve: failed himself because his obsession was not, finally, proof against all evidence, failed the audience because his choice of color was not proof against fading. My bluish print seemed to prove that the aura was evanescent, its transience conditioned by the chemistry that had created it. Later I learned that the same fade into blue afflicted the original that had been copied and released around the country in 1983. The scholars I consulted—preeminently Robert A. Harris, one of the two collaborators on the restoration print released in 1996—confirmed that the technicolor three-color process in which *Vertigo* was shot, though more durable than any other, was not permanent in part because, as John Belton reports, in the early 1950s Technicolor "shifted" [from black and white negatives] to Eastmancolor negatives "which did fade." By the 1980s the original negative *had* faded, principally the cyan or yellow tint, which elements the green we see, leaving an excessively bluish hue.[43] The degradation would seem to vindicate Barthes, who like Scottie disparaging Midge's labors in the underwear department, dismissed color "as an artifice, a cosmetic (like the kind used to paint corpses). What matters to me," he added, "is not the photograph's 'life' (a purely ideological notion) but the certainty that the photographed body touches me with its own rays and not with a superadded light" (*CL*, p. 81).

Hitchcock selected the color of everlasting nature for one of his most artful scenes, a green that would assure the viewer that whatever human calamity ensues, the idea has been realized. The color's decay, however, may have been just what Hitchcock intended. He surely knew that Technicolor was not immortal: it would fade, and the iconic green would be the first color to pass away. Hitchcock surely envisioned the fading of his rhetorical colors even as he invoked them as the condition of his art. Belated though we be, it would be perverse not to save the phenomena by reading the hotel scene as the negation of the empire of the symbol, as the allegory of its own temporality. If, as Gilberto Perez has argued, cinema is the medium that brings to the screen a "material ghost," *Vertigo* uniquely brought to the screen an apparition haunted by an elemental awareness of its own dematerialization. It may be that when the first attentive viewers reflected on "Madeleine's" complaint, "I don't like it. Knowing I will die," it was impossible to identify that "I" as Judy playing Madeleine or Judy as Judy or Judy as Kim Novak. The passage of time, however, has conferred the credit on Madeleine herself, dressed in black and white and speaking as the film itself, haunted by the certain loss of its living colors and expressing "a tragic knowledge of the conditions of its own existence."[44]

Despite her beauty, despite her fancy accessories, and despite the wishes of her lover, Madeleine, because she will die, is not a work of art. *Vertigo* is a film whose greatness as a motion picture is to recognize that despite all the skill lavished on its creation, unlike art it will die. Yet *Vertigo* is also a motion picture whose greatness as art is to have faith that it will be restored. The narrative, of course, is a recipe for restoration, though not by some wandering Scot, paralyzed by his own yearning.[45] Hitchcock's own provisions for the movie prepared for restoration. Throughout his career, Hitchcock had shown faith in those with expertise, both on the production end—the camera men and set and costume designers—and on the consumption end, British, American, and French critics. That faith would eventually be vindicated, as auteurist, feminist, and psychoanalytic critics would give Hitchcock's reputation a revolutionary uplift and as, with astonishing ingenuity, James C. Katz and Robert A. Harris, would use computer technology to resurrect a *Vertigo* in all its sonic clarity and visual vividness.[46] Its DNA digitally altered, the film has finally become *Vertigo sempervirens* and achieved the permanence of art. It persists as a rebuttal to the formalism it interrogates.

There are reasons to distrust corporate empires as much or more than Madeleine distrusts the sequoia: artificial persons constructed for the convenience of hidden persuaders that exist outside of one's control and that persist beyond one's own mortal span. But there is equally good reason to distrust an independence that will always be crippled by the qualifier *fairly*. The difference between trees and empires is that you can make a deal with a mogul. There would have been no underwear department and no resurrection without the capital provided by Universal Classics, lineal descendant of MCA and MCA Revue, subsidiary of Universal Studio. Hitchcock did not put his faith in the studio system or in independence or in a museum but in the institutional genius and the monopolistic imagination of Lew Wasserman. Ultimately, Hitchcock's corporate faith betrayed him. As Thomas Schatz compellingly argues, after the departure of his key collaborators and despite his own relocation from "hotel" studios to a home studio, Universal, where his wishes were law, Hitchcock's work declined. The director learned that formal independence was no substitute for Robert Burks, Bernard Herrmann, Edith Head, Saul Bass, and his other long-standing department heads—a lesson that *Vertigo* teaches (*GS*, 491). That betrayal does nothing to invalidate the power of *Vertigo*, however, which may not have prevented Hitchcock's decline but which uncannily scripts the narrative of its own restoration, from the original vision through a mortal fading to a freshly green illusion. We should credit the author of that process as Lew Wasserman, the corporate architect of the push-pull between perception and representation, production and consumption, agency and ownership that Hitchcock would initially imitate, then meditate, and in which he would ultimately participate.

Saving Warner Bros.
Bonnie and Clyde, the Movements, and the Merger
(1964–1968)

> To be white and a radical in America this summer is to see horror and feel impotence.
>
> Andrew Kopkind

> Everything is given, without provoking the desire for or even the possibility of a rhetorical expansion. . . . We might (we must) speak of an *intense immobility*: linked to a detail (to a detonator), an explosion makes a little star on the pane of the text or of the photograph.
>
> Roland Barthes, *Camera Lucida*

Because Warner Bros. paid to make it and because the familiar Warners shield precedes its title card, *Bonnie and Clyde* is generally talked about as a Warner Bros. movie. But *Bonnie and Clyde* was never in fact a Warner Bros. product. As the closing credits declare, the movie was released in the summer of 1967 under the copyrights of two new and short-lived companies, Warner Bros.–Seven Arts and Tatira-Hiller, after Warner Bros. Motion Picture Corporation had ceased to exist. The regime had changed at Warners on November 14, 1966, when Jack Warner, the last surviving brother, sold his 1,573,861 million shares in the company for twenty dollars a share to Seven Arts Production, a company that *Variety* described as "basically a distributor of old pictures to television stations." The terms of the takeover, which would be completed the following July, "stipulated that [Jack] would remain an independent producer and the company would finance his pictures." One recent beneficiary of Jack Warner's support was Warren Beatty, who, earlier in 1966, had secured financing for the David Newman and Robert Benton script of *Bonnie and Clyde*, which he planned to produce. Warners was not Beatty's first choice. He had contacted the studio only after he had been turned down at Twentieth-Century Fox and toyed with by United Artists. Beatty eventually struck a deal with Warners that guaranteed a remarkable ownership share of 40 percent of the adjusted gross to Tatira-Hiller, a production company formed by Beatty and named after his parents.¹

The chief executives at Warners never wanted to make the movie. According to legend, Beatty had to crawl on his knees to Jack Warner and plead for the $10 million dollars he needed. According to Beatty, "Warners didn't understand the movie at all. They wanted us to shoot it on the back lot. There's a letter in the studio archives where Jack Warner says: "What does Warren Beatty think he's doing? How did we [sic] ever get us into this thing? This gangster stuff went out with Cagney."[2] Beatty's anecdote suggests that Warner is mistaken about "gangster stuff." Yet it's not clear *how* Warner was supposed to have been mistaken: by assuming that "gangster stuff" no longer had a market, or by thinking that *Bonnie and Clyde* was in fact "gangster stuff"? If *Bonnie and Clyde* had not appeared under the Warners shield but at United Artists or Fox, it would have been seen for what it is: a bandit picture like the original Bonnie and Clyde movie, *You Only Live Once*, a 1937 United Artists release, which was produced by Walter Wanger, not Warners, or like *Jessie James*, made in 1939 at Fox, not Warners.[3] No one in the company except Jack Warner mistook *Bonnie and Clyde* for gangster stuff: the pressbook attests to the movie's peculiarity by coining for it a new category: "oddball action picture," which fits, though the moniker was not a good bet to attract mobs.[4]

i. The New Sentimentality and the Old Put-On

Arthur Penn confirmed that Jack Warner didn't like the movie at all.

> Beatty tried to explain the picture to Warner. He spoke with painful deliberation, his sentences swallowed by the ominous silence that filled the room. Finally, grasping at straws, he said, "You know what, Jack. This is really kind of a homage to the Warner Brothers gangster films of the '30s, you know?" Warner replied, "What the fuck's a homage?"[5]

Whether or not the anecdote is true, there is no doubt that in accepting the job to direct *Bonnie and Clyde*, Penn, at least, had an idea about making an homage, though not to Warner Bros. He was replacing his hero, Francois Truffaut, David Newman and Robert Benton's choice to direct the self-consciously avant-garde film, which they had written in part as an homage *to* the avant-garde, a movement, which, according to the partners, was reverent toward its forbears. In an article "The Movies Will Save Themselves," which appeared in *Esquire* in October 1968, more than a year after the release of *Bonnie and Clyde*, the screenwriters observed that it "is possible for the most avant-garde film to be, at least to the filmmaker, partly a synthesis of and a reverence for the work of other directors. Which is only natural. Our script for *Bonnie and Clyde*, for example, is consciously influenced by Hitchcock, Hawks, Truffaut, Godard, Bergman, and who knows how many others, as well as by its own director Arthur Penn."[6] Newman and Benton do qualify their cineast's piety somewhat. "But if today's movies are full of yesterday's," they add, "it still seems to most observers that there is a new something in them, and to our mind what that is his [the filmmaker's] personal statement" ("MWST," p. 186). The screenwriters followed the critical consensus by illustrating their statement with reference to the "unmistakable signature" identifiable in the films of well-known directors: in a "Griffith film" and "of a Ford, a Hitchcock, a Hawks, a Siegel, etc." Auteurism assimilates the new personal statement, the past personal statement, and the future personal statement, his, yours, and mine, as aesthetic *variants* of each other. The deliberate enactment of that aestheticization is the signature of Arthur Penn in *Bonnie and Clyde*.

Penn's signature is legible in the movie's bravura opening scene, which he identified as his favorite.⁷ The scene begins with a dissolve from the credit card that introduces Clyde Barrow to an extreme close-up of a woman's vividly red lips just as the last touch of lipstick is applied. Then a lick. And then the lips press together to seal the color. The blond head turns, and a quick pan reveals the face of an attractive woman in a mottled mirror. She tests a smile and leans closer as if to penetrate the pretty face to whatever might be behind. A sequence of quick cuts to agitated close and medium shots of the woman increase our sense of her anger and frustration. Then, as she moves behind a dressing screen, the camera cuts to an objective high-angle shot, through a window screen, of a man inspecting a car. Cut back to the woman, and a pan as, still naked, she moves toward the window. Reverse cut to a close-up of her framed by the window screen.⁸

Bonnie, at the window, looks down, and we see the first shot from her point of view: man inspecting a car. Reverse to her in close-up as she calls out, "Hey, boy, what you doin' with my momma's car?" Reverse to Clyde as he looks up to the source of the voice, shielding his eyes with the brim of his hat. Reverse again to a shot from his point of view that closes the distance between them and frames her torso through the screen, as she leans on the top of the lowered windowpane that obscures her nakedness down to her waist (Figure 5.1).

Figure 5.1

Clyde gazes at the picture in surprise and delight. In Penn's words, they have "locked on to each other." The spectator's balance is restored by the end-stopping of the jarring New Wave syntax with an iconic shot of a woman in a window: a framed portrait of a classicized, modestly nude female figure, softened and flattened by the medium of the screen. Clyde has never seen anything like it. As a matter of fact, neither have we: we see through Clyde's eyes the figure that has been assembled from those pieces like an epiphany, the material elements of screen and wooden window frame dematerialized into media for the effective presentation of the image of beauty in repose. When, without its subject's premeditation, the momentarily transfixing portrait is hung on a blistering white wall, we are invited to regard the serene picture as an artful transformation of the nervous, intimate, allusive montage signed, "Arthur Penn, postmodernist."

By announcing what Newman and Benton call "a new thing," the opening sequence functions as what Fredric Jameson would later refer to as a "periodizing hypothesis"—a term he ventured in order to apprehend the postmodern *nouveau déjà vu* as a historically specific successor to modernism that distinguishes itself by dissolving historical specificity. Alan Liu subsequently enfolded Jameson's "periodizing hypothesis" in the figure of the "historicism paradox" as a defining feature of the debates over postmodernism in the 1980s and 1990s. "On the one hand," Liu writes, "postmodern experience has been described as the aestheticization of historical reality. Where once things mattered, historical matter (economic, social, political, cultural) now appears indistinguishable from the phantasmic." Our example is the frustrated, perspiring working-class woman who is transformed into an aloof lovely image, framed and screened. As Liu writes with reference to the other side of the paradox, "the fierce debate over whether . . . this transformation of matter into a phantasm is something *really* new or just another feat of style . . . proceeds precisely on the grounds of economic, social, political, and cultural matter—that is, on the presumption of a substrate able to determine the rise of the new world order of indeterminacy."[9] We shall ask how novel a "feat of style" must be to qualify as a substrate. How does style matter?

Newman and Benton betrayed no anxiety about a substrate in which to anchor *Bonnie and Clyde*. In an arch essay published in *Esquire* in January 1964, they had proposed as a catchphrase for a new era, "the New Sentimentality," a label as superficial as the phenomena it was meant to synthesize. The renovation, they assert, had gone unnoticed by "the wise people and the intellectuals," who believed that "there was no more sentimentality in them," but who, in fact, had "merely exchanged Old Sentimentality for New Sentimentality."[10]

Some "wise people and intellectuals," such as David Riesman and the multitude of readers of *The Lonely Crowd*, had, of course, noticed the change fifteen years earlier: the old and the new sentimentalities are nicknames for "the inner-directed" and the "other-directed" character types that, according to Riesman, had successively dominated American society. Newman and Benton would not have been touched by such criticism, however. Attention to historical precedent is part of the old sentimentality; repackaging the types of *The Lonely Crowd* needs no justification under a dispensation in which packaging is all. The *Esquire* piece makes its contribution by boiling sociological concepts down to popular affect and by providing illustrations—that is, photographs—of the representative figures in what Douglas B. Holt calls, the contemporary "myth market," where obsolete icons can be exchanged for the current models.[11]

On their established principle that neither values nor meaning count in contemporary culture, that it is instead the mobility, immediacy, and the style of feeling that matters, Newman and Benton reject every notion that people have concocted to explain what *Bonnie and Clyde* "was *really* about: 1) Lee Harvey Oswald; 2) the riots in Watts; 3) police brutality (anti, of course); 4) the Hippie movement; and 5) Vietnam. And sometimes people got mad," they recall, "when we said, or director Arthur Penn said, that it really wasn't about any of those things, it was about Bonnie and Clyde and a lot of other ideas and theories and themes that we had." What "ideals and theories and themes" they actually held is not quite spelled out. Newman and Benton's indifference to events in the world outside the cinema does not mean that they dismiss history or interpretation, however. On the contrary, they are excited by the cultural phenomenon of impassioned readings of the movie by contemporary college students, which are so different from the studious interpretations produced according to the clinical "precepts, concepts, and practices" of the New Criticism in which they were schooled:

> Now, the students are responding with real fervor to works of art (and movies most often) only when they can somehow relate the movies to their own *outside* experiences, ideas, life. They bring *outside* interpretations to films or force films to correspond with preconceived notions, and then, if it seems to work, they dig the movie. The advantage of this to the film maker is that he can't do anything about it (if he does, it will probably look forced) and so much just be as good and inventive as he can, send the picture out into the world and *see what the reverberations are*. ("MWST," p. 186)

When, in her landmark review of *Bonnie and Clyde* in the *New Yorker* in October of 1967, the pre-postmodern Pauline Kael wrote that "violence is its meaning," she may have had such an aesthetic in mind. Or Newman and Benton may have thought she did. And they may very well have had her famous review in mind as they retrospectively formulated their artistic project according to a "kiss kiss bang bang" poetics.[12] Yet even with Kael's endorsement, the word *reverberations* was hardly innocent in 1967. Amid the news reports of riots at home and war abroad, Benton and Newman must have looked irresponsible even to some readers of *Esquire* for promoting the notion that motion pictures should be lit, shot, and detonated around the globe just to watch the reverberations.

Of course, it is unlikely that Benton and Newman actually intended to place *Bonnie and Clyde* in the incendiary context of, say, the illustrated recipe for a Molotov cocktail that appeared on the August 24, 1967, cover of the *New York Review of Books*, which reverberated in the nation's editorial pages during the "Vietnam summer." They would have agreed with Kael that their movie is different from other kinds of provocations because it is art. Like Clement Greenberg specifying the potency of modern painting, Newman and Benton identify the interpretive fervor that the cinema arouses in terms of its distance from literature. "It is safe to assume," they write, that "the cinema lends itself to such a variety of interpretations because visual images tend to be more ambiguous than words in a book. The director can make his setup and call his shot, but you just might get a fix on a table lamp in the corner of the frame and decide that's the real meaning of the image." They add that "this quest for ambiguity has, to a great extent, been encouraged by filmmakers in the last few years. Odd juxtapositions of subject matter or of images themselves have been so freely used that audiences have become educated to expect the shattering of 'continuity'" ("MWST," p. 187). That's a change, all right. The students of the New Criticism were educated to expect an ambiguity constrained by convention and the demands of coherence. The students of the new ambiguity are educated or, as Eisenstein might say, conditioned in the movie theater to expect that the next moment will be nothing like the one before or the one to come. They learn the idiom and the attitude of what Liu would later call "the stubbornly noncognitive *and* noninstrumental aesthetics . . . that Walter Benjamin . . . dubbed 'reception in a state of distraction' . . . and that postmodern theory has updated into a whole aesthetics of everyday distraction." Liu inventories postmodern theorists who are connoisseurs of what he calls "the microstylistics of sensation: Lyotard's 'feeling' for the 'unpresentable'; Deleuze and Guattari's 'pure intensities'; Baudrillard's 'ecstasy'; Haraway's 'pleasure in the confusion of boundaries'; de Certeau's 'almost invisible pleasures, little extras'; Jameson's 'boredom as an aesthetic response'" ("RSG," p. 265).

I want to add to that list a microstylistic of manipulation: Pauline Kael's "put-on." In her review of *Bonnie and Clyde*, Kael declared,

> It is a peculiarity of our times—perhaps it is one of the few specifically modern characteristics—that we don't take our stories straight any more. . . . *Bonnie and Clyde* is the first film demonstration that the put-on can be used for the purposes of art. . . . *Bonnie and Clyde* keeps the audience in a kind of eager, nervous imbalance—holds our attention by throwing our disbelief back in our faces. To be put on is to be put on the spot, put on the stage, made the stooge in a comedy act. People in the audience at *Bonnie and Clyde* are laughing, demonstrating that they're not stooges—that they appreciate the joke—when they catch the first bullet right in the face. The movie keeps them off balance to the end. . . . Instead of the movie spoof, which tells the audience that it doesn't need to feel or care, that it's all just in fun, that "we were only kidding," *Bonnie and Clyde* disrupts us with "And you thought we were only kidding." (*KKBB*, p. 62)

Kael's observation that "we do not take our stories straight anymore" anticipates Lyotard's famous assertion that the abandonment of grand narratives is the salient characteristic of the postmodern condition, but the point of the put-on for Kael is to tease those who would make such a portentous claim. Kael's put-on contributes to the capricious pluralism of postmodern art by lowering the brow of art lovers from the elevation achieved by postwar modernism. Unlike either a deception or a hoax, the put-on cannot be carried off without humor and often involves a moment of enlightenment by the victim and, perhaps, a moment of deliberate self-exposure by the perpetrator.[13] The put-on mothballs irony in favor of a new kind of kidding that is not "only kidding." When Kael invokes that moment in the movie when the fun first stops being funny, she has in mind the sequence of the gang's first bank robbery. After the comically labored success of C. W. Moss (Michael J. Pollard) in parking the getaway car in a tight space jeopardizes the gang's escape, the panicked Clyde fires his pistol into the eye of the teller, who has climbed on the running board. The shot shatters the window, shatters the lens of the man's glasses, and, of course, shatters the light-hearted mood induced by the musical soundtrack and C.W.'s clumsiness, which had distracted the audience from the seriousness of the business of armed robbery. We may have been hip enough to expect some kind of discontinuity but not this *violent* discontinuity. Yet even the focal violence in this scene is a distraction from the reality of murder that the vulgar might take it to represent, since, as every reader of the *New Yorker* or *Esquire* should know, it invokes the shot of the old woman spectacularly shot through the lens of her glasses during the Odessa steps sequence of Eisenstein's *Potemkin*. The violence of the shot in *Bonnie and Clyde* is aestheticized by Penn's punctilious framing of an imitation of another image embedded in a montage sequence that also aimed to shock but which had a political valence that is completely absent from the sentimentalizing American motion picture.

For Kael, the cultural disposition that favors the put-on is the eagerness of moderns to put history off by remembering it as legend. And "part of what makes a legend for us Americans," she argues, "is viewing anything that happened in the past as much simpler than what we are involved in now"—which, Kael neglects to add, is also a convenient way of viewing anything in the *present* as much simpler than what we are involved in now, including the self-interested effort of heavily capitalized organizations to mobilize resources to produce a seamlessly simplified past for our viewing pleasure (*KKBB*, pp. 64–65). The capitalist backstory is addressed in a surprisingly complementary review of *Bonnie and Clyde* by Peter Collier, which appeared in the left-wing journal *Ramparts*. Collier argues that Bonnie and Clyde's

> celluloid lives make no real criticism of the status quo that supposedly oppresses them. It is a myth of pop nihilism; it is Andy Warhol's serial put-ons packaged in a dramatic context with all of Hollywood's savvy behind it. . . . Periodically, the gang meets up with people who have the slack-jawed bewilderment and gutted stares of the faces in a Dorothea Lange photo album; there is even a fleeting attempt to suggest Clyde's sympathy for those dispossessed and vicariously broken by Wall Street, heading West to stagnate in despairing Hoovervilles. It is all there—but as window-dressing for fantasia. . . . The setting is used in much the same way that the world of advertising uses backgrounds: to create more or less subliminal presumptions in favor of what they're trying to sell."[14]

Like Kael, Collier observes that *Bonnie and Clyde* simplifies history as legend or myth and makes no real critique of the status quo. They agree that the poor people whom Bonnie and Clyde meet are merely stereotypes flattened into a backdrop for the vivid escapades of its "gorgeous" heroes. And, finally, they conceive of the movie as a series of put-ons, which identify it as a species of contemporary art—that is, Collier implies, if you think that what Warhol does is art.

Collier could have made more of his observation about the connection between advertising and the depiction of poor folks who are practically a different species from Bonnie and Clyde. Clyde's declaration to the dispossessed farmer, "We rob banks," is an affirmation of purpose to which he has recourse not out of sympathy but only to extricate himself from the embarrassment of *not* sympathizing with the farmer's predicament. When, during the later scene at the lakeside shantytown, an older man, who looks like he has just been working in the fields, reaches into the rear window of the getaway car, Clyde lifts a bloody hand just high enough that the man can barely flick one of his outstretched fingers across the ontic distance that separates the famous from the abject. That gap is apparently crossed during the couple's visit with Bonnie's family in the barren sand pits, but in order to convene the two worlds of the family and the gang Penn cagily chooses to transform "the material into the phantasmatic," shooting the scene through a window screen, which produces the effect of an uncanny animation of a faded family photograph. Jack Shadoian nicely captures the peculiar isolation that the other-directed band of outlaws paradoxically bear: "Penn lets his characters run away with the film as if the world they moved through was of no consequence, as if, in fact, the characters were not part of that world at all but actors who have been asked to impersonate certain temperaments that can be potent in combination with others—the world become a stage."[15]

The world is not, however, divided simply between the properly named actors and the anonymous folk. Unlike the eerily bland Chicago of *The St. Valentine's Day Massacre* (Los Altos, 1967), the walls of the West Texas towns are dotted with numerous colorful signs advertising Coca-Cola, Pepsi, Clabber Girl Baking Powder, Philip Morris cigarettes, Camels cigarettes, and Franklin Delano Roosevelt, signs whose sharp contrast with the peeled paint on the walls where they are tacked distracts the eye. The signs too inhabit another plane of reality from the anonymous "folks." For one thing their historical authenticity is indisputable. The same advertising was there on the same walls when Dorothea Lange and Walker Evans came through snapping their photos. Such signs, small and large, affixed to walls, brandished over storefronts, or looming along the highways were often photographed by the artists of the WPA, who captured the local ironies inadvertently produced by the relentlessly cheerful corporate interpellations of folks without two nickels to rub together.[16] The pervasive advertisements do not convey irony in *Bonnie and Clyde*, however. Just as the visual quotations from Dorothea Lange and Walker Evans familiarize the folk, the ads for Coke, Pepsi, Philip Morris, and Clabber Girl dissipate the alterity of the past.

Looking back at the movie in 2000, David Newman endorsed the anachronistic feel of the main characters that troubles Collier and Shadoian as the key to the picture's relevance:

> *Bonnie and Clyde* is about style and people who have style. It is about people whose style set them apart from their time and place so that they seemed odd and aberrant to the general run of society.... What first attracted us in the mythology was hearing about the photos Bonnie and Clyde took of each other and mailed to the news-

papers, the doggerel poetry that Bonnie wrote, the business of Bonnie posing with a cigar, and so on.... It was Andy Warhol's "fifteen minutes of fame" long ahead of its time, for surely their skill as bank robbers was pathetic. But their skill at creating "images" for the public could have gotten them the Coca-Cola account today.[17]

Bonnie and Clyde conspicuously advertises the ability of movies to sell. In the scene that follows the killing during the botched hold-up, the trio takes refuge in a movie theater. Clyde and C.W., absorbed in apologies and recriminations, do not even notice the movie screen. Bonnie is engrossed by a Warners musical, though it is unlikely that she knows or cares who made the movie. Newman and Benton care little more. *Gold Diggers of 1933* is introduced but as an advertisement of the costumes of the showgirls, who are exulting, "We're in the money," while stylishly wearing jewelry that *looks* like gold coins. After the cut away from the movie screen, we see Bonnie once again looking in a mirror, this time putting on a necklace strung with discs that also look like gold coins. Unlike Judy Barton simulating Madeleine, who, when she looks at her ruby necklace in the mirror, sees the blood that bonds her to a possessive male, Bonnie is in her *own* money—she integrates the showgirls' jewelry into *her* look. The possibility of being a gold digger is out of Bonnie's reach. Whose gold would she dig in this dingy world far from Hollywood and New York? When Bonnie's photogenic good looks are matched with her reputation as a desperado, however, she will become a personality that has a right to a picture in the newspaper.

Bonnie's manipulation of the press to enhance the gang's celebrity and, later, to publish their story aligns her with what Bosley Crowther, esteemed movie critic for the *New York Times*, notoriously denounced as the "raw and unmitigated campaign of sheer press-agentry [that] has been trying to put across the notion that Warner Brothers' *Bonnie and Clyde* is a faithful representation of the desperado careers of Clyde Barrow and Bonnie Parker, a notorious team of bank robbers and killers who roamed Texas and Oklahoma in the post-Depression years" (quote in *FBC*, p. 22).[18] Bonnie had to perform as her own press agent. Faye Dunaway was luckier: she got the press with little push on her part. In an interview edited into a documentary on the anniversary two-DVD release, Dunaway recalls her surprise that, when she attended the London opening, "everybody there looked like me!"[19] All the girls were wearing their new berets, imitating Faye as Bonnie, just as Bonnie imitated the chorines. Rarely does someone want to buy Newman and Benton's "lamp in the corner," even if it does trigger an interpretation. The beret, however, like the necklace, is one of those metonyms of a star that enables the pleasure of consumption to stand in for the work of interpretation. To buy a beret *is* to understand *Bonnie and Clyde*—not because its success depends on profits from the sale of hats, but because, just as Bonnie interpellates her readers as the medium of the couple's legend, the movie interpellates the spectator as the medium for the transmission of its brand.

As creator with Benton of *Esquire*'s original "Dubious Achievement" awards, Newman had impeccable credentials to designate Bonnie and Clyde as forerunners of the Warholian dispensation. But for Newman to praise the couple's ability to snag the Coca-Cola account suggests that he has not watched his movie closely.[20] *Bonnie and Clyde* is keenly interested in Coke, but neither the characters nor the motion picture have any interest in *representing* the product, even though it is the case that Coca-Cola signs are prominent among the many simple, colorful advertising signs mentioned above (Figure 5.2). Unlike Penn's portrayal of Bonnie and Clyde, which glamorizes Bonnie's mythmaking, and his depiction of the itinerant dispossessed, which flatters Dorothea Lang and Walker Evans, the historical authenticity of the signs in the movie is not in doubt. They are the same ones that the Farm Security Administration photographers would have seen had they passed through snapping their photos. Crucially, *Bonnie and Clyde*'s advertising signs are *not* product placements, even—indeed *especially*—for Coca-Cola, which is singled out for mention before we see any signs at all.[21] In the opening scene, after Bonnie descends from her room and mocks Clyde by saying that he does not have enough money to buy a car, he replies, "I've got money for a Coca-Cola." But at the end of their stroll he does not buy a Coca-Cola. The bottles from which he and Bonnie drink a brown beverage are generically shaped and unlabeled (Figure 5.3). Now it may be that Clyde had the money for one Coke but not for two. Or it may be

Figure 5.2

Figure 5.3

that the store was out of Coke. Or it may be that he was using the name Coca-Cola generically to apply to all soda pop. Or it may be that in their refusal to have the characters represent Coca-Cola, the filmmakers were here as mindful of Andy Warhol's precedent, that is, his famous painting of the Coca-Cola bottle—as elsewhere they were of the directors of the New Wave.

Warhol's breakthrough painting is swathed in anecdote. Arthur C. Danto has recalled Emile de Antonio's legendary account of a visit to Warhol's apartment in the summer of 1960:

> One night . . . I went over and had a bunch of drinks and he put two large paintings next to each other against the wall. Usually he showed me his work more casually, so I realized this was a presentation. He had painted two pictures of Coke bottles about six feet tall. One was just a pristine black-and-white Coke bottle. The other had a lot of abstract expressionist marks on it. I said, "Come on, Andy, the abstract one is a piece of shit, the other one is remarkable. It's our society, it's who we are, it's absolutely beautiful and naked and you ought to destroy the first one and show the other."

Danto comments that "the Coke bottle is one of the classic shapes of modern sensibility, and archeologists of the future will surely see inscribed in its silhouette the narrow-waisted female form, and infer from its form its function, to hold some sweet elixir of arousal and fulfillment."[22] As Danto reads D'Antonio, Warhol's pristine black-and-white painting of a Coke bottle momentously shifts interest from the representation to the represented, whether as the "we" of D'Antonio's "who we are" or as Danto's "elixir." *Bonnie and Clyde*, however, insistently displays advertisements that represent no products at all: no one in the movie smokes a Camel, drinks a Coke, or bakes a cake with

Clabber Girl. *Bonnie and Clyde* depicts a world in which there is no abundance of anything except signs of an economy not quite sunk by the Depression: an economy of representations.[23] While *Bonnie and Clyde* may distract the viewer from the actual social and economic conditions that historians tell us contributed to the Depression, the movie nonetheless accurately reads the legend of Bonnie and Clyde as having a historical tendency that the filmmakers aspired to fulfill. In *Bonnie and Clyde* the Coke signs represent, not what Bonnie and Clyde want to buy or what they might want to sell, but what they want to *be*, not products or ad agents for a product but an iconic brand, like Coca-Cola or like Warner Bros. Moreover, the stylish Bonnie and Clyde, precursors of Tatira-Hiller, know that the prospects for a potent brand are dependent on the organization that constructs and manages it, not the particular products that the brand may encompass.

That's the *organization*, not the director. Newman and Benton would not have agreed. As faithful adherents of the *Cahiers du Cinema* line, and stalwart in their support of Penn's auteurship, they insisted that "if there is one thing we have learned beyond any question in the movie business it is this: once there is a director, he is the boss. . . . There can only be one general, in spite of all the theories advanced by non-directors promulgating the notion of 'film-making by committee.'"[24] Kael, however, whose faint praise stops just short of damning Penn, implicitly nominates another candidate when she approvingly quotes Beatty's comment that "there's not one scene that couldn't have been improved by another day's shooting," which she interprets as evidence of the producer's refinement of his sense of timing by the pressure of financial responsibility (*KKBB*, p. 72). Of course the comment also suggests that Penn did not get any scene just right, and that it was Beatty alone who knew what improvements could have been made. Warner Bros. may have been reluctant to take ownership of *Bonnie and Clyde*, but Beatty did not hesitate to do so at any stage of production, distribution, or exhibition. He indulged his collaborators' pious objectives of making a statement, rolling out a style, paying homage, or pursuing a "quest for ambiguity"; but he shared these objectives only insofar as they advanced his own heretical objective of transforming Bonnie and Clyde, the faded legend, into *Bonnie and Clyde*, the "iconic brand."

According to Holt, "brands become iconic when they perform identity myths: simple fictions that address cultural anxieties from afar, from imaginary worlds rather than from the worlds that consumers regularly encounter in their everyday lives." He adds that "the source materials for American myths exist wherever populism takes its most authentic form. Populism thrives wherever people are thought to act according to their own beliefs rather than have their actions shaped by society's institutions: on the frontier, in bohemia communities, in rural backwaters, in immigrant and African American neighborhoods, in youth subcultures." The people who consume these myths rarely inhabit the populist world. The myth and the iconic brand it subtends provide consumers with an imaginary connection to such worlds. Holt argues that "iconic brands function like cultural activists, encouraging people to think differently about themselves. The most powerful iconic brands are prescient, addressing the leading edges of cultural change. These brands don't simply evoke benefits, personalities or emotions. The value of a particular myth resides not in the myth itself, but in its alignment with society's incipient identity desires" (*BM*, p. 9). Holt's account of the iconic brand's genesis and social function— its populist origins, its mythic dimensions, its satisfaction of widespread cultural anxieties—corresponds with the insights that shaped the script of *Bonnie and Clyde*, which combined the élan of the New Wave with a true-life crime story in order to renovate populist legend as contemporary myth. Of course, Newman and Benton did not talk about their movie as an ambitious marketing enterprise. They just wanted to get it made. Yet even if the marketing techniques for branding were unfamiliar to the pair (a dubious hypothesis), the concept of a work of art as an icon was not. As students of the New Criticism they would have known something about *verbal* icons from the work of W. K. Wimsatt, whose aspirations for literature and for literary theory could hardly have been more remote from the world of getting and spending. Still, Newman and Benton could have found something to take away from *The Verbal Icon*: specifically, the relation of iconicity to a dynamic form, which Wimsatt calls the "concrete universal."

In the essay by that name, Wimsatt observes "that literary theorists have from early times to the present persisted in making statements which . . . seem to mean that work of literary art is in some peculiar sense a very individual thing or a very universal thing or both." His purpose is to inquire "what that paradox can mean" and "by the inquiry to discuss not only a significant feature of metaphysical poetics from Aristotle to the present day but the relation between metaphysical poetics and more practical and specific rhetorical analysis."[25] That may sound like an arcane pursuit, but an entire generation of ambitious undergraduates, students of literature who were unscarred by the Depression or by combat, followed Wimsatt's lead and learned that it was a short step from inquiry into what a paradox can mean to insight into how a paradox can be managed. And it was just another step from mating poetics with rhetorical analysis to applying that analysis to a rhetorical practice that succeeds on Madison Avenue or, as in the cases of David Newman and Robert

Benton, in the pages of *Esquire*. It paid, then, to pay attention to Wimsatt. Following Steven Knapp's analysis of Wimsatt's argument, in *Literary Interest: The Limits of Anti-Formalism*, I hope to show that it still pays—even if our goal is not, like Newman and Benton's, to write the script for a movie but the more modest objective of interpreting one.

Knapp connects the problem of the concrete universal to the problem of reference. Any universal will be a generalization, referring to some shared idea or attribute. Contrarily, the concreteness of the particular literary object or symbol or poem as symbol involves detachment from reference. To explain the literary symbol as a concrete universal requires that we understand "what it means to be *more* interested in a representation than in what it represents."[26] Knapp quotes Wimsatt's attempt to specify what it is about Shakespeare's Falstaff and Cleopatra that makes them instances of the concrete universal. "A kind of awareness of self," Wimsatt argues, "with a pleasure in the fact, is perhaps the central principle which instead of simplifying the attributes gives each one a special function in the whole, a double or reflex value. Falstaff or such a character of self-conscious 'infinite variety' as Cleopatra are concrete universals because they have no class names, only their own proper ones, yet are structures of such precise variety and centrality that each demands a special interpretation in the realm of human values" (*VI*, pp. 78–79). Knapp observes that mere self-reflection is not sufficient to account for the concreteness of Falstaff as symbol, because he reflects only on shared attributes and because self-reflection is just another form of reference. Knapp shrewdly focuses on the "pleasure in the fact" of that self-awareness as the critical element in Wimsatt's formulation because it suggests that "to imagine the existence of a concrete universal in Wimsatt's sense might consequently be to treat a symbol as if it could itself have—or perhaps as if it could *be*—an experience, which would amount to treating it as if it could have or be a body" (*LI*, pp. 63–64). To rephrase Knapp's proposition: to be interested in the representation or symbol rather than what is represented or symbolized is as if one were to imagine (oneself as?) a character in a play, as if that character were embodied in order to experience pleasure in the sheer fact of that embodiment, a pleasure and a fact that are empty of semantic content and without referential orientation. We'll return to the mechanics of this operation later, but it is worth noting here that Wimsatt's "reflex" and Knapp's "as ifs" both involve a movement of the attention or the imagination that is decisive, and, moreover, that movement of attention is not conditional on the use of verbal language; it could just as easily be carried out in a live action movie such as Godard's *Breathless* or an animated movie such as Pixar's *Wall-e*.

Wimsatt's theory of the concrete universal corresponds fairly closely to the theories of experiential marketing and iconic brands proposed a half-century later by marketing theorists who regarded the brand as a symbol that involves consumers in embodied experiences, which create brand-loyal customers who take pleasure in the fact of that embodiment. In the relentlessly ingenious discipline of marketing theory, the brand icon currently stands at the apex of what Mark Batey calls the four levels in "the evolution" of the brand. The phases progress from (1) unbranded commodities that lack any differentiation: for example, soap, lords, cellophane, officers, mouthwash, carriers, Travelers, and Attendants; to (2) the use of the brand as "differentiation of products primarily along functional lines, identifying their utilitarian benefits with a distinctive name": for example, Windex, Westmoreland, Scotch tape, Mortimer, Bromo Seltzer, Poins, Listerine, Gadshill. That phase is subordinate to the process of (3) deliberately building "emotional appeal into their brands, endowing them with personalities of their own and fleshing them out in advertising": for example, Chevrolet, Hotspur, Mr. Clean, Domitius Enobarbus, Lucky Strikes, Owen Glendower, Charmin, Dame Quickly. In that third stage, "a closer affinity starts to develop between consumer and brand, with the consumer becoming an active participant in the relationship and the molding of the brand's meaning." Finally, (4) "with time and consistency some brands become meaningful symbols to large groups of people. They become iconic brands": for instance, Falstaff, Coca-Cola, Cleopatra, McDonald's. "Icons are beacons of meaning within a society. . . . By the time this stage is reached, where the brand has come to represent something bigger than itself and its meaning is predominantly symbolic, the brand has effectively become decoupled from the product life cycle as traditionally defined."[27]

My assertion of a congruence between the evolution of mere commodities into brand icons and the transformation of mere words into verbal icons follows from Knapp's suggestion that we "treat a symbol as if it could itself have—or perhaps as if it could *be*—an experience, which would amount to treating it as if it could have or be a body" (*LI*, p. 64). I would add the marketer's codicil that such a treatment need not entail the existence of an *individual* flesh-and-blood body or, indeed, the need for any *real* flesh-and-blood bodies at all. By design, many people could have (or could believe they were having) virtually the same experience by, say, flipping open the magnetic cover of an Apple iPad2, and could take pleasure in that fact without any reference to the significance or function of the experience, even if they were in no contact with each other. Such a conclusion deducts from the equation all the grossness of fat men and women that, as Knapp notes, disgusted Socrates in the *Ion*, for if any symbol could be treated *as if* it could have an experience, and any experience could be treated *as if* it had a body, and any body could be treated *as if* it were flesh and blood, then any flesh-and-blood body could be treated as if it were without any grossness, without any matter at all except for the minimum of surmise that would provide what Liu calls "a substrate" for the imagination's construction of the concrete universal. Batey and Holt, I take it, would wholly accept this development of Wimsatt's logic, for the fecund productivity of the imaginative "as if" is what Batey, at least, means when he asserts that "these brands, decoupled from the product cycle, "break out of their category and into the culture" (*BM*, 203). An iconic brand sponsors an interest in representational *practices* and poetics, not in what is represented or in representations as such. To get into the icon business is to get out of the reference business altogether.

If the crucial turn for conceptualizing the concrete universal is to imagine the symbol as having an experience that is tantamount to having a body, marketing theorists would agree that one of the most visible and convincing examples of an iconic brand identity achieved through a brand that seems to acquire a body and take pleasure in the fact of that embodiment has been the sight of a group of middle-aged and mostly middle-class men and women of no other particular affiliation rollin' down the highway on their Harleys, each wearing a muscle shirt that exposes a Harley-Davidson tattoo on his or her arm in a collective experience of "Harleyness." Holt, Batey, Pines, and Gilmore among others, venerate Harley-Davidson as the company that has had remarkable success in crafting a brand icon that incorporates consumers' "total experience" (Figure 5.4).[28] As the logo-bearing consumers congregate and collaborate, "the brand's center of gravity gradually shifts from manufacturer to consumer. By the time the brand has escaped from category into the culture, its passage into consumer ownership is complete" (*BM*, p. 204). In Harley culture, "what it means to be *more* interested in a representation than in what it represents" is that you have joined a brand community by virtue of your embodied experience of a symbol, a membership which—crucially—does not depend on your making any kind of a purchase but does entail your participation in a shared representational practice.[29] The sentimentality of the new sentiment consists in the return of that experience to a filmic text that has been emptied of its semantic content, or, as Friedrich Schiller might say, the new sentiment is the imagination of the avant-garde motion picture as one that reflexively takes itself as a naïve pretext for pleasure in the sheer fact of its own embodiment.

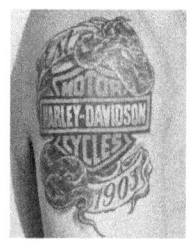

Figure 5.4

The autotelic dynamic that Wimsatt and Knapp adumbrate and that Batey and Holt would later apply is realized in *Bonnie and Clyde*.[30] As we have seen, from their polar positions on the critical spectrum Kael and Collier agree that, unlike the photos of Dorothea Lange, which the filmmakers imitate, *Bonnie and Clyde* is not an authentic document of the Depression in part because it shows more interest in Lange's representation of the poor than in those people she sought to represent. Unlike Collier, Kael does not regard the lack of authenticity as a fault; she reveres no category except the undefined honorific, "art." With an eye on the devices that the movie manipulates to achieve its effects, Kael shrewdly observes that in the shantytown scene the audience is embodied in picture by being "transformed into the poor people, the Depression people of legend—with faces and poses out of Dorothea Lange and Walker Evans and *Let Us Now Praise Famous Men*" (*KKBB*, p. 65). Kael does not consider the moral or political implications of the transformation of the historically actual poor people of the Depression into the "legendary poor"; for her what matters is the transformation of the audience into that peopled legend. Lange and Evans's familiar "faces and poses" serve as vehicles for an audience identification that provides the feel of social solidarity as we, like them, witness the passion of Bonnie and Clyde.

Our observation is mediated, of course, but that is not a meaningful criticism, for it is the first lesson of Postmodernism 101 that all observation is mediated and all positions posed. The viewers of *Bonnie and Clyde* can reasonably believe that they occupy the same legendary space as the poor who are watching Bonnie and Clyde because these figures are provided solely in order that we can put them on. We may differ about whether the viewers' belief is true, whether the scene actually produces the transformation that Kael describes, but it can hardly be doubted that the scene is *about* how transformations from a collective that shares only dire material conditions, a table, firewood, and beans, into an audience in which each individual may have his or her own embodied experience while sharing a common object of attention, namely the sight of the suffering Bonnie and Clyde. Arguably (and *Bonnie and Clyde* is that argument), such a sentimental semiotics, when practiced by an expert production team, can produce a stronger feeling of connection among people who are remote in time and place than economic conditions could ever generate.

The scene at the lakeside camp begins with a high-angle shot of a two-toned sedan approaching an odd lot of the dispossessed in a tent, tending a campfire, and seated around a table in a barren tract of land alongside a lake—a landscape that is the objective correlative of the "the human erosion" of the time.[31] When the car stops, a shirtless C. W. Moss gets out (Figure 5.5). From the extreme long shot that barely shows a mark on Moss's chest, the camera cuts to a view from behind the boy. But, without our seeing it closely in this scene, we know exactly what the poor people see on his chest, because in an earlier scene

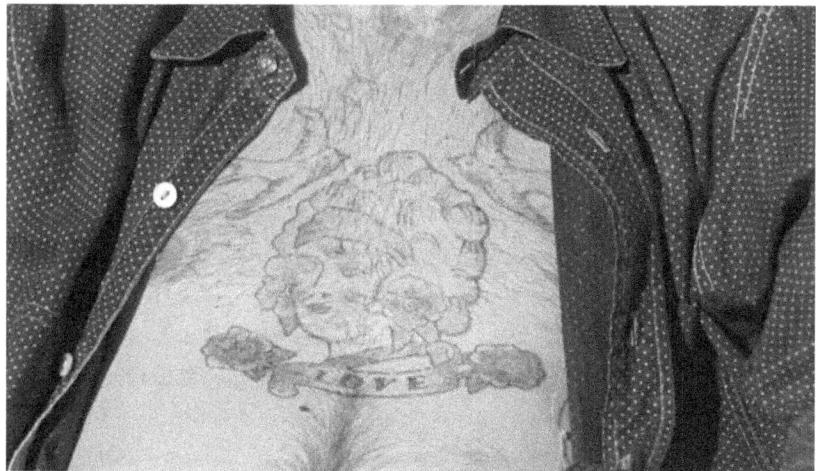

Figure 5.5

in Bonnie and Clyde's motel room we were introduced to C.W.'s tattoo. There Buck studied the new design on C.W.'s chest, a picture of two birds facing each other and hovering over the head of a woman, which has "LOVE" written underneath it (Figure 5.6). Buck fingers the tattooed image of the woman's head: "Who is this there? Is that your girlfriend?" C.W. shakes his head. Buck spells out, "L-O-V-E" and asks, "Well, whose idea was it to get Bluebird?" C.W. takes off his gas mask and points to Bonnie sitting at the vanity: "Bonnie's. Bonnie picked it out." The smiling Buck persuades Blanche to touch the tattoo. When she does, she screams in repulsion. Bonnie lashes out, "If you two want to play with C.W., why don't you take him outside." The tattoo by now has become a flashpoint for smoldering resentments among the gang, the first example of a reverberation catalyzed by the brand of "Bonnie and Clyde." In persuading C.W. to get tattooed, Bonnie has used him to devise, promote, and control the

Figure 5.6

public image of the gang as Bonnie and Clyde bonded by love, not Bonnie and Clyde and Buck and Blanche bonded by blood and marriage. With the inscription of the logo on his chest, which is the embodiment of his special intimacy with Bonnie and Clyde, C.W. becomes the incorporating trademark of "Bonnie and Clyde" and the medium for projecting that product to the public, a realm to which Buck and Blanche have been suddenly assigned.

As we see at the shantytown, the sign of a love that enfolds the socially and sexually deviant in a brand community has considerable power in the legendary world of *Bonnie and Clyde*. When the bare-chested C.W. steps out of the car and exposes his tattoo, he is fulfilling his functional identity as the bearer of the trademark of a corporation that is now, after the deaths of Buck and Blanche, held together not by blood but by "LOVE." When C.W. crouches at the fire he asks, "Can you spare us some drinking water?" A man responds, "Who are you boy?" C.W. replies, "The name's Moss." It cannot be the name that moves the man, for, as we will learn when the trio returns to the Moss home, that name has never been in the newspaper. As we see when the man rises and goes over to a crowded table where all eyes are trained on Moss's exposed chest, what grasps their attention is the tattoo (Figure 5.7). Everyone at the table stares at the branded Moss, except for one woman, whose eyes shift from him to the car. When Moss returns to the car with water the man had given him, the woman rises and follows him at a distance to the vehicle. The shot is held on Moss as he climbs into the car and pours water into the cup for Bonnie (Figure 5.8). Captured in that frame is the inquisitive woman, who appears in the rectangular frame of the rear window, shading her face from the sun, peering through the glass at Bonnie. She looks as if she has fit together the vehicle with the tenor and

Figure 5.7

Figure 5.8

experiences a recognition of the whole, independent of any semantic content. She is a symbolic placeholder, having the embodied experience the spectators in the audience have not quite attained.

When the trio arrives at the Moss homestead, C.W.'s father, Malcolm (Dub Taylor), immediately recognizes his son's tattoo as Bonnie and Clyde's mark, an inscription that makes his boy the nameless medium of their brand. After Clyde tells C.W. that he ought to be glad that the newspapers always refer to him as an "unidentified suspect," Malcolm angrily confronts his son in the kitchen:

> *Malcolm*: You look like trash, all marked up like that. Cheap trash!
>
> *C.W.*: Bonnie says it looks good.
>
> *Malcolm*: What does Bonnie know? She ain't nothin' but cheap trash herself. Look what they do to you. You don't ever get your name in the paper. You just get those pictures painted on your skin by Bonnie and Clyde. Ssshoot, they ain't nothin' but a couple of kids.

C.W. may think that the tattoo is a mark of Bonnie's partiality for him, but the derisive Malcolm correctly identifies the tattoo as the mark of the firm named "Bonnie *and* Clyde," which, in exploiting the docile body of his son, is feeding its urge to monopolize the publicity it relentlessly generates.

Because of Malcolm's treacherous deal with the Texas Ranger, C.W. survives the massacre. So does the tattoo. And so does the other medium of the Bonnie and Clyde brand, the nameless bodies of the spectators, who will suffer the stunning beauty of the slow-motion montage of gun blasts that twitch and twist and perforate and, finally, still the bodies of the couple. When the gunfire is done the posse leaves its hiding place in the bushes to cross the road. In extreme long shot two black men run toward the camera, which tracks sideways, momentarily acquiring the frame of the car door; then, slipping the frame, it slides opaquely across the bullet-riddled metal. The point of view is subtly transformed from third to first person as the lens forcibly contrives a subjectivity by restricting its view to no more than its position, *my* position, allows. The camera settles at the back of the car, looking through the back window, a perspective that reverses the point of view of the woman in the camp scene who had peered through the same window at the wounded fugitives. This window is centered, however, by a bullet-hole that focuses my field of vision on the lawmen, who, in looking at the corpses of their victims, seem almost to see me clearly, "intensely immobile," through the puncture in the protective screen (Figure 5.9).

"I" have lost the theatrical distance of the spectator that the poor woman's merely vicarious watching metaphorized, which does not mean that I have become complicitous or a participant: nothing I could do or say would have changed the outcome of this story or its pattern of bursts of alternating high jinks and (increasing) violence, spasms of sex and death—a pattern that resists identification and disables those vicarious affiliations that have been formed. In the final scene we find our point of view *within* the motion picture, unattached to any surrogate, as if the final shot required our embodied experience to give the motion picture its uniquely thrilling shape. As Knapp writes, "The only thrill inseparable from this particular configuration of metaphors is the thrill produced by encountering this particular configuration of metaphors, a thrill—that is, an experience—whose contours are uniquely defined by the particular cognitive and emotive effects of these metaphors and the temporal order in which they succeed each other" (*LI*, p. 67). By focusing through a

Figure 5.9

unique lens, the camera transforms what is seen in the familiar third-person narrative syntax into a scene that only this *particular* spectator is experiencing—a perspective that thrillingly absorbs each spectator in the theater into the picture suddenly with no memory of Eisenstein or Truffaut or Godard and no conditions except that she must have a point of view that refers back to the "semantically empty" cinematic representation called *Bonnie and Clyde*. To put it in Wimsatt's terms, the spectator has been imaginatively re-created as the embodied referent of the moving picture which "absorbs the interest of its referents into itself and contains it in an impractical stasis" (*LI*, p. 50), as the brand of Bonnie and Clyde has absorbed the interest of its referents—C.W. Moss, Buck and Blanche, Sheriff Hamer, Malcolm, the dispossessed.

ii. The New Left and the Postmodern Style

By the time *Bonnie and Clyde* was released in August 1967, at the tail end of the Summer of Love and little more than a month after the release of the Beatles' album *Magical Mystery Tour*, which included the anthem "All You Need is Love," the choice of the trademark tattoo during the shooting the previous winter must have seemed inspired.[32] But that choice also makes the movie vulnerable to charges of complicity with the so-called "cultural turn" of the student movement that, according to Michael Szalay and Sean McCann, occurred in 1967, when "the movement cut itself off both from older traditions of organized dissent" and embraced "a new political vision built in large part on the appeal of the spontaneous, the symbolic, and ultimately, the magical."[33] Szalay and McCann restate the thesis of an older generation of consensus liberals, such as Seymour Martin Lipset, who, as Wini Breines observes, distinguished between "youth groups" and "adult political organizations by their emphasis on what Max Weber has called 'the ethic of absolute ends,' as contrasted with 'the ethic of responsibility.'" Breines quotes Lipset: "Their politics is often expressive rather than instrumental. The New Left groups also have no clear concept of any road to power, of a way of effecting major social change."[34] Perhaps. Nonetheless, stress on the irrationalist urge of the many has obscured the political work undertaken by the few before and during the summer of 1967, those who organized tens of thousands student volunteers to lead "'teach-outs' instead of 'teach-ins' in order to organize workers, professionals, housewives, clergy, and anyone else in their communities who had doubts about the war."[35] Consequently, like their liberal forebears, Szalay and McCann "fail to recognize the degree to which the new left sought to discover organizational forms and instrumental mechanisms that could be both effective within the given political arena and consistent with the so-called anti-political motifs of the movement" (*GR*, p. 5).

One unforeseen consequence of the Vietnam Summer Project was its key role in modeling the social psychology of the antiwar movement by way of Kenneth Keniston's *Young Radicals*, published in 1968. After interviewing a group of radical leaders in the National Office of Vietnam, Keniston felt able to distinguish these community organizers from "the old New Left," with its emphasis on electoral politics and coalition building and "the new New Left," which included the more militant and anarchist elements of Students for a Democratic Society (SDS). Keniston also contrasts these "radicals," who "systematically attempt to reform and change their society," to the "hippies [who] turn their backs on society in their effort to find meaning through an intensification of personal experience." Both radicals and hippies, however, share an opposition to violence, a hostility toward institutions, and, most important, a "postmodern style," which involves "a focus on process rather than on program, which reflects a world where flux and change are more apparent than direction, purpose, or future."³⁶ Keniston does not diverge ideologically from Liu or Szalay and MacCann; he is just more discriminating, particularly in his avoidance of the politics-culture divide of the liberal commentators and of the materiality-versus-mere-style opposition that Liu invokes. That Keniston foregrounds style as the hallmark of the New Left does not foreclose the conceptualization of a substrate. Keniston announces the arrival of "a postmodern world," which is a strikingly innovative periodizing hypothesis: not only because he is one of the first writers in English systematically to apply the term *postmodern*, but also because his hypothesis is based, not on something concrete or tangible, but on something temporal and transitory. Drawing on the psycho-historical work of Erik Erikson, Keniston associates the postmodern style with a new developmental period of "postadolescence," which is "an emergent state of life that intervenes between adolescence and adulthood" and which has been made structural by a developmental time lag between the achievement, first, of psychological maturity and, later, of sociological maturity that has been generated by the so-called automatic affluence of postindustrial society (*YR*, pp. 263, 260; italics in the original). Wini Breines's subsequent analysis is similar to Keniston's, except that what Keniston calls a "postmodern style" she names "prefigurative politics," recognizable in "counterinstitutions" that were the vehicles for the organized but "essentially anti-organizational politics characteristic of the movement." The young radicals endeavored "to create and sustain within the live practice of the movement, relationships and political forms that 'prefigured' and embodied the desired society" (*GR*, p. 6).

According to J. Hoberman, *Bonnie and Clyde* was embraced by leftist critics in *The Guardian* and *New Left Notes*, where it was called a movie that "defines a revolutionary's lot." As Hoberman suggests, at this much later date it may seem to be more sensible to read the free-swinging flick as a parody of the outlaw wing of the antiwar movement, ideologues without a program, which had already begun its helter-skelter dash toward violence and despair.[37] Ironically, however, the Barrow gang's cultural activism did eventually result in something they would recognize as a notable outcome: a motion picture—and one that takes the politics of prefiguration seriously. The shantytown scene may transform the movie audience into the Depression poor, but it only does so by first transforming the Depression poor into an audience—a maneuver that, as I have tried to show, prefigures the final scene, which immures the spectator within the movie as fully as Falstaff is immured in Henry IV. *Bonnie and Clyde*'s relative effectiveness depends on a strategic choice that one would think the radicals would have repudiated: the motion picture exploits the correlation between prefigurative politics and modern marketing as that practice was defined by Peter F. Drucker in the mid-1950s. Effective marketing must begin, Drucker argued, with the recognition that "there is only one valid definition of business purpose," which is not to make a profit but "*to create a customer.*"[38] The marketer must *prefigure* a customer in order to create him or her as a consumer with needs that his business will satisfy. Drucker's management theory is programmatically indifferent to the objective of institutionalizing a business on the model of a Metropolitan Life or an AT&T. Drucker urges that good managers proceed under the guidance and security of the *concept* of the corporation not under allegiance to any particular manifestation. Consequently, each manager who understands the core importance of marketing to assuring profitability must ask herself each morning, "What business are we in?" and be ready to alter her answer in response to the changing needs of the customer whom she and her colleagues are continually re-creating.

Beatty had created Jack Warner as his initial customer, but the effort was almost wasted: neither Jack nor other top executives followed through by deploying the company's capacity to market *Bonnie and Clyde*: the institution could not imagine customers for the movie because it had not "grown up" sufficiently to recognize the new sociological reality of a youth audience immune to the allure of Jack's vanity picture, the lackluster *Camelot* (Warners, 1967). The radicals of the 1960s cherished the hope that the egalitarian communities they formed while marching, sitting in, and burning their draft cards collectively were the type of a transformed society in which people could realize their productive potential untrammeled by repressive bureaucracies. *Bonnie and Clyde* represents a prefigurative "politics" that is indistinguishable from marketing a brand—the closest thing to an institution in which those precocious cultural activists could believe. The motion picture represents itself as the antitype that fulfills the ambitions of the type of the outlaw and his admirers: the people's yearning for a community devoted to something greater and more glorious than themselves could be satisfied, not by the NRA, the WPA, the FAA, SDS, or PLP, but by participation in an iconic brand, itself prescient of a future in which a new America or—in the case of Tatira-Hiller—a new Hollywood could be created.

iii. The New Wave and an Old Opposition

Keniston's sympathetic reflections on the radicals' quixotic adherence to their political ideals have an air of melancholy. Newman and Benton's contemporaneous jubilant reflections on the success of *Bonnie and Clyde* are well-nigh messianic. There could hardly be a more grandiose expression of confidence in the power of cultural activism than the title of Newman and Benton's article in the November 1968 issue of *Esquire* that poses on its cover the question, "Can We Salvage the Twentieth Century?" Newman and Benton's answer, "The Movies Will Save Themselves," invokes neither the political culture of the New Left nor the counterculture of the hippies, but movie culture. Not only does the claim of self-sufficiency deny a need for help, it also presupposes a disavowal of any political or social responsibility as a condition for survival. To grasp the character and scope of the team's ambition, we need to return once again to the 1930s: not that decade as represented by the imagery of FDR and the New Deal, or of Dorothea Lange and Walker Evans, or even Coke and Clabber Girl, but as indicated by the eventful publication in 1939 of Clement Greenberg's article "The Avant-Garde and Kitsch," in the *Partisan Review*.

According to Serge Guilbaut, Greenberg's essay broke the impasse in which leftist artists of the Popular Front found themselves as their commitment to a politically engaged art was undermined by the news of Soviet brutality and treachery. Greenberg accepted Trotsky's diagnosis of "the causes of the crisis of Western culture . . . namely, the crisis of capitalism and the decline of a ruling class," while carrying "Trotsky's defense of a critical art that remained 'faithful to itself' one step further, maintaining that while the avant garde did indeed do critical work, it was criticism directed within, toward the work of art itself, toward the very medium of art, and intended solely to guarantee the quality of the production."[39] Greenberg distilled the threat of capitalism into the menace of kitsch, ersatz, "popular commercial art," which appeals to the "insensibility" of the "new urban masses" by exploiting the availability "of a fully matured cultural tradition, whose discoveries, acquisitions and perfected self-consciousness kitsch can take advantage of for its own ends."[40] "By making kitsch the target," Guilbaut argues, "Greenberg gave artists who were at a loss for what to do next the means to act. By fighting through art against mass culture, artists enjoyed the illusion of actively fighting against repugnant regimes, using the weapons of the elite.... Greenberg's position led to a complete break with the political approach taken during the Depression. He appealed to socialism to save the dying culture so as to be able to carry on the artistic tradition" (*HNYS*, p. 37).

Greenberg does not foreground conservation, however, when he distinguishes avant-garde art from a pious Alexandrianism that evades controversy. "The avant-garde moves," he declares, "while Alexandrianism stands still" ("AGK," p. 10). Greenberg's strategic decoupling of culture from the vicissitudes of politics and of the avant-garde from rigid academic approaches to art in the name of an imperative *movement* engaged the 1960s generation of self-creating avant-garde auteurs among American filmmakers: men such as Penn, Robert Altman, Hal Ashby, and Bob Rafelson, who may not have been Greenbergian modernists in their tastes or tools but who struggled to respond to another artistic initiative headquartered in Paris, led this time by Truffaut and Godard, not Picasso and Matisse, and who struggled to resist Hollywood's pressure to conform.[41] When Greenberg asserts that in the past "the true and most important function of the avant-garde was not to 'experiment,' but to find a path along which it would be possible to keep culture *moving* in the midst of ideological confusion and violence," he might have been prefiguring *Bonnie and Clyde*'s manic repudiation of both generic decorum and political content. Perform the substitutions: "the true and most important function of the Barrows gang was not to 'experiment,' but to find a path along which it would be possible to keep their vehicle *moving* in the midst of ideological confusion and violence" ("AGK," p. 8). The same might be said about the production company under the prod of Beatty, who pressed Penn to maintain a high velocity of distractions that would render the spectator breathless as he was sped past the posters of FDR and the signs of dispossession to the retardant death scene, which is as vivid a presentation of a picture moving fatally toward what Wimsatt had called an "impractical stasis" as there had been in the history of Hollywood.

If Greenberg, a cultural activist by anyone's definition, would have projected his prescience into the postmodern world, his article might have been entitled, with a nod to Newman and Benton, "Art Will Save Itself," and subtitled, with a nod to Serge Guilbaut, "By Stealing the Idea of Modern Art." By stealing the idea of postmodern filmmaking from Paris, Benton and Newman came to occupy the one available position that the modernists left uncovered:

"the avant-garde *as* kitsch." Greenberg had stigmatized the *New Yorker* as being "fundamentally high-class kitsch for the luxury trade, [which] converts and waters down a great deal of avant-garde material for its own uses" ("AGK," p. 13). Newman and Benton could imagine, however, that *Esquire* performed the same function for avant-garde movies in the new sentimentality of the 1960s as the *Partisan Review* performed on behalf of avant-garde painting and literature in the obsolete sentimentality of the 1930s, although to a much larger readership, which is flatteringly represented in the advertisements for Johnny Walker scotch, Hathaway shirts, and Marlboro cigarettes that almost crowd out the prose. Drawing this analogy may be interpreted as betraying Greenberg by attaching his prestige to "artists" whose main effort is not to save art but to commandeer a defense of art on behalf of a commercial enterprise that continues to be art's worst foe. Greenberg would hardly be in a position to dispute that survival justifies radical measures, however. Moreover, even if, especially if, Newman and Benton's own policy conflicts with Greenberg's agenda for paintings (in "The New Sentimentality" Newman and Benton expressly ally with Lichtenstein, not Pollock), it does so by renovating Greenberg's own categories, that is, by accepting that movies *are* kitsch and trying to work out a defense of them in those terms.

iv. The New Hollywood and Corporate Avant-Gardism

By the time Newman and Benton published "The Movies Will Save Themselves" in October 1968, *Bonnie and Clyde* had become the iconic brand that its narrative had designed. The movie was, according to Robert Sklar, "a cultural phenomenon. . . . Bad press did not kill the film. . . . It was as if audiences understood better than either the distributor or the critics the emotional power of the film's anarchic individualism." He celebrates its success in the absence of any media prompting as a populist victory.[42] The studio was even less help. Warner and Kalmanson smothered its release by burying it in the sticks in August. After taking over from Jack Warner, Hyman, head of Warner-Seven Arts, resisted re-releasing *Bonnie and Clyde* even after the recantations among the reviewers during August and September 1967, after the *Time* magazine cover devoted to *Bonnie and Clyde* in December, and after the extraordinary Paris debut, when the movie proved its myth-marketing power by selling berets to the French. The only pressure that ultimately worked on Hyman was Beatty's inspired threat of a lawsuit—not on any specific grounds, but on his suspicion that the executive had been involved in shady operations sometime or other and would himself suspect that Beatty knew more than the nothing he did. Warners-Seven Arts took the all but unprecedented step of re-releasing the movie in January 1968, just in time for it to receive ten Oscar nominations (*PR*, p. 370). If breaking free of the product cycle is the criterion for capturing the status of iconic brand, *Bonnie and Clyde*'s exceptional re-release in response to the demand of an audience that Jack Warner did not even suspect existed proved that by forging its own myth of its singularity, the movie had become the iconic brand it had imagined.

"Entering into the culture" does not entail establishing an institution organized either to achieve an articulated objective or to endure for an indefinite future. From the liberal perspective of Riesman, Bell, and Lipsett, *Bonnie and Clyde*'s culturalist orientation is politically inconsequential. Nonetheless, despite the successful efforts of cultural activists to exploit anarchic enthusiasm, the iconic brand is not intrinsically *anti-*institutional. Prefigurative politics invests in *institutionality* as the placeholder that spans (or patches) the gap between a psychological break with the past and the advent of new social or economic institutions adequate to the populist cultural impulse. The brand icon is not falsifiable. I argued earlier that participation in the Boys Town brand is creedal: just as Father Flanagan's plans for the future can be falsified by a default on his loan, so is the proposition in which we believe "there is no such thing as a bad boy" falsifiable in principle. Falsifiability makes the creedal commitment appear to be on a rational basis; that is, it makes sense to believe in something that is falsifiable and absolute. And if you do, if you cannot falsify the proposition, you must believe in everything that follows from it: which is how Father Flanagan gets more donations, more mortgages, more buildings. The brand icon is also creedal, but it requires something more like the willing suspension of disbelief that constitutes poetic faith. If you do not believe in Harley gear or stock up on iPhone accessories you just do not experience the affective solidarity of the Harley-Davidson or Apple brand communities, even if you buy a Harley cycle or a Macintosh computer. The creedal brand is related to the iconic brand as a conviction about reality is to the sentiment of really belonging.[43] MGM had been a studio committed to institutionalizing its values and eminence—a trope of authority—whether by means of autotelic figuration, as in *The Grand Hotel* and *Singin' in the Rain* or by means of analogy, as in *Boys Town* and *Executive Suite*. Warners' gangster and gold-digger movies make claims for the legitimacy of marginal, even criminal modes of living by force of their critique of prevailing social and economic institutions—the police, the courts, the banks—as frozen violence. *Bonnie and Clyde* mounts no critique of institutions. By imagining violence as a vehicle for the manifestation of style, the motion picture dissolves and dissipates both the facts of history and the conventions of realism in order that they may be re-created as an icon that achieves institutionality by appealing over the heads of the producers and arbiters of mass culture to the demos as an incipient market for a new mode of social organization and as a body that can be absorbed in the brand. The act: a corporate takeover. The result: impractical stasis.

Beatty was not the first actor to produce and star in his own motion picture. Burt Lancaster worked as producer and coproducer, credited and uncredited, on a handful of films made by Lancaster and Hecht in the 1950s.[44] Kirk Douglas earned executive producer credits on *Spartacus* and *Grand Prix* in the 1960s. But it is fair to say that no actor-producer since Chaplin had been as intimately involved with all aspects of a Hollywood production—including distribution and exhibition. And unlike Chaplin, who was a partner in United Artists, Beatty had to negotiate every step of the way, from acquiring the initial financing, to acquiring a 40 percent stake in the profit, and, ultimately, to get the picture on the screen so the audience that wanted to see it could see it. As producer he innovated an organizational style that departed dramatically from the studio-mimetic productions of postwar independents and that successfully adapted to the instability in the post-Paramount industry. His dominance has not been sufficiently acknowledged in part because he exercised it rarely. Robert Towne, who served both as Beatty's collaborator in rewrites and as mediator between Beatty and Penn in their daily "discussions," commented to Mark Harris that "the fact that Warren had nursed this material, that it was within his control, paradoxically allowed him to give up control more easily to a director" (*PR*, p. 247). And yielding control to Penn meant yielding more control to the actors, who were allowed more opportunity to improvise. Yielding control also meant increased responsibility for the novice art director Dean Tavoularis, and costume designer, Theadora van Runkle—both of whom rose to the challenge. Beatty's major responsibility was to protect the project from Jack Warner's thoughtless interference or, what would be equally damaging, his disdainful neglect. Warner may have only been thinking of himself as he made the deal with Seven Arts, but during the last year of his authority at the studio, thinking of himself meant thinking of *Camelot*. After the extraordinary success of *My Fair Lady*, Warner had been confident that another Lerner and Loewe musical would be the kind of glorious success that would inevitably invite Arthurian comparisons with his own decision to end his long reign over his kingdom of make-believe. *Camelot* quickly proved to be a failure with the critics and at the box office and therefore an uncrowning disappointment to Warner (*PR*, p. 357). Jack had never wanted to be just one of the Warner brothers; he wanted to be *the* Warner brother—an impossible, self-nullifying wish. Beatty's ambition was large but more restricted: he not only wanted to establish *Bonnie and Clyde* as a Warner Bros. motion picture but to identify Warner Bros. with *Bonnie and Clyde*—not with either Jack Warner or Seven Arts.

For Beatty, owner and operator of Tatira-Hiller, the only politics worth playing was studio politics. He adroitly manipulated the means at his disposal to displace the corporate line of succession at Warner Bros. and to project a fundamental change in its corporate structure. In Newman and Benton's redemptive terms, *Bonnie and Clyde* undertook to save the motion picture industry by demonstrating how a declining major anchored to a failing business model could be rebranded as a cultural icon of substantial value to corporate managers who understood their financial success to be bonded with their cultural and political role; the Tatira-Hiller's motion picture prefigures a new Hollywood and, in doing so, projects a new model of citizenship, which I have called corporate populism, as an alternative to the lapsed consensus that liberals esteemed or the participatory democracy of which radicals dreamed.

Beatty preempted Newman and Benton's argument that "the movies will save themselves" by executing a marketing strategy presupposing that the movies could only save themselves if they also saved the studios from the death wish that gripped every executive office in Hollywood. Warners' unloading of the studio had devalued Warner Bros.: he did not appear to care what it was worth. Warner's handling of *Bonnie and Clyde* also devalued the studio: he did not know what it meant. He was intent on casting away the opportunity that Beatty had presented him of rejuvenating the Warner Bros. brand for the new era that, by the fall of 1967, many foresaw. Hyman stuck to his objective, which was to sell the studio not to manage it. Once he took charge, he further degraded the brand by shopping the studio for buyers, by cutting back on production, and by abandoning the traditional Warner Bros. shield for the pseudocool, modernist mark that visually integrated the Warner Bros. "W" with a "7"—telecommunications lite (Figure 5.10).

Figure 5.10

Tatira-Hiller saved Warner Bros. for the sake of *Bonnie and Clyde* and, incidentally, for the sake of the "undertaker," played in real life not by Gene Wilder but by Steve Ross, who had begun his business career as a funeral director in his father-in-law's company and would end it as co-CEO and undisputed leader of Time Warner Inc. Ross would prove the accuracy of Beatty's periodizing hypothesis, which, though not trumpeted like Newman and Benton's "New Sentimentality," matches Keniston's: the key to the spirit of the age was not the Vietnam War or the civil rights movement, the young radicals or the counterculture, but the uneven development between the precocious artistic maturity of filmmakers like Warren Beatty, Robert Altman, and Hal Ashby and the industry's sudden confrontation not with its death but with its sociological immaturity, its failure to develop the institutions that would exploit talents that had already become too sophisticated for the classical format. Postmodern filmmaking explored the poetics of the put-on, which for Beatty, as for Steve Ross after him, was the essential technique in the art of the deal.[45] In pursuit of a record company, Steve Ross, the almost unknown chief executive of Kinney Corporation, a miscellaneous corporate assemblage of funeral homes, parking lots, and so on, would come in 1968 to bury the studio but then would praise it, having recognized its value as an iconic brand and the ideal base from which to launch a multiplatformed media corporation that would provide the fitting institutional format for the postmodern style developed by the New Wave, the New Left, the New Sentimentality, and the New Hollywood (*MG*, pp. 48–58). Beatty prepared the way by taking advantage of the peculiar circumstances of the studio, orphaned by Warner and un-integrated by Seven Arts, that made it available for a symbolic takeover that would replenish the company's brand and revalue it as one of the few indispensable studios over the next forty years.

Beatty announced his corporate takeover of Warner Bros. in the form of a put-on that has become legendary. In an interview recorded for the special features section on the fortieth anniversary reissue DVD of *Bonnie and Clyde*, Beatty, recounting his struggles with Jack Warner to get his way, retells the story of a confrontation that occurred during the production: "There was a terrific moment when Jack Warner was telling me that I was wrong about something and we were having an argument and we were in his office and he said, 'Well, You see whose name is on the water tower, don't you?' And, uh, it occurred to me as he said it that I thought I remembered that it was the initials. And I went over to the window, and I looked, and uh I said, 'Well, it's my initials.' And, uh, that was a good moment."[46]

Beatty, of course, was referring to the large "WB" centered in a shield, the company's trademark, which at the time was emblazoned on the studio's peaked water tower. Beatty's joke has bite because it exploits the weakness of Warner's position as the superannuated founder and head of a studio by mocking not only his loss of authority but his contingent relation to the name "Warner Bros.," which, through his own actions, has suddenly become the groundless caption to the initials "WB" emblazoned on the studio's water tower. Warner's decisions to sell and to concede a 40 percent share of the adjusted gross on *Bonnie and Clyde* to Tatira-Hiller are the enabling conditions for Beatty's double-edged put-on, which severs the studio from its founder and former owner while reinforcing its status of the studio as an iconic site of identification, either through the initials W.B. (if you have them) or the name Warner Brothers (if it means something to you in a way that it no longer does to the man whose name it formerly was). From here on Jack Warner becomes merely J.W., an elderly man who will have to satisfy his residual identity aspirations by going to the movies like everyone else. And for the time being, if there is to be a Warner Bros., WB has a greater claim to ownership than J.W. because he does know something: to have an ownership stake in the phenomenon of *Bonnie and Clyde* is to have a stake in a Warner Bros. that no longer belongs to Jack Warner, who founded the studio, or to Kenneth Hyman, who bought it, but belongs instead to the culture at large and to anyone in particular whose experience of the movie has marked him or her. Recall that when Dore Schary was challenged by Mayer regarding his decision to take a producing credit on *Battleground*, unlike Thalberg and himself, who shunned that ostentation, Schary replied that Mayer could afford to be modest in the credit roll because his surname was embedded in the name of the studio and offered to forsake future producer's credits if "Schary" were to be added to the sequence Metro-Goldwyn-Mayer.[47] Schary's wry suggestion was met with indignation by Mayer, and, of course, it was a doomed claim, first, because Schary's timing was wrong and, second, because he had insufficient corporate capital to compel a change. Beatty marked his time as right by putting his initials on the icon and, in the vacuum of authority, thereby signing himself as the auteur of the Warner Bros. that would be.

One must remember that whatever else changes in Hollywood, both prominence and power depend on credit: credit where credit is due, and credit where credit is not due. The credits at the beginning and end of a motion picture include the prescribed acknowledgment of artistic, technical, and financial contributions; the statement of copyright, which identifies the formal owner of the narrative representation imprinted on the reel of celluloid; and the formal opportunity for the display of the studio logo, which represents the corporate brand that subsumes all residual symbolic revenue that the motion picture generates, whether or not the studio has sold the copyright, whether it owns any print of the motion picture, or whether it collects royalties from future screenings. Beatty had right of approval with *Bonnie and Clyde*, and rights to the sequence, size, font, color, sound, and pacing of the credits. As a consequence, he was involved in a protracted fight with the studio, in the person of production head Walter MacEwen, over the size and placement of the credit for Faye Dunaway, who wanted equal billing with Beatty, who, after much prodding, "conceded Dunaway 100% above the title."[48] Beatty also struggled with the studio over the credit sequence at the beginning of the movie: objections were raised by Jack Warner and others to the graininess of the snapshots, the intrusiveness of the camera click, and the color of the sequence: the studio wanted the photographs to match "the beige or off-white color which was one of the samples made up of the WB Shield." Apparently at Beatty's insistence, the letters of the title and the featured performers were slightly off-white—the color of the letters crediting Tatira-Hiller—and quickly filled to red. The WB shield stayed a darker sepia: an antique.[49] Apparently, there was never any question that it would be the Warner Bros. trademark and not a freshly minted Warner Bros.–Seven Arts logo. As we have seen with *The Fountainhead* and will see again in *Batman* and *You've Got Mail*, the Warner Bros. logo was and is malleable and therefore available for exploitation by interested parties on behalf of changing relations of power and provenance. The logo usually graced the motion picture at the beginning, before the credits; occasionally and significantly, as in the case of *The Fountainhead*, it appeared at the end. Rarely, did the logo appear alone and centered on the screen at the beginning *and* the end. The logo always had been conspicuous, but excessive obviousness was not part of the script.

The verbal icon, by definition, is constructed of words. That construct might imply an author but it does not require that the author be named. Anonymity does not diminish a poem's capacity to achieve the status of a concrete universal. But an iconic brand must be anchored in a graphic image, a claim of provenance that is the condition of the brand's possibility. *Bonnie and Clyde* is a sterling example of studio authorship because, although the owners, executives, and employees had a hand in making the motion picture, by the time the credits were added to the final print the existence of the studio named Warner Bros. had become strictly symbolic, a formal condition for the appearance on the screen of a motion picture that would reinvigorate the brand by giving it a new meaning. And thus alone of all the credits, the "Warner Brothers" shield appears in sepia. A relic of antiquity, it blazons the narrative that will confect its past (Figure 5.11). The movie concludes with this version of the studio logo,

Figure 5.11

Figure 5.12

infrequently used since the 1930s, which is the same version that was imprinted on the water tower in the 1960s, Warren Beatty's final put-on (Figure 5.12). There is none of Greenberg's and Wimsatt's disfavored subject matter or semantic content here. Transferred from the water tower to the screen, the WB is a possessory credit that declares that ownership of the brand has been dislodged from the family that invented its form, built its stature, and, for many years, carefully maintained its value. Its appearance here marks the transfer of ownership from the studio to a new wave of stars: producers, agents, actors, even directors. Ultimately, the severance of the logo from biological persons will enable Warner Bros. to thrive as the brand identity of a fully corporatized culture. If the initial Warner Bros. logo shields us from forgetting the past, the "WB" formally promises the survival of the "living culture that [for better or worse] we now have," if only because the postmodern filmmaker, like his modernist forebears, "derived [his] chief inspiration from the medium"—that is, corporate art—he "works in" ("AGK," 22–23).

6 Post-Warners Warners
Batman and *JFK*; *You've Got Mail* (1989–1998)

i. Mind the Gap

The space between the last chapter, which ends with the detachment of the famous WB from reference to any Warner brother, living or dead, and this chapter, which begins with an analysis of the use to which the inventive and persuasive Steve Ross put Warners pictures as he refined the art of the deal, represents a leap across twenty years of Hollywood history, which are associated with the emergence and dissolution of the so-called New Hollywood. Those turbulent decades were characterized by the dispersal of authority, by the blossoming of a "renaissance" of smart, stylish, and subversive motion pictures brought to the screen by star directors, such as Martin Scorsese, Francis Ford Coppola, Robert Altman, Bob Rafelson, and Peter Bogdanovich, and by the countervailing force of corporate consolidation of multiple entertainment platforms, the emergence of the blockbuster mentality, and the rise to preeminence of the marketing model of filmmaking under the concept of the high concept, which presupposes, as Justin Wyatt has argued, that "the logic of the marketplace is clearly the author of [a movie's] style."[1]

The academic historiography of the period continues to debate the relative continuity of the New Hollywood with the Hollywood of the studio era or even with the global extravaganzas that Columbia, Warners, and Paramount have since become. For our purposes, it is important to keep in mind the picture that Thomas Schatz saw in 1993 as he looked out on a landscape where the acquisition of Twentieth Century Fox by Rupert Murdoch's News Corporation in 1985, the formation of Time Warner in 1989, and the takeover of MCA by Japan's Matsushita Electric Industrial Company in 1990 loomed large. Schatz concluded that the refashioning of the industry was not merely a matter of new production and marketing strategies; it involved the conglomeration of film companies into larger entertainment corporations and of entertainment corporations into global media giants. A major reorientation had occurred as "the vertical integration of classical Hollywood, which ensured a closed industrial system and coherent narrative, has given way to 'horizontal integration of the New Hollywood's tightly diversified media conglomerates which favors texts strategically 'open' to multiple readings and multimedia reiteration."[2] The steady growth of film-related income from ancillary and secondary markets has made it possible for Warners or Sony to absorb the risk that a $150 million movie will bomb at the box office, because the company is all but certain to recover its costs at Blockbuster or on cable television or at Toys "R" Us or at a neighborhood theater in Bangkok.

Schatz aptly quotes Eileen Meehan's description of the vanishing of the integrity of narrative as blockbuster motion pictures are expertly exploited as "commercial intertexts" among various media platforms. He singles out her shrewd observation that *Batman* "is best understood as a multimedia, multimarket sales campaign." Meehan's essay on *Batman* is an excellent account of the marketing strategies that made *Batman* such a perfect symptom of the complex and far-flung synergistic merchandising campaigns of the entertainment behemoths of the New Hollywood. In what follows I want to take on board Meehan's analysis and especially her closing admonition that "we must be able to understand [capitalist media] as always and simultaneously text and commodity, intertext and product line."[3] I shall, however, add another innovation that enhances the palette of the artist of the deal: the use of *Batman* as an allegory specifically designed to market Warners to Time Inc. During the negotiations over the merger, Warners executives deployed *Batman* as a weapon to puncture the equilibrium enjoyed by the communications and entertainment industries behind their traditional partitions in order to create what Carl Laemmle might have called "a new species" of entertainment corporation, one expressly designed to acquire the future.

ii. The Time Warner Conspiracy

> Think about the future!
>
> The Joker, *Batman*

Formed in 1989, the year the Wall fell that had segregated rival versions of the truth, Time Warner, the corporate merger of fact and fiction, was deeply invested in a vision of American democracy gone sour and sore in need of rescue. That investment is most salient in two films: *Batman*, released in 1989 during the merger negotiations between Time Inc. and Warner; and *JFK* (Warners, 1991), the signature film of the new organization. *Batman* and *JFK* are corporate expressions: the former an instrumental allegory contrived to accomplish corporate objectives, the latter a scenario that effectively expands the range of what counts as a corporate objective. *Batman* addresses savvy corporate insiders.

JFK aspires to turn everyone into an insider by inducting its viewers into a new American mythos geared for an age in which successful corporate financial performance presupposes a transculturalist politics: corporate populism. Corporate populism responds to the inchoate political dissatisfaction of the legacy rebels of the 1960s by using new cinematic tools to translate politics as spectacle by the insertion of a brand where once there might have been an idea. Under corporate populism, the old, corporate liberal agencies for integrating a *pluribus* of individuals into a social *unum* are to be superseded by a mass entertainment complex capable of projecting a riveting logo that summons all people's attention, that offers membership in an invisible body by virtue of collective participation in a spectacular event or cathexis of a corporate person or enthrallment in a sublime virtuality, and that substitutes for credal affiliation a continuously renewable identification with logo, trademark, slogan, or brand. The means for deploying corporate populism as technology for producing branded citizens had been available since the emergence of the broadcast networks in the 1920s. But it was not until the fall of the evil empire, with the explosive expansion of international markets, the expiration of ideological contestation, and the sudden obsolescence of the national security state as sovereign system for the production of loyal subjects that conditions became ideal for the suasive elaboration of an extragovernmental, postideological matrix of corporatized citizenship.

JFK was universally recognized as a bold, innovative political film, although the exact orientation of its politics was hotly disputed. Upon its release in 1991, *JFK* provoked attacks from center, left, and right—a proper posthistorical confusion of tongues. The left divided against itself. Some left-wing writers applauded the film as a potent critique of governmental covert action and cover-up, one crediting Oliver Stone with having produced a film that works to "delegitimate the national security state."[4] Others derided the film as a conspiratorial myth that irresponsibly forecloses informed historical analysis. Michael Albert, the editor of *Z*, attempted to save *JFK* for leftist taste by reconstituting a distinction between a right-wing explanation of events, which imputes causation to conspiratorial activity, and a left-wing analysis grounded in institutional imperatives. According to Albert, a conspiratorial theory entails a "claim that a particular group acted outside usual norms in a rogue and generally secretive fashion. It disregards "structural features of institutions" by insisting that an "outcome would not have happened had not the *particular* people with their particular inclinations come together and cheated." Institutional theories, he argues, "claim that the *normal* operations of some institutions generate the behaviors and motivations leading to the events in question." They "address personalities, personal interests, personal timetables, and meetings only as facts about the events needing explanation, not as explanations themselves, as causal agents" ("Conspiracy?... Not!" *JFK*, pp. 358–59).

Albert acknowledged that *JFK* liberally scatters charges of conspiracy, and he deplored Stone's glorification of Kennedy. Yet he found those melodramatic excesses to be incidental to Stone's fundamental, praiseworthy political achievement: the mounting of a commercial movie that convincingly represents the assassination of an American president as a coup d'état. In Albert's judgment, *JFK* counts as a leftist film because "Stone's 'bad guy' is a *system* oriented to war and profitability" (*JFK*, p. 364). Maybe so. But if so, it is hard to understand why Albert credits *Stone* with the achievement, when, according to the terms of his analysis, he really ought to praise Warner Films and its parent company, Time Warner. Why praise the person as cause when all we know about the operations of capitalism would lead us to believe that *JFK* came about through the normal operations of the corporate institution?

To claim that the business of a business "normally" involves institutional critique of American business and the American state seems counterintuitive, leftist in form only. And Albert certainly never got around to saying it. If he had, Albert might have been induced to examine his obsolete distinction between persons and institutions—an obsolescence accomplished in large part by the concordat executed under the canopy of the brand between the inhuman plasticity of the corporate form and the sociocultural monstrosity called a star. In the absence of a threat of state interference, the constructions of corporate populism exercise power through the exploitation of that hybridity. That was so especially in the case of Time Warner: accounts of the merger agree that the negotiation between institutional commitments and personal prerogatives, between acquisitive managers and a charismatic executive, drove the deal between Time Inc. and Warner Communications in 1989.[5]

Albert was not prepared to see the connection between the rhetorical strategy of *JFK* and a corporate strategy of Time Warner because, although he eagerly followed Stone in his rejection of the suspiciously simplistic lone gunman theory of the assassination, he strangely adhered to the equally simplistic lone-crusader theory—if not Kennedy, struck down in his prime, or Garrison, stonewalled by government bureaucracy, then Stone himself, pilloried by a mainstream press unwilling to tolerate challenges to its prerogatives. Albert did not feel the pinch of the contradiction because he was a victim of theory—not political theory but film theory. Despite his able critique of persons as causes, he embraced the explanatory model of the auteur theory, which proposes the director as agent of the distinctive vision of the motion picture, a person whose detectable signature authorizes the commercial product as a meaningful artifact. Albert rightly believed that films are meaningful. And he had no way of explaining how institutions make films. No one does. But this is not important. As I have argued throughout this book, institutions do not make films; corporations do. Hollywood films are corporate speech—a claim validated by the Supreme Court in *Citizens United v. Federal Elections Commission*, January 21, 2010.

Peter F. Drucker used General Electric as his favored example of a company that builds "customer and market appeal into the product from the design stage on."[6] There's no reason to doubt his assertion. Nonetheless, it is reasonable to wonder why he did not choose Warner Bros. instead. At its best, General Electric merely approximated the marketing mentality that saturates the motion picture industry, where the marketing appeal is not merely built into the product (which is not and never was perforated strips of exposed celluloid) but *is* the product. We can hypothesize that the motion picture industry *might* have epitomized Drucker's progressive business enterprise, because he makes clear why, writing in 1954, he ignored it. For Drucker, successful economic performance presupposes that the manager has the capacity to act with a virtually free hand to realize the customers he or she imagines. But in 1954, as Drucker notes, managerial imagination was subjected to constraints that had nothing to do with "economic performance." "A 'Cold War' of indefinite duration," he writes, "demands the ability to satisfy the country's military needs while building up, at the same time, an expanding peacetime economy. It demands, indeed, an unprecedented ability of the entire economy to shift back and forth between peacetime and defense production, practically at an instant's notice. This demand, on the satisfaction on which our survival may well depend, is above all a demand on the competence of the managements, especially of our big enterprises" (*PM*, p. 5). Those imperious demands deformed management's function within the business enterprise, for "managing a business must be a creative rather than an adaptive task. The more a management creates economic conditions or changes them rather than passively adapts to them, the more it manages the business" (*PM*, p. 47). The Cold War's demand on the competence of managers was not dictated by the objective of creating new customers but by the strategic requirements of an old customer, the national security state. In requiring spasmodic shifts from peacetime to wartime production, the national security state elevated political advantage above economic performance. Under the Cold War dispensation the motion picture industry was doubly disabled: by ideological constraints imposed by Congress at just the time when the Supreme Court had relieved the legal impediments to free expression; and by the strategic doctrine of the national security state, which prioritized massive industrial capitalization for defense, just as the financially pressed studios were forced to discount their investments in studio lots and sound stages. Nonetheless, the motion picture industry's plight was only a relative disadvantage. Under the rules of the waiting game, big enterprises such as Lockheed, Boeing, and even General Electric were privileged, but that privilege came at a price: these enterprises were not permitted to ask the fundamental question that Drucker calls the key to innovation, "What is our business?" (*PM*, p. 50).

However larded with illustrations from the business world, Drucker's account of managerial practice was an idealization, because the demands of the Cold War introduced an impediment to managerial freedom. As we have seen, that impediment had a temporal dimension. Indeed, Drucker encourages the inference that the theory of managerial authorship would remain mere theory until the end of the Cold War and the expiration of the hegemony of the national security state over the economy. No industry would benefit from the end of the Cold War, which included the relaxation of censorship, more than the entertainment industry, which was poised to exploit the new markets that would be created. The purchase of Hollywood studios by Gulf+Western, Transamerica, and Kirk Kerkorian in the 1960s was an expression of confidence in the future of a diversified entertainment industry. The company best poised to exploit the unnerving of the state's strong hand was a company formed in 1968, Warner Communications Inc. (WCI), for under the leadership of its charismatic CEO and president, Steve Ross, the question "What is our business?" *was* asked by Warner management every business day. The improvisational character of Warner was caught by a Time Inc. executive during the merger talks, begun in 1988, when he sarcastically commented that WCI was "basically a collection of deals smartly banded together" (*TET*, p. 205).[7] The remark was revealing, both about WCI and, reflexively, about Time. WCI radicalized Drucker's version of the modern business enterprise by introducing marketing into every aspect of a business understood as its own most important product. That is another way of saying that WCI was no longer Jack Warner's company and never became Warren Beatty's. It was Steve Ross's. In every other company that Ross had run, the identity of the company had always been subject to ceaseless negotiations, as in one deal after another he acquired and relinquished companies, mutating from the funeral parlor business to the parking lot business to the music and motion picture business, to the entertainment and information business. Time, however, had always considered itself to be something other than the negotiations in which it engaged. Although under Time's CEO, Richard Munro, the company had begun to experiment with expansion into the communications and entertainment fields, it sought to protect a nonnegotiable core identity in which journalistic integrity and public spiritedness elevated its business above the mere pursuit of profit. By and large, Time's experiments had not proved successful. Although the company had steadily increased its profits, its stock remained consistently undervalued. It had developed HBO and had launched the enormously lucrative *People* in the mid-1980s, but the forays into cable and satellite television transmission had been disappointments (Time Inc. regularly lost out in a head-to-head competition with WCI for cable contracts). A strategic study in early 1982 discovered a company "identity crisis" (*TET*, p. 70). In brief, although the company had expanded and diversified sufficiently that its magazine business generated only one-third of its revenues, Time Inc. remained locked into the journalistic identity that had been established by its founder, Henry Luce.

During the merger talks between Time Inc. and Warner, certain premises remained constant: (1) Time would acquire WCI in a stock for stock swap, and the name of the new company would reflect Time's preeminence; (2) Time would preserve its identity within the new corporation, an identity that was itself based on the preservation of journalistic integrity and editorial independence; (3) the executive succession of Time's management would be assured, and a Time executive, namely Nicholas Nicholas, would, subsequent to the retirement of Munro, be appointed as the sole CEO of the new company within five years.

Batman was released in mid-June 1989, just months after the March announcement of the merger of Time Inc. and Warner Communications Inc., and at a time when Time management had good reason to feel skittish. In response to the notice of the planned merger Martin Davis, CEO of Paramount, had, on June 6, tendered a hostile takeover bid for Time designed to appeal to the company's stockholders. Time management did not swerve from its commitment to Ross, who had sweetened the deal by agreeing to unprecedented compensation packages for Time's upper management. In order to turn back Davis, Time's opportunistic management persuaded the board of directors to approve a restructured deal that had two salient features: it replaced the original stock for stock transfer with a cash transaction, which would involve taking on a $14 billion debt, and it bypassed a vote by the shareholders. Management had good reason to fear a vote, since Davis had first offered 175 dollars a share for stock valued at only 135 dollars before the offer and later raised his bid to 200 dollars—considerably in excess of the return Time's stockholders could expect on a deal with Ross that would involve incurring a gigantic debt. Davis sued in a Delaware Court. The case of *Paramount vs. Time Inc.* was engaged, Chancellor William Allen presiding.

On June 23, 1989, threatened by a hostile takeover bid, a court challenge, and a congressional inquiry, Dick Munro, then Time's CEO, went to the movies for the first time in ten years. The movie? The first showing of *Batman*. The place: not New York, model for *Batman*'s Gotham and home to both Time and Warner, but Washington, DC. The venue made sense. Washington had figured importantly in the recent travel schedules of a number of high Time and Warner executives, who had been summoned to testify regarding the proposed merger before various congressional subcommittees and had filed briefs with the FCC, FTC, and Justice Department during the spring of 1989. In that context the Washington opening of *Batman* makes the picture look like another brief presented to another DC audience on behalf of the merger. Of course, the event had been planned well before the Davis bombshell. Who knows if Munro would have gone if he hadn't been in Washington to file a suit against Paramount for "threatening the first amendment rights of Time journalism"? (*TET*, p. 238). But he did go, accompanied by Steve Ross, CEO and president of Warner Communications. And Munro must have been reassured, for *Batman* spoke to his predicament.

Like the later *JFK*, *Batman* is a civic rescue fantasy: the masked crusader rescues a bleak, crime-ridden Gotham from the terrorism of psychotic gangsters. But more to the point for Munro, it is also a *corporate* rescue fantasy that casts Time in the role of the maiden in distress. The connection is explicit: when the eye-catching Vicki Vale (Kim Basinger) introduces herself to the intrepid reporter (Robert Wuhl) in the newsroom, he replies, "Yeah, yeah, the photographer: *Vogue, Cosmo*, yeah, yeah. Look if you want me to pose nude, you're going to need a long lens." She smiles and answers, "Actually, I was in the Corto Maltese." Cut to a close-up of a copy of *Time* magazine, which she has placed on the desk for him to see (Figure 6.1). On the cover is a photo of a corpse on a barren hilltop bisected by the headline, "Corto Maltese Revolution," and the

Figure 6.1

credit, "pics by Vicki Vale." The *Time* photos are invoked twice more in the film. In her first interview with Bruce Wayne, Vale mentions she's working on a story on Batman, and he mockingly voices a concern that may have been troubling a journalist or two at Time Inc.: "Batman? That's a little light after the Corto Maltese, isn't it?" Later, when the Joker (Jack Nicholson) paws through Vale's portfolio, he slams one colorful fashion pic after another ("Crap! Crap!") until he gets to the *Time* cover followed by the black-and-white Corto Maltese photo (Figure 6.2). "Ah, that's good work," he proclaims. "The skulls, the bodies, you give it such a glow. I don't know if it's art, but I like it." Both men appreciate Vale's journalistic work but for different reasons. Wayne credits it with gravity. Why not? Even though the earnest Wayne contrasts Batman and the Corto Maltese as subjects, the effect of Vale's journalistic experience is reflexively to elevate Batman as subject, who is endowed with weight by Vale's attention. As a self-proclaimed "homicidal artist," and champion of a new aesthetic, the Joker recognizes in Vale a kindred spirit and, therefore, a suitable subject for the performance of his art.

If Vicki Vale is explicitly linked with Time, the character of disguised hero Bruce Wayne–Batman strongly suggests an impersonation of Warners. Batman is primarily associated with the privatized technological space of the Bat Cave, set up as a television control booth. His eventual triumph over the forces of evil involves the installation in the heart of Gotham of a projection system that evokes the apparatus used by a motion picture studio during production or at premieres. Climactically, the image of the projected bat sign against the night sky visibly rhymes with the enskyed Warner Bros. trademark that opens the film (Figures 6.3 and 6.4).

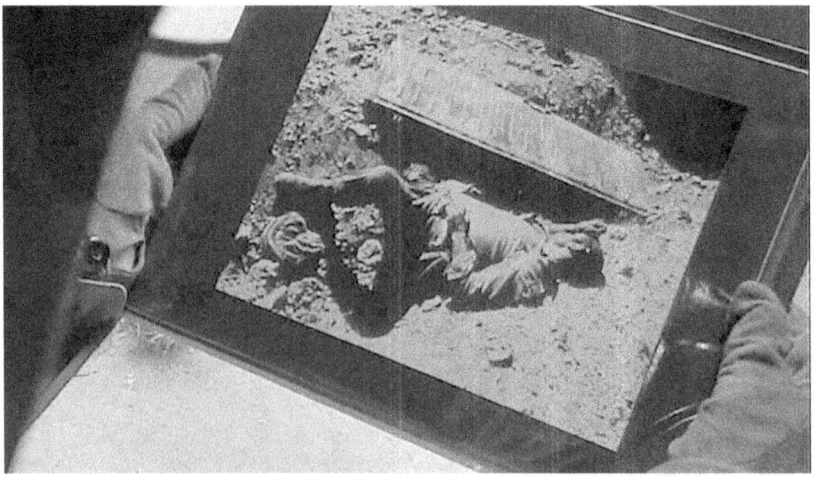

Figure 6.2

Figure 6.3

Figure 6.4

The Joker suggests a demonized Martin Davis. First, it was Davis who threatened to seize Time from Warner's grasp. In the film the Joker gives his coercion a dealer's twist: when told that Vicki is "dating some guy named 'Wayne,'" he quips: "She's about to trade up." The film also devotes some time to dramatizing the Joker's seizure of power from Boss Grissom (Jack Palance), whom he had loyally served as chief enforcer. Davis had only recently come into power at Paramount (at the time named Gulf+Western) after the death of the infamous Charles Bludhorn. Notorious in the industry for his zeal to perform Bludhorn's most cold-blooded commands, Davis had acquired the nickname of "hatchet man" (*TET*, p. 223). Now it is true that Bludhorn died of a heart attack—not, as Grissom does, by a gunshot from his former hatchet man. The point of the allegory is not, however, to represent what actually happened to Bludhorn, but hyperbolically to stigmatize Davis (recently described as "possibly one of the most unpleasant bosses in the annals of business"),[8] as a usurper and to activate those fears regarding breaks in the continuity of executive succession that had obsessed Time management and shaped their negotiating posture from the very outset of the talks with Ross. Finally, the nearest that the Joker comes to success is during the city's street festival, when he stages a spectacular appearance on a float, tethering giant balloons, and fulfills his advertised promise to prove his fitness to rule the city by going over the heads of the constituted powers and directly showering the populace with millions of dollars (Figure 6.5). The corporate allegory is compelling: the Joker's promise of instant wealth to the citizens of Gotham evokes Davis's promise of instant wealth to the shareholders of Time. And the admonition is clear: Davis's benefaction, like the Joker's, would be followed by a poison that would destroy those who accept his lure.

But there is a problem with this reading: the timing seems all wrong. Davis had made his surprise offer just the week before the premiere of *Batman*. The movie, of course, had been in production well before.[9] But the problem is only apparent, for the pertinence of the film is not as a commentary on or record of the takeover bid but as a scenario devised in order to control contingencies that might follow the launching of the merger. That such planning could occur is certain: Davis had been a contender for a deal with Time well before management settled on Warners (*TET*, p. 146). The movie attests that such planning *did* occur. If *Batman*, unlike the reformatted deal, could be explained, not as an overnight response to the tender from Paramount, but as an *anticipation* of a hostile move from Davis (or from a studio executive a great deal like Davis), it became critical evidence that could defend Time management and its board

Figure 6.5

against the charge that they had betrayed their fiduciary responsibility by reformatting the deal with Warner in what Michael Albert would call "a rogue and secretive fashion" that wrongfully bypassed a stockholder vote. Seen from a tower in Gotham, secrecy was necessary to protect shareholders from a threat to which their avarice had blinded them.

Time's defense in the Delaware case depended in part on the company's persuasiveness that its managers had foreseen the potential of hostile bids as part of their strategic planning and had taken reasonable measures to protect themselves against those bids. The scenario of *Batman* qualifies as Warners' contribution to the set of defensive measures (a staggered board, long notice of shareholder motions at meetings, a poison pill preferred stock rights plan, etc.) that Time had earlier introduced in order to ward off takeover bids. Crucial to the case was the determination of the scope of managerial foresight and managerial authority to act on that foresight even to the extent of overriding the so-called "efficiency of the market." Could managerial projections of a future valuation of a stock legally outweigh the valuation that the market had already placed on it?[10] That question could not be resolved by determining which valuation was accurate (even the court did not have privileged access to the future), but by assessing whether management did in fact *believe* that its prospective valuation was accurate. The judge's decision for the defense strongly emphasized what he called "the subjective intentions" of the board and the managers; and he assessed that their intention was to choose "less current value in the hope . . . that greater value would make that implicit sacrifice beneficial in the future" (Allen, 13). *Batman*'s conjunction of easy money with poison looks like evidence of an intention to prevent the shareholders from accepting a deal immediately gratifying but eventually fatal to them and to the company.

However important, the question of market valuation was not paramount, for no merely financial measurement proved decisive. As Chancellor Allen observed, although Time sought to establish a vertically integrated, global enterprise, attaining such a financial goal was not "a transcendent aim of Time management or its board. More important to both, apparently, has been a desire to maintain an independent Time Incorporated that reflected a continuation of what management and the board regarded as distinctive and important 'Time culture.'" Note the phrase, "what the management and the board regarded." Not only is the preservation of Time's culture the responsibility of the management and the board, the *definition* of what counts as Time culture was up to them. This made it possible for both Time's management and Chancellor Allen to identify preservation of the power of Time's managers, bearers of benign subjective intentions, with the preservation of Time culture. Allen is explicit: "effectuation of the reformatted transaction" would "afford the company a video production capacity of recognized talent, it would extend the company into global markets in a substantial way, and it would continue the Time identity and the Time 'corporate culture' (i.e., in this instance, it would assure that Mr. Nicholas ultimately will serve as the CEO of the enterprise" (Allen, p. 11). Chancellor Allen goes on to deliver an opinion no less influential for being framed as a double negative: "I am not persuaded that there may not be instances in which the law might recognize as valid a perceived threat to a 'corporate culture' that is shown to be palpable (for lack of a better word), distinctive and advantageous" (Allen, p. 14). Culture trumps economics. And the defense of culture is the defense of Nicholas's claim to succeed Munro and eventually become CEO of Time Warner.

The culture defense is the legacy of *Paramount vs. Time* to corporation law. Although its radical resolution of the prerogatives of management was eventually moderated, the decision nonetheless validated the virtual indifference of the board and the managers to both shareholders' rights and the efficiency of the market on the grounds that they were custodians of a culture subject solely to their definition and of a corporate identity indistinguishable from their personal identity. Chancellor Allen identified the corporation, especially its governing *structure*, as a culture; described that culture as the signature of a great man, Henry Luce; and ascribed its preservation to named individuals. Drucker's vision of corporate organization imagined every manager as creator of the customer who would direct his practice; but that practice, however responsive to society, was still to be described and appraised as "economic performance." By revoking the constraint of "economic" on managerial "performance," the successful culture defense of Time made some managers embodiments of the corporation, auteurs indifferent to market concerns and antagonistic to institutional checks. By protecting corporate governance from actual politics—the will of the stockholders as expressed in a ballot—and making it a matter of culture, which existed and could exist only in the minds of those *particular* managers and directors, rogue or not, the court not only sustained the merger of Time and Warner but also endorsed a merger of corporate structure with managerial personality, an implicit affirmation of conspiracy as legitimate managerial practice.

Returning to *Batman*, we can see that not only does it anticipate the hostile takeover attempt by Davis, it lays out a version of the culture defense that would be mounted by Time's attorneys in *Paramount Communications v. Time Inc.* We have seen that the Joker peruses Vicki Vale's portfolio. He has the opportunity do so because at his request she has brought the portfolio to a dinner engagement that he, pretending to be Bruce Wayne, has arranged with her at the

Gotham Art Museum. The raucous entrance of the Joker and his goons into the museum dramatizes his threat to the high culture that the museum displays but cannot protect. The Joker and his men prance through the hall, knocking down sculpture and spray painting and butchering the canvasses of the old masters. The takeover/makeover maniac greets Vale with this ominous compliment: "Beautiful—in an old fashioned kind of way. But I'm sure we can make you more *today*." Then, to demonstrate what he means by "more today," the self-described "homicidal artist" reveals his own work of art, the acid-scarred face of Grissom's former mistress, as the failed prototype for a defacement for which he covets Vale in order to perfect. The identification of Vale, Time photo-journalist, with old-fashioned high culture as objects of the Joker's vandalism is clear.

Everything I have said thus far would support the thesis that *Batman* could have been submitted to the court as evidence for management's defensive intentions. But, for good reason, it was not. Although the film anticipates the culture defense, it anticipates that strategy in a context predictive of the ultimate failure of Time to preserve its identity. If it is a defensive measure, *Batman* is a defense conducted by Warners for Time, which, like tempting target Vicki Vale, cannot defend itself. And what do we know about the motivation of the hero? First of all, unlike the Joker, he wears a disguise. The Joker vandalizes a museum; Bruce Wayne lives in one. Wayne relates to the artifacts that surround him not as aesthetic objects meriting disinterested regard but as property, inherited or acquired, arousing no form of interest. Wayne is more at home in the Bat Cave among his high-tech toys than in the house that is the burden of his past. Batman's indifference to the tradition that surrounds him bodes ill for Time's enterprise, for, his attraction to Vale notwithstanding, Batman's self-realization occurs only when he understands himself as the twig once bent by the traumatic murder of his parents to be forever the resolute antagonist of the Joker. Vicki Vale becomes incidental to an increasingly mimetic rivalry. Batman's climactic rescue of her from the grip of the Joker is a metonymy for his symbolic rule over a corporatized Gotham. In the end, as the Joker complains, Batman does not win because he is right or good but because he has better "gadgets"—a studio with multiple cameras and remote surveillance screens, a costume that works like a second skin to incorporate and strengthen his merely human body, and, finally, a device to project his image to the citizenry of Gotham—the kind of gadgets that attracted Time management to Warners in the first place. You would think that Dick Munro could not miss the final irony. *Batman* does not narrate the victory of traditional culture; it represents the triumph of a technologically more powerful spectacle over a weaker one; in doing so, the movie both exercises the comic book's capacity to innocuously deface high cultural pretension and proves the entertainment corporation's ability to artfully perform its populist ministry unaided by any state. That's the real joker in the story: Batman argues that Time needs to acquire Warners so that Warners can remake Time in its own image.

As evidence for this we can note that the day after *Batman* opened to record-breaking grosses, Steve Ross called Mark Canton, head of production at Warners, from Washington: "Congratulations," he told Canton. "You may be responsible for making the merger happen" (*HR*, p. 173). What could he have meant? Sure, it was nice to bring in so much money; but cash flow could scarcely affect the deal one way or another at that point. The boffo box office would certainly have no effect on *Time*'s stock price. More likely, Ross was referring to the effect of the movie on Munro. Munro understood enough of the deal to be reassured about his future, but not enough to perceive its meaning for the company he headed. We can infer that the same blindness applied to the film. At Warner it was widely understood that, for Ross, making a deal depended on Ross's opponent not understanding it. Introducing an allegorical opacity into his deals was fundamental to Ross's managerial practice. Here is an anecdote told by one of Ross's subordinates: "His financial acumen was amazing. He'd come into the office and say, Let me do a deal. He would have pieces of paper that sometimes he'd worked on all night long. He always carried a little spiral notebook. He'd go through the deal with all its permutations and variations. Then he'd say, Do you get it? Do it for me. You mean *you* understood it! Every paper would then be ripped up. If you understood it, he'd say, *they* will understand it, so that's not the deal I'm going to go with" (*TET*, p. 331). Ross could tell that Munro didn't get the point of the deal—and therefore that the deal would succeed—because he didn't get the film. Or, to look at it from another angle: Munro's failure to take Ross seriously as a disguised and formidable adversary is of a piece with his failure to appreciate *Batman* as anything more significant than a glitzy, pumped-up comic book. For it is difficult to believe that an interested observer would not notice that *Batman* is candid about its aspiration to save Time for life in a world supervised by a Warner superhero. Recall that *Batman* does not end with a romantic clinch between the masked crusader and Vicki Vale. The *Time* photo-journalist is whisked away to the background prior to the concluding shot, which, as we have seen, isolates Batman loftily overlooking a city that gratefully projects his brand. Munro, in short, failed to be sufficiently paranoid. When the deal had been settled, Time had received little from it except money for its managers.[11] Its board and managers failed to secure the contractual guarantees of unbroken managerial succession or of the governance structure that would assure its continued independence within the merged company. Within three years, Steve Ross alone would rule a corporation in which appeal to a bygone Time culture might have a rhetorical use but would no longer have substantive standing.

In March 1991 Steve Ross used the occasion of his first postmerger press conference to rhapsodize on Time Warner's future in interactive broadcasting, "the third age of television." Its greatest importance, he announced, would derive from its ability "to teach students according to their individual abilities, interests, and educational needs." Although Ross admitted that "these scenarios and others may be a few years off . . . they're signals in the wire waiting to be launched." Ross continued to discourse on his vision—Time Warner's vision—of education in the imminent future:

> One of the ways you have to educate is to make it entertainment. If you don't make it entertaining, if you are unable to get the right equipment in the home to sell education, we will not be able to educate America. How do we do that? No one will buy education. What they will buy is entertainment and certain information. Through that you will get the right equipment into the home. If you can make education entertaining, they will tune in and interact. (*TET*, pp. 321–22)

This would become a concrete scenario. The devices for a pilot project in interactive television were scheduled to be installed in a cluster of homes in Orlando by 1995. The system for introducing entertainment-driven educational TV into the public schools was in the process of being implemented as Ross spoke, and *JFK* would be the vehicle for it.

JFK makes a forceful argument for a revisionary interpretation of the past; but *JFK* was also a manifestation of corporate power designed to affect the future by floating credible scenarios. Scenario thinking was introduced into U.S. strategic planning early in the Cold War by Herman Kahn, who developed military strategic studies for Rand Corporation. Ute von Reibnitz observes of such military scenarios: "Similar to a theater production where stage set and scenery create a backdrop, the accent here was on creating a background for certain scenes and setting up a framework for possible future activities by showing future environmental situations. The military planners' task consisted of operating as well as possible within these set conditions and of coming through even in adverse circumstances."[12] The hegemony of the military-industrial complex meant that corporations could acquire special access to the future by investing in the scenarios developed by government strategic planners, who set the parameters for what counted as background and what counted as foreground, for who would be actors and who would be mere spectators. Scenario writing modeled on military planning entered the business environment in the early

1970s, largely through the agency of the Dutch-based but internationalist Shell Oil Corporation, "which became the first corporation to use scenarios in order to position itself to be able to take advantage of contingencies it could not fully control."[13] Shell's first notable success was in developing scenarios in 1972 for a projected Mideast oil crisis, which, of course, soon followed.

Shell's equivalent to the culturalist moment of *Paramount v. Time* was the 1992 hiring of an English professor, Dr. Betty S. Flowers, as its "editor for myths." Flowers's self-described task was to challenge the economistic bias of Shell stories of possible futures by inducing "Shell managers to think mythologically and causally, to see every major local or world event as potentially located in a story, and to make on-the-spot business and policy decisions based on what they know about where that story would lead if allowed to play itself out." The well-constructed myth is not simply a managerial guide but an effective modeling of the future, for, according to Flowers, "when you tell stories about the future, even if you're not claiming to forecast, there's some sense that actually, the future is the story you *choose*. Now that is very uneconomic in its basis. It's not the 'invisible hand' working out invisibly, like a machine. It's human beings coming in and saying, I choose scenario A, not scenario B. It's a different emphasis—it puts the human being more in the center, in very nuanced ways, instead of these huge impersonal forces" (quoted in "SCF," p. 151). By "huge impersonal forces," Flowers means economic determinants, not corporations, which are personalized as the "you" who create scenarios that solicit choice from "you" the customer. Just as scenario making abandons the economistic model of "straight-line forecasting," which presupposes a future continuous with the present ("SCF," p. 148), so does it blur the line separating those customers of the scenario who are inside the corporation from those who are outside. The choice of a future entails the human being's participation in a corporate narrative and thus her self-identification as a customer created by the scenario—a customer who contributes to the success of the business enterprise whether or not she actually ever consumes the product of the corporation. For the scenarist, "the future is what you use to create the present, and the present that you then create will create the future that you want" ("SCF," p. 160). That "very strong cognitive feedback loop" of corporate self-confirmation can successfully unfold in a global environment where "the myth of economics," also known as capitalism, prevails without substantial challenge, whether from competing ideologies or from the nation-state itself.

Global capitalism is the effective corporate imagination of the world as a cognitive feedback loop. No industry has taken advantage of the opportunities of that system more than the entertainment industry. And Time Warner has been the leader of this trend. Certainly Oliver Stone's comments in interviews suggest that he understood his role in terms strikingly similar to Flowers's. When Stone was asked by Ken Auletta how he justified putting words into the mouths of famous men, as he does in *JFK*, Stone replied, "It comes out of context. If you examine the movie, you'll see that nothing is factually put. It's surmised. Donald Sutherland [who played the character X] describes a scenario: 'This could have happened. And that is possible.' And he lays out a paradigm of possibilities. And you choose."[14] That justification neatly epitomizes Ross's idea of interactive edutainment. In a *Time* interview, Stone elaborates on the *JFK* enterprise: "So I'm giving you a detailed outlaw history or counter-myth. A myth represents the true inner spiritual meaning of an event. I think the Warren Commission was a myth, and I think the movie, hopefully, if it's accepted by the public, will at least move the people away from the Warren Commission and consider the possibility that there was a coup d'etat that removed President Kennedy" ("Plugging into the Labyrinth," in *JFK*, p. 298). Stone articulates the delegitimation that is the consequence of his scenario's specific form and force, which is not performative (the release of *JFK* will not, in and of itself, delegitimate the state) but recursive. Like Shell's scenarios, Time Warner's puts the human being at the center: success requires that the myth be "accepted by the public" in the present as a past in order to predict a future.

Time Warner needed Stone in the same way that Stone needed X, and as Shell needed Flowers—not as an author, because insofar as the author is imagined as cause, that function belongs to the corporation and to those like Steve Ross and Gerald Levin who capably impersonate it—but instead as a source of scenarios that Time Warner could float and, depending on public acceptance, elect to develop. The role of Stone was as restricted in the corporate enterprise that owns *JFK* as was the featured role occupied by John Fitzgerald Kennedy in the nation's theater of power. Indeed, the pathos of Kennedy as produced in *JFK* is exactly the pathos of the auteur. Recall that for Stone the chief act that conferred on Kennedy his moral authority was his affixing his signature to National Security Action Memorandum 263, which reports the approval by the president of plans to remove one thousand United States troops from Vietnam by Christmas 1963. That document accomplished nothing except to register an individual intention and sadly to evince that such intentions—even presidential ones—are subject to institutional imperatives that require no signatures or judicial validation.

Pathos apart, *JFK* was oriented not to the past but to the future. And its stance was educational. The catechism by Agent X on the Capitol Mall is only the most conspicuous of a series of pedagogical moments that build to the climactic courtroom scene. The visual power of the film has impressed all viewers; and it is the power of visual imagery on which Garrison relies in his prosecution, as, deploying the hottest visual aids in history, he turns the very courtroom into a classroom. The primo visual aid is, of course, the Zapruder film clip, the kernel of documentary fact that supports *JFK*'s prosecution of the state's conspiratorial abuse of power (Figure 6.6). The use of the Zapruder film in *JFK* accomplishes the merger of certain tendencies in film history: the documentary reality of the Lumieres (for them, a party of French bourgeoisie boarding a ship; for Stone, the street scene of the assassination of a president) transformed by Méliès' fantastic arsenal of tricks of the camera and the editing room. The Zapruder clip is the capital basis for the accumulation of *JFK*'s mutating speculations—capital directly analogous to the journalistic core of the Lucean corporation that the Warner entertainment empire had colonized.

JFK advanced Ross's scenario by providing a pretext for Time Warner to lay claim to an educational mission in direct competition with the institution of public education. Warner Bros. distributed Stone's *JFK Study Guide* to high school and university history departments at the time of the movie's release. Some critics saw this as evidence of a sinister design. One, David Belin, accused the company of spreading "disinformation" into the public schools, "in effect brainwashing students through the power of commercial film and rewriting history the Hollywood way" ("Earl Warren's Assassins," in *JFK*, p. 465). Such retrograde paranoia missed the point. What was important to Time Warner was not teaching *JFK* but using the film to justify the corporation's prerogative to teach the Time Warner way—by providing a curriculum and commanding a certain portion of the school day for corporate-sponsored edutainment in order to re-create the public as customer.

The *JFK Study Guide* was just one foray in the educationist strategy of Time Warner. By 1992 the corporation was half-owner of Whittle Communications, which made it a partner in Chris Whittle's Edison Project, an initiative to build

Figure 6.6

a national profit-generating school system to replace public education. In the short term, Time Warner could get its logo across to captive audiences in public school classrooms through its sponsorship of Whittle's Channel One, a "news" channel offered "free" to public schools for direct transmission into the classroom. Channel One proved irresistible to many poor urban and rural districts because it offered the loan of classroom television monitors connected to a satellite dish that would beam in the full menu of cable channels in exchange for a contractual agreement that each class would quietly view the twelve-minute "news" program broadcast daily by Channel One. The news programming at Channel One was notable not only for its submersion in commercials for Pepsi and Fritos but also for its conception of news as largely entertainment news, and entertainment news as stories by and about Time Warner magazines, films, filmmakers, and musicians. Oliver Stone's films were not only promoted in the news portions of the program, but the man himself was introduced as an advisor to youth, repeating his oft-told tale of parental divorce, disillusionment at Yale, self-realization in Vietnam and, eventually, meteoric success in Hollywood. Stone's potted biography was represented as educational not despite but because of its corporate provenance. Corporate packaging of American history and its penetration of the public school classroom aimed to usurp democratic processes by creating school systems as customers for entertaining curricula. At the end of the line, students would be reconstructed as consumers of education, just as jurors in *JFK* became an audience for Garrison's performance, and as the motion picture audience for *JFK* became jurors in the imaginary appellate theater of history.

So, what would be the climax of this plot, told the Hollywood way? It is easy to imagine a scenario, let's call it *Invasion of the Student Snatchers*, which would end with a triumphant corporate takeover of the educational system. The final scene would be a classroom captivated by a media-driven curriculum that has transformed students into robotic consumers of Time Warner products. But again, that's history the Hollywood way—the old, classical, pre-*JFK*, pre-Ross way. Channel One continued to rule the airwaves in many public schools. The Edison Project refashioned its business model under former Yale president Benno Schmidt. Yet Time Warner lost interest. In 1994 it divested both companies as Ross had divested the funeral parlors and parking lots that had been the revenue machines of his original Kinney Corporation. Unlike the state, hamstrung by the antiquated obligation to govern, the postmodern corporation can casually divest itself from unprofitable enterprises. From the perspective of the boardroom the state as government looks like a bad version of the corporation, its managers overly responsive to shareholders, its board only as stable as the next election returns. Recall that the scenario of *JFK* renders the state's potency as *nothing but* a monopoly on violence—a monopoly that, after the end of the Cold War, could seem generally pointless and occasionally dangerous. Who really wants a monopoly on violence when one can make motion pictures like *Natural Born Killers* (Warners, 1994), films that, by symbolizing violence, effectively master the imaginary according to which people lead their lives? Whether considering short-run profits or long-run leverage, it is much smarter to shoot *JFK* than to shoot JFK.

Under the dispensation of the mass-entertainment complex, as under the military-industrial complex, "black is white and white is black," as Garrison says. But the diagnosis is incomplete without the corollary stated by the abject David Ferry: "everybody's flipping." The moral: he who flips best wins. And he who wins had better keep flipping. That moral is a guide to the way that Ross acquired and consolidated power within the newly formed Time Warner and the way in which *JFK* worked as an exercise of that power. Under the leadership of Dick Munro and laboring under its Lucean past, Time Inc. had understood itself as an institution constrained by its ethos of governance and its established place within the political and cultural landscape. Steve Ross and his confreres cared only about making money and acquiring power. If Luce created Time, Ross imaginatively recreated it as the perfect customer for Warner Communications. In negotiating the deal, Ross cannily took advantage of the institutional mentality of the Time executives, which blinded them to Time's financial interest and Time's considerable corporate power. Ross was able to pacify the vaunted concern for the continuity of institutional identity by personalizing the issue, soothingly and emptily reassuring its management and board that the status and power of Time's CEO-apparent, Nicholas Nicholas, would be preserved under a plan for orderly executive succession. There would be no usurpation of the chief executive. Steve promised.

But that is not how things worked out. As Bruck reports, during the negotiations the Warners side developed a contempt for the Time people, who had used their preening reverence for journalistic principle as an alibi for turning the stronger negotiating position into a net loss in money and power. That contempt is brandished in *JFK* as an act of intracorporate humiliation. Here again the Zapruder tape is the core weapon. For just as *JFK* uses the Zapruder film to expose the conspiracy of the otiose military-industrial complex, it also deploys the clip in order to delegitimate the anachronistic journalistic policies of Time Inc. and to destabilize the authority of Nicholas, nominally Ross's co-CEO. *JFK* pointedly gives Jim Garrison the opportunity to blister *Life* magazine for publishing on its cover a doctored photo of Lee Harvey Oswald and, even more scandalously, for locking away the Zapruder tapes in its vaults. Zapruder's eight-millimeter clip had been the property of Time Inc. from 1963, when *Life* purchased the film from the Zapruders for 150,000 dollars, until 1975, when it returned the film to the family for one dollar. It was a bad investment, but *Life* imagined itself as custodian of the values that legitimated American institutions and sought to do its best to maintain the Lucean fiction of corporate service in the public interest. By using the Zapruder film in *JFK*, Time Warner, simulating public-interestedness, humiliated Time Inc. (didn't those guys realize the entertainment value of what they had?) and in the same gesture redeemed the long immurement of the Zapruder clip by dramatically displaying the dated film as if it were breaking news. To Ross loyalists the unhindered global expansion of the entertainment conglomerate Time Warner entailed the delegitimation of both the national security state and of Time Inc., anachronistic institutions that, in the name of ideology or tradition, would set limits to corporate ambition.

The exercise in delegitimation was no empty gesture. For Ross to rule Time Warner meant the abandonment of governance as an issue of abiding concern within the corporation. Aggrandizing power within the corporation and aggrandizing corporate power within the polity were mutually implicated policies. *JFK*'s humiliation of Time, Inc. publicly sealed the remarkable feat by which the smaller and weaker Warner, which, once acquired by Time, had, through Ross's shrewd management of the merger, gained the upper hand in all substantive areas of corporate decision making. As Connie Bruck notes, "The Time Warner deal may well signal the first time in corporate history that one company has acquired another and put in place a governance structure suggesting that the opposite has occurred" (*MG*, pp. 272–73). Black was turned to white. In the language of David Ferry, Ross had successfully flipped the positions of Warners and Time and laid the groundwork for a coup d'état.

That coup d'état was completed when Nicholas Nicholas was suddenly fired as joint CEO of Time Warner in February 1992. Nicholas was shocked. He shouldn't have been, however, since *JFK*, released a few months before, had told his story. Nicholas fell, if not by a magic bullet then certainly by a conspiracy of power-savvy Warner executives under the leadership of Ross but crucially aided by the man whom Nicholas had elevated to second in command on the Time side, Gerald Levin. Converted by Ross from a Time loyalist to a Warners conspirator, Levin, if not the architect of the coup, was certainly, in the words that Jim Garrison applies to LBJ, "an accomplice after the fact." *JFK* shows us how such conspiracies work; and the subsequent success of Gerald Levin, as compared to LBJ, proves that they work better when executed by corporate insiders, unchecked by anything more than the fungible abstraction called stockholders, than they do when undertaken by politicians, hounded by the media in the name of the people. If the leftist Michael Albert was a victim of auteurist film theory, Nicholas Nicholas was defeated in part because he did not have the film theory that I have been laying out in these pages. He couldn't read the writing on the wall because he couldn't interpret the story on the screen. He failed to understand that *JFK* was something more than filmed history; it was a corporate scenario that effectively projected his own undoing. But we should not shed tears for Nicholas. For although he was caught in the strong cognitive feedback loop of the Warner scenario, he certainly could be said to have gotten the future he chose, if never articulated.

According to Bruck, "the Time Warner deal, in the end, stood not as a testament to any model of corporate governance but, rather, to the triumph of personality" (*MG*, p. 278). That conclusion requires only the amendment that the deal was pivotal just because the triumph of personality at Time Warner meant that the rule of personality had become all of corporate governance that mattered. That commitment to personality and to the postmodern entertainment conglomerate as the medium for the global restructuration of personality explains better than does National Security Action Memorandum 263 the fetishizing of Kennedy by Time Warner's *JFK*. In the Time Warner coup d'état a president was munificently severed not killed, and anyway, no one would mistake the dour Nicholas Nicholas for Jack Kennedy. In the end we do not have to choose left or right, black or white. For in the best postmodernist manner the Time Warner deal saved all the phenomena that *JFK* embraces: the system, a conspiracy, and, if not the *particular* person who was Kennedy, then his personal charisma. According to the iron law of Hollywood, star power was preserved, as Kennedy's personality returned in the person and the institution of Steve Ross, who was, for a time, the posthistorical corporation in *propria persona*.

iii. Mail on the Screen, Money in the Mail

> Think back to the Warner Brothers movie *You've Got Mail*, nicely promoted jointly with AOL.
>
> Gerald Levin, Chairman and CEO, Time Warner, at the news conference on CNN announcing the merger of AOL and Time Warner, January 10, 2000

While driving to my office on the morning of January 10, 2000, I heard the report on NPR that the entertainment conglomerate Time Warner, under the leadership of its CEO Gerald Levin, had negotiated a merger with the leading Internet service provider America Online (AOL), headed by its founder Steven M. Case.

Merger in this instance meant that Time Warner had been bought out by AOL, a company which, floating high on the dot-com bubble, then had a market valuation double that of the largest media company in the world. I stopped off in the office of Drayton Nabers, a colleague who had read with some skepticism a draft of an essay I'd been writing on the Time Warner merger, passed on the news, and then half-jokingly added, "There's got to be a movie about this merger." Five minutes later I had an e-mail from him with the message "There is," and a link to Timothy Noah's "Chatterbox" column in that morning's *Slate*.[15]

Noah begins with the question, "Is Nora Ephron responsible for AOL's proposed acquisition of Time Warner?" He then invites his readers to consider that the massive deal had been not only anticipated but prepared by the 1998 Warner Bros. film *You've Got Mail* (co-written and directed by Ephron), which, he speculates, could have been "an attempt to soften the ground for AOL's lastest acquisition." Writing to deadline, Noah only suggests a reading. "Although the film doesn't portray AOL-the-corporation in any particular light," he writes, "it does portray Tom Hanks, scion of another giant communications empire (in this case a Borders/Barnes & Noble–type book superstore chain) as being sweet and misunderstood, even though he puts Meg Ryan's independent bookstore out of business!" Noah proposes this allegorical payoff: "When Ryan and Hanks finally smooch at the film's end, you can think of it as a consummated romance; or, you can think of it as . . . a merger!" He quickly backs off from the merger option, however, confessing that he is "engaging in the same sort of paranoid logic" practiced by the technophobic journalist in the film.

Noah's double move, attributing responsibility to Ephron as co-writer and director and ritually invoking "paranoid logic," expresses a resistance to assigning authorial agency to the corporate organization that is in fact responsible for the film. The atavistic veneration for the original, individual artist as fount of meaning is familiar enough. Yet there is more to this resistance than retrograde auteurism. The reluctance to acknowledge the corporate authorship of low and high cultural artifacts immunizes such activity from judgment. It is as if the legal charter that has made it possible for entertainment corporations to act as persons in the market, and the legal decisions that have granted or conceded entertainment companies the citizen's first amendment rights to free speech in the public sphere, have had the paradoxical effect of exempting the articulate commodities those persons produce from being suspected of advancing corporate objectives, whether by making a case or by managing a brand.

Is Noah's sketch of an allegorical reading plausible? Not if we restrict ourselves to Nora and Delia Ephron's "2nd final white revised" script, dated February 2, 1998.[16] The script is entitled "You've Got Mail," which is, of course, the familiar alert that America Online subscribers receive from their PCs (used by Joe Fox, the character played by Hanks) or their Macs (laptop of choice for Kathleen Kelly, played by Ryan). The alternate title "You've Got *M@il*" had been considered in January, and "You Have Mail" was apparently still a candidate when shooting began.[17] When, exactly, the title was set is unclear (one source puts the date on May 30).[18] All variations of the title more or less mimicked the characteristic AOL alerts. The shift from one title to another may have reflected concern about the legal status of the phrases: although none of the phrases was registered as a service mark or trademark, a distinctive or suggestive phrase may acquire trademark status without formal registration by the United States Patent and Trademark Office. The vacillation almost certainly signaled changing attitudes regarding the relationship between the Time Warner picture and AOL.

Divergent attitudes toward AOL are discernable in the Ephrons' final script. Early on, a corporate defense against a possible charge of trademark infringement is adumbrated in an exchange between Kathleen, owner of the children's bookstore called The Shop Around the Corner, and the predatory Joe Fox at a cocktail party:[19] Kathleen says, "I am your competition. Which you know perfectly well or you would not have put up that sign saying 'Just around the Corner.'" To which Joe responds, "The entrance to our store is around the corner. There is no other way to say it. It's not the name of our store, it's where it is. You don't own 'around the corner.'"[20] Kathleen naïvely inflates her standing by calling herself Joe's competition, perhaps out of pride (mistaking the business for the personal) or prejudice (misunderstanding the value of professional growth). During the narrative she will progress to the realization that she is stronger when bonded to him than she ever was as an independent proprietor. But at this point, as if outfacing a potential lawsuit, Joe interprets Kathleen's remark as an implicit accusation of trademark piracy and mounts the rebuttal that she has no property right in "around the corner"—a descriptive phrase which, like generic phrases such as, say, "You have mail" and "You've got mail," belongs to the "linguistic commons" and therefore cannot be owned.

Earlier in the script there is a scene among the clerks in Shop Around the Corner, in which the elderly Birdie is asked whether she has had cybersex. To the unlikely question she gives an unlikely answer: "I tried to have cybersex once but I kept getting a busy signal."

A clerk named Christina responds, "I know, I know. One Saturday night I was really depressed about not having a date, so I thought, no problem, I'll go on and I won't be lonely, but I couldn't get on, there were hundreds of thousands of people who didn't have dates trying to get on. (You have to wonder which is harder, getting a date or getting online when you don't have a date.)" The joke is not only that the busy signal betrays the cyberpromise of immediate sexual gratification, but in the wry allusion to the notorious difficulties that AOL subscribers were known to chronically suffer when trying to get online. The joke is developed fully in only the script, however. In the film, perhaps as a courtesy to an AOL much more integrated into the commercial neighborhood that the movie embraces, Christina's response is muffled, and the final joke is omitted.

Joe and Kathleen are in pursuit of something much purer than cybersex. And neither has to wait to get online. Late in the story Joe praises the potency of the AOL phrase:

> *Kathleen*: We only know each other—oh God, you're not going to believe this—
> *Joe*: Let me guess. From the Internet.
> *Kathleen*: Yes.
> *Joe*: You've Got Mail.
> *Kathleen*: Yes.
> *Joe*: Very powerful words.

The viewer's readiness to credit that observation is in part owed to Joe's superior knowledge, which duplicates the viewer's own perspective on the action, in part due to an awareness of the force that the common phrase has in almost everyone's lives, and in part owed to a somewhat distant invocation of the increasingly pervasive corporate presence of America Online in American society. The finished movie welds those parts together by making the link between the Warner Bros. motion picture and the corporate fate of AOL explicit, by signaling that the corporate affiliation is the very condition for the existence of the narrative, by intimating that the generic acquires its distinctive force primarily through corporate mediation, and by demonstrating that the power of the AOL slogan is enhanced through its partnership with Time Warner.

If the particular allegory of the merger—AOL acquiring Time Warner—that Noah floats is missing from the Ephron text, the script nonetheless signals an allegorical intention on behalf of Time Warner. For although Starbucks and Zabars are given their proper names, the bookstore chain is not. Most reviewers have identified the chain as a thinly disguised Barnes & Noble. Both the script and the movie name it "Fox"—they name it and model it (Figure 6.7). When Joe takes his young aunt and young brother to Shop Around the Corner), Joe even spells it out: "F-O-X." For the reader or viewer who knows something about Time Warner (an audience segment with special but not occult knowledge, given the print and pixels devoted to the vicissitudes of the media giant in the press and online), choosing the name of Fox for a corporation that is aggressively invading New York City should invoke Fox Broadcasting, just as the many-times-married,

Figure 6.7

cynically predatory, dynastically determined head of the bookstore chain should invoke Rupert Murdoch. There is a history of conflict between the two entertainment companies. The antagonism between Murdoch and Ted Turner (on the Time Warner board in 1998) goes back at least to an *X-Files* episode entitled "Wetwired," which aired on May 10, 1996, in which *Fox* Mulder traces the source of signals provoking people to commit homicide to videotapes of cable news broadcasts—a dig at CNN.[21] In 1996 Fox News filed a $2 billion antitrust lawsuit "less than 18 hours before the first of two shareholders meetings . . . to vote on Time Warner's purchase of Turner Broadcasting."[22] In November of that year Time Warner Cable of New York won its suit against the City of New York to prevent the city from compelling the company to carry Fox News as part of its cable programming.[23] The companies would patch up relations briefly in 1999, but not before Warner Bros. tweaked the Time Warner rival in *You've Got Mail*.

So far as the script goes, then, there is reasonably good evidence that the canny Ephron embedded an insider's allegory. But a reading of the script alone provides no persuasive evidence of corporate allegory in the strong sense: that the film is an intentional form designed by a corporate enterprise to address distinct audiences in order to achieve one or more business objectives. In the finished film, however, released on December 18, 1998, it is a different story. Before the credit there appears a commemorative version of the familiar Warner Bros. logo projected against the sky, with the subscript "A Time Warner Entertainment Company" (Figure 6.8). In a seamless optical transition the sky-like background is replaced by a field of blue (Figure 6.9). Then the logo recedes to reveal what appears as a computer desk top (Figure 6.10). I say "appears as" because it is not quite accurate to say that this is the *image* of a computer screen. There is no border to the blue field; all that makes it resemble a com-

Figure 6.8

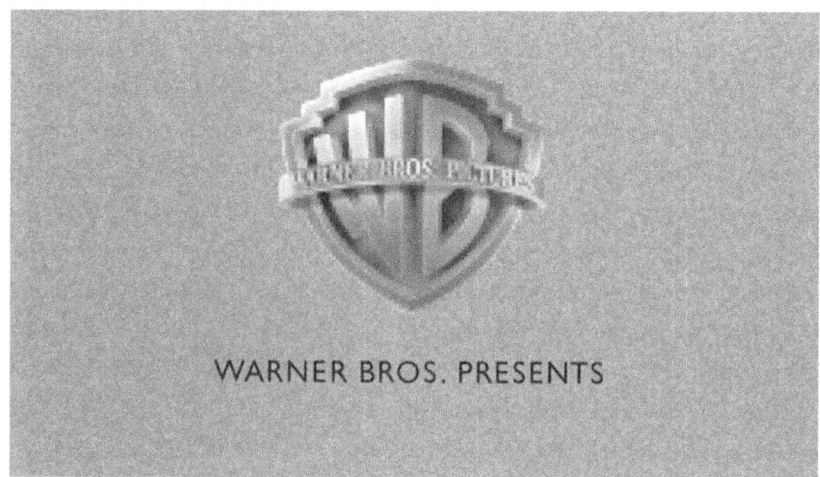

Figure 6.9

Figure 6.10

puter screen is an array of generic Microsoft desktop icons. And then, of course, there are the logos, native to no known desktop. In the upper-left corner is the Warner Bros. logo; in the lower-right corner, on a direct diagonal with the WB logo is the logo of AOL. Because there is no perceptible difference between the motion picture screen and the computer screen, it seems appropriate to say that the two screens have *merged*. WB and AOL share, not divide, exactly the same screen real estate. The seamlessness of the connection is represented in the credit sequence, which begins with "A Lauren Shuler Donner Production," appearing on the blue field, followed by a mouse point, followed in turn by a click that triggers an animation sequence which begins in outer space and then gradually closes in on the Upper West Side of New York before it dissolves from a computer-generated image to a filmed image of an apartment building.

The pairing of the corporate logos precedes any other credit as well as the introduction of the pair of unlikely lovers. A logo is not just another visual image: federally registered and legally protected against duplication, the logo is the graphic representation of a distinctive corporate brand. Each logo claims corporate ownership of the space it occupies, and each asserts an unambiguous corporate identity. While a writer can refer to a logo in a script with impunity, the logo itself cannot be reproduced without someone having secured the right to do so. The coexistence of the logos on the merged screen is, therefore, not a mere fiction: it attests to a formal relationship between the corporate persons Warner Bros., a Time Warner subsidiary, and AOL that exists in the world of contracts as well as on the screen. The opening screen shots brandish the Warners logo as the source of the message that this film about sending and receiving messages is and situate AOL in the position of both receiver of the message (reading the screen left to right) and partner in a marketing communication to the viewer (apprehending the screen as a whole). The credit sequence that superintends the narrative raises Ephron's scattered references to AOL to a new level by framing her metropolitan romance as a message from one corporation to another, a message that projects a new brand identity.

By initially representing the appearance of the paired logos that establish the identities of the corporate characters, the film invites the viewer to make an allegorical connection between them and the characters of Joe and Kathleen when they appear. That connection would have looked different in 1998, when Time Warner still dwarfed AOL, than it did to Timothy Noah subsequent to the merger in January 2000, when a bloated AOL had acquired the media giant. On balance, Joe fits best with Time Warner: he runs a large diversified business (books, yes, but cappuccino, coffee mugs, and various knickknacks) and whose revenue, as he spitefully points out to Kathleen, beggars that of Shop Around the Corner. Kathleen, the addressee of the single most important message in the film: "Should we meet?" is, like AOL (if you don't count its acquisition of the now deceased Compuserve), an independent, and, like AOL, she is all about interface and customer service. What she has that Joe wants is a customer base: about 20 million for AOL at the time, somewhat less for Shop Around the Corner.

That does not mean that Noah is wrong in his essential premise that *You've Got Mail* softened the ground for the merger, only that there was more ground to cover than he noticed and that the softening of it was a complicated process. As Jim Hu and Dawn Kawamoto reported on February 9, 1999, during 1998 Time Warner was softening the ground because, as had "long been rumored," the corporation was "in the market for a major Internet acquisition." After the announcement on January 10, 2000, that AOL had acquired the larger, more profitable, and more diversified company, it was natural to think that AOL had softened up its target in order to close the deal, but in fact Time Warner had started the job in 1998. Hu and Kawamoto reported that during the previous week, in a conference call about quarterly earnings, CEO Gerald Levin had said that the company would use its existing assets instead of cash or stock, as currency in joint ventures or combinations. While Levin was vague on specifics about those investments, a media-industry source said Time Warner might be looking to use its "soft money" through currency-free promotion and distribution via its holdings, which also include the WB television network, Warner Music, and Turner Entertainment Networks—in exchange for a stake in an Internet company. It appears that Time Warner is not willing to pay cash or trade its stock for internet companies, largely because of their high valuations.[24]

Levin's approach is clear: you soften the ground by soaking it with soft money. But what Hu and Kawamoto do not report is that Time Warner had already concluded the first phase of Levin's soft-money strategy, which centered on the use of *You've Got Mail* as a lure for AOL. In the spring of 1998 someone—perhaps Ephron, perhaps Shuler—approached AOL about a closer relationship with the film. There is, so far as I have been able to ascertain, no public record of that meeting, but it almost certainly occurred before April 20, the date that AOL filed twice with the U.S. Patents and Trademarks Office to register "You Have Mail" as a trademark. That filing was followed by four others in May: for "You've Got Mail," for the graphic of the mailbox, and so on. The flurry of filings is evidence of a desire to seek protection of phrases and images that AOL had long ignored but that it now recognized were going to escalate in value as a result of the motion picture and therefore would become targets for predatory competitors. By filing for trademark protection AOL also enhanced the justification for Time Warner to license the trademarks from AOL, an agreement that not only enabled Time Warner to begin promotion of the movie but that provided some corroboration that AOL owned them.[25] We know that Time Warner did license the trademarks, but it remains obscure as to when the licensing agreement was reached. Despite speculation regarding the magnitude of AOL's expenditure to acquire an unprecedented amount of screen real estate in a Hollywood feature film, we lack any evidence that AOL paid anything to Warner Bros. to place its product in the motion picture.[26] Given Levin's remarks about soft money, it seems unlikely that AOL paid a dime. Time Warner did get some advertising for the movie on the AOL portal in exchange for advertising the Internet company in the film. From an AOL perspective the deal was an advertising swap, similar to the kind of deal that AOL regularly engineered before the merger (not wholly unlike those subsequently investigated by the Securities and Exchange Commission) and one that was also practiced among the divisions of Time Warner before and after the merger. Indeed, the cashless advertising swap was in form if not in magnitude similar to the nontaxable stock swap by which the merger would eventually be accomplished.

Yet the barter was incidental to the main deal from the perspective of Time Warner. For what AOL received from Time Warner's promotion of its brand in *You've Got Mail* was wholly incommensurable with whatever paltry millions might have been paid or written off as payment. The film was not a vehicle for exchanging dollars or passing along soft money; the film *was* the soft money that Levin lavished on AOL to impress Steve Case with the power of his company to generate market value. And Case must have been impressed (Table 6.1). AOL's stock had been steadily rising during October and November 1998: it increased ten dollars on a twelve-dollar price in the space of seven weeks. And then the stock hovered around twenty-two dollars from November until December 21, the first Monday after the opening of *You've Got Mail*, on December 18, when the stock spiked fourteen points in ten days. It's not just the increase in price that's impressive. Look at the trading volume. There were other busy days during the fall, but nowhere was there the sustained level of trading as that we see at the end of the month. *You've Got Mail* was soft money—lots of it—that went right into the portfolios of the shareholders in time for the holidays. The windfall was, of course, a special gift for Steve Case. Just multiply his holding of 20 million shares by fourteen; it's a wonderful message. Nothing personal, just business.

After that spike the stock settled down until March, when it renewed its astonishing climb to the peak it reached in early January 2000, just in time for the conclusion of the merger. Now, I'm not arguing that *You've Got Mail* caused that spike in December 1998, or even that Levin planned it. It's enough for me to solicit the reader's belief that Case and Levin could have believed that the movie

Table 6.1 AOL Prices from December 1–31, 1998[a]

Date	Volume	Ask	High Bid	Adj. Close
12/01/98	94,666,000	22.50	20.40	22.46
12/02/98	39,627,200	22.68	21.78	21.87
12/03/98	50,710,000	22.50	20.87	21.00
12/04/98	44,594,000	21.96	21.20	21.93
12/07/98	27,724,800	22.43	21.93	22.40
12/08/98	42,242,400	23.00	22.18	22.59
12/09/98	38,679,600	23.46	22.64	23.23
12/10/98	38,613,200	23.46	22.01	22.48
12/11/98	32,947,600	23.04	22.10	22.98
12/14/98	32,811,200	22.68	22.09	22.25
12/15/98	38,867,600	23.31	22.65	23.21
12/16/98	68,135,600	24.32	23.62	24.06
12/17/98	43,837,600	24.92	24.00	24.68
12/18/98	49,604,800	26.25	24.90	26.15
12/21/98	72,788,800	29.84	27.06	29.12
12/22/98	90,378,800	31.09	28.62	30.70
12/23/98	110,757,200	35.12	33.50	34.57
12/24/98	27,463,200	34.75	33.87	34.15
12/28/98	102,285,600	39.93	34.87	39.28
12/29/98	72,880,000	39.87	36.75	38.50
12/30/98	111,528,000	38.50	33.50	36.95
12/31/98	152,473,600	40.00	35.75	40.00

[a] AOL Personal Finance Forum, keyword "stocks." See the same chart at www.google.com/search?hl=en&lr=&ie=UTF-8&oe=UTF-8&prev=/search%3Fq%3DAOL%2BPrices%2Band%2Bvolumes%2Bhistory%26hl%3Den%26lr%3D%26ie%3DUTF-8%26oe%3DUTF-8&q=stocks:AOL+.

caused the sudden climb. It's enough that we can tender the belief that those insiders, such as Steve Case, and would-be insiders, such as the day-trading wise guys, who saw the movie and—signaled by the credits—decoded the barely veiled allegory of corporate romance, could have believed that the film signaled a corporate intent to complete a merger that would raise the stock even more, or that they believed the signal of a merger would be enough to raise the stock value for a time whether or not the merger ever took place, or that they believed that others would believe the stock value of AOL would leap in response to the film and bought stock themselves in order to be the elusive first-one-in. We'll never know what any one or two or thousand or million stock purchasers actually believe, which is why we speak of what the market thinks, fears, hopes. No matter. It is not the inference of an amorphous market psyche that is at stake here, but the suasive evidence of a determinate corporate intention which was legible in the film and which made it credible that the film was used as soft money in order to achieve a specific corporate objective—thereby proving Time Warner's value to AOL by demonstrating how it could dramatically increase AOL's value to its shareholders.

By the time Levin publicly talked about using soft money to buy an Internet company in February 1999, Time Warner had already munificently bestowed such money on AOL—Time Warner, not Levin. For it is just as likely that Levin inferred the corporate strategy after he perceived its plausible success as it is that he deliberately planned that course of action. Levin has certainly never said that he plotted the strategy, and those who have read either Connie Bruck's *Master of the Game* or transcripts of Levin's press conferences know that the "visionary" CEO was neither shy about taking credit nor reluctant to spread the blame when deal-making credit was swamped by postdeal debit. Like Ephron, Levin was an agent of a corporate intention that he could impersonate but for which he was not solely responsible. Still, if my story is to be believed, it needs to be explained why the merger did not occur in January 1999. It could be argued that *You've Got Mail* succeeded too well. Indeed, the case could be made that the whole enterprise backfired, for by jacking up the stock value of AOL, Time Warner had elevated it to a level that completely changed the basis on which negotiations could be conducted. Whatever the prospects for acquisition were early in 1998, after *You've Got Mail*, Time Warner could not hope to buy AOL at its January valuation. So AOL bought Time Warner the following year.

That seems ironic. But it is only ironic if you believe Levin's public statements that it was in fact his objective to acquire an Internet company. The fact was that the "soft money" approach—which came down to buying a major corporation with free advertising—did not sound ludicrous when Levin formulated it only because the idea of Time Warner, which was still wallowing in the debt that it had taken on in the last merger, spending the kind of real money it would take to acquire a robust Internet company, was a highly unlikely and extremely risky strategic move.[27] As Paul Farhi, who reported on the Time Warner connection for the *Washington Post* in 1998–99, suggested to me, it is likely that Levin's press conference in February 1999 was a "head fake" designed to plant the impression that Time Warner was in an acquisitive disposition while, having deterred hostile moves, the company could ready itself to be acquired, exploiting the merger to move to another level where its debt would be absorbed in the greater whole. That strategy would be completely consistent with Levin's deal-making model, the Time Warner merger engineered by Steve Ross in 1989. By the time that Levin and Case "met cute" at a Global Business Dialogue which they co-chaired, not only had the marketing principle been proved, it had also been "proved" that AOL would hold and even increase its value. After the meeting and a romantic trip that Case and Levin made to China together, it was only a matter of a few months before the Levin flip was accomplished, and Steve Case, assuming the Tom Hanks role, contacted shop girl Levin to say, "I think this would be an extraordinary merger, a merger of equals."[28] With that call the merger was assured, and Timothy Noah's reading of *You've Got Mail* as persuasively anticipating AOL's acquisition of Time Warner would become not only inevitable but right.

Money matters, of course. But what is money? According to Levin there is hard money and soft money—and the latter, which includes motion pictures and other forms of advertising is, he attested, a medium of exchange preferable to cash. If readings in the history of the global operations of multinationals and of the merger mania of media conglomerates in the late decades of the twentieth century teach us anything, it is that to level the charge that a chief executive officer's reasoning is circular does not disconfirm aggressive arguments for investment, merger, diversification, or takeover that are backed by sufficient political, cultural, or financial capital. Scenario thinking worked for Shell and Time Warner as it had worked for the National Security Council, because it was devised to absorb all contingencies into a feedback loop. In the case of AOL and Time Warner, the initial affiliation of the companies involved a deal in which AOL agreed to advertise a Time Warner film that advertised AOL and suggested a possible merger. That promotion raised AOL's market value by inducing stock purchases based on the belief that the stock would ascend to a new level due to others' purchases made in the belief that the stock would ascend to a new level. And that bubblicious increase in stock value created AOL as a customer for the purchase of Time Warner, which was acquired when, in payment for an utterly illusory share of power in the merged company ("See, our name comes first!"), AOL returned to Time Warner shareholders an incommensurate portion of the value that *You've Got Mail* had created. That value, the very concept of value, promulgated by Case and Levin was, it turned out, equally illusory.[29] Three years later, after all the machinations and promotions, stock rising and stock falling, Levin was gone and Case as good as gone. It turns out that the only thing of value associated with *You've Got Mail* that persists is *The Shop Around the Corner* (MGM, 1940)—not the store owned by Kathleen Kelly but the film made by Ernst Lubitsch, who had the good fortune to work for MGM, in 1940, not Warner Bros., which had become the fountainhead of senseless splurges, in the 1990s.

7. The Conscience of a Corporation
Toys United the Disney-Pixar Merger, and the Assertion of "Cultural" Authorship (1995–2010)

i. Corporate Speech, Corporate Liability

At the end of Walt Disney's 1939 feature *Pinocchio*, an animated, artificial person, proven to be a money machine for the gypsy impresario Stromboli, becomes, thanks to the intervention of the Blue Fairy, a real boy. In 2006 Pixar, the little company that had demonstrated its capacity to be a money machine to new Disney CEO Robert Iger, became, thanks to the negotiating skills of Steve Jobs, CEO of Pixar, a real conscience for Walt Disney Productions. I shall argue that the terms of Disney's acquisition of Pixar (consistently called a merger by the two parties), terms that commit Disney to "help maintain Pixar's corporate 'culture,'" reflect Pixar's reading of *Pinocchio* as an allegory of corporate transformation and the development of something very much like a theory of the function of "culture" as a creative technology within Disney.

To pursue this argument requires a revision of the studio authorship thesis, which is anchored by two claims: (1) an adequate understanding of the historical development and contemporary importance of the Hollywood entertainment business demands an understanding of what still remains its preeminent product, motion pictures; (2) many of those motion pictures cannot be fully understood without interpreting them as corporate texts. The thesis unfolds as a series of entailments: no interpretation without meaning, no meaning without intention, no intention without an author, no author without a person, no person with greater right to or capacity for authorship than a corporate person, no corporate person who can act without an agent, whether executive, board of directors, or employee.[1] This chapter adds a clause formulated to fit the circumstances of the transformative Disney-Pixar merger in 2006: the agent of a corporate principal may be its "culture," acting as the conscience of the corporation.

The critical issue for corporate theory is no longer whether a corporation may speak as freely as any other person, just as Pinocchio magically does when first touched by the fairy's wand. The U.S. Supreme Court has settled the question with its judgment for the plaintiff in *Citizens United v. Federal Election*

Commission, 130 S.Ct. 876 (2010). This judgment was made in the context of a suit regarding the release by Citizens United, a nonprofit corporation, of a critical documentary, *Hillary*, in January 2008, to be broadcast within thirty days of the Democratic primary elections, in violation of the rules established by the Court in *Austin v. Michigan Chamber of Commerce*, 494 U.S. 652, which held that such speech could be banned based on the speaker's corporate identity. *Citizens United* conferred the First Amendment right to freedom of speech on all corporations, profit-seeking and nonprofit, so corporations can now speak as freely as any other person in the United States. As we shall see, however, whether a corporation is the kind of person who, like Jiminy Cricket, can intend as an author, tell right from wrong, and accept the consequences of its actions, are questions that the U.S. Supreme Court obliquely raises but fails to answer. There are good reasons why a corporation might be happy to speak but be unhappy to be burdened with intention. Speaking in the form of political advertising can be hugely influential. Speaking in the form of financial contributions to lobbyists and even legislators can guarantee access and influence. Speaking in the form of motion pictures enables entertainment corporations not only to reach a global audience but also to shape it and the social conditions in which such speaking means. Adding the capacity to intend would make it possible for the corporation to be an author who speaks copyrightable utterances rather than merely purchasing them. There may be a drawback, however. The people, the Congress, or the Supreme Court might decide that the corporate author should be held responsible for its works, even so far as to be held liable for criminal acts executed on its authority.

That a corporation could actually intend to make *Batman* or *Grand Hotel* has always been a difficult sell. Yet it would not be so had there not been a certain amount of professional interference from literary theorists, committed to preserving creativity for individuals or, conversely, intent on denying to any persons at all what Samuel Taylor Coleridge once called the esemplastic power. Corporate lawyers overall have cooperated with those academic agendas, since it is generally in the interest of their clients to cover any tracks that would make a corporation's intention legible. And for good reason. The problem of corporate intention has been critical in two distinct but affiliated areas of the law that bear on studio authorship: antitrust and criminal liability. In both areas attempts by prosecutors to attach liability to the corporation have often foundered on the implications of using terms traditionally applied to biological persons for identifying the subjectivity of artificial persons. As we have seen, since the passage of the Sherman Antitrust Act in 1890, corporate intent has been critical to the determination of the guilt or innocence of an alleged monopolist.

Proving the existence of a corporate intent to restrain trade has always been difficult, but directly prosecuting corporations for acts that do not involve strict liability or negligence has been almost impossible because liability for criminal acts traditionally depends on evidence of *mens rea*, a guilty mind, and few jurists have been convinced that the corporation as such is in possession of the subjective capacity to apprehend guilt. Consequently, criminal liability must be derived from the actions of people, not from an artificial entity supposedly incapable of forming motives. Peter A. French has, however, influentially argued that a corporation's capacity to select a right course of action over a wrong one is enabled by the Corporate Internal Decision structure, or CID, which distributes policy decisions throughout the executive hierarchy so that the corporation can pursue its strategic objectives without placing ultimate authority on any individual. According to French, the existence of the CID provides the means for assessing whether a corporate action is the offspring of policy and the grounds for judging whether that policy is moral or immoral.[2]

Nonetheless, behaving illegally is not the same as knowing right from wrong. To close the gap, activists in the 1990s, especially in the Commonwealth nations, adopted *culture* as their name for a nonindividualized corporate subjectivity with a sense of right and wrong, a trope designed to enable the legal system to dispense "with any necessary connection between corporate and individual liability. The aim," according to Eric Colvin, "is to construct a scheme of liability for the organizational conduct and fault of the corporation, regardless of whether or not any individual would have committed an offense."[3] One systematic approach, which Colvin examines, is the Australian Model Criminal Code of 1994, which recognizes "a distinctive corporate form of recklessness, based upon the presence of a corporate culture favoring the commission of offenses" ("CP," p. 34). Even though the "physical element of the offense" might involve "the conduct of officers, employees, and agents acting within the scope of their authority or employment," the "fault element" of the offense could be attributed to the culture of the corporation, which

> may have caused the offense to occur, either because the offense was actually directed or because the nature of the culture led to its commission [or because it] may have given psychological support for the commission of the offense. . . . The common bond between these various modes of participation is some positive feature of the culture that can be said to favor the commission of the offense. A corporation would be held responsible for an offense involving subjective fault because of this positive feature, just as an individual would be responsible because of some positive state of mind. ("CP," p. 37)

The Australian Code locates intent nowhere and everywhere: no person is charged with the construction of policy, although every informal practice presupposes a policy that anyone attuned to the culture may, perhaps *must*, infer. Therefore, Colvin concludes, "a corporation ought not to conduct its operations in such a manner that the inference of intent to commit a criminal offense can be drawn" ("CP," p. 35). A *Wall Street Journal* editorial posted by e-mail from the chief accounting officer to the entire accounting department that objects to the prosecution of corporations for backdating stock options could lead an employee to infer that she may be called upon to acquiesce in an implicit company policy to backdate stock options. Crucially, it is not the employee's fault for drawing such an inference. The culture's failure to prevent an employee from making the inference is evidence that the corporation either fosters or tolerates a criminogenic environment, which is tantamount to a violation of the code.

Bad behavior is supposedly caused by bad culture. Bad culture presupposes bad intentions, even though such intentions are nowhere avowed or even suggested in statements of policy or procedure. Bad culture motivates deviation from sound business practices; it is answerable for their commission and their omission. Under the Australian Code, the surest way for a corporation to protect itself from suspicious inferences regarding features of its culture would be to subject all conduct and practices to a code monitored by a specialized agency: a list of dos and don'ts that would leave no ambiguity about what was encouraged or tolerated in the corporation. The existence of that agency would be the best possible evidence that the company complied with its obligation to prevent bad things from happening. In sum, the Australian Code projects the need for corporate equivalents of a "Hays office," the agency established by the motion picture industry in the 1920s to institute a code of dos and don'ts and an enforcement procedure regulating what was seen or heard on the screen. Thus equipped with an officially objective monitor of business practices, a corporation's intention to comply with the law would be formally established—although, as the history of Hollywood's self-censorship shows, even scrupulous regulators would be subject to capture by the culture they are charged with policing: eyes would wink, heads would turn away, rules would be stretched. We may infer from experience that a code of dos and don'ts is no better than a transparent CID as a substitute for a conscience.

Given the implication that a conscience presupposes the subjective capacity for consideration of moral options, the likelihood or even the possibility that a corporation might develop one is not widely credited. That sentiment is entirely reasonable. The culturalist legal movement and this study of studio authorship share the premises that a corporation, considered as an organization, is irreducible to a group of biological individuals, and, considered as a person, is irreducible to a single biological, psychologically complex individual. Consequently, as legal reformers have argued, a positive criminal act committed by a corporation that is equivalent to an act by an individual with *mens rea* could be accepted as evidence of liability for a crime without adverting to the mental state of the corporation.[4] The converse position, however, has received little attention. If the sheer positive act, without reference to a mental state, is sufficient for conviction of a corporation, why could it not be sufficient for any person? It would seem to follow from the logic of the culturalist theory as from the logic of the evolution of the corporate form that people who are persons are not reducible to biological individuals any more than corporate entities are. It's not clear that we, the people, want to suffer the consequences associated with such a conclusion.

We may have no choice. The U.S. Supreme Court implicitly endorsed that logic of equivalence between corporations and people in *Citizens United v. Federal Election Commission*, which overruled the Court's recent decision in *Austin v. Michigan Chamber of Commerce*, 494 U.S. 652, upholding the Election Commission's rule prohibiting electioneering by corporations within thirty days of a primary for election to a federal office. The Roberts Court extended full First Amendment rights to both nonprofit and profit-making corporations on the grounds that the First Amendment of the U.S. Constitution protects political speech, and that speech is speech, regardless of the identity of the speaker. An important, if implicit corollary of that decision is the Supreme Court's confirmation that there is no constitutional distinction between political speech and commercial speech, and therefore none between speech and money. The superficial plausibility of the Court's argument depends on a calculated inconsistency: sometimes it calls corporations "persons," sometimes "speakers," sometimes "citizens." The terms that the majority opinion deploys to identify what exactly distinguishes corporate speech also vary widely: they veer from "funding" to "facts" to "opinions" and "views." At times the decision is so loosely phrased and indifferent to both *stare decisis* and the basic professional obligation to quote earlier decisions candidly that the majority opinion in *Citizens United* seems less the handiwork of disciplined ideologues than the outburst of a renegade judicial subculture. That would be a dangerously comforting conclusion to embrace. The majority's discourse may be called an "opinion," but like the speech of the corporations that the majority zealously serves, its opinion is also an agenda.

The most immediate though not the only connection that *Citizens United* has to the history of the motion picture industry is its citation of a case to which free-speech cases have infrequently adverted: the Supreme Court's 1952 decision for the plaintiff in *Joseph Burstyn Inc. v. Wilson*, 343 U.S. 495, which rejected state censorship of a politically controversial motion picture on the grounds that the "importance [of motion pictures] as an organ of public opinion is not lessened by the fact that they are designed to entertain as well as to inform" (*Burstyn*, p. 501), thus reversing *Mutual Film Corp. v. Industrial Commission of Ohio* 236, U.S. 230 (1915), which found that expression tainted by commercial objectives, as in the film industry, could not qualify for constitutional protection. Building on *Burstyn* as well as *First National Bank of Boston v. Bellotti* 435 U.S. 765 (1978) and other recent decisions, the majority opinion deploys what might be called the "opinion effect" of any and all corporate speech in order to overturn *Austin*, which deserves reversal because that decision has "the purpose and effect" of preventing corporations, including small and nonprofit corporations, "from presenting both facts and opinions to the public" (*Citizens*, p. 39).

In his forceful dissent to the majority opinion, Justice John Paul Stevens states that "it is an interesting question 'who' is even speaking when a business corporation places an advertisement that endorses or attacks a particular candidate" (*Citizens*, p. 77). After eliminating various possibilities, including the shareholders, the directors of the corporation, and its employees, he concludes that if you take away "the ability to use general treasury funds for some of those ads, no one's autonomy, dignity, or political equality has been impinged upon in the least" (*Citizens*, p. 86). No harm to an individual, no foul on the corporation. Stevens's question regarding the source of corporate speech emphatically departs from Foucault's rhetorical question (quoting Samuel Beckett),"What does it matter who is speaking?"[5] For Justice Stevens it does matter; for Justices Kennedy, Roberts, Scalia, Thomas, and Alito it does not. Foucault called that "indifference" "ethical," but the Roberts Court more accurately calls it political, for if it does not matter who is speaking, then, as Stevens suggests, the corporation will speak for all—whether by making propaganda or by paying people to do its bidding.

Is corporate speech authored? The Supreme Court does not directly address the question. Nonetheless, apart from the infamous *Hillary* "documentary" that provoked the suit, the majority opinion's single concrete example of how corporate speaking works, which introduces the final section of the Court's opinion, suggests that corporate speech can indeed be authored and Hollywood movies are one important result:

> When word concerning the plot of the movie *Mr. Smith Goes to Washington* reached the circles of Government, some officials sought, by persuasion, to discourage its

distribution. Under *Austin*, though, officials could have done more than discourage its distribution—they could have banned the film. After all, it, like *Hillary*, was speech funded by a corporation that was critical of Members of Congress. *Mr. Smith Goes to Washington* may be fiction and caricature; but fiction and caricature can be a powerful force. (*Citizens*, p. 56)[6]

The Court not only validates the studio-authorship thesis, it gets there by a foray into film history that successfully distorts every "fact" it blithely mentions. We know that because Justice Kennedy's industrious clerk supplied citations. In fact, Frank Nugent, film reviewer for the *New York Times*, reported in October 1939 that persuasion was initiated by no official but by Pete Harrison, an author of a trade journal, who, offended by *Mr. Smith*'s scornful representation of the U.S. Senate, lobbied for the retaliatory passage of the Neely antiblock booking bill, which was then making its way through Senate committees. His advice to the Senate, however, was not that *they* act on the bill, which was virtually certain of passage, but to "tell the members of the House of Representatives that [*Mr. Smith*'s widespread distribution] is only a sample of the impotence of the exhibitors to reject a picture that has been sold on the block-booking system, and that Congress must therefore make it possible for them to reject such a picture and similar other pictures which may offend the sensibilities of the American public" ("CCO," p. X5). Harrison's objective, then, was not to censor *Mr. Smith* (an option that was, of course, available to numerous state and local censorship boards), but to encourage the Senate to persuade the House to pass antitrust legislation that would prohibit block booking: the film industry's systematic policy of requiring exhibitors to take all the films offered in a package or to get none, thereby making it financially suicidal to refuse *Mr. Smith* or any other offensive pictures forced upon them by a studio. Passage of the Neely bill might have meant that exhibitors would have rejected *Mr. Smith*; or they might have welcomed the film. Defeat of the bill meant they would continue to have no choice. Lobbying on behalf of the bill was not a free-speech issue. Even today, the First Amendment has not yet been interpreted by the Supreme Court as requiring exhibitors to screen or citizens to watch the *Hillary* documentary or making it mandatory for anyone to sit still for any other corporate propaganda.

If any senators did organize their own lobby in response to the article in the trade journal, members of the House of Representatives either didn't listen or didn't care. As it routinely did during the Second New Deal, the House repelled any steps to stop block booking. So if an objective of the movie was to blunt the momentum to regulate the industry by burnishing the vanity of the junior chamber, it achieved a tactical victory. That victory was soon followed by a strategic defeat, however. The legislative rejection of Neely triggered the filing by the Roosevelt Justice Department of *United States v. Paramount*, a frontal assault on the industry's anticompetitive practices, the following year. So the Roberts Court is mistaken about the facts, but once again, its indifference to reference is political. By casting this brief dispute from the 1930s as a potential First Amendment issue, the Court cannily identifies governmental attempts to eliminate oligopolistic business practices in Hollywood with policies designed to regulate an individual's free speech and, without saying it, to associate, correctly, corporate intention in the sphere of distribution with corporate intention as manifest on the screen. It turns out that the 1930s are pertinent to contemporary developments in corporate law only insofar as progressive political efforts to dilute the concentration of power in the motion picture industry can be revised to look like a contemporary contest about the First Amendment rights of corporate persons. Indeed, it is just a slight exaggeration to assert that the 1930s are only invoked by the Roberts Court so that the Second New Deal can be succinctly annulled.

The majority may have gotten its history wrong, but it accurately concluded that the business of the studio's narrative is the studio's business. If corporate speech is indeed political (and who doubts that?), in a democratic society such speech is liable to have a political response from the people's elected representatives. Despite the majority's gesture of supporting disclosure requirements, the subsequent and partisan defeat in the U.S. Senate in October 2010 of HR 5175, the "Democracy Is Strengthened by Casting Light on Spending in Elections" Act, commonly called the DISCLOSE Act, which would have required such disclosure of the identities of corporate and union contributors to political campaigns, is widely regarded as flowing from the Court's decision in *Citizen United*, especially from Justice Thomas's concurring opinion. Whatever the Court's expressed views, the *Citizens* decision has given crucial impetus to lowering an impenetrable veil to protect corporations from a political response to their funding of the expression of political opinions.[7]

From the perspective of a film historian, the most telling aspect of the Court's invocation of *Mr. Smith* is its conspicuous omission of the name of Frank Capra, who directed the picture and who was one of the few directors whose name appeared in the credit "above the title." Capra's name was all over the newspaper accounts of the *Mr. Smith* controversy. He is not mentioned by the majority opinion, which imagines that credit and blame for celluloid speech is applicable solely to the corporation, Columbia Pictures, that "funded" the production and distribution of the picture. Although the title card does say "Frank Capra's" *Mr. Smith Goes to Washington*, that credit was negotiated with

Columbia Pictures, which displayed its own credit for ownership on a separate card preceding the title. Evidently, in the majority's serene mind, where ownership and authorship seamlessly combine, Columbia, not Capra, is author of the movie, has full responsibility for the picture, and should, therefore, be the target for those offended by an insult against senatorial dignity. In getting the facts of the news event wrong, the Roberts Court gets the spirit of the political event right by recognizing that Columbia had better reason for releasing a movie satirizing the Senate, for promoting the movie nationally, and for premiering it in Washington, DC, than Capra did. Moreover, in its political imaginary the Roberts Court appreciates that the Senate may have had excellent reason to retaliate, that is, to hold Columbia *liable* for its actions, since *Mr. Smith* is political speech, and in the real world of power politics that the Roberts Court plays so well, you are liable to be punished politically for your aggressive speech to the extent that the assailed party is capable. With that jeopardy in mind, the majority's retrospective defense of Columbia renders the First Amendment as a shield law protecting the corporation from both the legal and political consequences of its political speech—funding and action. It matters not to the majority that Columbia's speech could only reach the screen because the company had the assurance of profit provided by the systematic anticompetitive practices that the Neely bill aimed to abolish.

To put the issue in slightly different language, by suppressing the role of Capra or of any other person besides the studio in bringing *Mr. Smith* to the screen, the Court is able to exploit the linkage of corporate ownership with financing and slide the funding by the studio into the author position. In doing so, the Court brazenly represents a presumptive intent by Columbia to restrain trade as evidence of the studio's intent to satirize those who would attempt to outlaw its monopolistic practices. The Court thereby introduces an astonishing judicial trope that is comprehensive enough to render any attempt at regulation of corporate economic activity as an unconstitutional abridgment of free speech. The only political response open to this essay is to urge that critics and theorists do what they can do: take advantage of the Court's wily subterfuge by using the cover of authorship, with its presumption of a controlling mind, to slide liability right back. Rendering corporate speech as equivalent to corporate authorship may reinforce its claims on protection, but authorship can be used to introduce deliberation and discretion into the construction of the corporate subject—that is, to attribute to the corporation the capacity to distinguish between a right and wrong way of doing things as the basis for holding corporations criminally liable for the harm that they do, just like real people.

ii. Pixar's Logic: Corporate Liability, Culture, and Conscience

The Roberts Court was by no means the first collection of legal experts to connect the issue of liability for what corporations put on motion picture screens with antitrust prosecution by the federal government. The threat of antitrust prosecution, along with the danger of boycotts and censorship, motivated the industry's formation of the Hays Office, in 1922, the subsequent formulation of the Production Code, and voluntary submission to policing by the Production Code Administration. The studios were impelled to deal not only with moral issues, such as the exposure of people to sexual imagery and language, but also with tortious issues such as the measurable harm that many accused motion pictures of causing to its audience, particularly children. That vulnerability was addressed in the unusual prologue to *Frankenstein* (Universal, 1931), in which Edward Van Sloane, who plays the upright and earnest Dr. Waldman in the movie, appears on a stage as an agent of Mr. Carl Laemmle, head and owner of Universal Studios:

> Mr. Carl Laemmle feels that it would be a little unkind to present this picture without just a word of friendly warning. We're about to unfold the story of Frankenstein, a man of science who sought to create a man after his own image, without reckoning upon God. It is one of the strangest tales ever told. It deals with the two great mysteries of creation: life and death. I think it will thrill you. It may shock you. It might even horrify you. So if any of you feel you do not care to subject your nerves to such a strain, now is your chance to . . . Well, uh, we warned you.

No doubt the warning is about as sincere as a carnival barker's admonitions outside the tent of Little Eva. Still, Van Sloane's address seems to have fulfilled the minimum requirements for the speech act called "warning" and therefore potentially the conditions for the legal protection called "disclaimer" or "alibi." Whether or not the warning had any effect on the audience, it did little to appease all critics, some of whom had developed data to prove that the newly named "horror film" had bad effects on the children in attendance. Indeed, Henry James Forman's "popular summary" in *Our Movie Made Children* of the results of the investigations by the Committee on Educational Research of the Payne Fund, carried out during 1929 to 1933 at the request of the Motion Picture Research Council, reports the alarming results of movie going as disclosed by the application of a "hypnometer" to sleeping children, a "psychogalvometer," to boys and girls at the theater, an interview with a "theater nurse," who attests that *The Phantom of the Opera* "caused . . . eleven faintings and one miscarriage in a single day," and interviews of children disturbed by their exposure to "horror and fright pictures"[8]—all of which does not prove that

Frankenstein harmed anyone, only that Laemmle–Van Sloane's product warning prologue had little effect on sociologists who were conducting their studies at the time. Laemmle's intervention was a classic example of the power of the Hollywood mogul to override the Corporate Internal Decision structure of his company by forcibly binding ownership and authorship. The performative effect of this stagecraft was to subordinate the contributions to the picture of both the producer, Carl Laemmle, Jr., and the director, James Whale—who were warned by this segment, which neither had mandated, that this mogul reserved the power to trump rivals to his authority.

The reign of the founding Hollywood moguls was remarkably stable but not even close to eternal. After the transformation, decline, or extinction of the major studios in the late 1950s and 1960s, a new model of authority and, therefore, responsibility, adapted to the dramatic rise to prominence of the director as auteur, emerged, a model much more personalized and much less capitalized than the studios that financed, marketed, and distributed the auteur's creations. The most notorious instance of criminal prosecution of a filmmaker in the employ of a major studio for criminal negligence occurred in the trial of John Landis, director of two segments of the anthology picture *The Twilight Zone* (Warners, 1983). Landis was indicted for involuntary manslaughter for his role in the accidental deaths of the veteran actor Vic Morrow and two Vietnamese child actors, who were decapitated and crushed by a falling helicopter during the night shoot of a battlefield rescue in a Vietnam sequence. Landis was famous both for self-identifying as an auteur with the standing of a Steven Spielberg or a Francis Ford Coppola, subsequent to his taste-breaking success directing the blockbuster *Animal House* (Universal, Oregon Film Factory, and Stage III Productions, 1978), and for a zeal to push the boundaries of acceptable risk during his productions. Whatever other infractions of safety standards allegedly occurred during the shooting of *The Twilight Zone*, there could be no question that the child actors were on the set deep into the night in violation of California's child labor laws. The catastrophe and its aftermath dramatized the perilous consequences of the anticorporate auteurist model for those captivated by its allure, for despite Warners' funding and ownership of the motion picture, the studio was never indicted for any crime. Unlike the Supreme Court's erasure of Capra's name from its account of *Mr. Smith Goes to Washington*, the California justice system, sensitive to the glow of celebrity, featured Landis as its headliner, implicitly accepting the studio's self-exculpation. As Stephen Farber and Marc Green, the authors of the engrossing *Outrageous Conduct*, observe, "When civil suits were filed naming the studio as a defendant . . . the studio clung to the belief that it was Landis's movie.

The creative freedom that he and other directors had won as a result of two decades of growing directorial autonomy meant the he should take responsibility for mistakes he made without the studio's knowledge." Whether the studio's self-proclaimed ignorance was a reasonable excuse was never subjected to challenge in the courtroom from which studio executives, busy with other things, prudently absented themselves. Warners' own morality could not be tested because auteurism was the perfect alibi for the malfunctioning of what remained of the studio's CID (corporate internal decision structure) and a justification for its scapegoating of Landis. In his testimony, Landis tried to dissociate himself as auteur from control over anything except aesthetic issues. He blamed everyone else for everything else, including Warners and the "experts" responsible for explosives, helicopters, and live children. Almost everyone else in court blamed Landis as director–producer and boss. It was a standoff that worked. Landis escaped jail for the criminal charge and the studio escaped bad publicity while quietly settling the civil suits by the families of the victims.[9] By reducing authorship to a single, biological individual and failing to consider the negligence of the studio, the LA district attorney made it impossible to successfully prosecute a crime that in its complexity mirrored the corporate reality of the New Hollywood.

Warners escaped, but it was a messy business. The construction of shell companies to absorb the blame for any person or action that might incur liability makes a much cleaner studio alibi, in part because it does not depend on auteurist scapegoating. Disney, long unruffled by the antics of auteurs, understands these things. When, according to David A. Price, Disney partnered with Pixar to make *Toy Story* in 1993, they formed a "joint venture called Hi Tech Toons... to shield the two companies from liability and to simplify production accounting." Hi Tech Toons was a one-off company with a separate management that the principal firms could use to hire employees and to process salaries and other expenditures. If something happened during the production that damaged people or property, Hi Tech, which had no assets except the money to pay its employees, would be a very bad bet for a litigant seeking a settlement or a prosecutor seeking an indictment. The device also prevented conflict between Disney's unionized workers and Pixar's nonunionized employees by making both temporary employees of a third company.[10] Notably, the arrangement diminished liability but did not entail taking additional precautions to prevent unforeseen calamities. The addition of Hi Tech Toons had the appearance of modifying the CID, even as its true function was to employ a legal accounting maneuver to cordon off Disney, Pixar, and their executives from moral responsibility and legal liability for bad things that might happen.

Against that background of chronic concern about exposure to liability, Disney and Pixar's shell-less merger contract of 2006 is a striking innovation. "Culture" is the key. Once the concept of the corporation had been expanded to include the institutionalization of a way of doing things that invests all functions, such as planning, purchasing, allocating, producing, accounting, hiring and firing, reporting, ordering, marketing, and, of course, speaking with meaning for the stakeholders in a company, the rickety CID could be renovated as a CCD (corporate cultural decision) structure that explicitly binds authority and identity. No corporation in America was more prepared for this transformation than Disney, because no company takes culture as seriously as Disney, whether it involves culture that the company markets or the culture that the company is. Culture is Disney's business and its brand. That new CCD is invoked in Exhibit 99.1 of merger contract, "Policies for Management of the Feature Animation Businesses." The pertinent section of the exhibit reads,

> Upon the effective date of the Disney-Pixar merger, a Committee ("Committee") shall be immediately established to help provide oversight to the Feature Animation Businesses of Disney and Pixar. The principal objectives of the Committee are: (i) to help maintain the Pixar "culture," (ii) to help supervise Pixar and Disney Feature Animation, (iii) to oversee Pixar compensation practices and (iv) to approve the film budgets of Pixar, all subject to final approval by Disney's Chief Executive Officer.[11]

That promise to help maintain the Pixar "culture" that is expressively and uniquely framed by quotation marks, probably sealed the deal.

Michel Foucault accurately stipulated that "a contract may have a guarantor—it does not have an author" ("WIA," p. 108): no single subject is responsible for originating the contract, nor can the language of the contract be copyrighted or plagiarized. By so calling the culture that Disney promises to maintain, the contract enunciates a practice of "cultural" authorship identified by its warding off the connotations that culture usually bears—when, for example, it is used by a cynical Time management as an alibi to protect its prerogatives, or when it is codified by Australian legislators, or when it is preached by Disney in its self-promotions.

No doubt the scare quotes are an awkward gesture. In her history of ballet, Jennifer Homans illustrates how such awkwardness signifies:

> Many of today's dancers, for example, have a revealing habit: they attack steps with apparent conviction—but then at the height of the step they shift or adjust, almost imperceptibly, as if they were not quite at ease with its statement. This is so common-

place that we hardly notice. But we should: these adjustments are a kind of fudging, a way of taking distance and not quite committing (literally) to a firm stand. With the best of intentions, the dancer thus undercuts her own performance.[12]

The problem here is not a lack of talent, or will, or imagination. It is a problem of cultures: the weighty cultural capital of ballet tradition and the specific cultural conditioning that contemporary dancers undergo as part of their training. For Homans the dancer's adjustment does not express an individual subjectivity daunted by a challenge and escaping into the familiar. Her fudging of the last step is the almost imperceptible sign of a contemporary ballet culture that uniformly induces in dancers the uneasy adjustment to a statement of artistic conviction as its inadvertent signature.

Pixar's scare quotes fudge by instituting a position at a distance from a contractually frank and open statement of affiliation with a dominant culture, which, in this case, is not the culture of Petipa or Balanchine but the culture of Disney. Culture is Disney's business. The company not only has a prescriptive corporate culture but it produces culture homologous with its company culture, which it packages for the screen, vends on the shelves in Disney stores, and imparts to both visitors and employees of its theme parks. As Janet Wasko reports, "new employees learn about the 'Disney Culture'—defined in company literature as 'the values, myths, heroes and symbols that have a significant meaning to the employees.'"[13] Pixar, however, is effectively distanced from a potentially destabilizing avowal of the priority of its own culture by quotation marks that imply that the word *culture* properly belongs to the dominant partner, as part of its corporate identity. Whether the quotation marks were imposed by a condescending Disney, by a strategic Pixar, or in an ironic collaboration, its authorship belongs to whatever set of norms, practices, and personalities that make Pixar not what it is but what it does, and which thereby constitute not its identity but its *value*. Like the dancer adjusting herself to the core, doctrinal statement of the classical ballet, Pixar's assertion of "cultural" authorship is the enactment of a mild but definite form of apostasy. The "cultural" author becomes what it does as it intentionally falls away from complete fidelity to the dominant creed in order to make no statements, only movies.

As you will recall from the introduction to this volume, in a 1932 profile of MGM *Fortune* magazine announced its expectation of a corporate art. What went unmentioned was that just two years later *Fortune* named the studio that had fulfilled its expectations. It was not MGM, or Warners, or Paramount, MGM's chief competitors for market share. It was the Walt Disney Studio, a privately held corporation, whose size and revenue were dwarfed by the tiered establishments of the members of the Motion Pictures Producers and Distributors Association cartel.[14] Despite its size and specialization, Disney, which had never put a star under contract, built a sound stage, or owned a theater, had nonetheless brought forth something new into the world. The Disney studio, *Fortune* writes, is organized as "a factory.... But the result is no simple product like cigarettes or razor blades; it is myth.... In Disney's studio a twentieth-century miracle is achieved: by a system as truly of the machine age as Henry Ford's plant at Dearborn, true art is produced."[15] No early assessment of Disney's work and of the Disney studio would prove as compatible with contemporary judgments of Disney's organizational acumen or as prescient of the focal role that Disney would play in synthesizing mythmaking with what has come to be called "experiential marketing."

Work on *Pinocchio* began in December 1937, upon the completion of *Snow White*, Disney's first feature, when studio morale was high and artistic invention inspired. This was the golden age venerated by Lasseter's team at Pixar, the period when Disney animation was presided over by Walt and the "nine old men," who gave Disney features their entrancing look and feel, when the Disney Company still retained some of the effervescent, egalitarian community spirit of the late 1920s and the early 1930s, and when Walt was still able to ignore the financial pressures that his brother Roy had to face every day. All that would change by the end of 1941. Agitation for unionization led to violent conflicts between management and labor. The disappointing revenues from *Pinocchio* and *Fantasia* (1940), which contributed to the mounting debt at the Bank of America, compelled the Disney brothers to take their company public and distribute ownership to anonymous shareholders. The studio was also forced to desist from making features until the financial health of the company could be restored. Moreover, the onset of the war curtailed the studio's access to markets overseas, forced rationing essential chemicals at home, and required diversion of its diminished financial, physical, and human resources to government projects, that is, to propaganda, serving the war effort (*BC*, pp. 139–40).

Disney's travails in the 1940s would steel Walt to make riskier investments in the postwar period so as to exploit changing audiences that were developing new habits of pursuing entertainment. Disney had some inherent advantages over the other Hollywood studios. Although Walt bridled at his inability to mount live-action movies, that inhibition actually benefited him in relation to his larger peers, especially the stodgy MGM, whose star-constellating strategy, which had elevated MGM to industry leadership in the 1930s, had begun to raise its costs enormously (Mickey Mouse never collected a paycheck or signed a contract) and, consequently, to limit its scope. People joked about

Clark Gable's ears; no fans bought caps to display them. As a company uniquely responsive to consumer demand, Disney early on became an innovative and efficient licenser of its cartoon figures, which, unlike MGM's stars, could not object to any use to which the studio put them. *Steamboat Willie* marketed Mickey to merchandisers around the globe, who, in turn, produced towels, caps, and pajamas that extended the reach of Disney's marketing deep into the domestic life of multitudes. In the 1950s, more than any other studio, Disney successfully exploited the marketing opportunities offered by television and, with the opening of Disneyland, the burgeoning superhighway system. After Walt's death and a fallow interregnum, Disney, ruled by Michael Eisner, resumed its marketing leadership among entertainment conglomerates in part by even more aggressive cross-platformed theming, which reached its peak with Eisner's reckless decision in 1994 to theme America in a new park near Manassas Junction in Maryland, site of the First Battle of Bull Run on July 21, 1861. The plan was, surprisingly, defeated by opponents of the "Disneyfication" of American history.[16] Nevertheless, although Eisner did not succeed in becoming the titled impresario of "America," his merchandising touch remained nearly infallible.

Disney's assumption of the role of mythmaker to the nation's children has been attacked by cultural critics. For example, Wasko quotes Frances Clarke Sayers, who charges that Disney's "treatment of folklore is without regard for its anthropological, spiritual, or psychological truths. Every story is sacrificed to the 'gimmick' of animation.'" Sayers adds that "there is nothing to make a child think or feel or imagine."[17] More recently, Michael Budd has argued that Disney's synergism erases any distinction between mythmaking and brand management by ensuring that every "Disney product is both a commodity and an ad for every other Disney commodity."[18] Sayers's and Budd's complementary critiques of the blurring of the boundaries between high and low culture as the malign effect of the Disneyfication of childhood are, of course, deeply indebted to Theodor W. Adorno's somber analysis of the manipulative techniques and homogenizing impact of the culture industry,

> which fuses the old and familiar into a new quality. In all its branches, products which are tailored for consumption by masses, and which to a great extent determine the nature of that consumption, are manufactured more or less according to plan. The individual branches are similar in structure or at least fit into each other, ordering themselves into a system almost without a gap. This is made possible by contemporary technical capabilities as well as by economic and administrative concentration. The culture industry intentionally integrates its consumers from above.[19]

Another way of putting it, keeping in mind *Citizens United*'s supreme indifference to the source of popular culture, would be that indifference "as to who speaks" solicits the corporation to speak to and for us.

Adorno's perspective has ruled in academic criticism of Disney, and *Pinocchio* has been a touchstone for that criticism. Jack Zipes's landmark Adornovian essay, "Toward a Theory of the Fairy-Tale Film," takes *Pinocchio* as the chief example of Disney's ideologically driven adaptations of fairy tales, here with the aim of Americanizing an edgy European story by celebrating the transformation of a willful puppet into a socially conforming young boy. Zipes's zeal to expose the repressive project of *Pinocchio* leads him to distort the symbolic significance of that transformation, however. He remarks that "Pinocchio is the perfect charming good boy when he awakes on his bed, but he is almost too perfect to be true. Like a doll that has been mass-produced and is ready to be taken home from the shelf of a store, he is the dream toy that Geppetto has wished for, prefabricated by the fairy's instructions and endowed with a moral conscience also supplied by the fairy."[20] Zipes may regard the child as a dream toy, but apparently no one else did. Although merchandizing was vital to the Disney corporate enterprise, which needed to squeeze out as much revenue as possible to make up for the costliness of *Pinocchio*'s production, I can find no evidence that Pinocchio, the real boy, ever became a toy displayed on shelves for sale. Instead, Pinocchio, the stringless puppet with the telltale white gloves, was mass-produced and stocked in shops.

Indeed *Pinocchio*'s narrative contrives a cul-de-sac: the final version of Pinocchio may represent a real boy, but the figure we see is still a cartoon. *Pinocchio*'s transformational logic sets an objective that the picture cannot achieve except extradiegetically, by repudiating animation for live action—a choice that Walt happily made in the postwar era, when he seized the opportunity to produce *Treasure Island* in the United Kingdom in 1950. Consequently, the most blatant of the Walt-centric allegories that *Pinocchio* offers is the identification of Geppetto on his knees, praying that Pinocchio will become a real boy, with Walt praying to the same star that in his next movie, cartoon figures will be replaced by real live boys. From that perspective, the movie's dead end deliberately forecloses not just sequels to *Pinocchio* but any more animated features—an objective that Eisner would also later embrace.

Instead of following Zipes's example by imagining a shelf in the store where Geppetto's dream toy sits, we might instead repeat Jiminy Cricket's more helpful tour of Geppetto's "shop," on the walls and shelves of which are displayed "the most fantastic clocks you ever laid your eyes on, and all carved out of wood. Cute little music boxes, each one a work of art. Shelf after shelf of toys"

(Figure 7.1). None of those intricate artifacts bears either a price destining it for the market or a trademark connecting it to Geppetto. They have no exchange value and, therefore, in Geppetto's world, no use value: when he wants to know the time, he ignores the chiming, cuckooing, cawing, and buzzing clocks that surround him and consults his brass pocket watch. So what kind of place is this? A store, a home, a workshop? Proprietor, father, craftsman—which narrative function is most important? "Proprietor" doesn't take us far, for not only are the other artifacts literally priceless, Pinocchio, who is connected to Geppetto as artifact to maker, fulfillment to wish, is never displayed on a shelf. He is, as Jiminy says, when he first sees him set apart on the workbench, "something else . . . , a puppet, you know, one of those marionette things, all strings and joints." Although the newly stringless Pinocchio is sold to Stromboli, who knows exactly how to exploit his unique capacities, the sale occurs without Geppetto's knowledge, and without him profiting from it. If we stress *father*, we will inevitably invoke Walt as either benevolent parent or anxious son and join the psychoanalytic critics of the movie in a debate about what it means for Disney to induce the wish that the father's wish could be the living puppet's wish and that both wishes could be gratified by the puppet's dramatic transformation into a virtuous boy. If we prefer *craftsman* it may be because Geppetto appears less as a woodcarver than as an animator (the only tool we see him wield is a paintbrush); therefore he reads as a figure for the formidable collection of talents at Disney, who often modeled their characters in three dimensions, and even acted them out for each other. The parallel between Geppetto's shop in the movie and the animators' shop at either Disney's Hyperion or Burbank studio partially explains the curious exemption that Geppetto is imagined to have from market considerations.[21] Of course, the Disney animators were not so naïve as to ignore either the proximity at the studio of exuberant fun and donkeylike drudgery or their own participation in the creation of a money machine that would enrich the Stromboli who owned the studio. Disney's "nine old men" fetishized decommodification and were as contemptuous of mass production as Zipes or Adorno. Because to think "father" you must think Walt, and to think "craftsmen" you must recall a group of highly talented men who labored almost anonymously under Walt's supervision and were forcibly assimilated to his paternal image, the movie should be

Figure 7.1

read, as it surely was by Pixar, as an early sign of the acrimonious conflict over credit, salary, and unionization that almost destroyed the heavily indebted Disney studio in 1941. Recall that Hi Tech Toons was formed as a device to avoid both liability and the threat of unionization.

Jiminy Cricket was the first visitor to Geppetto's shop to call attention to the difference between the toys and a puppet; Pixar was the second. That difference is the crux of *Toy Story 2*, Pixar's most extended engagement with *Pinocchio*. After deciding to make *Pinocchio*, the first question that Walt asked himself, his animators, and his writers was how they could effectively adapt Collodi for the screen. Although he had a vexed relation with Collodi's story, Walt accepted the basic narrative arc of stringed puppet to stringless puppet to real boy. *Toy Story*, however, was an original script idea. According to a well-worn anecdote, "Once [John] Lasseter and the rest of the team asked themselves a key question. '"If a toy were alive, what would it want?'—the answers came flooding out. Toys are manufactured to be played with by children, they reasoned, so that is what they want more than anything else in the world" (*IB*, p. 85). A puppet is not crafted to be a toy. Its purpose is neither to be played with nor to become a real boy but to perform for an audience as the instrument of a master entertainer intent on accumulating wealth. From Pixar's perspective, Geppetto *should* have sold the puppet to the gypsy impresario, who is the only character able to exploit this unique expression of the puppet form, this artificial person, by realizing its true potential to be a money machine: Pinocchio Inc., privately held and controlled by Stromboli. Alive or not, toys are toys and not some other thing—least of all unevolved children. No toy pines for a conscience, that's for sure. Toys are not crafted by a loving maker. They are trademarked objects, manufactured in plastic with standardized characters and devised to fit into a marketing niche, their names and functions prescribed. Mass production and consumption are manifestly the conditions for the existence of every toy in Pixar pictures, and relentless, centralized, top-down merchandising is the only way any toy could get into the toy box of Andy, the chief executive officer of the privately held bedroom.

Toy Story does not challenge that system. Its answer to *Pinocchio*'s nostalgia is the same as its answer to Adorno's critique: mass culture is, indeed, centralized and fully commercialized, but the administration of culture stops at the playroom door, where another culture forms. The toys are manufactured for a purpose but if the purpose is play, how play *happens* is, according to *Toy Story*, *Toy Story 2*, and *Toy Story 3*, the prerogative of the child's imagination, not the manufacturer's design: in the exercise of that prerogative the child can be smirkingly sadistic, like Sid, or noisily exuberant, like Andy. Who wouldn't prefer to be owned by Andy? Straight out of the box Andy singles out all the toys for a role in play at some variance with their manufactured and marketed characters; and even that role is no constraint on toy creativity, for each toy has a distinctive personality developed through conversation, conflict, and, above all, cooperation in the pluralistic culture that thrives under Andy's benign corporate canopy. Toy "culture" works fine for a toy as long as the toy can stay out of a box and off of a shelf; and that depends on Andy's continued, reasonably attentive ownership. Pixar has a deeply corporatist vision: no distinctive, satisfying way of doing things can be formed without the institutional framework of Andy's bedroom or Disney's boardroom; no culture can be held together without Andy's mark or Disney's brand. The sense of belonging at Pixar was cultivated in two specific ways. First, the company fostered a distinctive culture that blends techies with creative types and places as high a valuation on idiosyncratic personalities as on specialized expertise. Second, that sense of belonging was cultivated by a technology of corporate identity formation. The initial device was the agreement to co-brand with Disney, a division of screen credit which was institutionalized in the second contract. That co-branding relationship is thematized in *Toy Story* by the scrawl of "Andy" on the bottom of the boots of Woody, Buzz (and, eventually, Jesse). Pixar's avowed dream had always been to be a productive, creative community thriving within the institution of a studio and protected by a strong brand. As Michael Szalay has suggested, *Toy Story* has the shape of an allegory that dreams of the merger between the bygone Disney's older characters, represented by Woody, and the new, techno-driven figures, represented by Buzz Lightyear, that are generated by Pixar's creative computer experts. The Andy brand is not, then, the correlative of "Pixar" but the sign of Disney, the matrix of narrative animation to which Pixar, a company of talents that had weathered business crises and employee attrition, had long aspired to pledge its allegiance.

 Pixar did not, however, pledge this allegiance to the Disney of Michael Eisner, who, like his surrogate Al, owner of the Toy Barn in *Toy Story 2*, always put money first. It is true that when, after many fallow years, in 1984, Eisner assumed control of the Walt Disney Company, the company once again began to think seriously about toys and even animation, but always within what Eisner called the "box." Eisner famously enunciated this management philosophy: "I have always believed that the creative process must be contained in what we call 'the financial box'—financial parameters that creative people can work in—but the box is tight, controlled and responsible. Finance," Eisner declared, "has the key to the box" (*UD*, p. 29). And, of course, every aspect of "finance" answers to Eisner, in whose office the financial box is shelved. It's a vivid metaphor made more so by the prominence of the shelved and then boxed toys in *Toy Story 2*, a movie that systematically repudiates Eisner's corporate philosophy as it moves from the crisis of a damaged Woody being shelved in Andy's bedroom, when the boy goes off to cowboy camp, to his confinement in a display case readied for sale to a Japanese museum, to the sublime scene in Al's Toy Barn, where Buzz Lightyear confronts the colossal array of boxed replicas of himself, stacked to the ceiling and stretched to infinity and beyond—a shot in stark contrast to the view of the individualized clocks and knickknacks stocked on the shelves in Geppetto's shop (Figure 7.2).

Indeed, *Toy Story* erases Geppetto altogether. There is no maker of Woody, Buzz, or any of the other toys; and there is no father for Andy.[22] Stromboli returns, however, in the guise of Al, proprietor of Al's Toy Barn, the villain of *Toy Story 2*, who boxes up Woody because of his value just as Stromboli had caged Pinocchio. Unlike Stromboli, who has no contact with Pinocchio's home life, Al's commercial world impinges on Andy's household, first through the television set in Andy's room and then during the yard sale that Andy's mother sets up. This sale is the occasion of Woody's return to the realm of exchange value, when he is boxed by Al and spirited away in his Cadillac. The episodes in Al's office and on the display floor are all about boxes: the Lucite case in which Woody is displayed and which, the Old Prospector attempts to convince him, is the vehicle of his emancipation (Figure 7.3), the opaque cardboard boxes from which Jesse and the Prospector yearn to escape (Figure 7.4), and the imagery of the mathematical sublime that nearly overwhelms him as he comes across the display of the new models of Buzz Lightyear.

Separated from his friends, Buzz discovers that the multitude of boxed and shelved star rangers that stretch to infinity and beyond are identical to him in every

Figure 7.2

Figure 7.3

respect except for their subjection to the advertising copy with which the culture industry has defined their identity. Each is, of course, utterly ignorant of the experiences that Buzz has shared with the rest of Andy's toys, whose conversation and example had encouraged him to test his fantasies of omnipotence against a reality that does not conform to the generic scenarios recorded on the looping tape that dictates his character. When released from the box into the social world of the playroom, Buzz painfully learns the disparity between the ad copy on his box, which endows him with super powers, and the real world in Andy's bedroom, which is a web of interdependence. Buzz must learn the crucial importance of belonging, of being owned and of being loyal. He constructs his own personality by interacting with his peers, the way that Pixar encourages each employee from Lasseter on down to construct his and sometimes her own corporate personality.

Figure 7.4

Unlike Buzz, Woody is completely outfitted with a personality when he appears in *Toy Story*. We do not see him in his naïve state, that is, in full conformity with his manufactured character until the scene in *Toy Story 2* when Stinky Pete, the Old Prospector, plays the tape of the 1950s television show *Woody's Round-Up* on the most seductive of all the boxes, the TV (Figure 7.5). Here the mythic function of the media narrative does not, as Sayers complains of Disney, replace some more authentic story; the video recording provides the illusion of a biographical

Figure 7.5

narrative and a continuous identity where there is none. *Woody's Round-Up* does not revive memories: it makes them. The television adventures never happened to *this* Woody but to another Woody, who is not only a distinct article, like each boxed and shelved Buzz Lightyear, but a different species, as different as a puppet is from a toy. What is peculiar about the video is that our Woody so easily identifies with someone else, who is living the same story over and over again, imprisoned in the video box, as if it really were an earlier version of a self that had evolved, metamorphosed, or somehow acquired a personality. But it isn't and it hasn't. There's no video of a Blue Fairy appearing to transform Woody the puppet into Woody the toy. Cultural memory is false memory. Watching *Woody's Round-Up*, our Woody revels in the fact that "Woody" (now in scare quotes) was once a performer, who, like Pinocchio in the hands of Stromboli, was a money machine for the various companies whose products he advertised. Had Woody actually made the *Pinocchio* connection, as Pixar does, however, he would have noticed that, unlike the toy he is, the Woody on the *Round-Up* is a puppet—and there he is bested by Pinocchio, for the performing Woody has strings and the performing Pinocchio does not. The video representation of Woody the puppet so effectively mediates lapsed time and distance that regression would be as easy as turning on the remote and as appealing as climbing back into a Lucite box to be shipped abroad and then displayed on a shelf in a museum, where, abstracted from the culture that has given him personality, a toy could fantasize that he will forever enjoy the regard of people to whom he is a pristine relic of another world and time, guaranteed value by his rarity, immortality by his value, and sterility by his box.[23]

As we have seen, in *Citizens United* the majority opinion equates corporate authorship with corporate speech and corporate speech with corporate funding. The Supreme Court's verdict put American political culture in the box called finance and slammed the lid. I have countered that under the corporatist regime, authorship, considered not as a sign of subjectivity but as the supervening intentional function of the organization, differs from speaking in the capacity not only to take responsibility for what it makes but to accept liability for its making. Where do we find the model for such a corporate author? As a child of Disney, I have had an answer ready for a long time: let our conscience be our guide. If, according to the Roberts Court and Michel Foucault, it makes no difference who is speaking, it might as well be a homuncular cricket who can tell right from wrong and who can convincingly impersonate the corporate author. *Pinocchio* is ultimately Jiminy Cricket's story. The movie begins and ends with his direct address to the audience (the first in Disney's history) and with his physical framing of the narrative, which he initiates by opening a book, and which he concludes by closing the window frame to set the stage for his departure to other venues where he can carry out the office conferred on him by the Blue Fairy. Unmistakably, the significance of Jiminy as conscience is that he is *not* internalized by Pinocchio or by the narrative. Indeed, he was only given prominence in Disney's feature when the narrative authored by Collodi was jettisoned in favor of a narrative authored by Disney. *Pinocchio* and *Citizens United* have pretty much demonstrated that an artificial person cannot internalize a conscience (although there is a contrary view articulated by Steven Spielberg and Stanley Kubrick's riposte to *Toy Story 2: Artificial Intelligence: AI*, which travels deep into the valley of the uncanny to sentimentalize artificial persons, even as it abandons human beings to the deluge of history). Jiminy Cricket is not the part that stands for the Disney whole: *no* part can legitimately stand for the corporate whole; that's what logos are for. A corporation, however, can acquire a conscience by incorporating it, just as Disney did with Jiminy Cricket and, much later, with Pixar.

Figure 7.6

Although Pinocchio the puppet is not shelved during the movie, the narrative named *Pinocchio* is, in the form of the large red book with a silhouette of Pinocchio on the cover, propped up on a table (Figure 7.6). When Jiminy opens its cover he discloses a new species of book. It has no title page, no frontispiece, no acknowledgment of Collodi, no words at all: just a framed image of a sleeping village within the frame of the book's page (Figure 7.7). This book is remarkably different from any volume in which Collodi's story might appear; it is a book that only Disney could produce, with its animators, its multiplane technology, and its license from Technicolor. Just as Walt had to dispose of the first script that in its fidelity to Collodi weakened the native force of Disney's animation, so Jiminy usurps the writer of the tale by impersonating the figure of an author who can incorporate

Figure 7.7

fairy tales while fully reimagining them, who can break with tradition even while celebrating it, who can visualize a book of visuals without needing to write one—and who, ideally, would not just receive credit and revenue for his products, but would also accept liability, if something (Blue Fairy, help us!) should go wrong. Jiminy Cricket may not have the high cultural authority that Adolf Berle deploys when, in *The 20th Century Capitalist Revolution*, he exemplifies how corporations might be invested with a conscience by invoking medieval Norman Law and the right of the convicted to appeal to the conscience of the king for equity; but each age has its convenient myths, and Jiminy has turned out to have more relevance to at least one major corporation than William the Conqueror.[24]

Jiminy Cricket was invented by the Disney animators to right a narrative gone wrong and, incidentally, to teach an artificial person with no inner voice how to recognize the right way of doing things from the wrong way. Disney featured the personality over the years as the image, if not the agent of the company's conscience, its acknowledgment of a right and a wrong that cannot be written into charters or expressed on a spreadsheet. Had Berle but known what was bred into Pixar's bones, that Jiminy Cricket, who became the spokesman for the Disney empire, was a figure with more potential to persuade the corporation to behave than to assure the social conformity of the kids in the TV audience, he would not, I think, have demurred from putting him to theoretical use in 1954, as Pixar did in its business model in 2006.

Pixar always wanted to be owned, whether by George Lucas of Industrial Light and Magic, who was a neglectful father, or by brotherly Steve Jobs, who redeemed Pixar from neglect and eventually arranged the merger that would attach Pixar to Walt Disney under terms that would maintain its "culture" and enable it to fulfill the obligations of belonging. But, it is fair to ask, what about Pixar's "culture" makes it worth maintaining? Why would Disney, which under Eisner was notorious for breaking its contractual promises, keep its promise to Pixar? In a thoughtful analysis of the deal, Victor Fleischer is skeptical that the company will in fact keep its promises. He does not believe that what he calls Pixar's "bottom up culture" can be maintained under a contract that subjects the execution of all agreements to the authority of the executive at the top of the Walt Disney Company. Fleischer warns that the omission of any mention of the well-publicized Pixar University has been adduced as evidence that distinctive elements of Pixar's culture were already being abandoned before the contract was signed. Only the reification of Pixar's culture as bottom-up, however, impels Fleischer to inventory what is in the Disney basement. Indeed, it was Fleischer who first pointed to the importance of the quotation marks around *culture* in Exhibit 99.1 and who astutely associated that form with the way that the intangible managerial capital called "goodwill" was once represented in contracts.[25] The association of "culture" with "goodwill" is telling, both because the quotation marks around goodwill were eventually dropped as accounting methods were adopted that made that capacious intangible accountable, and because, by asserting itself as author, Pixar "culture" claims to be able to generate both good products and goodwill—neither a moral good. For Iger to squeeze out that "culture" would be, Eisner-like, to deliberately destroy that value, both by driving away indispensable talent and by disabling the institutionally specific protocols shared by techies and creative types, who combine to author the motion pictures that generate goodwill. The insistence on the maintenance of the contract is the assertion of a cultural authorship of incalculable value, because as long as Pixar continues to be able to tell right from wrong and conscientiously does things right, one must trust that its "culture" will be indefinitely productive of more value. Indeed, rather than facilitating the imposition of Disney ideology on Pixar, the merger has been followed by influence heading the other way—and, significantly, not only on the animators. Lasseter is now principal creative adviser for the imagineers, who have the responsibility for planning the future of Disney in all areas of its enterprise. In 2010 it was reported that Iger has invited Lasseter and other Pixar directors and writers to conferences on live-action productions with the aim exploiting their narrative expertise so that Disney can get its stories right.[26] We may congratulate Pixar executives on their success as consultants on the Disney side, but such missionary work is not always welcomed by the supposed beneficiaries, and in this case Pixar's willingness to advise inevitably comes with liability for advice that may not save or may even sink the project in which they intervene. The chances for failure always exceed the chances for success in Hollywood, and Pixar's institutional capital, namely its astounding record of continuous successes, is put at risk not only by each new feature but with each consultation.

We can skip an inventory of the assorted policies, practices, properties, and personalities that constitute Pixar "culture," for although many of them are important, none is either necessary or sufficient. My construction of Pixar's self-understanding has exploited the peculiar appearance of a framed culture in the merger contract to avoid what I believe Pixar was avoiding: being boxed in by a Hobson's choice between the demystification of Pixar as ultimately the studio of John Lasseter, creative genius, whose vision is served by zealous, talented acolytes, and the alternative hypostasis of Pixar culture as a prescriptive way of doing things, a medium for the formation of a collective identity, and a technology for enforcing brand discipline. "Cultural" authorship cannot thrive at either extreme. Extremes must meet—not, however as formal collaborations or task-dedicated teams, but as studio functions that mutually inform each other and figure a cultural identity as a maneuver, not a subject position. I can't imagine how that relationship could be empirically verified, whether from the bottom or the top. No reason to try. The framing of culture in Exhibit 99.1 invites an allegorization of Pixar Animation Studio as structured by the always potential conflict between the freewheeling creative types, authors of meaningful, character-driven narratives, and the cubicled techies, ingenious writers of code who make dew glisten, hair tousle, and Buzz tango. That allegory was first invoked by John Lasseter as the chiasmus that figures the engine of Pixar culture: "the art challenges the technology, and the technology inspires the art" (*IB*, p. 43).

What matters, then, is not culture as another version of goodwill, intangible but quantifiable managerial capital fabricated by the expert manipulation of the corporation's two bodies, but culture as *figurative* capital. "Culture" is the framing of a word that would refer to and be uttered by what is casually called corporate culture, could such a culture find a voice adequate to the figure of the chiasmus by which this "culture" recognizes itself, assures its dynamism, takes responsibility for corporate projects, gets things right, and, crucially, accepts liability for what goes wrong. Liability is crucial because Pixar cannot claim to be a conscientious author without accepting liability for the consequences of its actions, even if those consequences prove that the corporation has no real conscience at all.

Notes

Introduction

1. *Fortune*, December 1932, in *The American Film Industry*, ed. Tino Balio, rev. ed. (Madison: University of Wisconsin Press, 1979), pp. 318–19. This source hereafter will be cited in the text as *AFI*.

2. See Morton J. Horowitz, *The Transformation of American Law, 1870–1960* (New York: Oxford University Press, 1992), pp. 69–70.

3. John Sedgwick and Michael Pokorny, "The Risk Environment of Film Making: Warner Bros. in the Inter-War Years," *Explorations in Economic History* 35, no. 2 (1998): 196–97.

4. Leo Rosten, *Hollywood: The Movie Colony, the Movie Makers* (New York: Harcourt, Brace, 1941), pp. 81–82. This source hereafter will be cited in the text as *H*.

5. See Jared Gardner, "Covered Wagons and Decalogues: Paramount's Myths of Origins," *Yale Journal of Criticism* 13, no. 2 (Fall 2000): 361–89; Paul Grainge, "Branding Hollywood: Studio Logos and the Aesthetics of Memory and Hype," *Screen* 45, no. 4 (Winter 2004): 354–60.

6. Peter F. Drucker, *The Concept of the Corporation* (New York: John Day, 1946), pp. 8, 15, 7.

7. Roland Marchand, *Creating the Corporate Soul: The Rise of Public Relations and Corporate Imagery in American Big Business* (Berkeley: University of California Press, 1998), see esp. pp. 130–201.

8. Thurman Arnold, *The Folklore of Capitalism* (New Haven, CT: Yale University Press, 1937), pp. 350–53.

9. Suman Gupta, *Corporate Capitalism and Political Philosophy* (London: Pluto Press, 1988), p. 102. This source hereafter will be cited in the text as *CC*.

10. Will Hays, *See and Hear* (1929; rpt., New York: Arno Press, 1970), p. 4.

11. For a splendid account of this theoretical spectrum see Robert Spadino, "Geniuses of the System: Authorship and Evidence in Classical Hollywood Cinema," *Auteurism Revisited, Film History* 7, no. 4 (Winter 1995): 362–85. Spadino begins with a judicious response to Thomas Schatz's groundbreaking study of Irving Thalberg's authorship at MGM in *The Genius of the System: Hollywood Filmmaking in the Studio Era* (New York: Pantheon Books, 1988); he then gives an enlightening account of both the power and constraints of the formalist paradigm elaborated in David Bordwell, Janet Staiger, and Kristin Thompson, *The Classical Hollywood Cinema* (New York: Columbia University

Press, 1985), surveys auteurism, and concludes by proposing a more pluralist theory of authorship, which does not, however, include among its eligible authors the corporate person.

12. Richard Maltby, "'Nobody Knows Everything': Post-Classical Historiographies and Consolidated Entertainment," in *Contemporary Hollywood Cinema*, ed. Steve Neale and Murray Smith (London: Routledge, 1998), pp. 25–26.

13. Howard T. Lewis, *The Motion Picture Industry* (New York: D. Van Nostrand, 1933), 1.

14. Mae D. Huettig, *Economic Control of the Motion Picture Industry: A Study in Industrial Organization* (Philadelphia: University of Pennsylvania Press, 1944), p. 67; hereafter *EC*.

15. Schatz, *Genius of the System*, p. 5; Richard Maltby and Ian Craven, *Hollywood Cinema: An Introduction* (London: Blackwell, 1995); Douglas Gomery, *The Hollywood Studio System: A History* (1986; new ed., London: British Film Institute, 2005); Charles Harpole, gen. ed., *A History of the American Cinema* (Berkeley: University of California Press, 1994–2006); John Thornton Caldwell, *Production Culture: Industrial Reflexivity and Critical Practice in Film and Television* (Durham, NC: Duke University Press, 2008), pp. 197–274, 13, 9.

16. Bordwell, Staiger, and Thompson, *Classical Hollywood Cinema*, pp. 3, 88; hereafter *CHC*.

17. Dirk Eitzen, "Evolution, Functionalism, and the Study of the American Cinema," review of *Classical Hollywood Cinema*, in *Velvet Light Trap* 28 (Fall 1991): 76; hereafter "E" (emphasis added).

18. M. E. Porter, *Competitive Strategy* (New York: Free Press, 1980), p. 5.

19. *The Grand Design: Hollywood as a Modern Business Enterprise, 1930–1939*, ed. Tino Balio, vol. 5 of *A History of the American Cinema*, gen. ed. Charles Harpole (Berkeley: University of California Press, 1995), pp. 25–26.

20. Martin J. Sklar, *The Corporate Reconstruction of American Capitalism, 1890–1916* (Cambridge: Cambridge University Press, 1988), p. 12.

21. William Roy, *Socializing Capital: The Rise of the Large Industrial Corporation in America* (Princeton, NJ: Princeton University Press, 1997), p. 6; hereafter *SC*. See also Charles Perrow, *Organizing America: Wealth, Power, and the Origins of Corporate Capitalism* (Princeton, NJ: Princeton University Press, 2002).

22. See the earlier discussion of corporate structural power in Carl Kaysens, "The Corporation: How Much Power? What Scope," in *The Corporation in Modern Society*, ed. Edward S. Mason (1959; rpt., New York: Atheneum, 1966), pp. 84–105.

23. David Riesman, in collaboration with Reuel Denney and Nathan Glazer, *The Lonely Crowd: A Study of the Changing American Character* (New Haven, CT: Yale University Press, 1950). For influential developments of Riesman's categories, see Warren Susman, *Culture as History: The Transformation of American Society in the Twentieth Century* (New York: Pantheon Books, 1984); and Jackson Lears, *Fables of Abundance: A Cultural History of Advertising in America* (New York: Basic Books, 1994).

24. Alfred D. Chandler, Jr., *Strategy and Structure: Chapters in the History of the Industrial Enterprise* (Cambridge, MA: MIT Press, 1962), pp. 13,14, 15.

25. Kenneth R. Andrews, *The Concept of Corporate Strategy* (1971; 3rd ed., Homewood, IL: Irwin, 1987), pp. 13, 18, 15.

26. Barry King, "Articulating Stardom," *Screen* 26, no. 5 (September–October 1985): 31. See also Leo Braudy's influential discussion of "role-playing and type-casting," in Braudy, *The World in a Frame: What We See in Films* (Chicago: University of Chicago Press, 1976), pp. 201–12.

Chapter 1: The Rackets

1. Quoted in Richard Maltby, "The Production Code and the Hays Office," in *Grand Design: Hollywood as a Modern Business Enterprise, 1930–1939*, ed. Tino Balio, vol. 5 of *A History of the American Cinema*, gen. ed. Charles Harpole (Berkeley: University of California Press, 1995), p. 43; hereafter *GD*.

2. Quoted in Scott Eyman, *The Lion of Hollywood: The Life and Legend of Louis B. Mayer* (New York: Simon and Shuster, 2005), p. 139; hereafter *LH*.

3. The only prior article was "The Case of William Fox," in May 1930, which, in the words of the caption, "dissected, rearranged, and spread out in coherent and comprehensible form" the origins, conduct, and conclusion of the litigation between Fox, and Harold Stuart of Halsey, Stuart, and Co., Inc., and John Otterson of Electrical Research Products, Inc., over ownership of 150,101 shares in Fox Film and Fox Theaters. The case had been concluded with a surrender by Fox and loss of control of his company (*Fortune*, May 1930, pp. 48–49 ff.

4. *Fortune*, December 1932, in *The American Film Industry*, ed. Tino Balio, rev. ed. (Madison: University of Wisconsin Press, 1979), p. 312; hereafter *AFI*.

5. See Terry Smith, *Making the Modern: Industry, Art, and Design in America* (Chicago: University of Chicago Press, 1993), for a splendid account of *Fortune*'s strategies for acquiring prestige and influence (pp. 173–89); hereafter *MM*.

6. Cf. Douglas Gomery, *The Hollywood Studio System: A History* (1986; new ed., London: British Film Institute, 2005), pp. 99–107; and John Izod, *Hollywood and the Box Office, 1895–1986* (New York: Columbia University Press, 1988), p. 89 (hereafter *HBO*): these represent MGM strictly as a subsidiary of Loew's and subservient to its corporate strategy, with an authority structure that flows from Schenck to Mayer to Thalberg. That is a reasonable perspective after the diminishment of Thalberg's authority in 1933, but to account for product differentiation at MGM and the toleration of ideological conflict requires the attribution of authority to Thalberg. See *LH*, p. 33.

7. See Janet Staiger's article "Announcing Wares, Winning Patrons, Voicing Ideals: Thinking About the History and Theory of Film Advertising" *Cinema Journal* 29, no. 3 (Spring 1990): 3–15, on pitching to mass audiences from 1910 to 1940.

8. In a statement that he later drafted in response to the pressure on the industry to amend its practices, Thalberg professed a much more modest cultural role for the motion picture industry: "We do not create the types of entertainment. . . . We merely present them" (*GD*, p. 43).

9. Bernays, *Propaganda* (New York: H. Liverwright, 1928), p. 18; hereafter *P*. On contemporary responses to the book, see Larry Tye, *The Father of Spin: Edward Bernays and the Birth of Public Relations* (New York: Henry Holt, 1998), pp. 98–99.

10. The marketing objective of making customers would be featured as first prin-

ciple in Peter F. Drucker's landmark *The Practice of Management* in 1954. Drucker does not refer to Bernays's earlier statement of the problem.

11. For a brief account of some of the "techniques to manufacture consent" used by Bernays and Ivy Lee, see David Miller and William Dinan, *A Century of Spin: How Public Relations Became the Cutting Edge of Corporate Power* (London: Pluto Press, 2008), pp. 35–37.

12. On Thalberg's use of previews and his idea that the script was, as Walter Wanger attested, "a blueprint [which meant] you could always improve it," see Mark A. Vieira, *Irving Thalberg: Boy Wonder to Producer Prince* (Berkeley: University of California Press, 2010), pp. 180–83; hereafter *T*.

13. For an excellent analysis of the production transcripts of *Grand Hotel* and their implications for evidence of Thalberg's authorship, see Thomas Schatz, *The Genius of the System: Hollywood Filmmaking in the Studio Era* (New York: Pantheon Books, 1988), pp. 108–20; and Robert Spadino, "Geniuses of the System: Authorship and Evidence in Classical Hollywood Cinema," *Auteurism Revisited, Film History* 7, no. 4 (Winter 1995): 362–85.

14. Paul Vinogradoff, "Juridical Persons," *Columbia Law Review* 24, no. 6 (June 1924): 595.

15. See Gregory A. Marks, "The Personification of the Business Corporation in American Law," *University of Chicago Law Review* 54, no. 4 (Fall 1987): 1478–83; John Dewey, "The Historic Background of Corporate Legal Personality," *Yale Law Journal* 35, no. 6 (April 1926): 673.

16. Roland Marchand, *Creating the Corporate Soul: The Rise of Public Relations and Corporate Imagery in American Big Business* (Berkeley: University of California Press, 1988), esp. pp. 7–47.

17. The Hollywood majors had never been attentive to the concerns of their shareholders. Since their formation, it was from the banks on each coast that they raised most of the capital they needed for technological innovation and geographical expansion. For the consequences of that dependence in the 1920s and 1930s, see *HBO*, pp. 50–51, 53, 96–97.

18. Despite the inclusion of his own surname in the name of the studio, Louis B. Mayer's jealousy of Thalberg's reputation as a "genius," which was cultivated by his coterie at MGM, was well-known. See, for example, Bosley Crowther, *Hollywood Rajah* (New York: Holt Rinehart and Winston, 1960), pp. 159–60. Scott Eyman attributes both the beginning of "the Thalberg legend" and Mayer's jealousy to the *Fortune* article, which relegates Mayer "to the rear of the piece" (*LH*, pp. 152–53).

19. *The Crowd* was written and directed by King Vidor, but it would not have been made except for the personal intervention of Irving Thalberg, who greenlit *The Crowd* despite doubt that it would return a profit. Thalberg supported the film not because it was the kind of film he liked but because he admired Vidor and because, as Bob Thomas reports him saying, "MGM can afford to take a loss on an experimental picture now and then." *Thalberg: Life and Legend* (1969; rpt., Beverly Hills, CA: New Millennium Press, 2000), p. 72.

20. Donald Crafton, *The Talkies: American Cinema's Transition to Sound, 1926–1931*, vol. 4 of *A History of the American Cinema*, gen. ed. Charles Harpole (Berkeley: University of California Press, 1997), p. 207.

21. King Vidor, interviewed by Nancy Dowd, ed. Edward Schilling in the unnumbered series *A Directors Guild of America Oral History* (archive/manuscript, University of California, Los Angeles, 1980), p. 101.

22. "The Motion Picture Industry as a Basis for Bond Financing," May 27, 1927, in *The American Film Industry*, ed. Tino Balio (Madison: University of Wisconsin Press, 1979), pp. 211–12.

23. Walter Lippmann, *Public Opinion* (1922; rpt., New York: Free Press, 1997), p. 81; hereafter *PO*.

24. Robert Lang, *American Film Melodrama: Griffith, Vidor, Minnelli* (Princeton, NJ: Princeton University Press, 1989), pp. 120–21.

25. One of several moments in the movie where one can see in James Murray's performance as John the prototype for Dick Powell's character in Preston Sturges's *Christmas in July* (Paramount, 1940).

26. Miriam Hansen, "Ambivalence of the 'Mass Ornament': King Vidor's *The Crowd*," *Qui Parle* 5, no. 2 (1992): 102–19, p. 103. Generalizing causality, Raymond Durgnat describes the Sims's daughter as a "victim of the city's weight and speed." Raymond Durgnat and Scott Simmon, *King Vidor, American* (Berkeley: University of California Press, 1988), p. 78; hereafter *KV*.

27. According to Vidor, the initial upward-panning shot of the building where John works was taken of the entrance to the Equitable Life Insurance Building in New York City. King Vidor, *A Tree Is a Tree* (New York: Harcourt Brace, 1952), p. 150; hereafter *TIS*.

28. Michael Szalay, *New Deal Modernism and the Rise of the Welfare State* (Durham, NC: Duke University Press, 2000), pp. 127–28. Both Szalay and Durgnat call attention to John's employment at an insurance company.

29. Allan Young, *The Harmony of Illusion: Inventing Post-Traumatic Stress Disorder* (Princeton, NJ: Princeton University Press, 1995), p. 5; quoted by Kirby Farrell, *Post-Traumatic Culture: Injury and Interpretation in the Nineties* (Baltimore: Johns Hopkins University Press, 1998), p. 9.

30. F. Kennedy, "The Mind of the Injured Worker: Its Effects on Disability Periods," *Compensation Med* 1 (1946): 19–21; quoted by George Mendelson, whose study resulted in statistical evidence that "of the 264 subjects who were not working at the time of litigation and who could be traced, 198 (75 percent) were not working after an average of 23 months following the finalization of their cases" (Mendelson, "Compensation Neurosis Revisited: Outcome Studies of the Effects of Litigation," *Journal of Psychosomatic Research* 39, no. 6 [1995]: 695).

31. "Many wage earners go through life without being the victims of industrial accidents, without serious illness, never lacking for work, and not living long enough to become superannuated. These are all risks to which wage earners are exposed, not certain needs which they can clearly foresee. The average wage earner does not believe that he will be overtaken by any of these evils. He is an optimist. He believes in his luck. It is easy to make him see that collective provision for these needs is desirable, because he knows that others are unlucky. It is not easy to convince him that he personally should insure himself against them, because he thinks that he personally is immune" (Henry Rogers Seager, *Social Insurance: A Program of Social Reform* [New York: Macmillan, 1910], pp. 21–22).

32. "Metropolitan Life Insurance Company," *Fortune*, August 1934, p. 122.

33. See Rick Altman, *The American Film Musical* (Bloomington, IN: Indiana University Press, 1989), p. 228, on the "performance myth" of "the happy clown."

34. On the various endings, see *KV*, pp. 80–81.

35. Eyman reports that "Mayer hated the picture," and "campaigned against it at the nascent Academy Awards in 1928," which was won by Howard Hughes's *Wings* (*LH*, p. 138).

36. Preston Sturges would later follow this path in his comical *Christmas in July*.

37. Walter Lippmann, *The Phantom Public* (New York: Macmillan, 1927), p. 77. See Stuart Ewen, *PR! A Social History of Spin* (New York: Basic Books, 1996), p. 153.

38. Reinhold Niebuhr, "Catastrophe or Social Control," *Harpers Monthly*, June 1932, p. 118.

39. Jeffrey R. Lustig, *Corporate Liberalism: The Origin of Modern American Political Theory, 1890–1920* (Berkeley: University of California Press, 1982), p. 128.

40. Richard Maltby, *Harmless Entertainment: Hollywood and the Ideology of Consensus* (Metuchen, NJ: Scarecrow Press, 1983), pp. 21–22; hereafter *HE*.

41. I take the language of scaling from Reinhold Martin, *The Organizational Complex: Architecture, Media, and Corporate Space* (Cambridge, MA: MIT Press, 2003), p. 114. "Theatrical topography," however, is my substitution for a topography of landscape in Martin.

42. Adolf A. Berle and Gardiner C. Means, *The Modern Corporation and Private Property* (1932; rev. ed., New York: Harcourt, Brace and World, 1968), p. liii.

43. Scott Eyman remarks that "Hearst's deal was a gold mine for him, wildly expensive for MGM. MGM financed all Cosmopolitan pictures and Hearst got a third of the profits. Hearst also got 40 percent of the profits from any MGM pictures made from stories in his *Cosmopolitan* magazine, in addition to being paid for the rights to the stories." The salary of Marion Davies, Hearst's mistress, "was set at $10,000 a week, $6,000 of it paid by the studio, $4000 paid by Hearst." In return, MGM had "complete run" of the Hearst Press—twenty-two daily newspapers, fifteen Sunday papers, and nine magazines, with a total circulation of nine million—"to publicize its pictures" (*LH*, pp. 114–15).

44. Under the head "Mayer Tells MG Execs to Work Only; Cut Costs and No Prima Donnaing," *Variety* (hereafter *V*) reports on January 10, 1933, from Culver City that when

> Mayer took charge of active production at Metro, due to the illness of Irving Thalberg last week it did not take long for every one on the lot to know that the big boss meant business. He called in the associate producers, supervisors and executives for the second time in a week, and in no uncertain terms again told them that the thought they possessed that they were all prima donnas must be discarded.

Mayer insisted they get to work by nine and that "when they got on the lot that they would have to try and accomplish things, instead of talking about bridge and parties of the night before. They must realize . . . that Metro was paying for their time, and because of the hectic conditions in the industry he would expect them to give value received for it" (p. 4).

Mayer's fury with the Thalberg who was his intimate colleague and the Thalberg of the *Fortune* profile, for whom talk was work, who paid his producers for their ideas, not their time, *boils* throughout the article.

45. Matthew Bernstein, *Walter Wanger: Hollywood Independent* (Berkeley: University of California Press, 1994), p. 84; hereafter *WW*.

46. Louis Pizzitola, *Hearst over Hollywood: Power, Passion, and Propaganda in the Movies* (New York: Columbia University Press, 2002), pp. 293–99; hereafter *HH*.

47. *WW*, pp. 82–89; Charles Higham, *Merchant of Dreams: Louis B. Mayer, M.G.M., and the Secret Hollywood* (New York: Dell, 1993), pp. 222 and 227 (hereafter *MD*); and Samuel Marx, *Mayer and Thalberg: The Make-Believe Saints* (New York: Random House, 1974), pp. 204–5.

48. Henry Luce was Mussolini's foremost publicist in the United States. "Il Duce" appeared on the cover of *Time* magazine five times, and the July 1934 issue of *Fortune* was devoted to a multifaceted analysis of the Italian experiment in fascism.

49. R. H. Coase, "The Nature of the Firm," *Economica* 4, no. 16 (1937): 387; hereafter "NF." Coase is quoting Sir Andrew Salter's statement of the first principle of laissez-faire economics.

50. Coase is quoting Sir Andrew Salter's statement of the first principle of laissez-faire economics.

51. See Bob Jessop, "Institutional re(turns) and the strategic-relational approach, *Environmental and Planning A* 13 (2001): 1215–16. Coase's argument was developed at length by the economist Oliver Williamson, who, as Kenneth Lipartito and David B. Sicilia write in the introduction to their useful collection of essays, *Constructing Corporate America: History, Politics, Culture* (New York: Oxford University Press, 2004), viewed firms as "vast transactions cost-reducing machines, complex perhaps, and subject to periodic breakdown, but like any technology, useful tools" (p. 6). Lipartito and Sicilia cite Williamson's *Markets and Hierarchies, Analysis and Antitrust Implications: A Study in the Economics of Internal Organization* (New York: Free Press, 1975); and "The Modern Corporation: Origins, Evolution, Attributes," *Journal of Economic Literature* 19, no. 4 (1981): 1537–68.

52. Alfred D. Chandler, Jr., *The Visible Hand: The Managerial Revolution in American Business* (Cambridge, MA: Harvard University Press, 1977), p. 8.

53. Albert O. Hirschman, *Exit, Voice, and Loyalty: Responses to Decline in Firms, Organizations, and States* (Cambridge, MA: Harvard University Press, 1970), p. 15; hereafter *EVL*.

54. As we review these assumptions by Coase, it would be prudent to keep in mind their limitations. For example, one way that consumer's dissatisfaction with price or product is neutralized is by marketing: either by advertising that invents qualities of the product previously imperceptible to the customer or by brand management, which has as its objective the construction of customer loyalty that is relatively indifferent to marginal cost differentials. Brand management enables firms to acquire a virtual monopoly on certain perhaps imaginary qualities, sufficient to acquire what John Kenneth Galbraith, after Karl Marx and Carl Kaysen, calls "market power," which enables them to override automatic fluctuations in the market. Galbraith, *The New Industrial State* (Princeton, NJ: Princeton University Press, 1967), p. 60 and *passim*.

55. Thurman Arnold, "Law Enforcement: An Attempt at Social Dissection," *Yale Law Journal* 42 (November 1932): 15.

56. Benito Mussolini, *The Corporate State* (2nd ed., Florence: Vallechi, 1938).

57. Lippmann, "The Underworld," in *Interpretations, 1931–1932*, ed. Allan Nevins (New York: Macmillan, 1932), p. 315.

58. The initials stand for the Racketeer Influenced and Corrupt Organizations Act, an unwieldy title surely chosen to produce the acronymic homage to the "hero" of Warners' *Little Caesar*.

59. David E. Ruth, *Inventing the Public Enemy: The Gangster in American Culture, 1918–1934* (Chicago: University of Chicago Press, 1996), p. 51; hereafter *IPE*.

60. For a thorough and penetrating study of the reception of the gangster cycles of motion pictures in the late 1920s and early 1930s, see Richard Maltby, "The Spectacle of Criminality," in *Violence and American Cinema*, ed. J. David Slocum (London: Routledge, 2000), pp. 117–52.

61. Mark H. Haller, "Illegal Enterprise: A Theoretical and Historical Interpretation," in *Organized Crime*, ed. Nikos Passas (Aldershot, Eng.: Dartmouth Press, 1993), pp. 218–19; hereafter "IE."

62. Chester I. Barnard, *The Functions of the Executive* (Cambridge, MA: Harvard University Press, 1938), p. 235.

63. The scene is dramatically different from its depiction in the novel, where Big Boy is crude and animalistic. When Rico visits, "The Big Boy sat opposite . . . his derby on the side of his head, . . . 'See that picture over there?' He pointed to an imitation Velasquez. 'That baby set me back one hundred and fifty berries.'" In the movie, Big Boy, played by the suave Sidney Blackmer, would be unlikely to be mistaken for a gangster by anyone not in the know. His mansion is decorated in Louis Quatorze. He informs Rico that the painting cost him fifteen thousand "dollars," not "berries." Gerald Peary, "Rico Rising: Little Caesar Takes Over the Screen," in *The Classic American Novel and the Movies*, ed. Gerald Peary and Roger Shatzkin (New York: Frederick Ungar Publishing, 1977), pp. 287–88.

64. See the "rule of reason" laid out by the Supreme Court's chief justice Edward White in 1911: "Two distinct categories, for which two different tests of restraint of trade were required. First were those contracts or combinations whose 'inherent nature of effect' was to restrain trade. This category included combinations involving more than one individual or corporation, such as gentlemen's agreements, pools, and other types of cartels. These combinations were illegal per se; that is, the Sherman Act applied literally to them." Naomi R. Lamoreaux, "Partnerships, Corporations, and the Limits on Contractual Freedom in U.S. History: An Essay in Economics, Law, and Culture," in *Constructing Corporate America*, ed. Kenneth Lipartito and David B. Sicilia (New York: Oxford University Press, 2004), p. 49; hereafter "PCLCF."

65. *Variety*, January 14, 1931, np., p. 3; January 21, 1941, pp. 3, 5. At this point, when Hays was clearly spinning things toward peace and goodwill, the official answer to the question of Warners' possible violation of the rules was "no." *Variety* reported that position, but happened to print a small item adjacent to Hays's denial: "Kay Francis Grows Ill When Given Maid Role in Par Feature." The brief notice mentions that she "produced a doctor's certificate that she was unable to appear"; it also mentions that "Miss Francis has entered into an agreement with Warners following her Par term, shortly expiring" (*V*, April 8, 1931, p. 3).

66. *Hold-up* is a term applied in business to the way one interest group within a

firm may effectively extort cooperation from another. As Lamoreaux shows, holding up was relatively difficult in a partnership where the oppressed partner could dissolve his connection to the firm and retrieve his portion of the firm's assets ("PCLCF," p. 49). Holding up minority shareholders in a corporation by management or a board became increasingly easy and convenient, especially when bylaws allocated votes not to individual shareholders but to individual shares, which, of course, made it possible for an owner-management team like the Warners to maintain control of their business. The Big Five formed an association, not a corporation, but they were vulnerable to Warners' strategy because they could not openly appeal to a gentlemen's agreement that had no legal status.

67. "Warners, MGM Break," *Variety*, July 24, 1931, p. 1: "All booking relations between Metro-Goldwyn-Mayer and Warners have been broken off, with MGM selling their product to opposition house. The break was caused by Warners refusing to play the MGM pictures on percentage over their entire circuit."

68. Mae D. Huettig, *Economic Control of the Motion Picture Industry: A Study in Industrial Organization* (Philadelphia: University of Pennsylvania Press, 1944), pp. 114–15; hereafter *EC*.

69. The term *cutthroat competition* belongs to the same trade-association discourse that, according to Ellis W. Hawley, "generally regarded a price cutter as a 'chiseler' and price competition as immoral." *The New Deal and the Problem of Monopoly: A Study in Economic Ambivalence* (1966; rpt., with new intro., New York: Fordham University Press, 1995), p. 11; hereafter *NDPM*.

70. Douglas Gomery, "Rethinking U.S. Film History: The Depression Decade and Monopoly Control," *Film and History* 10 (May 1981): 36.

71. Thomas Schatz describes the secrecy in which Zanuck conducted the adaptation, which began in mid-November 1932. He planned to announce the remake of *The Gold Diggers* after the release of *42nd Street* so that it could come "like a big news break" (*GS*, p. 151). In April 1933 Warners took out a two-page ad in *Variety* to announce the early release and explaining the urgency as the studio's acceptance of "a major share of the responsibility for restoring prosperity to this industry" (*V*, April 11, 1933, 14–15).

72. Crawford—then Lucille Lesuer—was discovered in the chorus line at the Winter Garden by Howard Dietz, who recommended her to Harry Rapf, a producer at the studio (*T*, p. 53).

73. The classic essay on the issues of the commodification of women in *The Gold Diggers of 1933* and the Warners Busby Berkeley musicals in general is Patricia Mellenkamp, "The Sexual Economics of *Gold Diggers of 1933*," in *The Hollywood Musicals: The Film Reader; in Focus*, ed. Steven Cohan (New York: Routledge, 2002).

74. The reference to the "Spanish-American war stuff" is also a dig at Hearst, who was, as we have seen, a power at MGM and was forever associated with journalistic drum beating on behalf of the 1898 war with Spain.

75. *Fortune* promotes Warners' sensationalism in its profile of 1934. In *his* comparison of MGM and Warners, Scott Eyman suggests that "MGM's influence was so pervasive that a studio like Warners basically defined itself as the antithesis of MGM." Eynman quotes the telling recollection of Warners' writer-producer Jerry Wald: "I remember distinctly being called in once and [being told] that we could not compete with

Metro and their tremendous stable of stars, so we had to go after the stories, topical ones, not typical ones. The stories because the stars.... We used to say 'T-T-T: timely, topical, not typical.'" (*LH*, 189; quoting from Neil Gabler).

76. John O. Thompson, "Screen Acting and the Commutation Test," in *Stardom: Industry of Desire*, ed. Christine Gledhill (New York: Routledge, 1991), p. 191.

77. Charles W. Eckert, "The Anatomy of a Proleterian Film: Warner's *Marked Woman*," *Film Quarterly* 27, no. 2 (Winter 1973–74): 10–12.

78. "Metro-Goldwyn Mayer," *Fortune*, December 1932, *AFI*, pp. 311–33; "Metropolitan Life Insurance Company," *Fortune*, August 1934, p. 48; hereafter "MLIC."

79. Quoted in *MM*, p. 162. For a history of Metropolitan, see Olivier Zunz, *Making America Corporate, 1870–1920* (Chicago: University of Chicago Press, 1990), p. 230, nn. 101, 103; hereafter *MAC*.

80. On Metropolitan's response to the Armstrong Commission as an example of the way big business could co-opt the reformers' program, see *MAC*, pp. 91–92.

81. On Metropolitan's attempt to substitute policy holding for the support system of fraternal organizations, see *MAC*, p. 96.

82. Thurman Arnold, *The Folklore of Capitalism* (New Haven, CT: Yale University Press, 1937), p. 215.

83. For two useful and sharply divergent accounts of this debate among a large inventory, see Morton J. Horwitz, *The Transformation of American Law, 1870–1960: The Crisis of Legal Orthodoxy* (New York: Oxford University Press, 1996), pp. 65–109; and Gregory A. Mark, "Personification of the Business Corporation in American Law," *University of Chicago Law Review* 54 (1987): 1441–83.

84. Thurman Arnold, "Law Enforcement," *Yale Law Journal* (November 1932): 23. Neither the intent nor value of Arnold's analysis was strictly critical. In *Hollywood's New Deal* (Philadelphia: Temple University Press, 1997), Giulana Muscio argues that Arnold's analysis amounted to an implicit recommendation that the New Dealers effort to "reappropriate the folklore of capitalism in order to make innovative practices appear 'traditional,' by formulating associations and analogies, which would supply the 'New Organizations' with mythico-symbolic roots and thus reactivate the mechanisms of consensus" (p. 17).

85. "Crime and the New Deal," *Fortune*, August 1934, p. 59n; hereafter "CND."

86. I am indebted to Drayton Nabers's forceful case on behalf of the importance and complexity of *Bullets or Ballots*, presented in a graduate seminar paper at Johns Hopkins University in March 1996.

87. Ruth Vasey, *The World According to Hollywood, 1918–1939* (Madison: University of Wisconsin Press, 1997), 125.

88. On Willie Bioff and George S. Browne crooked management of the IATSE, see Michael Woodiwiss, *Organized Crime and American Power: A History* (Toronto: University of Toronto, Press, 2001), pp. 156–58.

89. The contest is replayed at Warners in *The Amazing Dr. Clitterhouse* (1938), in which Robinson's and Bogart's characters vie for supremacy. Once again Bogart dies at the hands of Robinson, who, however, escapes the gallows.

90. F. Raymond Daniell, "The Big Business of the Racketeers," *New York Times Magazine*, April 27, 1930, p. 5; qtd. in *IPE*, p. 46.

91. Raymond Moley, "The Racket, Most Elusive of Crimes," *New York Times*, August 8, 1931; qtd. in *IPE*, p. 61.

92. Michael Rogin, "Blackface, White Noise," in *Blackface, White Noise: Jewish Immigrants in the Hollywood Melting Pot* (Berkeley: University of California Press, 1996), pp. 73–120; hereafter *WN*.

93. In his otherwise useful discussion of the motion picture in *Harmless Entertainment*, Richard Maltby erroneously claims that Detective Blake introduces the numbers racket to the city (*HE*, p. 110).

94. "Presidential Statement upon Signing the Social Security Act; August 14, 1934," in *The Public Papers and Addresses of Franklin D. Roosevelt, with a Special Introduction and Explanatory Notes by President Roosevelt*, compiled by Samuel I. Rosenman, vol. 4 of *The Court Disapproves, 1935* (New York: Random House, 1938), p. 324.

95. "Social Security by Any Other Name," *Fortune*, March 1935, pp. 83–84.

96. Ralph Cassady, Jr., "Some Economic Aspects of Motion Picture Production and Marketing," *Journal of Business of the University of Chicago* 6 (April 1933): 127–28.

97. "U.S. Corporate Management," *Fortune*, June 1933, p. 104.

98. Kenneth Davis, *FDR: The New Deal Years, 1933–1937; A History* (New York: Random House, 1979), p. 267.

99. Quoted in James McGregor Burns, *Roosevelt: The Lion and the Fox* (New York: Harcourt, Brace, 1956), pp. 228–29.

100. "Warner Brothers," *Fortune*, December 1937, p. 213; hereafter, "WB."

101. Franklin Delano Roosevelt, "Praising the First Hundred Days and Boosting the NRA (7/24/1933)," in *FDR's Fireside Chats*, ed. Russell D. Buhite and David W. Levy (1992; rpt., New York: Penguin Books, 1993), p. 33.

102. Pressbook for *Boys Town*, Billy Rose Collection, New York Public Library. For a detailed account of the approach that Warner Bros. adopted when assembling pressbooks in the late 1930s, see Mark S. Miller, "Helping Exhibitors: Pressbooks at Warner Bros. in the Late 1930s," *Film History* 6, no. 2 (Summer 1994): 188–96.

103. Morris's business is not explicitly identified as a pawnshop, although it serves the function of a pawnshop. Nor is Morris explicitly identified as a Jew, although the real person on whom he was based was Jewish.

104. *Management Past and Present: A Casebook on the History of American Business*, ed. Alfred D. Chandler, Jr., Thomas K. McCraw, Richard S. Tedlow (Cincinnati, OH: Southwestern Publishing, 1996), case 5, p. 23.

105. Arthur M. Schlesinger, *The Politics of Upheaval*, vol. 3 of *The Age of Roosevelt* (Boston: Houghton Mifflin, 1960), p. 405. On the penetration of Keynesianism in the Second New Deal during 1937–38, see Ellis W. Hawley, "The Discovery and Study of a 'Corporate Liberalism,'" *Business History Review* 52, no. 3 (Autumn 1978): 277–80.

106. According to Mark Daniels, collections associate at the Hall of History and Father Flanagan House, the statue represented in the film "was called 'The Homeless Boy' and was created by former Boys Town resident Jimmy Webster in 1933. He had polio, and lived here for several years before moving to Chicago. The statue was modeled after a nine year old boy named John Rushing. It appeared in the film and was used as Boys Town's logo during the 1930's, until Fr. Flanagan adopted the 'Two Brothers' logo in the early 1940's. Unfortunately it was constructed out of Plaster of Paris and was placed

outside, where it did not survive the Nebraska weather" (e-mail message to the author from Mr. Daniels, December 5, 2002).

107. On Mayer's protection of the MGM trademark from the Marx brothers' "irreverence" in 1935, see *MD*, p. 264.

108. Erving Goffman, *Essays on the Social Situation of Mental Patients and Other Inmates* (New York: Doubleday, 1961), pp. 5–6.

109. David F. D'Alessandro, *Brand Warfare* (New York: McGraw-Hill, 2001), p. xiv. In his preface, D'Alessandro mentions that he is the first CEO of a Fortune 500 company to have ascended to the position from the marketing division.

110. "Social Security," *Fortune*, March 1935, p. 116.

111. See *MD*, pp. 311–12.

112. Because Le Roy's salary of three hundred thousand dollars eclipsed that of the other producers at the studio, Mayer tried, unsuccessfully, to keep it secret so as to avoid having to deal with the claims of other producers at the studio for equivalent pay. Aljean Harmetz, *The Making of the Wizard of Oz* (New York: Hyperion, 1977), p. 14.

113. Compare Margaret Hamilton's appearance as a social worker in *Babes in Arms*, where her insistence that the children of the itinerant show people should stay in school is treated as though it were as arbitrary and tyrannical as an order by Stalin to ship the youngsters off to Siberia.

114. Aljean suggests such a correspondence by the title of her third chapter, "The Brains, the Heart, the Nerve, and the Music," which describes the roles of Freed, Arlen, and Harburg in the production.

115. *V*, January 29, 1947, p. 4.

Chapter 2: MGM and the Postwar Era

This section is Copyright © 2000 The Johns Hopkins University Press. This article first appeared in *English Literary History* 67 (Winter 1999): 257–92. Reprinted with permission by The Johns Hopkins University Press.

1. Clayton R. Koppes, and Gregory D. Black, *Hollywood Goes to War: How Politics, Profits, and Propaganda Shaped World War II Movies* (Berkeley: University of California Press, 1987), pp. 83–84; hereafter *HGW*.

2. Dwight David Eisenhower, *Crusade in Europe* (Garden City, NY: Doubleday, 1948), p. 68; hereafter *CE*.

3. Warren F. Kimball, *The Juggler: Franklin Roosevelt as Wartime Statesman* (Princeton, NJ: Princeton University Press, 1991). When Henry Morgenthau announced the sale of Defense Bonds in April 1941, he not only advocated their purchase so that in the face of war, each citizen would "have the right to say to [himself], 'I am doing something to help,'" he promoted them for their defense against a possible postwar recession, what he calls a "postwar adjustment period." (Morgenthau, "Inauguration of the Sale of Defense Bonds," CBS Radio, April 30, 1941).

4. I am indebted for this insight to Drayton Nabers.

5. Charles Higham draws the connection between Mayer's interest in horses and the "disastrous venture" of *Florian* in *Merchant of Dreams: Louis B. Mayer, M.G.M., and the Secret Hollywood* (New York: Dell, 1993), pp. 334–35. See also his discussion of Mayer's absorption with horse breeding in 1940, pp. 352–53.

6. In point of fact, as the correspondent for *The Film Daily Annual* reported in 1941, the surviving operating movie theaters in Great Britain (eight hundred had been damaged by aerial attack during the year) remained open during blackouts and served the distraction hungry populace well as impromptu fallout shelters.

7. William O'Neill, *A Democracy at War: America's Fight at Home and Abroad in World War II* (Cambridge, MA: Harvard University Press, 1993), p. 167.

8. Jan Herman, *A Talent for Trouble: The Life of Hollywood's Most Acclaimed Director, William Wyler* (New York: Da Capo Press, 1997), p. 232; hereafter *TT*.

9. "Loew's, Inc.," *Fortune*, August 1939, in *The American Film Industry*, ed. Tino Balio (Madison: University of Wisconsin Press, 1976), pp. 334–50; hereafter "L."

10. Stanley Cavell concludes his influential analysis of *The Philadelphia Story* by indulging in a "daydream" in which the marriage of Tracy and Dexter is referred to as the American covenant as adumbrated by the Declaration of Independence and the Constitution (*Pursuits of Happiness: The Hollywood Comedy of Remarriage* [Cambridge, MA: Harvard University Press, 1981], pp. 153–59). If we are to refer the studio allegory to more general considerations, we would, as Drayton Nabers has argued, start with Ronald Coase's contemporary essay "The Firm" (1937).

11. See Stanley Cavell, *Pursuits of Happiness: The Hollywood Comedy of Remarriage* (Cambridge, MA: Harvard University Press, 1981), pp. 135–60.

12. Alfred Sloan, *My Years at General Motors* (Garden City, NY: Doubleday, 1963), p. 308; quoted in Richard S. Tedlow, *New and Improved: The Story of Mass Marketing in America* (Cambridge, MA: Harvard Business School Press, p. 168).

13. See Tedlow, "The Great Cola Wars," chap. 2 in *New and Improved*, 22–106. The "Pepsi Colas" of Hollywood were the poverty-row studios, such as Monogram and Republic, whose programmers provided Depression-era audiences with double-bill entertainment for the same price as an MGM feature.

14. "Coca-Cola," *Fortune*, July 1931, p. 65.

15. Of course, Coca-Cola did actually produce something you could purchase: you got to drink the Coke and keep the bottle until you claimed your deposit. MGM produced nothing you could touch or keep.

16. See Thomas Schatz's *The Genius of the System: Hollywood Filmmaking in the Studio Era* (New York: Pantheon Books, 1988), pp. 41–57, for a fine account of the consequences of the "high cost of quality" at MGM in the late 1930s and the war years.

17. The British film industry had not expired, but it was mortally wounded, diving from a prewar level of over two hundred films a year to a 1942 level of approximately fifty—and most of those subsidized by Hollywood through their affiliated British production wings.

18. See, for example, the contemporary *White Cliffs of Dover* (MGM, 1944) and the more recent *The War of the Roses* (Gracie Films / Twentieth Century Fox, 1989).

19. Edmund Burke, *Reflections on the Revolution in France* (Harmondsworth, Eng.: Penguin Books, 1969), pp. 175–76.

20. Henry Agard Wallace, *America Must Choose: The Advantages and Disadvantages of Nationalism, of World Trade, and of a Planned Middle Course* (New York: Foreign Policy Association, 1934), p. 24.

21. Douglas Gomery notes that *Mrs. Miniver* earned best gross and best profit of

any MGM film to that time. Gomery, *The Hollywood Studio System: A History* (1986; new ed., London: British Film Institute, BFI, 2005), p. 107. Gomery gives the credit to Schenk, who made numerous canny business decisions on behalf of Loew's, not to Mayer, who bred a marvelous stable of stars for MGM.

22. Mason Wiley and Damien Bona, *Inside Oscar: The Unofficial History of the Academy Awards* (New York: Ballantine Books, 1996), p. 130.

23. See Thomas Schatz, *Boom and Bust: American Cinema in the 1940s*, vol. 6 of *A History of the American Cinema*, gen. ed. Charles Harpole (Berkeley: University of California Press, 1997), pp. 188–91; hereafter *BB*.

24. Scott Eyman, *The Lion of Hollywood: The Life and Legend of Louis B. Mayer* (New York: Simon and Schuster, 2005), p. 425; hereafter *LH*.

25. Jeanine Basinger, "The World War II Combat Film: Definition," from *The World War II Combat Film: Anatomy of a Genre* (New York: Columbia University Press, 1960), rpt. in *Hollywood and War: The "Film" Reader*, ed. J. David Slocum (New York: Routledge, 2006), pp. 174–82. See also *BB*.

26. Captain Lassiter: "Any time you get an idea while we're together on this job, give your orders to the men. You don't have to waste time asking me first, trying to make me look good. And any time I give an order that seems wrong to you, tell me why. We'll get things done better and easier that way."

27. J. F. C. Fuller, *Training Soldiers for War* (London: Hugh Rees, 1914), p. 19; quoted in Hew Strachan, "Training, Morale and Modern War," *Journal of Contemporary History* 41, no. 2 (2006): 218.

28. "The ability to identify with a group and the past history of such identification are probably the most important components of good motivation for combat." Wessely, quoting Roy Grinker and John Spiegel, *Men Under Stress* (Philadelphia: Blakiston, 1945), p. 278.

29. Samuel A. Stouffer, Edward A. Suchman, Leland C. DeVinney, Shirley A. Star, and Robin M. Williams, Jr., *The American Soldier*, vol. 1, *Adjustment During Army Life* (Princeton, NJ: Princeton University Press, 1949), p. 82; hereafter *AS*.

30. A version of this exchange famously occurred between General Omar Bradley and an overeager soldier, who challenged Bradley with the question, "What is the capital of Illinois?" When Bradley answered, "Springfield," the soldier replied, "No, Chicago," and put the general under arrest.

31. That is a theme in *Go for Broke* (MGM, 1951), also written and, unfortunately, directed by Robert Pirosh, which follows the fortunes of the 422nd Regiment, recruited from Hawaiian Japanese-Americans, from boot camp to the frontline. When one soldier expresses the desire to be assigned to the Pacific theater so he can fight the "Japs" who killed his parents at Pearl Harbor, his friend assures him it will never happen since there's no way to guarantee that even in an American uniform he would not be mistaken for the enemy and shot by American troops.

32. Hew Strachan, "Training, Morale, and Modern War," *Journal of Contemporary History* 41, no. 2 (2006): 211; hereafter "TMMW."

33. Wessely, quoting Grinker and Spiegel, *Men Under Stress*, p. 278.

34. Walter Wanger, "The Role of Movies in Morale," *American Journal of Sociology* 47, no. 3 (November 1941): 378; hereafter "RMM."

35. For a detailed account see "The 101st Airborne During WW II," 101st Airborne Division Web site, www.ww2-airborne.us/18corps/101abn/101_overview.html (accessed April 6, 2011).

36. See Catherine Jurca, "*Mildred Pierce*, Warner Bros., and the Corporate Family," *Representations* 77 (Winter 2002): 30–51.

37. Samuel Goldwyn, "No New Jazz Age," *This Week* magazine, December 12, 1943; reprinted in *Appendix to the Congressional Record* (Washington, DC: Government Printing Office, 1943), December 13, 1943, V. 89 78–1.

38. For a concise, authoritative survey of the period, see *BB*, pp. 329–52.

Chapter 3: "'Til the Stars Go Cold"

1. Quoted in Scott Eyman, *The Lion of Hollywood: The Life and Legend of Louis B. Mayer* (New York: Simon and Schuster, 2005), p. 401; hereafter *LH*.

2. Hepburn is the example that Simon Watney chooses to represent what he calls "the cinema of chastisement." My genre nomination is not meant to compete with his, only to shift the emphasis to a kind of studio policy that comprises the rebuke of Hepburn in *The Philadelphia Story* and the deconstruction of Astaire at the opening of *The Band Wagon* and of Bette Davis throughout *The Star*. See Watney, "Katherine Hepburn and the Cinema of Chastisement," *Screen* (September–October 1985): 52–65.

3. Dore Schary, *Heyday: An Autobiography* (Boston: Little, Brown, 1979), pp. 198–202; hereafter *H*.

4. Robert A. Brady, "The Problem of Monopoly," *Annals of the American Academy of Political and Social Science* 254 (November 1947): 132; hereafter "PM."

5. Thalberg's name appeared on a screen only once: when he gave himself a writer's credit for the scenario of *Dangerous Little Demon*, which he produced at Universal in 1922. Roland Flamini, *Thalberg: The Last Tycoon and the World of MGM* (New York: Crown Publishers, 1994), p. 39.

6. Carol J. Clover, "Dancin' in the Rain," *Critical Inquiry* 21 (Summer 1995): 723; hereafter "DR."

7. Stephen M. Silverman, *Dancing on the Ceiling: Stanley Donen and His Movies* (New York: Alfred A. Knopf, 1996), p. 142.

8. Steven Cohan, *Incongruous Entertainments: Camp, Cultural Value, and the MGM Musical* (Durham, NC: Duke University Press, 2005), p. 222; hereafter *IE*.

9. Hugh Fordin, *MGM's Greatest Musicals: The Freed Unit* (New York: Da Capo Press, 1975), pp. 361–62; hereafter *GM*.

10. Ernest Borneman, "Rebellion in Hollywood," *Harpers*, October 1946, pp. 337–38.

11. In his strikingly different account of the scene in which Don and Cosmo share *Variety* with the "cannibal," Cohan emphasizes the way that the representation of the introduction of sound works to efface Warner Bros. from the subsequent evolution of that technological innovation: self-reflexiveness invites a teleological reading that not only sees MGM as the endpoint of that history but regards MGM's trope of self-reflexiveness as the engine of evolution.

12. My interpretation of the French Revolution theme in *Singin' in the Rain* is heavily indebted to Charles Dove, who was the first to illuminate the significance of Lina's role as a faux aristocrat, her revolutionary challenge to Monumental Studio, and her

positioning as a scapegoat of the studio's counterrevolution. Dove also disclosed the relation between that revolutionary theme and the persistent priority given to technology over the stars that are manufactured and maintained by the studio's fixed capital. Dove's brilliant, unpublished dissertation chapter is the single best reading of *Singin' in the Rain* I have encountered; it is woven into the fabric of my argument. Charles Dove, "Sleep No More: Mass Culture and the Uncanny in the Postwar Cinema," Ph.D. diss., Johns Hopkins University, 1994.

13. See Cohan's comment on the "sissy joke" Don was to make to "Cosmo" in the original script: "Great, what are you doing this evening?" The joke was censored by the PCA. *IE*, p. 240.

14. Hal Draper, "Neo-Corporatists and Neo-Reformers," *New Politics* (Fall 1961): 87–106, in *Government-Business Cooperation, 1945: Corporatism in the Post-War Era*, ed. Robert F. Himmelberg (New York: Garland Publishing, 1994), pp. 79–98. This section of Chapter 3 was originally published as Jerome Christensen, "Neo-Corporate Star-Making: The Band Wagon and the Charismatic Margin," *Law and Literature* 20, no. 2 (Summer 2008): 213–27. © 2008 by The Cardozo School of Law, Yeshiva University.

15. Adolf A. Berle, discussion in W. H. Ferry, *The Economy Under Law* (Santa Barbara, CA: Center for the Study of Democratic Institutions, 1959), p. 54; hereafter, *EUL*.

16. Adolf A. Berle, *The 20th Century Capitalist Revolution* (New York: Harcourt, Brace, 1954), pp. 65–70; hereafter *20th CCR*.

17. See Margaret M. Blair, *Ownership and Control: Rethinking Corporate Governance for the Twenty-First Century* (Washington, DC: Brookings Institution, 1995); and Kent Greene, *The Failure of Corporate Law* (Chicago: University of Chicago Press, 2006).

18. Max Weber, *Economy and Society*, vol. 1, trans. Talcott Parsons et. al., ed. Guenther Roth and Claus Wittich (1925; rpt., Berkeley: University of California Press, 1978), p. 241; hereafter *ES*.

19. Alan Bryman, *Charisma and Leadership in Corporations* (New York: Sage Publications, 1992), p. 24.

20. Thurman Arnold, *The Folklore of Capitalism* (New Haven, CT: Yale University Press, 1937), p. 350.

21. See Peter F. Drucker, *The Concept of the Corporation* (New York: John Day, 1946), pp. 234–36, hereafter *CC*; and *The Practice of Management* (New York: Harper and Row, 1954), pp. 37–41.

22. Others have put the quintessential quality of the star in different terms. There is "it," for example. There is also the "*x* factor," which is the term for that indescribable quality which Jeanine Basinger employs in her richly detailed study, *The Star Machine* (New York: Alfred A. Knopf, 2007), pp. 8–9.

23. Mark Fenster, "The Symbols of Governance: Thurman Arnold and Post-Realist Legal Theory," *Buffalo Law Review* 51 (2003): 1053.

24. Adolf A. Berle, *The American Economic Republic* (London: Sidgwick and Jackson, 1963), p. 202; hereafter *AER*.

25. John Mickelthwait and Adrian Wooldridge, *The Company: A Short History of a Revolutionary Idea* (New York: Modern Library, 2003), p. 108.

26. Burleigh B. Gardner and Sidney J. Levy, "The Product and the Brand," *Harvard Business Review* (March–April 1955): 39; hereafter "P and B."

27. See David F. D'Alessandro, *Brand Warfare* (New York: McGraw-Hill, 2001), p. xiv.

28. Marty Neumeier, *The Brand Gap: How to Bridge the Distance Between Business Strategy and Design* (Berkeley, CA: Aiga, 2006), p. 19; hereafter *BG*.

29. Barry King, "Articulating Stardom," *Screen* 26, no. 5 (September–October 1985): 31.

30. Leo Rosten *Hollywood: The Movie Colony, the Movie Makers* (New York: Harcourt, Brace, 1941), 81–82; *BG*, pp. 62–64.

31. Phillip Rieff, *Charisma: The Gift of Grace and How It Has Been Taken Away from Us* (New York: Pantheon Books, 2007), 28–31.

32. Oscar Grusky, "Administrative Succession in Formal Organizations" *Social Forces* 39 (December 1960): 105–6.

33. *Executive Suite*'s importance was registered at the time by the handful of Oscars it claimed, by its appearance on the covers of both *Time* and *Newsweek*, and by its prominent place in *Fortune*'s twenty-fifth anniversary issue in January 1955.

34. Internet Movie Database (IMDB). Oliver Stone erroneously identifies the narrator as Edward R. Murrow in his commentary on the film on the recently released DVD.

35. Max Weber, *Theory of Social and Economic Organization*, trans. A. B. Henderson and Talcott Parsons (1947); excerpted in *Max Weber on Charisma and Institution Building*, ed. S. N. Eisenstadt (Chicago: University of Chicago Press, 1968), p. 57; hereafter *MWC*.

36. "'Management control' is a phrase meaning merely that no large concentrated stockholding exists which maintains a close working relationship with the management or is capable of challenging it.... Thus they need not consult with anyone when making up their slates of directors, and may simply request their stockholders to sign and send in a ceremonial proxy. They select their own successors." Adolf A. Berle, *Power Without Property: A New Development in American Political Economy* (New York: Harcourt, Brace, 1959), p. 73.

37. Eric Larrabee and David Riesman, "The Executive as Hero," *Fortune*, January 1955, p. 134; hereafter "EH."

38. Herryman Maurer, "The Age of the Managers," *Fortune*, January 1955, p. 84; hereafter "AM."

39. Joseph A. Schumpeter, *Capitalism, Socialism, and Democracy* (1942; rpt., New York: HarperPerennial, 1975), p. 83. I have substituted "innovation," the preferred term of business pictures, for Schumpeter's "mutation."

40. Gareth Morgan, *Images of Organization* (Thousand Oaks, CA: Sage Publications, 1997), p. 146.

41. Douglas Gomery, *The Hollywood Studio System: A History* (1986; new ed., London: British Film Institute, 2005), pp. 81–86, 99–107.

42. "Whereas brand image is a concept originated and 'owned' by marketers and advertising specialists, the idea that a brand has equity that exceeds its conventional asset value," Biel claims, "is a notion developed by financial people." Biel adds that, "In the case of a brand acquisition, it is the expectation of the future cash flow that commands a premium over the cost of developing the plant and infrastructure required to bring a new, competing brand to the market." Alexander L. Biel, "Converting Image into Equity," in *Brand Equity and Advertising: Advertising's Role in Building Strong Brands*, ed. Alexander L. Biel and David A. Aaker (Hillsdale, NJ: Laurence Erlbaum Associates, 1993), p. 69.

43. Eric Larrabee and David Riesman, "Company-Town Pastoral: The Role of Business in 'Executive Suite,'" in *Mass Culture: The Popular Arts in America*, ed. Bernard Rosenberg and David Manning White (Glencoe, IL: Free Press, 1957), p. 326; hereafter "C-TP."

44. Eames Demetrios, *An Eames Primer* (New York: Universe Publishing, 2001), p. 36; hereafter *EP*.

45. Pat Kirkham, *Charles and Ray Eames: Designers of the Twentieth Century* (Cambridge, MA: MIT Press, 1995), pp. 221–23; hereafter *CRE*.

46. Edward Shils, "Charisma, Order, and Status," *American Sociological Review* 30, no. 2 (April 1965): 202; hereafter "COS"; italics in original.

47. As Schary notes, the studio "assembled a cast of stars, most of them under contract, whom most likely we could never have corralled on the open market for the price we charged to our production." He adds that "the success of *Executive Suite* strengthened Schenck's resolve not to bow to the agents who were yelling, 'Let my people go.'" But those stars did go once their contracts expired, joining "independent setups" in part because "Schenck was still opposed to giving stars a piece of the action" (*H*, p. 276).

48. John Houseman, *Front and Center* (New York: Simon and Schuster, 1979), p. 419.

49. Alan Liu, *The Laws of Cool: Knowledge Work and the Culture of Information* (Chicago: University of Chicago Press, 2004), pp. 45–62.

50. Herman Miller (Firm), *The Herman Miller Collection* (rpt., New York: Acanthus Press, 1995), p. 71; hereafter *HMC*.

51. According to Hugh Fordin, who adds that "Comden and Green maintain that Dore Schary, having replaced L. B. Mayer, gave his go-ahead to the production. However, Mayer was still at the studio and it was he who said, 'O.K.'" Fordin notes that "Mayer resigned June 22, 1951, three days after *Singin' in the Rain* went before the camera." *GM*, pp. 352–53.

52. So natural that it tells us nothing about the person who sings it—which is the point of having the sadistic character played by Malcolm McDowell sing the song in *Clockwork Orange* (Warners, 1971).

Chapter 4: Ownership and Authorship

The opening section of this chapter was first published as "Studio Authorship, Warner Bros., and *The Fountainhead*," by Jerome Christensen, in *Velvet Light Trap* 57 (Spring 2005): 17–35. Copyright © 2006 by the University of Texas Press. All rights reserved.

1. Quoted in George H. Marcus, *Functionalist Design: An Ongoing History* (New York: Prestel-Verlag, 1995), p. 16; hereafter *FD*.

2. Alfred D. Chandler, Jr., *The Visible Hand: The Managerial Revolution in American Business* (Cambridge, MA: Harvard University Press, 1977), pp. 6–7.

3. Jeffrey Meyers, *Gary Cooper: An American Hero* (New York: William Morrow, 1998), pp. 214–21; hereafter *GC*.

4. After Frank Lloyd Wright asked too much money to provide drawings for the models, the studio hired its own "architect" to design the models to be used in the film. George H. Marcus comments, "The buildings that represented Roark's architecture for the 1949 film that Rand adapted from the novel were unfortunately mere pastiches of modernist designs" (*FD*, p. 132).

5. Kenneth R. Andrews, *The Concept of Corporate Strategy* (1971; 3rd ed., Homewood, IL: Irwin, 1987), p. 14.

6. David F. D'Alessandro, former CEO of John Hancock, defines a brand as "whatever the consumer thinks of when he or she hears your company's name." *Brand Warfare: 10 Rules for Building the Killer Brand* (New York: McGraw-Hill, 2001), p. xiv.

7. Robert Spadoni, "Guilty by Omission: Girding *The Fountainhead* for the Cold War," *Literature/Film Quarterly* 27, no. 3 (1999): n.p.; hereafter "GO."

8. Jerrold Levinson, *The Pleasures of Aesthetics: Philosophical Essays* (Ithaca, NY: Cornell University Press, 1996), p. 178.

9. Clement Greenberg, "Towards a Newer Laocoon," in *Clement Greenberg: The Collected Essays and Criticism*, ed. John O'Brian, 4 vols. (Chicago: University of Chicago Press, 1986), 1: 37; hereafter "TNL."

10. See Rem Koolhaas, *Delirious New York: A Retroactive Manifesto for Manhattan* (New York: Monacelli Press, 1994), pp. 9–11; hereafter *DNY*. I'm grateful to Mark Goble for bringing Koolhaas's text to my attention.

11. "What Do They Mean by Monopoly?" *Fortune*, March 1938, p. 77.

12. Harry Aubrey Toulmin, Jr., *The Trade-Mark Act of 1946 Analyzed, Annotated, and Explained* (Cincinnati: W. H. Anderson, 1946), pp. 7–8.

13. Leo C. Rosten, *Hollywood: The Movie Colony, the Movie Makers* (New York: Harcourt, Brace, 1941), pp. 81–82.

14. The case for a Kantian defense of the right of publicity adumbrated in *The Fountainhead* is made directly by Alice Haemmerli in her article "Whose Who? The Case for a Kantian Right of Publicity" (49 *Duke Law Journal* 383 [November 1999]), where she argues that "property is inseparably associated with one's 'personhood' because property grows out of freedom and freedom is essential to personhood" (p. 418).

15. See Jane M. Gaines, *Contested Culture: The Image, the Voice, and the Law* (Chapel Hill: North Carolina Press, 1991), pp. 224–27.

16. The original *Skyscraper Souls*, starring Warren William, was a low-budget, Wall Street version of *Grand Hotel*, produced for MGM by Cosmopolitan Pictures in 1932. It treats executive financial malfeasance as the moral equivalent of sexual peccadilloes.

17. In the novel not only does Wynand not commit suicide after closing *The Banner* and commissioning the Wynand Building, but in his commission Wynand stipulates that the building "will be used, [that] it will house the *The Clarion* and all the offices of the Wynand Enterprises now located in various parts of the city. The rest of the space will be rented." Ayn Rand, *The Fountainhead* (1943; rpt., New York: Penguin Books, 2005), p. 690.

18. The cursive script on Roark's office door that is replaced here by the block letters is nearly identical to the script that is used for Vidor's credit as director, producer, and co-screenwriter on the 1941 MGM feature *H. M. Pulham, Esq.*

19. Donald Spoto, *The Dark Side of Genius: Alfred Hitchcock* (Boston: Little, Brown, 1983), p. 393; hereafter *DFG*.

20. See Jonathan Freedman, "From *Spellbound* to *Vertigo*: Alfred Hitchcock and Therapeutic Culture in America," in *Hitchcock's America*, ed. Jonathan Freedman and Richard Millington (New York: Oxford University Press, 1999), pp. 77–98. Freedman explores the way that Hitchcock in *Vertigo* engages the so-called "triumph of the thera-

peutic" in postwar America, including his own contribution, *Spellbound*. What Freedman calls Freud's ahistoricism does not, I would argue, characterize Hitchcock, however, whose turn to the late Freud coincides with an especially incisive elaboration of his exploration of a specifically postwar American culture.

21. Robin Wood, *Hitchcock's Films Revisited* (New York: Columbia University Press, 2002), p. 110; hereafter *HFR*.

22. David Riesman, Reuel Denney, and Nathan Glazer, *The Lonely Crowd: A Study of the Changing American Character* (New Haven, CT: Yale University Press, 1950), p. 239; hereafter *LC*.

23. On the terms of art in this scene, Deborah Linderman describes Madeleine as "a fully objectified image, [who] walks up behind the point of Scottie's seat and, stopping there, into a frame that perfectly delimits her as a form of desire." "The Mise-en-Abîme in Hitchcock's *Vertigo*," *Cinema Journal* 30, no. 4 (Summer 1991): 63. Robert Baird has a somewhat similar take on Hitchcock's uses of profiles, but unlike Linderman, he separates their use from the domain of psychoanalysis. Robert Baird, "Hitchcock's Uses of Profiles in *Vertigo*," *Images Journal* Web site, www.imagesjournal.com/issue02/features/vertprof.htm (accessed April 6, 2011).

24. On the castration theme and its relation to the paintings in *Vertigo*, see Tania Modleski, *The Women Who Knew Too Much: Hitchcock and Feminist Theory* (New York: Methuen, 1988), p. 92; and Brigitte Peucker, "The Cut of Representation: Painting and Sculpture in Hitchcock," in *Alfred Hitchcock Centenary Essays*, ed. Richard Allen and S. Ishi Gonzales (London: British Film Institute, 1999), pp. 149–51.

25. See Steven Knapp, *Literary Interest: The Limits of Anti-Formalism* (Cambridge, MA: Harvard University Press, 1993), pp. 51–60.

26. In an essay on Hitchcock on the MoMA site, the curator comments that "Hitchcock engaged his audience the way an artist absorbs his viewer—through process, both instinctive and methodical. He disdained the notion that he tricked his public, but won their confidence through technique in the way—he told more than one interviewer—a painter convinces through the strokes of his brush" ("Alfred Hitchcock, April 16–June 13, 1999," www.moma.org/interactives/exhibitions/1999/hitchcock/curator_essay1.html [accessed April 6, 2011]). That may be generally true, but in *Vertigo* Hitchcock proves his integrity not by mimicking the painter but by exposing the tricks by which painters and curators absorb their public.

27. Like the villains of Vance Packard's contemporary best seller, Elster is an expert in public relations who indoctrinates himself "in the lore of psychiatry and the social sciences in order to increase [his] skill at 'engineering' consent to [his] propositions." *The Hidden Persuaders* (New York: David McKay, 1957), pp. 4–5.

28. It is entirely relevant to this reading of the motion picture that the actual *Portrait of Carlotta* was painted as a prop for the movie by the abstract expressionist John Ferren, who, like Midge, was freelancing for a fee. Unlike Ferren's other works, there is no evidence that this one survived (Dan Auiler, *"Vertigo": The Making of a Hitchcock Classic* [New York: St. Martin's Press, 1998], p. 83; hereafter *VMHC*).

29. Cf. William Rothman's somewhat different account in "Some Thoughts on Hitchcock's Authorship," in *Alfred Hitchcock Centenary Essays*, ed. Allen and Gonzales, p. 31.

30. Thomas Schatz, *The Genius of the System: Hollywood in Filmmaking in the Studio Era* (New York: Pantheon Books, 1988), p. 486; hereafter *GS*.

31. Thurman W. Arnold, *The Bottlenecks of Business* (Washington, DC: Beard Books, 1940), p. 111.

32. Dennis McDougal, *The Last Mogul: Lew Wasserman, MCA, and the Hidden History of Hollywood* (New York: Crown Publishers, 1998), pp. 252–53, 297–302.

33. Thomas M. Leitch, "The Outer Circle: Hitchcock on Television," in *Alfred Hitchcock Centenary Essays*, pp. 65–69; hereafter "OC."

34. Mark Caro, "Filmmakers and Writers Get Possessive About Lines of Credit," *Chicago Tribune*, November 19, 2000. See also "Possessory Credit Timeline," in *DGA Magazine* Web site, February 2004, www.dga.org/news/v28_6/news_pc-timeline.php3 (accessed April 6, 2011).

35. Patrick McGilligan, *Alfred Hitchcock: A Life in Darkness and Light* (New York: HarperCollins, 2003), p. 412.

36. Andrew Sarris, "Note on the Auteur Theory in 1962," in *Auteurs and Authorship: A Film Reader*, ed. Barry Keith Grant (Malden, MA: Blackwell, 2008), pp. 42–45.

37. The argument with the museums is not finally an aesthetic one: Hitchcock was actually treated with all but unparalleled respect by the Museum of Modern Art: the museum began collecting his films and associated advertisements in 1935, when he first gave a lecture under the museum's sponsorship. MoMA's support continued throughout his life (see "Alfred Hitchcock," www.moma.org/interactives/exhibitions /1999/ hitchcock/curator_essay1.html). It's not that Hitchcock wants access to a museum, he wants to develop a company that has the advantages of a museum but which he can curate and from which he can profit.

38. In 1951 the motion picture industry shifted from cellulose nitrate base to acetate safety film. See the brief history of film preservation by David Francis, "Motion Picture Conservation at the Library of Congress," Library of Congress Web site, www.loc.gov/rr/mopic/mppresdf.html (accessed April 6, 2011).

39. See Francis, "Motion Picture Conservation," on the advantage that prestige gives to those institutions intent on the conservation of restoration and preservation of paintings.

40. Virginia Wexman acutely observes that "Hitchcock's obsession with controlling his leading ladies, which grew as his career in films progressed, can be seen as an adaptation that for a long period of time enabled him to function more effectively in the environment of commercialized eroticism that defined the Hollywood style." Wexman, "The Critic as Consumer: Film Study in the University, *Vertigo*, and the Film Canon," *Film Quarterly* 39, no. 3 (Spring 1986): 34.

41. Roland Barthes, *Camera Lucida*, trans. Richard Howard (New York: Hill and Wang, 1987), p. 126 and *passim*; hereafter *CL*.

42. Samuel Taylor Coleridge, *Lay Sermons* (1917), ed. R. J. White, *The Collected Works of Samuel Taylor Coleridge*, gen. ed. Kathleen Coburn, 19 vols. (Princeton, NJ: Princeton University Press, 1972), 6: 30.

43. I am indebted to the generosity and expertise of John Belton, who tutored me on the effects of the switch from Technicolor to Eastmancolor negatives in an e-mail message on November 16, 2009, and who consulted with Robert A. Harris, who authori-

tatively confirmed Belton's hypothesis that "the original color negative had faded and was not fully corrected for the re-release," with the testimony that "the yellow layer fade on the OCN [original color negative] would have made it [the 1983 release print] more blue than green" (e-mail exchange between John Belton and Robert A. Harris, November 17 and 19, 2009).

44. Gilberto Perez, *The Material Ghost: Films and Their Medium* (Baltimore: Johns Hopkins University Press, 1987).

45. See Murray Pomerance's take on the recipe in his essay "The Man Who Wanted to Go Back," in *The End of Cinema as We Know It: American Film in the Nineties*, ed. Jon Lewis (New York: New York University Press, 2001), pp. 42–45.

46. Some sounds were criticized as too clear. As Belton notes, "there was a 'scandal' attached to the restoration in that Harris and Katz re-recorded all the sound effects and added some [such as the sound of gulls during Madeleine's staged suicide attempt in the bay] that were never there" (e-mail message, November 16, 2009). See James C. Katz's comments on the controversy in *VMHC*, p. 1.

Chapter 5: Saving Warner Bros.

1. Mark Harris, *Pictures at a Revolution: Five Movies and the Birth of the New Hollywood* (New York: Penguin Books, 2008), pp. 192–94; hereafter *PR*. Mark Harris's remarkably well-researched and shrewd study has been a valuable resource throughout this chapter.

2. Patrick Goldstein, "Blasts from the Past," *L.A. Times-Calendar*, August 24, 1997, n.p.

3. *The St. Valentine's Day Massacre*, produced by Roger Corman for Los Altos and Fox and released less than a month before *Bonnie and Clyde*, made the most striking gangster statement of the 1960s by explicitly connecting criminal gangs and corporate America in its voiceover prologue. *The St. Valentine's Day Massacre* would beget Paramount's *The Godfather*, directed by the American International Pictures alum Francis Ford Coppola. *Bonnie and Clyde* spawned Robert Aldrich's gruesome *Grissom Gang*, Corman's *Red Hot Mama*, and, illustriously, Sam Peckinpah's *The Wild Bunch*.

4. Billy Rose Collection, New York Public Library, reel no. 221, no. 14.

5. Peter Biskind, *Easy Riders, Raging Bulls: How the Sex-Drugs-and-Rock 'N' Roll Generation Saved Hollywood* (New York: Simon and Schuster, 1998), p. 35.

6. Robert Benton and David Newman, "The Movies Will Save Themselves," *Esquire*, thirty-fifth anniversary issue, *Can We Salvage the Twentieth Century?*, November 1968, pp. 182–87; hereafter "MWST."

7. I am generally indebted to insightful readings by John Cawelti, "The Artistic Power of *Bonnie and Clyde*," in *Focus on Bonnie and Clyde*, ed. John G. Cawelti (Englewood Cliffs, NJ: Prentice-Hall, 1973), pp. 40–84; hereafter *FBC*; Matthew Bernstein, "Perfecting the New Gangster: Writing *Bonnie and Clyde*," *Film Quarterly* 54, no. 4 (Summer 2000): 16–31; and Robert Kolker, *A Cinema of Loneliness* (3rd ed., Oxford: Oxford University Press, 2000), pp. 30–47.

8. "I wanted the film to have a certain rhythm, a nervous montage." Jean-Louis Comolli interview with Arthur Penn, *FBC*, p. 15.

9. Alan Liu, "Remembering the Spruce Goose: Historicism, Postmodernism, Romanticism," *South Atlantic Quarterly* 102, no. 1 (Winter 2003): 272–73. Liu quotes (p. 273)

from Fredric Jameson, *Postmodernism; or, The Cultural Logic of Late Capitalism* (Durham, NC: Duke University Press, 1991), p. 3; hereafter "RSG."

10. David Newman and Robert Benton, "The New Sentimentality," *Esquire*, January 1964, pp. 25–31.

11. Douglas B. Holt, *How Brands Become Icons: The Principles of Cultural Branding* (Cambridge, MA: Harvard Business School Press, 2004), pp. 56–61; hereafter *BM*.

12. Pauline Kael, "*Bonnie and Clyde*," in *Kiss Kiss Bang Bang* (1968; rpt., New York: Bantam Books, 1969), p. 69; hereafter *KKBB*. This mutual concern can be assumed because, as Mark Harris reports in his indispensable study *Pictures at a Revolution*, Kael interviewed Newman and Benton before she wrote her lengthy panegyric, which gives special praise to the screenwriters (*PR*, p. 346). That praise comes mostly at the expense of Arthur Penn. Kael did not mention the interview during the course of her review.

13. See Denise Mann's discussion of *The Hucksters*, in *Hollywood Independents: The Postwar Talent Takeover* (Minneapolis: University of Minnesota Press, 2008), pp. 110–11.

14. Peter Collier, *Ramparts*, May 1968; quoted in John G. Cawelti, ed., *FBC*, p. 29.

15. Jack Shadoian, *Dreams and Dead Ends: The American Gangster Film* (Cambridge, MA: MIT Press, 1977), p. 302.

16. See Stuart Ewen, *PR: A Social History of Spin* (New York: Basic Books, 1996), p. 281, for photos of advertising-laden business in the 1930s.

17. David Newman, "What's It Really All About: Pictures at an Execution," in *Arthur Penn's "Bonnie And Clyde*," ed. Lester D. Friedman (New York: Cambridge University Press, 2000), pp. 38–39; hereafter *APBC*.

18. It is strange that Crowther, in a bid for custodian of the nation's history, would call the early 1930s (Bonnie and Clyde were killed in 1934) "post-Depression years."

19. *Bonnie and Clyde*, fortieth anniversary ed., DVD (Warner Home Video, 2008).

20. Newman and Benton did study Godard, however, who, as Katie Trumpener has reminded me, includes conspicuous references to Coca-Cola in both *Breathless* and *Masculin Feminine*.

21. Although Beatty tried to get many more brand names into the movie, the legal department at Warners did their best to keep out all of them. In a memo of November 3, 1966, Curtis Kenyon, a representative of Jack Warner's, listed a dozen brand names that Beatty had kept in the script despite agreeing to eliminate them. He concludes: "As you know, J.L. feels very strongly about the use of any names which might appear to be plugs, and we would therefore like you to find substitutes for the above-mentioned items, in line with our earlier understanding." Curtis Kenyon to Warren Beatty, November 3, 1966, Warner Bros. Archive, University of Southern California. We must conclude that either the Warners eyes trained on the film did not see the Coca-Cola, Pepsi, and other signs or, more likely, that they did not see them as plugs but as integral to the townscape of West Texas in the early 1930s.

22. Arthur Danto, *Beyond the Brillo Box: The Visual Arts in Post-Historical Perspective* (New York: Farrar, Straus and Giroux, 1992), p. 139.

23. "During 1930, the name Coca-Cola was brought to the attention of the public 500,000,000 times in letters varying from one-sixteenth of an inch to sky-written characters one mile in height. It was written in glass, paint, gold, fiber, cardboard, leather,

bone, wood, and flowers. Coca-Cola advertisements were painted on 20,000 walls and 160,000 posters; more than 5,000,000 Coca-Cola glasses were sold (at cost) to U.S. fountains; 400,000,000 magazine and newspaper pages carried the Coca-Cola 'message.'" "Coca-Cola," *Fortune*, July 1931, pp. 108–10.

24. Newman and Benton essay, in *The Bonnie and Clyde Book*, ed. Sandra Wake and Nicola Hayden (New York: Simon and Schuster, 1972), p. 139.

25. W. K. Wimsatt, Jr., "The Concrete Universal," in *The Verbal Icon: Studies in the Meaning of Poetry* (Lexington: University of Kentucky Press, 1954), p. 69; hereafter *VI*.

26. Steven Knapp, *Literary Interest: The Limits of Anti-Formalism* (Cambridge, MA: Harvard University Press, 1993), p. 49; hereafter *LI*.

27. Mark Batey, *Brand Meaning* (New York: Routledge, 2008), pp. 191–92.

28. In the words of Pine and Gilmore: "The company that is perhaps most successful in embedding its goods into a total experience is Harley Davidson. How many other company logos do you find tattooed on users' bodies?" (B. Joseph Pine II, James H. Gilmore, *The Experience Economy: Work Is Theater and Every Business a Stage* (Cambridge, MA: Harvard Business School Press, 1999), p. 18; hereafter *EE*.

29. On the process by which "the means of differentiating the product (the star) became an end in itself," see Jane M. Gaines's indispensable *Contested Culture: The Image, the Voice, and the Law* (Chapel Hill: University of North Carolina Press, 1991), pp. 37–41. On the process by which "the sign increasingly replaces the product itself as the site of fetishism" and "the focus of commodity fetishism shifts from the product to the sign values invested in products by corporate imagery and marketing's structures of meaning," see Rosemary Coombe, *The Cultural Life of Intellectual Properties: Authorship, Appropriation, and the Law* (Durham, NC: Duke University Press, 1998), pp. 55–57.

30. I am using *dynamic* in place of both the word *process* and a word that would be likelier, given Nicholas Luhmann's academic importance: namely, *system*. My master is Thurman Arnold, iconoclastic law professor at Yale in the early 1930s and head of the antitrust division of the U.S. Justice Department during the Second New Deal, whose work of ironical realism, *The Folklore of Capitalism* (New Haven, CT: Yale University Press, 1937), has infused this study. Arnold's term for his never completed project was *political dynamics*. In this supplement to that project, I would stipulate that the use of *dynamic* here means a form that performs as if an autotelic system but that does not run on autopilot. A dynamic is a process motivated by intention, energized by agency, and subject to the contingencies of time, place, politics, and finance.

31. *New Yorker*, note on Dorothea Lange's photographs, in Anne Whiston Spirn, *Daring to Look: Dorothea Lange's Photographs and Reports from the Field* (Chicago: University of Chicago Press, 2008), p. 37.

32. No description of the tattoo appears even in the much revised final version of the script that Newman and Benton had first completed in 1964.

33. Michael Szalay and Sean McCann, "Paul Potter and the Cultural Turn," in *Countercultural Capital, Yale Journal of Criticism* 18, no. 2 (2005): 209–20. Paul Potter was the leader of the Students for a Democratic Society during a decisive period in the ramping up of the Vietnam War.

34. Wini Breines, *The Great Refusal: Community and Organization in the New Left, 1962–1968* (New York: Praeger, 1982), p. 1; hereafter *GR*. Breines ably summarizes the

critique of the liberals such as Edward Shils, Daniel Bell, Nathan Glazer, and Lipset, who first leveled the indictment against the New Left that Szalay and McCann echo. They

> accused the students of having no real interests in any specific demands, of being indifferent to legality and of ignoring the conventional channels by which . . . the students could have attained these demands. The rules by which they are accused of refusing to play were (1) compromise, (2) representation (a two-party system preferably), and (3) a commitment to the rules. The rules, in the sociologists' view, were more important than democracy, which is as clear an example of formal rationality as any. (p. 5)

35. Terry H. Anderson, *The Movement and the Sixties: Protest in America From Greensboro to Wounded Knee* (Oxford: Oxford University Press, 1994), p. 166.

36. Kenneth Keniston, *Young Radicals: Notes on Committed Youth* (New York: Harcourt, Brace, and World, 1968), pp. 15–16; hereafter *YR*.

37. J. Hoberman, *The Dream Life* (New York: New Press, 2003), pp. 172–85.

38. Peter F. Drucker, *The Practice of Management* (New York: Harper and Row, 1954), p. 37; italics in original.

39. Serge Guilbaut, *How New York Stole the Idea of Modern Art: Abstract Expressionism, Freedom, and the Cold War* (Chicago: University of Chicago Press, 1987), pp. 29, 33–35; hereafter *HNYS*.

40. Clement Greenberg, "Avant-Garde and Kitsch," in *Clement Greenberg: The Collected Essays Pollock and After*, ed. J. O'Brien, 4 vols. (Chicago: University of Chicago Press, 1986), 1: 12; hereafter "AGK."

41. There is some justice in this "theft" insofar as it depends on the regulative idea of the priority of the director as author in the interpretation of serious film. As Janet Staiger argues, "The notion of looking for a signature did not, however, necessarily, or even likely, come from French criticism. The director-as-author was a potential discourse within American intellectual circles from at least the 1920s," when programming of foreign movies was organized by "the director's name." Janet Staiger, *Interpreting Films: Studies in the Historical Reception of American Cinema* (Princeton, NJ: Princeton University Press, 1992), p. 188.

42. Robert Sklar, *Movie Made America: A Cultural History of American Movies* (1975; rpt., New York: Vintage Books, 1994), p. 301.

43. Note how tortuous becomes the proposition at the end of *The Wizard of Oz*, "I'll know that if it's not there I won't have lost it anyway." We can say that the absence of "it" cannot be contradicted and the existence of it cannot be falsified.

44. Hecht-Hill-Lancaster Productions and later Lancaster-Hecht are the subject of Denise Mann's sustained attention in her splendid *Hollywood Independents*.

45. That equation is, I think, a fair summary of the theme of Bruck's study of Ross's career. Connie Bruck, *The Master of the Game: Steve Ross and the Creation of Time Warner* (New York: Penguin Books, 1994); hereafter *MG*. See pp. 44–45.

46. For another version of Beatty's anecdote, see *PR*, p. 92. For Arthur Penn's suspiciously novelized version, see *AFBC*, p. 27.

47. Dore Schary, *Heyday: An Autobiography* (Boston: Little, Brown, 1979), p. 209.

48. Memorandum from Walter McEwen to Warren Beatty, May 25, 1967, Warner Bros. Archive, University of Southern California, p. 1.

49. The plasticity of the logo was, as Paul Grainge observes in *Brand Hollywood*,

one shift among the many smaller-scale shifts and changes that marked the movement from the Old to the New Hollywood. Grainge gives a brief history of "three variations of [a logo] design that reflected transitions in ownership and the formation of Warner Bros.–Seven Arts in 1967 and Warner Communications Inc. in 1972," but he overlooks the dramatic inflection of existing logos through the agency of Warren Beatty's Tatira-Hiller in 1967, which occurred *during*, even *as* the transition—a change that assigned more significance to *Bonnie and Clyde* than anyone has ever thought to confer on the productions introduced by the apparition of the logo for Warner Bros.–Seven Arts. Paul Grainge, *Brand Hollywood: Selling Entertainment in a Global Media Age* (New York: Routledge, 2008), pp. 72–79.

Chapter 6: Post-Warners Warners

An earlier version of the first section in this chapter appeared as "The Time Warner Conspiracy: *JFK, Batman*, and the Manager Theory of Hollywood Film," *Critical Inquiry* 28, no. 3 (Spring 2002): 591–617. © 2002 by The University of Chicago. All Rights Reserved. "The Time Warner Conspiracy" section of this chapter appeared in an earlier version as "Taking It to the Next Level: *You've Got Mail*," *Critical Inquiry* 30, no. 1 (Autumn 2003): 198–215. © 2002 by The University of Chicago. All Rights Reserved.

1. Justin Wyatt, *High Concept: Movies and Marketing* (Austin: University of Texas Press, 1994), p. 34. See pp. 65–108 for Wyatt's detailed account of that market logic.

2. Thomas Schatz, "The New Hollywood," in *Film Theory Goes to the Movies*, ed. Jim Collins, Hilary Radner, and Ava Preacher Collins (New York: Routledge, 1993), pp. 34 and *passim*. For a trenchant and comprehensive analysis of the "new system" organized in the 1990s and consolidated early in the first decade of the new century, see Edward Jay Epstein, *The Big Picture: Money and Power in Hollywood* (New York: Random House, 2006).

3. Eileen R. Meehan, "'Holy Commodity Fetish, Batman!': The Political Economy of a Commercial Intertext," in *The Many Lives of the Batman: Critical Approaches to a Superhero and his Media*, ed. Roberta E. Pearson and William Uricchio (New York: Routledge, 1991), pp. 62 and 52.

4. Michael Parenti, "Morte D'Arthur," *Nation*, March 9, 1992; collected in *JFK: The Book of the Film*, ed. Oliver Stone and Zachary Sklar (New York: Applause Books, 1992), p. 478; hereafter *JFK*.

5. The two chief accounts are Richard M. Clurman's *To the End of Time: The Seduction and Conquest of a Media Empire* (New York: Simon and Schuster, 1992); hereafter *TET*; and Connie Bruck's *Master of the Game: Steve Ross and the Creation of Time Warner* (1994; rpt., New York: Penguin Books, 1995); hereafter *MG*. My version of the negotiations is completely indebted to Clurman and Bruck, unless otherwise indicated.

6. Peter F. Drucker, *The Practice of Management* (New York: Harper and Row, 1954), p. 39; hereafter *PM*.

7. For a fine-grained, lucid account of the deal-making frenzy that afflicted Hollywood in the post–*Bonnie and Clyde* years beginning with the attempt by Kirk Kerkorian, CEO of MGM, to acquire control of Columbia Pictures in 1979 to the struggles between Gerald Levin, CEO of Time Warner, with Rupert Murdoch, see Jon Lewis, "Money Matters: Hollywood in the Corporate Era," in *The New American Cinema*, ed. Jon Lewis (Durham, NC: Duke University Press, 1998), pp. 87–121.

8. Kim Masters, *The Keys to the Kingdom: How Michael Eisner Lost His Grip* (New York: William Morrow, 2000), p. 131. See *Keys*, pp. 126–38, for a detailed account of the transfer of power at Gulf+Western (then the umbrella company of which Paramount was a subsidiary) and of Davis's tenure as head of the corporation in the 1980s.

9. In *Hit and Run* Nancy Griffin and Kim Masters describe the continual revisions of the film script and interference with Tim Burton's direction by one of the coproducers, Jon Peters, right up to the last minute. After the record-breaking opening Peters "blustered to anyone who would listen that he had written, directed, cast, and single-handedly marketed the film." *Hit and Run: How Jon Peters and Peter Guber Took Sony for a Ride in Hollywood* (New York: Simon and Schuster, 1996), pp. 158–74; hereafter *HR*.

10. *Paramount Communications Inc., and KDS Acquisition Corp., Plaintiffs v. Time Incorporated*, Court of Chancery of Delaware, New Castle. Decided July 14, 1989, judge: William T. Allen, Chancellor (p. 13); hereafter Allen.

11. "The guarantees that the Time board members had insisted on from the beginning had slipped away without their knowing it. The controlling Time Warner by-laws say it in plain language: 'Any officer may be removed, either with or without cause, by the Board at any meeting called for the purpose'" (*MG*, p. 190).

12. Ute von Reibnitz, *Scenario Techniques* (New York: McGraw-Hill, 1988), p. 12.

13. Robbie E. Davis-Floyd, "Storying Corporate Futures," in *Corporate Futures: The Diffusion of the Culturally Sensitive Corporate Form*, ed. George E. Marcus (Chicago: University of Chicago Press, 1998), p. 142; hereafter "SCF." For a detailed discussion of scenario thinking at Shell, see Art Kleiner, *The Age of Heretics: A History of Radical Thinkers Who Reinvented Corporate Management* (San Francisco: Jossey Bass, 2008), pp. 226–69.

14. Ken Auletta, *The Highwaymen: Warriors of the Information Superhighway* (San Diego: Harcourt Brace), p. 76.

15. Timothy Noah, "Did Nora Ephron Broker the AOL–Time Warner Deal?" *Slate*, http://slate.msn.com/id/1004341 (accessed April 6, 2011). While Noah's column was the inspiration for this analysis of *You've Got Mail*, the actual stimulus was the challenge of Peter Havholm and Peter Sandifer in their essay "Corporate Authorship: A Response to Jerome Christensen," *Critical Inquiry* 30, no. 1 (Autumn 2003): 187–97. This section of the chapter is a revision of my answer, published in the same issue of *CI*: "Taking it to the Next Level: *You've Got Mail*, Havholm, and Sandifer (*CI*, pp. 198–215).

16. Tomhanksweb.com, www.tomhanksweb.com/media/mail/ygmscrpt.txt.

17. Internet Movie Database, http://us.imdb.com/Title?0128853 (accessed April 6, 2011).

18. At www.darkhorizons.com/1998/youhave/youhaven.htm.

19. All quotations from the script of *You've Got Mail* are taken from this unpaginated draft, which can be accessed at www.tomhanksweb.com/media/mail/ygmscrpt.txt.

20. This is the language of the Appeals Court as it ruled in favor of AT&T's defense against America Online's suit accusing it of trademark infringement (*America Online, Inc. v. AT&T Corp.*, United States Court of Appeals for the Fourth Circuit, February 28, 2001, p. 13). AOL commenced its action on December 22, 1998, four days after the opening of *You've Got Mail*.

21. I am indebted to Michael Szalay both for pointing out the pervasive use of cor-

porate allegory in the Fox series and for calling my attention to the specific episode that tweaks CNN.

22. Farrell Kramer, AP, 1996, n.d. (www.google.com/search?q=Fox+News+antitrust+lawsuit&hl=en&lr=&ie=UTF-8&oe=UTF-8&start=10&sa=N).

23. *Time Warner Cable of New York v. City of New York*, United States District Court for the Southern District of New York, November 6, 1996 (Communications Media Center at New York Law School; www.nyls.edu/cmc/uscases/timewnyc.htm).

24. Jim Hu and Dawn Kawamoto, "Is Time Warner Next in Merger Mania?" CNET News.Com, February 9, 1999, http://news.com/2100-1040-221449.html.

25. AOL's concern was warranted. Just after the release of the film AT&T began using "You Have Mail," "Buddy List," and the mailbox logo "in connection with its email service. AOL was upset, and filed suit in federal court alleging various trademark and unfair trade competition." "Summary of *America Online v. AT&T*," *Tech Law Journal* Web site, n.d., www.techlawjournal.com/courts/aolvatt/Default.htm (accessed April 6, 2011). AOL eventually lost its suit on appeal.

26. In November 1998 *Wired News* quoted a comment by Evan Neufeld, "practice director for online advertising strategies at Jupiter Communications," that "you could typically see a deal like this in the US $3 to 6 million range." But Neufeld "cautions that much of the value of the deal could exist only on paper: AOL gets brand placement in the film; in return, Warner Bros. gets heavy promotion through AOL's online properties" ("You've Got Product Replacement," *Wired* Web site, November 4, 1998, www.wired.com/news/culture/0,1284,16046,00.html [accessed April 6, 2011]). The day before the film was released Paul Farhi reported in the *Washington Post* that "no money changed hands" (*Washington Post*, December 17, 1998).

27. Time Warner investors, who were burned in the earlier merger, were regarded as being opposed to enormous expenditures for overpriced internet companies. See the comments of David Simons, managing director of Digital Video Investments, reported by Hu and Kawamoto.

28. "In the Money," CNN, transcript no. 00011001FN-I04, January 10, 2000. Perhaps there was an omen for AOL Time Warner in Case's choice of a phone rather than an e-mail to ask his question, "Do you want to merge?"

29. Here's just one example of the line that Case incessantly spun at the time of the merger: "But there is another reason why this merger is so important, and it is not its size, it is really the company's potential for innovation and creation of new value and new choice for consumers" (*In the Money* news conference, January 10, 2000). As events would soon prove, "innovation" meant little, "choice" meant less, and "value" meant nothing.

Chapter 7: The Conscience of a Corporation

1. For an elaboration of this theory in relation to contemporary debates about intentionalist interpretations, see Jerome Christensen, "Studio Authorship, Corporate Art," *Auteurs and Authorship: A Film Reader*, ed. Barry Keith Grant (Malden, MA: Blackwell Publishing, 2008), pp. 167–79.

2. Peter A. French, "The Corporation as a Moral Person," *American Philosophical Quarterly* 16, no. 3 (July 1979): 211–15.

3. Eric Colvin, "Corporate Personality and Criminal Liability," *Criminal Law Forum* 6, no. 1 (1995): 2–3; hereafter "CP." See also Pamela H. Bucy, "Corporate Ethos: A Standard for Imposing Corporate Criminal Liability," *Minnesota Law Review* 75 (1990–91): 1095–1184.

4. See Celia Wells, *Corporations and Criminal Responsibility* (2nd ed., Oxford: Oxford University Press, 2001), esp. pp. 63–83; and James Gobert and Maurice Punch, *Rethinking Corporate Crime* (London: LexisNexis Butterworths, 2003), pp. 46–81.

5. Michel Foucault, "What Is an Author," *The Foucault Reader*, ed. Paul Rabinow (New York: Pantheon Books, 1984), p. 101; hereafter "WIA."

6. Cited as sources in text are Eric Smoodin, "'Compulsory' Viewing for Every Citizen: *Mr. Smith* and the Rhetoric of Reception," *Cinema Journal* 35 (Winter 1996): 3, 19, and n. 52, which cites Frank Nugent, "Mr. Smith Riles Washington," *Time*, October 30, 1939, p. 49; and "Capra's Capitol Offense," *New York Times*, October 29, 1939; hereafter "CCO."

7. See Ben W. Heineman, Jr., "Hidden Election Expenditures After *Citizens United*," *Atlantic*, July 14, 2010, www.theatlantic.com/politics/archive/2010/07/hidden-election-expenditures-after-citizens-united/59756/ (accessed April 6, 2011); and Charlie Cray, "*Citizens United v. America's Citizens*: A Voters Guide," *CorpWatch*, October 22, 2010, www.corpwatch.org/article.php?id=15635 (accessed April 6, 2011). Jill Jusko, "DISCLOSE Opponents Gain a Victory," *Industry Week*, November 1, 2010, p. 12.

8. Henry James Forman, *Our Movie Made Children* (New York: Macmillan, 1933). See chap. 5, "Movies and Sleep," pp. 69–89; chap. 6, "Other Physical Effects, pp. 90–104; and chap. 7, "Horror and Fright Pictures," pp. 105–20.

9. Stephen Farber and Marc Green, *Outrageous Conduct: Art, Ego, and the "Twilight Zone" Case* (New York: Morrow, 1988), pp. 156–57, 196–97, and *passim*.

10. David A. Price, *The Pixar Touch: The Making of a Company* (New York: Vintage Books, 2009), p. 133, and in private correspondence with the author.

11. Exhibit 99.1, "Policies for Management of the Feature Animation Businesses," www.sec.gov/Archives/edgar/data/1001039/000119312506012082/dex991.htm (accessed April 6, 2011).

12. Jennifer Homans, *Apollo's Angels: A History of Ballet* (New York: Random House, 2010), p. 541.

13. Janet Wasko, *Understanding Disney* (Cambridge Mass: Polity, 2001), p. 92; hereafter *UD*.

14. The company that was formed in 1923 was named the Disney Brothers Studio. The name was changed at Roy Disney's suggestion to the Walt Disney Studio when the company, still a partnership, moved to a new location on 2719 Hyperion Avenue in the Silver Lake district of Los Angeles in 1925. It was incorporated as Walt Disney Productions in 1929. Walt Disney Incorporated was formed by Walt as an independent company to finance the planning stages for Disneyland in 1953. Concerned that the stockholders might "be disturbed over possible conflict of interest between Walt Disney Productions and Walt Disney, Incorporated, [Roy] suggested that Walt change "the name of his company, and it became WED Enterprises, the initials of Walt's name." Bob Thomas, *Building a Company: Roy O. Disney and the Creation of an Entertainment Empire* (New York: Hyperion, 1998), pp. 48, 52, 139; hereafter *BC*.

15. "The Big Bad Wolf," *Fortune*, November 1934, p. 88.

16. James B. Stewart, *Disney War* (New York: Simon and Schuster, 2005), pp. 147, 190.

17. Frances Clark Sayers and Charles M. Weisenberg, "Walt Disney Accused," *Horn Book Magazine*, November–December 1965, p. 610; quoted in *UD*, p. 126.

18. Michael Budd, introduction to "Private Disney, Public Disney," in *Rethinking Disney: Private Control, Public Dimensions*, ed. Mike Budd and Max H. Kirsch (Middletown, CT: Wesleyan University Press, 2005), p. 1.

19. Theodor W. Adorno, "Culture Industry Reconsidered," in *The Culture Industry: Selected Essays on Mass Culture*, ed. J. M. Bernstein (New York: Routledge, 1991), p. 98.

20. Jack Zipes, "Toward a Theory of the Fairy-Tale Film: The Case of *Pinocchio*," *Lion and the Unicorn* 20, no. 1 (1996): 20.

21. For an account of Lasseter's veneration of the "nine old men" and the golden era of Disney animation, see Karen Paik, *To Infinity and Beyond: The Story of Pixar Animation Studios* (San Francisco: Chronicle Books, 2007) pp. 30–31; hereafter *IB*.

22. In *Toy Story 2*, however, the figure of the ancient touch-up artist (a figure recycled from Pixar's earlier short *Geri's Game* [1998]), who repairs and rejuvenates Woody, evokes the near obsolete craftsmen who specialized in hand-drawn animations.

23. A condition which seems to be endorsed by the epical transfixion of the robot boy David through millennia of frozen adoration of the carved figure of the Blue Fairy in Dreamworks' apocalyptic version of the Pinocchio story: *Artificial Intelligence: AI* (2001), directed by Steven Spielberg.

24. Adolf A. Berle, *The 20th Century Capitalist Revolution* (New York: Harcourt, Brace, 1954).

25. I'm indebted to Victor Fleischer, University of Colorado Law School, for providing me with his invaluable, unpublished draft manuscript, "Protecting Pixar's Culture in the Disney Merger." For his comment on the peculiarity of the quotation marks surrounding "culture" in Exhibit 99.1, see "Steering Culture," *Conglomerate* (January 27, 2006), www.theconglomerate.org/2006/01/steering_cultur.html (accessed April 6, 2011).

26. Jeffrey Leins, "Disney Picks Pixar Brains on New Muppets Movie," NewsinFilm.com, *The Hollywood Reporter*, July 27, 2010, www.hollywoodreporter.com/hr/content_display/news/e3i4c15c030a696fa14c0791f2acbc0e09b (accessed April 6, 2011). Leins mentions the involvement of "the Pixar Brain Trust" in discussions of plans for *The Greatest Muppet Movie* and the reshoot of *Tron: Legacy* at the invitation of Rich Ross, newly appointed Disney Studios chairman in 2009.

Index

Academy of the Motion Picture Arts and Sciences, 17, 19, 346n35; Oscars, 113, 116, 125, 132, 158, 159, 187, 207, 273, 357n33
Actors Studio, 179, 195
Adorno, Theodor W., on the culture industry, 313, 319, 329–30, 331, 332
advertising, 237–38, 260, 310, 312, 347n54, 363n23; in *Bonnie and Clyde*, 252, 253–54, 255, 256–57; in *The Crowd*, 34, 41, 43; institutional advertising, 177–78, 203, 208–9; vs. marketing, 9, 218
Albert, Michael, 291, 302; on *JFK*, 282–84
Aldrich, Robert, 158, 362n3
All About Eve, 157
Allen, William, 286, 291
Allyson, June, 190
Altman, Robert, 271, 275, 280
Alton, John, 173
Amazing Dr. Clitterhouse, The, 350n89
American Civil War, 129–30
American in Paris, An, 159, 181, 201, 207
American popular culture, 22, 42, 146, 152, 208
American Soldier, The, 137, 138, 143, 146, 152
America Online (AOL), 308–13, 368n25; merger with Time Warner, 13, 23, 268n25, 302–3, 304–5, 306–13, 367n20, 368nn27–29; and *You've Got Mail*, 13, 23, 268n25, 302, 304–5, 308–13, 367n20
Ames, Leon, 147
Andrews, Dana, 129
Andrews, Kenneth R., 20–21; *The Concept of Corporate Strategy*, 212
Andy Hardy series, 95, 115, 166
Animal House, 324
anti-Semitism, 6
AOL. *See* America Online
Apple, 273
Arlen, Harold, 104, 352n114
Arnold, Thurman, 111, 175, 350n84; *The Bottlenecks of Business*, 233–34; on capitalized earning power, 176–77, 178; on personification, 29, 72, 168; on political dynamics, 364n30; on Sherman Antitrust Act, 233–34; on social adjustment, 51, 72; *The Folklore of Capitalism*, 10, 71–72, 177, 364n30
Arthur, Harry, 86
Artificial Intelligence: AI, 337, 370n23
Ashby, Hal, 271, 275
Astaire, Fred, 63, 171, 177, 197; in *Band Wagon*, 158, 173–74, 180, 181, 182–83, 184, 185, 186, 355n2
A Star Is Born, 18–19
AT&T, 367n20
audiences, 225, 227, 229–30, 239, 242–43, 315, 343n7, 353n13; of *Bonnie and Clyde*, 250, 251, 262, 266–67, 269, 272, 273; of Disney pictures, 323, 328; *Fortune* on, 26–27, 31; of Hitchcock pictures, 360n26; of MGM pictures, 8, 9, 22, 25, 26–27, 38, 41, 42, 44, 109–10, 115, 116–17, 119, 130, 134, 135, 136, 142–43, 150, 152–54, 156, 166–67, 169, 170, 171–72, 174, 185, 189, 194, 196, 197, 201; as middle class, 9, 115, 194, 208; as multiple, 7, 116, 167, 306; after World War II, 22, 152–54, 163

371

Auletta, Ken, 297
Australian Model Criminal Code, 316–17, 326
auteurism, 40–41, 302, 303, 341n11; defined, 13; and directors, 235–36, 244, 247, 257, 271, 283–84, 324–25; and Hitchcock, 235–36, 244; and Penn, 247, 257, 271
avant-garde, the, 246, 270–72

Babes in Arms, 90, 98, 124, 166, 170, 201, 352n113
Bad and the Beautiful, The, 187, 188
Baird, Robert: on *Vertigo,* 360n23
Balaban, Barney, 196
Balio, Tino: *The Grand Design,* 17
Bancroft, George, 55, 56
Band Wagon, The, 12, 180–85, 187, 201; Astaire in, 158, 173–74, 180, 181, 182–83, 184, 185, 186, 355n2; "Girl Hunt," 172, 182–85, 186; and movie stars, 22, 182, 185, 186, 202–3
banks, 170–71, 344n17
Barnard, Chester I., 54
Barrymores, the, 179
Barthes, Roland, 240, 242, 243, 245
Bartholomew, Freddie, 90, 107, 108
Basinger, Jeanine: on *Bataan,* 133–34; *The Star Machine,* 356n22
Basinger, Kim, 287
Bass, Saul, 244
Bataan, 133–35, 136, 144, 149, 286–87, 315
Batey, Mark, 260, 261
Batman, 7, 8, 367n9; Meehan on, 281; and Steve Ross, 13, 287; and Time-Warner Communications merger, 13, 23, 281, 286–91, 292–93
Battleground, 135–56, 354n26; and *The American Soldier,* 137, 138, 143, 146, 152; passwords in, 139–42, 354n30; and rebranding, 153–54, 155–56; and Schary, 12, 22, 132, 133, 152, 153–54, 155–56, 159, 277
Baudrillard, Jean, 250
Beatty, Warren, 271, 272; on *Bonnie and Clyde,* 257; relationship with Jack Warner, 9, 13, 21, 245–46, 269, 274–75, 276–78, 363n21, 365n46
Beau Geste (1939), 149

Beavers, Louise, 78
Beckett, Samuel, 319
Beckett, Scotty, 139
Belin, David, 298
Bell, Daniel, 273, 365n34
Belton, John, 243, 262n46, 361n43
Benjamin, Walter, 250
Bennett, Constance, 55, 56
Benton, Robert, 254, 255, 363n20; on *Bonnie and Clyde,* 248, 258, 270; on directors, 257; on the New Sentimentality, 248–49, 272, 275, 276; script of *Bonnie and Clyde,* 245, 246, 363n12, 364n32; "The Movies Will Save Themselves," 246–47, 249–50, 258–59, 270, 271–72, 275
Bergman, Ingmar, 246
Berkeley, Busby, 63, 69, 349n73
Berle, Adolf A., 174–76, 183; *The American Economic Republic,* 177–78; on conscience creation, 175; on consensus application, 174, 175, 178; on constitutionalism, 174–75; *The Corporate Revolution in the 20th Century,* 175; on management control, 357n36; on political scientists, 175; on stakeholders, 174–75; *The 20th Century Capitalist Revolution,* 338; *The Modern Corporation and Private Property,* 44, 174; on transcendental margin, 175, 177–78
Bernays, Edward, 99, 145; *Propaganda,* 26
Bernstein, Sidney, 234
Best Years of Our Lives, The, 129
Biel, Alexander L., 196, 357n42
Big Parade, The, 133, 137, 152
Big Sleep, The, 7, 151
Bioff, Willie, 76
Black, Gregory D.: *Hollywood Goes to War,* 105, 106
blacklisting, 171
Blackmer, Sidney, 348n63
Blessed Event, The, 59
block booking, 84–85, 320–21
blockbuster pictures, 280, 281
Blondell, Joan, 62, 66, 74, 81
Blonde Venus, 27
Bludhorn, Charles, 289–90
Boardman, Eleanor, 33

Bogart, Humphrey, 73, 76, 89, 90, 350n89
Bogdanovich, Peter, 280
Bonnie and Clyde, 245–58, 261–67, 268–70, 272–79, 362n3, 366n48; audiences of, 250, 251, 262, 266–67, 269, 272, 273; and Beatty-Jack Warner relationship, 9, 245–46, 269, 274–75, 276–78, 363n21, 365n46; Coca-Cola in, 254, 255–57, 363n21; Collier on, 252, 253, 261–62; credits for, 277–78; Crowther on, 254, 363n18; C. W.'s tattoo, 262–64, 265, 364n32; and Great Depression, 257, 262, 269; Hoberman on, 268–69; as iconic brand, 272–74; Kael on, 249–50, 251–52, 257, 261–62, 363n12; and New Hollywood, 8, 23, 270, 275; Newman on, 248, 253–54, 255, 258, 270; and Penn, 246, 247–48, 249, 252, 253, 255, 257, 271, 274, 362n8, 363n12
bonus marchers, 44, 49
Bordwell, David: *The Classical Hollywood Cinema,* 15–17, 341n11
Borneman, Ernest: "Rebellion in Hollywood," 163
Boys Town, 5, 8, 49, 61, 87–100, 119, 188, 201, 351nn103,106; and brands, 93–95, 99, 273; and marketing, 91, 92, 95, 97; and New Deal, 88, 89, 90–91; and Schary, 90–91, 155; vs. *Wizard of Oz,* 87, 104
Bradley, Omar, 354n30
Brady, Robert A., 159, 163
Brando, Marlon, 179
brands, 10–12, 70–71, 76, 114, 139, 212, 240, 257, 359n6, 363n21; and *Boys Town,* 93–95, 99, 273; brand equity, 196–97, 357n42; brand management, 23, 164, 178–79, 208–9, 303, 329, 347n54; and corporate populism, 282; creedal brands, 94–95, 273; Disney as brand, 326, 329, 333; Hitchcock as brand, 235, 236; iconic brands, 257–58, 260–61, 269–70, 272–74, 276, 278; MGM as brand, 2, 11–12, 27, 31, 40, 94, 159, 166–67, 173–74; Paramount as brand, 7–8; rebranding, 153–54, 155–56; relationship to personifications, 21; Time Warner as brand, 308, 310;

Warner Bros. as brand, 9, 13, 275, 276, 277–79. *See also* logos; marketing; trademarks
Breathless, 259, 363n20
Breen, Joseph, 75, 107, 120, 151
Breines, Wini, 267, 268, 364n34
Brent, George, 61
Broadway Melody, 163, 164
Brown, Denise Scott, 210–11
Brown, George, 76
Brown, Nacio, 160, 162
Browning, Todd: *Freaks,* 26
Bruck, Connie, 300, 301, 302; *The Master of the Game,* 312, 365n45, 366n5
Bryman, Alan, 176
Buchanan, Jack, 181
Budd, Michael, 329
Bullets or Ballots, 8, 73–84, 350n86; and New Deal, 73, 78, 90; and racketeering, 73–75, 78–80, 82–84, 85, 86–87, 351n93
Burke, Billie, 102
Burke, Edmund, 126, 127; on British culture, 208
Burks, Robert, 213, 244
Burton, Tim, 367n9

Cagney, James, 64, 76, 90
Caldwell, John Thornton: *Production Culture,* 15
Caldwell, Orville, 88
Calhern, Louis, 190
Camelot, 269, 274
camp style, 161, 166–67, 172–73
Canton, Mark, 294
capitalism, 71–72, 195, 252; and corporations, 1–2, 29, 167–68, 283, 296–97; and media, 281
Capone, Al, 52, 53, 56, 77
Capone, Ralph, 53
Capra, Frank, 236, 321, 322, 324
Captains Courageous, 7, 49, 90, 95
Carol, Lewis: *Alice in Wonderland,* 131–32
Casablanca, 211
Case, Steven M., 23, 302, 310–11, 312–13, 368nn28,29
Cassady, Ralph, Jr., 84–85
Cavell, Stanley: on *The Philadelphia Story,* 113, 353n10

Cawelti, John: on *Bonnie and Clyde*, 362n7
Center for the Study of Democratic Institutions, 174
Certeau, Michel de, 250
Chandler, Alfred D., Jr., 210; *Strategy and Structure*, 19–20; *Visible Hand*, 17–18, 47
Chaplin, Charley, 274
charisma, 47, 90; charismatic margin, 175–76, 177, 178–79, 180, 185, 186, 202, 208; and *Executive Suite*, 187, 188, 190, 193, 195, 201–3; of movie stars, 5, 177, 182, 185, 186; of Steve Ross, 13, 283, 285; Weber on, 175–76, 190, 194, 201–2
Charisse, Cyd, 181, 184, 185
Chatterton, Ruth, 55, 56
Cheat, The, 8
choice, 110–11, 116–18, 121–22, 125, 130
Christensen, Jerome: "Studio Authorship, Corporate Art," 368n1
Christmas in July, 8, 345n25, 346n36
Churchill, Winston, 111
Cinemascope, 19
Citizen Kane, 121, 182
Citizens United v. Federal Election Commission, 23, 284, 314–15, 318–22, 324, 330, 336, 337
class, 22, 64, 68, 84, 107, 117–19, 126, 171, 172; middle class, 26, 109, 113, 115, 117, 122, 127–28, 130–31, 166, 194, 198, 200, 261; working class, 117–18, 124, 127
classical economic theory and the corporation, 45–46, 50, 52
classical era of Hollywood, 3–4, 8, 15, 280–81
Clayton Act, 85
Clockwork Orange, 209, 358n52
Clover, Carol: "Dancin' in the Rain," 160–61
Clurman, Richard M.: *To the End of Time*, 366n5
Coase, Robert: on conscious power, 46, 47, 50, 219, 347n51; "The Nature of the Firm," 45–47, 48, 50, 347n49, 353n10
Coca-Cola, 114, 115, 260, 353n15, 363nn20,23; in *Bonnie and Clyde*, 254, 255–57, 363n21

Cohan, Steven, 202; *Incongruous Entertainment*, 163, 165–66, 356n13; on *Singin' in the Rain*, 163, 165–66, 355n11, 356n13
Cohn, Harry, 240
Colbert, Claudette, 18
Cold War, 22, 148, 150, 177, 213, 284–85, 295, 300
Coleman, Ronald, 55
Coleridge, Samuel Taylor: on esemplastic power, 315; on symbols, 242
Collier, Peter: on *Bonnie and Clyde*, 252, 253, 261–62
Columbia Pictures, 3, 107, 211, 236, 240, 280, 321–22, 366n7
Colvin, Eric, 316–17
Comden, Betty, 160, 173, 207, 358n51
Comolli, Jean-Luc, 75
competition, 3–4, 21–22, 52, 85, 89; as cutthroat, 58, 78, 349n69; in *Mrs. Miniver*, 119–20, 125, 126, 127
concrete universals, 258–61, 267, 278
conscience creation, 174, 175
consensus application, 174, 175
Considine, Tim, 204
constitutionalism, 174–75
consumerism/conspicuous consumption, 117–18, 119, 120, 122–23, 125, 167
Coombe, Rosemary: *The Cultural Life of Intellectual Properties*, 364n29
Cooper, Gary, 7, 211, 212, 217–18
Coppola, Francis Ford, 280, 362n3
Corman, Roger, 362n3
corporate authorship. *See* studio authorship thesis
corporate culture: as conscience, 314, 317–18, 337, 338, 339–40; cultural authorship, 23, 314, 317–18, 326–27, 338–40; of Disney, 326–27; and *Executive Suite*, 196–97, 204; and *Paramount vs. Time Inc.*, 292–93; of Pixar, 326–27, 333, 338–39, 370n25; relationship to corporate intention, 316–17
corporate intention, 2–3, 20–21, 236, 321, 322; of MGM, 8, 156, 166, 195–96, 207; relationship to corporate culture, 316–17; relationship to studio authorship, 8, 14, 76–77, 311–12, 314, 315–17, 336; of Time Warner, 305, 306, 314;

of Warner Bros., 8, 76–77, 311–12. *See also* corporate personhood

corporate liability, 23, 315, 322, 323, 324–26, 336, 338, 340; in Australian Model Criminal Code, 316–17, 326; and Hi Tech Toons (Pixar-Disney), 325, 332; relationship to Corporate Cultural Decision (CCD) structure, 326; relationship to Corporate Internal Division (CID) structure, 316, 317, 324, 325; relationship to corporate personhood, 317–18

corporate personhood, 8, 9–11, 17, 177–78, 188, 215–16, 342n11, 350n83; and *Citizens United* decision, 23, 284, 314–15, 318–22, 324, 330, 336, 337; and due process clause, 1; integrationists vs. aggregationists regarding, 167–68; of motion picture studios, 3, 13–14, 25; relationship to corporate liability, 317–18; and Santa Clara case, 1. *See also* corporate intention; personifications; studio authorship thesis

corporate populism, 275, 282, 283

corporate power: types of, 18–20

corporate scenario thinking, 295–97, 313

corporate strategy, 2–6, 19–21; vs. ideology, 2–3; of MGM, 2, 3–5, 7, 8; of Warner Bros., 2, 5–6

Cosmopolitan Pictures, 8, 44, 346n43, 359n16

Covered Wagon, The, 8

Craven, Ian: *Hollywood Cinema,* 15

Crawford, Joan, 21, 59–60, 63, 65, 125, 157, 158, 179, 349n72

credits: for *Bonnie and Clyde,* 277–78; and MGM, 160–63, 169, 277, 355n5; and Warner Bros., 211–12

Crime School, 89–90, 95, 97

Croly, Herbert, 42

Crowd, The, 31–44, 98, 99, 136, 152, 345nn25–28; accident in, 32, 35–39, 41, 42, 49; insurance in, 36–37, 39–40, 41, 42; and traumatic neurosis, 38–39, 42

Crowther, Bosley: on *Bonnie and Clyde,* 254, 363n18; *Hollywood Rajah,* 344n18

Cukor, George, 18–19, 112

Cummings, Joe, 159

Dailey, Dan, 177

Daily Mirror, 55

D'Allesandro, David F., 95, 352n109; on brands, 359n6

Dancing Lady, 4, 5, 59–64, 65, 68, 170, 171

Dangerous Little Demon, 355n5

Daniell, F. Raymond, 77

Daniels, Bebe, 56, 61

Daniels, Mark, 351n106

Danko, Betty, 102

Danto, Arthur C., 256

D'Antonio, Emile, 256

David Copperfield, 130

Davies, Marion, 346n43

Davis, Bette, 124, 157–58, 179, 355n2

Davis, Martin, 286, 287, 289–91, 367n8

Dead End, 89, 90

Deleuze, Gilles, 250

Demetrios, Eames, 199

de Mille, Cecil B.: *Ten Commandments* (1923), 7; *Ten Commandments* (1956), 7

democracy, 144

DePree, Dirk Jan, 198, 199

DePree, Hugh, 198

Destination Unknown, 59

Deutsch, Armand: on Freed unit, 157

Dewey, John, 29, 97

Dietrich, Marlene, 7, 27, 157

Dietz, Howard, 61, 349n72

Dinner at Eight, 59, 62

Disney, 3, 325, 369n14, 370n21; corporate culture of, 326–27; fairy castle logo, 7; marketing by, 329, 330; merger with Pixar, 23, 314, 326–27, 332, 333, 338–40, 370nn25,26; vs. MGM, 328–29; Mickey Mouse, 328–29. *See also* Pinocchio

Disney, Roy, 328, 369n14

Disney, Walt, 328, 329, 330, 331, 332, 337, 369n14

Disneyland, 329, 369n14

Donat, Robert, 111

Donen, Stanley, 162, 173, 207

Double Indemnity, 151

Douglas, Kirk, 274

Douglas, Paul, 190

Douglas, Robert, 214

Dove, Charles: on *Singin' in the Rain,* 165, 355n12

Draper, Hal: on neocorporatism, 174
Dreamworks, 8, 370n23
Drucker, Peter F., 193; on General Electric, 284; on innovation, 285; on management, 72, 191, 269, 284, 285, 292; on managerial power, 177; on marketing, 269, 285, 343n10; on mass production, 200; *The Practice of Management*, 344n10; *The Concept of the Corporation*, 8, 9, 11, 13
Duck Soup, 27
Duel in the Sun, 211
Dumont, Margaret, 27
Dunaway, Faye, 254, 277
Dunne, Irene, 166
Durgnat, Raymond, 40–41, 345nn26,28

Eames, Charles, 197, 198–200
Earmes, Ray, 198–99
Eastmancolor, 240, 243, 361n43
Eckert, Charles, 68
Edens, Roger, 173, 206
Edison Project, 298–99
education: as entertainment, 295, 298–99; and television, 295, 298–99
efficiency, 17–18, 79
Eisenhower, Dwight D.: *Crusade in Europe*, 105–6, 110, 129
Eisenstein, Sergei, 250, 267; *Potemkin*, 124, 251–52
Eisner, Michael, 329, 330, 333–34, 338
Eitzen, Dirk, 16
Ephron, Delia, 303–4
Ephron, Nora, 303–4, 306, 308, 309
Epstein, Edward Jay: *The Big Picture*, 366n2
Erikson, Erik, 268
Esquire's "Dubious Achievement" awards, 255
Evans, Walker, 253, 255, 262
Evening World, 55
Executive Suite, 12, 22, 174, 187–209, 273, 358n47; *Fortune* on, 192, 193, 194; Larrabee on, 192, 193, 194, 197, 200, 203; Riesman on, 192, 193, 197, 200, 203; and Schary, 187, 188, 196, 201, 207, 208, 209, 358n47; and teamwork, 204–6
extortion, 52–53, 73–74, 76, 77, 78–80, 82, 86

Eyman, Scott, 159, 201, 344n18, 346n35, 349n75

Fairbanks, Douglas, Jr., 81
Fallen Angel, 151
falsifiability, 94–95, 273
Fantasia (1940), 328
Farber, Stephen: *Outrageous Conduct*, 324–25
Farhi, Paul, 312, 368n26
Farley, James, 85
fascism, 45, 52, 347n48
Ferren, John, 360n28
Ferry, David, 300, 301
Film Daily Annual, The, 353n6
film noir, 149, 151–52
First Amendment, 315, 318–19, 320, 321, 322
Flamini, Roland, 355n5
Flanagan, Fr. Edward, 5
Fleischer, Victor, 338–39, 370n25
Fleming, Victor, 100, 102
Florian, 108, 352n5
Flowers, Betty S., 296, 297
Ford, Henry, 15, 48, 113, 328
Fordin, Hugh, 358n51
Forman, Henry James, 323
Fortune, 16, 19, 60, 217, 343n5; on antitrust laws, 85; on audience taste, 26–27, 31; on Coca-Cola, 115; on corporate management, 193; corporate profiles in, 24–25, 29, 343n3; on *Executive Suite*, 192, 193, 194; on Fox, 343n3; on Lowe's, 111; on Metropolitan Life, 39, 69–71, 83; on MGM, 1–2, 3, 4, 9, 22, 24–27, 28–31, 44, 55, 69, 111–13, 114, 115–17, 132, 169, 196, 344n18, 346n44; on organized crime, 72–73, 77–78; on proprietary monopoly, 216; on Social Security, 100; on studio morale, 116–17; on Thalberg, 2, 9, 22, 24–27, 30, 31, 44, 55, 169, 344n18, 346n44; on Walt Disney Studio, 327–28; on Warner Bros., 58–59, 63, 85, 349n75
42nd Street, 6, 59, 61, 62, 63, 64, 349n71
Foucault, Michel, 319, 326, 336
Fountainhead, The, 8, 22–23, 211–21, 236, 358n4, 359n14; and credit, 159–60, 211–12, 220–21, 236, 278; and func-

tionalism, 211, 214, 215, 216–17, 219; ideological motivation in, 213–14; vs. *Singin in the Rain,* 159–60
Fourteenth Amendment's due process clause, 1
Fox, William, 343n3
Fox Broadcasting, 305–6
Foy, Gloria, 63
Francis, David, 361nn38,39
Francis, Kay, 56
Frankenstein (1931), 6, 186, 323–24
Freaks, 26
Freed, Arthur, 160, 206, 352n114; Freed unit at MGM, 5, 12, 22, 104, 157, 159, 161, 162, 166–67, 170, 171, 173, 187, 196, 201, 207; and "Good Mornin,'" 169; relationship with Mayer, 100, 104, 159, 201; relationship with Schary, 173, 201, 209; and "Singin' in the Rain," 161–63, 208, 209; and *Wizard of Oz,* 5, 104
Freedman, Jonathan, 359n20
French, Peter A., 316
Freudian psychology, 222, 223, 229, 360nn20,24
Fuller, J. F. C.: on morale, 136, 143; *Training Soldiers for War,* 136, 143
functionalism: in architecture, 210–11; and the corporation, 211; functionalist film scholarship, 15–18, 19–20; and *The Fountainhead,* 211, 214, 215, 216–17, 219

Gable, Clark, 18, 21, 62, 63, 64, 106, 112, 166, 177, 179, 180, 186, 329
Gabriel over the White House, 8, 44–52, 58, 61; as fascist, 44, 52; and gangsters, 50–51, 52, 54, 57; and Great Depression, 45, 49; and Louis B. Mayer, 45; and Roosevelt, 44, 45
Gaines, Jane M.: *Contested Culture,* 364n29
Galbraith, John Kenneth, 347n54
Garbo, Greta, 106, 125
Gardner, Burleigh H., 208–9
Garland, Judy, 87, 90, 108, 159
Garnett, Tay, 133, 151
Garson, Greer, 109, 111, 122, 125, 127, 132, 157, 166

General Electric, 58, 284
General Motors, 2, 113–14, 178
Geri's Game, 370n22
Gibbons, Cedric, 21, 200
Gigi, 201
Gilbert, John, 158, 164
Gilmore, James H., 261, 364n28
Gish, Lillian: on MGM, 24
Glazer, Nathan, 365n34
G-Men, 76
Goble, Mark, 359n10
Godard, Jean-Luc, 246, 260, 267, 271
Goetz, William, 211
Goffman, Erving, 94
Go for Broke, 354n31
Gold Diggers of 1933, 59, 61–62, 63, 64–69, 170, 273, 349nn71,73; "Forgotten Man," 68–69, 174; "We're in the Money," 64–65, 254
Goldwyn, Samuel, 129, 153, 161
Gomery, Douglas: on *Mrs. Miniver,* 353n21; *The Hollywood Studio System,* 15, 196, 343n6, 344n17, 353n21
Goodbye Mr. Chips, 111
Good News, 159
Good Sam, 211
goodwill, 5, 10–11, 177, 179, 202, 339, 340
Grable, Betty, 140, 141, 143
Grainge, Paul: *Brand Hollywood,* 365n49
Grand Hotel, 7, 8, 27–28, 30, 31, 60, 273, 315, 344n13, 359n16
Grand Prix, 274
Grant, Cary, 112, 226–27, 234
Grapes of Wrath, The (1940), 8
Great Britain, 120; Campbell Act of 1846, 38; during WWII, 105, 106, 107, 108–11, 125, 128, 129, 130, 353n6, 353n17
Great Depression, 1, 6, 21–22, 69–70, 100–101, 114, 118, 145, 271, 353n13; and *Bonnie and Clyde,* 257, 262, 269; crash of 1929, 3–4, 24, 32, 44; and *Gabriel over the White House,* 45, 49
Greatest Muppet Movie, The, 370n26
Green, Adolph, 160, 173, 207, 358n51
Green, Marc: *Outrageous Conduct,* 324–25
Greenberg, Clement, 131, 213, 250, 279; "The Avant-Garde and Kitsch," 270–72
Griffin, Nancy: *Hit and Run,* 367n9

Grinker, Roy: *Men Under Stress*, 143, 354n28
Grissom Gang, 362n3
Grusky, Oscar, 188
Guardian, The, 268–69
Guattari, Félix, 250
Guilbaut, Serge, 270–71
Gulf+Western, 285, 289, 367n8
Gunga Din, 149
Guzik, Jack, 53

Haelan Laboratories Ind. v. Topps Chewing Gum Inc., 218
Haemmerli, Alice, 359n14
Hagen, June, 158, 160
Haller, Mark. H., 53
Halsey, Stuart and Co., 32, 42
Hamilton, Margaret, 90, 101, 102, 352n113
Hamilton, Walton H.: "Our Social Responsibilities," 1
Hanks, Tom, 303, 304
Hansen, Miriam, 345n26
Haraway, Donna, 250
Harburg, Yip, 104, 352n114
Harley-Davidson, 261, 273, 364n28
Harmetz, Aljean, 102, 352n112,114
Harris, Mark, 274; *Pictures at a Revolution*, 362n1, 363n12
Harris, Robert A., 243, 244, 361n43
Harrison, Joan, 236
Harrison, Peter, 320
Havholm, Peter: "Corporate Authorship," 367n15
Hawk Films, 209
Hawks, Howard, 152, 246; and *The Big Sleep*, 7; and *Scarface*, 2
Hawley, Cameron, 187–88
Hawley, Ellis W., 349n69, 351n105
Hays, Will, 14, 145, 348n65; and *Gabriel over the White House*, 45; Hays Code, 62, 75, 76, 323; on motion picture studios, 12; and MPPDA, 3, 17, 56, 57
Hays Office, 21, 58, 75–76, 78, 317, 356n13
HBO, 286
Head, Edith, 238, 240, 244
Hearst, William Randolph: and fascism, 52; and MGM, 44, 45, 57, 62, 346n43, 349n74
Hearst newspapers, 19, 57, 346n43

Hecht, Harold, 274
Hecht-Hill-Lancaster Productions, 365n44
Hell's Highway, 59
Hemingway, Ernest: "The Killers," 151
Hepburn, Katherine, 112, 157, 355n2
Herman Miller Furniture Co., 188, 198–200, 203, 205, 206, 207, 209
Herrmann, Bernard, 244
Higham, Charles: *Merchant of Dreams*, 352n5
Hillary, 315, 319, 320
Hirschman, A. O., 68; *Exit, Voice, and Loyalty*, 47–49
His Glorious Night, 158, 164
History of the American Cinema, 15
Hitchcock, Alfred, 246, 361n40; and *Alfred Hitchcock Presents*, 234–35, 236, 237; contract with Paramount, 234, 236, 237; and hotels, 232–33, 241; independence of, 23, 217, 222, 234–37, 244; and *Notorious*, 234; relationship with Wasserman, 23, 217, 222, 233, 234–35, 236, 237, 244; and *Rope*, 234, 235–36; and San Juan Batista Mission, 238–39; and *Vertigo*, 23, 226–27, 230, 232–33, 234, 237, 238, 239, 240, 241–42, 243, 244, 359n20, 360nn23,26
Hi Tech Toons, 325, 332
H. M. Pulham, Esq., 359n18
Hoberman, J.: on *Bonnie and Clyde*, 268–69
Hodiak, John, 140, 177
Holden, William, 188, 195
hold-ups (in firms), 348n66
Hollywood Reporter, The, 19
Holt, Douglas B.: on iconic brands, 257–58, 261; on the myth market, 249
Homans, Jennifer, 326–27
Hoover, Herbert, 45, 49, 58, 118
Hopwood, Avery: *The Gold Diggers*, 59
horror pictures, 6, 26, 323–24
Houseman, John, 166, 187, 206, 207, 208
house style: and MGM's Freed unit, 159, 166–67, 173; vs. corporate art, 2, 13–14
House Un-American Activities Committee (HUAC), 212, 213
Hu, Jim, 309
Hudson, Rock, 19

Huettig, Mae, 57–58; *Economic Control of the Motion Picture Industry*, 14, 15
Hughes, Howard, 133, 346n35
Hume, David: on causality, 36
Huntley, Chet, 189
Huston, Walter, 49
Hyman, Kenneth, 272, 275, 277

I Am a Fugitive from a Chain Gang, 59
Iger, Robert, 314, 339
Ince, Thomas, 186
independent production companies, 163, 164, 233, 274, 365n44
International Alliance of Theatrical Stage Employees (IATSE), 76
international markets, 281, 282
Invasion of the Body Snatchers (1978), 8
Is My Face Red?, 59
Ivanhoe, 206
Izod, John: *Hollywood and the Box Office*, 343n6

Jackdaw Strut, 56
Jagger, Dean, 190
Jameson, Frederic: on boredom as an aesthetic response, 250; on the periodizing hypothesis, 248
Jaws (1975), 8
Jazz Singer, The, 8, 31, 66, 82, 96, 163, 164
Jessie James (1939), 246
Jezebel, 124, 157
JFK, 281–84, 287, 295–302; Albert on, 282–84; and corporate scenario thinking, 295–97; and Steve Ross, 298, 301, 302; and Stone, 282, 283–84, 297
JFK Study Guide, 298
Jobs, Steve, 314, 338
Joe Smith, American, 133
Johns, Glynis, 157
Johnson, Nunnally, 211
Johnson, Van, 140
Jolson, Al, 31, 96, 97
Journal of Business, 84
Julius Caesar (1953), 187

Kael, Pauline: on *Bonnie and Clyde*, 249–50, 251–52, 257, 261–62, 363n12
Kahn, Herman, 295
Kalmenson, Ben, 272

Kant, Immanuel, 215, 359n14
Katz, James C., 244, 362n46
Kawamoto, Dawn, 309
Kaysen, Carl, 347n54
Keeler, Ruby, 62, 66
Kelly, Gene, 158, 159, 161, 162, 171, 173, 177, 207
Kelly, Grace, 227, 242
Kendall, Cy, 89
Keniston, Kenneth, 275; on postmodernism, 268; *Young Radicals*, 268, 270
Kennedy, F., 345n30
Kennedy, John, 235
Kenyon, Curtin, 363n21
Kerkorian, Kirk, 285, 366n7
Keynes, John Maynard, 92, 175, 351n105
Kibbee, Guy, 61
Kimball, Warren F.: *The Juggler*, 352n3
King, Barry, 21, 179
King, Joseph, 74
Kinney, Corporation, 299
Knapp, Steven: *Literary Interest*, 259, 260–61, 266
Kolker, Robert: *A Cinema of Loneliness*, 362n7
Koolhaas, Rem, 214, 218–19
Kopkind, Andrew, 245
Koppes, S. Clayton: *Hollywood Goes to War*, 105, 106
Korda, Alexander, 130
Kubrick, Stanley, 209, 337

Laemmle, Carl, 281, 323, 324
Laemmle, Carl, Jr., 324
Lamoreaux, Naomi, 348n64, 349n66
Lancaster, Burt, 274
Lancaster-Hecht, 365n44
Landis, John, 324–25
Lang, Fritz, 151, 152
Lang, Robert, 34
Lange, Dorothea, 252, 253, 255, 262
Langley, Noel, 104
Lanham Act, 216, 217
Lanza, Mario, 159
Larrabee, Eric: on *Executive Suite*, 192, 193, 194, 197, 200, 203; "The Executive as Hero," 192, 193, 194, 200
Lasseter, John, 328, 332, 335, 339, 340, 370n21

Lassie Come Home, 107, 133
LeRoy, Mervyn, 100
Leins, Jeffrey, 370n26
Leitch, Thomas M., 235
LeRoy, Mervyn, 7, 104, 352n112
Let Us Now Praise Famous Men, 262
Lever Brothers Building, 210
Levin, Gerald, 297, 301–2, 366n7; and AOL–Time Warner merger, 13, 20, 23, 302, 309, 310–11, 312–13
Levy, Sidney J., 208–9
Lewis, Howard T.: *The Motion Picture Industry,* 14
Lewis, Jon, 366n7
Lichtenstein, Roy, 272
Life, 112, 179, 300–301
Linderman, Deborah: on *Vertigo,* 360n23
Lipartito, Kenneth, 347n51
Lippmann, Walter: on organized crime, 52; *The Phantom Public,* 41; *Public Opinion,* 33, 41; on stereotypes, 33, 35
Lipset, Seymour Martin, 267, 273, 365n34
Little Caesar, 4, 5, 6, 7, 8, 53, 56, 64, 77, 87; vs. *Bullets or Ballots,* 80, 81, 232; and RICO law, 348n58; Rico's audience with Big Boy, 54–55, 67, 80, 348n63
Liu, Alan, 261, 268; on the historicism paradox, 248; *Laws of Cool,* 204; on postmodern aesthetics, 250; on teams, 204
logos: Disney's fair castle, 7; Fox's searchlights, 7; MGM's lion, 7, 21, 61, 62, 94, 127, 161; Paramount's mountain, 7; RKO's radio tower, 7; Warners' shield, 7, 275, 276–79, 280, 288–89, 306–8, 365n49
Lombard, Carole, 106
Look, 19
Los Altos, 362n3
Lost Patrol, The, 149
Love Me Tonight, 8, 38
Lubitsch, Ernst, 313
Lucas, George, 338
Luce, Henry, 52, 286, 292, 300, 301, 347n48
Luce Corporation, 112
Luhmann, Nicholas, 364n30
Lumière brothers, 298
Lustig, Jeffrey R., 42
Lyotard, Jean-François, 250, 251

MacArthur, Douglas, 49, 110, 134, 135
MacEwen, Walter, 277
MacLane, Barton, 73
MacMahon, Aline, 62, 66
Madam Curie, 49
Magical Mystery Tour, 267
Maltby, Richard, 14–15, 75; *Harmless Entertainment,* 44, 351n93; *Hollywood Cinema,* 15; "The Spectacle of Criminality," 348n60
Mann, Denise: *Hollywood Independents,* 365n44
Man Who Knew Too Much, The, 232, 234
March, Frederic, 188, 190
Marchand, Roland: *Creating the Corporate Soul,* 9, 29
Marcus, George H., 358n4
Marie Antoinette, 7
marketing, 4, 8, 11, 12, 13, 19, 23, 151, 177, 181, 212–13, 235, 258, 260, 275, 280, 281, 284, 313; vs. advertising, 9, 218; and *Boys Town,* 91, 92, 95, 97; and brand management, 178–79; by Disney, 329, 330; Drucker on, 269, 285, 343n10; experiential marketing, 260, 328; as making customers, 9–10, 26–27, 30–31, 145, 195, 269, 343n10, 347n54; and market segmentation, 114–15; as protection, 84–85; rebranding, 153–54, 155–56. *See also* brands; logos; trademarks
Martin, Reinhold: *The Organizational Complex,* 346n41
Marx, Karl, 175, 347n54
Masculin Feminine, 363n20
Massey, Raymond, 214
mass production, 15–16
Masters, Kim: *Hit and Run,* 367n9
Matsushita Electric Industrial Co., 280
Maurer, Herryman: "The Age of the Managers," 193–94
Mayer, Louis B., 4, 5–6, 7, 11–12, 22, 25, 30, 59, 64, 107, 108, 155, 203, 354n21; and *Boys Town,* 87, 99–100, 155, 201; and The Crowd, 346n35; and *Gabriel over the White House,* 45; and horse breeding, 108, 352n5; on motion pictures, 99–100; and *Mrs. Miniver,* 111, 122, 125, 126, 132; as personification

of MGM, 21, 133; and *Philadelphia Story*, 112, 113; and propaganda, 111, 116; relationship with Freed, 100, 104, 159, 201; relationship with Gilbert, 158; relationship with Schary, 104, 133, 152, 153, 154, 158–59, 160, 163, 188, 208, 277; relationship with Schenck, 8, 44, 54, 111–12, 113, 115, 133, 201, 343n6; relationship with Thalberg, 54, 343n6, 344n18, 346n44; resignation of, 104, 207, 208, 358n51; and *Wizard of Oz*, 5, 100, 104, 352n112

Mayor of Hell, 90

MCA. *See* Music Corporation of America

McCann, Sean, 267, 268, 365n34

McCarey, Leo, 211

McDowell, Malcolm, 358n52

McDowell, Roddy, 107

McHugh, Frank, 81

Means, Gardiner: *The Modern Corporation and Private Property*, 44, 174

media conglomerates, 280–81, 313

Meehan, Eileen: on *Batman*, 281

Meehan, John, 90

Meet Me in St. Louis, 22, 165

Méliès, Georges, 298

Mellenkamp, Patricia, 349n73

Mendelson, George, 345n30

method actors, 179, 195

Metro-Goldwyn-Mayer. *See* MGM

Metropolitan Life, 39, 69–71, 83, 269

MGM, 13, 59, 70, 234, 349n67, 353n15; allegory in pictures of, 5, 7, 49, 50–51, 104, 111, 112–13, 116, 125, 172, 173, 185, 201; "ars gratia artis" slogan, 61, 62; as brand, 2, 11–12; and breeding, 22, 107–9, 124–25, 130, 352n5; commitment to quality, 4, 5, 9, 25, 27, 31, 104, 112, 114–17, 118, 126, 159, 196, 200, 207, 353n16; corporate strategy of, 3–5, 7, 8; and credit, 159–63, 169, 170, 277, 355n5; vs. Disney, 328–29; *Fortune* on, 1–2, 3, 4, 9, 22, 24–27, 28–31, 44, 55, 69, 111–13, 114, 115–17, 132, 169, 196, 344n18, 346n44; vs. Fox, 100–101, 133, 139, 151; Freed unit, 5, 12, 22, 104, 157, 159, 161, 162, 166–67, 170, 171, 173, 187, 196, 201, 207; and William Randolph Hearst, 44, 45, 57, 62, 346n43, 349n74; lion/Latin motto logo, 7, 21, 61, 62, 94, 127, 161; and musical comedy genre, 4, 5, 12, 158, 159, 162, 202; vs. Paramount, 4, 5, 27, 106, 115, 116, 151, 154, 164; personifications of, 21, 24–26, 29–31, 115, 133, 167; relationship with Loew's, 3, 4, 6, 8, 22, 24, 25, 44, 54, 109, 115, 158, 187, 196, 201, 343n6; and self-reflexiveness, 9, 22, 27, 63, 152–53, 155–56, 158, 163–64, 167, 195, 355n11; and social adjustment, 22, 51, 61, 64, 82, 103, 124, 127, 152–53, 156, 171–72; and star-punishment pictures, 157, 158, 355n2; as studio of stars, 4–5, 22, 25, 60, 63, 106, 115, 125, 159, 163, 171, 172, 177, 202–3, 328, 354n21, 358n47; vs. Warner Bros., 2, 4, 5–6, 7, 8, 9, 12–13, 21–22, 54–55, 57, 60, 61–64, 67, 77, 82, 89–90, 97, 115, 151, 154, 159–60, 164, 180, 313, 349n75; during WWII, 106, 107, 108–11, 120. *See also* *Band Wagon, The*; *Battleground*; *Boys Town*; *Crowd, The*; *Dancing Lady*; *Executive Suite*; *Gabriel over the White House*; *Grand Hotel*; *Mrs. Miniver*; *Philadelphia Story, The*; *Singin' in the Rain*; *Wizard of Oz, The*

Midsummer Night's Dream (1935), 64

Mildred Pierce, 151–52

Miller, Mark S., 351n102

Minnelli, Vincente, 173, 207

Minority Report, 8

Mitchell, Billy, 51

Mitchell, Thomas, 134

modernism, 189, 211, 219, 248, 251, 271

Moley, Raymond, 79

Monogram, 107, 353n13

Monsky, Henry, 91

Montalban, Ricardo, 140

Montgomery, Robert, 106

morale, 136, 143–45, 152

Moran, Bugsy, 56

Morgan, Frank, 87, 104

Morgan, Gareth, 196

Morgenthau, Henry, 352n3

Morocco, 7

Morrow, Vic, 324

Motion Picture Herald, 56
Motion Picture Producers and Distributors Association (MPPDA), 3, 6, 17, 19, 21, 56, 107, 328
Motion Picture Production Code Administration/Hays Office, 21, 58, 75–76, 78, 317, 356n13; Production Code, 62, 75, 76, 323
Motion Picture Research Council, 323
movie stars, 12, 55–56, 356n22; and *The Band Wagon*, 22, 182, 185, 186, 202–3; charisma of, 5, 177, 182, 185, 186; and MCA, 233–34; as monopolies on themselves, 5, 10–11, 177, 179–80, 217–18; star-punishment pictures, 157–58, 355n2
Mrs. Miniver, 7, 8, 108–11, 116–32, 145, 150, 353n21; and breeding, 22, 108–9, 124–25, 130; competition in, 119–20, 125, 126, 127; and Louis B. Mayer, 111, 122, 125, 126, 132; and MGM's commitment to quality, 116–17, 118, 126
Mr. Smith Goes to Washington, 236, 319–20, 321–22, 324
Muni, Paul, 179
Munro, Richard, 285, 286–87, 292, 293, 294, 300
Murdoch, Rupert, 280, 306, 366n7
Murray, James, 31, 345n25
Muscio, Giulana, 350n84
Museum of Modern Art, 198, 199, 360n26, 361n37
Music Corporation of America (MCA), 23, 217, 222, 233–35, 244, 280
Mussolini, Benito, 347n48; *The Corporate State*, 52
My Fair Lady, 274

Nabers, Drayton, 75, 303, 350n86, 352n4, 353n10
Narboni, Paul, 75
National Industrial Recovery Act (NIRA), 58, 85
National Recovery Administration (NRA), 58, 78, 85
National Velvet (1944), 107
Natural Born Killers, 300
Nazi Germany, 6
Nelson, George, 198–99, 200

neocorporatism, 174–76, 178, 180
Neufeld, Evan, 368n26
Neumeier, Marty, 178, 179
New Criticism, 249, 250, 258
New Deal, 216, 350n84; First New Deal, 58, 103, 174; and planning, 130; Second New Deal, 70, 72–73, 78, 85, 86, 88, 89, 90–91, 103, 106, 130, 320–21, 351n105, 364n30; Szalay on, 37; and Warner Bros., 6, 22, 73, 78, 85, 86, 90
New Hollywood, 8, 23, 270, 275, 276, 280–81, 325, 366n49
New Left, 23, 267–70, 276, 364n34
New Left Notes, 268–69
Newman, David, 363n20; on *Bonnie and Clyde*, 248, 253–54, 255, 258, 270; "Can We Salvage the Twentieth Century?," 270; on directors, 257; on the New Sentimentality, 248–49, 272, 275, 276; script of *Bonnie and Clyde*, 245, 246, 363n12, 364n32; "The Movies Will Save Themselves," 246–47, 249–50, 258–59, 270, 271–72, 275
News Corporation, 280
New Sentimentality, 23, 248–49, 272, 275, 276
newspaper pictures, 6
Newsweek, 193
New Wave, 23, 256, 258, 276
New Yorker, 272
New York Review of Books, 250
New York State, 218; insurance code of, 69–70, 71
New York Times, 77
New York Times Magazine, 77
Ney, Richard, 109
Nicholas, Nicholas, 286, 292, 300, 301–2
Nichols, Dudley, 100
Nicholson, Jack, 288
Niebuhr, Reinhold, 41–42
Nitti, Frank, 53
Nixon, Richard, 190
Noah, Timothy: on *You've Got Mail*, 303, 305, 308, 309, 313, 367n15
No Highway in the Sky, 157
Nolan, Lloyd, 134
North by Northwest, 227, 231–32, 234, 242
Novak, Kim, 238, 240, 241, 242
Noyes, Betty, 160, 161, 169, 173

Noyes, Eliot, 198
Nugent, Frank, 320
Nuisance, The, 49

O'Connor, Donald, 158, 161
Office of War Information, 19, 106, 120
Okay America, 59
O'Neill, Henry, 74
Otterson, John, 343n3
Our Daily Bread, 170
Out of the Past, 151
Owen, Reginald, 109

Packard, Vance: *The Hidden Persuaders*, 360n27
Palance, Jack, 289
Paramount Pictures, 3, 59, 86, 103, 170, 196, 211, 280, 289, 362n3, 367n8; as brand, 7–8; contract with Paramount, 234, 236, 237; vs. MGM, 4, 5, 27, 106, 115, 116, 151, 154, 164; mountain logo, 7; Paramount Decree/*United States v. Paramount*, 132, 164, 179, 186, 187, 213, 215, 216, 233, 321; and Warner Bros., 6, 55, 56–57, 86
Paramount vs. Time Inc., 286, 291–93, 296
Partisan Review, 270, 272
Pasternak, Joe, 159
Pathe, 55
Payne Fund: Committee on Educational Research, 323
Peary, Gerald, 348n63
Peckinpah, Sam, 362n3
Penn, Arthur: as avant-garde, 271; and *Bonnie and Clyde*, 246, 247–48, 249, 252, 253, 255, 257, 271, 274, 362n8, 363n12
People, 286
Perez, Gilberto, 243
personifications, 10, 17, 72, 177, 179; of MGM, 21, 24–26, 29–31, 115, 133, 167
Peters, Jon, 367n9
Phantom of the Opera, The, 323
Philadelphia Story, The, 112–13, 227; Cavell on, 113, 353n10; Hepburn in, 112, 157, 355n2; relationship to MGM's intention, 8
Photoplay, 19, 179
Pidgeon, Walter, 109, 128, 190

Pine, B. Joseph, II, 261, 364n28
Pinocchio (1940), 8, 330–32; Jiminy Cricket as conscience, 336–38; and Pixar, 23, 314, 328, 332, 334, 336; transformation in, 23, 314, 330; Zipes on, 330, 331
Pirate, The, 159, 160
Pirosh, Robert, 138, 354n31
Pixar: corporate culture of, 326–27, 333, 338–39, 370n25; merger with Disney, 23, 314, 326–27, 332, 333, 338–40, 370nn25,26; and *Pinocchio*, 23, 314, 328, 332, 334, 336. See also *Toy Story*; *Toy Story 2*
Pizzitola, Louis, 57
Plato's *Ion*, 229, 237, 260
Pokorny, Michael, 4
Polan, Dana, 76–77, 81–82
Pollard, Michael J., 251
Pollock, Jackson, 272
Porter, Cole: "Be a Clown," 160
Postman Always Rings Twice, The, 151–52
postmodernism, 210, 248, 251, 262, 268, 271–72, 276, 279
Potemkin, 124
Potter, Paul, 364n33
Powell, Dick, 62, 66
Powell, Eleanor, 159
Powell, Michael, 125
Powell, William, 55, 56
Pressberger, Emeric, 125
Price, David A., 325
Proctor and Gamble, 178
profit, 1, 4, 5, 11–12, 120, 145, 190, 192–94; maximization of, 2, 15–16, 47, 177, 188, 192–93, 195–96
prohibition, 50, 53, 72–73
propaganda, 110–11, 116, 146, 328
Psycho (1960), 8, 232, 234, 236, 237, 242
psychoanalysis, 222, 223, 229, 360nn20,24
Public Enemy, 4, 57
public opinion, 19, 41, 110, 116, 153

racketeering, 58, 63–64, 66–67, 72–75, 77–80; and *Bullets or Ballots*, 73–75, 78–80, 82–84, 85, 86–87, 351n93; extortion, 52–53, 73–74, 76, 77, 78–80, 82, 86; RICO law, 53, 348n58
Rafelson, Bob, 271, 280

Rainbow Productions, 211
Rand, Ayn, 22, 210, 212; *The Fountainhead*, 191, 211, 213, 218, 358n4, 359n17
Rand Corporation, 295
Random Harvest, 49
Rankin, Eleanor, 90
Rapf, Harry, 349n72
Rear Window (1954), 227, 234
Red Hot Mama, 362n3
Reibnitz, Ute von, 295
religion, 147–49, 153
Republic Pictures, 107, 353n13
Revue, 233, 234, 244
Reynolds, Debbie, 158, 160, 161, 169, 172
Richards, Addison, 88
RICO law, 53, 348n58
Rieff, Phillip, 182
Riesman, David, 186, 273; on *Executive Suite*, 192, 193, 197, 200, 203; on other-directed vs. inner-directed persons, 225–26, 227, 249; "The Executive as Hero," 192, 193, 194, 200; *The Lonely Crowd*, 19, 222, 225, 249
Rivera, Diego, 2
River Rouge Plant, 210
RKO Radio Pictures, 3, 86, 149, 151, 154, 157, 160, 170, 180, 186, 234; radio tower logo, 7; Selznick at, 6, 59, 133
Roach, Bert, 33
Road to Utopia, 8
Robinson, Edward G., 7, 56, 57, 74, 76, 350n89
Rogers, Ginger, 61, 65, 184
Rogin, Michael: "Blackface, White Noise," 82, 96–97
Rohde, Gilbert, 199
Rooney, Mickey, 87, 90, 95, 97, 100, 106, 107, 159
Roosevelt, Franklin, 59, 65, 73, 85, 86, 97, 103, 106, 108–9; and *Gabriel over the White House*, 44, 45, 52; and Hays Code, 58; and *Mrs. Miniver*, 111; on Social Security, 84. See also New Deal
Rope, 234, 235–36
Ross, Rich, 370n26
Ross, Steve, 275, 276, 280, 297, 299, 365n45; and *Batman*, 13, 287; charisma of, 13, 283, 285; and *JFK*, 298, 301, 302; and Time-Warner Communications merger, 13, 23, 286, 290, 294–95, 300, 301, 312
Rosten, Leo, 4–5, 177, 179, 217; *Hollywood*, 14
Roy, William G.: on corporate power, 18–19; *Socializing Capital*, 18–19
Ruth, David, 53, 55, 77
Ryan, Edmon, 140
Ryan, Meg, 303, 304
Ryan, Patricia, 214

Saarinen, Eero, 198
Salter, Sir Andrew, 347nn49,50
Samuel Goldwyn Inc., 13
Sanders, Claire, 109
Sandifer, Peter: "Corporate Authorship," 367n15
Sarris, Andrew, 236
Saturday Review, 53
Sayers, Frances Clarke, 329, 335
Scarface (1932), 2, 5, 53, 57, 76
Scarlet Street, 151
Schary, Dore, 115, 146, 166; and *Battleground*, 12, 22, 132, 133, 152, 153–54, 155–56, 159, 277; and *Boys Town*, 90–91, 155; and *Executive Suite*, 187, 188, 196, 201, 207, 208, 209, 358n47; *Heyday*, 158; on Paramount Decree, 187; relationship with Freed, 173, 201, 209; relationship with Mayer, 104, 133, 152, 153, 154, 158–59, 160, 163, 188, 208, 277
Schatz, Thomas, 244, 280–81; *The Genius of the System*, 15, 341n11, 349n71, 353n16
Schenck, Nicholas, 25, 30, 154, 158, 187, 188, 196, 209, 354n21, 358n47; relationship with Mayer, 8, 44, 54, 111–12, 113, 115, 133, 201, 343n6
Schiller, Friedrich, 261
Schmidt, Benno, 299
Schumpeter, Joseph, 195, 357n39
Scorsese, Martin, 280
Screen Actors Guild, 233
Seager, Henry Rogers: *Social Insurance*, 345n31
Sedgwick, John, 4
Selznick, David O., 21, 107, 188, 211, 234; at MGM, 59, 107, 133, 154; at RKO, 6, 59, 133

Selznick, Myron, 234
Selznick International, 13
Seven Arts Productions, 245, 274, 275, 276
Severn, Christopher, 109
Shadoian, Jack: on *Bonnie and Clyde,* 253
Shakespeare, William: Cleopatra, 259, 260; Falstaff, 259
Shamley Productions, 8, 232, 234, 237
Shearer, Norma, 24, 27
Shell Oil Corp., 296, 297, 313
Sherman Antitrust Act, 56, 58, 85, 86, 233–34, 315, 348n64
Shils, Edward, 201–2, 365n34
Shop Around the Corner, The, 313
Show Boat, 201
Shrek, 8
Shuler, Lauren, 308, 309
Sicilia, David B., 347n51
Sidney, George, 152
Silverman, Stephen, 161
Simons, David, 368n27
Sinatra, Frank, 159
Sinclair, Ronald, 107
Singin' in the Rain, 8, 158, 159–74, 182, 185, 187, 201, 207–8, 273, 355n12; Clover on, 160–61; Cohan on, 163, 165–66, 355n11, 356n13; and credit, 159–63, 169, 170; Dove on, 165, 355n12; vs. *The Fountainhead,* 159–60; and Freed, 12, 161–63, 207, 208, 209; "Good Mornin'," 168–69, 172; "Make 'em Laugh," 160, 165, 172; "Singin' in the Rain," 161–63, 172, 173, 208, 209, 358n52; as star-punishment picture, 22, 180; "You Are My Lucky Star," 163; "You Were Meant for Me," 172, 195
Sirovich, William Irving, 57
Sklar, Martin J., 17–18
Sklar, Robert, 272
Skouras company, 85–86
Skyscraper Souls, 194, 359n16
Slate, 303
Sloan, Alfred, 113–14, 178
Smith, C. Aubrey, 107
Smith, Edward H., 77
Smith, Kent, 214
Smith, Terry: *Making the Modern,* 343n5

Snow White, 328
social adjustment: Arnold on, 51, 72; and MGM, 22, 51, 61, 64, 82, 103, 124, 127, 152–53, 156, 171–72
social consciousness, 118–19, 120, 127
social intelligence, 41–42, 61
social responsibility, 173–74, 175, 182
Social Security Act, 84, 100, 103
sound technology, 16, 106, 158, 169, 170, 171, 172–73; and Warner Bros., 6, 163–64, 355n11
Spadino, Robert, 341n11, 344n13
Spadoni, Robert: on *The Fountainhead,* 212, 213–14
Spanish-American War, 62, 349n74
Sparks, Ned, 61, 65
Spartacus, 274
Spellbound, 222, 360n20
Spiegel, John: *Men Under Stress,* 143, 354n28
Spielberg, Steven, 337, 370n23
Spitz, Leo, 211
Spoto, Donald, 222, 241
Staiger, Janet, 365n41; "Announcing Wares, Winning Patrons, Voicing Ideals," 343n7; *The Classical Hollywood Cinema,* 15–19, 341n11
stakeholder participation, 174–75, 196
Stanwyk, Barbara, 189–90
Star, The, 157, 355n2
star-punishment pictures, 157–58, 180, 355n2
Starr, Irving, 133
Steamboat Willie, 329
stereotypes, 33, 35, 36, 37, 39, 40
Stevens, John Paul, 319
Stewart, Donald Ogden, 113
Stewart, James, 106, 112, 113, 217, 222, 226–27, 234
Stone, George E., 81
Stone, Oliver, 299; and *JFK,* 282, 283–84, 297
Strachan, Hew, 143–45
Strasberg, Lee, 179
Street with No Name, 151
Stuart, Harold, 343n3
Students for a Democratic Society (SDS), 268, 364n33
Studies in Social Psychology, 137

studio authorship thesis, 13–22, 219–21, 236, 285, 305, 336–37, 368n1; and *Bonnie and Clyde*, 278–79; and *Citizens United*, 319–20, 321–22; and cultural authorship, 23, 314, 317–18, 326–27, 338–40; relationship to corporate intention, 8, 14, 76–77, 311–12, 314, 315–17, 336; and *You've Got Mail*, 303, 311–12. *See also* corporate personhood

Sturges, Preston, 345n25, 346n36

St. Valentine's Day Massacre, The, 253, 362n3

Sullivan, Louis, 214, 218; "The Tall Office Building Artistically Considered," 210

Summer Holiday, 159

Sunset Boulevard, 7, 8, 170

Sun Tzu's *Art of War*, 133

Sutherland, Donald, 297

Swope, Gerard, 58

Szalay, Michael, 267, 268, 333, 365n34; *New Deal Modernism*, 37, 345n28

Tatira-Hiller, 245, 257, 270, 275, 276, 278, 366n48

Taurog, Norman, 90–91

Tavoularis, Dean, 274

Taylor, Dub, 265

Taylor, Elizabeth, 107

Taylor, Robert, 134, 157

Technicolor, 240, 243, 361n43

Tedlow, Richard S., 114

television, 132, 152, 174, 186, 209, 286, 329, 335–36; *Alfred Hitchcock Presents*, 234–35, 236, 237; and education, 295, 298–99; motion pictures on, 114, 115, 239, 281

Ten Commandments (1923), 7

Ten Commandments (1956), 7

Tennessee Johnson, 129–30

Thalberg, Irving, 4, 5–6, 11–12, 28, 41, 44–45, 54–55, 64, 87, 104, 107, 111, 125, 132, 133, 200, 236; and credit, 160, 277, 355n5; and *The Crowd*, 344n19; *Fortune* on, 2, 9, 22, 24–27, 30, 31, 44, 55, 169, 344n18, 346n44; and *Grand Hotel*, 344n13; legacy of, 7, 167, 196; on motion pictures as entertaining, 24, 54, 343n8; as personifying MGM, 21, 24, 25–26, 167; relationship with Mayer, 54, 343n6, 344n18, 346n44; on the script, 344n12

That's Entertainment, 186

They Died with Their Boots On, 149

Thomas, Bob, 344n19, 369n14

Thompson, John, 64

Thompson, Kirsten: *The Classical Hollywood Cinema*, 15–17, 341n11

Thompson, Marshall, 139

Thoroughbreds Don't Cry, 107–8

Time, 19, 193, 272, 287–88, 347n48

Time, Inc., 285–95, 298, 300–301, 326; merger with Warner Communications, 13, 23, 280, 281, 283, 286–93, 294–95, 300–301, 312, 366n5, 367n11

Time Warner Inc., 275, 280, 281, 283, 292, 296–97, 298–303, 366n7, 367n11; merger with AOL, 13, 23, 302–3, 304–5, 306–13, 367n20, 368n25, 368nn27–29; and *You've Got Mail*, 13, 23, 268n25, 302, 304–5, 308–13, 367n20. *See also JFK*; *You've Got Mail*

To Catch a Thief, 232, 234

Toland, Gregg, 121

Tone, Franchot, 61, 171

Too Hot to Handle, 7

Toulmin, Harry Aubrey, 216

Towne, Robert, 274

Toy Story, 8, 23, 325, 332–33, 334, 335

Toy Story 2, 8, 23, 332, 333, 334–36, 337, 370n22

Toy Story 3, 332

Tracy, Spencer, 87, 88, 95, 100, 166

trademarks, 96, 97, 139, 155, 178, 235, 264, 282, 332; vs. brands, 95; MGM trademark, 5, 7, 21, 44, 61, 62, 94, 127, 161, 352n107; Trademark Act, 216, 217; U.S. Patents and Trademarks Office, 304, 309; Warner Bros. trademark, 7, 221, 275, 276–79, 278, 280, 288–89, 306–8, 365n49; and *You've Got Mail*, 304, 309–10, 367n20

Transamerica, 285

Transatlantic Productions, 234

traumatic neurosis, 38–39, 42, 345n30

Travers, Henry, 109

Treasure Island (1950), 330

Tron: Legacy, 370n26

Trotsky, Leon, 270
Trouble with Harry, The, 234
Truffaut, Francois, 246, 267, 271
Trumpener, Katie, 363n20
Turner, Lana, 151
Turner, Ted, 306
Twelve O'Clock High, 8, 139
Twentieth-Century Fox, 3, 5, 8, 13, 59, 115, 154, 157, 245, 246, 280, 343n3; vs. MGM, 100–101, 133, 139, 151; searchlights logo, 7
Twilight Zone, The (1983), 324–25

Under Capricorn, 236
United Artists, 8, 245, 246, 274
Universal Classics, 244
Universal International Pictures, 211, 234, 235, 236, 237, 244
Universal Pictures, 3, 6, 8, 26, 59, 107, 222, 234, 323
U.S. Justice Dept., 85, 103, 108–9, 111, 216, 235, 287, 321, 364n30
U.S. Patents and Trademarks Office, 304, 309
U.S. Supreme Court, 12, 85; *Austin v. Michigan Chamber of Commerce,* 315, 318, 319, 320; *Citizens United v. Federal Election Commission,* 23, 284, 314–15, 318–22, 324, 330, 336, 337; *First National Bank of Boston v. Bellotti,* 319; *Joseph Burstyn Inc. v. Wilson,* 319; Justice Alito, 319; Justice Kennedy, 319, 320; Justice Roberts, 319; Justice Scalia, 319; Justice Thomas, 319, 321; Justice Edward White, 348n64; *Mutual Film Corp. v. Industrial Commission of Ohio,* 319; Paramount Decree/*United States v. Paramount,* 132, 179, 186, 187, 213, 215, 216, 233, 321; Santa Clara case, 1
U.S. War Department: Research Branch, Information and Education Division, 137, 138, 153–54

Valenti, Jack, 14
Van Dyke, W. S., 7
Vanguard Pictures, 133, 211, 222
Van Runkle, Theadora, 274
Van Sloane, Edward, 323

Variety, 19, 55, 56, 58–59, 163, 245, 346n44, 348n65
Vasey, Ruth, 75
vaudeville, 166, 169
Veblen, Thorstein, 197
Veiller, Anthony, 151
Venturi, Robert, 210–11
verbal icons, 258, 260, 278
Vertigo, 222–44, 254, 359n20, 360nn23,28; and bilateral monopolism, 222; color green in, 240–44, 361n43; and Freudian psychology, 222, 223, 229, 360nn20,24; and Hitchcock's independence, 23, 222, 234, 237, 244; responsibility in, 224–25
Vidor, King: and *The Crowd,* 31–32, 35, 40–41, 344n18, 345n27; and *Duel in the Sun,* 211; and *The Fountainhead,* 22, 211, 212, 213, 217, 359n18
Vinogradoff, Paul, 28–29
Virginian, The (1929), 8
Volstead Act, 52, 77
Von Sternberg, Josef, 7

Wald, Jerry, 349n75
Wallace, Henry A.: *America Must Choose,* 130, 131
Wall-e, 259
Wallis, Hal, 64, 154, 211
Walt Disney Productions. *See* Disney
Wanger, Walter, 44, 45, 246, 344n12; "The Role of Movies in Morale," 144–45
Warhol, Andy, 252, 254, 255, 256
Warner, Abe: "Warner Brothers," 222
Warner, Albert, 54
Warner, Harry, 54, 56, 85–86, 107, 212
Warner, Jack, 6, 9, 12–13, 54, 64, 157, 211–12, 221, 273; on film cycles, 6, 58–59; relationship with Beatty, 9, 13, 21, 245–46, 269, 274–75, 276–78, 363n21, 365n46; Warner Bros. sold by, 3, 23, 245
Warner Bros., 13, 209, 235–36, 280, 349n67, 351n102; allegory in pictures of, 6, 281, 290; as brand, 9, 13; and commutability, 22, 64–65, 66, 67–68, 77, 82; corporate strategy of, 2, 5–6; and credit, 159–60, 211–12, 220–21, 236, 278; *Fortune* on, 58–59, 63, 85,

349n75; and gangster genre, 4, 5–6, 53–57, 76–77, 246, 273; vs. MGM, 2, 4, 5–6, 7, 8, 9, 12–13, 21–22, 54–55, 57, 60, 61–64, 67, 77, 82, 89–90, 97, 115, 151, 154, 159–60, 164, 180, 313, 349n75; and monopoly, 215–16; and New Deal, 6, 22, 73, 78, 85, 86, 90; and Paramount, 6, 55, 56–57, 86; relations with Skouras theater chain, 85–86; shield logo, 7, 275, 276–79, 280, 288–89, 306–8, 365n49; and sound technology, 6, 163–64, 355n11; and star-punishment pictures, 157, 158; as studio of genres, 4, 5–6. *See also Batman; Bonnie and Clyde; Bullets or Ballots; 42nd Street; Fountainhead, The; Gold Diggers of 1933; Jazz Singer, The; Little Caesar; Time Warner Inc.; Warner Communications Inc.; You've Got Mail*

Warner Communications Inc. (WCI), 285–95, 298, 366n48; and *Batman*, 13, 23, 281, 286–91, 292–93; merger with Time, 13, 23, 280, 281, 283, 286–93, 294–95, 300–301, 312, 366n5, 367n11

Warners-Seven Arts, 3, 23, 245, 272–73, 278, 366n48

War of the Roses, The, 353n18

Wasko, Janet, 327, 329

Wasserman, Lew, 23, 217, 222, 233, 234–35, 239–40, 244

Watney, Stanley: on the cinema of chastisement, 355n2

Weber, Max, 18, 195; on bureaucratic authority, 201; on charisma, 175–76, 190, 193, 194, 201–2; on the ethic of absolute ends, 267

Webster, Jimmy, 351n106

Weekly Variety, 55

Wexman, Virginia, 361n40

Whale, James, 324

Whatever Happened to Baby Jane?, 158

When Ladies Meet, 157

White Cliffs of Dover, The, 107, 206, 353n18

Whitmore, James, 139

Whittle, Chris, 298–99

Whittle Communications, 298–99

Whitty, Dame May, 109

Wilcoxon, Henry, 111

Wild Bunch, The, 362n3

Wilder, Billy, 151

William, Warren, 66, 359n16

Williams, Esther, 159

Williamson, Oliver, 347n51

Wimsatt, W. K., 279; on the concrete universal, 258–61, 267; on impractical stasis, 271, 274

Wings, 346n35

Wizard of Oz, The, 49, 61, 90, 100–104, 170, 352n114, 365n43; vs. *Boys Town*, 87, 104; and Freed, 5, 104; and Louis B. Mayer, 5, 100, 104, 352n112

Wood, Robin, 223, 227–28

Words and Music, 159

World War I, 50, 69, 137, 144–45

World War II, 105–6, 137, 144–45, 352n3, 354nn31, 32; audiences after, 22, 152–54, 163; Great Britain during, 105, 106, 107, 108–11, 125, 128, 129, 130, 353n6, 353n17; MGM during, 106, 107, 108–11, 120

Wright, Frank Lloyd, 210, 214, 358n4

Wright, Teresa, 109, 132

Writers Guild of America, 235

Wuhl, Robert, 287

Wyatt, Justin, 280

Wyler, William, 111, 120–21, 124, 129

X-Files, 306

Young, Allan, 38

You Only Live Once, 246

You're My Everything, 160

You've Got Mail, 8, 303–13, 368n26; and AOL–Time Warner merger, 13, 23, 268n25, 302, 304–5, 308–13, 367n20; Noah on, 303, 305, 308, 309, 313, 367n15; and trademarks, 304, 309–10, 367n20

Zanuck, Darryl F., 64, 100, 154, 349n71

Zapruder film, 298, 300–301

Zipes, Jack: on *Pinocchio*, 330, 331; "Toward a Theory of the Fairy-Tale Film, 330

 Announcing a new series: **Post•45**
Florence Dore and Michael Szalay, Editors
Post•45 Group, Series Board

Post•45 publishes groundbreaking work on U. S. culture after the Second World War. Our goal is to question rather than reproduce critical orthodoxies—to ask basic questions about how to read and categorize American writing since 1945. Though the series will gravitate toward literature, we welcome writing on a wide range of popular and avant-garde culture, including film, drama, music, graphic arts, and computer-based forms.

The authorized representative in the EU for product safety and compliance is:
Mare Nostrum Group
B.V Doelen 72
4831 GR Breda
The Netherlands

www.ingramcontent.com/pod-product-compliance
Lightning Source LLC
Chambersburg PA
CBHW080723300426
44114CB00019B/2472